The New York Times
Guide to
New York City
2001

The New York Times
New York, New York

Please send all comments to:
The New York Times Guide to New York City
122 E. 42nd St., 14th Floor
New York, NY 10168

Published by:
The New York Times
229 W. 43rd St.
New York, NY 10036

ISBN 0-9668659-8-7
Printed in Canada
First Printing 2000
10 9 8 7 6 5 4 3 2 1

For the New York Times: Mitchel Levitas, Editorial Director, Book Development; Thomas K. Carley, President, News Services Division; Nancy Lee, Director of Business Development. Elliott Rebhun and the staff of NYToday.com provided essential help and cooperation.

Correspondents: Randy Archibold, James Barron, Ben Brantley, Barbara Crossette, Leslie Eaton, Grace Glueck, Abby Goodnough, Laurel Graeber, Clyde Haberman, Anemona Hartocollis, Amanda Hesser, Bernard Holland, Leslie Kaufman, Randy Kennedy, Michael Kimmelman, Anna Kisselgoff, Douglas Martin, Herbert Muschamp, Robin Pogrebin, Rita Rief, Tracie Rozhon, Susan Sachs, Jennifer Steinhauer, Anthony Tommasini, Amy Waldman.

Maps: Charles Blow.

Prepared by Elizabeth Publishing: *General Editor:* John W. Wright. *Senior Editors and Writers:* Alice Finer, Alan Joyce, Richard Mooney. *Writers:* Charles Suisman and the staff of *The Manhattan Users Guide* (Hotels), Kurt Hettler (Sports and Recreation), Terry Golway, Jerold Kappes, Gloria Levitas, Susan McMichaels, Amber Morgan, Ed O'Donnell, Elda Rotor, Nicole Weinstein. *Data Entry:* Arlene Jacks.

Design and Production: G&H SOHO, Inc., Hoboken, N.J.: Jim Harris, Gerry Burstein, Ian Wright, Mary Jo Rhodes, Christina Viera, Gerald Wolfe.

Cover Design: Barbara Chilenskas, Bishop Books

Distributed by Publishers Group West

Table of Contents

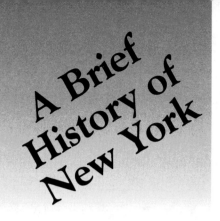

A Brief History of New York

The first European explorer to reach what would be known as New York harbor was Giovanni Verrazano in 1524. He liked what he saw, but bad weather forced him out to sea after only a few hours. Others followed, but it wasn't until 1609 that Henry Hudson (the Englishman in the employ of the Dutch East India Company) arrived to conduct the first detailed survey of the region. Several expeditions of Dutch fur traders came and went in succeeding years until 1624, when the ship *New Netherland* arrived to establish a settlement with 30 families. Two years later, according to local legend, the Dutch Director General Peter Minuit purchased the island from the local Indians for 60 guilders worth of goods.

The colony of New Netherland and its main town, New Amsterdam, grew slowly and returned virtually no profit to the investors of the Dutch West India Company. The colony suffered from a series of poor governors (either incompetent, corrupt, or both), unruly settlers, and conflict with local Indians. In 1647, following a disastrous war with the Indians, Peter Stuyvesant took over as Director General. Autocratic but effective, he restored order and a measure of prosperity to New Amsterdam. No sooner had he done so, than a squadron of British ships sailed into the harbor in 1664 and demanded that Stuyvesant surrender. Unwilling to do so even though he had virtually no soldiers, he was overruled by the merchants and property owners of the town. After only 40 years of Dutch rule, New Amsterdam passed into British hands without a shot being fired. The latter promptly renamed it New York, in honor of the Duke of York, King Charles II's brother.

Colonial New York grew and prospered as a key trading port in the British Empire and its population reached 20,000 by 1760. Yet when England sought to assert control over the colonies in the 1760's, New York became a leading center of anti-Crown sentiment and activity. The British invaded New York shortly after the Revolution broke out in 1776, intending to split the colonies north and south. They succeeded in taking New York City from George Washington, but failed in their larger goal.

New York was in a sorry condition when the Revolutionary War ended in 1783. A great fire in 1776 had devastated much of lower Manhattan and the population slipped below 20,000. Nonetheless, by 1815 its deep and protected harbor with access to the rich hinterland up the mighty Hudson River, coupled with a diverse population and pervasive entrepreneurial spirit, enabled the city to surpass Boston and Philadelphia in both population and economic clout. The opening of the Erie Canal in 1825, connecting the Hudson River to Lake Erie, propelled New York far ahead of its rival cities. For the rest of the century, nearly 70 percent of the nation's imports and exports passed through the Port of New York.

After 1830 the city experienced unprecedented growth in population, largely due to the onset of massive immigration from Europe. In the 1850's, more than two million immigrants, mostly from Ireland and Germany, landed in New York. As the population soared, innovations in mass transit such as the steam railroad and horsecar allowed the city to spread northward along the narrow island of Manhattan, while ferries spurred settlement in the independent city of Brooklyn. With growth came problems. A professional police force was established (1845) to deal with a sharp rise in crime and the frequent outbreak of rioting. The threat of fire and cholera prompted the city to construct a 44-mile aqueduct into the mountains north of the city (1842) to supply fresh water. And to make up for the lack of open space, city officials purchased a vast tract of land in the middle of Manhattan island to begin construction of Central Park (1858).

By the Civil War the city had developed a different sort of institution—the political machine. While there were several machines, the one that eventually outlasted its rivals was the faction of the Democratic party known as Tammany Hall. The power of the machine derived from its ability to provide vast numbers of poor voters with jobs, charity, and mass entertainment in exchange for their votes. Tammany's most infamous leader was William "Boss" Tweed. He reigned supreme from the early 1860's to 1871 when a massive corruption scandal sent him and his henchmen to jail. Despite this setback, Tammany recovered and eventually became went on to dominate city politics until the early 1930's.

By the late 1870's the city's population surpassed one million, just as the sources of immigration began to change. Over the next four decades millions of Italians, Eastern European Jews and countless other groups arrived to once again transform the cultural character of the city. Most of them would pass the Statue of Liberty (unveiled in 1886) as they entered the harbor on their way to the new immigrant receiving center on Ellis Island, which opened in 1892.

In the 1890's, at the behest of merchants, property owners and real estate developers, the New York State Legislature approved a plan to consolidate the independent cities of New York and Brooklyn (then the nation's third largest city) with dozens of smaller municipalities in what now constitute the Bronx, Queens and Staten Island. On January 1, 1898, the City of Greater New York was born—a colossal 320 square miles and 3.2 million people. No American city would ever challenge its supremacy again.

In 1904 the city's first subway line opened. It would grow to a peak of 722 miles, spurring development wherever tracks were laid. The early twentieth century also witnessed the emergence of Times Square—named for *The New York Times*—as home of American theater, popular music, media and advertising. With consolidation and continued immigration, New York grew as never before, reaching a population of 8 million by the 1930's. Increasingly, with the advent of steel, new engineering methods, and the elevator, the city grew upward, a trend epitomized by the completion of the Empire State Building in 1931.

The Twenties were in many ways a golden era for New York. Despite the passage of Prohibition, alcohol flowed freely in the city's many clubs and speakeasies. So too did the new and innovative sounds of jazz, a product of the city's soaring African-American population, especially in Harlem. But the good times ended with the Crash of 1929 on Wall Street. When Fiorello LaGuardia was elected mayor in 1933, he brought a spirit of reform, innovation and enthusiasm to city government during the most trying years of the Great Depression. His close relationship with President Franklin Roosevelt helped him garner millions in federal funds for relief and construction programs. The World's Fair at the end of the decade (the remnants of which can still be seen in Queens) helped to stimulate the economy and to publicize the city's greatness around the world.

In the first two decades following World War II, New York enjoyed both stability and prosperity. A building boom in the 1950's saw the construction of dozens of modern skyscrapers, hundreds of miles of highways, and major institutions like the United Nations and Lincoln Center. These were also the glory years for the famed New York Yankees who won ten World Series between 1945 and 1962. The opening of the second World's Fair in 1964 epitomized the confidence shared by most New Yorkers.

Yet like the nation as a whole, the second half of the 1960's brought unanticipated turmoil and despair. Increased crime, rising racial tensions, and decaying infrastructure convinced more and more middle-class New Yorkers to join the great national movement to the suburbs. The subsequent loss in taxes and consumer spending hurt local business and brought the city to the verge of bankruptcy in 1975. Movies like "The French Connection" and "Taxi Driver" popularized the image of the city as an anarchic and violent place.

The city's condition stabilized somewhat in the 1980's, in no small measure due to the booming national economy. Still crime, racial tensions, and pessimism about the city's future remained high. Then in the early 1990's, for reasons still not yet fully understood, urban America, led by New York City, made a stunning comeback. The city's notorious crime rate dropped 70 percent, while tourism, job creation and construction hit record highs. For the first time in memory, the city ran a budget surplus, allowing it to undertake long-overdue improvements to its infrastructure.

Great challenges still confront the city, from overcrowded and underfunded public schools, to high rates of poverty in several areas. Still, as New York enters the 21st century, it does so with a renewed spirit of optimism that has consistently run through its long and storied history.

—Edward T. O'Donnell
Department of History
Hunter College

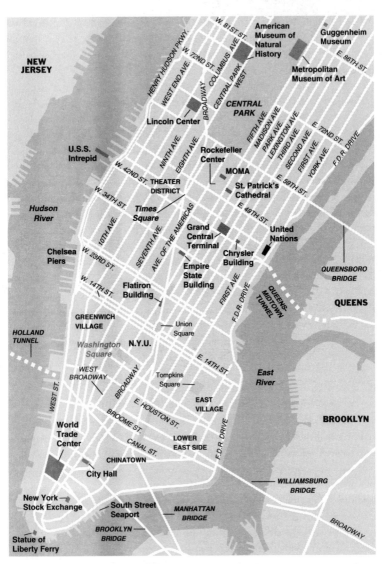

Manhattan Highlights

Visiting New York

GETTING IN AND OUT
By Car

Before you decide to bring your car into Manhattan consider these simple facts: tolls for turnpikes, bridges and tunnels are the highest in the nation, traffic is horrendous in the daylight hours and parking fees are four or five times what they are anywhere else. If you need to drive, call your hotel beforehand and find out how much they'll charge you for parking so there are no surprises.

Directions From the South and West: From the New Jersey Turnpike (I-95) to midtown Manhattan take exit 16E to the Lincoln Tunnel which will bring you to 42nd St. and 9th Ave. If you are staying downtown, you can go to exit 15W and take the Holland Tunnel which will leave you on or near Canal St. You can also use exit 13 and take the Goethals Bridge onto the Staten Island Expressway which goes to the Verrazano Bridge. From here you follow the signs to the Shore Parkway to the Gowanus Expressway to the Brooklyn Battery Tunnel which will bring you out right near the World Trade Center.

Directions from the West: I-80 is the major highway leading to the George Washington Bridge, which will take you onto the Cross Bronx Expressway unless you exit almost immediately. For the east side of Manhattan, look for the exit to the Harlem River Drive (this leads to the FDR Drive); for the west side take the Henry Hudson Parkway or Riverside Drive (south).

Directions from the North: The New York Thruway (I-87) becomes the Major Deegan Expressway as you enter the Bronx. If you wish to go to Manhattan's west side, exit at the Cross Bronx Expressway (west) and quickly exit at the Henry Hudson Parkway (south); this turns into the West Side Highway. If you want the east side of Manhattan, stay on 87, go past Yankee Stadium to the Third Ave. Bridge, or a little farther to the Triborough Bridge. Both lead to the FDR Drive.

From New England: Take I-95 to the Bruckner Expressway (I-278) to the Triborough Bridge to the FDR Drive (for the east side); for the west side take the Bruckner to the Cross Bronx Expressway (west) to the Henry Hudson Parkway.

By Train or Bus

Major Terminals

Penn Station, 32nd St. at 7th Ave.
Grand Central Terminal, 42nd St. at Park Ave.
www.grandcentralterminal.com
Schedules: (212) 532-4900
Port Authority Bus Terminal, Between Eighth and Ninth Aves., 40th to 42nd
St. Schedules: (212) 564-8484

Rail Lines

Amtrak

www.amtrak.com
Departs from: Penn Station
Major areas served: In addition to service to Florida and nationwide, there are
frequent trains to Washington, D.C. and Boston—including the new high-
speed (extra fare) Acela.
Phone: (800) 872-7245

Long Island Rail Road (LIRR)

www.mta.nyc.ny.us/lirr
Departs from: Penn Station, Jamaica Center Station, Flatbush Avenue Station
Major areas served: Points throughout Long Island
Phone: (718) 217-LIRR (5477), (718) 558-3022 (TTY), (516) 822-LIRR
(5477) or (516) 231-LIRR (5477)

Metro North

www.mta.nyc.ny.us/mnr
Departs from: Grand Central and 125th Street Station (all lines);
Fordham (Fordham Rd. at Webster Ave.—New Haven and Harlem lines only);
other stations in the Bronx serve individual lines.
Major areas served: Westchester, Putnam and Dutchess Counties in New York
State; Fairfield and New Haven Counties in Connecticut with connections to
the rest of the state.
Phone: (212) 532-4900), (800) METRO-INFO, (800) 724-3322 (TTY)

New Jersey Transit

www.njtransit.state.nj.us
Departs from: Penn Station
Major areas served: Points throughout New Jersey, including Atlantic City;
Philadelphia
Phone: (800) 626-7433, (973) 762-5100

Bus Lines
Greyhound
www.greyhound.com
Departs from: Port Authority (Eighth Ave. at West 42nd St.), Queens Village
(219–17 Hillside Ave.)
Major areas served: United States (points throughout the country); Canada;
Mexico
Phone: (800) 231-2222

Peter Pan Trailways
www.peterpan-bus.com
Departs from: Port Authority (Eighth Ave. at West 42nd St.)
Major areas served: Points between Boston and Washington, D.C., including all
of New England.
Phone: (800) 343-9999

Regional Buses
Depart from: Port Authority (Eighth Ave. at West 42nd St.)
Phone: (212) 564-8484

New Jersey Transit
www.njtransit.state.nj.us
Departs from: Port Authority (Eighth Ave. at West 42nd St.), George Washington
Bridge Bus Station (at 179th St., between Broadway and Ft. Washington Ave.)
Major areas served: Points throughout New Jersey, including Atlantic City and
the Jersey Shore; Philadelphia; Wilmington, Delaware and Washington, D.C.
Phone: (800) 626-7433, (973) 762-5100

MTA Long Island
www.mta.nyc.ny.us/libus
Departs from: Flushing (at Main St. and Roosevelt Ave.), Jamaica
Center, 179th St. (at Hillside Ave., Jamaica)
Major areas served: Points in Nassau and Suffolk Counties, including Jones
Beach, Roosevelt Fields, and Walt Whitman Mall
Note: Free transfer with Metrocard
Phone: (516) 766-6722, (516) 228-4000 (Paratransit)

Hampton Jitney
Departs from: 86th St. between Lexington and Third Aves; 69th St. and Lex-
ington Ave.; 59th St. and Lexington Ave; 40th St. and
Lexington Ave.
Major areas served: Points between Manhattan and Montauk, including the
Hamptons
Phone: (800) 936-0440, (516) 283-4600

Navigating the Airports

Traveling to the metropolitan area's three major airports continues to require patience and lots of extra time. Here are some suggestions for getting to La Guardia Airport, Kennedy International Airport and Newark International Airport—some ways are cheaper. Limousines are more expensive—and more convenient (*see "Limousines"*).

By Subway or Train and Bus

To La Guardia—Take the E, F, G or R subway to the Roosevelt Avenue-Jackson Heights subway station or the No. 7 to the 74th Street-Broadway stop. Then get the Q-33 at the bus terminal located at street level or jump in a cab. Estimated time from midtown to the airport is 50 minutes . . . Take the A, B, C, D or Nos. 2, 3, 4, 5 or 6 subway to 125th Street, or the Nos. 1 or 9 trains to Adam Clayton Powell Jr. Blvd. and 116th Street. Then take the M-60 bus. It runs every half hour and stops at most avenues along 125th Street . . . Take the N train to Astoria Boulevard, where you can catch the M-60 bus.

To Kennedy (JFK)—Take the A train marked Far Rockaway to the Howard Beach-JFK Airport station, then get the free shuttle bus to JFK terminals. Estimated time from midtown to the airport is 70 minutes . . . Take the E or F subway to Union Turnpike, then get the Q-10 Green Bus . . . Take the F subway to 179th Street-Jamaica, where you can get the Q-3 bus . . . Take the No. 3 subway to New Lots Avenue, where you get the B-15 bus to Kennedy. Metrocards allow you free transfer to the buses in Queens. For more information call the M.T.A., 718-330-1234.

To Newark Airport—Take the PATH train from the World Trade Center to Newark Penn Station. It costs $1. In Newark, take the Air Link bus (No. 302) run by NJ Transit. It runs every 20 minutes or so and costs $4. (PATH: 800-234-7284; NJ Transit: 973-762-5100 or 800-626-7433.) The ride lasts about 42 minutes (22 on PATH, 20 on the bus) . . . From New York's Penn Station, take the NJ Transit train to Newark Penn Station ($2.50), then get the No. 302 bus (as above) to the airport, $4. Estimated ride: 40 minutes (20 on train, 20 on bus).

It is advisable to leave extra time when traveling by any bus or rail connection to the airport, especially if you expect to be traveling during morning or evening rush hours. Transportation agencies in the metropolitan area offer lots of additional route and schedule information on the Web to help you get to the airports using their transit systems.

By Private Bus or Van

To Newark Airport—Olympia Airport Express (212-964-6233) leaves from three places in Manhattan and charges $10 for the trip to Newark Airport. From Penn Station (at the northwest corner of 34th Street and Eighth Avenue), buses leave every half hour from 5:10 to 7:10 A.M., then every 20 minutes until 11:10 P.M. Travel time is approximately 35 minutes. From the Grand Central Terminal area (at 120 E. 41st St., between Park and Lexington Aves.), every half hour from 5 A.M. to 7 A.M., then every 20 minutes until 11 P.M. Approximate travel time is 45 minutes.

At the Port Authority Bus Terminal (212-564-8484), purchase your ticket at the Airport Bus Center on the 42d Street side of the building. Service starts at 4:15 A.M., then every half hour from 5 to 7 A.M, then every 20 minutes until midnight, then at 1 A.M. and 2:45 A.M. Approximate travel time is 35 minutes. From 1 World Trade Center (next to the Marriott Hotel on West Street), buses leave at 6:15 A.M., then every half hour until 8 P.M. Approximate travel time is 25 minutes. Even with express bus lanes, leave extra time in rush hours. *To La Guardia and Kennedy*—New York Airport Service (718-706-9658) has service from the Port Authority Bus Terminal, Grand Central and Penn Station, and you can make arrangements to be picked up at some midtown hotels. Approximate travel time is 45 minutes to one hour. It costs $10 to La Guardia and $13 to Kennedy.

To All Airports—Gray Line NY (212-315-3006). Call 24 hours ahead to reserve a pickup at some midtown hotels between 23d and 63d Streets from 5 to 7 P.M. La Guardia ($16); Kennedy and Newark Airports ($19) . . . Call the blue Super Shuttle (212-209-7000) vans a day ahead to arrange for the service to pick you up at your home or office and take you to the airport. A van may make up to three pick-ups. La Guardia ($14–$15); Kennedy ($15–$24); Newark Airport ($17–$28). The least expensive fares are from the Battery and the most expensive are from the northern end of Manhattan. You can also arrange to meet the shuttle at the airport for the trip home. Super Shuttle service is available in Manhattan only.

By Helicopter
To All Airports—Helicopter Flight Services (212-355-0801) charges $595—more outside of normal business hours—for a helicopter trip to the three airports. It carries four people with one bag to check and one carry-on each. Once there, a van transfers you to the airline terminals. Make arrangements at least a day in advance. Approximate travel time is 10 minutes. Helicopters leave from West 30thStreet, East 34th Street, and the Wall Street heliport (which is three blocks south of where Wall Street meets the East River).

By Ferry
To La Guardia—New York Waterway (800-533-3779) runs ferry services to the Marine Air Terminal at La Guardia from Wall Street's Pier 11 (one block south of where Wall Street meets the East River), the East 34th Street heliport, and a pier at East 62d Street. Ferries, which run Monday to Friday during business hours, are timed to meet the shuttle flights to Washington, D.C. and Boston that operate from that terminal. Approximate travel time is 25 minutes from East 34th Street. The fare is $15 one-way, $25 round-trip. If you're not flying the

Delta Shuttle, you will have to take the Route A shuttle bus from the Marine Air Terminal to the other terminals. The shuttle buses run every 20 minutes.

Renting a Car

Renting a car in New York can be an expensive hassle if you're not careful. You'll need to decipher a dizzying, somewhat confusing collection of rules and rates. Your age, your driving record and where you live may all factor into how much it will cost you to rent a car.

Age: It is illegal in New York State to discriminate against young drivers (25 and under), according to the New York State Bureau of Consumer Fraud and Protection. But car rental companies are allowed to tack on a steep surcharge that covers the cost of the additional insurance they must provide for younger drivers.

Driving Record: In New York State, a car's owner (in this case the car rental company)—not the driver—is financially and legally liable in the event of an accident. Many national chains now check your driving record with the New York State Department of Motor Vehicles when you give them your license at the counter. If you've had serious driving violations, they may decide not to rent to you; however, rules vary by company.

Getting Around

New York has quite a few places that can help you find your way. Web sites like **New York Today** provide up-to-the-minute information about city events and locations. There are two visitor information centers, one in Times Square and the other nearby. Both centers have bus and subway maps, and much more. Also, the agency that runs the city buses and subways—the Metropolitan Transportation Authority (MTA)—has a 24-hour Travel Information Center where you can get directions by telephone at (718) 330-1234. Subway toll booths have subway maps, too; some buses have bus maps.

New York Today (www.nytoday.com) is *The New York Times'* online service. It offers a wealth of information about New York City events, arts and entertainment, restaurant reviews, shopping, sports, news, weather, traffic conditions and a customizable calendar of city activities and events. New York Today is updated daily, giving users access to the latest news and reviews from the respected writers of *The New York Times*. Features of the site include the **Around Town** section, with overviews, attractions and current events listings for specific neighborhoods in all five boroughs; comprehensive, searchable databases of *New York Times* restaurant, hotel and movie reviews; and **newyork.urbanbaby.com,** with helpful information on living in or visiting New York with children. **Note:** Visitors with some brands of handheld computers can also download **Vindigo** (www.vindigo.com), which gives users access to descriptions and walking directions for thousands of restaurants, bars and stores, plus current movie listings and showtimes, all drawn from New York Today's online database.

The Times Square Visitors Center
Broadway at 47th St. (212) 869-1890

The center has an information desk where help is available in five languages, racks and racks of brochures about things to do, an MTA booth for Metrocards and information, a row of computer terminals where you can spend 10 free minutes on the Internet and send e-mail, an out-of-town newspaper stand with U.S. and foreign papers and magazines, a full-price theater ticket desk, Times Square's history on closed circuit TV, a free video game, a sightseeing tour desk (by bus, boat and helicopter), a New York City souvenir counter, an Automatic Teller Machine (ATM), a machine that exchanges 10 foreign currencies for dollars, discount coupons for shopping and clean bathrooms. A free tour of Times Square begins at the center every Friday at noon.

New York City & Co.
810 Seventh Ave. (betweem 52nd and 53rd Sts.) (212) 484-1222 and 1-800-692-8474

This center, operated by the New York Convention and Visitors Bureau, has an information desk where they speak seven languages, several touch screens for the day's events and tickets to Broadway shows, museums and tours, more racks and racks of brochures—here including restaurants, hotels and shopping—an ATM machine, a Metrocard machine, a one-hour photo developer and discount coupons for shopping. You can also call or visit the bureau online (www.nycvisit.com) to order their Official NYC Visitor Kit, which includes a pocket-size guide to New York, a fold-out map, a newsletter about upcoming events and brochures from various New York attractions. Delivery is $9.95 for rush delivery, $5.95 for nonrush, or free for the city guide only.

Public Transportation

New York has three public transportation systems—not counting your own two feet.

1. Subways are the fastest way to get around, which is why the natives use them. They are safe, too, but you should always be alert to what is going on around you. A $1.50 fare will take you to the far ends of the city—including both baseball stadiums, both city airports and Coney Island. (See **METRO-CARDS** for best fare deals.)

2. Buses tend to be slow, but they have advantages—no stairs to climb, and bus stops are closer together than subway stations, so buses can put you closer to where you are going. Buses also give you picture window views of the street scene. Riding the bus costs the same as riding the subway.

3. TAXIS are better than buses at weaving through and around sticky traffic, and they take you from wherever you hail them to wherever you want to go. There are taxi stands at LaGuardia and Kennedy airports, and in Manhattan at

Penn Station, Grand Central Terminal and the Port Authority Bus Terminal. Otherwise, taxis cruise the streets looking for cutomers. Taxis are, of course, more expensive than public transit, starting at $2 the minute the meter starts running. Yellow cabs are regulated by the city, which makes them a safer bet than unmarked gypsy cabs for tourists. The gypsies usually charge lower fares, but may fleece the unsuspecting.

There are also dozens of **LIMOUSINE** services *(see below)*.

The Subway System

The New York subway system may be one of the oldest in the world, but it is also one of the most efficient. It runs 24 hours a day, 365 days a year and covers every area of the city except Staten Island. There are over 722 miles of track and 469 stations.

While it is true that parts of the subway are a bit run down, and the screeching noise from the few remaining older trains can cause jangled nerves, one look at the traffic jams in midtown and at the bridges and tunnels leading to the outer boroughs will tell you why millions of New Yorkers ride the subway every day.

Manhattan

West Side: served by the A, B, C, D, 1, 2, 3 and 9 trains. The A, 2 and 3 are "express" lines with relatively few stops. The C, 1 and 9 are "local" trains, stopping more frequently. B and D service is mixed. E and F lines run local north–south service south of 50th St., then head east for crosstown stops on 53rd. The N and R run north–south below 57th St., then head east for crosstown stops on 60th St.

East Side: served by the 4, 5 and 6 trains. Trains run under Lexington Ave. north of 42nd St., and under Park Ave. to the south. The 4 and 5 are express trains; the 6 is local. They all have interchanges with the E, F, N and R, and with the 42nd St. Shuttle (S) and the 7 line.

Bronx:
Served by the B, D, 1, 2, 4, 5, 6 and 9 trains. *(see "The Bronx")*

Brooklyn:
Served by the A, B, C, D, F, G, M, Q, R, 2, 3, 4 and 5 trains. *(see "Brooklyn")*

Queens:
Served by the B, E, F, G, J, M, N, R, Z and 7 trains. *(see "Queens")*

Some Advice From the Natives

Subways are safe, but visitors to New York City are advised to be alert, especially when packed tight on a crowded train. Beware of pickpockets, a crafty lot. Keep your hands on your purse and your wallet. Don't wear flashy jewelry. At night, don't ride in the last car, which tends to be the emptiest and riskiest. If you are nervous, seek out the middle car where the operator is positioned to open and close the doors.

For comfort, hold onto the poles and overhead rods that are there to steady you when the train lurches.

Take note of posted signs that tell you which trains will not run on Saturday and Sunday. Loudspeaker announcements are almost always unintelligible. Don't hesitate to ask someone for directions.

The Metropolitan Transportation Authority has a 24-hour Travel Information Center which you can telephone at (718) 330-1234, but it is not always completely informed about weekend service. It can, however, give directions to where you want to go. The MTA also posts weekly service notices on its website: **www.mta.nyc.ny.us**

The Bus System

Note well: you **must** have a token, a Metrocard or $1.50 in coins when you board a bus. The driver does not handle money. You pay your fare with coins or a token, or by dipping a Metrocard in the fare box. If you are paying cash and do not have the right coins, you may find someone on the bus who can make change for your paper money or pay for you with his Metrocard and take your cash—or you may not, in which case you must get off.

City bus lines run the length and breadth of Manhattan. They are especially useful for getting across town. The route numbers for all routes within Manhattan begin with the letter M. Many of the crosstown routes have the same number as the street on which they cross. Traffic on the principal crosstown streets runs in both directions; all the rest are one-way. As a general rule, even-numbered streets are one-way from west to east, and odd-numbered streets run east to west.

Here are the crosstown routes:

M 8 runs on 8th and 9th Sts. from Avenue D and 10th St. to Christopher St.

M 14 operates on 14th St.

M 16 and **M 34** operate on 34th St.

M 23 operates on 23rd St.

M 27 and **M 50** operate on 49th St.; the 27 goes to Penn Station.

M 31 crosses 57th St., then up Madison Ave. and across East 72nd St.

M 42 operates on 42nd St.

M 66 operates on East 67th St. westbound and crosses Central Park at 66th St.; eastbound it operates on West 65th St. until it crosses Central Park, then continues on East 68th St.

M 72 operates on West 72nd St. and East 72nd St., crossing Central Park at 65th St eastbound and 66th St. westbound.

M79 operates on East 79th St. east of Central Park and West 81st St. west of the park.

M 86 operates on 86th St. and crosses Central Park on that street.

M 96 operates on 96th St. and crosses Central Park on that street.

M 106 operates on 106th St. east of Central Park, and 96th St. west of the park.

M 100, M101 and **Bx 15** operate on 125th St.

M 116 runs across 116th St. to Manhattan Ave., then down to West 106th St.

Metrocards

Metrocards are the smart way to pay for riding subways and buses. They are always convenient and often a bargain. You can buy them in subway stations and at 3,000 other locations—newsstands, restaurants, hotels, pharmacies and wherever an orange-and-blue Metrocard sign is posted.

A "Funpass" Metrocard for $4 permits unlimited rides on buses and subways for one day. Funpasses may be purchased from machines in subway stations—not from token clerks—and at both the two tourist information centers.

A $17 weekly Metrocard permits unlimited rides during the seven days after you first use it. A monthly $63 card permits unlimited rides for 30 days after the first use.

Otherwise, you can buy a Metrocard for $3 (two rides) or any higher amount you want. If you buy one for $15 (10 rides) you automatically get an eleventh ride free.

The use of a Metrocard is usually simple, just swipe it through the slot at a subway turnstile or dip it into a bus fare box. But sometimes a turnstile will tell you to swipe the card again . . . and again . . . and again. The key is to place the card all the way down in the slot, hold it firmly and run it all the way through quickly and smoothly. If all else fails, go to the token clerk, who should then let you through the "special entry" turnstile.

Transfers: A Metrocard permits transfers between subways and buses and vice versa, and between buses and buses, so long as you do not transfer to the same route you started on. After you use your card at the start of a trip, you have two hours to transfer to another route, not necessarily connecting with the first leg of your trip, at no extra charge. (The card "knows" when your two hours has expired.)

Note: When you pay a bus fare with cash or a token the fare box will give you a transfer for another bus ride within two hours. It will not work for the subway.

HELPFUL HINTS

All of the major tourist destinations are within a short walk of subway and bus stops. The **World Trade Center** is on four different subway lines. The **Metropolitan Museum of Art** is one block from four uptown bus routes on Madison Ave.—seven or eight blocks from subways. Buses running downtown on Fifth Ave. and crosstown on 34th St. stop near the **Empire State Building,** and two subway lines (1/9 and 6) have stops three blocks away. Three bus routes and two subway lines take you close to the boat to the **Statue of Liberty** and **Ellis Island.**

Times Square: The intersection of Broadway and 42nd St. has more subway and bus service than anyplace in the whole city. Most of its subway and bus lines serve the West Side of Manhattan, but some swing over to the East Side. **Grand Central Terminal** on the East Side is also well served, mostly by subways and buses running uptown and downtown. Both Times Square and

Grand Central are also on 42nd St. crosstown bus routes, and the Shuttle (the S train) and No. 7 subway lines. Both places are good starting points when you feel lost.

Taxis

A taxi's roof light will tell you if it is available. Look for cabs with the center section of the light lit. They are empty, looking for customers. If the center section is off and the two ends are lit, they say "OFF DUTY" and the driver is not interested in you. If the entire light is off, don't bother with frantic waving—the cab has a passenger. Unlike some other cities, cabs with passengers do not stop to pick up more. (Hailing taxis in the rain is maximum frustration. Consider some other way to go.)

Hailing a cab: There is a knack to this which you can learn by watching how experienced taxi riders do it: stick your arm out and all the way up, and don't be shy. Yell "taxi" if necessary—no one in New York will look strangely at you for yelling. Get off the sidewalk if there is a lot of traffic or if parked cars will prevent the taxis from seeing you. Remember to be watchful of cars and trucks swerving into the lane where you may be standing.

Rules and Traditions: First of all, you should always remember that a New York taxi driver is *required* by law to take you anywhere within the city—even to the far ends of Brooklyn or Staten Island—as well as to Newark Airport and Westchester or Nassau counties. Most drivers today are natives of India, Pakistan and the Middle East and many are religious Muslims. While a small percentage have less than adequate skills with English, most New Yorkers will tell you that they are far more courteous and respectful than drivers of earlier periods. Unfortunately, like their predecessors, the long hours and low pay often lead to aggressive and reckless driving, so:

- Buckle your seat belt
- Tell the driver to slow down if you become fearful (he knows his tip is dependent on your satisfaction and that you can file a complaint if you are unhappy)
- Take a fare receipt from the cab driver when you get out. It gives the trip number and the taxi's official medallion number—information you need if you want to make a complaint or trace something you may have left in the cab. It also shows the 24-hour consumer hotline telephone: (212) NYC-TAXI, which is the same as (212)-692–8294.

Fares: Yellow cab fares start with an initial charge of $2. The fare rises by 30 cents for every 1/5 mile traveled, and by 20 cents for every 90 seconds in stopped or slow trafic. From 8 P.M. to 6 A.M. there is a surcharge of 50 cents per trip.

On trips to Westchester and Nassau Counties you pay the metered amount to the city line plus double the metered amount from the city line to your destination, as well as round-trip tolls. Cabs are required to pick you up if you have a Seeing Eye dog or are in a collapsible wheelchair.

Airports: From JFK airport there is a flat fee of $30 to any point in Manhattan, plus bridge or tunnel tolls. This is the only one of the three major airports in the metropolitan area for which a flat rate is charged. Fares to and from LaGuardia are on the meter, and may hit $20 or more. Fares to and from Newark Airport are higher—the metered amount and another $10, plus the driver's round-trip tolls.

Tipping: Compared with many other cities, New York's taxi charges are not out of line, i.e. riding in a taxi is one of the few services in New York that is not outrageously priced. So we urge visitors to tip generously if the ride is satisfactory since the drivers depend on this to raise their pay to a decent level. Some rules of thumb: never tip less than a dollar, $2 when the fare is over $6, $3 if over $10. For trips to the airports tip $6 to $10, more if the driver helps with your luggage.

Limousines

There are dozens of limousine services, from long white Lincolns and Cadillacs equipped with bars and TV to short black sedans. They cost more than taxis, but will come when you want them. You must arrange for them in advance. Here are a few:

Tel Aviv (212) 777-7777 and 1-800-222-9888
Carmel (212) 666-6666
Sabra (212) 777-7171 and 1-800-722-7122
Allstate (212) 333-3333 and 1-800-453-4099

For the latest information on restaurants, hotels, concerts, nightlife, sporting events and more, check online at New York Today, the *New York Times* website devoted entirely to life in New York City: www.nytoday.com.

Exploring New York

Like all the great cities of the world, New York opens up much more of its inner self to those visitors who take the time to walk its streets. There is no other city, at least not in America, that is more inviting to see on foot because no other place has New York's variety of buildings, shops and people.

Only by taking long, leisurely (if still purposeful) strolls can you begin to sense that energy and drive so many visitors to New York have written about for over 200 years. It may not be a tangible thing but it *is* palpable—you will feel it. Even people born and raised here acknowledge its existence, if only because they feel its absence when they travel elsewhere.

So if you can do it, plan to walk somewhere at least once a day; if you can take the time to walk for five or six hours one day you won't regret it and you will learn much more about New York than you will from the top of a tour bus.

Helpful Hint: Don't stand in the middle of the sidewalk while you are talking, studying a map or looking up at a tall building. Always step back toward the buildings.

Be Careful: Most first-time visitors have never experienced the hazardous traffic conditions found in New York. Cars, trucks, busses, and bicycle messengers all compete for a favored place on the road and people on foot are seen as just another impediment to their halting progress through the city.

The traditional pedestrian's right of way is, as Shakespeare says, "more honored in the breach than the observance." So walk defensively: assume that a taxi will jump the red light, a truck or van will turn rapidly into the crosswalk in an attempt to beat you into the center of the street so he doesn't have to wait for all the pedestrians to cross.

You will notice almost immediately that New Yorkers pay no attention whatsoever to "Walk" "Don't Walk" signs (it is just a part of that New York "state of mind," the part that stresses independent thinking, self-reliance, and asks: why trust a sign? I have eyes!). But if you are new here you should obey them at least for a few days, until you get the hang of crossing when it's safe.

Crime safety

New York is much safer now than it was only a few years ago but crime, the Mayor's p.r. machine notwithstanding, does still exist so it pays to err on the side of caution. Here are some common-sense rules:

- avoid desolate areas at night.
- don't walk in Central Park at night unless there is a major event or you've attended a play at the Delacorte Theater.
- always try to walk in groups.

- keep your money in an inconspicuous place; women should grasp their pocketbooks or wear them across the body; men should be sure a wad of money is not bulging conspicuously in their pants pocket.
- don't wear valuable necklaces (especially in the warm weather months) that can be ripped off with ease by street thugs.

Public Bathrooms

New York City has been laggard in providing public bathrooms at curbside. At the turn of the century there were none, but there may be some by the time you read this. Otherwise, here are places where you will surely find relief as you stroll around the city:

- Department stores
- Hotels (commonly on the same floor as the ballroom)
- Bryant Park (behind the Public Library on the 42nd St. side)
- Mid-Manhattan Library (across 40th street from the Public Library)
- Donnell Library (across 53rd St. from the Museum of Modern Art)
- Grand Central Terminal
- Pennsylvania Station
- Port Authority Bus Terminal
- Central Park Boathouse.

Finding Your Way

Although New York City proper is made up of five boroughs and stretches for 10 to 20 miles in several directions, the focal point of virtually every new visitor is the island of Manhattan. If you can plan to spend more than a few days in New York by all means take the time to visit such wonderful places as the Bronx Zoo (especially if you are traveling as a family) or the Brooklyn Botanic Garden. These are world famous institutions and should not be regarded as inferior by reason of location. You will find descriptions, directions, hours and prices for these as well as other wonderful sites in the specific borough entries later in this chapter.

As the accompanying maps make clear, Manhattan—or "the city" as the natives call it—is one of the easiest places in the world to visit. The island is only 13 1/2 miles long and 2 1/3 miles wide at the center (not even a mile at the southern tip). The basic facts to keep in mind are:

Avenues: run north–south

Streets: run east–west

East Side-West Side: the dividing line is Fifth Avenue. All addresses on the east side of Fifth begin at 1 East; on the west side of Fifth they begin 1 West.

Streets are for the most part numbered consecutively and laid out in a grid. From 8th St. north to 181 St. (and beyond) you will always know where you are relative to, say, 42nd St. South of 8th St. the streets have names and you will need to consult the maps for each neighborhood to keep your bearings. (In Greenwich Village, be forewarned, even a map can be confusing especially in the area where W. 4th St. crosses W. 10th St.!).

Avenues (again these run north–south) are also mostly numbered with First, Second, Third being on the East Side (Lexington, Park and Madison follow); after Fifth Ave. comes Avenue of the Americas (still called 6th Ave. by almost everyone), then 7th Ave. and Broadway (which heads East at 34th St.); in midtown you'll find 8th, 9th, 10th, 11th and 12th Avenues but uptown they assume new identities as Central Park West, Amsterdam, Columbus, West End and Riverside Drive.

NEW YORK'S
TOP 25 ATTRACTIONS

American Museum of Natural History
Brooklyn Bridge
Bronx Zoo
Brooklyn Botanic Garden
Central Park
Chrysler Building
Columbia University
Empire State Building
Grand Central Terminal
Grant's Tomb
Guggenheim Museum
Lincoln Center
Metropolitan Museum of Art
Museum of Modern Art
New York Botanical Garden (Bronx)
New York Public Library
Radio City Music Hall
Rockefeller Center
Saint Patrick's Cathedral
Statue of Liberty
Times Square
United Nations
Yankee Stadium
Wall Street (The Stock Exchange)
World Trade Center

SUGGESTED WALKING TOURS

Below are four short walks you can easily fit into your schedule. Each begins at one of New York's premier attractions: Battery Park, Lincoln Center, the Empire State Building and the Metropolitan Museum of Art.

Lower Broadway: Battery Park north to City Hall Park

A trip to the Statue of Liberty lands you back at Battery Park, the natural start-ing point for a walk up historic lower Broadway, the canyon of ticker tape parades. Along the way you will pass No. 39, site of the house where George and Martha Washington lived in his first year as President. You will also see where Alexander Hamilton was buried after his fateful duel with Aaron Burr, and the offices where John D. Rockefeller ran Standard Oil.

In Washington's time Manhattan Island began at what is now the northern edge of Battery Park. No. 1 Broadway is the building with blue awnings across the street. One entrance says "Cabin Class," and the other "First Class." Now a Citibank branch, this was where travelers of an earlier day booked passage on the United States Lines. The bank has preserved the hall as it was, a grand space befitting a great steamship company.

Across Broadway the massive building with four sculptures out front is the **Alexander Hamilton U. S. Customs House,** a national landmark. It houses the Museum of the American Indian now, but the building itself is remarkable. The large oval in the cavernous rotunda is where importers declared their wares, back when most government revenue came from customs collected in New York. Overhead is a gallery of maritime murals commissioned as a WPA project during the Depression.

The Customs House faces on **Bowling Green,** the city's oldest park. In colo-nial times it had a gilded equestrian statue of King George III, toppled by a mob in 1776 when the colonies were in revolt. The fence, erected in 1771, is still there.

No. 26 Broadway is the **Standard Oil Building.** Across Broadway, the **Post Office** at No. 25 was the booking office of the Cunard Lines, and pre-Cunard the site of the famously fashionable Delmonico's Hotel. Cunard's great vaulted hall is one of the grandest. Now cluttered with postal paraphernalia, it is worth viewing anyhow. They don't build them like that any more.

A few blocks uptown is historic **Trinity Church,** once the tallest building in the city. The first Trinity Church was wooden, built in 1697 and destroyed in the great fire that leveled much of the city in 1776. A map inside the church, behind the last pews on the left, shows where Hamilton, Robert Fulton and others are buried. Directly across Broadway at 1 Wall St. is the **Bank of New York** with an eye-popping Art Deco lobby of red and gold mosaic.

Up four blocks is **St. Paul's Chapel,** where Washington worshiped on the day of his inauguration in 1789. He continued to attend during the months when New York was the capital. His pew is to the right as you enter.

You are now at the foot of **City Hall Park.** Branching to your right is **Park Row,** where Greeley, Pulitzer, Hearst, Ochs and other newspaper titans held forth for most of the 19th and some of the 20th centuries. No. 41 was the origi-nal "New York Times" building, now part of **Pace University.** Messrs. Currier and Ives made their prints behind it at 152 Nassau Street.

Finally, take in the **Woolworth Building** on Broadway facing City Hall Park. This, too, was tallest for a while, and the view from the top was a magnet for tourists. The critic Brendan Gill called it "a romantic confection," and described the lobby as "one of the most sumptuous in the country . . . a bedazzlement of marble walls and gilt bronze doors with a vaulted ceiling of blue and gold mosaics." Don't miss it, and while inside don't miss the architect's jest, a whimsical carving of Woolworth counting his money.

Midtown: 34th St.–59th St.

Fifth Ave., Walking north from 34th St.: This walk is only a little more than a mile and could be done after a visit to the **Empire State Building.** Diagonally across the street from the Empire State is the new branch of the **City University** (formerly a famous department store, B. Altman, built in 1906). As you walk north there are small stores, coffee shops, a Yankees store, and the popular department store **Lord & Taylor** (on the west side of the avenue at 37th St.). Just across the street is the former **Tiffany Building** (409 Fifth Ave.), designed in 1906 by Stanford White who based it on a 16th century Venetian palazzo.

At 42nd St. you'll reach the magnificent **New York Public Library** (see "Midtown West"). Weather permitting, you could stop for lunch in beautiful **Bryant Park** right behind the library. There are two outdoor restaurants and an upscale indoor one called the **Bryant Park Grill** (see the section on "Restaurants").

Heading north you will find many more stores and several interesting buildings especially the **Fred F. French Building** (at the northeast corner of 45th St.). Built in 1927, its arcade and lobby are wonderful examples of the Art Deco style. Only a few blocks north are two of the most popular attractions in New York: **St. Patrick's Cathedral** and **Rockefeller Center.** All through the 40's and 50's you'll find the heart of New York's fanciest shopping district with such stores as **Saks Fifth Avenue** (which dates from 1924), **Tiffany's, Bergdorf Goodman, Henri Bendel,** and at 59th St. **F.A.O. Schwartz,** reported to be the nation's largest toy store. (You can learn more about these stores in the section on "Shopping.")

Upper West Side:
Lincoln Center to 86th St.

Broadway, Walking north from 65th St.: This short walk will take you through an interesting cross section of Manhattan. The Upper West Side is an area where young professionals, families and older New Yorkers reside and commingle with ease, strolling broad sidewalks that run past a wide variety of stores including the dazzling food emporia **Fairway Market** (74th St., west side of Broadway), **Citarella** (next door) and **Zabar's** (81st St., also the west side) All are described in the section, "Shopping."

When you reach the busy intersection of 72nd St. and Broadway (where Amsterdam Ave. crosses Broadway) you can enjoy a well-known New York treat, a couple of **Gray's Papaya** franks and a drink for only $1.95. At 73rd St. on the east side of Broadway, the wonderful Apple Bank building, erected in 1928, is a great favorite of architects. At 74th Street on the west side of Broadway is the old **Ansonia Hotel** which was built by a French firm in 1904. Recently cleaned, restored and converted to apartments, its ornamental facade will dazzle you from every angle. Only four blocks up the street is the 1908 **Apthorp,** a huge apartment house that occupies a full city block; midblock between 78th and 79th is a huge arched entrance leading to a vast interior courtyard.

To get a true sense of this community you should walk down any of the side streets for a few blocks. If you head west you'll pass West End Ave. and then Riverside Drive. The park that runs along the Drive is one of the highlights of the neighborhood and well worth a visit. You'll find views of the Hudson River, wonderful flower gardens and, quite often, families, dogs and picnickers. At 87th St. and Riverside Drive the impressive **Soldiers and Sailors Monument** is a terrific place to sit and relax. At 79th St. you can walk down by the river to the outdoor **Boat Basin Cafe** for a delightful snack while watching the boats and barges pass by.

If you head east from Broadway you'll be heading toward Central Park. On 72nd St. and Central Park West you'll find the famous **Dakota** apartment building, built in 1884. It has always been a symbol of New York opulence but it became world famous in 1980 when John Lennon, a resident of the building, was shot to death in the entryway. A well-visited memorial to Lennon, **Strawberry Fields,** is located just across the street at the entrance to Central Park.

To return to midtown you can take an enjoyable walk through the park or stay on Central Park West and see some of the finest apartment houses in the city.

Upper East Side: Fifth Avenue

The Metropolitan Museum Neighborhood: As you leave the **Metropolitan Museum of Art,** look straight across Fifth Ave. to the southeast corner of East 82nd St. and the former mansion home of Benjamin Duke. Born to a tobacco farming family in North Carolina, Duke and his younger brother James were founders of the American Tobacco Company and the principal benefactors of a little college that became Duke University. With this elegant home as a starting point, you are on your way to a revealing walk up or down what was once called "millionaire's row," the stretch of Fifth Ave. first settled a century ago by such legendary men as Vanderbilt, Carnegie and Whitney. Most of their homes are now museums, schools and charitable organizations, or offices of foreign embassies. A few are subdivided as apartments. Many are city landmarks. If you head downtown you will see the block-long **Frick Mansion,** the immodest digs of the publisher Joseph Pulitzer, and the double townhouse Sara Delano Roosevelt built for herself and her son Franklin—a closeness that made FDR's wife Eleanor understandably uncomfortable. If you head uptown you will see Andrew Carnegie's mansion, Frank Lloyd Wright's **Guggenheim Museum** and the homes of bankers Otto Kahn and Felix Warburg. Here are the highlights.

Walking downtown from the museum:

The Benjamin Dukes bought their place from a developer who built it on spec in 1901. They later sold it to his brother James, who lived there until he built his own nearby. Members of the Duke family and their relatives the Biddles lived in the Benjamin Duke house until recently.

The French Gothic palace on the southeast corner of 79th St., property of several millionaires at different times, belongs now to the **Ukrainian Institute of America.** The onetime home of the millionaire financier Payne Whitney between 78th and 79th Sts. now serves as French Embassy's cultural offices.

James Duke's place, modeled on a chateau in Bordeaux, rose on the northeast corner of 78th St. in 1912. A leading critic calls it "one of the most magnificent mansions in New York." Duke's widow and their daughter, Doris Duke, lived there until the late 1950's when they gave it to New York University. It is now **N.Y.U.'s Graduate School of Art History.**

At 75th St. on the northeast corner, the **Commonwealth Fund** occupies the home of Edward Harkness, son of one of John D. Rockefeller's original partners in the Standard Oil Company. Edward Harkness built most of the undergraduate dorms at Harvard and Yale. The Commonwealth Fund, founded by his mother, devotes Harkness millions to health and medical research.

Halfway into the first block of East 73rd St. is the house Joseph Pulitzer built—No. 11, the one with lots of columns—now subdivided by 13 less affluent tenants. Pulitzer, German-born publisher of the *New York World* and the *St. Louis Post-Dispatch,* had lived briefly at 9 East 72nd St., which he bought from Henry Sloane, son of one of the founders of the W. and J. Sloane furniture stores.

The mansion of coke and steel tycoon Henry Clay Frick stretches from 70th St. to 71st St. Frick, once chairman of Carnegie Steel, was an avid collector of art, especially of the Italian Renaissance. The mansion was designed by the same architects who designed the New York Public Library and planned from the start as both home and gallery. Frick left the house and the art to the city. (See the section "Museums" for tours and other information.)

The Roosevelts' twin townhouse is worth a final two-block walk from Fifth Ave. to No. 47–49 East 65th St. It has just one front door. Inside the vestibule were separate entrances to FDR's domineering mother's quarters on the left, and her son's on the right. Small wonder that Eleanor didn't like it. The FDR's lived there in 1920–21 when he was convalescing from polio and stayed there when they were in the city. The house is now a student center for **Hunter College,** which is nearby on Park Ave.

Walking uptown from the museum:

Two blocks north of Benjamin Duke's place on 82nd St. is the **Marymount School** at 84th St., spread through three houses—the house at the southeast corner and two adjacent on Fifth Ave.—once owned by three different families. At the southeast corner of 86th St. is a former Vanderbilt mansion, now home to the **Serge Sabarsky Foundation,** which exhibits the art collection of a noted dealer-collector who died in 1996.

The **Guggenheim Museum** at 88th St. is Frank Lloyd Wright's major work in

New York City, as notable for its architecture as for its art. Even if you're not up for another museum today, step inside for a moment to see what the American Institute of Architects calls "one of the greatest Modern interiors in the world."

Andrew Carnegie's mansion at 91st St. reflects his grand style and great wealth. While his peers were clustered farther down the avenue, he bought a large piece of empty acreage uptown so he could decide who his neighbors would be. After putting up his 64-room house with its large garden he built something smaller next door at 9 East 90th St. for his daughter and sold land across 91st St. to Otto Kahn.

Carnegie gave away millions of his fortune in steel for thousands of public libraries, Carnegie Hall, various Carnegie foundations and many other good causes. His mansion is now the Smithsonian Institution's **Cooper-Hewitt Museum of National Design.** Kahn, a partner in the Kuhn, Loeb investment house, was a leader in philanthropic promotion of the arts and chairman of the Metropolitan Opera for a quarter century. His mansion at No. 1 East 91st St. copied the 15th century Pallazo della Cancellaria in Rome. It is now a school and faculty housing for the **Convent of the Sacred Heart.**

No. 7 and No. 9 East 91 were built by William Sloane and his wife, Emily—a Vanderbilt—for their daughters. The founder of the Vanderbilt fortune, Commodore Cornelius Vanderbilt, was a notorious tightwad, but he left a bundle for generations of his descendants to build impressive shelter for their children. There is another Vanderbilt place at 56 East 93rd St.

Two more neighborhood mansions are distinguished museums. The Gothic chateau that houses the **Jewish Museum** at the northeast corner of 92nd St. was the home of Felix Warburg, another Kuhn, Loeb partner, and his wife, Frieda, a Schiff, who donated it to the museum. The museum doubled its size in the 1990's. The **International Center of Photography** at the northeast corner of 94th St. was originally the home of Willard Straight, a diplomat and financier, and his wife Dorothy, a Whitney. The Straights founded the *New Republic* magazine.

GUIDED SIGHTSEEING TOURS

The Department of Consumer Affairs estimates the current number of sightseeing licensees, including bus, boat, building and walking guides, at well over a thousand. Tour-takers range from native New Yorkers to empty-nest suburbanites reconnecting with the city to out-of-towners of every description. The people leading the tours include historans, enterpreneurs, nonprofit institutions, licensed guides, unlicensed guides and rank amateurs who are pretty much talking through their hats. The best guides blend the skills of historian, teacher, showman and safety guard as they shepherd their charges through streets teeming with traffic.

There are John Lennon walks, Jacqueline Kennedy Onassis itineraries, pub crawls, celebrity and movie-location jaunts and "gourmet" visits to neighborhood restaurants. There are self-guided tours providing rented compact disk players. And despite the demise of "America's Sitcom," there are now two *Seinfeld* tours: a ride-and-walk effort led by Kenny Kramer, the real-life inspiration for Cosmo

Kramer, and an upstart tour by Gotham Walk. Unlike bus tours, walking excursions allow for greater interaction with people in the neighborhoods.

"New York is a city of small villages, and there is an infinite number of possible tours because New York is endlessly fascinating," says tour guide Joyce Gold, who has a library of 500 books on New York and has read 500 more. "Right at the corner of Wall Street and Broadway, you could talk for three hours and you wouldn't need to take a single step."

Boat, bus, and other "vehicular" tours tend to have reasonably regular schedules, but some seasonal change can occur. Schedules, prices, and meeting places for most of the walking tours listed here can vary wildly throughout the year, so call well in advance or check Web sites to avoid surprises. Do-it-yourselfers can have a wealth of self-guided tourbooks to choose from, or they can contact Talk-a-Walk Sound Publishers (212-686-0356), a publisher of audiotaped, self-guided tours of Manhattan. *The New York Times* also carries a list of tours every Friday, and NYToday.com's "Around Town" section offers more listings.

Walking Tours

Adventure on a Shoestring (212) 265-2663. This group offers 90-minute tours of New York and the surrounding areas. Most trips focus on areas in lower Manhattan, but tours of Astoria, Hoboken, and Roosevelt Island are also available. Special tours also take place each year on the "birthdays" of the Brooklyn and George Washington bridges. Tours include chats with members of the community when possible, and some walks are followed by luncheons at local restaurants. **Prices:** $5, cash only (luncheons not included). **Schedule:** 90-minute tours, most on Sat. and Sun.

Architecture City Tours (800) 557-2176 www.artandarchitecture.com/ newyork.htm Architectural historians and local writers lead these easy, educational tours. No previous knowledge of architecture is expected, and highlights include the Chrysler Building, the United Nations, and Rockefeller Center. **Prices:** $18 ($15 per person for more than 50 participants).

Architecture City Tours (800) 557-2176 www.artandarchitecture.com/ newyork.htm Architectural historians and local writers lead these easy, educational tours. No previous knowledge of architecture is expected, and highlights include the Chrysler Building, the United Nations, and Rockefeller Center. **Prices:** $18 ($15 per person for more than 50 participants).

Big Apple Greeter (212) 669-2896 www.bigapplegreeter.org Offers very personal tours for very small groups, such as a family or two. The itinerary can be set by the group if they want, and tour guides are volunteers who love to show off their city. **Prices:** Free. Reservations required.

Big Onion Walking Tours (212) 439-1090 www.bigonion.com Big Onion offers two-hour tours every weekend and holiday. Themes range from simple neighborhood tours to in-depth historical and ethnic surveys, like "Historic

Burial Grounds of Lower Manhattan" or "Immigrant New York," to special holiday and eating tours. All guides are licensed by the city and hold advanced
degrees in American History.

Prices: $10, adults; $8, students and seniors; special tours, $11–$16. **Features:**
Student and adult group tours for 1 to 200 participants available year-round;
Lectures.

Central Park Conservancy (212) 360-2727 www.centralparknyc.org The
Central Park Conservancy sponsors one-hour tours that explore the history,
ecology, design, or simply the beauty of Central Park. Routes and meeting
places vary, and some tours require registration. Guides are New York City Park
Rangers, skilled birders and other park experts.

Prices: Free. **Features:** Group tours (call 360–2726).

Citywalks (212) 989-2456. Citywalks offers private tours on the history and
architecture of lower Manhattan, especially Chelsea, Greenwich Village, the
Lower East Side and the Financial District.

Prices: $100 for a two-hour tour for one or two people; price drops to around
$15 per person for groups of 15–20.

Discover Harlem (917) 763-8051. Four tours of upper Manhattan are available through this group, exploring everything from jazz clubs to churches to the
Morris-Jumel Mansion, Washington's headquarters in 1776. Some tours are
expensive, but they include some great extras, like an evening of jazz or a meal
at Sylvia's restaurant.

Prices: Vary, up to $77.

Foods of New York Walking and Eating Tours (732) 636-4650. Over the
course of this two-hour tour of the food, landmarks, music and culture of Greenwich Village, you'll visit 18 eating establishments and sample food from 6 of them.
The tour specializes in restaurants and local food shops that New Yorkers visit and
emphasizes that "you can eat affordably in those areas if you know where to go."

Prices: $20 (min. 15 people); $18, students (min. 30 students). Cash only.
Includes food and tour. **Schedule:** Tours 7 days a week at 11:30 A.M., reservations required.

Grand Central Terminal (212) 818-1777. Free tours of the renovated Grand
Central Terminal are held every Friday at 12:30 P.M. Participants meet on 42nd
Street at the Philip Morris/Whitney Museum, across the street from Grand
Central.

Prices: Free. **Schedule:** Fri. 12:30 P.M.

Harlem Spirituals Gospel and Jazz Tours (212) 391-090
www.harlemspirituals.com Despite the name, Harlem Spirituals offers tours of
every New York borough. But the Harlem walking tours make it stand out, featuring everything from Sunday church services to Saturday night soul food and
jazz tours.

Prices: $15–$80, adults; $12–$80, children.

Heritage Trails (212) 466-3600 www.heritagetrails.org Heritage Trails is a not-for-profit group that promotes the history and attractions of Downtown New York. You can request a free "TrailsMap" that guides you to 40 site markers erected by the group around lower Manhattan, or take advantage of several guided tour options, including one that visits the New York Stock Exchange.

Prices: (For World of Finance tour) $15, adults; $10, seniors, students with ID and children under 12. **Schedule:** World of Finance, Fri. 10 A.M.; Destination Downtown (free), Thur. at noon.

Joyce Gold History Tours (212) 242-5762 www.nyctours.com All of these tours are conducted by Joyce Gold herself, an instructor of Manhattan history at the New School University and New York University and author of several walking guides to New York City. Ms. Gold boasts an extensive list of neighborhood tours heavy on history, with titles like "East Village—Culture and Counter-Culture" and "The New Meat Market—Butchers, Bakers, and Art Scene Makers."

Price: $12, no reservations needed. **Schedule:** Sat.–Sun., 1 P.M. (2–3 hours). **Features:** Lectures, slide shows, and private tours also available.

Municipal Art Society Tours (212) 935-3960 www.mas.org The MAS program "Discover New York" sponsors these diverse, year-round tours of New York's neighborhoods, history, and culture. Some special tours, like "Cast in Iron: Manhole and Chute Covers" have companion lectures and slide shows that delve farther into the subject of the walk.

Prices: Weekdays: $10; $8, students, seniors and MAS members. Weekends: $15; $12 MAS members. Lecture fees vary. **Features:** Bus and private tours also available.

New York City Cultural Walking Tours (212) 979-2388 www.nycwalks.com Alfred Pommer has been researching and conducting a wide array of tours for over fifteen years. Featured walks include multi-ethnic "heritage" tours, as well as staples like the "Bohemian Walking Tour of Greenwich Village" and the unusual "Gargoyles in Manhattan ." There is a different tour each month, March-December

Prices: Public tours: $10. Private tours: $25/hour, groups of four or more; $15/hour, groups of three or fewer. **Features:** Over 25 private tours available (prices vary).

New York Talks and Walks (888) 377-4455 www.newyorktalksandwalks.com Dr. Philip Schoenberg offers a multitude of seasonal, ethnic and historical tours, including the "Hidden Treasures of Chinatown," the "Jewish Gangster Tour" and the "Multiethnic Heritage Tour of the East Village."

Prices: Most tours, $12–$15. **Features:** Lectures and child-friendly tours available.

92nd Street Y Tours (212) 996-1100. There are hundreds of walks to choose from here, covering aspects of the city from arts and architecture to history and more.

Prices: $20–$25. **Schedule:** Weekends, times vary. **Features:** The Y also offers bus tours and international travel.

NYC Discovery Tours (212) 465-3331. NYC Discovery offers over 60 different tours, most emphasizing the city's history. The group covers major attractions as well as lesser known, but equally important sites in the city. Special themes include "Historic Taverns," "Art History New York," "The Civil War" and "John Lennon's New York."

Prices: $10–$12. **Schedule:** Year-round; tours last 2 hours, days and starting times vary. **Features:** Private tours available by appointment.

Radical Walking Tours (718) 492-0069 www.he.net/~radtours/ These tours are led by historian Bruce Kayton. Walks explore significant sites in New York's history of political activism, with special attention to topics like civil rights and gay and lesbian rights. Kayton also offers special private group tours focusing on these topics and others like labor, black history and women's history.

Prices: $10; children 12 and under free. Private group tours, $150. Cash only. **Schedule:** Tours Sat.–Sun., Mar.-Dec.; office open 24 hours.

Savory Sojourns (212) 691-7314. These tours can be expensive, but for your money you get a five- to six-hour eating tour of one of the city's neighborhoods, complete with cooking demonstrations, kitchen tours, food, beer and wine.

Prices: Vary according to neighborhood, from $100 for Little Italy and the Lower East Side to $250 for Union Square. $50 deposit is required at time of reservation. **Schedule:** By reservation only. **Features:** Customized tours available.

Urban Explorations (718) 721-5254. Patricia Olmstead's operation covers many neighborhoods and themes, including trips through gay and lesbian Greenwich Village and tours of private artists' lofts.

Prices: $12, adults; $10, students and seniors; $5, children. Discounts for repeat customers. **Features:** Coach, limo, and group tours available.

Wildman Steve Brill's Food and Ecology Tours (718) 291-6825. Steve Brill, once arrested for eating dandelions in Central Park, now offers four-hour tours of city parks teaching identification and applications of a wide variety of wild plants. Walkers are encouraged to bring bags and containers to carry home wild herbs, mushrooms, and berries.

Prices: $10, adults, $5, children (suggested donation). Checks accepted. **Schedule:** Mar.-Dec. **Features:** School programs, birthday parties, private tours and lectures available.

Bus Tours

As Scene on TV Tours (212) 410-9830. This tour shuttles visitors to sites used as exterior settings for a number of TV shows. All tours depart from the Times Square Visitors Center on Broadway (between 46th and 47thSts.)

Prices: $15, adults; $8, children 6–12. **Schedule:** Sat.–Sun., 10 A.M., 12 noon, 2 P.M., and 4 P.M.

Gray Line (212) 397-2600. Hop-on, hop-off tours of Manhattan, the boroughs, and beyond. "Total New York" tour includes two-day bus ticket and free admission to the Statue of Liberty, plus the World Trade Center and Empire State Building observation decks.

Prices: $22–$112 (for bus plus helicopter tour). Packages outside New York are more expensive.

Hassidic Tours (718) 953-5244. This group "hopes to educate, inspire, and familiarize people with the ideals of Hassidic Jewry," as seen in the Crown Heights area. Bus tours leave from Midtown every Sunday, and women are advised to dress "modestly" in keeping with the community's standards.

Kramer's Reality Tour (800) KRAMERS www.kennykramer.com Kenny Kramer, the real-life inspiration for the Kramer character on TV's "Seinfeld," hosts these three-hour "multi-media" tours of the Seinfeld universe. See locations like the "Soup Nazi" shop, Joe's Produce Store, and Monk's Restaurant, and feast on the "Real Kramer's Original Famous Pizza."

Prices: $37.50, reservations required. **Schedule:** Sat.–Sun., 12:00–3:00 P.M.

Cruises

Circle Line (212) 563-3200 www.circleline.com Tours leave from Pier 83 at the west end of 42nd St. and Pier 16 at the South Street Seaport. The three-hour "Full Island" cruise draws the most people here, but be warned: complete circumnavigation of Manhattan may be a novel idea, but you'll see just as many major sights on the shorter cruises. Stick with the 1-hour "Liberty Cruise," the Beast speedboat ride or perhaps one of the themed trips. Arrive 45 minutes before departure time.

Prices: $15–$22, adults; $16–19, seniors; $10–$12, children. **Schedule:** Cruises 7 days, times vary. Closed Tues.–Wed. in Jan. and Feb., Dec. 24–25, or Jan. 1. **Services:** Group tours; snack bar on all cruises.

New York Waterways (800) 533-3779 www.nywaterway.com Tours depart from Pier 78 at the west end of 38th St. and Pier 17 at the South Street Seaport. This is the Circle Line's biggest competitor, offering a similar variety of cruises on their new, clean boats. Besides the standard harbor cruises, they also run special baseball cruises to Yankees and Mets games and a number of cruises to scenic destinations up the Hudson.

Prices: Harbor Cruises: $11–$18, adults; $6–$9, children. Other cruises: $10–$60, adults; $5–$60, children. **Schedule:** Cruises 7 days, times vary. No Harbor Cruises Mon.–Wed. from Jan. to mid-March., Dec. 24–25, or Jan. 1.

Express Navigation Cruises (800) 262-8743. These 75-minute harbor tours depart twice daily, Monday through Saturday.

Prices: $15, adults; $13, seniors; $8, children under 12; children under five, free. **Schedule:** Mon.–Sat., 12 P.M., 2 P.M.

Seaport Liberty Cruises (212) 630-8888. Jazz and dance cruises depart from Pier 16 at the South Street Seaport every evening.

Prices: $15–$25. **Schedule:** 6:30 P.M., 9:30 P.M.

Spirit Cruises (201) 867-8307. Another catch-all cruise operator, offering a variety of packages that take in the major sites of New York's harbor and rivers. Tours depart from Chelsea Piers on the Hudson at West 23rd Street.

Prices: $30–$70, depending on day and time of cruise. **Schedule:** Lunch cruises, Mon.–Sun., 11:30 A.M.–2 P.M.; dinner cruises, Mon.–Thur., 7 P.M.–10:30 P.M., Fri.–Sat. 8 P.M.–11:30 P.M., Sun. 6:30 P.M.–10 P.M.

Helicopter Tours
These are expensive and brief tours, but they do offer a unique perspective on the city. Trips tend to range from 5 to 20 minutes and take in most of the major sights, from the Statue of Liberty, to the World Trade Center, to Central Park.

Island Helicopter Sightseeing (212) 564-9290
Price: $44–$129. **Schedule:** Mon.–Fri. 9 A.M.–9 P.M., weather permitting. Closed Christmas. **Features:** Multilingual staff, night flights available.

Liberty Helicopter Tours (212) 967-6464 www.libertyhelicopters.com
Prices: $46–$159. **Features:** Same-day reservations available at (212) 967-4550.

Other Transportation
(See also *Sports & Recreation* for biking)

Carriage Rides These rides, which depart from Central Park South, are a romantic idea, but the reality—high prices, itchy blankets and the smell of manure—is rarely so perfect. Still, for some, this is an essential New York experience. Buggy rides are available year round, with fewer carriages operating in very cold and very hot weather.

Prices: $34, 25-minute ride; $54, 45-minute ride; $10 each additional 15 minutes.

Central Park Bicycle Tour (212) 541-8759. These guided tours hit major park locations like Belvedere Castle, Jacqueline Kennedy Onassis Reservoir, and Strawberry Fields. Prices include bicycle rental.

Prices: $30, adults, $20, children. **Schedule:** Tours depart every day at 10 A.M., 1 P.M. and 4 P.M.

Crypt Keeper Tours (888) EXHUMED www.cryptkeepertours.com Visit sites of famous people's deaths (including John Lennon, Sid Vicious, Jackie Onassis, Andy Warhol and Typhoid Mary) in a vintage hearse.

Price: $45, reservations required. **Schedule:** Mon.–Thurs., 7–10 P.M.

NEW YORK CITY SEASONAL EVENTS

Winter

The Nutcracker New York State Theater at Lincoln Center (212) 870-5570. The New York City Ballet performs this famous work each year with students from the School of American Ballet. It's a special treat for the kids.

November-December *www.nycballet.com*

Christmas Spectacular Radio City Music Hall, 1260 Sixth Ave. (at 50th St.) (212) 247-4777. The Radio City Christmas Spectacular features the famed Rockettes in Santa hats kicking alongside larger-than-life Nutcracker soldiers.

November-early January *www.radiocity.com*

Christmas Window Displays Along Fifth Avenue in Midtown marvel at the tiny winter scenes in department store windows. (Lord & Taylor and Saks Fifth Ave. are the most popular). Check out the Cartier building wrapped for Christmas in an enormous red bow and the doormen at FAO Schwarz dressed as wooden soldiers.

December

Christmas Tree Lighting Ceremony Rockefeller Center, Fifth Ave. (between 49th and 50th Sts.) (212) 632-3975. One of the tallest Christmas trees in the country is mounted in Rockefeller Center where it is strung with five miles of lights and lit by the mayor in a ceremony that includes an ice-skating show and other entertainment.

Early December

Lighting of the Hanukkah Menorah Grand Army Plaza, 59th St. and Fifth Ave. (718) 778-6000. Just a few blocks from one of the country's largest Christmas trees in Rockefeller Center is a 32-foot-tall Menorah, reportedly the world's largest. An electric candle is lit for each day of Hanukkah.

December

Kwanza Holiday Expo Jacob K. Javits Convention Center, 655 W. 34th St. (at 11th Ave.) (212) 216-2000. To celebrate this African-American holiday 300 vendors from around the country gather at the convention center to sell crafts, jewelry and food. There is dancing and musical entertainment, as well as storytelling in the youth pavilion. It's a multicultural celebration that is open to all.

Third weekend in December

Messiah Sing-In Avery Fisher Hall, Lincoln Center (212) 333-5333. The National Chorale Counsel organizes this sing-a-long of Handel's "Messiah" led by 20 conductors with an audience of up to 3,000 including four trained soloists to rescue the arias. No experience is necessary and lyrics sheets are provided. Everyone from amateurs to professionals to entire high school choirs participate.

Mid-late December *www.lincolncenter.org*

New Year's Eve Ball Drop Times Square (212) 768-1560. It's not the New Year until the ball drops over Times Square. The new and improved ball is now adorned with a stunning 12,000 rhinestones and 180 75-watt bulbs. The ball drop is televised all over the world, but if you want the folks back home to see you, arrive early. The area is packed with revelers hours before midnight.

New Year's Eve Fireworks Central Park. Spectators gather at Tavern on the Green and other spots throughout the park for views of the annual fireworks display. Festivities begin at 11:30 P.M.

New York National Boat Show Jacob K. Javits Convention Center, 655 W. 34th St. (at 11th Ave.) (212) 216-2000. 100,000 people show up each year to see 400 of the world's leading manufacturers show off 1,000 of the latest power-boats—from small craft to yachts—and marine accessories. Seminars on fishing and boating are also offered.

Nine days in early January

Winter Antiques Show Seventh Regiment Armory, Park Ave. (at 67th St.) (718) 292-7392. The city's premier antiques fair—featuring collections ranging from ancient to Art Nouveau—is also a benefit for East Side House Settlement.

Mid-late January   *www.winterantiquesshow.comy*

Outsider Art Fair The Puck Building, 295 Lafayette St. (at Houston St.) (212) 777-5218. This three-day event draws an international crowd of dealers, collectors and art aficionados. Thirty-five dealers exhibit self-taught, visionary and art brut pieces to crowds in the thousands. It's a good place for celebrity sightings and the occasional star-studded seminar. Prices range from about $300 to $75,000.

Last Thursday of January

Chinese New Year Chinese Cultural Center, (212) 373-1800 Tourist Info, (212) 484-1222. Celebrate the year of the dragon in 2001 (or snake in 2002) in Chinatown on and around Mott Street. Five days of celebrating culminate in a lively and colorful procession of lions and dragons made from wood and silk that wind their way through the narrow and festively decorated streets. Fireworks were banned in 1997, which has taken some of the bang out of the festivities, but the colors, lights, dancing and food still make it quite an experience.

Begins first full moon after January 21

Valentine's Day Marriage Marathon Empire State Building, 350 Fifth Ave. (at 34th St.) (212) 736-3100, ext. 377. Fifteen couples marry atop the Empire State Building in back-to-back 15-minute ceremonies every Valentine's Day. Couples vie for the honor each year. The deadline for entry is December 31 and each couple is limited to 10 guests who then gather in the Sky Lobby on the 80th floor for champagne and photographs.

February 14   *www.esbnyc.com*

Westminster Kennel Club Dog Show Madison Square Garden, Seventh Ave. (at 33rd St.) The nation's oldest and second largest animal event after the Kentucky Derby features 3,000 dogs that are pared down to seven finalists and eventually a single winner. About 30,000 spectators show up for the two-day event.

Mid-February   *www.westminsterkennelclub.org*

The Art Show Seventh Regiment Armory, Park Ave. (at 67th St.)
(212) 766-9200. Sponsored by the Art Dealers Association of America, this is
New York's foremost art fair. Seventy of the nation's leading galleries gather to
exhibit works that span five centuries from 17th-century masters to contemporary artists in a range of media that includes painting, drawing, print, sculpture,
photography and video. Proceeds benefit the Henry Street Settlement, a long-
standing social service agency in the Lower East Side.

Mid-late February   *www.artdealers.org*

Empire State Building Run-Up 350 Fifth Ave. (at 34th St.) (212) 860-4455.
On a Wednesday in February 150 runners race up the 1,576 steps of the Empire
State Building from the lobby to the observation deck on the 86th floor, all
vying for the record-breaking time. The current time to beat is 10:49 for the
men and 12:19 for the women. Afterward the runners and their families gather
on the 80th floor for an awards ceremony and refreshments.

Late February   *www.esbnyc.com*

Manhattan Antiques and Collectibles Triple Pier Expo 12th Ave.
(between 48th and 51st Sts.) (212) 255-0020. 900 dealers take over Piers 88, 90
and 92 along the Hudson River to sell everything from posters, toys, textiles,
fashions and furniture to silver, porcelain, fine china, paintings, jewelry and
glassware. The prices range anywhere from $2–$75,000.

Last two weekends of February, and Mid-November   *www.antiqnet.com/stella*

Spring

International Cat Show Madison Square Garden, Seventh Ave. (at 33rd
St.) (212) 465-6741. The International Cat Show draws 35,000 people to the
Garden where they can watch as 800 felines covering 40 breeds compete for
the Best of Show award with all the composure for which cats are famous.
Afterwards you can shop for cat accessories at the cat supermarket or listen
to cat-related lectures with topics like cat acupuncture, massage and feline
aerobics.

March

St. Patrick's Day Parade Fifth Ave. (44th-86th St.) (212) 484-1222. In one
of the city's oldest annual events, over 150,000 Irish Americans and other revelers draped in green join the festivities along Fifth Avenue from 44th Street to
86th Street (starting at 11 A.M.) and fill bars throughout the city well into the
night. You can find green beer, green bagels and virtually everything in the
shape of shamrock as New York City goes Hibernian for a day. For best views of
the parade you have to line up early.

March 17

International Asian Art Fair Seventh Regiment Armory, Park Ave. (at 67th
St.) (212) 642-8572. Top dealers from around the world gather at the Armory
to sell art from South East Asia and the Middle and Far East. The art, sculpture,

ceramics and textiles typify the talent and skills of Eastern Artists over the centuries. Fourteen thousand people come to browse and buy items that range anywhere from $200 to hundreds of thousands of dollars.

Late March   *www.haughton.com*

New Directors/New Films Museum of Modern Art, 11 W. 53rd St. (between Fifth and Sixth Aves.) (212) 875-5610. This film festival, sponsored by the Museum of Modern Art and the Film Society of Lincoln Center, features works by emerging, overlooked and new directors. Such notables as Wim Wenders, Spike Lee and Steven Spielberg have screened films in past years.

Late March-early April   *www.filmlinc.com*

Ringling Bros. and Barnum & Bailey Circus Madison Square Garden, Seventh Avenue (at 33rd Street) (212) 465-6741. Kicking off its New York run each spring the circus's lions, tigers and bears (and elephants) parade along 34th Street to Madison Square Garden at midnight on the night before the first performance. The spectacular procession of animals is a great way to get a free peek at "The Greatest Show on Earth."

Late March-early May   *www.ringling.com*

Whitney Biennial Whitney Museum of American Art, 945 Madison Ave. (at 75th St.) (212) 570-3600. Every two years since 1932, the Whitney has presented an exhibition of what it regards as the most influential contemporary American art, often highlighting works by innovative and vanguard artists.

Late March-early June   *www.whitney.org*

Easter Parade Fifth Avenue (44th-57th Sts.) (212) 484-1222. One of the older New York traditions that dates back to the Civil War era, the Easter Parade draws crowds of bonneted spectators sporting everything from the classic bowler to the more extravagant flowering bonnets. The best perch is the platform at St. Patrick's Cathedral, if you can get near it.

Easter Sunday

New York International Auto Show Jacob K. Javits Convention Center, 655 W. 34th St. (at 11th Ave.) (800) 282-3336. North America's first and largest auto show features hundreds of the newest cars, trucks and SUVs as well as classics from automotive history. In 2000 the show celebrated its 100th anniversary.

Mid April   *www.autoshowny.com*

New York Antiquarian Book Fair Seventh Regiment Armory, Park Ave. (at 67th St.) (212) 777-5218. 180 international book dealers offer rare books, manuscripts, autographs, fine bindings, maps, modern firsts, illustrated books, children's books and more. Prices range from $25–$25,000.

Mid April

Macy's Flower Show 34th St. (at Broadway) (212) 494-2922. Celebrate the arrival of spring when Macy's department store turns into a botanical paradise with over 30,000 varieties of flowers, plants and trees from around the world. And if you're too rushed to go inside, walk on by and glimpse the floral window displays along Broadway.

Last two weeks of April

The Cherry Blossom Festival Brooklyn Botanic Garden (718) 622-4433. To celebrate the blooming of the Garden's 200 cherry trees in 40 varieties, this festival features classical Japanese dance performances accompanied by bamboo flutes and taiko drums. There is storytelling as well as lessons in calligraphy, flower arranging, oriental brush painting, block painting and origami.

Late April or Early May   *www.bbg.org*

You Gotta Have Park Parks throughout the five boroughs (212) 360-3456. Look for free activities and events in city parks throughout May during the Parks Department's kickoff to summer. Check the Department's web site for details.

May   *www.ci.nyc.ny.us/html/dpr*

Bike New York: The Great Five Boro Bike Tour (212) 932-BIKE. America's largest bicycling event includes 30,000 riders who traverse 42 miles (68k) and five boroughs. The tour starts in Battery Park with a sendoff by the Mayor and ends with a ride across the Verrazano-Narrows Bridge to Staten Island. A post-ride festival and picnic given by sponsors features food, concessions and activities.

Early May

Lower East Side Festival of the Arts Theater for the New City, 155 First Ave. (at 10th St.) (212) 245-1109. This annual festival featuring more than 20 theatrical troupes and local notables celebrates the culture of the Lower East Side, where such iconoclasts as Allen Ginsberg and Andy Warhol drew inspiration.

First weekend of May

Ninth Avenue International Food Festival Ninth Ave. (37th-57th Sts.) (212) 581-7029. Hundreds of stalls are set up along Ninth Avenue for two days to serve every type of ethic food you can imagine—from Thai to Italian. Musicians and vendors hawking plants, crafts and T-shirts join in the festivities while over a million people sample the gamut of New York's ethnic cuisines.

Mid-May

Bird Watching in Central Park Central Park (212) 427-4040. With 275 species sighted at last count, Central Park is one of the 14 best bird watching places in North America. From parrots to bald eagles to the red-tailed hawks that nest along Fifth Avenue, all manner of birds show up for springtime in the park. Many of the more exotic species arrive en route from the Southern States, Mexico and even the tropical rain forests.

May-June

Fleet Week Sea, Air and Space Museum, U.S.S *Intrepid* (46th St. at 12th Ave.) (212) 245-0072. Fifteen to 20 battleships, aircraft carriers and other ships from the U.S. Navy and Coast Guard as well as foreign fleets sail up the Hudson, past the Statue of Liberty, and dock at Pier 86 where 10,000 uniformed personnel disembark and make room for curious New Yorkers to go on for free. During the week there are also parachute drops and air displays that are sure to impress the kids.

Late May

Washington Square Outdoor Art Exhibition Washington Square Park (212) 982-6255. For nearly 70 years, the 20 blocks in and around the park are transformed into an arts and crafts fairground on Memorial Day and continuing for the three following weekends. Around 600 exhibitors participate each day of the fair from noon until sundown.

Memorial Day (and the three following weekends)

Summer

Metropolitan Opera Parks Concerts Various locations (212) 362-6000. Each year the Met presents free performances of two operas in Central Park and other locations throughout the city. Bring a picnic and grab a patch of grass early if you want to get a good view.

June

Bryant Park Free Summer Season Sixth Ave. (at 42nd St.) (212) 922-9393. Lunchtime concerts and performances are a favorite of midtown workers throughout the summer. The free classic movies under the stars on Monday evenings are a New York City summertime must. Bring a blanket and a picnic and be sure to arrive early for some prime lawn space.

June-August

Celebrate Brooklyn! Performing Arts Festival Prospect Park Bandshell, 9th St. (at Prospect Park West), Park Slope (718) 855-7882. Around 25 free outdoor performances in music, dance, film and theater are offered for nine weeks in this Prospect Park venue. The city's longest-running free performing arts festival attracts top-notch acts from around the country and the world. Check the web site for a schedule of events.

June-August   *www.bkny.net/celebrate*

Central Park SummerStage Rumsey Playfield, Central Park (at 72nd St.) (212) 360-2777. Since its founding in 1986, SummerStage has presented over 500 free weekend afternoon concerts and performances for over 5 million people. Everyone from the latest pop stars to up-and-coming artists have graced the stage. Occasional benefit shows charge admission to help fund the program.

June-August   *www.summerstage.com*

Hudson River Festival World Financial Center, West St. (at Vesey St.) (212) 945-0505. The World Financial Center's Winter Garden presents free outdoor performances as the sun sets over the Hudson as well as indoor arts events.

June-August   *www.worldfinancialcenter.com*

New York Shakespeare Festival Delacorte Theater, Central Park (at 81st St.) (212) 539-8750, (212) 539-8500. Sponsored by the Joseph Papp Public Theater, this is the quintessential summer activity in New York. Celebrity performers often join the cast for free outdoor performances of two plays each summer—one by Shakespeare and one by another famous dramatist. Available at the Public Theater and the Delacorte Theater, tickets can be difficult to come by when the cast is particularly star-studded.

June-August

Puerto Rican Day Parade Fifth Avenue (44th-86th St.) (212) 484-1222, (718) 401-0404. With lively music and an enthusiastic crowd, this is one of New York's most festive parades.

First Sunday in June

New York Jazz Festival Various locations (212) 343-8805. Taking the name of its corporate sponsor each year, this festival presents hundreds of acts running the gamut of jazz styles from classic to avant-garde. The two-week series run by the Knitting Factory occupies 10 of the city's smaller venues as an alternative to the more mainstream JVC Jazz Festival.

Early June   *www.jazfest.com*

Toyota Comedy Festival Various locations (800) 331-4331. Thirty venues throughout the city host over a hundred acts.

Early-mid June

Museum Mile Festival Various locations (212) 606-2296. For one day a year you can get into nine of New York's major museums for free. Coupled with the street entertainment along Fifth Avenue (82nd-104th St.) it's quite a bargain.

Second Tuesday in June

JVC Jazz Festival Various locations (212) 501-1390. From small clubs to Carnegie Hall and Lincoln Center, jazz takes over most of the city's major music venues for about two weeks each year. World-class jazz musicians as well as lesser-known artists take to New York's stages for performances and jam sessions.

Mid-late June   *www.festivalproductions.net/jvc/ny*

Mermaid Parade Boardwalk at Coney Island (W. 10th-16th St.) (718) 372-5159. To kick off summer and the official opening of the Atlantic Ocean, hundreds of mermaids, as well as mermen, merchildren and other sea creatures march down the boardwalk in a colorful display. Elaborate floats and outlandish costumes make this one of the most unique parades the city has to offer.

Saturday after summer solstice   *www.coneyisland.brooklyn.ny.us*

Gay and Lesbian Pride Parade Fifth Ave. (Columbus Circle-Christopher St.) (212) 807-7433. To commemorate the 1969 Stonewall riots, thousand take to the streets to celebrate the birth of the gay liberation movement in the world's largest gay pride parade. A week of events surrounds the parade with an outdoor dance party at the West Side Piers, a film festival, club events throughout the city and many other activities.

Late June

Restaurant Week A prix-fixe lunch at over 100 of the city's top restaurants is only $20 for a week in June. For a list of participating restaurants send a self-addressed stamped envelope to NYCVB, 810 Seventh Avenue, New York, NY 10019 or check local papers.

Late June   *www.restaurantweek.com*

Midsummer Night Swing Lincoln Center Plaza (212) 875-5766. Nothing can quite compare to dancing under the stars with Lincoln Center's famed fountain as a backdrop while top dance bands play everything from swing to salsa. Dance lessons, which are included in the price of admission, begin at 6:30 P.M. and the featured band goes on at 8:15 P.M. (Tues.–Sat.).

Late June-late July

Lincoln Center Festival Lincoln Center (212) 875-5928. This relatively new program, begun in 1996, showcases dance, theater, music, opera in and around Lincoln Center's several venues, with performances by the Center's regular companies and other artists from around the world. Tickets to special symposia about and inspired by the festival's performances are also available.

July   *www.lincolncenter.org/festival*

Summergarden Museum of Modern Art, 11 W. 53rd St. (between Fifth and Sixth Aves.) (212) 708-9491. This free concert series in the museum's sculpture garden features classical performances by graduate students and alumni of the Jiulliard School of Music. Concerts are held for nine weekends at 8:30 P.M.

July-August   *www.moma.org/programs/summergarden*

Macy's Fireworks Display East River, (212) 494-4495. The FDR Drive is closed to traffic for a few hours so pedestrians can get a better look at the 30-minute display launched from two points on the East River. The fireworks start at around 9 P.M.

July 4

New York Philharmonic Concerts in the Parks Various locations (212) 875-5656. For 10 days the Philharmonic presents evening concerts in parks throughout the city.

Late July-early August

Mostly Mozart Avery Fisher Hall, Lincoln Center (212) 875-5030. The Mostly Mozart Festival Orchestra—accompanied by world-class soloists and other guest performers—presents around 30 concerts in four-week period every summer.

Late July-late August

Lincoln Center Out-of-Doors Lincoln Center (212) 875-5108. Everything from classical music to dancing to children's puppet shows can be found at this popular festival on the plazas of Lincoln Center.

August   *www.lincolncenter.org/outofdoors*

Harlem Week Throughout Harlem (212) 862-8477. The Taste of Harlem food festival, the Black Film Festival and a lively street fair along Fifth Avenue (125th-135th St.) are highlights of the largest Black and Latino festival in the world. Look for museum open houses, block parties, outdoor concerts and special events at area jazz clubs during this festival which last two to three weeks.

Starts early August

Hong Kong Dragon Boat Festival The Lake at Flushing Meadows-Corona Park, Queens (718) 539-8974. Local teams race these traditional 39-foot boats decorated like Chinese dragons in a spectacular display.

Mid August   *www.hkdbf-ny.org*

Greenwich Village Jazz Festival Throughout Greenwich Village (212) 929-5149. Most of the Village's jazz venues participate in 10 days of performances topped off by a free concert in Washington Square Park.

Late August

Wigstock Pier 54 (12th-13th St.) (800) 494-8497. With up to 10,000 bewigged spectators and around 60 performers, this drag festival may be the city's most colorful. The festival benefits the Gay Men's Health Crisis.

Labor Day weekend   *www.wigstock.nu*

West Indian Day Carnival Eastern Parkway (Utica Ave.-Grand Army Plaza), Brooklyn (212) 484-1222, (718) 625-1515. A crowd of nearly 2 million revelers turns out to celebrate Carribbean culture in New York's biggest and most energetic parade. The parade of extravagant costumes and colorful floats caps a weekend of festivities beginning Friday evening with reggae, salsa and calypso at the Brooklyn Museum.

Labor Day

Autumn

Broadway on Broadway 43rd and Broadway (212) 768-1560. For a couple of hours each year Broadway is accessible to everyone. On a stage erected in the middle of Times Square, a free concert of highlights from the season's biggest shows gives a taste of what Broadway has to offer.

Mid September

Brooklyn BeerFest Brooklyn Brewery, 79 N. 11th St. (between Berry and Wythe Sts.) (718) 486-7422. This outdoor festival in Williamsburg offers food, music and, of course, a whole lot of beer. Each year nearly 100 brews from around the world are there for the tasting to mark the first day of Oktoberfest.

Mid September   *www.craftbrewers.com*

Downtown Arts Festival Various locations (212) 243-5050. What better place for an arts festival than SoHo? Art lovers come from far and wide for three days of exhibitions, performances and lectures at dozens of SoHo locations.

Mid September

Atlantic Antic Atlantic Ave. (Flatbush Ave.-East River) (718) 875-8993. With music, food, arts and crafts, a children's circus and over 450 vendors the Antic is one of Brooklyn's largest street fairs drawing crowds of nearly 1 million each year.

Last Sunday in September   *www.atlanticave.org*

Columbus Day Parade Fifth Ave. (44th-86th St.) (212) 484-1222. Columbus may have landed far from New York on a Spanish ship, but he was born in Italy. That's enough for the city's Italian-Americans who are front and center for this parade up Fifth Avenue.

Columbus Day, second Monday in October

Big Apple Circus Damrosch Park, Lincoln Center (212) 268-2500, (800) 922-3772. With its local roots, intimate one-ring big top and kid-friendly mission, the Big Apple Circus has staked out its own ground between the glitz of the Ringling Brothers circus and the adults-only artistry of the Cirque du Soleil.

November-January   *www.bigapplecircus.org*

Feast of San Gennaro Mulberry St. (Houston-Worth St.) (212) 764-6330. Since 1926 Little Italy's main drag, Mulberry Street, is transformed into a fairground for 11 days in September. Three million people turn out each year for food and fun at this festival honoring the patron saint of Naples.

Third week of September   *www.nyclittleitaly.com*

New York Film Festival Alice Tully Hall, Lincoln Center (212) 875-5610. Approximately 20 independent, foreign and big studio films are screened in a two-week run at Lincoln Center's Alice Tully Hall. Held annually since 1965, the festival has premiered films by directors such as Martin Scorsese, Jean-Luc Godard and Robert Altman.

Late September-early October   *www.filmlinc.com/nyff*

Next Wave Festival Brooklyn Academy of Music, (718) 636-4100. BAM showcases experimental works by both established and lesser-known contemporary artists from around the world in music, theater and dance.

October-December   *www.bam.org*

Halloween Parade Sixth Ave. (Spring-23rd St.) (212) 475-3333, ext. 4044. Over 25,000 participants take to the streets of Greenwich Village for the most famous Halloween parade in the country. Join the crowd of elaborately costumed revelers or have nearly as much fun watching from the sidelines.

October 31   *www.halloween-nyc.com*

New York City Marathon Starts Staten Island side of the Verrazano-Narrows Bridge (212) 860-4455. The 26.2-mile race finishes at Tavern on the Green in

Central Park at West 67th Street as a crowd cheers on the 35,000 participants each year. Spectators line the streets handing out drinks all along the course which hits each of the five boroughs.

Last Sunday in October or first Sunday in November *www.nycmarathon.org*

Macy's Parade Central Park West (at 77th St.) to Macy's (Broadway and 34th St.) (212) 494-4495. From 9 A.M to 12 P.M. on Thanksgiving a procession of floats and huge cartoon character balloons marches to Macy's in this children's favorite. Catch the inflating of the balloons the night before at Central Park West and 79th Street (6–11 P.M.).

Thanksgiving Day *www.macyparade.com*

For the latest information on restaurants, hotels, concerts, nightlife, sporting events and more, check online at New York Today, the *New York Times* website devoted entirely to life in New York City: www.nytoday.com.

MANHATTAN NEIGHBORHOODS
World Trade Center and Battery Park

The twin towers of the **World Trade Center** have become an icon of New York City—at least to out-of-towners. But to the millions of New Yorkers (and New Jerseyites) who work there or pass through the place every year, the trade center is simply a really big office building. Which is to say, not terribly interesting.

Okay, not every big office building has so many subway stations. Or sits on top of a mall you might find in Milwaukee. Or has a huge, windswept plaza which, despite a recent refurbishment, remains about as inviting as a polar icecap.

But the area does have its definite attractions, and tourists are more clued in than New Yorkers to a big one: the views from the top of 2 WTC. They really are spectacular when the weather cooperates. Unfortunately, there always seems to be people thronging the upper level of the lobby, waiting to take the elevators up to the top, which may explain why more New Yorkers don't make the trip. They are notorious for their reluctance to stand, as they say, "on line." The views are just as grand from **Windows on the World** or **Wild Blue** at the top of No. 1, but you have to shell out for the food.

To rub elbows with the natives, cross Church Street to **Century 21,** the discount department store. Around lunch time, it is packed with New Yorkers buying everything from black socks in bulk to Italian outfits in silk. Or, on Thursdays (and Tuesdays, June through December), stroll through the farmers' market on the eastern side of the Trade Center.

Or cross the bridge over the West Side Highway to the **World Financial Center.** At first glance, this might seem even less "New York" than the Trade Center; palm trees indoors do not immediately spring to mind as appropriate symbols for the Big Apple. Originally dismissed by some city dwellers as "Dallas without the parking," the WFC remains very, well, shiny. But it has clearly begun to grow on people. There is a changing array of shops and restaurants, and that rarest of New York amenities, clean public bathrooms.

The big attraction is the outdoor **esplanade,** a long walkway along the river, backed by immaculately maintained flower beds. Even on cold days, there are runners panting down the paths; on nice days, every available seat is taken before, during and after lunch. Shoals of strollers appear; young families have flocked to **Battery Park City,** south of the WFC. You may see sailboats and kayaks in the river, and the only panhandlers are gray squirrels.

In the evenings, the sunsets over New Jersey are fabulous; young stock brokers fill the bars, slapping each others' backs and snapping each others' suspenders. On the weekends, in-line skaters compete with bikers and dog-walkers for space on the lower pathway (the upper one is reserved for pedestrians).

If you are walking with children, head north along the river; there's a wonderful playground, and a sculpture garden kids find entrancing. Head south for a heart-stopping view of the **Statue of Liberty,** the entrance to the **Museum of Jewish**

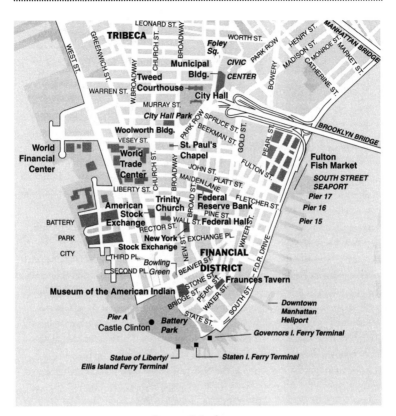

Lower Manhattan

Heritage, and the lush **Wagner gardens.** You can even walk all the way around the tip of the Battery and ride the **Staten Island Ferry**—it's free.

—*Leslie Eaton*

HIGHLIGHTS OF THE NEIGHBORHOOD

Battery Park Battery Place (212) 732-0756. Need a reminder that Manhattan is an island? Try windswept Battery Park. Wedged between skyscrapers and New York Harbor, the park reminds visitors that the city's history is based on commerce and seafaring. Built entirely on landfill, the park is filled with historic landmarks, including **Castle Clinton,** (212) 344-7220, designed in 1811 as a fort to protect against British invasion, and later converted into an opera house, an immigration center and the New York Aquarium. It's now the ticket center for boat trips to Ellis Island and the Statue of Liberty. The park is a popular weekend spot for tourists and locals alike.

Bowling Green Broadway and Whitehall Sts. Bowling Green, a small triangle at the foot of Broadway, was Manhattan's first park—no small claim to fame in a city with more than 1,500 parks. It was once used as a cattle market and later as a bowling lawn. A statue of King George III stood in the park until 1776, when it was destroyed as a symbol of oppressive British rule. The statue's remains were then melted down and turned into ammunition, but some pieces remain in historic collections. At the south end is the elegant **U.S. Customs House,** which houses the **National Museum of the American Indian.** A farmers' market operates here daily.

Ellis Island Information: (212) 363-3200 Ferry schedule: 269-5755 www.nps.gov/stli Even if you do not trace your roots to an ancestor who arrived in the United States through Ellis Island—and these days, fewer than 40 percent of Americans do—you may well feel a kinship with the 12 million anxious immigrants who shuffled through the echoing halls of this red-brick way station between 1892 and 1954 on their way to a new life in a new land. All through the impressively restored building, there are bigger-than-life sepia photos of the evocative faces that passed through Ellis Island to become symbols of the American experience. Among them: a young boy in a jauntily angled embroidered cap, his lips pursed as if he is trying to suppress a grin of pure exultation. Two Dutch brothers, each with a processing number pinned to his shirt and each with a determined gaze already directed far beyond New York harbor. A pair of dignified young black women coming from Guadeloupe in 1911, both in ankle length lace-trimmed dresses and tiny hats shaped like a handful of rose petals.

The main processing center is the only part of the original compound that is open to the public. Displays on its three floors use film, photos, turn-of-the-century posters and the voices of reminiscing immigrants to show a broader story of immigration. You discover where people of various national origins live in the United States today. You hear immigrants tell their stories of adjustment, discrimination, poverty and success. You learn about the nativist movements that feared immigrants; a 1902 political cartoon shows them as the personification of "filth" and "disease." And you see how popular culture was enriched by immigrants—as in the old song, "Hello Wisconsin, Won't You Find My Yonnie Yonson?"

Renovations of the long abandoned site, completed in 1992, recreated the processing center as it looked in the first decades of the 20th century, when each day saw up to 5,000 immigrants, fresh from a two-week ocean voyage in steerage, herded inside and inspected for disease, deformities and destitution. For first-class and second-class passengers, only their paperwork was processed at Ellis Island; the passengers themselves were inspected on their ships and dispatched directly to Manhattan.

A few rooms on the third floor give a taste of what the dormitories and detention cells were like. But, other than the thoughtful museum exhibits, there is little left in the second-floor Registry Room to recall the millions of human dramas that it witnessed. Unless, that is, you are lucky enough to have Charles A. Walker, National Park Service Ranger, as your guide for a free tour of the building. Mr. Walker, after giving a dramatic reading of Emma Lazarus's poem "The New Colossus" and acting out the imaginary interrogation of a timorous immigrant, will point out that one of your own grandparents might well have waited on the same hard wooden bench you are sitting on right now.

Although many visitors to Ellis Island expect to be able to search for information about their own immigrant backgrounds, the long-awaited Family History Center has not yet opened. The latest official projection is that sometime in 2001, you will be able to look up the immigration records of anyone who arrived by way of Ellis Island up to 1924. *—Susan Sachs*

Hours: 8:45 A.M.–5:45 P.M. daily, extended hours during summer (call for information). **Price:** Admission is free. Round trip ferry tickets: $7.00 adults, $3.00 children, $6.00 senior citizens.

Museum of Jewish Heritage—A Living Memorial to the Holocaust
18 First Pl., Battery Park City (at West St.) (212) 968-1800. Strongest on the social history of European Jews and Israel, this museum on the water's edge is dedicated to living history, and to recording and preserving the memories of Holocaust survivors, rescuers and witnesses. The roof design of its impressive granite structure forms a Star of David. Opened in 1997, it is a dignified reminder of New York's important place in Jewish history.

Price: $7, general; $5, students and seniors; children under 5, free.

National Museum of the American Indian
1 Bowling Green (between Whitehall and State Sts.) (212) 668-6624. The basis of the museum's permanent collection is the unsurpassed collection assembled by George Gustav Heye. Now located in the former U.S. Customs House, a spectacular domed Beaux-Arts landmark at the foot of Broadway, this branch of the Smithsonian Institution is the model for a new national museum, scheduled to open in 2002 on the Mall in Washington, D.C.

New York City Police Museum
25 Broadway (between Morris and State Sts.) (212) 301-4440. With interactive exhibits, computer simulations, vintage uniforms and antique badges, the New York City Police Museum presents a multifaceted view of the rigorous, clearly dangerous, at times political and often tedious life of a police officer. In one room, visitors pretend to be police officers and are suddenly confronted by a gunman who fires at them, on film, with the unfaltering aim of a desperate criminal. In another room, they watch as brainstorming police chiefs, speaking from multiple video monitors, grill a precinct commander about a rising burglary rate. Down the hall, at a mock crime scene, visitors examine the broken glass, forgotten crowbar and grimy carpet of an apartment where there has been a burglary to test their analytical skills against those of veteran detectives. And around the corner they pause at a wall of tributes to several of the 580 New York City officers who have died in the line of duty.

Shrine of St. Elizabeth Ann Seton
7 State St. (between Whitehall and Pearl Sts.) (212) 269-6865. This 1793 Federal-style building is dedicated to Elizabeth Ann Seton, the first American-born saint of the Catholic Church. Seton, who founded the American Sisters of Charity, the first order of nuns in the U.S., lived here from 1801 to 1803. The building is one of the few surviving mansions in lower Manhattan. The adjoining church was built at the same time.

Price: Free.

Staten Island Ferry SE end of Battery Park (212) 225-5368. Historically, there have been few better bargains in New York than a ride on the Staten Island Ferry. For many decades, it cost only a nickel. That changed in the mid-1970's, when the first of several fare increases took effect, inching the price up eventually to 50 cents for the round trip between Battery Park in Manhattan and St. George, Staten Island.

But these days a ferry ride is absolutely the best deal in town. It costs nothing, part of a new system of free mass-transit transfers.

The ferry is a lifeline to the city for many Staten Islanders; some 30,000 people ride it each midweek day. But it also provides as romantic a journey as the city can offer.

The ferry operates 24 hours a day—every 15 minutes during rush hours, every 30 minutes the rest of the day and evening, and once an hour at night. It is operated by the city's Department of Transportation.

To truly appreciate the grandeur of New York, ride the ferry at sunrise, starting with the 25-minute trip from Manhattan to Staten Island and then reversing the journey on the next boat back. At dawn, the first rays of the sun strike the glass towers of lower Manhattan. Off to the left, the Statue of Liberty's torch still burns bright in the vanishing darkness. How can anyone's heart not leap at the sight?

—*Clyde Haberman*

Statue of Liberty Information: (212) 363-3200 Ferry schedule: 269-5755 www.nps.gov/stli These days, nothing more inspiring than the baggage claim area at John F. Kennedy International Airport greets most visitors and immigrants to the United States. But a century ago, the exhilarating sight of the towering Statue of Liberty at the entrance to New York harbor signaled to shiploads of travelers, both the bedraggled and the bejeweled, that they had reached the shores of a new land.

Inspired by the colossal monuments of Egypt and an outsized 19th-century French fascination with American egalitarian ideals, the Statue of Liberty still has the power to take your breath away, just as it thrilled the 12 million immigrants who passed it on their way to Ellis Island in the first decades of the twentieth century.

Resolute and stern, the massive female figure, 151 feet high from her toes to the top of her torch of freedom, rests on a 150-foot-high pedestal at the tip of a tiny landscaped island in New York Bay. Gardens around the base, dotted with dozens of white wrought-iron chairs, offer a sumptuous view of the skyscrapers of Lower Manhattan.

The idea for a grand statue to celebrate friendship between France and the United States, originated in 1865 around the Parisian dinner table of Edouard de Laboulaye, a scholar of the American Constitution. (A great-grandson of de Laboulaye spearheaded fundraising in France for restoration of the statue 100 years after it opened). Alexis de Tocqueville, another admirer of American democracy, is said to have been a guest at the dinner. So was the sculptor who would design the statue, Frédéric-Auguste Bartholdi.

For many visitors, no trip to Liberty Island is complete without a 354-step

James Estrin/The New York Times

Statue of Liberty

climb up a narrow twisting staircase to the statue's crown, where glimpses of the New York and New Jersey coasts are visible on clear days through smallish Plexiglas windows. Because of overheated conditions in the stairwell, only passengers on the first morning ferries during the summer months are allowed in the crown.

But there is a better view from the skinny outdoor walkway around the base of the statue. It can be reached by an elevator, or up four flights of steps.

Inside the pedestal, an informative museum shows the evolution of

Bartholdi's vision of what the statue should look like, the engineering used to keep it stable in the tricky harbor winds, and the lasting impressions it made on generations of immigrants. Visitors also can gaze on a full-scale copper replica of one of Miss Liberty's feet, which sports toenails the size of truck tires. A delightful collection of old Statue of Liberty kitsch, as opposed to the new collection in the gift shop downstairs, concludes the exhibit, demonstrating the monument's enduring role as both icon and huckster.

—*Susan Sachs*

Hours: 8:45 A.M.–5:45 P.M. daily, extended hours during summer (call for information). **Price:** Admission is free. Round trip ferry tickets: $7.00 adults, $3.00 children, $6.00 senior citizens.

World Financial Center and Winter Garden 1 World Financial Center (between Albany and Liberty Sts.) (212) 945-0505. Built on landfill along the Hudson River, this commercial development includes shops, restaurants, gallery space, a yacht harbor and the glass-covered Winter Garden, which hosts concerts, dance performances and other cultural events . The complex of four office towers are interconnected and joined to the World Trade Center by a series of walkways and pedestrian bridges. The Winter Garden is a gigantic, glass-vaulted public space, complete with a monumental arced staircase and an arrangement of tall desert palm trees. Outside, a promenade circles the yacht harbor, and the proximity of the water reminds visitors and residents alike that they are indeed on an island.

Price: Free. **Subway:** 1, 9, N, R to Cortlandt St.

World Trade Center www.wtc-top.com They have survived a terrorist bombing and the disdain of many New Yorkers, who hardly ever rank the twin towers of the World Trade Center among favorite—and shorter—monuments to commerce like the Empire State Building, the Chrysler Building or the Woolworth Building. Too sleek. Too boxy. But there is something exhilarating about standing outdoors on the observation deck on the 102nd floor of 2 World Trade Center. Could it be the idea of looking *down* on the Statue of Liberty? The urge to reach out and touch passing airliners? The view of New Jersey? (Nah.) Perhaps it is the mere thought that there are two of these things— 1,350-feet-tall—that, for their stature, oddity, modernist appeal, whatever, have become a symbol of New York. They are after all the tallest buildings in New York City, never mind that there are taller in Chicago and Malaysia. Some 40,000 people work here daily and another 150,000 come for business and leisure, some to the 70-store shopping mall down below. Designed by Emory Roth & Sons and completed in 1973, the towers are owned by the Port Authority, which is headquartered there. Commercial office space fills the rest—except for the pricey, spectacular Windows on the World restaurant and two bars at the top of No. 1.

—*Randy Archibold*

Subway: N, R, 1, 9 to Cortlandt St.; A, C, E to Chambers St.; 4, 5 to Fulton St. **Bus:** 10 (Broadway) to West St.; 6 (Broadway) to Fulton St.; 15, 101, 103 to Park Row.

Lower Manhattan: World Trade Center,
Woolworth Building and City Hall Park

Highly Recommended Neighborhood Restaurants
(See "Restaurants" section for reviews)

American Park	☆	$ $ $	NEW AMERICAN
Hudson River Club	☆ ☆	$ $ $ $	NEW AMERICAN
Wild Blue	☆	$ $ $	NEW AMERICAN
Windows on the World	☆ ☆	$ $ $ $	NEW AMERICAN

Wall Street/Financial District

The Wall Street denizens of film and fiction—brash stockbrokers, icy investment bankers and hair-trigger traders—really do exist. But catching a glimpse of
them is hard, even when you are strolling on Wall Street itself.

That's partly because many of the big stock and bond firms have abandoned the traditional financial district and opened offices all over Manhattan.
Those that remain tend to keep odd hours. Most financial types like to be at
their desks at dawn. Some flee as soon as the stock market closes at 4 P.M.
Others work till all hours of the night and take private taxis home. If you are
out late enough, you can see the "black cars" lined up outside **Goldman Sachs**
(85 Broad Street). Almost everyone who works on Wall Street thinks he or
she is far too important to take a break for lunch, except when celebrating a
deal.

Still, there are a few good spots for Wall Street watching. Outside the **New
York Stock Exchange** building on both Wall and Broad Streets, you will see
men and the occasional woman (this is still a male-dominated business), wearing brightly colored jackets and smoking. These are the brokers and traders who
work on the floor of the exchange. To see them in action, go to 20 Broad Street
for a ticket to the visitors' gallery overlooking the trading floor (stop by early,
because all tickets are often gone by noon).

Some traders still swill martinis at **Harry's Hanover Square** (downstairs at 1
Hanover Square between Stone and Pearl Streets), though the younger crowd
seems to opt for the **Wall Street Kitchen and Bar** (70 Broad St.). And as long
as they can put the meal on an expense account, executives eat lunch at **Delmonico's** (56 Beaver Street between William and Broad).

The cliché that Wall Street guys love cigars turns out to be true; you can see
them buying 'em by the box at **Barclay Rex** (7 Maiden Lane) and **JR Cigars**
(corner of Wall and Pearl).

For a sense of what Wall Street used to be like before the days of skyscrapers,
take a stroll through the twisty little streets just north of Broad: Stone Street,
Mill Lane and South William Street, which intersects with William Street.

The **Museum of American Financial History** (28 Broadway), is more interesting than it may sound. Nearby, two wonderful old buildings that housed
steamship companies have been put to other uses but still bear traces of their
glory days. At One Broadway, just west of **Bowling Green,** the door for first-class
passengers now leads to a Citibank branch. Up the block, the old **Cunard Line
Building** (25 Broadway) now serves as an ugly Post Office, but it's almost worth
standing in line for stamps when you can gaze at the amazing original ceiling.

There are three places that Wall Street regulars seldom visit, but that are
worth a quick stop: the statue of the charging bull by Arturo di Modica at the
north end of Bowling Green (great place for photos); **Federal Hall** (dull
exhibits, nice view) and **Trinity Church.** If you think a church makes an odd
symbol for an area long associated with Mammon, think again. Trinity once
owned most of lower Manhattan, made big bucks from the island's development, and remains a major commercial landlord to this day. St. Paul's Chapel, a

short distance up Broadway, is linked to Trinity Church. Washington worshiped there as President and his pew has been preserved.

— *Leslie Eaton*

HIGHLIGHTS OF THE NEIGHBORHOOD

Federal Hall National Memorial Wall St. at Nassau St. (212) 825-6888. Wall Street's version of the Parthenon, Federal Hall stands on the site of George Washington's inauguration in 1789, which explains his statue on the front steps. One of the finest Greek Revival buildings in the city, the former U.S. Customs House and early Federal Reserve branch was designed in 1834 and built in 1842. Behind its portico of severe Doric columns and five-foot walls, the building houses a museum of constitutional history.

Hours: Mon.–Fri., 9 A.M.–5 P.M. **Price:** Free.

Federal Reserve Bank 33 Liberty Place (between Nassau and William Sts.) (212) 720-5000. Five stories below Liberty Street, the Federal Reserve's New York branch houses a substantial share of the world's gold reserves behind jail-like bars. The bank offers tours of the underground vaults, which store approximately $100 billion worth of gold ingots for some 60 countries. A government bank for banks, the Federal Reserve regulates U.S. currency, supervises commercial banks and has considerable impact on the economy through its influence on the money supply and interest rates. The New York branch, which dominates the other 11, covers a trapezoidal city block. Its rusticated limestone building is reminiscent of a Florentine Renaissance palazzo.

Ruby Washington/ The New York Times

Wall Street

Fraunces Tavern Museum 54 Pearl St. (at Broad St.) (212) 425 1778.
The18th-century Fraunces Tavern has been substantially rebuilt since it was the
haunt of George Washington and the Sons of Liberty. It is now a small museum
of American history. The Long Room, where Washington made his farewell
address to his Revolutionary War officers, is one of the several period rooms
where displays are located. The Museum offers tours, lectures and performances
coordinated with current exhibitions, as well as special events on Washington's
Birthday and Independence Day.
Prices: Adults, $2.50; children, students and Seniors, $1.

New York Stock Exchange 11 Wall St. (between New and Broad Sts.)
(212) 656-3000. On a good day—a day when the stock market is soaring—you
can almost smell the money in the air outside the New York Stock Exchange. If
you go inside, you can see it being made (or lost). To visit the exchange, go to
the little booth on Broad Street and pick up a free ticket. You will be sent
around to the back of the building, through a lobby, up an elevator to the third
floor, and into the "Interactive Education Center." You can skip all the propa-
gan . . . er, educational exhibits . . . though there is a lively video clip that helps
to explain exactly what it happening on the floor of the exchange.

From the glassed-in visitors' gallery, you can gaze at the main trading floor.
The effect is rather like watching a really fancy ant farm. Hundreds of strangely
dressed people bustle about, bark at each other, gab on phones, peer at computer screens and drop little bits of paper all over the floor. Most of them are
brokers carrying big buy and sell orders to the specialists, auctioneers of a sort.
Each specialist handles trading in several stocks.

Peer past the web of wires and pipes and cables to see the turn-of-the-century ceiling, all carved ivory and gold. In a few years, the exchange is slated to
leave this old building for a new complex to be built across the street. But some
seers predict that before that happens, the whole kit-and-caboodle will have
moved to cyberspace.

—Leslie Eaton

St. Paul's Chapel 211 Broadway (between Fulton and Vesey Sts.)
(212) 602-0874. New York City's oldest church building, the chapel served
uptown parishioners of Trinity Church as the colonial city expanded northward.
Completed in 1766, the church is a New York brownstone version of London's
St. Martin-in-the-Fields, a marble Georgian church that greatly influenced
American ecclesiastic architecture. George Washington worshiped here on the
day of his inauguration and during the 18 months New York was the nation's
capital. The tree-filled graveyard behind the church preserves a parcel of the
18th-century countryside. In conjunction with Trinity Church, St. Paul's offers
a well-attended lunchtime concert series.

Trinity Church and Museum Broadway (at Wall St.) (212) 602-0872. At
the foot of Wall Street in downtown Manhattan stands Trinity Church, once
the tallest structure in Manhattan. The first Episcopal church in New York, the
parish was chartered in 1697. The Gothic-style church on the site now was
built in 1846 by Richard Upjohn. Two earlier churches on the site were

New York Stock Exchange

Fred R. Conrad/The New York Times

destroyed by fire. Many prominent New Yorkers, including Alexander Hamilton and William Bradford, are buried in the graveyard next to the church. During the summer months, they share the spot with office workers on their lunch breaks, enjoying the sun in this rare downtown patch of open space. The church hosts a popular lunchtime concert series and houses a museum featuring changing exhibitions and a permanent collection of artifacts.

Highly Recommended Neighborhood Restaurants
(See "Restaurants" section for reviews)

Bayard's	☆☆	$ $ $	NEW AMERICAN
Delmonico's	☆	$ $ $	ITALIAN/NEW AMERICAN
14 Wall Street	☆	$ $ $	FRENCH/NEW AMERICAN
Wall Street Kitchen and Bar		$ $	NEW AMERICAN

South Street Seaport/City Hall

For several hundred years, the **South Street Seaport** was a thriving commercial dockland of warehouses and markets handling great ships from all points: China clippers, schooners, ferries and fishing boats. Barges floated down from the Erie Canal bearing cargo from middle America. This busy East River port became obsolete in the late 19th century, however, as bigger ships powered by steam docked at new and larger piers on the Hudson River.

When restoration of the area began in the 1960's, a jewel of a neighborhood was recreated to evoke a great age in New York's maritime history. There were cobbled streets free of traffic and piers open to wind and water. Alas, over recent years the seaport has turned into something of a theme-park shopping mall, where busloads of tourists clamber over each other on their way to boutiques and vast restaurants bearing no relationship to a seafaring life. Still, it remains an unusual corner of the city, and a pleasant place to spend a sunny day away from skyscrapers and stark, perpendicular avenues.

The restoration of the South Street district has included the construction of a large new pier, too, but one built for pleasure, where a stroll offers a bracing breeze and a view across to Brooklyn. Nearby are the original **Fulton Fish Market,** with a restaurant and other facilities in a dockside building once known for its fish and produce. The fish market is still the place where restaurants and retail fish markets buy their daily fare in the wee hours of the morning. Moored at the port is a four-masted sailing barque, the **Peking,** part of the **South Street Seaport Museum.** The *Peking*, launched in 1911 even as its breed was doomed, is one of the largest sailing vessels ever built. Visitors can board her and go below decks to learn her history.

At the Water Street entrance to the Seaport is the **Titanic Memorial Lighthouse** built in 1913 to commemorate the disaster. On Fulton Street between South and Front Streets is **Schermerhorn Row,** a series of early 19th-century Georgian-Federal-style buildings once used as warehouses by leading merchants.

To the west where Fulton Street meets Broadway is **Park Row,** the street that borders the east side of **City Hall Park** and leads to the entrance of the **Brooklyn Bridge.** Among the sights in and around the park are **City Hall,** the **Woolworth Building** and the **Municipal Building** (see highlights) as well as the **African Burial Ground** (Duane St. at Elk St.) where approximately 20,000 African-Americans were laid to rest during the 18th century. The site was uncovered in 1991 during construction of the Federal office tower across the street. The **Tweed Courthouse,** just north of City Hall, was the old New York County Courthouse made famous by the corrupt dealings of politician William "Boss" Tweed in the late 1800's. With its Italianate design and stunning interiors the building is worth a visit.

Farther north along Centre Street are today's active court buildings. At 40 Centre Street is the **United States Courthouse,** a mid-1930s Classical Revival skyscraper topped with a golden pyramid. The **New York County Courthouse** moved to its current location at 60 Centre Street in 1927. This hexagonal, Roman classical building is a frequent backdrop for "Law and Order" and countless films and television shows. At the **Criminal Courts Building** (100 Centre Street) arraignments are held 24 hours a day, seven days a week. The 5:30 P.M. to 1 A.M. shift ("night court") is real-life theater. It is mostly pantomime, robbed of its dialogue by bad acoustics, but it offers the curious visitor a hard look at New York life.

South Street Seaport: Fulton St. at South St. on the East River. (212) 748-8600 www.southstseaport.org

Subway: A, C, 2, 3, 4, 5, to Fulton St., walk east to the river.
Bus: 1, 6 (Broadway) or 15 (2nd Ave.) to Fulton St.

HIGHLIGHTS OF THE NEIGHBORHOOD

Brooklyn Bridge Manhattan entrance: Park Row at Centre St. Brooklyn entrance: Washington St. at Adams St. One of the grandest and most potent symbols of New York City since the day it was opened in 1883, the Brooklyn Bridge still provides probably the best free tourist activity in the whole city— walking across it toward the Manhattan skyline.

To start on the Brooklyn side, climb the three flights of stairs on Washington Street. (The closest subway stop is the High Street station on the A line). You will be following in the steps of President Chester A. Arthur, who led the first group of pedestrians across. And you will thank John A. Roebling, who designed the bridge in 1867 and put the elevated walkway in the center, above other traffic, so that pedestrians could "enjoy the beautiful views and the pure air."

From end to end, it is more than a mile—6,016 feet. The portion over the East River soars 135 feet above mean high water.

But long before you thread through the massive keyholes of the bridge's second Gothic-arched tower (at the time they were built, the towers were taller than anything on either shore), you will easily understand why the bridge has loomed so large in the nation's imagination.

Over the years, it has loomed indeed. It has been painted by everyone from George Bellows to Georgia O'Keeffe. Its glories have been sung in poetry and prose by thousands, including Hart Crane, the poet who asked: "How could mere toil align thy choiring strings!"

—*Randy Kennedy*

Subway: 4, 5, 6 to Brooklyn Bridge (Manhattan end).

City Hall Broadway and Chambers St. (212) 788-6865. Topped by a cupola that once offered commanding views of the countryside, City Hall is now

Brooklyn Bridge pedestrian walkway

dwarfed by office towers. An amalgamation of French Renaissance and Federal design completed between 1802 and 1812, it houses the offices of the mayor and the City Council. Official receptions for winning teams, astronauts and other dignitaries take place on the steps outside. The interior has a remarkable pair of cantilevered stairs under a central rotunda.

Fulton Fish Market South St. and Fulton St. (212) 748-8590. The nation's largest fish market becomes hectic around 4 A.M., but is largely deserted during the day. Still, a fishy odor lingers in the air long after the pandemonium of fork-lifts and trucks has delivered the day's catch to wholesalers, retailers and chefs from the city's finest restaurants. As a federal prosecutor in the 1980's, Rudolph Giuliani began a crackdown against Mafia influence and, in 1995, the city stepped in to take control of the market. Nearby, the renovated 19th-century Fulton Market holds upscale food stalls, but it has been overtaken in popularity by neighboring Pier 17, which juts into the East River. One of the last working areas of the Manhattan waterfront, the fish market adjoins bars and restaurants that guarantee a lively snack break in the middle of the night.

Municipal Building 1 Centre St. (at Chambers St.). Best known as the place where thousands of couples get married every year, the Municipal Building is coincidentally crowned by a round, colonnaded tower that resembles a wedding cake. Instead of two colossal newlyweds, however, the top of the building houses a monumental gilt sculpture called "Civic Flame." Roughly a decade after the merger of the five boroughs in 1898, the city held a competition for an office building to house various city agencies under one roof. The resulting Beaux-Arts skyscraper—designed by McKim, Mead & White and completed in 1914—stands guard over the approach to the Brooklyn Bridge. The building's entrance, which incorporates a Roman triumphal arch, boldly straddles Chambers Street.

Surrogates Court Hall of Records 31 Chambers St. (at Reade St.) (212) 374-8286. One of the most impressive downtown monuments, the Hall of Records was constructed in 1899 at a time when civic monuments were inten-tionally grandiose. Built by John R. Thomas and the firm of Hogan & Slattery, it possesses a particularly beautiful central hall. Whether or not citizens' records merited such splendor is another matter altogether, but the building itself is def-initely worth the visit.

Woolworth Building Broadway opposite City Hall Park. View this dramatic structure from a distance far enough to take in the Gothic flourishes of intri-cately carved buttresses capped by a summit that sits like a medieval castle 792 feet above lower Broadway. The building is truly from another era, when corpo-rate barons like F.W. Woolworth, of five-and-dime fame, battled for skyscraper supremacy. Designed by the celebrated architect Cass Gilbert, the Woolworth Building was the tallest skyscraper until the Chrysler Building (and countless others subsequently) conquered it in 1930. It remains a standout among the more contemporary glass-and-steel boxes of the nearby financial district. Some-where inside are a swimming pool and a storeroom of Gothic ornaments to replace the ones adorning the exterior. The only area open for casual visitors is the lobby, a sight itself to behold with its vaulted ceilings of tiled mosaics, murals, marble splendor and, on a windy day, a moaning, eerie whistle befitting the building's style.

—Randy Archibold

Subway: N, R to City Hall
Bus: 1, 6 to Park Place

Chinatown

Geography, New York style: China shares a border with Italy, and has for more than a century. The boundary is fluid, to be sure, and Chinatown's expansion in recent years across the traditional demarcation line of Canal Street has whittled Little Italy down to Tiny Italy. The area has Vietnamese, Cambodian and Hispanic communities too, and some traces of a once vibrant Jewish culture.

The Chinese population grew slowly from about 150 residents in the mid 1800's to around 4,000 just before the repeal of the Chinese Exclusion Act in 1943. Since 1965 the population has exploded and it is now the largest Chinese community in the Western Hemisphere. With about 150,000 documented residents (and many more undocumented), this is one of the most densely populated sections of the city.

A self-sufficient community with a large population of non-English speakers, many residents never have to leave the area. On narrow streets, fishmongers and greengrocers spill onto the sidewalks. In late January or early February the **Chinese New Year** is marked by a raucous street festival (Mayor Giuliani has taken some of the sizzle out of this celebration ever since 4695 when he banned firecrackers). The **Museum of Chinese in the Americas** (70 Mulberry St.) offers exhibits celebrating Chinese-American culture and history.

To the outsider searching for the perfect egg roll, Chinatown may seem changeless. Yet along with the infusion of Hong Kong capital has come a shift in the economic center from Mott Street to the **Bowery** and **East Broadway,** while the traditional dominance of immigrants from China's Guangdong Province is being ceded to those from Fujian.

There are an estimated 300 restaurants in the area focusing on any of several Chinese cuisines. After dinner or dim sum (traditional lunch of dumplings and other specialties) try the **Chinatown Ice Cream Factory** (65 Bayard St. between Mott and Elizabeth Sts.) for a scoop of green tea ice cream. The **Pearl River Mart** at Canal St. and Broadway carries a huge selection of Chinese imports—dishes, traditional costumes and decorations, housewares and food. Along with smaller import shops, most Chinatown streets (particularly Canal Street) are lined with little storefronts and sidewalk stands selling everything from cheap electronics and batteries to Rolex knockoffs and discount luggage.

Just south of the **Manhattan Bridge** entrance (at Bowery and Canal St.) past **Confucius Plaza,** one of the area's newer housing developments, is **Chatham Square.** Here the **Kimlau Arch** honors Chinese soldiers killed in American wars.

Where Catherine Street meets East Broadway is the **Republic National Bank,** the quintessential Chinatown building designed with the flourishes of a pagoda.

HIGHLIGHTS OF THE NEIGHBORHOOD

Asian American Arts Center 26 Bowery (between Bayard and Pell Sts.) (212) 233-2154. The Asian American Arts Center, founded in 1974, presents exhibits of both traditional and contemporary Asian and Asian-American art. The center examines the historical and cultural context of Asian arts, and supports contemporary Asian artists working in traditional media.

Columbus Park Mulberry St. at Bayard St. This mostly concrete plaza in the heart of Chinatown seems like a lush oasis when you enter it from some of the narrowest and most congested streets in the city. The park's benches and stone chess tables are usually occupied, from dawn to dusk, by elderly Chinese women and men playing cards and mah-jongg. The park is located on the site of the Mulberry Bend, an infamous tenement slum of the 1800's, and one of the most dangerous places in the city. The buildings were torn down at the urging of the reformer Jacob Riis, who wrote a scathing report on the area's disgraceful condition.

Museum of the Chinese in the Americas 70 Mulberry St. (at Bayard St.) (212) 619-4785. This is the only professionally staffed American museum focused on Chinese-American history. Located on the second floor of a century-old school building in the heart of Chinatown, it offers educational and community programs and facilities for research on Chinese American and Asian American studies.

Subway: N, R, J, M, Z or 6 to Canal St.; B, D, Q to Grand St.
Bus: M15, M101, M102, M103 to Chinatown.

Recommended Inexpensive Neighborhood Restaurants
(See "Restaurants" section for reviews)

Big Wong	CHINESE
Evergreen Shanghai	CHINESE
Goody's	CHINESE
Grand Sichuan	CHINESE
Joe's Shanghai	CHINESE
New York Noodle Town	CHINESE
Nha Trang	VIETNAMESE
Sweet-N-Tart Café	CHINESE

Lower East Side

The Lower East Side has a charm that much of Manhattan has lost. And though the area has seen its share of rent hikes and gentrification in recent years, it remains a tapestry of cultures and a celebration of New York's diversity. Since the mid-19th century it has been the gateway to America for countless

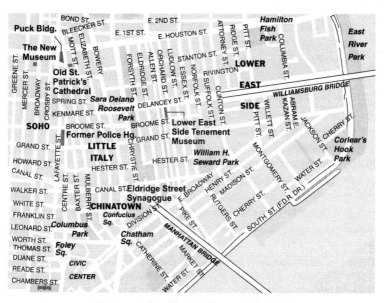

Chinatown/Little Italy/Lower East Side

generations of immigrants. Waves of families from Eastern Europe, Italy, Ireland, Germany, and more recently China, Puerto Rico and the Dominican Republic, have passed through here leaving their stamp on the neighborhood's cultural landscape. In the last two decades an influx of artists and hipsters have made the Lower East Side, not only a cross-cultural mecca, but also a thriving center for art, fashion and nightlife.

In the storefronts on blocks like **Essex Street** (between Canal and Grand Sts.) the Lower East Side of the past and present converge, epitomizing the real allure of the area. Asian-owned electronics stores abut old Jewish businesses like **Guss' Pickles.** Guss', with its open front and barrels lining the sidewalk, has been scooping pickles by hand for 90 years. (The green tomatoes are excellent). Signs in Yiddish alternate with signs in Chinese along this stretch; locals pack **Kossar's Bagelry** (some the best bagels in the city), as others settle down for a Sichuan lunch a few doors away.

To the north **Delancey Street** bisects the area, beyond which residents are largely Hispanic with a strong showing of younger newcomers. This thoroughfare offers mostly discount goods and cheap knock-offs and an occasional shaved-ice snow cone vendor. But while the Lower East Side may be changing, **Ratner's** soldiers on, serving Jewish dairy food with a snarl since 1905—only now it shares a building with **Lansky Lounge,** hot spot for nostalgic hipsters (see the section "Nightlife"). For a real cheese blintz, go to **Ratner's. Rivington Street,** one block north of Delancey, is dotted with Puerto Rican and Dominican businesses and home to **ABC No Rio,** one of several area cultural centers. But it also has **Schapiro's Kosher Wines,** the last functioning winery in the city, family-run since 1899, and **Streit's Matzos,** one of the premier suppliers of matzo and other Jewish staples for over 75 years.

On the block to the west, the **Orchard Street Bargain District** (see the section "Shopping"), where peddlers with pushcarts once crowded the streets, shoppers still come for discount leather goods, luggage and clothing. **Orchard** and **Ludlow Streets** are home to some of the most fashionable shops and a slew of chic bars and lounges (see the section "Nightlife"). A few paces away are some of the Lower East Side's longest standing eateries. **Katz's Deli-catessen,** an area artifact and originator of the World War II slogan, "Send a salami to your boy in the Army," still carves pastrami and corned beef by hand. The kitschy Borscht Belt party atmosphere of **Sammy's Roumanian,** the enormous garlic-rubbed beef tenderloins and the bowls of schmaltz—rendered chicken fat—on every table are a nostalgic paean to the days before cholesterol consciousness. Also don't miss **Russ and Daughters** for smoked fish and other deli specialties and **Yonah Shimmel,** supplying the neighborhood with knishes since 1910.

HIGHLIGHTS OF THE NEIGHBORHOOD

ABC No Rio 156 Rivington St. (between Clinton and Suffolk Sts.) (212) 254-3697. This rock club has sponsored punk rock concerts, political discussions, film showings and poetry readings as well as art exhibitions. The name is a rearrangement of some letters that fell off a sign outside a lawyer's office across the street; the sign originally read, "Abogado y Notario Publico."

Eldridge Street Synagogue 12 Eldridge St. (between Canal and Division Sts.) (212) 219-0888. Even in a state of disrepair, the Eldridge Street Synagogue's intricate carved facade and stained glass windows stand out amid the tenements. Built in the late 1800's by immigrants from Eastern Europe, it was the first large-scale Orthodox synagogue in New York. It is being restored under the stewardship of the Eldridge Street Project, which offers tours of the building, lectures, and educational programs including rugelach baking lessons and genealogy workshops.

First Shearith Israel Graveyard 55–57 St. James Pl. (between Oliver and James Sts.). Located in Chinatown, this small cemetery is the oldest surviving burial ground for the first Jewish congregation in North America. The congregation was mostly comprised of Spanish and Portuguese Jews. The oldest stone dates from 1683.

Henry Street Settlement—Abrons Arts Center 466 Grand St. (at Pitt St.) (212) 598-0400. In its century or so of existence, the Henry Street Settlement has been unsurpassed in bringing a multitude of cultural and community-related activities—including opera, music, dance, theater, talks and work-shops—to the residents of the Lower East Side. The hub of the Settlement, which occupies a row of handsome Greek Revival town houses, is the Abrons Arts Center. The majority of performances take place in the 350-seat Harry De Jur Playhouse, a national historic landmark. There is also a smaller theater, a recital hall and an outdoor amphitheater as well as classrooms, studios and art galleries.

Lower East Side Tenement Museum 90 Orchard St. (at Broome St.)
(212) 431-0233. If a museum is meant to be a place where things are displayed
to teach us who we are and where we've come from, then the grimy and dank
building at 90 Orchard Street may prove to be more intimately meaningful for
many than the Louvre or the Metropolitan. From beneath the floorboards of
this 130-year-old house and between many layers of wallpaper have come notes
and artifacts to illuminate the experiences of more than 1,300 people who
passed through the building's 22 units.

Admission: $8; $6, students and seniors. **Credit cards:** All major. **Hours:**
Tues.–Wed., Fri., noon–5 P.M.; Thur., noon–9 P.M.; Sat.–Sun., 11 A.M.–5 P.M.
Services: Tours, gift shop, lectures.

Schapiro's Wine Company 126 Rivington St. (between Essex and Norfolk
Sts.) (212) 674-4404. The grapes are grown upstate, but the wine is fermented
and bottled in ancient barrels on the premises. On Sundays from 11 A.M. to 5
P.M., Norman Schapiro, a real old-time character, offers free tours of the winery
and tastes of his wines, ranging from the treacly sweet to the dry. For more
information, visit their Web site: www.schapiro-wine.com.

Williamsburg Bridge Delancey St. and East River. The Williamsburg Bridge
was born of a dare. Could Leffert Lefferts Buck, the city's chief engineer, build a
bridge that was longer than the Brooklyn Bridge, in half the time and with less
money? He could, and did. When it opened in 1903, the Williamsburg was the
world's longest suspension bridge, with a span of 1,600 feet, 5 feet more than the
Brooklyn Bridge. At a cost of $24,188,090, it was $906,487 under its rival. And
it was built in seven years; the Brooklyn took 13.

Selected Restaurants and Food Shops

Guss' Pickles
35 Essex Street (between Hester and Grand Sts.)   (212) 254-4477

Katz's Delicatessen
205 East Houston St. (at Ludlow St.)   (212) 254-2246

Kossar's Bagelry
39 Essex St. (between Hester and Grand Sts.)   (212) 387-9940

Ratner's
138 Delancey St. (between Norfolk and Suffolk Sts.)   (212) 677-5588

Russ and Daughters
179 East Houston St. (between Orchard and Allen Sts.)   (212) 475-4880

Sammy's Roumanian
157 Chrystie St. (between Delancey and Houston Sts.)   (212) 673-0330

Streit's Matzos
150 Rivington St. (at Suffolk St.)   (212) 475-7000

Yonah Shimmel Knishes
175 East Houston St. (between Eldridge and Forsythe Sts.)   (212) 477-2858

Little Italy/NoLiTa

Historically, Little Italy was a family neighborhood, home to several waves of immigrants who settled in its five- and six-story tenement buildings. Some of them moved up and out, but others turned into the gray-haired grandmothers who still sit out on the stoops in pleasant weather.

The Italians moved in during the 1850's. In the first half of the 20th century nearly everyone was of Italian descent. Since the late 1960's, when the United States opened its doors to Chinese immigrants, Chinatown has been creeping northward, crossing over its traditional Canal Street boundary. Although many Italian restaurants and stores remain, much of Little Italy proper—the blocks between Canal and Kenmare Streets—has the feel of Chinatown.

Along **Mulberry Street** there are still dozens of Italian restaurants and cafes serving such specialties as coal-oven pizza and chocolate cannoli. **Ferrara Pastries** (195 Grand St.) has been producing traditional Italian desserts for over 100 years. Try **Puglia** (189 Hester St.) for a unique, family-style dining experience. **Mare Chiaro** (176 1/2 Mulberry St.), with its Sinatra photos and authentic feel, is the place to go for a drink (see the section "Nightlife"). For a taste of the area's Mafia past, go to the former site of **Umberto's Clam House** (149 Mulberry St.) where mobster Joey Gallo was gunned down in 1972. A couple of blocks north was the **Ravenite Social Club** (247 Mulberry St.), now a boutique, which served as John Gotti's unofficial headquarters until he was arrested there in 1990.

The big annual event is the **Feast of San Gennaro,** which starts the Thursday after Labor Day. For 10 days several streets are open to pedestrians only.

Old St. Patrick's Cathedral on Prince Street (at Mulberry St.) was founded by Irish immigrants in 1809. The cathedral became a parish church in 1879 when it was eclipsed by the new St. Patrick's Cathedral on Fifth Avenue. The old church achieved a measure of cinematic fame as the childhood parish of Martin Scorsese and as a backdrop for several movies, including two in Francis Ford Coppola's *Godfather* series. Another area building worth seeing is the **New York City Police Headquarters** (240 Centre St. between Broome and Grand Sts.). This domed Edwardian Baroque building completed in 1909 was converted into a luxury apartment building in 1988.

NoLiTa (which stands for **No**rth of **Li**ttle I**ta**ly) is the extension of Little Italy north to Houston Street. It attracts a young and trend-setting clientele of artists and professionals. As they set up shop and home, they are recasting the neighborhood with an up-to-the-minute mix of retailing and nightlife. Boutiques, galleries, cafes and nightclubs have sprouted in once-vacant storefronts, and several midsize apartment houses have gone up.

TriBeCa

At night and on weekends, TriBeCa can look and feel rather desolate. There is little activity on the streets, compared with SoHo and other trendy downtown neighborhoods. It's hard to tell which of the many cast-iron loft buildings have apartments tucked inside, and which are long abandoned.

But if you look hard enough, you can find signs of life no matter when you visit TriBeCa, a patch of lower Manhattan bounded to the north by Canal Street, to the east by Broadway, to the south by Chambers Street and to the west by the Hudson River.

TriBeCa was a bustling commercial and manufacturing center in the 19th century. Since the neighborhood was near the river and several shipping piers, wealthy merchants built warehouses there to hold agricultural goods, as well as spices, nuts and coffee. Factories and warehouses dominated the neighborhood well into the 20th century, but most were abandoned by 1970. That's when artists began trickling in, transforming space in many empty lofts into studios, galleries and living quarters.

Savvy real estate developers came up with the name TriBeCa, from **Tri**angle **Be**low **Ca**nal Street. By the early 80's, the neighborhood was drawing investment bankers who liked its proximity to Wall Street, celebrities who liked its relative privacy, and anyone else who could afford the vast loft apartments whose values were shooting up.

A well known landmark is **Odeon,** the sleek and cavernous restaurant that played a leading role in *Bright Lights, Big City,* Jay McInerny's novel about the hedonistic nightlife of young New Yorkers in the 80's. Odeon still serves American and French bistro food and stays open until 2 A.M. on weekdays, 3 on weekends. TriBeCa is also home to several hip eateries owned by Robert DeNiro and Drew Nieporent, including **Nobu,** a sushi restaurant, and **Layla,** a Middle Eastern restaurant complete with belly dancers (see the section "Restaurants").

Mr. DeNiro, who opened the **TriBeCa Film Center** (375 Greenwich Street), is one of the neighborhood's most famous residents. John F. Kennedy Jr. was another. After he and his wife died in a plane crash in 1999, hundreds of mourners placed flowers and notes in front of 20 North Moore Street, where they lived.

Reade Street between Broadway and Church has some fine examples of the marble and cast-iron buildings that the neighborhood is known for, as does Duane Street between Church and West Broadway. Franklin, White and Walker Streets are also good places to check out the local architecture.

For green space, TriBeCa has **Duane Park,** a triangular patch of land that was a formal garden in the early 1800's. An overpass leads pedestrians across the West Side Highway at Chambers Street, past the prestigious **Stuyvesant High School,** to **Hudson River Park.** Starting just north of the World Financial Center, the riverside park is eventually supposed to stretch all the way to midtown. For now, you can walk along the river from just north of Chambers Street, up to Gansevoort Street in Greenwich Village.

TriBeCa's eastern fringes are its most commercial, particularly along Church Street, where coffee shops, discount stores and fast food restaurants abound. One worth checking out is **Pakistan Tea House** (176 Church Street), a crowded but cozy little place that serves generous portions of tasty and surprisingly inexpensive food, drawing equal numbers of cab drivers, office workers and hip TriBeCa residents.

—Abby Goodnough

Highly Recommended Neighborhood Restaurants
(See "Restaurants" section for reviews)

Bouley Bakery	☆ ☆ ☆ ☆	$ $ $ $	FRENCH
Chanterelle	☆ ☆ ☆	$ $ $ $	FRENCH
Danube	☆ ☆ ☆	$ $ $ $	EAST EUROPEAN/GERMAN
F.illi Ponte	☆ ☆	$ $ $ $	ITALIAN
Layla	☆ ☆	$ $ $	MIDDLE EASTERN
Montrachet	☆ ☆ ☆	$ $ $ $	FRENCH
Next Door Nobu	☆ ☆ ☆	$ $ $ $	JAPANESE
Nobu	☆ ☆ ☆	$ $ $ $	JAPANESE
Odeon	☆ ☆	$ $	BISTRO/NEW AMERICAN
Salaam Bombay	☆ ☆	$ $	INDIAN

Recommended Inexpensive Restaurants

Sosa Borella	LATIN AMERICAN
Tiffin	INDIAN/VEGETARIAN

SoHo

"I really want those Gucci shoes," the good-looking young man told two friends as they walked across Prince Street. But one of them, a woman, was distracted. Pulling out her Nikon, she clicked away at a line of clean white laundry flapping from a line between two nearby brick tenements.

Art and commerce coexist in SoHo more fiercely, perhaps, than anywhere else in New York City, yet still have managed not to drive each other out. (Artists who can't afford million-dollar lofts are a different matter.) There is impromptu art, like the clothes line panorama in black and white, the fetchingly arranged baskets of unbelievably yellow tomatoes at **Dean & DeLuca** (see the section "Shopping"), the small Italian cheese purveyor turned prototypical luxury food mogul, or the plumage of an elegant woman stepping down restaurant row on West Broadway. And then there is the more institutional art: the 200-odd galleries that have colonized the neighborhood since four prominent uptown dealers, **Leo Castelli, Ileana Sonnabend, John Weber** and **Andre Emmerick** settled in the big loft building at 420 West Broadway in 1971 (see "Galleries" in the section "The Arts").

The arrival of the big-four dealers signalled the transformation of the once gritty warehouse neighborhood populated, often illegally, by penniless artists into the chic scene it is today, with limousines idling outside stores where a deceptively minimalist esthetic—lots of space, little merchandise—telegraphs old-money taste to new-money patrons.

Mr. Castelli, who used to put artists on a payroll whether they produced or not, introduced Andy Warhol's Campbell's Soup cans to SoHo. The neighborhood went on to nurture the wiggly post-graffiti art of Keith Haring and Jean Michel Basquiat. Mary Boone, a Castelli protégé who promoted Julian Schnabel

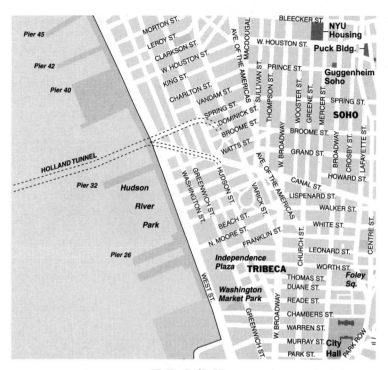

TriBeCa/SoHo

and David Salle, has since moved her gallery north of 58th Street, where she was arrested for handing out 9-millimeter cartridges to visitors the way coffee shops offer mints. Maybe she would have gotten away with it if she had stayed downtown.

In SoHo, almost nothing is ordinary, from the gorgeous art and architecture books of **Rizzoli** (454 West Broadway) to the ornate brackets at upscale hardware store **Anthropologie** (375 West Broadway), to the handmade note papers at **Kate's Paperie** (561 Broadway), to the french fries with lemony mayonnaise at **Balthazar** (80 Spring Street). Trendy clothing and accessory designers like **Anna Sui** (113 Greene St.), **kate spade** (454 Broome St.) and **Agnes B.** (79 Greene St.) also have shops here. To the south is Canal Street, on the border with Chinatown, where jeans are both hip and functional, lucite is still cool and a bit of haggling will get you the cheapest watch in town.

But cheap rents are as quaint in SoHo these days as the sweatshops that once occupied the 26 blocks of the historic cast-iron district, when it was called Hell's Hundred Acres, because of the frequent fires fueled by cloth and chemicals. Since Jill Clayburgh became a painter and drank at the **Spring Street Bar** (corner of Spring and Mulberry St.) in Paul Mazursky's 1978 movie, *An Unmarried Woman*, the anonymous artist homesteaders have been replaced at various times by celebrity denizens like "Maus" cartoonist Art Spiegelman, sculptor Claes Oldenburg, art critic Robert Hughes, actor Willem Dafoe, paleontologist Stephen Jay Gould and monologuist Spalding Gray.

Would they, let alone the original artists, have discovered SoHo without its architecture? From the **Puck Building** (295 Lafayette Street), with its gilded homage to *A Midsummer Night's Dream*, on East Houston, SoHo's northern border, to the **Haughwout Building** (488–492 Broadway), to the **Marble House** (southern edge of Mercer and Canal), the area is filled with distinctive buildings. The most famous, of course, are the post-Civil War cast-iron buildings, their Italianate elegance belying their seminal role as the grandfather of prefab architecture, the Sears catalog of building design, with owners choosing a Doric capital from column A and a Corinthian from column B. The bottle-glass sidewalks once allowed sunlight to illuminate the storage vaults below. Some streets are still paved with Belgian brick (not cobblestone) brought over as ship's ballast.

On Sullivan Street there are still some remnants of the Italian population that once called this area home. **Joe's Dairy** (156 Sullivan Street) and **Pino's Prime Meats** (149 Sullivan Street) are classics.

For children, a cast-iron tour can be almost as much fun as the **New York City Fire Museum,** with its collection of old firefighting equipment. Just buy a pack of cheap magnets; they'll help you tell the authentic cast-iron facades from the ringers.

—*Anemona Hartocollis*

HIGHLIGHTS OF THE NEIGHBORHOOD

(For **Alternative Museum of the Arts, Guggenheim SoHo, Museum for African Art** and **New Museum of Contemporary Art** see "Museums" in the section "The Arts"; for **Children's Museum of the Arts** see the section "New York for Children.")

New York City Fire Museum 278 Spring St. (between Hudson and Varick Sts.) (212) 691-1303. Located in a 1904 firehouse, the New York City Fire Museum displays historic firefighting equipment and traces the history of New York's bravest from the 1600's to the present. The permanent collection includes a horse-drawn firefighting carriage and an exhibit on the "bucket brigade." In addition to all the items related to putting out fires, the museum focuses on what secretly interests many of the museum's visitors: big fires. An exhibit of photographs records the nation's most serious fires, including New York's Triangle Shirtwaist fire of 1911 and the Chicago fire of 1871.

Highly Recommended Neighborhood Restaurants
(See "Restaurants" section for reviews)

Alison on Dominick	☆☆	$ $ $	FRENCH
Balthazar	☆☆	$ $	BISTRO/FRENCH
Honmura An	☆☆☆	$ $ $	JAPANESE/NOODLES
Provence	☆	$ $ $	FRENCH
Quilty's	☆☆	$ $ $	NEW AMERICAN
Woo Lae Oak	☆☆	$ $	KOREAN
Odeon	☆☆	$ $	BISTRO/NEW AMERICAN

Recommended Inexpensive Restaurants

Jean Claude   BISTRO/FRENCH
Pao   PORTUGUESE
SoHo Steak   BISTRO/STEAK

NoHo

It's easy to forget that NoHo, wedged between the West Village, the East Village
and SoHo, is a neighborhood in its own right. But while it shares many qualities
with its better-known neighbors, NoHo—which stretches from Houston Street to
Astor Place, and from Mercer Street to the Bowery—has its own quirky history.

Some of the city's glitziest families, including the Astors and the Vanderbilts,
were drawn to the neighborhood in the 1830's. They lived in the Greek Revival
town houses known collectively as **Colonnade Row,** on Lafayette Street between
Astor Place and Great Jones Street. Only four of the nine mansions remain, and
although the city has designated them landmarks, they are in shabby shape.

One of them houses the **Astor Place Theater** (434 Lafayette Street) where
the ever-popular performance troupe called Blue Man Group has been putting
on a wacky show involving Twinkies and marshmallows since 1991. But NoHo's
most venerable performance venue is the **Joseph Papp Public Theater** (425
Lafayette Street). The big old Italian Renaissance-style building originally
belonged to John Jacob Astor, the city's first multimillionaire and one of
NoHo's most famous residents. He donated the building to the city in 1854, and
it became New York's first free public library.

The building was set to be demolished in the 1960's, but at the last minute it
was renovated and reopened by Joseph Papp, founder of the New York Shakespeare Festival. There are actually six theaters inside, and altogether they seat
more than 2,500 people. "Hair" and "A Chorus Line" opened there, and the
Public now stages about 25 productions a year.

The city designated much of NoHo a historic district in 1999, after a three-
year crusade by residents to preserve the largely intact rows of 19th-century loft
buildings scattered throughout the neighborhood. The buildings, with facades
of marble, cast iron, limestone and terra cotta, once housed retail stores topped
by manufacturing spaces or warehouses.

Artists began moving into the area in the early 1970's, trickling north from
SoHo in search of cheaper rents. They adopted the name NoHo—for North of
Houston—and in 1976 got the city to rezone the neighborhood similarly to
SoHo, allowing artists to live and work in the same space.

NoHo has no park, school or library, but trendy bars and restaurants abound.
One popular dinner spot is the **Time Café** (380 Lafayette Street), an 1888
building designed by Henry J. Hardenburgh, architect of the Plaza Hotel and
the Dakota apartment house on Central Park West. In the basement is **Fez,** a
neo-Moroccan lounge with Persian rugs, plenty of couches and performances
that range from folk music to poetry readings.

Marion's Continental (354 Bowery) is a retro-chic supper club with good cocktails and 50's decor. And **NoHo Star,** (330 Lafayette St.) a laid-back neighborhood favorite, offers a mix of Asian and American fare.

—Abby Goodnough

East Village

Almost since it stopped being Peter Stuyvesant's "bouwerie" (Dutch for "farm") and grew up into a neighborhood, the East Village has been the city's place for bold statements.

It was there, at **Cooper Union,** in what is now the city's oldest auditorium, that Abraham Lincoln delivered the famous anti-slavery speech that helped him win the Republican nomination in 1860. It was on St. Marks Place that Leon Trotsky started talking about revolution and later went to join one in Russia. And it was in the smoky music clubs around the Bowery, most notably **CBGB** (see "Rock Clubs" in the section "Bars & Nightlife"), many decades later, that punk rock got its deafening start.

Now, with skyrocketing rents and new $12-a-drink bars opening on every other corner, the only revolution is the kind practiced by young Internet pioneers, who have found a way to get rich without ever punching a clock.

But the East Village—stretching from the East River to the Bowery, and from 14th Street to Houston Street—has not completely lost the rough edges it acquired back in the early 1960s, when radicals, musicians and artists flocked there when they were priced out of Greenwich Village. Stroll, for example, past the **Hell's Angel's** headquarters on East Third Street, where most of the members are middle-aged now, but the plaque near the door still offers this youthful advice: "When in doubt, knock 'em out."

Or get a mug of beer at **McSorley's** (E. 7th St. near Third Ave.), which was male-only until just 30 years ago and which looks as if no one has mopped since the first mugs were filled there in 1854 (or 1862, depending on whose version of New York bar history you believe.)

There are also still a few traces left of the neighborhood's multifarious ethnic past. Beginning after World War II, the East Village—back then it was known, less glamorously, as the Lower East Side—became the center of the city's Ukrainian community, as immigrants fleeing Soviet oppression joined others who had settled in the neighborhood around the turn of the century.

On Second Avenue you can still spot old men reading Svoboda, the Ukrainian-American newspaper. You can also grab a blintz at **Kiev,** a quick and cheap diner near Seventh Street, or a bowl of borscht at **Veselka,** a trendier, recently renovated Ukrainian restaurant at the corner of 9th Street.

Practically all evidence has disappeared of the days when a stretch of Second Avenue was known as the Jewish Rialto, the Broadway of Yiddish theater. But a quick side trip on East Tenth Street takes you to the **Russian and Turkish Baths,** a cavernous, tiled throwback to a time when the neighborhood was filled with "shvitzes," Yiddish slang for sweat or steambath. For $20, there's an endless supply of steam and for a little more, a vigorous oak-leaf scrub is available, designed to draw out the body's toxins.

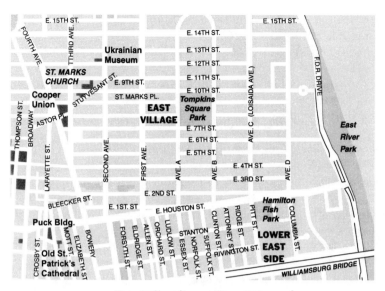

East Village/Lower East Side

Little India (E. 6th St.between First and Second Aves.) offers a cluster of lit-tle Indian restaurants with nearly identical menus and decor. These are great places to stop for a cheap tasty meal. For dessert grab a cannoli at **Veniero's** (342 East 11th St.) or **De Roberti's** (176 First Ave.) around the corner. These turn-of-the-century shops are two at two of the city's oldest Italian pasticcerias.

The best example of the East Village's bohemian credentials can be found on **St. Marks Place,** which—despite the arrival of a Gap and a Subway sandwich shop and the recent loss of a popular rock club, Coney Island High—still man-ages to attract nightly crowds of the heavily pierced and the colorfully coifed to its scrappy stores, bars and cafes. The street is not, however, quite as scrappy as it used to be: If you decide you would like a tattoo, there are places to get one while you sip a cappuccino.

St. Marks dead-ends at another of the neighborhood's raucous landmarks, **Tompkins Square Park,** where in 1988 riots erupted when the police moved in impose a curfew. Three years later, the police cleared out homeless people and self-styled anarchists and closed the park for extensive renovations and clean-up. Today, the loudest place in the park is usually near the concrete chess tables, where speed players shout to throw off their opponents' concentration.

The easternmost part of the East Village, from Avenues A to Avenue D, was known until only a decade ago mostly for its abundance of drug dealers and crime. But this area—called **Alphabet City** by some and **Loisaida** (Low-ee-SIDE-ah) by others because of its identification as the Hispanic center of the Lower East Side—has been undoubtedly the most changed by the neighbor-hood's rapid gentrification.

On the same corner where heroin sales were once the main commercial activity, upscale bakeries are doing a brisk business in blackberry scones. Buildings once called tenements now offer $1,500-a-month, closet-sized studios with superfast Internet connections. So what about all the radicals, musicians and artists who came to the neighborhood in search of lower rents? They are searching elsewhere.

—*Randy Kennedy*

HIGHLIGHTS OF THE NEIGHBORHOOD

Cooper Union 30 Cooper Square, East 8th St. and Fourth Ave.
(212) 254-6300. At one end of Cooper Square in the East Village sits Cooper Union, New York's first free nonsectarian college, housed in the city's first steel-frame building. The school was founded in 1859 by Peter Cooper, the industrialist who built the first U.S. locomotive. Cooper wanted to offer students the technical education that he himself had never received and to create a center for open discussion. The school's Great Hall is just that. Inaugurated in 1859 by Mark Twain, it served as the site for Lincoln's "right makes might" speech in 1860. The hall later became a meeting place for reformers, and today you can still attend lectures and concerts there. In the triangle south of the building is a statue of Peter Cooper by Augustus Saint-Gaudens. The gallery features exhibitions of fine art, architecture and graphic design. Cooper Union still offers a college degree in engineering, architecture and the graphic arts, and tuition is still free—but you have to compete to get in.

Grace Church 802 Broadway (at 10th St.) (212) 254-2000. This Gothic-style Episcopalian church, built in 1846, was designed by James Renwick, later the architect of St. Patrick's Cathedral. Later in the century, a marble spire was added to the white limestone church, as were several adjacent Gothic Revival buildings. A longtime center for the evangelical Low Church movement, Grace Church in recent years has operated overseas missions and a shelter for the homeless.

Merchant's House Museum 29 East Fourth St. (between Lafayette St. and Bowery) (212) 777-1089. If you get a charge out of looking at Architectural Digest and seeing how the other half lives, you'll enjoy this small town-house museum in the East Village. It provides a historically accurate glimpse of the lifestyle of an affluent 19th-century family, with original furnishings and exhibitions related to the period. Lectures and readings are held throughout the year. **Admission:** $3, general; $2, students and seniors.

Nuyorican Poets Cafe 236 East 3d St. (between Aves. B and C)
(212) 505-8183. Since the 1970's, the Nuyorican Poets Cafe has been a veritable warehouse of Lower East Side culture. A product of the black and Latino liberation movements, the Cafe spawned the spoken-word poetry slams popularized by MTV in the early 1990's. The slams, contests in which the audience judges poets in game show fashion, still take place in the high ceilinged space, as do featured reader nights, Latin big-band music blowouts and occasional theater productions. The black and Latino liberation movements' notion of street

poetry—full of humor and sass, a little rough around the edges, but honest and perceptive—still holds forth at the Nuyorican, though the poets now come from a wide range of backgrounds.

Russian and Turkish Baths 268 East 10th St. (between First Ave. and Ave. A) (212) 473-8806 There is nothing particularly remote or serene about the Russian and Turkish Baths, in a timeworn tenement on East 10th Street. A visit there offers a different kind of escape, a voyage to an era when the Lower East Side bustled with peddlers and Yiddish-speaking immigrants. Before the arrival of sushi and $10 martinis, the neighborhood's dozen or so public bathhouses were basic amenities for people deprived of indoor plumbing. Today, only the 10th Street Baths remain. Aside from the steep $20 admission charge and a juice bar—which still serves pierogen and pickled herring—little seems to have changed at what regulars still call "the shvitz," a temple to the art of sweating. The subterranean Russian Room, heated to 200-plus degrees, still sears the lungs. The kiddie-sized swimming pool is still cold enough to cause cardiac arrest. The chaotic locker room is strewn with soggy towels, and patrons still pad from floor to floor in cheap sandals and turquoise hospital gowns. And most of the clientele is refreshingly oblivious to late 20th-century notions of fitness. Bellies are ample and folds of flesh droop without apology, unintentional reminders of a time when, among poor immigrants, a full figure boasted a full cupboard.

St. Marks Church in the Bowery 131 East 10th St. (between Second and Third Aves.) (212) 674-6377. Tilted on a true east–west axis, this Episcopal church sits on land that was the farm of New Amsterdam's Gov. Peter Stuyvesant. A Federal-style fieldstone building completed in 1799, the city's second-oldest church (after St. Paul's Chapel) was later outfitted with a Greek Revival steeple and a cast-iron portico. Following a devastating fire in 1978, the interior was restructured into a versatile open space that functions as a venue for the performing arts as well as religious services. In addition to its ongoing Poetry Project, the socially progressive East Village church hosts an outdoor pop music series. Stuyvesant and his wife are buried under the church.

Ukrainian Museum 203 Second Ave. (between 12th and 13th Sts.) (212) 228-0110. The East Village is home to a small but thriving Ukrainian population. The Ukrainian Museum houses permanent and changing exhibitions of native arts and crafts, including photos, documents, coins, stamps, textiles, costumes, Easter eggs and rare books.
Admission: $1, general.

Highly Recommended Neighborhood Restaurants
(See "Restaurants" section for reviews)

Bambou	☆☆	$$$	CARIBBEAN
Bond Street	☆☆	$$	JAPANESE
I Coppi	☆☆	$$	ITALIAN

Recommended Inexpensive Restaurants

Acquario	MEDITERRANEAN
Boca Chica Latin	AMERICAN
Cyclo	VIETNAMESE
First	NEW AMERICAN
Flor's Kitchen	LATIN AMERICAN
Frank	ITALIAN
Habib's Place	MIDDLE EASTERN
Holy Basil	THAI
Lavagna	MEDITERRANEAN
Le Tableau	MEDITERRANEAN
Moustache	MIDDLE EASTERN

Greenwich Village

This neighborhood is compelling not only for its curving side streets and quaint charm, but because it embodies both New York City's historic past and its hip present. On the one hand, there are the regal Greek revival row houses that line **Washington Square,** built in the mid-1800's. But there are also the lively coffee houses and music clubs filled with New York University students and other locals.

Bounded to the north by 14th Street, to the east by 4th Avenue and the Bowery, to the west by the Hudson River, and to the south by Houston Street, the Village is one of the city's oldest and most diverse residential neighborhoods. Originally laid out in the late 18th century, the neighborhood began to be urbanized in the 1820's. By the early 19th-century, people moved to the Village to escape crowding and epidemics in the more densely populated areas to the south. Federal style row houses were built of brick or wood with brick facades, purchased by middle-class households.

In the 1830's, wealthy New Yorkers began moving to the Village, particularly the area between Fifth Avenue and Sixth Avenue north of Washington Square. Later, the population changed as middle-class families moved to newer neighborhoods uptown and poor immigrants crowded into single-family row houses which were converted into multiple dwellings. Then Italian and German immigrants moved in. Apartment buildings went up. And, in the early 20th century, the neighborhood's low rents and heterogeneous population began to attract artists and political and social radicals. The nontraditional character of the Village also began to draw a large number of gay men and lesbians, establishing Greenwich Village as a center of gay life in New York.

Now Greenwich Village has became a magnet for tourists where the crush of traffic makes it is tough to navigate the narrow streets on weekends, let alone to find parking.

Among the sites to see are **St. Luke's Episcopal Church,** at 485 Hudson Street, one of most active and diverse congregations in the neighborhood; the former **Stonewall Inn** (53 Christopher St.)—now just called The Stonewall—

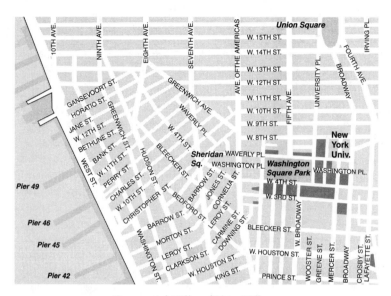

Greenwich Village/West Village

the gay bar that was raided by the police in 1969, setting off events that resulted in the birth of the modern gay and lesbian rights movement anniversary; **Jefferson Market Courthouse** (425 Sixth Ave.), now a branch of the New York Public Library; and the beaux-arts **Washington Memorial Arch** at Washington Square, completed in 1895. The arch was designed by Stanford White as part of the centennial anniversary of George Washington's inauguration as the first president of the United States.

Among the better places to grab a bite are **John's Pizzeria,** 278 Bleecker, for thin-crusted pizza from a brick oven and fat calzones; **Bruno Bakery,** on West Broadway, between Bleecker and Houston Streets for renowned cannoli and the **White Horse Tavern** at 567 Hudson for burgers and beer *(see Nightlife)*.

To simply have a cappuccino and people-watch, stop in at **Café Reggio** (119 MacDougal) or **Cafe Borgia** (185 Bleecker), where Allen Ginsberg and Jack Kerouac gave poetry readings during the 60's. —*Robin Pogrebin*

HIGHLIGHTS OF THE NEIGHBORHOOD

Church of St. Luke in the Fields 487 Hudson St. (between Grove and Christopher Sts.) (212) 924-0562. "'Twas the night before Christmas," the opening line of Clement Clarke Moore's famous Yuletide poem, has special meaning for parishioners at this enchanting Federal-style landmark church in the West Village. Moore was a founding warden of the church, which was built in 1822 as a satellite of Trinity Church and is Manhattan's third oldest. (The other two? St. Marks in the Bowery and St. Paul's Chapel downtown.) Strolling through the delightful gardens behind St. Luke in the Fields adds to the sense of being in a remote village, something the name itself suggests. In 1981, a devastating fire (the second in the church's history) destroyed the structure, later restored by the well-known architectural firm Hardy, Holtzman, Pfeiffer Associates, which captured its original simplicity. The church is extremely active in local neighborhood life and maintains a high musical profile: It's where the St. Luke's Chamber Ensemble was born, and where the West Village Chorale regularly performs.

Church of the Ascension Fifth Ave. and 10th St. (212) 254-8620. Among Richard Upjohn's legacy to New York City are several wonderful churches, among them the Church of the Ascension. Completed in 1841, the church was the first built on Fifth Avenue, which was then an unpaved track ending in a wooden fence at 23d Street. A Gothic Revival-style brownstone structure, the church relates closely to Upjohn's earlier (and better-known) Trinity Church in lower Manhattan. The beautiful interior is famous for its John LaFarge mural and stained-glass windows and exquisite marble statuary by Louis Saint-Gaudens. Music plays a particularly important role at the Church of the Ascension. Its 81-rank Holtkamp organ, installed in 1967, is a decent if not distinguished instrument. The extraordinary Voices of Ascension, a professional choir and orchestra, presents some of the finest choral concerts in town.

Forbes Magazine Galleries 5th Avenue at 12th St. (212) 620-2200. Malcolm Forbes, millionaire publisher, collected glamorous friends, Fabergé eggs, toy soldiers, toy boats, old Monopoly games, autographs and Presidental papers. It's all here—except the glamorous friends—tastefully exhibited on the ground floor of the Forbes magazine building, and it's free.

Judson Memorial Church 55 Washington Square South (between Thompson and Sullivan Sts.) (212) 477-0351. A Romanesque Revival building designed by McKim, Mead and White, this landmark Baptist church has long served as a center for social activism. In the 1960's and 70's, it served as a meeting place for antiwar and abortion-rights activists. Later, in response to the AIDS crisis, it offered space for drug trials. The yellow brick and limestone church, built in 1892 on the southern edge of Washington Square Park, is decorated with ornate details, including marble reliefs patterned on plans by Saint-Gaudens.

Meatpacking District The meatpacking district, a curious mix of commerce and community, is finally living down its reputation as a seamy, threatening segment of the Far West Village, a place where trade was in human flesh as well as animal. Certainly, some indelicate elements remain. But a crackdown on crime and the expansion of housing and small businesses have combined to make the area more desirable. The meat market itself, extending north from Gansevoort to West 15th Street, is zoned for light manufacturing. Because of this, few people live there. But the area is changing quickly, with a boom in restaurants, bars, art galleries, antiques stores and dance clubs.

New York Public Library—Jefferson Market Library 425 Sixth Ave. (between Ninth and 10th Sts.) (212) 243-4334. If you go anywhere near this building you'll notice it, and chances are you'll also like it. It's an eyeful of bright red stone and ornate pinnacles, towers, carvings and stained glass windows, all topped off with a clock tower that still keeps perfect time. These days it houses a branch of the New York Public Library, but it was originally built in 1877 as a courthouse, on the site of a public meat-and-produce market. The courthouse was part of a complex including a firehouse and a jail, which stood in the area now occupied by a lush community garden.

New York University Information Center, 40 Washington Square South (at Wooster St.) (212) 998-4636. Sometimes it seems as if everywhere you turn in Greenwich Village, you see a violet flag on a building telling you that you are looking at another part of New York University's sprawling campus. Washington Square Park is the de facto center of the campus, surrounded by university offices, student centers, dorms and libraries. Founded in 1831, NYU was designed to cater not only to the 19th-century penchant for the study of Greek and Latin, but also to feed the more practical needs of students wishing to pursue careers in science, business, industry, the arts, law and medicine. The school now hosts some 17,000 undergraduate and 18,000 graduate students, and boasts the nation's largest open-stack library. The university sponsors performance events at several of its auditoriums including the Loewe Auditorium, the NYU Theater and the Loeb Student Center.

Salmagundi Museum of American Art 47 Fifth Ave. (between 11th and 12th Sts.) (212) 255-7740. Also known as the Salmagundi Club, the Salmagundi Museum of Art is the oldest artists' club in the United States. Founded in 1870, it was moved to its current site on Fifth Avenue when the club purchased the Irving Hawley residence in 1917. Members of this private club have included famed artists Childe Hassam, William Merritt Chase and Louis C. Tiffany, as well as architect Stanford White. Painting exhibitions are held in a beautiful downstairs parlor. The museum is open to the public. The conference room and art reference library are open to members only. Whether you're interested in finding out about joining the club or simply dropping in to view an exhibition, the Salmagundi Museum is a charming, little-known jewel in Greenwich Village.

75 1/2 Bedford Street 75 1/2 Bedford St. (at Commerce St.). Only nine and a half feet wide and dating from 1893, this house is said to be the narrowest in the city. Edna St. Vincent Millay, Margaret Mead, William Steig and Cary Grant all lived in this tiny place at one time or another. The house fell into disrepair for several years, but it recently attracted a new owner who restored the place, named it the Millay House and rented it out for an astounding amount of money. Around the corner at 38 Commerce Street you can also visit the **Cherry Lane Theater,** opened by Millay and friends in 1924 in an old barn and still in operation.

Washington Mews Fifth Ave., between Washington Square North and East 8th St. This private street of two-story houses in Greenwich Village once functioned as stables and service quarters for the residents of the Greek Revival row houses along Washington Square North. These 19th-century structures were converted into private residences during the early 1900's, and were leased to

Sara Krulwich/The New York Times

Washington Square Park

New York University in 1949. Today, some of the buildings contain NYU offices, but this cobblestone street maintains its quiet charm.

Washington Square Park W. 4th St. at Macdougal St. (212) 387-7676. One of lower Manhattan's only large public spaces, Washington Square Park brings together downtown's diverse population. Musicians jam near the central fountain as skateboarders jump park benches. Students from nearby New York University lounge or shoot films, gay and straight singles swap canine tales as their dogs frolic and children swing in the fenced playground. The southwestern corner is also the proving ground for the city's most serious chess players. The park's identifying landmark is a large marble arch, constructed in 1895, which commemorates George Washington's inauguration. In the early part of the 20th century, the artists Marcel Duchamp and John Sloan climbed onto the arch to declare the secession of the neighborhood from the United States. A generation earlier, Henry James named a novel for the square. But as a public gathering place, the park also has its dark history, having served in the early 19th century as a graveyard and the site of public hangings. You would be excused for thinking it's haunted, as the gallows tree remains standing and many of the graves were left undisturbed when the park was established in 1827.

Highly Recommended Neighborhood Restaurants
(See "Restaurants" section for reviews)

Babbo	☆☆☆	$ $ $ $	ITALIAN
Blue Hill	☆☆	$ $ $	FRENCH
Clementine	☆☆	$ $ $	NEW AMERICAN
Gotham Bar & Grill	☆☆☆	$ $ $ $	NEW AMERICAN
Surya	☆☆	$ $	INDIAN

Recommended Inexpensive Restaurants

Bar Pitti	ITALIAN
Café Fes	MEDITERRANEAN
Drovers	NEW AMERICAN
Good	LATIN AMERICAN
Grange Hall	AMERICAN
Home	AMERICAN
Indigo	NEW AMERICAN
Le Gigot	FRENCH
Little Basil	THAI
Marumi	JAPANESE/SUSHI
Moustache	MIDDLE EASTERN
Pearl Oyster Bar	SEAFOOD
Pepe Verde	ITALIAN
Velli	NEW AMERICAN

Flatiron/Union Square/Gramercy Park

The neighborhoods that make up the broad swath of Manhattan between Sixth Avenue and the East River, from 14th to 27th Streets, contain some of the best preserved historical districts and landmarks in the city, as well as many of today's most fashionable spots for shopping, dining and nightlife. The area is dotted with little emerald oases—five parks whose importance far exceeds their acreage.

Madison Square (Fifth Ave. and 23rd St.), opened in 1847, was once home to a depot of the New York and Harlem Rail Road and two earlier incarnations of Madison Square Garden. It offers a front row view of two quintessential New York buildings: the **Flatiron Building** (175 Fifth Ave.) and the **Metropolitan Life Insurance Building** (1 Madison Ave.) whose 1909 tower with its four-faced clock and lantern is still intact despite substantial renovations. Also in the area are the exquisite **Appellate Division Courthouse** (27 Madison Ave.), the head-quarters of the **New York Life Insurance Company** since 1928 (51 Madison Ave.) and high-tech enterprises in **Silicon Alley** along Broadway and Fifth Avenue.

Union Square (14th-17th St. and Broadway) was once a rallying place for the organized labor movement, but it got its name as the union of the Bloom-ingdale Road (now Broadway) and the Bowery Road (now Fourth Ave.). By turns the province of aristocrats, anarchists and addicts, it has in recent decades felt more like a village green, thanks to the big **farmers' market** established there in 1977 (see "Greenmarkets" in the section "Shopping") and to a cleans-ing renovation that was completed in 1992. Between Madison Square and Union Square from Broadway to Sixth Avenue is **Ladies' Mile,** the post-Civil War shopping district that was the former home of Lord & Taylor (901 Broad-way) and B. Altman & Co. (615–629 Sixth Ave.) until department stores began to migrate uptown in the early decades of the 20th century. The recent rebound of the area extends throughout this district where the buildings that

Flatiron/Union Square/ Gramercy Park

housed the dry-goods emporiums of the Gilded Age have been restored to retail life as home furnishing stores, like **ABC Carpet and Home** on Broadway and **Bed, Bath and Beyond** on Sixth Avenue. Among Fifth Avenue's many shopping offerings are **Banana Republic,** the **Gap** and **Kenneth Cole.** Park Avenue South and other streets in the vicinity are lined with upscale restaurants such as **Tabla, Gramercy Tavern** and **Veritas.**

    Gramercy Park (Lexington Ave. and 21st St.) a fenced and locked enclave reserved for those who live on its perimeter, remains one of the most genteel squares in urban America, as it has been since 1831. The park is open to the public just three days each year for the Clean and Green celebration on a Saturday each May, Christmas Eve and the first night of Hannukah. A more expensive way to visit is to stay at the **Gramercy Park Hotel** (see the section "Accomodations"), which allows guests to use its keys to the park. One of the city's earliest high-rise apartment buildings stands on the park's southeast corner, while several townhouses with ornate wrought iron porches endure on the western side. Nearby is the **69th Regiment Armory** (68 Lexington Ave.) which hosted the celebrated 1913 "Armory Show" that introduced America to modern art and continues to hold various arts and antiques shows throughout the year. The area also includes several of the liveliest nightspots in town, like **Irving Plaza,** a concert hall at Irving Place and 15th Street (see the section "Nightlife").

    Straddling Second Avenue, **Stuyvesant Square** is home to a number of vital institutions, including Beth Israel Medical Center (one of many hospitals and infirmaries in the area, irreverently known along First Avenue as "Bedpan Alley"). The fifth area park is the gracious **Stuyvesant Oval**—a gathering place that is surrounded by the vast **Stuyvesant Town** housing project. Built to accommodate servicemen returning from World War II, this well-maintained complex and neighboring **Peter Cooper Village** have more than 11,000 apartments and remain among the more sought after addresses in a city starved for affordable housing.

HIGHLIGHTS OF THE NEIGHBORHOOD

Flatiron Building 175 Fifth Ave. (at 23rd St.). Originally known as the Fuller Building, the Flatiron Building took its nickname from its shape on a triangular block of land. The architect, Daniel H. Burnham, designed this early skyscraper, built in 1902, by overlaying an Italian Renaissance terra-cotta facade on a modern steel frame. The tall, wedge-shaped office building looks like a ship sailing uptown. Today the revitalized surrounding Flatiron District has taken on the building's name.

Friends Meeting House 15 Rutherford Place (between Second and Third Aves.) (212) 777-8866. Reflecting the Quaker love of simplicity, the Friends Meeting House, an 1860 landmark building, is beautiful in its austerity. It is a plain, red-brick structure in the Federalist style. Inside, the room is filled with rows of simple gray benches, with red cushions adding the only splash of color. On sunny days light pours through the tall windows, enhancing the room's subtle beauty. In addition to being used for Quaker meetings, the Friends Meeting House is often a venue of choice for concerts by small chamber ensembles.

National Arts Club 15 Gramercy Park South (between Park Ave. and Irving Pl.) (212) 477-2389. Established in 1898, the National Arts Club promotes various forms of American art. Over the past century, its membership has included notable painters, sculptors, architects, writers, musicians and philanthropists. The club's headquarters is a Gramercy Park brownstone, which Calvert Vaux— Frederick Law Olmstead's partner in the design of Central Park—renovated in a Victorian Gothic style for Governor Samuel J. Tilden. Behind the sumptuous clubhouse, which is a National Historic Landmark, stands a 13-story building used by members as studios. The organization awards art prizes and scholarships, hosts an assortment of public events and maintains several galleries open to the public.

School Of Visual Arts Museum 209 East 23rd St. (between Third and Fourth Aves.) (212) 592-2144. The School of Visual Arts was established in 1947 to train students as professional graphic and fine artists. The school's museum features changing exhibitions by students and established artists. Most of the work is contemporary, but shows span an array of mediums including illustration, fine art, sculpture, animation and photography. The school hosts film, music and lecture events throughout the year.

The Flatiron Building

Theodore Roosevelt Birthplace 28 East 20th St. (between Park Ave. South and Broadway) (212) 260-1616. This brownstone, which includes period rooms from 1865 and 1872, is a reconstruction of the four-story house where Theodore Roosevelt was born and lived until he was a teenager. During much of his childhood, Roosevelt was confined to the house with a variety of illnesses, including chronic asthma. There are 250,000 objects in the permanent collection, including T.R.'s christening gown and the stuffed Teddy bears that take his name. The site boasts the largest collection of the president's memorabilia anywhere, narrowly ahead of the collection at his home, Sagamore Hill, in Oyster Bay, Long Island. Displays from the permanent collection change regularly, and the museum hosts concerts and lectures throughout the year.

Highly Recommended Neighborhood Restaurants
(See "Restaurants" section for reviews)

Blue Water Grill	☆	$ $	SEAFOOD
Campagna	☆ ☆	$ $ $	ITALIAN
Eleven Madison Park	☆ ☆	$ $ $	NEW AMERICAN
Follonico	☆ ☆	$ $ $	ITALIAN
Gramercy Tavern	☆ ☆ ☆	$ $ $ $	NEW AMERICAN
I Trulli	☆ ☆	$ $ $	ITALIAN
Mesa Grill	☆ ☆	$ $ $ $	SOUTHWESTERN
Patria	☆ ☆ ☆	$ $ $	LATIN AMERICAN
Tabla	☆ ☆ ☆	$ $ $ $	PAN ASIAN
Veritas	☆ ☆ ☆	$ $ $ $	NEW AMERICAN

Recommended Inexpensive Restaurants

Chat 'n Chew	NEW AMERICAN
Mavalli Palace	INDIAN/VEGETARIAN

Chelsea

The formerly gritty neighborhood of Chelsea is better known these days for high rents, up-and-coming art galleries, a sprawling riverside sports complex and the hip clubs and restaurants springing up in the meatpacking district (see the section "Restaurants and Nightlife").

Chelsea stretches from Sixth Avenue to the Hudson River, roughly between West 14th Street and West 28th Street. Clement Clarke Moore, the scholar-poet who wrote "A Visit From St. Nicholas," developed the neighborhood in the early 1800's. His grandfather had bought the land in 1750 and named it after the Chelsea Royal Hospital in London.

These days, Chelsea's eastern end, along Sixth Avenue, is increasingly dominated by big-box stores like **Bed, Bath & Beyond** and **Old Navy.** For an outdoor shopping alternative, try the weekend **flea market** at the corner of Sixth Avenue and West 26th Street. It's a fun place to troll for kitschy treasures, although true bargain hunters will scoff at the prices. If you're looking for any sort of plant or blossom, the nearby **flower district** (around 27th St. and Sixth Ave.) is the place to find it.

For more breathing room, wander over to the residential cross streets between Seventh and Tenth Avenues, where 19th century brownstones proliferate and river breezes often take wanderers by surprise. West 20th, 21st and

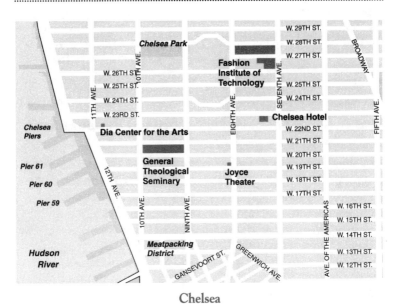

Chelsea

22d Streets between Eighth and Tenth Avenues are especially winsome blocks, perfect for meditative strolls. **Cushman Row** (408–18 West 20th St., between Ninth and 10th Aves.) contains some particularly notable Greek-Revival row houses (1839–40). One landmark worth glimpsing is the **General Theological Seminary,** which occupies the block between Ninth and Tenth Avenues, from 20th to 21st Street. The ivy-covered, Gothic-style buildings have a soothing effect on harried passersby.

Eighth Avenue in Chelsea is another heavily trafficked retail strip, where quirky boutiques mix with restaurants whose tables spill onto the sidewalks in the warmer months. There are also many bars and clubs catering to the area's large gay community (see the section "Nightlife").

One of Chelsea's most lively thoroughfares is West 23d Street, whose best known landmark is probably the **Chelsea Hotel** (see the section "Accomodations"), near the intersection with Seventh Avenue. In the past it was a beloved, if verging on decrepit, way station for artists, poets and rock musicians. You can still stay here, but a crop of new boutique hotels are providing stiff competition. If you're hungry, grab a chocolate-frosted doughnut from the **Krispy Kreme** shop down the block.

Athletic types would say that no tour of Chelsea is complete without a stop at the **Chelsea Piers** sports complex, which has taken over four piers on the Hudson River from 17th to 23d Street (see the section " Sports & Recreation"). There are ice and roller skating rinks, a health club, a fieldhouse for soccer and other sports, batting cages, a driving range and a bowling alley.

For those not inclined to exert themselves, Chelsea Piers also has benches on which to loaf an afternoon away, with views across the river to Jersey City and, if you linger long enough, the setting sun.

—*Abby Goodnough*

HIGHLIGHTS OF THE NEIGHBORHOOD

(see also the section, "The Arts in New York" for the **Bessie Schonberg Theater, Dia Center for the Arts, Joyce Theater** *and* **The Kitchen.***)*

Fashion Institute Of Technology Seventh Ave. and 27th St.
(212) 217-5779. The alma mater of the likes of Calvin Klein and Norma Kamali, the Fashion Institute of Technology (FIT) is the training ground for many of the players, and even more of the workers, in New York's garment industry. The school was founded in 1944 as the Central Needle Trades High School to meet the industry's demand for well educated and skilled workers. It has since expanded to become a community college campus of the State University of New York for students in all areas of design, fine arts, business and technology. The maze of buildings that make up the campus occupies a full block. You'll notice a proliferation of fashion-forward students in the neighborhood sporting their own exotic designs. The museum at FIT boasts one of the world's largest collections of costumes, textiles and accessories of dress from the 18th to 20th centuries, and it presents inventive fashion-related exhibitions. The institute's functional auditorium serves as home base to the Village Light Opera Group.

Highly Recommended Neighborhood Restaurants
(See "Restaurants" section for reviews)

Chelsea Bistro & Bar	☆☆	$ $ $	BISTRO/FRENCH
Frank's	☆	$ $ $	STEAKHOUSE
Periyali	☆☆☆	$ $ $	GREEK
The Red Cat	☆	$ $	NEW AMERICAN
The Tonic	☆☆	$ $ $	NEW AMERICAN
Vox	☆	$ $ $	LATIN/NEW AMERICAN

Recommended Inexpensive Restaurants

Bright Food Shop	NEW AMERICAN
Grand Sichuan	CHINESE
Gus's Figs Bistro & Bar	MEDITERRANEAN
Le Zie	ITALIAN
Royal Siam	THAI

Murray Hill

When the British landed in 1776 near importer Robert Murray's country estate (which stood near where East 37th Street crosses Park Avenue), Murray's wife and daughters are said to have invited British General Sir William Howe to tea, a respite which diverted Howe's forces long enough to allow George Washington's exhausted American troops to escape to Harlem.

The core of old Murray Hill—which stretches along the middle to upper 30s between Madison and Third Avenues—includes landmarks like the **Pierpont**

Morgan Library and the renovated carriage houses of **Sniffen Court** (150–158 East 36th St.). Side streets are lined with diplomatic missions, social and cultural clubs and mid-range hotels.

Murray Hill residents have long been wary of commercial development. When Benjamin Altman opened what was among the first luxury department stores on Fifth Avenue and 34th Street in 1906, he disguised it as an Italian palazzo in an effort to allay those fears. The landmark **B. Altman & Co.** building now houses the Public Library's high-tech Science, Industry and Business Library (188 Madison Ave. at 34th St.), the Graduate Center of the City University of New York (365 Fifth Ave. at 34th St.) and Oxford University Press. The west side of Fifth Avenue bustles with small retail stores, while a number of Asian and Middle Eastern restaurants line Third Avenue. On the northern edge of Murray Hill is **Tudor City,** completed in 1928, a middle-class "city within a city."

Anchoring the area on the south is the picturesque **Church of the Transfiguration** on 29th Street (between Madison and Fifth Aves.). It earned a place in the hearts of actors in 1870 when the minister at a nearby church refused to bury actor George Holland, and suggested instead "the little church around the corner."

HIGHLIGHT OF THE NEIGHBORHOOD

The Pierpont Morgan Library 29 East 36th St. (at Madison Ave.) (212) 685-0008. The world's most powerful financier in his day, J. P. Morgan started collecting medieval and Renaissance manuscripts, rare books, and English and American authors' manuscripts in 1890. Within a decade, his collection had grown to such an extent that he needed an entire building to house it. Designed by Charles McKim and completed in 1906, the neoclassical buildingthat houses the Library opened to the public in 1924. The library serves as both a museum and a center for scholarly research. In addition to drawings by Dürer, Blake and Degas, and the country's largest collection of Rembrandt etchings, the Morgan owns 1,300 manuscripts. The library's literary holdings include three copies of the Gutenberg Bible, letters by Jane Austen, Charles Dickens's manuscript of "A Christmas Carol" and Henry David Thoreau's journals. Musical texts include handwritten works by Bach, Mozart, Schubert and Stravinsky.

Admission: $7, general; $5, students and seniors.

Highly Recommended Neighborhood Restaurants
(See "Restaurants" section for reviews)

Asia de Cuba	☆	$ $ $	ASIAN/LATIN
Cinque Terre	☆ ☆	$ $ $	ITALIAN
Hangawi	☆ ☆	$ $	KOREAN/VEGETARIAN
Icon	☆ ☆	$ $	NEW AMERICAN

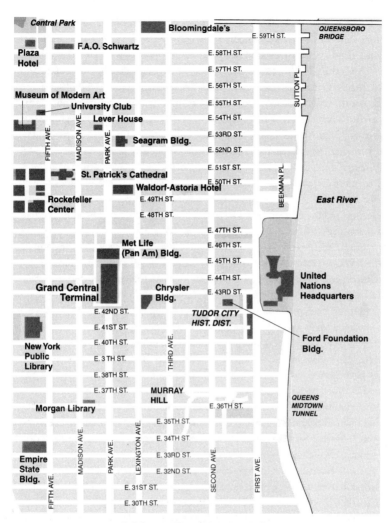

Midtown East/Murray Hill

Recommended Inexpensive Restaurants

Evergreen Shanghai   CHINESE

Wu Liang Ye   CHINESE

Midtown East

From the European jet set who browse posh shops along its affluent avenues, to
the diplomatic polyglot that is the **United Nations,** Midtown East is one of
New York City's most cosmopolitan areas. The annual tribute to St. Patrick and

a succession of parades that pass the Fifth Avenue cathedral named in his honor, reflect the strong connection many New Yorkers have to places like Ireland, Puerto Rico, Israel and Greece.

After the Civil War, New York society settled along Fifth Avenue from 34th to 59th Streets, then moved north as businesses arrived in the early 1900's. Today, the neighborhood is one of the city's largest business districts and hosts corporate headquarters filled each day by commuters who pass through the cavernous Beaux Arts concourse of **Grand Central Terminal.** Park Avenue and other neighborhood thoroughfares are lined with "glass boxes" like **Lever House** completed in 1952 (390 Park Ave. between 53d and 54th Sts.) and Art Deco marvels like the **Chrysler Building,** the **Waldorf-Astoria Hotel** (Park Ave. at 49th St.), a favorite stopover for U.S. presidents and other visiting dignitaries, and the **Chanin Building** on the southwest corner of 42nd Street and Lexington Avenue.

Saks Fifth Avenue, Henri Bendel and **Takashimaya New York** are among the several stylish stores in the area. Neighborhood streets and avenues are dotted with grand hotels and cultural institutions like the **Japan Society** and the **Dahesh Museum** (see the section "The Arts in New York").

At rush hour, pedestrians and drivers battle for control of the asphalt. It is hard to imagine Midtown East ever being the tranquil place it once was when turtles thrived near the quiet cove from which the **Turtle Bay** area takes its name. The most serene spots left are the affluent cul-de-sacs of **Beekman** and **Sutton Places.**

Second Avenue between 43d and 53d Streets is the commercial hub of Turtle Bay, lined with shops, businesses and a variety of eating establishments. The area is known for its steakhouses, such as **Sparks, Smith and Wollensky, Palm** and **Palm Too,** and a number of elegant restaurants, such as **Lutéce.** The **Amish Market** on 45th Street just off Second Avenue stocks a wide variety of produce, cheese and specialty items.

Turtle Bay's most charming side-street enclave is **Turtle Bay Gardens Historic District,** a stretch of 10 town houses on the north side of East 48th Street and 10 on the south side of East 49th Street between Second and Third Avenues. Gardens residents have included Katharine Hepburn, Stephen Sondheim and E. B. White, who wrote about the neighborhood for *The New Yorker*.

HIGHLIGHTS OF THE NEIGHBORHOOD

Chrysler Building 405 Lexington Ave. (between 42nd and 43d Sts.) (212) 682-3070. In late 1929 New Yorkers gawked as the Chrysler Building emerged from its construction scaffolding. The brilliant steel ornament and spire were unlike anything in New York, and at 1,046 feet, 4.75 inches high it was the tallest building in the world. The Chrysler Building is still unique, but until the recent cleaning of the metalwork, passers-by had become blasé about this Art Deco masterpiece. Now, people are again looking up.

Kenneth Murchison, an architect and critic of the time, admired the steel crown and "the astonishing plays of light which nature alone can furnish." While other buildings had been put up with distinctive spires, they were all in traditional

The Chrysler Building

materials: copper, terra cotta, iron, stone, brick. But on the Chrysler Building the entire upper section above the 61st floor—and much of the ornament below—is gleaming chrome-nickel steel, which reflects sunlight with dazzling brilliance.

From a distance the Chrysler Building seems like near kin to the Empire State Building, which took away its height record in 1931. But unlike the Empire State, which was proudly hailed by one of its architects as a building where "hand work was done away with," the Chrysler Building is like a giant craft project. The metal is generally soldered or crimped—all by hand—and the thick, wavy solder lines and the irregular bends all betray individual craftsmanship. The broad surfaces of metal, almost all stamped to form on the site, are wavy and bumpy, like giant pieces of hand-finished silver jewelry.

Just as surprising is the section just below the spire. So solid-looking from the outside, this part has no occupants and only intermittent flooring; only a few of the triangular openings have glazing. Inside, the wind rushes through what seems like a high, thin gazebo-shell of steel, at striking variance with the otherwise modernistic solidity of this continually fascinating building.

—*Christopher Gray*

Citicorp Center 153 East 53d St. (between Lexington and Third Aves.). The wedge-shaped spire of Citicorp Center, designed by Hugh Stubbins and Emery Roth, was designed to hold penthouse apartments, but residential zoning was denied. The aluminum and glass tower is headquarters for the Citigroup conglomerate, but it also has commercial, retail, mass-transit and even religious functions. The 915-foot building, supported entirely by four massive pillars, hovers over a sunken plaza that connects a multi-layered shopping mall, a subway crossroads and a church. St. Peter's, a starkly modernist replacement of the church that stood on the building site, holds Sunday jazz vespers and weekday concerts.

Grand Central Terminal 42nd St. at Park Ave. www.grandcentralterminal.com On its physical merits alone, Grand Central Terminal is one of New York's great treasures. Its main concourse is an immense, bustling space with a blue-green ceiling painted to resemble a starlit sky. But Grand Central is vastly important also as a historical and political symbol, for it lies at the heart of court decisions affirming the city's right to protect its architectural heritage. Opened in 1913, the Beaux-Arts monument was threatened in the 1960's by developers wanting to demolish the concourse and build office towers all around it. Preservationists took their case to court and to the public, with high-profile assistance from Jacqueline Kennedy Onassis. They won. In 1978, the United States Supreme Court ruled that the city had a right to protect Grand Central—and, by extension, other landmarks—from destruction. After falling into disrepair, the station got an expensive cleanup in the 1990's that restored much of its original grandeur. Above all, Grand Central remains what it has always been: one of the world's busiest train stations, with half a million people passing through it each day.

Trains serve suburban New York and Connecticut commuters, upstate New York and points west. The Municipal Arts Society conducts tours of the building, departing from the station's information booth every Wednesday at 12:30 P.M. Call (212) 935-3960 for tour information.

—*Clyde Haberman*

MetLife Building 200 Park Ave. (between 43rd and 45th Sts.) (212) 922-9100. Pan Am's former headquarters was the world's largest commercial office building when it was completed in 1963—its mammoth bulk effectively blocking the vista up and down Park Avenue. A team that included Emery Roth and Sons, Pietro Belluschi and Walter Gropius used concrete curtain walls to frame the building's structure. The lobby doubles as a concourse leading to Grand Central. Until a helicopter accident claimed five lives in 1977, a rooftop helipad provided quick airport access. In the 1980's Metropolitan Life Insurance bought the building from the financially troubled airline, and the MetLife logo supplanted Pan Am's globe as a landmark of Manhattan's skyline.

Park Avenue and 20th Century Architecture To a surprising number of architects and city-lovers, the so-called Park Avenue Corridor is the architectural heart of the 20th century. The corridor is the crystallization of the New York myth, the soaring city of work and ambition, where the sky is the limit and dreams are fulfilled. It symbolizes New York's displacement of Paris as the century's most vibrant City of Light.

The corridor contains several individual buildings of distinction from the 1950's to 60's, including the Seagram Building, Lever House, 500 Park Avenue (originally the Pepsi-Cola Building) and the Chase Building (originally the Union Carbide Building), the last three designed by the New York firm Skidmore, Owings & Merrill, and Philip Johnson's Russell Sage Foundation (originally Asia House). James Ingo Freed's Park Tower, completed in 1981, is a somber late addition to the group, while Frank Lloyd Wright's 1958 Mercedes-Benz (originally Jaguar) Showroom offers a quirky footnote to the ramp of the Guggenheim Museum's rotunda.

But much of the corridor's power lies in the aggregate, in the mix of lesser buildings with well-known landmarks. At the century's outset, long before the first curtain wall was actually hung, architects used to dream about the gleaming cities that glass would enable them to build. Here, the dream was realized.

The term International Style was coined by Philip Johnson and Henry Russell Hitchcock for an exhibition in 1932 at the Museum of Modern Art. In the postwar decades, the International Style became shorthand for the steel and glass towers like the Seagram Building, the supreme example of the genre, designed by Mies van der Rohe and Philip Johnson in 1957–58.

Mies described his own aesthetic as one of "almost nothing," a paring down of form to the discreet articulation of construction and enclosure. Walls were reduced to the transparent membrane of the glass curtain wall. Structure was expressed on the exterior by the application of non structural I-beams. This approach exemplified the architect's belief that less is more. It enlarged the artistic significance of proportion, scale, quality of materials and refinement of detail.

Not long ago, it was said that these buildings represented a rejection of history. In fact, the International Style was grounded in 19th-century historicism: the view that each epoch should produce a distinctive architectural style.

In the early 1960's, the International Style was a symbol of urban sophistication in many Hollywood movies, as accurate a barometer as we have of popular desires. In *Breakfast at Tiffany's, The Best of Everything* and even several Doris Day comedies, the glass tower epitomized worldly aspiration and success. In the reflections of the crystal canyon, the world of external reality merges with the subjective realm of ambition, fantasy and desire.

No design in recent years has given firmer shape to this idea than Christian de Portzamparc's **LVMH Tower** at 19–21 East 57th Street. Described by Mr. Portzamparc as an homage to the city of glass, the 23-story tower features a faceted glass skin that unfolds like a crystal flower. While the tower can't possibly be mistaken for an International Style skyscraper, LVMH responds to the context of the mythical New York where modernity took root. And it is the first blossom that this root has sent forth in many years.

—*Herbert Muschamp*

Seagram Building and Plaza 375 Park Ave. (between 52d and 53d Sts.) (212) 572-7000. For much of the past thousand years, the pendulum of Western architectural taste has swung between two esthetic poles: Gothic and classical, they eventually came to be called. Because it fuses elements of both positions in a supremely elegant whole, the Seagram Building is my choice as the millennium's most important building.

The 38-story Manhattan office tower was designed in 1958 by Ludwig Mies van der Rohe in association with Philip Johnson and is the most refined version of the modern glass skyscraper. It faces Park Avenue across a broad plaza of pink Vermont granite, bordered on either side by reflecting pools and ledges of verd antique marble. The tower itself is a steel-framed structure wrapped in a curtain wall of pink-gray glass. Spandrels, mullions and I-beams, used to modulate the surface of the glass skin, are made of bronze. The walls and elevator banks are lined with travertine.

Mies once defined architecture as the will of an epoch translated into space. For architects of his generation, this meant reckoning with the reality of the industrial age and the transforming power of machine technology. But it also meant overcoming the war of the styles, which had fragmented architecture into battling ideological camps.

In the Seagram Building, the classical elements are more obvious: the symmetry of its massing on the raised plaza; the tripartite division of the tower into base, shaft and capital; the rhythmic regularity of its columns and bays; the antique associations borne by bronze.

The building's Gothicism is subtler. It is evident in the tower's soaring 516 feet, the lightness and transparency of the curtain wall, the vertical emphasis conveyed by the I-beams attached to the glass skin and the cruciform plan of the tall shaft and the lower rear extension. Indeed, the Gothic cathedral was the prelude to the whole of modern glass architecture.

Today we recognize that Gothic and classical represent more than two architectural styles. They stand for two views of the world, neurologists have determined, that correspond to functions located in the left and right sides of the brain. The classical is rational, logical, analytic. The Gothic is intuitive, exploratory, synthetic. In hindsight, we recognize, too, that there's little to be gained by embracing one side at the other's expense. The business of civilization is to hold opposites together. That goal, often reached through conflict, has been rendered here by Mies with a serenity unsurpassed in modern times.

—*Herbert Muschamp*

St. Patrick's Cathedral Fifth Ave. (at 50th St.) (212) 753-2261 www.ny-archdiocese.org/pastoral St. Pat's is the Roman Catholic cathedral for

The Seagram Building

the Dioceses of New York, Brooklyn and several upstate regions and is generally recognized as a center of Catholic life in America. Constructed of granite, its design by James Renwick was based on the great cathedral in Cologne, Germany. The nave was opened in 1877, almost 20 years after the start of construction; the 330-foot twin spires were completed in 1888. At the time it stood on the northern edge of the city, visible from miles around. Architectural purists

St. Patrick's Cathedral

deride its mixed forms and the lack of flying buttresses, but it is a grand and elaborate statement nonetheless, surrounded now by city skyscrapers.

A magnificent rose window over the central portal measures 26 feet in diameter. The cathedral's 70 stained glass windows were crafted in studios in Chartres and Nantes in France, Birmingham, England and Boston—and not finally completed until the 1930's. The 14 stations of the cross were carved in Holland. The Pieta is three times larger than the Pieta in St. Peter's in Rome. There are three organs.

Chester Higgins, Jr./The New York times

The United Nations

The Fifth Avenue cathedral replaced the original and much smaller St. Patrick's Cathedral that was founded in 1809. Restored after a fire in 1866 and now called Old St. Patrick's Cathedral, it still functions downtown as a parish church in Chinatown at the corner of Mott and Prince Streets.

Subway: E, F to Fifth Ave.; 6 to 51st St. and Lexington Ave.
Bus: 1, 2, 3, 4 (on Fifth Ave.), 27 and 50 (crosstown)

United Nations First Ave at 42nd St. Tours: (212) 963-4440 www.un.org
Literally in a world of its own, United Nations headquarters and its grounds occupy a strip of international territory on the edge of Manhattan, running between First Avenue and the East River from 42nd to 48th Streets. The site was donated to the U.N. in 1946, a year after the organization's birth, by John D. Rockefeller, Jr. Three connected buildings—the boxy Dag Hammarskjold Library, the glass-walled Secretariat tower and the low-slung General Assembly—dominate the site. Erected between 1947 and 1953, they frame a central fountain crowned with a 21-foot-high bronze sculpture, "Single Form" by Barbara Hepworth, dedicated to the memory of Hammarskjold. He is the only Secretary General to have been killed in office, on a peace mission to the Congo in 1961. Daily public tours take in the most famous indoor chambers, including the Security Council and General Assembly halls. An eclectic collection of artwork donated by many countries is scattered throughout corridors and lounges. In the basement, shops sell jewelry and handicrafts from around the world, international books for adults and children and souvenirs of the U.N. itself. There are also outdoor attractions, especially when the weather is warm. Visitors stop to see the colorful array of flags from 188 nations flying along First Avenue or to enjoy walking on the riverside promenade and through the quiet formal gardens that form a two-block oasis of serenity north of the 46th Street visitors' entrance. The gardens form a back-

drop for several other monumental sculptures dedicated to the ideal of peace among nations.

—*Barbara Crossette*

Visitors can also eat at the Delegates' Dining Room Monday through Friday between 11:30 A.M. and 2:00 P.M., as tables become available. Reservations are a good idea and should be made in advance at (212) 963-7625.

Tour prices: Adults $7.50; senior citizens $6.00; high school and college students $5.00; students in grades 1–8 $4.00. 20% discount for persons with disabilities.

Subway: 4, 5, 6, 7 to Grand Central; walk east three blocks to First Ave.
Bus: 42 (42nd St. Crosstown); 15 (First and Second Aves).

Highly Recommended Neighborhood Restaurants
(See "Restaurants" section for reviews)

Restaurant	Stars	Price	Cuisine
An American Place	☆☆	$$$$	NEW AMERICAN
Bouterin	☆	$$$$	FRENCH
Brasserie	☆☆	$$$	BISTRO/FRENCH
Chianti	☆☆	$$	ITALIAN
Chola	☆☆	$$	INDIAN
Della Femina	☆	$$$$	NEW AMERICAN
Deniz a La Turk	☆☆	$$	TURKISH
Felidia	☆☆☆	$$$$	NORTHERN ITALIAN
Fifty Seven Fifty Seven	☆☆☆	$$$$	AMERICAN
The Four Seasons	☆☆☆	$$$$	NEW AMERICAN
Guastavino's	☆☆	$$$$	ENGLISH/FRENCH
Heartbeat	☆☆	$$	NEW AMERICAN
Il Valentino	☆☆	$$	ITALIAN
Kuruma Zushi	☆☆☆	$$$$	JAPANESE
La Grenouille	☆☆☆	$$$$	FRENCH
Le Cirque 2000	☆☆☆☆	$$$$	NEW AMERICAN
Le Colonial	☆☆	$$	VIETNAMESE
Lespinasse	☆☆☆☆	$$$$	FRENCH
Lutéce	☆☆☆	$$$$	FRENCH
March	☆☆☆	$$$$	NEW AMERICAN
Michael Jordan's	☆☆	$$$$	STEAKHOUSE
Oceana	☆☆☆	$$$$	SEAFOOD
Patroon	☆☆☆	$$$$	NEW AMERICAN
Peacock Alley	☆☆☆	$$$$	FRENCH
Rosa Mexicano	☆☆	$$$$	MEXICAN/TEX-MEX
Shun Lee Palace	☆☆	$$$$	CHINESE
Smith & Wollensky	☆☆	$$$$	STEAKHOUSE
Solera	☆☆	$$$$	SPANISH
Sushi Yasuda	☆☆☆	$$$$	JAPANESE/SUSHI
Zarela	☆☆	$$	MEXICAN/TEX-MEX

Recommended Inexpensive Restaurants

Jubilee	FRENCH
Katsu-Hama	JAPANESE
Meltemi Greek	SEAFOOD

Midtown West

There is probably more to see and do midtown in the West 30's, 40's and 50's than anywhere else in the city—not least the sizzling wattage of the newly booming **Times Square.** Long touted as "the crossroads of the world," it is fast becoming America's carnival midway. But midtown is also the tonier gleam of **Rockefeller Center,** the breathtaking pinnacle of the **Empire State Building,** the vigilant marble lions—Patience and Fortitude—guarding the Fifth Avenue entrance to the **New York Public Library.** Everything seems outsized.

Did someone mention shopping? Saks Fifth Avenue, Tiffany, Bergdorf Goodman, Brooks Brothers and more. Accommodations? Most of the city's most elegant hotels—The Plaza, St. Regis, Four Seasons, etc.—and any number of lesser establishments around **Penn Station** and the **Port Authority Bus Terminal.** By the way, "the world's most famous store"—**Macy's**—is just one block from Penn Station in **Herald Square.**

If you're a fan of the *Today* show or *Good Morning America* on the little screen, see them live and full-size through the plate glass of their street-level studios—in Rockefeller Center and Times Square, respectively. (For tickets to other TV shows see p. 101.)

MTV has studios behind glass in Times Square, too, not so easy to view because they are on the second floor; to find them, listen for squealing teeny-boppers. For music of a somehat finer calibre, there is **Carnegie Hall** on 57th St. For a corned beef sandwich that feeds two, there is the **Carnegie Deli** just two blocks away.

Broadway and 7th Avenue south of 42nd St. have been the main arteries of the **Garment District** for more than 100 years, home to the warehouses and workshops of the fashion industry. The **Theater District** runs north from 42nd St.—so-called "Broadway" theater on side streets east and west of Broadway, and a half-dozen "off-Broadway" houses on 42nd St. west of 9th Ave.

West of the Theater District is a residential neighborhood famed as **Hell's Kitchen,** the rough and tumble home of immigrant Irish in the second half of the 19th century—Senator Daniel Patrick Moynihan grew up there. Greeks, Eastern Europeans, Puerto Ricans and other groups moved in later. The politically sanitized name for the area now is **Clinton** (for DeWitt, not Bill) and its residents are young professionals, theater people and remnants of the old immigrant groups. **Restaurant Row** (46th St. between 8th and 9th Aves.) is a long block of restaurants side-by-side, all packed with theater-goers before curtain time—and half-empty after 8 P.M. New restaurants and bars along 9th Ave., often with lower prices, cater to the rapidly growing younger population.

HIGHLIGHTS OF THE NEIGHBORHOOD

Bryant Park Ave. of the Americas from 40th St. to 42nd St. (212) 983-4142. On warm weekdays, midtown workers descend on Bryant Park to shed ties and heels for some lunchtime relaxation. They arrange the park's folding chairs to gossip, or stretch out on the luxurious lawn for catnaps. Regulars play chess near a statue honoring the park's namesake, William Cullen Bryant, longtime editor of the *New York Post* and an early advocate of radical ideas such as abolition and public parks. Dotting its tree-lined boundaries are statues commemorating literary figures ranging from Goethe to Gertrude Stein, making the park a great place to read a chapter or two before heading back to the office. Probably the best time to go, though, is Monday nights in the summer, when HBO, headquartered across the street, presents movie classics on a huge screen.

Carnegie Hall Seventh Ave. and 57th St. (212) 247-7800. Can you imagine New York without Carnegie Hall? Probably not. But in 1960, its owners were ready to demolish Andrew Carnegie's shrine to music to make way for a new skyscraper. Violinist Isaac Stern almost single-handedly saved the world's most

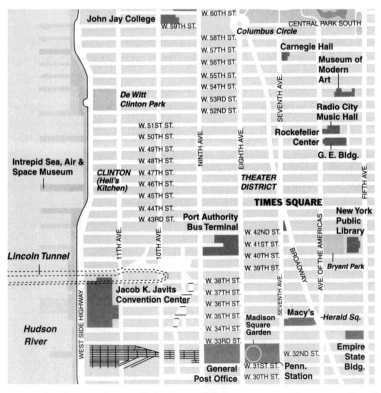

Midtown West

famous concert hall from becoming merely a fond memory. From the time it opened in 1891 (with Tchaikovsky conducting the inaugural concert) the 2,804-seat landmark has been synonymous with the greatest musicians of the 20th century, from Arturo Toscanini, Marian Anderson and Vladimir Horowitz to Ella Fitzgerald, Frank Sinatra and the Beatles.

Carnegie's acoustics are legendary, though some feel the sound was compromised after much-needed renovations were completed in 1986. (A concrete slab under the stage, discovered in 1995, didn't help matters and was later removed.) Once you get past the claustrophobic lobby, you're in for a visual and sonic treat. On the walls are photos and letters from famous composers, singers, instrumentalists and conductors. The seats are plush and the gilded décor ravishing. Even if a performance does not live up to your expectations, a visit to Carnegie always does.

During intermission, instead of squeezing into the lobby or the Cafe Carnegie, stop by the Rose Museum on the First Tier level, where interesting music-related exhibits give you a taste of the hall's illustrious history. On the same level are another cafe, the Rohatyn Room, and a gift shop. But beware: The shop is even more claustrophobic than the lobby.

Tickets: Carnegie Charge. **Credit cards:** All major. **Subway:** B, D, E to Seventh Ave.; N, R to 57th St.

Empire State Building 350 Fifth Ave. (between 33rd and 34th Sts.) (212) 736-3100. Known as the "Empty State" after it was completed in 1931, the Empire State Building remained half-rented during the Depression. Designed by Shreve, Lamb and Harmon, the Empire State was constructed at breakneck speed on the former site of the original Waldorf-Astoria Hotel. The Art Deco tower won a three-way competition with the Chrysler Building and 40 Wall Street to become the world's tallest skyscraper, a title it kept for more than half a century. The building's spire, immortalized as King Kong's perch, was designed—but used only once—as a mooring mast for dirigibles. Metal detectors were installed following a shooting spree in 1997 on the building's observation deck.

General Post Office 421 Eighth Ave. (between 32nd and 33rd Sts.) (212) 330-3601. When you're running to get a package postmarked before midnight, the main post office's staircase feels as monumental as it looks. The facility is open 24 hours a day. (Check out the scene on the night of April 15, when late tax filers race to meet the midnight deadline.) Built in 1914 and designed by McKim, Mead and White as a complement to the first Pennsylvania Station—a landmark that was demolished in the 1960's—the Classical Revival building stretches across two city blocks.

The post office's unofficial motto is spelled out above a parade of Corinthian columns: "Neither snow nor rain nor heat nor gloom of night stays these couriers from the swift completion of their appointed rounds." After a campaign by Senator Daniel Patrick Moynihan, plans are now being developed to turn a large part of the building into a new train station to replace the current, uninspiring incarnation of Penn Station.

The Empire State Building

Herald Square Broadway and Ave. of the Americas (at 34th St.). This mid-town shopping district is named for the headquarters of the defunct *New York Herald*, which was torn down in 1921. (A statue of Horace Greeley, the newspaper's founder, still stands in Greeley Square on the south side of 34th Street.) R. H. Macy opened the world's largest department store on the square in 1902. Others followed but eventually departed. By 1925, Saks had already moved uptown to Fifth Avenue. Gimbels gave way to a multilevel mall in the 1980's, and the district partially adapted to more suburban modes of shopping.

Jacob K. Javits Convention Center 655 West 34th St. (between 11th and 12th Aves.) (212) 216-2000. The convention complex, completed in 1986 at a cost of half a billion dollars, boasts over 17 acres of floor space. Named after the late New York Senator, the center was designed by the world famous architectural firm of I. M. Pei. The New York International Auto Show, held here each April, alone draws more than one million visitors.

Madison Square Garden 2 Penn Plaza (at 33rd St. and Seventh Ave.) (212) 465-6727. Few other sports arenas provide drama quite like Madison Square Garden. Unfortunately, to see the Knicks or the Rangers, you'll either need to know someone with season tickets, shell out your weekly paycheck to a ticket broker, or simply be extremely lucky. However, tickets to see the New York Liberty women's basketball team, the New York Cityhawks arena football team, or college basketball are much easier to come by. Visitors can also take a tour of the arena for $12. (See also *Sports and Recreation*).

The Museum of Television and Radio 25 West 52d St. (between Fifth and Ave. of the Americas) (212) 621-6600. This plain, midtown museum houses the some of the city's most fascinating and unlikely exhibits. Although the theaters show specials on TV and radio's most notable figures and events, the treasure of the museum is the archives in which you'll find a copy of almost anything from broadcast's past—old Jack Paar shows, Edward R. Murrow radio reports and even classic episodes of "Taxi" and other programs. Note: closed Monday.
Subway: E, F to Fifth Ave. (at 53d St.)

New York Public Library Fifth Ave. and 42d St. (212) 661-7220 www.nypl.org One of the world's greatest libraries, this two-block-long Beaux Arts palace of books has long been thought of as the main branch of the New York Public Library system, which includes 85 branches in the Bronx, Manhattan and Staten Island. But the building is actually the biggest of the system's four research libraries. Formally known as the Humanities and Social Sciences Library, no books are allowed to leave the building. Its 15 million items, from

AP Photo/Mark Lennihan

Rose Reading Room at the New York Public Library

rare illuminated manuscripts to pulp fiction to Cherokee literature, may be checked out and read in the library.

It is a place where leafing through a book takes on a whole new meaning. The Main Reading Room on the third floor, open again after a $15 million renovation stretches the length of a football field. Beneath its soaring ceiling murals of bright blue skies and clouds, readers can plug in a laptop, peruse a newspaper or just daydream.

Anyone can ask for a book to be fetched from seven floors of stacks underneath the room or two more floors concealed under the lawn of Bryant Park next door. There are about 132 miles of shelves in the stacks, not open to the public. (In order to maintain the proper hush, tourists are encouraged to take scheduled tours of the Reading Room.)

The library came along relatively late in the city's history—it is just 100 years old. A little known architecture firm, Carrere and Hastings, won a competition to build what was then the largest marble structure ever attempted in the country.

And the famous marble lions? They have stood guard at the Fifth Avenue entrance since the beginning. Mayor Fiorello LaGuardia's administration dubbed the one to the south Patience and the one to the north—you guessed it—Fortitude.

—*Randy Kennedy*

Radio City Music Hall 1260 Ave. of the Americas (at 50th St.) (212) 307-1000. Radio City Music Hall is Manhattan's version of a natural wonder. It's our Rainbow Arch, our Old Faithful, our Niagara Falls. After a $70 million restoration in 1999, the great hall's awesome beauty can be seen once again in the genius of its original conception.

Completed in 1932, the music hall is a tribute to the Rockefeller family's spirit of culturally progressive enterprise. Like Rockefeller Center, which surrounds it in midtown, the theater countered the Great Depression with a great infusion of hope in the city's future. Radio City! Live from Radio City!

Always seen as a place for families, the music hall opened at a time when family entertainment might include ballet, symphony and opera, along with comedy, popular song, acrobatics and the Rockettes. The vaudeville mix was recognizably of the radio age, when folks gathered round the Bakelite console to hear their favorite shows. The music hall gave them tunes and great visuals besides.

Three New York architectural firms are credited with the design of the theater. These firms brought to harmonious realization the unlikely alliance between the patrician Rockefellers and the plebeian Samuel L. Rothafel, known as Roxy, an impresario of movie palaces for the masses.

The building is a triumph of processional design. Its most dramatic aspect is an expanded version of an effect common in theater architecture: the disarming contrast between a small-scale exterior and an interior of epic proportions. The entrance and ticket lobby are lodged on the ground floor of an office tower that gives little sign of the grandiose space inside.

The ticket lobby is in keeping with the scale of the building's exterior, but the box offices anticipate the amplitude within. There are so many of them, and all for one theater: a soloplex. The box offices may remind some of passport-

Fred R. Conrad/The New York Times

Radio City Music Hall

control counters. The comparison is apt, for from here we proceed to a grand ocean liner of a space, the Grand Foyer. Moderne rather than modern, the foyer is one of the world's great Art Deco interiors, its length and height amplified by mirrors of gold-backed glass.

Entering the auditorium, we find ourselves on the deck of the ocean liner, gazing out to sea, precisely the image Roxy Rothafel wanted his architects to capture for his new 6,000-seat show palace. In time the showman's wish was conveyed to the young Edward Durell Stone, a draftsman in one of the three architectural firms responsible for the design. In later life Stone made his mark with Manhattan buildings like the Museum of Modern Art and the General Motors Building. At age 30 Stone found himself designing the most stupendous arch this side of Rome.

The auditorium's formal power is derived from the plain, unadorned half-circle of the proscenium, and from the projection of that shape from the front to the rear of the house. Like a dome, the design eliminates both walls and ceiling. This is why the auditorium is psychologically so overwhelming. No matter where you sit, you have the sensation of tumbling through the sky. This feeling is heightened by the broad strips of air-conditioning grilles, also used for lighting, that radiate longitudinally from the proscenium. These bands farther diminish the orientation that walls and ceiling usually provide. It's a cinematic effect, the architectural equivalent of the simultaneous reverse track and forward zoom in Hitchcock's "Vertigo."

For design historians the music hall is forever linked to Donald Deskey, responsible for the theater's iconic Art Deco interiors. Plate-glass vanity tables, metal tube chairs, mohair sofas, round mirrors, balustrades, light fixtures, theater seats: these are some of the classic pieces Deskey created for the hall.

—*Herbert Muschamp*

The G.E. Building at Rockefeller Center

Rockefeller Center Between 48th and 52nd Streets, Fifth to Seventh Avenues. This impressive complex in the heart of Manhattan includes some of New York's best known landmarks, including Radio City Music Hall and a sunken plaza that becomes an ice skating rink with a Christmas tree in wintertime. The Rainbow Room has dinner and dancing on the 65th floor of the G.E. Building (30 Rockefeller Plaza, between 49th and 50th Sts.), the sleek centerpiece of Rockefeller Center, but new owners are limiting public access to a few days a month.

The brainchild of John D. Rockefeller, the center is noteworthy for incorporating office buildings, stores, theaters and open space—including NBC Studios, where people can come to watch the live telecasts of *The Today Show* and tapings of *Conan O'Brien* and *Saturday Night Live* (tickets for tapings are usually gone well in advance, but there are standby tickets on the day of the show).

Rockefeller Center was the largest privately sponsored real estate venture ever undertaken in New York City when construction began in 1929. Originally intended to include a new Metropolitan Opera House, those plans were scrapped after the stock market crash that October. Mr. Rockefeller then reconceived the project as an entirely commercial complex.

—*Robin Pogrebin*

St. Thomas Church 1 West 53rd St. (at Fifth Ave.) (212) 757-7013. Fifth Avenue's Easter Parade first began at St. Thomas's in the 19th century, when congregants carried flowers to a nearby hospital. The church's current incarnation—a French Gothic building designed by Cram, Goodhue and Ferguson and completed in 1914—juxtaposes detailed sculptures and austere volumes on the tight corner site. The Episcopal parish maintains a boarding school for members of its renowned boys' choir and accommodates a medley of musical events.

Times Square Broadway and Seventh Ave., from 42nd St. to 47th St.
New Yorkers insist on calling it the Crossroads of the World. Of course, New Yorkers like to think of their city as the center of the cosmos, so it is hardly surprising that they attach mere global import to the dot on the hometown map where Broadway and 42nd Street collide. For once, however, the New York penchant for overstatement happens to be fact.

Times Square is, without a doubt, the most recognized intersection on the planet, and never is that more true than on New Year's Eve. Hundreds of thousands of people jam the square and tens of millions more watch on television as

Ozier Muhammad/The New York Times

Times Square

a glittering ball slowly descends, ticking off the final seconds of the dying year (the special ball manufactured to mark the year 2000 was made by Waterford Crystal, covered with 144 strobe lights and 12,000 rhinestones). By now, some are willing to believe that there would not be a new year, a new century, a new millennium without this communal gathering in the heart of New York.

It wasn't always like that. At the turn of the last century, the area was a humble place called Long Acre Square. The name was changed in 1904 when *The New York Times* moved there; the cachet of the Times Square name attracted people to the surrounding blocks, and the square became a neighborhood. For decades to come, Times Square would provide the country with some of its most enduring images, from the finger-snap pace of the crowds outside Jack Dempsey's restaurant to the strangers exultantly embracing on V-E Day. All it took was an overhead shot of the neon-bathed square to tell moviegoers that they were entering a world of sophistication.

Decay set in with the Great Depression; by the 1970's, Times Square had become synonymous with sleazy arcades and tawdry sex shows. The menace and sheer creepiness of the place, almost a vision of hell, was memorably captured by Martin Scorsese in his 1976 film, *Taxi Driver*. Historic theaters and hotels were sacrificed for office space, *The Times* moved around the corner and the terra cotta façade of the old building was replaced with faceless white marble.

But the '90's brought rebirth, with porno houses giving way to the likes of Disney and Warner Brothers stores. Some find the new attractions a tad too sanitized, but few truly mourn the passing of the dope dealers and pimps.

Today, there is no better place to people-watch than Times Square. Street performers, gawking tourists and get-out-of-my-way New Yorkers—they are all here, and are easily the most fascinating thing about the place. For show business, there's also no place like Times Square. In the early years of the century, a big show could earn an average of a million dollars in its first year. In the final year of the century, Broadway was still packing them in, with attendance a record 11.6 million and a box-office take of $588 million, also a record. There are also about 1,500 businesses and organizations here; 21 million square feet of office space and 2.4 million more being built; one-fifth of all New York City hotel rooms; 3.9 million overnight visitors each year, and 26 million day-trippers; more than 251 restaurants, 10 movie theaters and 22 landmarked Broadway theaters. And believe it or not, nearly 27,000 people actually live in the Times Square area; 231,000 folks go to work there every day.

Through the years, Times Square has evolved and is still evolving. Yet it remains the place to gather, whether to watch a televised space shot or protest a war or celebrate triumph over tyranny. It is far more than a neighborhood. It is America's town square.

—*Clyde Haberman*

U.S.S. Intrepid Sea-Air-Space Museum 46th St. at 12th Ave. (212) 245-2533 Launched in 1943 and decommissioned in 1974, the *Intrepid* once had more than 100 aircraft and a crew of over 3,000. The aircraft carrier was deployed in the Second World War, the Korean and Vietnam Wars and served as a recovery vessel for NASA capsules. There are jets and prop planes on the flight and hangar decks, and exhibits relating to the ship's history and undersea exploration. A flight simulator recreates the feeling of being inside an F-18 fighter during the Gulf War. The open-air flight deck allows access to the navigation bridge and wheelhouse, and close examination of planes, helicopters and gun galleries. The destroyer *Edison* and the submarine *Growler* lie alongside. All three vessels are open to visitors, but the 900-foot *Intrepid*, which occupies an area greater than a midtown Manhattan block, is the most impressive.

Admission: $10, general; $7.50, students and seniors; $5, children (6–11); $1, children (2 and under).

If You'd Like to Be Part of the Studio Audience . . .

From sitcoms to talk shows, New York has an abundance of programs that are taped before a live (and eager) audience. Here's your chance to take part, but take notice of the fine print. Some of these programs require commitments up to a year in advance. In most cases the lucky winners who can plan that far in advance— or are fortunate enough to win a lottery—will receive their tickets through the mail. For more programs that tape in the area check **www.nytoday.com.**

Saturday Night Live Saturdays at 11:30 P.M. No one under age 16 admitted. Tickets are decided by lottery based on postcards received during August. Winners are notified one to two weeks in advance with tickets for the dress rehearsal or the live show. Postcards can be sent to SNL, 30 Rockefeller Plaza, New York, NY 10112. Call (212) 664-3056 for more information. Standby tickets (one per person) are distributed at 9:15 A.M. on the mezzanine level of Rockefeller Plaza (49th Street side). These tickets do not guarantee admission.

The Cosby Show Thursdays at 4 and 7:30 P.M. No one under age 16 admitted. Tickets: call (718) 706-5389, (718) 706-5707 for groups, or send a postcard to Cosby Tickets, Kaufman-Astoria Studios, 34–12 36th St., Astoria, NY 11106. Specify the number of tickets and your preference for first or second taping.

The Daily Show with Jon Stewart Mondays through Thursdays from 5:45 to 7:30 P.M. No one under age 18 admitted. Tickets: call (212) 586-2477 or send a postcard with your preferred dates to The Daily Show, 513 W. 54th St., New York, NY 10019. Requests must be made four to six weeks in advance.

Late Night with Conan O'Brien Tuesdays through Thursdays from 5:30 to 6:30 P.M. No one under age 16 admitted. Arrive at 4 P.M. at the 49th Street entrance. Tickets: call (212) 664-3056/7, 664–3055 for groups, or send a postcard to Late Night with Conan O'Brien, 30 Rockefeller Plaza, Suite 9W, New York, NY 10112. Ticket reservations should be made four to five months in advance. Standby tickets are available at 9 A.M. at the page desk in the NBC Studios lobby.

The Late Show with David Letterman Mondays through Wednesdays at 5:30 P.M. and Thursdays at 5:30 and 8 P.M. Arrive at 4:15 for 5:30 tapings and 6:45 for tapings at 8. Tickets: call (212) 975-5853, order them through the CBS Web site or write to Late Show Tickets, Ed Sullivan Theater, 1697 Broadway, New York, NY 10019. Include your preferred date. For standby tickets, call (212) 247-6497 at 11 A.M. on taping days.

Live With Regis Philbin Mondays through Fridays at 9 A.M. No one under age 10 admitted. Tickets: send a postcard to Live Tickets, mation, call (212) 456-3054. Requests should be made one year in advance. For more info: P.O. Box 777, Ansonia Station, New York, NY 10023. Standby seats are available before 8 A.M. daily.

The Rosie O'Donnell Show Mondays through Thursdays at 10 A.M. and Wednesdays at 2 P.M. No children under age five. Tickets: call (212) 506-3288 or send a postcard to The Rosie O'Donnell Show, 30 Rockefeller Plaza, New York, NY 10112. There is a two-ticket maximum and currently an extensive wait. The standby line forms at 7:30 A.M. All tickets are drawn by lottery.

The View Mondays through Fridays at 11 A.M. No one under age 18 admitted. Arrive at 10 A.M. Send ticket requests to The View, Tickets, 320 W. 66th St., New York, NY 10023 or visit the ABC Web site. Requests should be made three to four months in advance. Standby tickets (first come, first serve) are available before 10 A.M.

Highly Recommended Neighborhood Restaurants
(See "Restaurants" section for reviews)

21 Club	☆☆	$ $ $ $	NEW AMERICAN
Aquavit	☆☆☆	$ $ $ $	SCANDINAVIAN
Chez Josephine	☆☆	$ $ $	BISTRO/FRENCH
Cho Dang Gol	☆☆	$ $ $	KOREAN
Christer's	☆☆	$ $ $	SCANDINAVIAN
Churrascaria Plataforma	☆☆	$ $ $	BRAZILIAN
Estiatorio Milos	☆☆	$ $ $ $	GREEK/SEAFOOD
Firebird	☆☆	$ $ $	RUSSIAN
Jack's Fifth	☆☆	$ $ $	FRENCH/ NEW AMERICAN
Joe's Shanghai	☆☆	$	CHINESE
Judson Grill	☆☆☆	$ $ $	NEW AMERICAN
Kang Suh	☆☆	$ $	KOREAN
La Caravelle	☆☆☆	$ $ $ $	FRENCH
La Côte Basque	☆☆☆	$ $ $ $	FRENCH
Le Bernardin	☆☆☆☆	$ $ $ $	FRENCH/SEAFOOD
Local	☆☆	$ $ $	NEW AMERICAN
Molyvos	☆☆☆	$ $ $	GREEK
Osteria Del Circo	☆☆	$ $ $	ITALIAN
Palio	☆☆	$ $ $ $	ITALIAN
Palladin	☆☆	$ $ $	NEW AMERICAN
Petrossian	☆☆	$ $ $ $	RUSSIAN
Quince	☆☆	$ $ $ $	FRENCH
Remi	☆☆	$ $ $	ITALIAN
San Domenico	☆☆☆	$ $ $ $	ITALIAN
Sea Grill	☆☆	$ $ $	SEAFOOD
Sugiyama	☆☆☆	$ $ $ $	JAPANESE/SUSHI
Thalia	☆☆	$ $ $	NEW AMERICAN
Viceversa	☆	$ $	ITALIAN

Recommended Inexpensive Restaurants

Carnegie Deli	DELI
Chimichurri Grill	LATIN AMERICAN
Garrick	NEW AMERICAN
Han Bat	KOREAN
Han Sung Garden	KOREAN
Havana NY	LATIN AMERICAN
Island Spice	CARIBBEAN
John's Pizzeria	ITALIAN/PIZZA
Los Dos Rancheros	MEXICAN
McHale's	BAR SNACKS/BURGERS
Puttanesca	ITALIAN
Rinconcito Peruano	PERUVIAN
Topaz Thai	THAI
Wu Liang Ye	CHINESE

Upper East Side

From the stately homes and manicured flower beds along **Park Avenue** to the art galleries and pricey boutiques on **Madison Avenue,** the Upper East Side has all the trappings of power and privilege (as well as 10021, the nation's wealthiest ZIP code in 1990). Walk along Park Avenue or its side streets on a weekday morning and you're likely to see professional dog walkers being tugged along in a tangle of pedigree pooches, or uniformed children traipsing off to Spence, Chapin and other exclusive private schools.

Historically the Upper East Side has been a place of privilege. Until the 1840's, it was primarily pastureland. That changed with the opening of Central Park in 1860. In the late 19th century, mansions rose on Fifth Avenue and brownstones lined the side streets. In 1906, when the New York Central Railroad converted from steam to electricity, the Park Avenue tracks were moved underground. In the 1950's the Third Avenue El was demolished, and within a few years that artery's tenements were vanishing, too.

But the Upper East Side has a more diverse population than its reputation suggests. On Lexington Avenue, neighborhood institutions such as **Bloomingdale's** department store, **Hunter College** and the **92d Street Y** lure shoppers, students and culture lovers from across the city. Farther east, middle-class families and young professionals who snagged rent-stabilized apartments in the early 1990's fill high-rise apartments that sprang up after World War II.

This area hosts some of the best known cultural institutions in the world. **Museum Mile** along Fifth Avenue has the **Metropolitan Museum of Art,** the **Solomon R. Guggenheim Museum,** the **Jewish Museum,** the **Museum of the City of New York** and **El Museo del Barrio.** The Frick and Carnegie mansions house the **Frick Collection** and the **Cooper-Hewitt National Design Museum,** respectively (see the section "Museums"). The mansions are two remnants of **Millionaire's Row,** where European-style grand residences overlooking Central Park were built in the early 1900s by super-rich industrialists competing to

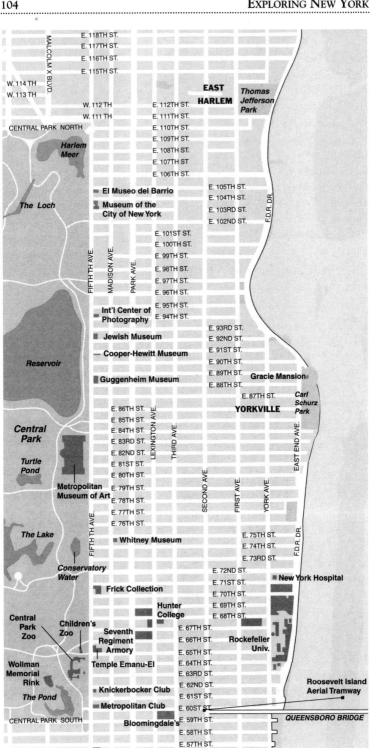

Upper East Side

outdo each other. Several institutions dedicated to world societies and cultures are also located here including the **Asia Society** and the **China Institute in America** (see "Institutes of World Culture" in the section "Museums").

Farther south is the **Seventh Regiment Armory** (Park Ave. and 66th St.), an 1879 medieval-style building that became the model for armories throughout the country. The armory, with its Tiffany interiors and enormous drill room, hosts frequent art and antiques shows . Also at the southern end of the neighborhood are several private clubs that are housed in historic buildings. Worth seeing are the **Metropolitan Club** (1–11 East 60th St.), designed by Stanford White in the 1890's, the **Knickerbocker Club** (2 East 62d St.) and the **Lotos Club** (5 East 66th St.). Other historical townhouses and carriage houses line the streets east of Park Avenue, particularly on 69th Street (between Third and Lexington Aves.) and in the **Treadwell Farm Historic District** on 61st and 62d Streets (between Second and Third Aves.).

In **Yorkville** (70th-96th St., east of Lexington Ave.), the Old World flavor of this once German and Hungarian (also Irish and Czech) enclave is fading. There are remnants such as **Schaller and Weber** (1654 Second Ave. between 85th and 86th Sts.) which has been selling authentic German sausage and other specialties since 1937. The **Heidelberg** (1648 Second Ave. near 86th St.) is the last authentic German restaurant in a neighborhood that was once home to more than two dozen of them. For the most part the old groceries and bakeries have been replaced by a more youthful spirit found in the cafes along Second and Third Avenues and bars that fill with exuberant drinkers on weekends. Joggers and the less harried take to the East River esplanade and **Carl Schurz Park** outside **Gracie Mansion,** the mayor's official residence.

Across the East River, just minutes away by aerial tram, lies tranquil **Roosevelt Island,** the site of a prison, an almshouse and an insane asylum from the early 1800's through the early 1900's. Today, the island is a mixed-income residential community that offers an escape from Manhattan's frenzy.

HIGHLIGHTS OF THE NEIGHBORHOOD

Abigail Adams Smith Museum 421 East 61st St. (between First and York Aves.) (212) 838-6878. This small museum sits well within earshot of the FDR Drive and in the shadow the Queensboro Bridge. You might find it hard to imagine that people used to flock to this setting for a peaceful escape from the hustle and bustle of downtown. But after an hour or so wandering through the museum's nine richly appointed period rooms and relaxing on a stone bench in the 18th-century-style gardens, it starts to seem more plausible. In the 1830's, wealthy New Yorkers would retreat to what was then called the Mount Vernon Hotel for the weekend. The Federal-style structure, built in 1799, is the only remaining building of its kind in Manhattan. The museum is named for Abigail Adams Smith, daughter of President John Adams, who originally built it as part of a planned 23-acre estate modeled after Mount Vernon. It was never completed. The museum offers guided tours, dramatic programs and lectures.

Admission: $3, general; $2, students and seniors; museum members and children under 12, free.

American Irish Historical Society 991 Fifth Ave. (between 80th and 81st Sts.) (212) 288-2263. The society features a substantial library and a gallery in its 100-year-old building, with small temporary exhibits highlighting Irish contributions to American society. There are frequent readings, lectures and concerts.

American Society of Illustrators 128 East 63d St. (between Park and Lexington Aves.) (212) 838-2560. You'll come away from this museum with a new respect for the artwork you see all around you every day, from soup-can labels to CD covers. The society has existed since 1901 to preserve the past and promote the future of illustration. The museum's permanent collection includes work by Norman Rockwell and J.C. Lyendecker.

Americas Society 680 Park Ave. (at 68th St.) (212) 249-8950. Founded in 1967 by Nelson Rockefeller to heighten economic, social and cultural awareness of all countries in the Western Hemisphere, the Americas Society features exhibitions, lectures and concerts. The neo-Federal building housing the Society was designed by McKim, Mead and White in 1909.

Carl Schurz Park East End Ave. at 84th St. (212) 360-1311. Named after a newspaper editor and reform politician who exercised great influence upon 19th-century elections, Carl Schurz Park is the site of Gracie Mansion, the mayor's official residence. Stretching along the East River, the park is also one of the city's quietest. Benches line a relaxing promenade that offers views of tugboats, Hell's Gate Bridge and the Roosevelt Island lighthouse. To the delight of loungers, the brick paths make the park a terrible place for in-line skating. The park has a basketball court and children's playground, too.

Museum of the City of New York 1220 Fifth Ave. (between 103d and 104th Sts.) (212) 534-1672 www.mcny.org If you accept the premise that New York is the world's greatest city, you will be at home at the Museum of the City of New York. Created in 1923 to collect and preserve the history of the city, the museum's intimate galleries are filled with a rich trove of artifacts from the 19th and 20th centuries. Its collections trace the development of the modern city and its people, from the skating ponds portrayed on Currier & Ives prints to the skyscrapers photographed by Berenice Abbott. Visitors can count on exhibits about the history of Broadway theater and American decorative arts. Kids will be drawn to the historic fire pumps and a gallery stuffed with toys. **Admission:** $5 (suggested); $4, students, children and seniors. **Credit cards:** All major; checks. **Hours:** Wed.–Sat., 10 A.M.–5 P.M.; Sun., 12–5 P.M. **Services:** Tours, gift shop, lectures, concerts.

New York Society Library 53 East 79th St. (between Madison and Park Aves.) (212) 288-6900. The Society Library is the oldest library in New York, dating from 1754. It has moved several times, but for 60 years it has been on East 79th Street. It is a membership library with nearly 200,000 volumes. Nonmembers can use the ground floor for reference or reading without charge. (Annual family membership is $135.) It feels and smells like an old-fashioned library with a wonderful, rich reading room filled with Audubon sketches.

Temple Emanu-El 1 East 65th St. (at Fifth Ave.) (212) 744-1400. The Temple Emanu-El is said to be the largest Jewish congregation in the world. The impressive limestone Moorish-Romanesque structure was completed in 1929 on the site of an Astor mansion. In size and beauty it rivals some of Europe's cathedrals. The sanctuary, which seats 2,500, has an extraordinary bronze ark in the shape of a Torah and is decorated with marvelous mosaics by Hildreth Meiere. The temple regularly hosts recitals and concerts, and, surprisingly enough (given its size), music sounds rather good here.

Highly Recommended Neighborhood Restaurants
(See "Restaurants" section for reviews)

Aureole	☆☆	$$$$	NEW AMERICAN
Café Boulud	☆☆☆	$$$$	FRENCH
Cello	☆☆☆	$$$	BISTRO/FRENCH
Circus	☆☆	$$$	BRAZILIAN
Daniel	☆☆☆	$$$$	FRENCH
Destinee	☆☆	$$$$	FRENCH
Etats-Unis	☆☆	$$$	NEW AMERICAN
JoJo	☆☆☆	$$$$	FRENCH
Lenox Room	☆☆	$$$	NEW AMERICAN
Little Dove	☆☆	$$$	NEW AMERICAN
Lobster Club	☆☆	$$$	NEW AMERICAN
Mark's	☆☆	$$$	AMERICAN
Match Uptown	☆☆	$$$$	PAN-ASIAN
Matthew's	☆☆	$$$	MEDITERRANEAN
Maya	☆☆	$$$	MEXICAN/TEX-MEX
Paola's	☆☆	$$	ITALIAN
Parioli Romanissimo	☆☆	$$$$	ITALIAN
Payard Pâtisserie	☆☆	$$$	BISTRO/FRENCH
Sushi Hatsu	☆☆☆	$$$$	JAPANESE/SUSHI

Recommended Inexpensive Restaurants

Bandol	FRENCH
Bistro Le Steak	BISTRO/STEAK
Donguri	JAPANESE/SUSHI
El Pollo	LATIN AMERICAN
John's Pizzeria	ITALIAN/PIZZA
L'Ardoise	FRENCH
La Forêt	BISTRO/FRENCH
Pig Heaven	CHINESE
The Sultan	TURKISH
Wu Liang Ye	CHINESE

Upper West Side

How to explain the Upper West Side? It has Columbus Circle at one end and Columbia University at the other. In between is a rectangle four miles long and one mile wide that is unlike any other neighborhood in the United States. Politicians who know the city by its ZIP codes know that 10023, 10024 and 10025—the Upper West Side—are three of the most liberal anywhere. But the rectangle is really a place of contrasts. It is a place of rich and poor, sometimes on the same block, of ethnic and religious variety, of churches and synagogues, and of culture that ranges from **Lincoln Center** to small neighborhood stages.

Where to begin an exploration? Not with a place but an idea: the Upper West Side is not old New York. It was farmland until well after the Civil War—the city, such as it was, covered only the lower third of the island of Manhattan. Before the proud apartment buildings began marching up Central Park West, Central Park's 843 acres were penciled off as a big green rectangle—"the grand-daddy of all American landscaped parks," the American Institute of Architects Guide to New York City called it. But Frederick Law Olmsted, principal designer of the park, did not want New Yorkers to think of the park as architecture. "What we want to gain is tranquility and rest to the mind," he said. The park is full of places where one can gain both. Runners circle the reservoir in endless laps. Rowers ply the lake in bulky rented boats. Zelda Fitzgerald, the wife of Jazz Age novelist F. Scott Fitzgerald, painted the bridge that bisects the lake.

From there, one can see the Dakota, an apartment building so spacious that Leonard Bernstein had no trouble fitting two grand pianos into his living room. The Dakota was also home to John Lennon, who was shot to death just outside the archway that leads to the building's elegant courtyard. His widow, Yoko Ono, still lives in the Dakota, only a short walk from **Strawberry Fields**, inside the park honoring his memory.

Up Central Park West, past the twin-towered San Remo apartments, are the museums. **The New-York Historical Society** has kept the hyphen that the rest of the city dropped more than a century ago. Next door is the **American Museum of Natural History**. The oldest section of the museum was designed by Calvert Vaux, Olmsted's collaborator on the design of the park just across the street. The museum's newest addition is the sleek glass box that encloses the **Hayden Planetarium** in the **Rose Center for Earth and Space**. Three blocks west is Broadway; between 72nd Street and 96th Street is a food shopper's paradise, with markets like Fairway, Citarella and Zabar's—and a sleek new Balducci's. Three stops beyond 96th Street on the No. 1 local is **Columbia University**. The campus was laid out by Charles Follen McKim, a partner in McKim, Mead & White, the legendary firm that satisfied the city's lust for carefully proportioned neoclassical creations at the beginning of the 20th century. The newest building on the Columbia campus is an $85 million student center, a gleaming glass box that opened in 1999, completing McKim's master plan.

—*James Barron*

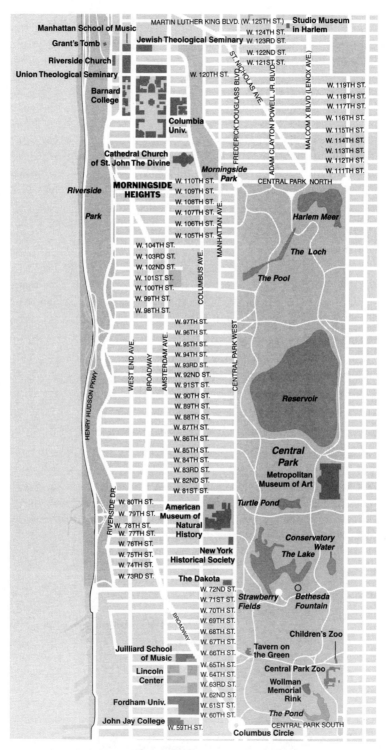

Upper West Side/Morningside Heights

HIGHLIGHTS OF THE NEIGHBORHOOD

The American Museum of Natural History Central Park West and 79th St. (212) 769-5100 www.amnh.org

  Holden Caulfield reported in *The Catcher in the Rye* that he loved this huge, hushed museum because "everything always stayed right where it was."

  But over the last several years, the Natural History Museum—the largest of its kind in the world, with about three-quarters of a million square feet of public exhibition space—has actually moved a lot of things around. The world-famous dinosaur halls were expanded and spruced up in the late 1990's, and the fossils themselves were rearranged to conform with new anthropological research. The towering Tyrannosaurus Rex was completely reshaped into a low stalking pose with its tail in the air. The Barosaurus, probably the first thing you will see when you walk in, still towers; at five stories, it is the world's tallest free-standing dinosaur exhibit.

  In February 2000, the museum opened the new **Rose Center for Earth and Space,** which encloses the rebuilt **Hayden Planetarium,** now the most technologically advanced planetarium in the world. The Rose Center includes a recreation of the birth of the universe in the Big Bang Theater, and a dazzling variety of exhibits relating to Mother Earth and outer space (see Rose Center description below.)

  But if you get tired of flash, the museum still has many reliable standbys to remind you of its origins. There's Akeley Hall, with its silent herds of stuffed elephants; the famous Star of India sapphire, the world's largest; and the 94-foot model of the Blue Whale, in whose shadow you might want to enjoy a smoked salmon sandwich in the Ocean Life Food Court.—*Randy Kennedy*

Admission (suggested): $9.50, adults; $7.50, students and seniors; $6, children.

The Ansonia 2109 Broadway (between 73d and 74th Sts.) (212) 724-2600. The thick, soundproof walls of the Ansonia have long harbored musicians. Enrico Caruso and Igor Stravinsky once lived upstairs in the Beaux-Arts apartment building, which dates from 1904, and Bette Midler launched her career singing downstairs in the Continental Baths, a gay spa that doubled as a cabaret in the 1970's. In more recent years, the building has been the site of fierce battles between the landlord and rent-regulated tenants, some of whom operate music rehearsal studios in their apartments. A confection of balconies, turrets and dormer windows, the restored 17-story facade gives its block of upper Broadway the look of a Parisian boulevard exaggerated on a New York scale.

Cathedral Church of St. John the Divine 1047 Amsterdam Ave. (At 112th St.) (212) 316-7540 www.stjohndivine.org The clerics at the Cathedral Church of St. John the Divine like to call it a medieval cathedral for New York City, not just in architectural style but in spirit and commitment. The cathedral is the seat of the Episcopal Diocese in New York; its bishop once said it combines all the life and struggle of the city. Peacocks strut across the bucolic 13-acre grounds, delighting the children who chase after them for tail feathers. Artists in residence haunt the basement vaults, rehearsing their pieces, then perform them in the eclectic splendor of the Gothic, Romanesque and Byzantine sanctuary. The cathedral tends to New York's forgotten homeless, at the same time it holds memorial services for many of the city's most famous citizens. About the only time you might see an elephant on Amsterdam Avenue is in the early fall, when St. John's clergy bless animals large and small in honor of St. Francis.

Neighborhood residents have affectionately nicknamed the cathedral, with its soaring Gothic arches, two luminous rose windows and carved stone figures, St. John the Unfinished. When its cornerstone was laid in 1892, on the site of a former orphan asylum, it was envisioned as a great acropolis on a hill, the rocky schist of upper Manhattan. Indeed, it is second in size only to St. Peter's Basilica in Rome, with more floor area than Notre Dame and Chartres combined, and still growing, mainly upward. Construction ceased during the iron and steel shortages of World War II. During the civil rights struggles of the late 1960's, the Diocese hesitated to lavish money on a building in a neighborhood filled with poverty, and dedicated itself to good works instead. Work has slowly resumed over the last few years.

On the vertiginous vertical tour, you can peer down from the crossway more than 100 feet above the floor—the real excitement of the cathedral for visiting schoolchildren. A guided tour through the interior helps uncover details from the whimsical (the prayer bay dedicated to sports, from polo to baseball) to the sobering (the bay dedicated to the healing arts, now dominated by a memorial to those who have suffered and died from AIDS). Among the profusion of icons, both sacred and mundane, are an ostrich egg, a symbol of meditation, donated by P.L. Travers, the author of "Mary Poppins," and a prominently displayed pair of menorahs donated by Adolph Ochs, former publisher of *The New York Times*. The bronze lights in front were salvaged from the demolished Penn Station. The bronze doors were fabricated in Paris by Ferdinand Barbedienne, who also cast the Statue of Liberty. St. John's is truly, as its founders hoped, a house of prayer for all nations.

—Anemona Hartocollis

Children's Museum Of Manhattan 212 West 83d St. (between Amsterdam Ave. and Broadway) (212) 721-1234.
(See the section, *New York for Children*.)

Christ And St. Stephen's Church 122 W. 69th St. (between Broadway and Columbus Ave.) (212) 787-2755. Nestled mid-block on a tree-lined street near Lincoln Center, behind a well-manicured patch of lawn (a rare sight in these parts), is Christ and St. Stephen's Church, a cozy brick chapel with some pretty turn-of-the-century stained glass. Built in 1880, the small church is a popular performance venue for musicians of all types. On any given day you might catch a recital, a chamber-music group, an orchestra or a choral concert. Thanks to the church's unusually low ceiling, the sound here is good.

Church of St. Michael Amsterdam Ave. and 100th St. (212) 222-2700. St. Michael's Church has a beautiful refurbished interior, with mosaics and Tiffany glass. The seven chancel windows, depicting St. Michael's victory over Lucifer, are among Tiffany's most notable works.

St. Michael's is also a wonderful place for music, and groups who perform here regularly, like the acclaimed early-music vocal quartet Anonymous 4, provide a compelling reason to venture this far uptown. The church is also home to an unusually fine organ, built by Rudolf von Beckerath in 1967, which, like the building itself, was recently restored and is considered to be one of the best in town.

Columbia University 116th St. and Broadway (212) 854-1754. Built on the site of a former insane asylum, Columbia University's main campus represents one of the most balanced expressions of Beaux-Arts urban design in America. Chartered as King's College before the American Revolution, New York's Ivy League university moved from Madison Avenue and 49th Street to Morningside Heights at the turn of the century. McKim, Mead & White designed a symmetrical quadrangle of Italian Renaissance-style buildings around the classical Low Library, whose monumental stone staircase has become a favorite warm-weather hangout for students. As Columbia expanded into a major research university, it overflowed its original four-block plan, creating tensions with the surrounding community. A stage for beatniks in the 1950's and student protests during the Vietnam War, Columbia has in recent years become a quieter place, both politically and culturally. Despite gentrification moving up the Upper West Side, the university's neighborhood—with its academic bookstores and antiquated coffee shops—maintains a certain detachment from the rest of the city.

Columbia University—Miriam and Ira D. Wallach Art Gallery Schermerhorn Hall (between Broadway and Amsterdam Ave.) (212) 854-7288. Scholars and curators will tell you that there is no substitute for contact with original art. With this in mind, Miriam and Ira D. Wallach donated funds in 1986 for a

Columbia University

gallery at Columbia University as both a resource for teaching and study and a public exhibition space. As its curators are often graduate students and faculty from the art history department, the gallery's exhibitions tend to be well researched and often have dense titles that require two sentences and a colon. The exhibitions are nevertheless treasure troves, drawing on Columbia's resources as well as public and private collections to present issues, methods and art that are not often seen elsewhere in the city. Catalogues are produced for each of the shows, which change every six to nine weeks.

Columbus Circle Broadway at Central Park South. At the southwest corner of Central Park, defined by wide avenues, open sky and the park, the traffic circle is well situated for civic grandeur. Yet it is filled with memorials to past schemes driven by self-interest. In the 1890's the city's growing Italian-American community outmaneuvered Spaniards to dedicate the statue of Christopher Columbus, which celebrates the 400th anniversary of the explorer's arrival in the New World. William Randolph Hearst financed the Maine Monument at the entrance to the park to commemorate the sinking of the ship that precipitated the Spanish-American War. As traffic increased, the circle began to look more like Times Square, with its large billboards and neon advertisements, than a Beaux-Arts pedestrian plaza. More recently, Donald Trump turned the former Gulf and Western building into a glitzy residential and hotel tower. The New York Coliseum was torn down in 2000.

Corpus Christi Church 529 West 121st St. (between Broadway and Amsterdam Ave.) (212) 666-9266. Located in the heart of seminary country (Union Theological and Jewish Theological Seminaries are nearby) is Corpus Christi Church, one of the many beautiful small churches that dot New York's neighborhoods. Built in the 1930's, this Roman Catholic church is the home of Music Before 1800, a highly acclaimed early-music series established in 1975, just before the period-instrument craze took the classical music world by storm. With its decorated ceiling and side galleries, intimate atmosphere and almost flawless acoustics, the 525-seat church is a wonderful setting for medieval, Renaissance and Baroque music.

The Dakota 1 West 72d St. (at Central Park West) (212) 874-8671 Located far uptown amid largely vacant lots when it was completed in 1884, the Dakota was said to be as remote as the Dakota Territory. An early luxury building in an era when rich New Yorkers had only just begun to move from town houses into apartments, the Dakota came equipped with steam-pumped elevators and ceilings that soar as high as 15 feet. In addition to John Lennon, who was fatally shot here in 1980, the building has housed a flock of arts and entertainment figures, including Judy Garland, Leonard Bernstein and Lauren Bacall, and provided the setting for the movie *Rosemary's Baby*. During the building's recent restoration, the mute yellow brick lost its brown patina. With its steeply gabled roof and massive structures—features that Henry J. Hardenberg, the architect, deployed in his later design for the Plaza Hotel—the Dakota stands like a fortress guarding the 72d Street entrance to Central Park.

Fairway Market 2127 Broadway (at 74th St.) (212) 595-1888.
(See "Food Markets" in the section "Shopping")

Grant's Tomb Riverside Dr. at 122nd St. (212) 666-1640 www.nps.gov
Quick! Who's buried in Grant's Tomb?

Don't groan at the old joke. It is asked only because most people give the
wrong answer, or at least an incomplete one.

Of course, the tomb contains the remains of Ulysses S. Grant, the great
Civil War general and perhaps not-so-great 18th president. But many are
unaware that next to him, in a matching sarcophagus of red granite, lies his
wife, Julia Dent Grant. Grant, who died in 1885, had wanted to be buried at
West Point, but his wife would not have been allowed to join him there. Thus
he became the only president buried in New York City, in a neoclassical granite
monument overlooking the Hudson.

For decades after its dedication in 1897, the tomb was among the most celebrated buildings in the country. Time dimmed its popularity. Over the years, the
memorial deteriorated into a graffiti-scarred drug hangout, until finally in the
1990's the National Park Service gave it a much deserved face lift. The cost was
$1.8 million—three times what it took to build it.

Visitors are few. That is good news for anyone interested in a tranquil refuge,
embodying Grant's epitaph, chiseled above the entrance: "Let us have peace."

—*Clyde Haberman*

Lincoln Center Broadway, between 62nd and 66th Sts. (212) 546-2656.
www.lincolncenter.org Hardly beautiful, but stunning in its comprehensive cultural offerings, Lincoln Center for the Performing Arts is a great stop on any visitor's itinerary. Even if you don't take in the myriad programs, from opera to ballet
to film to jazz, it is fun to sit and watch those who do. The winter season brings
the fur coat crowd to the Metropolitan Opera, its building their spectacular, glittering backdrop. In September, when the New York Film Festival is on, die-hard
film fans as well as directors and stars come here for everything from the first
screening of Woody Allen's latest to obscure films from Iran. It is almost impossible to get a ticket to these films, because they are sold in advance to members,
but you can almost always procure a pair from a member selling them outside
before the show. Lincoln Center also houses the New York Philharmonic, the
New York City opera, the New York City Ballet and the Juilliard School, which
frequently holds free or inexpensive concerts. Scores of different theater, music
and dance programs are also held at the center during the year. The fountain,
located in the center's plaza, is a great place to sit and sip a coffee, watch people
meet their dates, and try to conjure the day that ground was broken for the center—May 14, 1959, when President Dwight Eisenhower wielded the shovel and
Leonard Bernstein led the Philharmonic and Juilliard chorus in the "Hallelujah
Chorus." In the summer, there is outdoor dancing in that plaza, where New
Yorkers do everything from ballroom to square dancing under the stars.

—*by Jennifer Steinhauer*

Alice Tully Hall (212) 875-5050. Seven years after the official unveiling of
Lincoln Center, Alice Tully Hall opened. It was September 1969—the 67th

The Metropolitan Opera

birthday of its namesake, whose portrait dominates the large but underutilized lobby. The Chamber Music Society of Lincoln Center—which still calls the 1,096-seat hall home—played the inaugural concert of Bach, Schumann and Schubert, after which it was immediately apparent that, finally, after two acoustic failures (Philharmonic Hall and the New York State Theater), Lincoln Center had a concert hall it could be proud of. It's a wonderful stage for chamber music and recitals, as well as small-scale opera and orchestral concerts. Jazz and avant-garde artists play here, too, and there's even an occasional appearance by a pop star or two.

Avery Fisher Hall (212) 875-5030. When the New York Philharmonic relocated in 1962 from Carnegie Hall to Avery Fisher Hall (then called Philharmonic Hall), it found itself in a shiny new building with particularly appalling acoustics. What to do? Enter Avery Fisher—the electronics mogul and an amateur violinist—who gave great sums to improve the hall and attach his already well-known name to its portals. In the end, the results of these—and subsequent—renovations proved far from perfect. Nevertheless, the hall is, along with Carnegie, the city's premier concert venue. It's where an entire generation of baby boomers learned about classical music thanks to Leonard Bernstein's "Young People's Concerts," and where Kurt Masur now presides over the Big Apple's internationally acclaimed orchestra. Avery Fisher Hall also hosts the world's top visiting orchestras, instrumentalists, chamber groups and singers. Pop and jazz performers are frequent guests, too, especially when Jazz at Lincoln Center is on the calendar.

Adorning the 2,738-seat hall are photos and other historic memorabilia. Two restaurants in the lobby offer decent but pricey meals; the delectable pastries from Cafe Vienna are a better choice to tame the pre-concert appetite. The sprawling promenade directly off the orchestra level offers good views of the Lincoln Center plaza and the bustling surroundings—in the summer months, you can watch the would-be Fred Astaires and Ginger Rogerses learning to fox-trot, tango or samba at the popular Midsummer Night Swing series.

Library for the Performing Arts at Lincoln Center (212) 870-1630. This branch of the New York Public Library is a treasure trove of invaluable materials, boasting the largest reference, archival and circulating arts-related collection in the world. But after 32 years of growth, the library is bursting at the seams and in need of modernization. It was closed for renovations in July 1998 and will reopen in fall 2000 with a new information and welcome center, improvements to help speed material retrieval, centralized playback for the videotape archives and a much-needed central reading room.

Metropolitan Opera House (212) 362-6000. The second and current Metropolitan Opera House opened in September 1966 with the world premiere of Samuel Barber's *Antony and Cleopatra*. Leontyne Price sang. Thomas Schippers conducted. But none of them stood a chance that night, because the real star of the evening was the magnificent (some might say garish) theater that dominates the Lincoln Center plaza. It's the world's largest opera house, and even from a distance its grandeur is apparent. Five enormous glass arches overwhelm the eye. Behind them hang Marc Chagall's spectacular murals, "The Triumph of Music" on the south wall and "The Sources of Music" on the north.

Once inside the 3,900-seat house, the sweeping staircase ushers you into a glittering world of red velvet, gold leaf and gaudy crystal chandeliers that rise up to the ceiling at the beginning of each performance. Even in the nosebleed sections the sound is good, so it's not necessary to spend $150 or more for orchestra seats. You can even buy standing-room tickets for about $15, but they sell out fast.

Technically, the Met is a director's dream, equipped with a slew of mechanical wonders: Four huge stages with elevators and revolving platforms, a computerized lighting system and movable footlights. Every seat has the unique "Met Titles" screen, providing simultaneous translation. The large orchestra pit accommodates more than 100 musicians, and what musicians they are. James Levine, the artistic director, has turned the Met Orchestra into one of the best orchestras in or out of a pit.

Intermissions are usually rather long, giving you time to explore the Met's nooks and crannies. There are costume and art exhibits that impart a sense of the company's history. Or, if you prefer, have a drink, or dessert and coffee, which in balmy weather you can take onto the promenade terrace overlooking the plaza. (You can also have dinner in the Grand Tier Restaurant, but it must be ordered in advance.)

Lest we forget, the Met is also the home of the American Ballet Theater in May, June and early July.

New York State Theater (212) 870-5570. It may not be as posh as its sister opera house diagonally across the plaza, but in some ways, the New York State Theater is the more interesting building. Designed by Philip Johnson as a home for the New York City Ballet and the New York City Opera, the 2,800-seat theater's most striking feature is the grand, four-story foyer, flanked by two marvelous white marble Elie Nadelman sculptures and surrounded by balconies. Hundreds of long chains serve as draperies for a glass wall that opens onto a large terrace facing Avery Fisher Hall, with nice views of the Met's Chagall murals (and a place to smoke). Inside, a chandelier vaguely suggestive of a mirrored disco ball hovers overhead. The seats are comfortable, the sightlines good. Because the theater was built with dance in mind, acoustics are often a problem here. But recent additions of acoustical panels and other sound-absorbing materials have improved matters considerably, and now you can actually hear the singers.

Morningside Park Morningside Ave. at 110th St. (212) 360-1311. Morningside Park was built in 1887 atop the cliffs just to the east of the site, now occupied by Barnard College, where the Battle of Harlem Heights was fought in 1776. (A later battle over Columbia University's plans to build a gym in the park led to the student demonstrations and takeover of the campus in 1968.) The thin 31-acre park, which lies between Harlem and the Columbia campus, includes a concourse at the top of a tall stone wall built along Morningside Drive. The promontories on the concourse offer commanding views of spirited basketball and handball games in the courts below.

New-York Historical Society 2 West 77th St. (between Columbus Ave. and Central Park West) (212) 873-3400 www.nyhistory.org New York City's oldest museum in continuous operation, the society is an important institution for the study and preservation of the city's history and culture. The Society's art collection includes a number of landscape paintings by major artists of the Hudson River school of painters, 135 Tiffany lamps, and one of the largest collections of miniature portraits in the country. The building also houses a highly-regarded print collection with thousands of photographs, architectural drawings and ephemera (available by appointment only) and a research library with over two million manuscripts, 10,000 maps, and hundreds of photgraphs, prints and other materials.

Admission: $5, adults; $3, students and seniors.

Nicholas Roerich Museum 319 West 107th St. (between Broadway and Riverside Dr.) (212) 864-7752. Nicholas Roerich, the Russian-American star of this one-man museum, was a true Renaissance man, involved in a vast range of artistic, philosophical and spiritual pursuits. He worked with Stravinsky to design sets and costumes, studied Russian archaeology, wrote, painted and traveled extensively. The museum features a permanent collection of Roerich's works and personal memorabilia, including numerous paintings inspired by his interest in Buddhism and the Tibetan highlands. The museum also hosts concerts and poetry readings.

Riverside Church Riverside Drive and 120th St. (Claremont Ave. and 121st St.) (212) 870-6700. Built in 1930 and modeled after the cathedral in Chartres, France, this mammoth gothic-style church bordering Riverside Park has magnificent stonework and stained glass windows. The church's nearly 400-foot tower has an observation deck affording spectacular views of the city and the Palisades across the Hudson. At $1 to ascend, it's a true bargain. Aside from vistas of the landscape, there are unique views inside of the peregrine falcons that have taken up residence, as well as a close-up look at the innards of the famous carillon, a gift of the Rockefeller family. (It has 74 bells—one weighing 20 tons—making it the world's largest.) You can hear it played every Sunday at 3 P.M. And though 120th Street is not on the maps of most theatergoers, the resident Melting Pot Theater is worth a visit. It seats about 270, has great sight lines, an ample stage and first-rate lighting and sound systems. The theater used to present dance and music events, but now focuses on plays and musicals generally geared toward a family audience.

Rose Center for Earth and Space 79th St. and Central Park West (212) 769-5100 www.amnh.org/rose/ The $210 million Rose Center for Earth and Space opened in February 2000, offering visitors a virtual journey through time, space and the mysteries of the cosmos. The 333,500-square-foot, seven-floor, 120-foot-high exhibition and research facility includes the new Hayden Planetarium, the Cullman Hall of the Universe and the Gottesman Hall of Planet Earth. The Hayden Planetarium contains the Space Theater, presenting "Passport to the Universe," and the Big Bang Theater, featuring narrated visual and audio effects simulating how the universe began. The Cullman Hall of the Universe is a 7,000-square-foot permanent exhibition hall on the bottom level of the Rose Center, divided into four zones that illustrate the processes that led to the creation of the planets, stars, galaxies and universe.

The domed Space Theater offers synthetic views of the cosmos far more detailed than the most elaborate Hollywood productions. With the help of a supercomputer, a state-of-the-art Zeiss star projector, an advanced laser system, a gigantic database and, of course, the hemispheric Space Theater

The Rose Center for Earth and Space

Hayden Planetarium/The New York Times

itself, the builders have created a marvelous celestial playhouse. The 18-minute-20-second Space Theater show is a spectacular virtual ride through the universe. The audience seated under the dome whizzes past Mars, Jupiter and Saturn and on into interstellar space toward the constellation Orion. The recorded voice of Tom Hanks calls attention to points of interest along the way.

The sky show occupies the upper half of the center's 87-foot diameter sphere; the lower half is devoted to a very brief light and sound show depicting the Big Bang. Between the upper and lower levels of the Rose Center is a spiral walkway (reminiscent of the Guggenheim Museum) with a splendid gallery of 220 astronomical photographs arrayed in order of their distances in time and space from the Big Bang to the present.

The spiral ramp itself is one of many devices incorporated in the Rose Center to impart a sense of scale—in particular, an appreciation of the staggering dimensions of the universe. The length of the walkway, nearly 100 yards, represents a span of around 13 billion years, at the end of which is a single hair, the thickness of which represents the duration of human history. Some of the most interesting photographs along the walkway show the results of gravitational lensing, an effect not explained until we reach a little enclosure called the Black Hole Theater on the lowest level of the center, which gives viewers the flavor of relativity theory, of the genius of Einstein and of the bizarre distortions enormous masses cause in nearby space-time.

The Rose Center also contains curiosities, including a sealed ecosphere in which little crustaceans and various plants live isolated from the outer world, thriving on each other and the light that shines on their transparent globe, and the 15 1/2-ton Willamette Meteorite. Interactive television monitors are everywhere, and a remote-controlled robot entertains young visitors.

Shows in the Space Theater were sold out for months in advance when the Rose Center opened, and tickets are likely to remain a hot item for some time. Call well in advance to make reservations.

Hours: Sun.–Thurs., 10 A.M.–5:45 P.M.; Fri. and Sat. until 8:45 P.M. Space shows run throughout the day. **Admission** (suggested donation), for the American Museum of Natural History, which includes the Rose Center: $10; for students and the elderly, $7.50; children 12 and under, $6; under 2 free. Admission to the museum, the Rose Center and the new Hayden Planetarium Space Show: $19; for students and the elderly, $14; children 12 and under, $11.50.

Zabar's 2245 Broadway (between 80th and 81st Sts.) (212) 787-2000. (See "Food Markets" in the section "Shopping")

Highly Recommended Neighborhood Restaurants
(See "Restaurants" section for reviews)

Calle Ocho	☆	$ $	PAN-LATIN
Gabriel's	☆ ☆	$ $ $	ITALIAN
Jean Georges	☆ ☆ ☆ ☆	$ $ $ $	NEW AMERICAN
Nick and Toni's	☆ ☆	$ $ $	MEDITERRANEAN
Picholine	☆ ☆ ☆	$ $ $ $	MEDITERRANEAN/
			FRENCH
Ruby Foo's	☆ ☆	$ $	PAN-ASIAN

Recommended Inexpensive Restaurants

Alouette	BISTRO/FRENCH
Artie's	DELI
Avenue	BISTRO/FRENCH
Café Frida	MEXICAN/TEX-MEX
Dalia's	TAPAS
Gabriela's	MEXICAN
Isola	ITALIAN
John's	ITALIAN/PIZZA
Josie's	NEW AMERICAN
Luzia's	PORTUGUESE
Metisse	BISTRO/FRENCH
Metsovo	GREEK
Mughlai	INDIAN

Harlem

The Harlem Renaissance of the 1920's brought the world the likes of Langston Hughes, Countee Cullen, Dorothy West and Zora Neale Hurston. The Harlem renaissance now underway is bringing the community the likes of the Gap, a Disney store and Starbucks. It is an economic blooming as sure as the literary one of generations ago. And visitors will find plenty to satisfy their interest in both.

Harlem emerged in the 18th Century as an upper Manhattan getaway for wealthy downtowners, who gave way to a succession of immigrants—Jews, Irish and, in the early 1900's, blacks, who turned it into the capital of black America. Its exact boundaries are disputed; geography and emotion don't always mix. But Harlem's history and legend indisputably resonate today, particularly among black Americans. In its heydey in the 1920s and 30s, jazz and blues luminaries such as Ella Fitzgerald and Duke Ellington played long into the night at places like the Savoy and Cotton Club, now long gone. Langston Hughes gave poetry readings at the Harlem YMCA, one of the early cultural centers, and 125th Street bustled with the energy of any village main street.

Eventually, with the flight of the middle class and the scourge of drugs and crime, Harlem slid into a decay from which it is only now emerging. The middle and upper classes are moving back into its elegant brownstones and newer housing and the neighborhood once again has become a popular tourist attraction. Merchants complain, though, that visitors often do not get off the tourist buses.

The most popular destination remains **125th Street,** the main shopping strip. The **Apollo Theater** is the 86-year-old showplace where Billie Holiday, Aretha Franklin, Count Basie and many others graced the stage—and many more got the "hook" for disappointing feisty audiences. A weekly television variety program "It's Showtime at the Apollo" is produced there.

Famous places such as the Audubon Ballroom, where Malcolm X was assassinated in 1965, have disappeared. But many cultural and historic spots remain. The **Schomburg Center for Research on Black Culture,** the **Studio Museum** (see the section "The Arts in New York") and the **National Black Theater** (212-722-3800) all have deep roots in the community and offer frequent exhibitions and shows that testify to the importance of black culture. How such treasures will coexist with new development has been a source of debate in the community.

On 125th Street, a 285,000-square-foot shopping mall called Harlem U.S.A. houses a Magic Johnson nine-screen cinema, a Disney store, Old Navy and a branch of the New York Sports Club. Advocates say these will bring much needed dollars and jobs. Opponents lament what they see as the sanitizing and homogenizing of a vibrant community.

The new development has not reached much into nearby East Harlem, also worth a trek. **El Museo del Barrio,** a 30-year-old institution on Fifth Avenue at

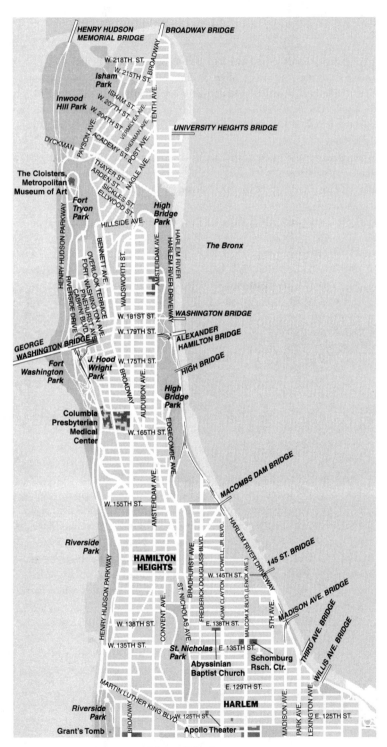

Upper Manhattan

104th Street, is among the many finds. Its focus is the Hispanic culture that defines East Harlem.

Other favored destinations for tourists are **Sylvia's Restaurant,** which serves soul food and has become a way station for politicians currying favor with black voters. Many other restaurants serve Caribbean, Latin American, African and continental cuisine. Harlem is also home to some of the city's best known jazz clubs.

—Randy Archibold

HIGHLIGHTS OF THE NEIGHBORHOOD

Abyssinian Baptist Church 132 West 138th St. (between Adam Clayton Powell and Malcolm X Blvds.) (212) 862-7474. The Abysinnian Baptist Church has become such a popular attraction that it has had to turn away tourists on Easter. Known for its rousing gospel choir, this 1923 Gothic church was home for many years to rousing sermons by Adam Clayton Powell, the charismatic preacher and Congressman. A memorial room displays artifacts from his life. Visit during Sunday services if you can, and afterwards head over for a soul food lunch at Sylvia's nearby.

Hamilton Grange National Memorial 287 Convent Ave. (between. 141st and 142nd Sts.) (212) 283-5154. A quaint country house built in 1802 that was once the country home of Alexander Hamilton—the first U.S. Secretary of the Treasury. Hamilton lived in Hamilton Grange with his family for only two years until he was killed in his duel with Aaron Burr in 1804. Given landmark status decades ago, the Grange now stands amid busy streets near the City College campus. The house features an interpretative program planned around themes of drama, music and colonial craft, as well as seasonal activities for children.

Schomburg Center for Research on Black Culture 515 Malcolm X Blvd. (at 135th St.) (212) 491-2200. The Schomburg Center's holdings are built on the personal collection of Arturo Alfonso Schomburg, a Puerto Rican black scholar and bibliophile who died in Brooklyn in 1938 at the age of 64. Schomburg's personal collection of materials was added to the Division of Negro Literature, History and Prints of the 135th Street branch of the New York Public Library in 1926. It became a research library of the Public Library system in 1972. The collections have grown to include more than 5,000,000 items—books, manuscripts, art objects, audio and video, and even sheet music, all documenting the history and culture of people of African descent throughout the world.

Sylvia's 328 Lenox Ave. (between 126th and 127th Sts.) (212) 996-0660. Tour buses pull up in front for a sanitized taste of Harlem. The food's not fabulous, but it offers everything you expect: fried chicken, collard greens and sweet potato pie. Best for the gospel brunch on Sunday.

Recommended Inexpensive Restaurants

(See "Restaurants" section for reviews)

Amy Ruth's	SOUTHERN
Bayou	CAJUN/SOUTHERN
Charles' Southern-Style	SOUTHERN
El Fogon	SPANISH
Emily's	SOUTHERN
Sylvia's	SOUTHERN

Washington Heights/Inwood

Dominican immigrants are only the latest arrivals in Washington Heights, an area that has been the first stop for many new Americans. In the early 1900's, the Irish poured into the area, especially to Inwood. In the period around World War II a large contingent of German Jews—including a young Henry Kissinger—made a home in the northern section near Fort Tryon Park.

Before the surge of immigration, Washington Heights was a rural retreat where the wealthy had country estates. It was this spaciousness that first attracted two major institutions: **Columbia-Presbyterian Hospital,** which opened in 1928, and **Yeshiva University,** which came in 1929. Other landmarks include the **Cloisters,** the Metropolitan Museum of Art's showcase for medieval art, which sits atop a hill in **Fort Tryon Park** and creates a sense of tranquility amid a noisy city. Long gone is the **Polo Grounds,** the former home of the baseball and football Giants, which overlooked the Harlem River at 157th Street.

At Manhattan Island's northernmost tip, the **Inwood** section lies between the Harlem River and **Inwood Hill Park,** where the borough's last stands of primeval forest remain. This neighborhood's newest arrivals are young professionals seeking affordable apartments in the Art Deco apartment buildings. On the banks of the Harlem River near Broadway, another dream lives on at **Baker Field,** where Columbia University's football team continues its often quixotic quest for glory.

HIGHLIGHTS OF THE NEIGHBORHOOD

American Academy of Arts and Letters 633 West 155th St. (at Broadway) (212) 368-5900. Though often criticized for elitism, the American Academy of Arts and Letters has honored an impressive and unarguably free-thinking group of architects, artists, writers and composers since its founding in 1904. Located in adjacent Beaux-Arts buildings, the Academy's activities for nonmembers are limited, but you can visit the galleries, featuring works by honorees, members and others.

American Numismatic Society Broadway (at 156th St.) (212) 234-3130. Filthy lucre looks wholesome and interesting in "The World of Coins," a permanent exhibition chronicling the history of units of exchange, including cowrie shells, beads, paper money and credit cards. Some of the earliest coins ever found are here: crudely shaped knife pieces dating to 1000 B.C., from China. Among the many oddities on view are a bronze coin struck with an unflattering portrait of Cleopatra and a 1,000,000,000,000,000,000-pengo bill from the inflation-ridden Hungary of 1946.

Dyckman Farmhouse 4881 Broadway (at 204th St.) (212) 304-9422
One of the few reminders that Manhattan was once farmland is standing its ground at the northern tip of Manhattan. The existing Dyckman Farmhouse, with a Dutch-style gambrel roof and field stone walls, was rebuilt in the 1780's after the original house was destroyed during the Revolutionary War. The museum features five period rooms, a reconstructed German military hut and a reproduction of a kitchen smokehouse.

Fort Tryon Park 741 Fort Washington Ave. (at 193d St.) (212) 360-1311.
Best known as the site of the Metropolitan Museum's Cloisters, Fort Tryon Park encompasses Manhattan's highest point, Linden Terrace, 268 feet above sea level. Surrounded by 66 hilly, wooded acres north of Washington Heights, the park's promenades offer unsurpassed views of the Hudson River and the Palisades. The site once held Fort Tryon, a Revolutionary War fort captured by the British and named for William Tryon, the last British governor of New York. During the 19th century, several large mansions were built in the area. John D. Rockefeller Jr. hired Frederick Law Olmsted Jr., son of the designer of Central Park, to turn his estate into a park, which he donated to the city in 1930. The Cloisters opened there eight years later.

The Cloisters Fort Tryon Park (near 190th St.) (212) 923-3700. The Cloisters at the northern tip of Manhattan is one of New York's most remarkable museums. Set atop a hill in Fort Tryon Park with stunning views of the Hudson River, the Cloisters houses much of the Metropolitan Museum of Art's extensive collection of medieval art. The building combines architectural elements from medieval monasteries, cloisters and secular buildings, with a collection that includes illuminated manuscripts, stained glass and tapestries. The Unicorn Tapestries, woven around 1500, depict a popular medieval legend. Surrounding the building are sprawling gardens filled with plants with medieval sounding names like bistort and mandrake. Opened in 1938, the majority of the Cloisters collection and the buildings themselves were purchased by the Metropolitan Museum with money donated by John D. Rockefeller Jr., who also gave the city Fort Tryon Park.

Admission: $8, general; $4, students and seniors; children under 12, free

George Washington Bridge Fort Washington Ave. at 178th St. The longest suspension bridge in the world when it opened in 1931, the George Washington Bridge remains New York City's only bridge across the Hudson. The bridge's towers were supposed to be sheathed in granite; as a result of the Depression, however, the steelwork was left exposed. With the postwar rise in automobile traffic, a lower level was added in 1962. Le Corbusier, the French proponent of modernist architecture, called the steel-cabled structure the most beautiful

The George Washington Bridge

bridge in the world. "It is blessed. It is the only seat of grace in the disordered city," he said.

Highbridge Park 172d St. and Amsterdam Ave. (212) 691-9510. Highbridge Park, designed in 1888 by Samuel Parsons Jr. and Calvert Vaux, begins in a thin spit called Coogan's Bluff that rises abruptly at West 155th Street and Edgecombe Avenue. In the swamps below, abutting the Harlem River, were the Polo Grounds, once home to the baseball and football Giants. Children who didn't have the price of admission could perch on the bluff and see part of the field. The southern zone of the park, stretching roughly 20 blocks uptown to the grand old High Bridge itself, was long impassable. But in 1997 the Parks Department began the arduous work of opening a trail along the route of the buried Croton Aqueduct, paralleling Edgecombe Avenue. Remarkably, three bridges—the Washington, the Hamilton and the pedestrian High Bridge—traverse the midpoint of Highbridge Park within seven blocks. Rather than being a fatal incursion, however, the spans with their warren of access ramps lend to this stretch of park beneath them an extra dimension of drama.

If you build up an appetite during a Highbridge hike, a dining opportunity beckons at the south end of the park, below Coogan's Bluff on the Harlem River Drive at 158th Street: **Guagua Amarilla,** or **Yellow Bus,** a school bus transformed into a roadside restaurant specializing in down-home Dominican fare.

Hispanic Society of America Broadway at 155th St. (212) 926-2234 www.hispanicsociety.org The Hispanic Society of America, in its atmospheric shabby-genteel Beaux-Arts setting on Audubon Terrace, is filled with fabulous paintings by El Greco, Goya and Velásquez, as well as fine examples of decorative arts, sculpture and textiles. There are some amazing pieces, like a breathtaking 10th-century Hispano-Moresque ivory box; the only comparable pieces of this kind locally are a few precious examples in the Met's collection. The Society also maintains a 250,000-volume research library (open to the public with photo ID) on all aspects of history and culture in Spain, Portugal, Latin America and the Philippines, as well as an extensive collection of rare books (contact the Society for viewing information). **Admission:** Free. **Hours:** Tues.–Sat., 10 A.M.–4:30 P.M.; Sun. 1–4 P.M.;

Inwood Hill Park Seaman Ave. at 207th St. (212) 304-2381. The most dramatic approach to the park is from the north, along 218th Street, a five-minute walk from the 215th Street subway station on the No. 1 or 9 local. You will come upon a complex vista unlike any other in Manhattan. To the north, on your right, is the Harlem River on its final leg before joining the Hudson in the swirl of Spuyten Duyvil. The sheer cliff on the far side, threaded at its base by Metro North tracks, defines Marble Hill, its heights studded with ungainly apartment buildings. Straight ahead is a tidal lagoon. Bordered by swamp grasses, it is the only accessible salt marsh in Manhattan and a magnet for water birds. Off to the left are low rolling athletic fields where soccer is the favored sport. Straight ahead, Inwood Hill itself juts into Spuyten Duyvil, which is spanned by the Henry Hudson Bridge to the Bronx, its steel gridwork painted bright red. Beyond that is the low-slung Amtrak bridge, part of the shoreline route to Albany. The final piece of this complex tableau is the noble New Jersey Palisades, looming up a mile away across the Hudson. Before heading into the forest, stop first at the park's ecology center on the lagoon. You can pick up a map and a schedule of tours led by urban park rangers all year. They even offer canoe expeditions.

Morris-Jumel Mansion 65 Jumel Terrace (at 161st St.) (212) 923-8008. In the midst of a citified neighborhood scenically situated on a high bluff, a delightful enclave suddenly opens up to the wanderer. In its center is a columned, white, two-story house, all peaks and gables, in a verdant acre-and-a-half setting of greenery. The Georgian-Federal mansion was built in the 1760's as a summer home by Roger Morris, a Tory who left during the Revolution. George Washington made it his headquarters in 1776 as his troops were being driven from the city. During that retreat he made the troops bite back in the Battle of Harlem Heights, in July 1776, when the British actually gave ground to the Americans. The mansion's name also recognizes a later occupant, Stephen Jumel, a wine merchant whose widow, Eliza, married Aaron Burr in the front parlor in 1833. The mansion's eight rooms, furnished in old-style elegance, are open for public visits.

Admission: Adults, $3.00; students, $2.00. **Hours:** Wed.–Sun., 10 A.M.–4 P.M. **Subway**: C to 163d St.

Trinity Cemetery Amsterdam Ave. (at West 153rd St.). Spread across a sloping hillside between Amsterdam Avenue and Riverside Drive from West 153d to West 155th Streets, Trinity Cemetery was opened in 1843 after a series of epidemics left the congregation's Wall Street churchyard dangerously overcrowded. Many of New York's most prominent citizens ended up on this rocky promontory, which overlooks the Hudson River and the New Jersey Palisades. As soon as you pass through the tall, wrought-iron gates on West 153d Street, the roar of Broadway is eclipsed by the cawing of ravens. A century-old canopy of ash and oak trees keeps the grounds appropriately shaded and somber. Trinity's monuments are richly varied in material, form and symbolism. Look for broken columns (died in the prime of life), sheaves of wheat (lived to a ripe old age), polished spheres and shrouded urns (symbols of the soul). There are Gothic-style marble mausoleums, towering steles of brownstone and simple slabs that conceal spacious subterranean vaults. Among those buried at Trinity are John Jacob Astor, the philanthropist; John Audubon, the naturalist, and Clement Clarke Moore, who wrote "A Visit From St. Nicholas."

Yeshiva University Museum 2520 Amsterdam Ave. (between 185th and 186th Sts.) (212) 960-5390. Begun in 1886 as an elementary yeshiva for Orthodox Jewish boys, the school expanded during the early 1900's to include a theological seminary and the first Orthodox Jewish high school in the United States. Yeshiva College, with its campus in Washington Heights, was formed in 1929, and in 1946 it was incorporated as a university. The museum features exhibits and cultural artifacts relating to Jewish history as well as some secular art.

Admission: $3, general; $2, seniors and children.

CENTRAL PARK

The miracle of Central Park is partly that it exists at all, but even more that it exists smack in the middle of a huge, throbbing city. The very incongruity of its charms—rolling meadows, jagged cliffs, graceful bridges and more than 26,000 trees—is what takes your breath away.

Central Park almost didn't happen. If the land had not been snapped up by City Fathers in the early 1850s, Manhattan would have quickly and inex-

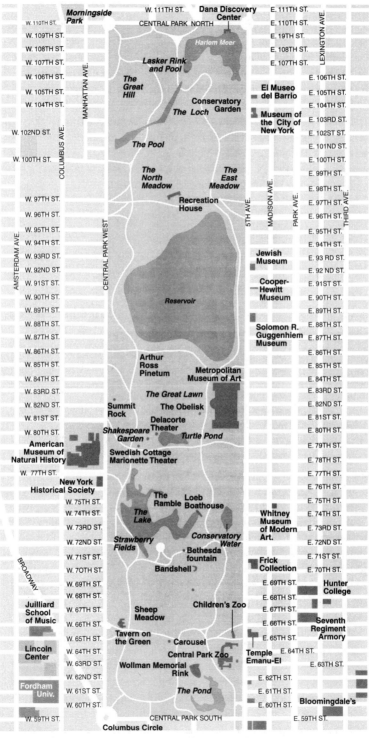

Central Park

orably become a single rectilinear street grid. Central Park was America's first major public park to be designed and built, as opposed to simply preserving nature. Frederick Law Olmsted and Calvert Vaux planned each square foot of the 843-acre park to create the effects of nature. A fake waterfowl here. A shrub placed there for almost painterly reasons. The goal was *rus in urb*, country in the city.

Olmsted and Vaux created an illusion of immense size by curving paths, carefully composed vistas and other landscaping techniques. From no point in the park can one see side to side or end to end. Illusion becomes reality. Not for nothing are the park's founders sometimes called precursors to Disney. For the visitor, the best place to get an idea of the original idea is to go to the **Ramble,** a 38-acre "wild garden" in Olmsted's words. The Ramble is located in the middle of the park between 73rd and 79th Streets and except for the underlying bedrock is a completely artificial creation. Paths twist and turn through the brush and there are scenic overlooks and rustic log structures. A tumbling stream called the gill gurgles coolly by.

The Ramble is one of the many great places for birdwatching in Central Park, a major stop along the Atlantic flyway. More than 275 species, from rare owls to hummingbirds have been spotted there. One of the park's more fascinating curiosities is located at the **Loeb Boathouse,** on the east side of the park between 74th and 75th Streets, where birders record their sightings in a looseleaf notebook that visitors are welcome to examine or add to. The Boathouse is located at the eastern entrance to the Ramble, where volunteers raise wildflowers to attract butterflies. So far 26 species have been spotted.

The Boathouse is on a 20-acre lake, the largest of seven bodies of water in the park. You can rent rowboats for $10 an hour ($30 deposit); a gondola for $30 an hour (seats six) or bikes for $14 for a tandem or $6 for a children's bike. It is one of the real pleasures of New York City to row in the shimmering duck-filled lake, marveling at the graceful cast iron Bow Bridge used in many movies, in the shadow of grand apartment buildings and skyscrapers.

But the best things in Central Park are free, and not just the obvious ones. One of the visual delights of the park, **Belvedere Castle,** a gothic fantasy, contains a nature center where would-be naturalists can borrow backpacks that contain binoculars, a bird guide and other reference material and notepaper. At the **Charles A. Dana Discovery Center,** a beautifully restored nature center on **Harlem Meer** at the northeast corner of the park, 50 bamboo fishing rods are lent out free of charge to fish for (and release) catfish, bluegills and other fish. Bait is also provided, either night crawlers or biscuit dough.

Central Park is a fabulous place for kids. The zoo in the southeast corner, with its underwater view of swimming polar bears—and adjacent children's zoo where kids can pet a Vietnamese pot-bellied pig—is worth a leisurely couple of hours. The carousel (mid-park at 64th Street) is the fourth generation of its genre—the first was turned by a blind mule and a horse—and whirls at a briskly invigorating pace. Nearby at 66th Street and the East Drive, the statue of Balto, the sled dog who took medicine to Nome, Alaska to squelch a diphtheria epidemic, has been polished by generations of loving, fascinated hands.

But there are also elements clearly for adults, and not just the **Tavern on the Green** restaurant with its fabulous Harvest Wild Mushroom Soup, among other treats. (You can also sip wine and dine elegantly in a restaurant at Loeb Boathouse, or go to the well-appointed snack bar there—or, more likely grab a hot dog for $1.50 from any of scores of vendors in the park.) Adults will also be drawn to the **Mall** on the east side between 66th and 69th Streets, where the elegant elm trees and lines of benches feel like Paris, especially in winter. The rougher terrain in the northern reaches of the park, with its pond and waterfall and outcroppings of 450-million-year-old Manhattan schist rock, are also best traversed by adults, or perhaps adults accompanied by children.

There is so much else of interest in Central Park: the elegant **Conservatory Garden** at 5th Avenue and 105th Street with its French, Italian and English floral treatments; the **Shakespeare Garden** on the west side between 79th and 80th Streets composed entirely of plant species mentioned by the Bard, including a red Mulberry said to be taken from Shakespeare's mother's garden; and, of course, **Strawberry Fields** on the west side between 71st and 74th Streets, built in memory of John Lennon by Yoko Ono. At its center is a mosaic, impressed with the world "Imagine," from a Lennon song. There are always fresh flowers and personal notes.

And don't forget the **Naturalist's Walk,** a new walk along the park's west side that celebrates biodiversity. Or the **Egyptian Obelisk** (east side of the park at 81st Street), a 71-foot tall stone needle that dates back to 1500 B.C. Or the **Pond** at the southeastern entrance, where J.D. Salinger's Holden Caulfield watched the ducks.

But the heart and soul of the park lay in the large places where people can come together and play ball, picnic and sunbathe—all kinds of people from all kinds of circumstances, exercising the democratic vision of parks so audaciously pioneered by Olmsted and Vaux. These are the **Sheep Meadow** on the west side of the park between 66th and 69th Streets, and the **Great Lawn** in mid-park between 79th and 86th Streets. You can fly kites, throw frisbees, stare into a lover's eyes and sip from a bottle of wine. Just be prepared for these pristine areas being at least partly closed, if there has been recent rain. These are the true backyards of New York City.

A last thought, which might well be a visitor's first. The Central Park Conservancy, which since 1980 has raised millions to restore and improve the park, runs a visitor's center in what was once the **Dairy,** which originally dispensed glasses of free milk. It is on the East Side at 65th Street. You can get directions, brochures and see exhibits that include a flip map showing how the park was built from the original landforms. *-Douglas Martin*

Transportation: West side of park: A, B, C, D, 1, 9 to 59th St.-Columbus Circle or any B/C subway stop or M10 bus stop between 59th and 110th Sts. East side of park: N, R to Fifth Ave. at 59th St.; any 4, 5, 6 subway or M1, 2, 3, 4 bus stop between 59th and 110th Sts.

Tours

Carriage Rides Central Park South. These rides are a romantic idea, but the reality—high prices, itchy blankets and the smell of manure—is rarely so perfect. Still, for some, this is an essential New York experience. Buggy rides are available year round, with fewer carriages operating in very cold and very hot weather

Prices: $34, 25-minute ride; $54, 45-minute ride; $10 each additional 15 minutes.

Central Park Bicycle Tour (212) 541-8759. These guided tours hit major park locations like Belvedere Castle, Jacqueline Kennedy Onassis Reservoir, and Strawberry Fields. Prices include bicycle rental.

Prices: $30 adults, $20 children. **Schedule:** Tours depart every day at 10 A.M., 1 P.M., and 4 P.M.

Park Attractions

The Arsenal 64th Street and Fifth Avenue. Originally built in 1848, the Arsenal is one of only two buildings in Central Park that were built before the park existed. This imposing structure resembles a medieval castle, with many architectural and artistic touches added over the years inside and out. It's worth visiting for its Depression-era murals and art exhibits focused on New York or Central Park. It also houses Olmsted and Vaux's original "Greensward Plan" for the park. This Landmark building is now the headquarters of New York City's Dept. of Parks and Recreation and the Central Park Wildlife Conservation Center.

Hours: Mon.–Fri., 9 A.M.–5 P.M.

Balto East Drive at 66th Street. This is one of the most sought-out sites in the park, and is the only park statue commemorating an animal. Balto was a heroic Siberian husky who braved a blizzard to bring diptheria antitoxin to Nome, Alaska; he was also the subject of a popular animated film. Created by Frederick George Richard Roth in 1925, Balto sports a golden back and snout, the patina and outer layer of bronze rubbed off by fingers, noses and backsides of thousands of worshipful children.

Belvedere Castle Mid-park at 79th Street. This impressive Victorian structure, perched atop the highest natural point in the Park, was occupied by the U.S. Weather Bureau from 1919 to the early 1960's, then fell into disrepair until the new Conservancy restored and reopened it in 1982. The site now offers good views of the park—especially Delacorte Theater, the Great Lawn, and the Turtle Pond—as well as excellent bird-watching. It also houses the Henry Luce Nature Observatory, where visitors can explore the plants and animals of the park through interactive exhibits. Also available are backpacks with information and binoculars to help budding scientists study the nearby Ramble or Turtle Pond (available Tues.–Sun., 10:00 A.M.–5:00 P.M.).

Bethesda Terrace and Fountain Mid-Park at 72nd Street. Olmsted and Vaux wanted nature to dominate the scene, but they did propose an architectural "heart of the park" overlooking the Lake. The split-level Terrace, decorated with detailed carvings of plants and animals, is one of the most popular areas of the park, affording gorgeous views of the Mall, the Lake, the Ramble, and all the human activity around the plaza. Bethesda Fountain itself, possibly the most-photographed monument in Central Park, commemorates the opening the Croton Aqueduct in 1842. It was the only sculpture called for in the original Park plan, and its creator, Emma Stebbins, was the first woman to be commissioned to produce a major piece of public art in the city.

Central Park Wildlife Center East Side, 63rd-66th Streets (212) 861-6030. Generations of New Yorkers have grown up with the Central Park Zoo. The oldest zoo in the city began in the 1860's as a menagerie to house animals given to the park, but has since been renovated many times and rechristened as the Central Park Wildlife Conservation Center. Divided into three zones—Arctic, rain forest and temperate—the center features animals in naturalistic settings. Its emphasis on public education is evident in the newly remodeled **Tisch Children's Zoo,** in which interactive nature exhibits have replaced kitschy storybook characters. Admission to the children's zoo is included in the general admission price, but make sure you bring along an extra pocketful of quarters for the feed dispensers. Kids love to feed the goats, cows, and potbellied pigs. Parents will also want to check on sea lion, polar bear, and penguin feeding times—all of which provide a fascinating spectacle for kids and adults. The beloved **George Delacorte Musical Clock,** between the Wildlife Center and the Children's Zoo, draws crowds on the hour and half-hour when a menagerie of motorized animals circle the clock to nursery-rhyme tunes.

Admission: $3.50 for adults, $1.25 for seniors, $.50 for children 3–12, and under 3 free. There are no group rates. **Hours:** Open 365 days a year, 10 A.M. until 5 P.M. on weekdays and 10:30 A.M.–5:30 P.M. weekends and holidays April-Oct; 10 A.M. until 4:30 P.M.. daily Nov-March. **Services:** Cafeteria, gift shop, handicapped accessible.

Chess and Checkers House East Side at 65th Street. This is the park's largest and most ornate wooden summer house. Playing pieces for the 24 indoor and outdoor tables here can be borrowed from the Dairy, and children's chess lessons are offered by the Central Park Conservancy in the summer.

The Concert Ground Mid-Park, 69th-72nd Streets (212) 360-2756. Music, theater, and dance performances are occasionally held at the neoclassical limestone **Naumberg Bandshell,** but strict regulations keep the number of shows down. Behind the shady Wisteria Pergola to the east of the bandshell, **Rumsey Playfield** plays host to Summerstage, a series of free rock concerts and opera performances, held June-August each year.

Conservatory Garden East Side, 104th-106th Streets. One of Central Park's best-kept secrets, these six acres of horticultural magnificence are tucked away behind the wrought iron gates that once served as the entrance to the Vanderbilt mansion at Fifth Avenue and 58th Street. This is the only formal garden in the park, with trees, flowers, statues, and fountains spread throughout three very different sub-gardens. To the north is a French-style garden, with concentric rings of flowers around a central fountain. Favorite sights here are the massive displays of tulips in the spring, chrysanthemums in the fall, and white roses in the summer. The central area is done in an Italian style, with a carefully tended central lawn and a simple fountain. The southern portion of the garden was created in an English style, and may be the most popular of the three. This may be due to the statuary fountain here, featuring characters from the children's book, *The Secret Garden*.

Conservatory Water East Side,72nd-75th Streets. The name of this popular pond comes from the conservatory, or greenhouse, that was meant to be built nearby. Most park patrons know it as the boat pond, due to the number of model ships floating in it on most good days. The **Kerbs Memorial Boathouse,** on the east side of the pond, rents out boats and sells refreshments beside a large patio. Other popular attractions are the red-tailed hawk watchers on the southwest edge of the pond and several statues along the pathways around the pond. In the summer, storytellers can often be found near the statue of **Hans Christian Andersen** to the west of the pond, and children love to climb on the **Alice in Wonderland** statue to the north.

The Andersen statue is also the best vantage point for one of the park's most remarkable wildlife dramas. For years, a pair of red-tailed hawks have been nesting on the 12th-floor ledge of a building just across from the pond, at Fifth Avenue and 74th Street. One most weekends, hawk watchers bring in telescopes and offer all passers-by close up views of the nest.

The Dairy East Side at 65th Street. During 19th-century "milk scandals" and diphtheria outbreaks, this Swiss-Gothic hybrid cottage served as a distribution center for fresh milk brought in from farms outside New York. It now serves as Central Park's Visitor Information Center and Recreation Building. The Dairy houses exhibits and information about the park, including an excellent flip map documenting the changes wrought on the landscape during park construction, as well as before-and-after photographs of the area.
Hours: Tues.–Sun. 10 A.M.–5 P.M. (Closes 4 P.M. in winter.)

Charles A. Dana Discovery Center Mid-Park at 110th Street. Central Park's newest building, on the north shore of Harlem Meer at the top of the park, offers general park information, conducts nature classes, showcases community projects and art, and loans out poles for catch-and-release fishing in the Meer (available Tues.–Sun., 10:00 A.M.–4:00 P.M. from April-Oct.). A deck outside the Center looks out over the Meer to the south, and an outdoor plaza, bordered by trees, hosts concerts and special public events throughout the year. Call for dates and times of the Harlem Meer Performance Festival (May-Sept.) or Dancing on the Plaza (Thursday evenings in August).
Hours: Tues.–Sun. 10 A.M.–5 P.M. (until 4 P.M. in winter).

Delacorte Theatre Mid-park at 80th Street (SW corner of Great Lawn) (212) 539-8655. For over 30 years, the Delacorte has offered free "Shakespeare in the Park" performances in July and August. With Belvedere Castle looming neaby, the Turtle Pond to the east, and the Great Lawn across a path to the north, an evening at the theater in Central Park can be unforgettable. New Yorkers and tourists line up for hours to get tickets, which are distributed at 1 P.M. the day of the performance (limit two per person). Tickets are also available from the New York Public Theater at 425 Lafayette Street, near Astor Place.

The Dene East Side, 66th-72nd Streets. Running between the Zoo and Conservatory Water, the Dene (which means "valley") is a peaceful, rolling landscape lined with shady trees and flowers. At the southern end, visitors can explore an old wooden shelter known as the summerhouse; to the north of the Dene, a meadow called the East Green has been restored to its original, pristine condition, after years of use as a cricket field.

The Friedsam Memorial Carousel65th Street Transverse and Central Drive. This is one of the largest merry-go-rounds in America, with 58 horses and two chariots. It's not the original carousel, however: the first was supposedly driven by a horse and a blind mule; this was replaced by a steam-powered carousel that burned down, as did its replacement in 1950. The present historic carousel was rescued from Coney Island by the Parks Department. It was built in 1908 by the firm of Stein and Goldstein, respected carvers from Brooklyn. Today the quaint building and calliope music draw over 250,000 riders per year.
Price: $.90 for adults, $.50 for children. **Hours:** Apr.-Nov. 10 A.M.–6 P.M.; Nov.-Apr. 10 A.M.–4:30 P.M., weather permitting.

The Great Hill West Side, 103rd-107th Streets. This green field offers picnic tables, a soft-surface walking or jogging path, and, in August, the "Great Jazz on the Great Hill" concert organized by the Central Park Conservancy.

The Great Lawn Mid-Park, 79th-86th Streets. Today the Lawn is one of the most popular areas of the Park, but until 1934 this was the site of the Croton Reservoir. When the city's water supply changed, the Reservoir became obsolete—until it was filled in with rubble from city construction to become the Great Lawn, a pond, and two playgrounds. These thirteen acres of grass, with eight softball fields, are used for all manner of private and public functions, especially after a massive restoration project in the mid-1990's. The Great Lawn has been the site of some of New York's largest outdoor events, including Paul Simon's 1991 concert and Pope John Paul II's 1995 mass (which drew 600,000 and 350,000 people, respectively); it also plays host to annual summer concerts by the Metropolitan Opera and the New York Philharmonic. All this use takes its toll, however, so the rules here are strict these days: no dogs, no bicycles, permits are required for ball games, and it is only open when the Keeper of the Great Lawn feels the lawn can handle public use.

Harlem Meer East Side, 106th-110th Streets. A walking tour of the 11-acre Meer (Dutch for "small sea") takes in an impressive array of plants and wildlife, including some impressive oak, beech, and gingko trees. The formerly fenced-off edge of the Meer has been restored to a more natural state, including a small sandy beach near the Charles A. Dana Discovery Center. At the southeast corner of the Meer, follow some steps to the water, where you will find yourself completely surrounded by flowers, with a private view of the water.

The Lake Mid-Park, 71st-78th Streets. After the Reservoir, this is the largest body of water in Central Park. Its meandering shoreline offers a great diversity of sights and attractions, from the wisteria arbor in the south, to Bow Bridge, the beautiful span in the center of the Lake, to the ornate Ladies' Pavilion on its northwest shore. Some of these sights may be best viewed from one of the rowboats available for rental at the Loeb Boathouse, at the northeastern edge of the Lake.

Hernshead (West Side, 75th-76th Streets). From Hernshead Landing, located just to the south along the Lake's edge, this rocky promontory is supposed to resemble a heron's head—hence the name, from an old English pronunciation of "heron." The Ladies Pavilion, a cast iron structure originally built to shelter horsecar passengers, sits in the middle of Hernshead, and a mass of rocks at the eastern end offers good views of the lake and opportunities for climbing.

Loeb Boathouse (East Side, 74th-75th Streets). The original Vaux-designed wooden building burned down long ago, but the current Loeb Boathouse has become a hub of park activity. The restaurant, **Park View at the Boathouse,** is a romantic, two-star favorite; more casual dining is possible at an outside café. Energetic visitors can rent bicycles and rowboats, while those in search of more relaxation can take a ride in a genuine Venetian gondola. Bird watchers come here to enter their sightings in the Bird Register, a large notebook stored in the Boathouse. And the Conservancy has installed a small wildflower garden, meant to attract butterflies, to the west of the Boathouse entrance.

Bike Rental: (212) 861-4137. Hourly rates from $6 for children to $14 for tandem bikes. March-Oct., 9 A.M.–5 P.M.

Rowboat Rental: (212) 517-2233. $10 per hour with $30 refundable deposit. mid-April-mid-October 10 A.M.-one hour before dusk.

Gondola Rental: (212) 517-2233. $30 per half hour (gondolas seat six). March-mid-Oct. 5:30–10 P.M.

Lasker Rink and Pool Mid-Park, 108th-109th Streets (212) 534-7639. As the name suggests, this facility offers skating in the winter on two oval rinks and free swimming in the summer. It occupies an area that was once part of the Harlem Meer—in fact, nearby Duck Island was created to replace an island formerly on the Lasker site, serving as a protected home to some of the Meer's flora and fauna.

Skating rinks: Admission: Adults $3, children and seniors $1.50. **Skate rental:** $3.50. **Dates:** Nov.-Apr. **Hours:** Mon-Thurs 10 A.M.–3 P.M.; Fri 10 A.M.–2 P.M., 5 P.M.–9 P.M.; Sat 11 A.M.–10 P.M.; Sun. 11 A.M.–6 P.M.

Pool: Admission: Free. **Dates:** July 1-Labor Day. **Hours:** 7 days a week, 11 A.M.–7 P.M.

Lawn Sports Center West Side at 69th Street (North of Sheep Meadow). Visitors can play croquet or lawn bowling on two tiny lawns from May 1st to October 1st. The New York Croquet Club (212-369-7949) offers free clinics on Tuesday nights and tournaments on weekends; the New York Lawn Bowling club (212-289-3245) also offers free lessons and regular club games.

The Mall (Literary Walk) Mid-Park, 69th-72nd Street. Four long rows of American elms, often the first park stop for spring warblers, form a cathedral-like canopy over the Mall. This grand promenade is one of only two formal elements remaining from Olmsted and Vaux's original park design (the other is Bethesda Fountain), and it contains many of the park's best known sculptures. Among them are William Shakespeare, Robert Burns, Victor Herbert, Beethoven, and Christopher Columbus. At the southern end of the walk is a non-sculptural tribute to Frederick Law Olmsted—a memorial flower garden surrounded by American elms.

Merchants' Gate and Maine Monument Southeast Park Entrance (Columbus Circle). Most of the original entrances to the park were dedicated to different professions, and Olmsted and Vaux insisted on very modest designs for the gates. Over time, however, the city added striking military monuments to the entrances along Central Park South, including this massive pylon commemorating the sinking of the battleship Maine in 1898. The monument honors the Americans killed in the Spanish-American War, and was partially funded with pennies and nickels collected from schoolchildren after the war. The Conservancy renovated the area around the gate in 1997, creating a well-lit public plaza with decorative paving and a seating wall.

Naturalists' Walk West Side, 77th-81st Street. This landscape was restored with the nearby American Museum of Natural History in mind: a dramatic variety of flowers, plants, and trees have been introduced to this area, attracting birds and butterflies and making it a natural destination after exploring the museum's Hall of Biodiversity and other exhibits.

The North Meadow Mid-Park, 97th-102nd Street. This is the largest grassy space in Central Park, divided only by 12 fields for baseball, softball, and soccer. Inside the Landmark **North Meadow Recreation Center,** the park Conservancy offers a wide range of programs for schoolchildren, from computer-based education to more physical activities. Any visitor with a photo ID can borrow one of the Center's Field Day kits, containing play items like balls, Frisbees, and jump ropes (available Mon.–Fri., 9:00 A.M.–7:00 P.M., Sat.–Sun., 10:00 A.M.–6:00 P.M.).

The Obelisk (Cleopatra's Needle) East Side at 81st Street. This 3,500-year-old stone obelisk was erected behind the Metropolitan Museum on January 22, 1881, after being uprooted from the city of Heliopolis, making a tumultuous ocean crossing, and crawling through the streets of Manhattan for four months. It remains the oldest man-made object in the park. Each corner is supported by a several hundred pound bronze replica of a sea crab—the originals of which are in the Met's Sackler Wing.

The Jacqueline Kennedy Onassis Reservoir Mid-park, 85th-96th Street. Until 1991, this 106-acre body of water still provided water to parts of Manhattan and the Bronx; now three huge tunnels bring water from upstate New York, but the Reservoir remains a good spot for jogging, bird watching, and observing the city skyline. The New York Road Runners Club (which organizes the New York City Marathon) holds weekly races on the 1.58-mile track—which is especially beautiful when the ornamental cherry trees bloom in the spring. Also worth a look are three elegant cast-iron pedestrian bridges that span the Bridle Trail, and three Vaux-designed gatehouses containing water flow-controlling and treatment equipment.

The Pond Southeast corner of park. Once an area of foul swampland, this is now one of the most attractive parts of Central Park, well shielded from street noise by trees and rocks. The small fenced-in area here is the Hallett Nature Sanctuary—four acres of park left untended, creating a haven for animals (like woodchucks, rabbits, and raccoons) and plants (including Black Cherry trees and many wildflowers). An excellent view of the Pond is available from Gapstow Bridge at the northern end of the Pond, or from the Cop Cot (Scottish for "little house on the crest of the hill"), located near the Sixth Avenue park entrance.

The Pool West Side, 100th-103rd Street. This body of water is a romantic place, sheltered by weeping willows and an impressive assortment of other tree species. A small peninsula on the south shore offers a good vantage point for duck feeding or for pictures of the Pool's foliage.

The Ramble Mid-park, 73rd-79th Street. It's hard to believe that this 38-acre sprawl of pathways, streams, cliffs and trees is entirely man-made—meticulously designed by Frederick Law Olmsted and carved out of a natural hillside. This may be the easiest place to get lost in Central Park, so entering with a map is advised. But the opportunity to lose yourself and escape from the crush of city life has also made it one of the most popular destinations in the park, a fact that has in turn led to an ongoing need for restoration. What many people don't know is that this is also one of the best sites for bird watching in the country, ranked among the top fifteen by the Audobon Society. Over 200 different species of birds have been seen here; the best time for birding is during spring and fall migration, in April and May and again in September and October.

The Ravine Mid-park, 102nd-106th Street. Stretching from the southern end of Lasker Rink to the Pool just above West 100th St., the Ravine is a peaceful destination filled with wildflowers, bird watching trails, and odd and beautiful bridges. One of the most impressive of these is Huddlestone Arch, a careful assemblage of rough boulders fitted together without any mortar or other binding material.

Arthur Ross Pinetum Mid-park, 84th-86th Street. This collection of twenty species of pine tree (plus elms and oaks) is the largest collection of evergreens in Central Park. Walking tours of the Pinetum meet at nearby Belvedere Castle,

The Sheep Meadow in Central Park

including a popular seasonal tour in early December. Birdwatchers also come here to spot owls in the pines, and there is a small playground that finds more use as a quiet picnic spot.

Shakespeare Garden West Side, 79th-80th Street. Once an extension of the Ramble, this area was dedicated to Shakespeare on the tricentennial of his death in 1916. This meandering, four-acre garden showcases about half of the 200 plants mentioned in the Bard's works, including a Mulberry tree said to be grown from a cutting from Shakespeare's mother's garden. Bronze plaques provide the quotations relevant to each plant.

Sheep Meadow Mid-park, 66th-69th Street. This 15-acre meadow was an actual grazing field for sheep until the 1930's, when the sheep were shipped out and their building became the Tavern on the Green restaurant. In the 1960's and 70's the field suffered from heavy use for sports, concerts, and hippie be-ins; but since the 1980's, the park Conservancy has exercised strict control over personal conduct and care of the meadow. Still, on warm summer days, this rolling lawn may attract thousands of walkers, sunbathers, and people-watchers. Radios, team sports, and dogs are prohibited, but often show up anyway. Just outside the northern fence is Lilac Walk, lined with 23 varieties of lilac. The Meadow is open mid-April to mid-October, dawn to dusk in fair weather.

Strawberry Fields West Side, 72nd Street. The landscaping of this area was made possible by Yoko Ono, who presented it to the city in memory of John Lennon, who was murdered outside the nearby Dakota apartment house in 1980. There aren't many strawberries here, but there is an incredible variety of plants and trees, all donated by countries around the world, forming what a plaque calls a "Garden of Peace." Over 161 species of plants, representing the countries of the United Nations, have been introduced to the park here, but most visitors come to view a gift from the city of Naples, Italy: a mosaic with the word "Imagine" at its center.

Summit Rock West Side, 81st-85th Street. At 137.5 feet, this is the highest point in Central Park. An ampitheater overlooks the south and east slopes, and a path leads up the southern slope to a beautiful green lawn that affords good views of the park and the Upper West Side. This and adjacent areas of Central Park were home to 5,000 New Yorkers before the city purchased the land and began park construction. At the time, there were nearly a thousand buildings on the land, including factories and churches. Seneca Village occupied this territory in the mid-1800s; this was one of the best known African-American communities in New York, composed mostly of free, black, landowning families.

Swedish Cottage Marionette Theater West Side at 79th Street. (212) 988-9093. Originally built for the 1876 Centennial Exposition in Philadelphia and used variously over the years as a storage shed, public toilets, an entomological laboratory, and a Civil Defense Headquarters, this replica of a 19th Century Swedish schoolhouse now hosts performances of children's stories, birthday parties, and other events year-round. The theater seats 100 children and features central air conditioning and a state-of-the-art stage. This is also the headquarters of the Citywide Puppets in the Parks program.
Suggested donation: Adults, $5; children, $4.

Turtle Pond Mid-park, 79th-80th Street. When the old Croton Reservoir was filled in with construction debris in the 1930's, becoming the Great Lawn, the southern end became Belvedere Lake and quickly attracted a wide range of aquatic life. The site was rechristened in honor of some of its more popular inhabitants in 1987, and a 1997 renovation altered the pond's shoreline, added new plants, and introduced Turtle Island, a new habitat for the turtles and birds that make their home here. A dock and nature blind offer great views of the pond and its denizens sunning themselves on dead tree trunks.

Wollman Memorial Skating Rink East Side at 62nd Street. To appreciate the beauty and calm of Central Park, head to the 33,000-square-foot Wollman Rink, near the park entrance at Sixth Avenue and Central Park South. Wollman also offers classes and guided tours around the park. After ice skating in the winter or rollerblading in the summer, you can relax on the terrace, patio or at the rink's cafe. During the spring and summer months, most patrons are tourists and novice skaters. Compared to the lanes in the park, the rink is fairly uncrowded, leaving plenty of skating room for New Yorkers.

Sports in Central Park
(See also the section " Sports and Recreation")

Baseball/Softball. The North Meadow diamonds are scheduled to reopen in spring 2000. The Great Lawn has seven softball fields; five more are at the

Heckscher Ballfields. Arsenal West (16 West 61st St.) is the place to go for permits, or call (212) 408-0226 for information.

Biking. Stick to the roads: park security may confiscate your bike if you ride on walkways or trails. Rental bikes are available near Loeb Boathouse, at 74th St. and the East Drive. Call (212) 861-4137.

Boating. Rowboats and gondolas can be rented at the Loeb Boathouse (call 212-517-2233 or see above for details).

Fishing. The Dana Discovery Center loans out poles and bait for catch-and-release fishing; fishing in the Lake is permitted, but may become more restricted in the future following the poisoning of some birds.

Horseback Riding. Horse rentals and riding lessons are available at the Claremont Riding Academy at 175 West 89th St.; call (212) 724-5100 for information. The park's bridle path runs around the Reservoir and northern quadrant of the park, and down the west side to 60th St.

Ice Skating. Available November through March at Wollman (212-396-1010) and Lasker (212-534-7639) rinks. See above for more information.

Inline Skating. The park drives are popular with skaters, but some prefer the area at the north end of the Mall and the driveway to the west of the Mall. From April to September, Wollman Rink is also open for inline skating. Call (212) 396-1010.

Running. There are designated running lanes on all park drives, and the entire road is closed to automobile traffic between 10 A.M. and 3 P.M. and after 7 P.M. on weekdays, and from 7 P.M. Friday to 6 A.M. Monday.

Swimming. Swimming is forbidden in all open bodies of water in the park, but the Lasker Rink becomes a free swimming pool in July and August. Call (212) 534-7639.

Tennis. The tennis center to the northwest of the Reservoir houses thirty courts; permits are required most of the time and are available at the Arsenal. Call (212) 360-8131 for details.

THE BOROUGHS

THE BRONX

"The Bronx is up" in more ways than one. Geographically, this is the northernmost part of the city and the only borough attached to the U.S. mainland. More
important is the Bronx's rise from the ashes of burning buildings and crime-rid-
den streets of the 1970's. Renewed vibrancy and pride have come to the borough that was a collection of rural villages—Mott Haven, Kingsbridge, Morrisania, et al.—in the 1890's, before being annexed into the expanding city.
Throughout the early decades of the 20th century the Bronx was mainly populated by waves of Irish and German immigrants seeking the open, green space of
the borough made available by the growth of the subway system. Early Bronx-
ites could watch D.W. Griffith making movies in a local studio and some spent
their summers living in tents on a rocky shoreline, where Robert Moses later
hauled in sand for Orchard Beach in the 1930's.

Perhaps best known as the home of the **Bronx Zoo** and **Yankee Stadium**,
the Bronx also features the green spaces of the **New York Botanical Garden**,
Van Cortlandt and Pelham Bay Parks, as well as **Wave Hill** in Riverdale. City
Island is a virtual New England village.

The Bronx is home to several colleges and universities: Fordham University
and Manhattan College; Bronx Community College, earlier the uptown campus
of NYU, with its Hall of Fame for Great Americans; Lehman College, formerly
Hunter College.

Many visitors to the Bronx travel to Woodlawn Cemetery to view its
grandiose mausoleums and especially the grave of Herman Melville. The man
at the gate is happy to tell you where to find it. Bronx visitors and residents
more interested in the living travel to Arthur Avenue in the Belmont section
of the borough. There they find lively food shopping and excellent Italian dining just down the street from the Zoo and opposite Fordham University's Rose
Hill campus.

How did the Bronx get its name? Yes, the Bronx River flows through the
borough, but the name probably goes back to the early Dutch settlers of the city
that was originally called New Amsterdam. The first Dutch inhabitants of the
area were Dutch farmer Jonas Bronck and his family, who owned a 500-acre
farm near what is now Morrisania. According to legend people would say they
were going to visit "the Broncks," thereby establishing the use of the definite
article in the borough's name, the only one with that distinction.

HIGHLIGHTS OF THE BRONX

Bartow-Pell Mansion Museum 895 Shore Rd. (718) 885-1461. A 150-year-
old Federal-style mansion with formal gardens, the Bartow-Pell house is all but
hidden in foliage several yards off the heavily traveled road to Orchard Beach.
The neo-classical stone mansion with a Greek Revival interior sits on property

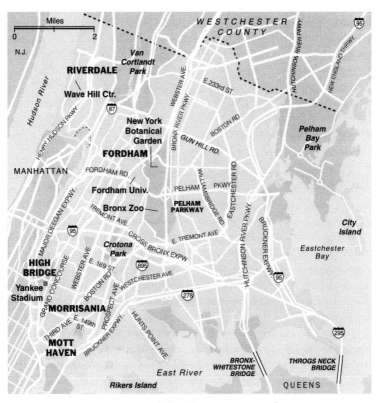

The Bronx

purchased from the Indians by Thomas Pell in 1654, in a nine-acre setting consonant with its original surroundings.

Admission: $2.50; $1.25, seniors and students

Bronx Museum of the Arts 1040 Grand Concourse (at 165th St.), Bronx (718) 681-6000. The only arts museum in the Bronx was established in 1961 and exhibits contemporary and historical art, particularly by Bronx artists or artists related in some way to the borough. Known for its high-quality, well-curated exhibitions, it's considered one of the many well-kept secrets in the Bronx. The permanent collection includes a strong collection of work by artists of African, Asian and Latin-American ancestry.

Admission: $3; $2, students with I.D.; free, children under 12. Free Wednesdays. **Credit cards:** All major; checks. **Hours:** Wed., 3–9 P.M.; Thur.–Fri., 10 A.M.–5 P.M.; Sat.–Sun., 12–6 P.M. Closed Monday and major holidays. **Programs for Children:** Workshops for families and groups. Phone the Education Department at the Museum for a calendar of events and additional information. **Services:** Tours, lectures, concerts.

Bronx Zoo Fordham Road and the Bronx River Parkway. (718) 367-1010
www.wcs.org

General Hours: Open every day of the year at 10 A.M. Closing times: Apr.-
Oct.: Mon.–Fri., 5 P.M.; until 5:30 P.M. weekends and holidays. Nov.-Mar.:
Daily, 4:30 P.M. Animals affected by weather may not always be on display.

General Admission: Wednesday daytime admission free, except during Holiday
Lights. **Apr. 1-Nov. 1:** Adults, $7.75; children 2–12 and seniors, $4.00. **Nov.
2–Jan. 3:** adults, $6; children 2–12 and seniors, $3. **Jan. 4–Mar. 31:** adults, $4;
children and seniors, $2. Children under 2, free.

Sprawled over 265 acres, the Bronx Zoo is the largest urban zoo in the United
States. With paths winding through lush greenery shaded by canopies of trees, it
can feel as much like a park as an animal repository. But turn any corner, and
you will be reminded exactly where you are. The zoo has more than 7,000 animals, of over 700 species, enough to make any skeptic marvel at nature's prolific
creativity. There are the exotic—cassowaries (flightless birds capable of killing a
person with their toenails); Mongolian wild horses, completely extinct in the
wild; a 24-foot-long reticulated python; black-necked swans. And there are the
routine but lovable—massive, placid elephants, vanilla-colored polar bears,
docile zebras.

The zoo has contrived all sorts of settings to let nature do its thing, and let
you watch. The "World of Darkness," for example, takes you through a dark-
ened building so you can see how nocturnal animals behave—bats spread their
wings, a gopher snake resolutely devours a mouse (conveniently delivered by a
zoo keeper). And some of the outdoor settings are lovely, such as the steep,
grassy hill that is home to gelada baboons and nubian ibex, with their baroquely
curled horns.

The zoo, in essence, brings not just the wild, but the world, to the city. Jun-
gleWorld, housed in a 37,000 square foot building, recreates four Asian habitats.
One of them is a mangrove forest, which most of us will never see, stocked with
animal inhabitants like bear cats, the black leopard and the Asian small-clawed
otter, the world's smallest otter species. The Bengali Express Monorail crosses
the Bronx River to take you on a leisurely, photo-friendly journey though Wild
Asia. There are antelopes, deer, wild cattle with their white-stockinged feet,
Indian rhinoceros—the largest land animal on earth—Asian elephant, and the
Siberian tiger.

Championed by, among others, Theodore Roosevelt, the Bronx Zoo opened
in 1899, and has not stopped growing since. The newest addition—and the
highlight of the zoo—is the Congo Gorilla Forest, which opened in 1999. It is
6.5 acres of a green playland, or homeland, for African rain forest animals, with
11 waterfalls, 55 artificial rain forest trees, misting machines and even jungle
sounds. The animals range from tiny, scampering colobus monkeys to brilliantly
vareigated mandrills to massive, lolling silverbacks. Some of the gorillas, who
group around male leaders, are lazy, some bawdy, some familially inclined, but
all are fascinating to watch. Only a layer of glass separates the masses from the
apes—close enough, it seems, to reach out and touch them.

AP Photo/Kathy Willens

Bronx Zoo

The gorilla exhibit includes a film on their threatened habitats, which is in keeping with the larger mission of the Wildlife Conservation Society, which runs the zoo: to preserve species and habitats around the world. The conservation message is ubiquitous, and effective. The diversity of species on display generates amazement—but also alarm, given the number that are on the edge of extinction. The zoo's educational mission succeeds as well, managing to teach, for example, about stork breeding habits. And the zoo is doing its part to promote procreation: more than 300 animals were born there in 1998.

But the best thing about any zoo—and certainly the Bronx Zoo—is serendipity: turning a corner to catch a glimpse of a giraffe's awkward beauty as it nibbles grass from a sun-bathed plain. Making a wrong turn that introduces you to the primeval-looking marabou stork. Looking up as you trudge toward the exit to see a North American brown bear standing atop a boulder, looking like the king of the wild, even if he no longer is.

Throughout, of course, there are ample opportunities to consume food, drink and souvenirs. Be warned that a day at the zoo will not necessarily come cheap, particularly for a family, given the extra charges for the Children's Zoo (where children can learn about the differences between human and animal behiavior, and among different kinds of animals), the Bengali Express Monorail, and the Congo Gorilla exhibit.

The crowds can be overwhelming as well, sometimes giving the zoo the feel of an amusement park. Be prepared, for example, to wait 45 minutes or more for Congo Gorilla Forest on a summer weekend.

But those gripes aside, it is a remarkably pleasant way to spend a day. That is not least because you get to see New Yorkers in nature themselves—for once, unhurried, and perhaps only mildly more aggressive than many of the animals they are contemplating.

—Amy Waldman

Special Hours: Holiday Lights: Nov. 26-Jan. 2; Sun.–Thurs., 5:30 P.M.–9:00 P.M.; Fri.–Sun. until 9:30 P.M. **Children's Zoo:** Tickets sold until 4 P.M., Mon.–Fri.; until 4:30 P.M., weekends and holidays. **Children's Theater:** 11 A.M.–4 P.M. Children's Zoo and all rides closed during winter.

Special Admission Costs: Congo Gorilla Forest: $3.00. **Holiday Lights:** adults, $6; children and seniors, $3. (Advance discounted group rates are available for ten or more people. Call 1–800-YES-2868.) **Children's Theater:** Adults, $2.00; children, $1.50. **Rides:** Bengali Express Monorail, Skyfari Aerial Tramway, and Zoo Shuttle, $2.00 each. Camel Rides: $3.00.

Services: Baby stroller rental at entrances (except Rainey Gate); adult strollers available by reservation at (718) 220-5188.

Restrictions: The Zoo is a smoke-free environment. No pets, radios, bikes, or skateboards. Blind, visually impaired and hearing-impaired visitors may be accompanied by harnessed guide dogs.

DIRECTIONS

By Car: (Parking for the Bronx Zoo is located just off exit 6 of the Bronx River Parkway.) **From Westchester County, NY:** Cross County Parkway to Bronx River Parkway south. **From Manhattan:** Triborough Bridge to Bruckner Expwy. east to Bronx River Pkwy. north. Or, west Side Highway to Cross Bronx Expwy. east to Bronx River Pkwy. north. **From Queens:** Bronx-Whitestone Bridge to Hutchinson River Pkwy. north to Cross Bronx Expwy west, to Bronx River Pkwy. north. **From Long Island, NY:** Throgs Neck Bridge to Cross Bronx Expwy west to Bronx River Parkway north. **From Connecticut:** New England Thruway (I-95) to Pelham Pkwy. west to Bronx Zoo. Or, Merritt Pkwy south to Cross County Pkwy west, then Bronx River Pkwy. south. **From New Jersey:** George Washington Bridge to Cross Bronx Expwy. east to Bronx River Pkwy. north.

By Subway: IRT #2 Express to Pelham Pkwy or IRT #5 Express to East 180 St and transfer to the #2 Express. Walk west to the Bronxdale entrance. Or IND D Express to Fordham Rd., then change to eastbound Bx12 Bus. Exit bus at Southern Blvd and walk east on Fordham Rd to entrance.

By Bus: Bx9 and Bx19 buses to Southern Blvd entrance. Or, Bx12 to Fordham Rd and Southern Blvd and walk east on Fordham Rd to entrance. Or, Q44 to 180 St and Boston Rd. Walk north to entrance. Liberty Lines' BxM11 express bus from Mid-Manhattan makes various stops on Madison Ave in Manhattan; call Liberty Lines at (718) 652-8400.

City Island Just off the northeastern edge of the Bronx, City Island is a quiet (except in summer) year-round virtual village of some 4,000 permanent residents, with one main drag, many boatyards and marinas, several newish condominium colonies and some dozen and a half mostly seafood restaurants. A mile and a half long and no more than half a mile wide, the island blends the forlorn mystery of a Hopper dreamscape with a cheerful blue-collar brawn and flashes of intriguing wealth: Sports cars behind gated walls; a gleaming black Mercedes convertible outside the bait shop.

Le Refuge Inn on City Island is a charming French provincial bed-and-breakfast that presents a weekly noontime series of chamber-music concerts in a setting reminiscent of the European salons of bygone days. The island's **North Wind Undersea Institute,** founded by a deep-sea diver to raise awareness of the serious plight of marine life surrounding City Island, is housed in a 125-year-old sea-captain's mansion and on a nearby tugboat. The **Boat Livery** is one of the best ways to explore City Island and nearby High Island. The Boat Livery rents small motorboats by the day ($45, weekdays; $55, weekends and holidays).

Directions: From Manhattan by car: Take the Triborough Bridge to the Bruckner Expressway. After I-95 joins the Expressway, take I-95 to Exit 8B (City Island/Orchard Beach); go to the first traffic light and make a right onto City Island Road; continue through the traffic circle to the City Island Bridge. From Manhattan by public transportation: take the Uptown No. 6 train to Pelham Bay Park (the last stop), then take the No. 29 bus.

Edgar Allan Poe Cottage 2640 Grand Concourse (between 192d and 193d Sts.) (718) 881-8900. Edgar Allan Poe moved to this cottage in Kingsbridge, the Bronx, from Manhattan in 1846, hoping that the country air would help his wife recover from tuberculosis. For three years, he lived in the tiny house, where he wrote "Annabel Lee." Three period rooms—a kitchen, parlor and bedroom—are filled with furniture from the 1840's, including Poe's own rocking chair and bed and the bed where his wife died not long after the move. At the museum you can watch a 20-minute film on Poe's life and the history of the house. A small gallery houses paintings, photographs and drawings from the 1840's.
Admission: $2.

Hall of Fame for Great Americans University Ave. at W. 181st St. (718) 289-5162. This landmark institution was founded in 1900 as part of the uptown campus of New York University (now Bronx Community College). The main attraction here is the 630-foot open air Colonnade, honoring Americans who have played a significant role in the nation's history—including Alexander Graham Bell, Eli Whitney and George Westinghouse. The Colonnade holds busts and commemorative plaques for nearly 100 honorees, representing occupations as diverse as authors, statesmen, scientists, and musicians. Admission is free.
Hours: 10 A.M.–5 P.M. daily.

New York Botanical Garden Opposite the Bronx Zoo (718) 817-8700 www.nybg.org Located at the northern end of Bronx Park along East Fordham Road, this elegant expansive garden was created in 1891, inspired by the success of the Royal Botanic Garden at Kew, England. The 250-acre garden was planted between 1895 and 1896, the landscape and construction work began in 1899. One highlight of the garden is the Enid A. Haupt Conservatory, a beautiful Victorian greenhouse, but the main attraction is of course the 47 gardens and plant collections and thousands of shrubs and trees. The Bronx River flows through the site, next to a stone mill dating from 1840. The rose garden was planned by Beatrix Farrand, the first American female landscape designer. There are 40 acres of the forest that once covered all of New York.

The garden runs hands-on discovery, craft and gardening activities for everyone on weekends. There are special events throughout the year, such as a holiday model train show and the Everett Children's Adventure Garden, with attractions like topiary bunnies. For live animals—including apes, elephants and monkeys—the Bronx Zoo is right next-door. For events info, call (718) 817-817-8777.

—Robin Pogrebin

Train: Metro North from Grand Central to "Botanical Garden."

Van Cortlandt Park Broadway and W. 240th St. (at Birchhall Ave.) (718) 430-1890. Frederick Van Cortlandt's stone mansion, built in 1748 and today the Bronx's oldest building, served as Revolutionary War headquarters for both George Washington and a British general. In the late 19th century, the Van Cortlandt family donated the house and the surrounding 1,146 acres to the city. The park's southern portion houses the Van Cortlandt House Museum, a lake, a golf course and playing fields for soccer, cricket, rugby, baseball and hurling. Meanwhile, the northern end of the park remains largely pastoral; along with a nationally renowned cross-country track, it features nature trails that wind through a 100-year-old hardwood forest populated by foxes, raccoons and pheasant.

Wave Hill House W. 249 St. and Independence Ave. (near Palisade Ave.) (718) 549-3200. Established in 1960 as a center for the arts and environmental studies, Wave Hill comprises 28 acres of land atop a hill overlooking the Hudson. The estate's mansion was built in 1843 of local stone. Theodore Roosevelt, Mark Twain and Arturo Toscanini all stayed at the Riverdale compound. Today, visitors can stroll through gardens and greenhouses, picnic in an enclosed courtyard, attend special events and concerts and view art exhibitions.

Yankee Stadium 161st St. (at River Ave.), Bronx (718) 293-4300. *(See the section "Sports & Recreation")*

BROOKLYN

If you're not a native, all you might know about Brooklyn is this: the Brooklyn Bridge is at one end, Coney Island the other, and the Dodgers used to play ball somewhere in between. Historically, though, Brooklyn has given more to the world than Jackie Robinson and Nathan's Famous hot dogs. The borough has been (and still is) a home to millions who were drawn to New York but found Manhattan life too hectic or expensive—and has been an inspiration to everyone from Walt Whitman to Spike Lee.

The original town of Bruecklen was chartered by the Dutch West India Company in 1646 and incorporated into Kings County in 1683. Despite British occupation during the Revolutionary War, the resident population continued to grow, reaching over 4,500 by 1800. By then, more than 30 percent of the county's residents were of African descent. When the Civil War broke out in

1861, Brooklyn found itself at the center of the abolitionist movement in America. Brooklyn was home to some of the first black landowners in America, as well as one of the first towns (Weeksville) settled by freed slaves.

At the start of the war, Brooklyn ranked as the third largest city in the U.S., and its dynamic population and proximity to New York had already sparked a major cultural renaissance. In 1855, a Brooklyn resident named Walt Whitman published *Leaves of Grass;* the next decade saw the creation of the Philharmonic Society of Brooklyn, the **Brooklyn Academy of Music**, and the National Association of Baseball Players—the first such centralized organization in the country. In 1867, Olmsted and Vaux completed work on Prospect Park, thought by some to rival Central Park in the beauty and genius of its design and execution. Eastern Parkway, another of the duo's designs, opened a year later, becoming the nation's first six-lane parkway.

The second major wave of immigrants began to arrive from eastern and southern Europe around 1880; the increased labor force helped Brooklyn to become the country's fourth largest producer of manufactured goods. In 1883 the Brooklyn Bridge opened, followed soon after by an elevated railroad and electric trolley service. Brooklynites had fought hard for years to retain the borough's identity and political independence, but in 1898, a close vote finally consolidated Brooklyn into Greater New York City. Brooklyn entered the 20th century as a borough of New York, with a population of over one million.

The Williamsburg and Manhattan bridges (as well as the IRT, New York's first subway) made the Manhattan-Brooklyn commute even easier, and funneled more arrivals across the East River. The "Great Migration" of African-Americans to Brooklyn began around 1915, adding to the steady influx of European immigrants. By 1930, half of the borough's residents were foreign born, and a substantial percentage remained African-American—but the Depression was tough on these immigrants and poor families from the rural South, and some of Brooklyn's beautiful neighborhoods turned into slums.

Lately, things are looking up. Business is growing again in the downtown Brooklyn area, especially the business district around Borough Hall and the Metrotech Center. The Brooklyn Academy of Music's Next Wave Festival, begun in 1983, has consistently drawn cutting-edge artists—as well as crowds from Manhattan. And as Manhattan rents creep skyward, more young professionals are drifting across the river, bringing new life (and money) to old neighborhoods, and making areas like Brooklyn Heights and Park Slope some of the more desirable addresses in New York. Brooklyn's population of over two million makes it (unofficially, of course) the fourth largest city in the U.S., and it seems poised for many more changes in the century ahead.

Coney Island

A seemingly endless stretch of sand, a boardwalk offering every imaginable variety of greasy food item, water-squirt games, a roller coaster that defines the term death-defying, a Ferris wheel you can see from miles away at night, carnival music, the world's best hot dog, cheap beer—no wonder Coney Island became

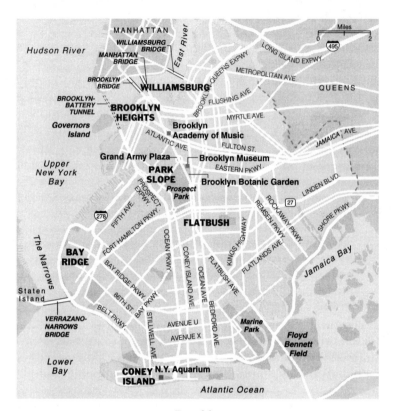

Brooklyn

the most famous beach in America. If you pay a visit today, however, be prepared to see an entirely different "Coney"—as the natives once called it—from the one of story and fable. The old bathhouses are crumbling, many buildings are run down and the Boardwalk vastly diminished from the days when crowds jammed the shops or huddled near the now silent Parachute Jump to marvel at the bravery of the men and women who soared 250 feet into the sky in an open seat.

Still, most out-of-towners report very positively about their journeys to the far reaches of Brooklyn. There's just enough left, it seems, to capture the spirit of one of New York's most recognizable symbols of a bygone era. The Boardwalk stretches from the community of Brighton Beach through Coney Island to Sea Gate, a strip that has known better and worse days. At the turn of the century, the eastern end was a high-society preserve, with oceanfront luxury hotels, restaurants, theaters and a race track. But anti-gambling sentiment closed the track in 1910, and by 1920 all the hotels were gone. To the west around Coney Island, more popular attractions developed, with the great amusement parks of Dreamland, Luna Park and George C. Tilyou's Steeplechase.

The arrival of the subway in 1920 created what was known as "a poor people's paradise" and soon hundreds of thousands of working class New Yorkers

were spending weekends at the beach. Decline set in during the social disloca-
tions of the 1960's. Changing populations and a series of fires in the flimsily
built fun parks brought decaying buildings, poverty and crime. Now, Russian
Jewish immigrants have established a thriving beachhead in Brighton, although
a promised Coney Island renaissance has not yet materialized.

Subway: B, D, F or N to Coney Island/Stillwell Avenue (about an hour from
Manhattan).

Amusement Park Rides:

B & B Carousel North side of Surf Avenue at West 12th Street. Complete
with painted horses carved about 1920 in the renowned workshop of Marcus
Illions, a Polish immigrant who established the fancifully flamboyant Coney
Island style of carousel horses.

Cyclone Surf Avenue at West Eighth Street. Fans scream their way through the
1927 landmark roller coaster's 100-second ride in cars that plunge from nine
thrill-packed hills. Like the Parachute Jump, this is on the National Register of
Historic Places and is landmarked by the state and the city.

Wonder Wheel West 12th Street between Surf Avenue and the Boardwalk.
The orange and green frame of the 78-year-old landmark Ferris wheel is 150 feet
in diameter. A leisurely ride, day or night, affords terrific views of the Brooklyn
landscape.

HIGHLIGHTS OF THE NEIGHBORHOOD

The Boardwalk From Brighton 15th Street and Brightwater Avenue in
Brighton Beach to West 37th Street and the private residential community of
Sea Gate in Coney Island. Rebuilt and extended intermittently, this inviting
promenade is now two and a half miles long and 80 feet wide. It is also the starting point of the annual **Mermaid Parade,** generally held on the first Saturday
after the summer solstice. Call (718) 372-5159 for more information.

Brighton Beach Baths Brighton Beach Ave. to Boardwalk, between Brighton
12th St. and Coney Island Ave. The Boardwalk affords a bird's-eye view of remnants of this once posh beach club, which opened in 1907 and closed a few
years ago. Until it is razed to make way for housing, its swimming pools, playing
courts and bandstand are nostalgic landmarks to those who spent youthful summers there.

Childs' Restaurant Boardwalk at West 21st Street. Coney Island's answer to
the Parthenon could be this ruin of a once splendid restaurant. Terra-cotta tiles
embossed with sea motifs are set into the Spanish yellow facade, and two florid
ceramic urns top twin turrets. Opened in 1923, it is now a graffiti-marred candy
factory.

Coney Island Museum 1208 Surf Ave. (at 12th St.) (718) 372-5159. This
museum is stocked with mementos from the great pay-one-price amusement

centers of Coney Island, like Luna Park, Dreamland and Steeplechase, that once ruled the shore. Chief among the antic artifacts are a fun-house mirror, an original wicker Boardwalk Rolling Chair and one of the rare wooden Steeplechase Horses. The display cases are filled with photographs of freak-show tents, including one with a sign promoting the "thrill of thrills": a man named Mortado "nailed to a tree." These serve as a nostalgic reminder of the place once known as Sodom by the Sea. The museum has a video loop of rare Coney Island film clips, which includes a bizarre 1904 film of an elephant being electrocuted, a stunt apparently engineered by Thomas Edison to persuade the public that the electric chair would be the most humane form of capital punishment.

Hours: Sat., Sun. Noon-Sundown. Price: $.99

Flea Market Surf Avenue between West Eighth and West 10th Streets. Open-front shops and alley stalls under the moving frieze of elevated trains display all sorts of new and used merchandise: kitchen utensils, tools, bric-a-brac, clothing, electronics, videotapes and CD's, a few genuine antiques and a lot of dusty junk. Most of the vendors are Russian immigrants who sometimes feign a language barrier when it suits them, but all bargain handily in English.

Handball Courts Boardwalk at West Fifth Street. These are said to be the busiest handball courts in New York, attracting the city's best players. Even midweek, six courts can be settings for vigorous doubles matches, always with kibitzers.

New York Aquarium for Wildlife Conservation
(See the section "New York for Children")

Parachute Jump Boardwalk at West 17th Street. Suggesting a miniature Eiffel Tower, this landmark 250-foot-high structure looks remarkably intact, leading to optimistic rumors of its restoration. Originally at the 1939–40 New York World's Fair, it was moved here in 1941.

Philips Candy Shop 1237 Surf Avenue, at the Stillwell Avenue train station. (718) 372-8783. Old-time sweets have been homemade here by John Dorman for 51 of the shop's 68 years. Delights include red-glazed candied apples, the whipped-cream-topped round of cake known as charlotte russe, glassily thin, crackly peanut brittle and the seaside classic, saltwater taffy.

Steeplechase Pier Boardwalk at West 17th Street. Out of season, you can walk 1,000 feet out into the Atlantic Ocean as tides lap beneath you and salty breezes blow, basking in the silence that is a precursor to the summer cacophony of salsa, bongos, hawkers and multicultural exuberance. Gaze out to sea, picnic on benches and watch fishermen hook herring.

Thunderbolt Boardwalk at West 16th Street. There's a haunting quality to the scorched skeleton of the 1925 roller coaster, which closed in 1983, an eerie reminder of a different time.

Brooklyn Heights/Cobble Hill/ Carroll Gardens

In 1965, **Brooklyn Heights** was designated the city's first historic district, assuring protection for brick and brownstone row houses on streets sometimes little altered since the Civil War. The area is now one of Brooklyn's most desirable (and expensive) residential areas, and remains a popular destination for architecture-lovers. Montague Street, the commercial core, is lined with shops, chain stores and restaurants and it is clogged with midday traffic.

Brooklyn Heights has played host to some impressive literary figures over the years, including Walt Whitman, who wrote *Leaves of Grass* while living here. Truman Capote, Arthur Miller, and W.H. Auden all lived here for a time, and Thomas Wolfe completed *You Can't Go Home Again* in a house on Montague Terrace. Today, Norman Mailer lives in one of the elegant brownstones on Columbia Heights.

One of the best reasons to visit, however, has to be the Brooklyn Heights Promenade. Stretching from Montague to Middagh Streets, it offers striking views of the lower Manhattan skyline and the Brooklyn Bridge. Lined by the lush gardens of picturesque town houses, the walkway and benches draw runners, families and—at night—romancing couples. The view of Manhattan is startling: You're far enough away to take it all in, but close enough that the buildings still loom large. If you lean over the railing a bit, you'll realize that the peaceful esplanade juts over the Brooklyn-Queens Expressway.

The best ending to a visit here is a stroll back across the Brooklyn Bridge. The footpath is accessible from Cadman Plaza Park, and the trip toward Manhattan offers the best views and photo opportunities.

If you want to venture a little deeper into Brooklyn, head south to the quiet neighborhood of **Cobble Hill,** most of which is part of a New York City Historic District designated in 1969 and slightly extended in 1988. In the 1930's, Thomas Wolfe lived here on Verandah Place. Jenny Jerome, the mother of Winston Churchill, was born on Amity Street in 1854. And Louis Comfort Tiffany in 1917 designed the windows, high altar and other appointments of the Episcopal Christ Church and Holy Family at 326 Clinton Street, a Greek Revival structure built in 1842.

Among merchants are a handful each of butchers, greengrocers and bakeries. Arabic restaurants and specialty food shops dot Atlantic Avenue in a section known as Little Arabia, offering Middle Eastern delicacies, particularly from Egypt, Yemen and Morocco. Atlantic Avenue is also well-known for its antiques stores.

Carroll Gardens, slightly farther to the south, has long had a strong Italian-American flavor, and that flavor is still very much in evidence. Court Street, the area's commercial district, has a high density of Italian restaurants and pizza stores. Part of the neighborhood was designated the Carroll Gardens Historic District by the New York City Landmarks Preservation Commission in 1973.

The district, which contains more than 160 buildings, includes houses on President and Carroll Streets between Smith and Hoyt Streets as well as adjacent parts of the four streets and a bit of First Street east of Hoyt. All the district's brownstone row houses were erected between 1869 and 1884.

Subway: A, C, F to Jay Street; 2, 3, 4, 5 to Clark St. or Borough Hall; N, R to Court St.

HIGHLIGHTS OF THE NEIGHBORHOOD

Borough Hall Court St. (at Joralemon St.) (718) 875-4047. This historic building won a Municipal Art Society award after its renovation around 1990. The plaza between Borough Hall and the nearby Supreme Court is the site of a large greenmarket on Fridays and Saturdays, and is a popular spot for rollerbladers and local office workers on their lunch breaks. Tours of the building are available on Tuesdays.

Brooklyn Historical Society128 Pierrepont St. (between Clinton and Montague Sts.) (718) 624-0890. While the rest of New York celebrated its consolidation as the world's second-largest city in 1898, Brooklyn mourned the end of over two centuries as an independent city. Even then, die-hard Brooklynites could turn to the Brooklyn Historical Society for consolation. Founded in 1863 as the Long Island Historical Society, the society has long housed the world's most extensive collection of Brooklynalia in its landmark building. Its collections range from fine paintings and sculpture to archeological artifacts, including an outstanding collection of ephemera on the lamented Brooklyn Dodgers.

Hours: Mon., Thur., Fri., Sat., noon–5 P.M.. **Price** : $2.50, general; $1, children under 12; Mondays admission is free. **Payment:** All major credit cards. **Services:** Tours.

New York Transit Museum Boerum Place and Schermerhorn St. (718) 243-3060. The entrance to the Transit Museum looks like that of any subway station, from the green-painted railing to the cement stairway. And as you head inside you go through the standard subway entry routine, paying your admission at a token booth (although there's an audible and eager-to-please staff member inside) and passing through a turnstile. But when you reach the lower platforms of this former subway station, you start exploring the past. Some of the old turnstiles are made of wood and ask for just five cents; the subway cars include magnificent wooden carriages from the early 1900's, with big windows and narrow wicker benches. And, unlike in so many museums, you and the kids can touch and play with nearly everything—you can even sit in a motorman's seat and operate a signal tower.

Hours: Tues.–Fri.,10 A.M.–4 P.M; Sat., Sun., noon–5 P.M.. **Price:** $3, general; $1.50, seniors and children under 17; MTA employees, free.

Plymouth Church of the Pilgrims75 Hicks St (near Henry St.) (718) 624-4743. This historic church was founded by Henry Ward Beecher, the

famous 19th-century abolitionist, and is sometimes referred to as the Grand
Central Terminal of the Underground Railroad. Plymouth Church also features
windows designed by Louis Comfort Tiffany.

Brooklyn Academy Of Music (BAM)

30 Lafayette Ave. (at Ashland Pl.), Brooklyn (718) 636-4100

It's the oldest performing arts center in the United States, yet it is also practically synonymous with the avant-garde. The main building houses the BAM
Opera House, which hosts programs like the innovative Next Wave Festival,
bringing the best in new music, dance, opera and theater to New York each year
(festival regulars include Laurie Anderson, Philip Glass and Robert Wilson).
Other annual Opera House performers include the Brooklyn Philharmonic and
BAM Opera.

Almost every Manhattan subway line stops at Brooklyn's Atlantic or Pacific
Avenue stations, both just one block away from BAM. The neighborhood
around BAM (Fort Greene) is a friendly, multicultural community, and there
are quite a few interesting shops and restaurants just around the corner on
Fulton Street. Less adventurous travelers can take the BAMbus between Manhattan and Brooklyn; call the main phone number above for prices and
reservations.

BAM Rose Cinemas Also housed in the main BAM building, the Rose Cinemas shows first-run independent and foreign films in four theaters with good
sightlines and good size screens. One of those screens is devoted exclusively to a
program featuring classic American and foreign films, documentaries, retrospectives and special festivals.

BAMcafé A good place for food and drinks before and after BAM performances. The café also hosts "BAMcafé LIVE" every Thursday, Friday and Saturday night, featuring a wide range of musical and spoken-word performances (no
cover, $10 food and drink minimum).

BAMcafé hours: Wed.–Sat., 4:30–11:30 P.M.; Sun., Noon–10:00 P.M.

BAM Harvey Theater 651 Fulton St. (between Ashland Pl. and Rockwell
Pl.). Built in 1904 as a legitimate theater and later used to show movies, the
Harvey Theater (formerly known as the Majestic but renamed in 1999 for
Harvey Lichtenstein, BAM's former president and executive producer) was
abandoned in 1968 and lay dark until its renovation in 1987. But don't be
fooled by the term "renovation": The building's shell, with exposed brick,
crumbling paint, chipped friezes and exposed ducts, was deliberately left more
or less intact. The theater has 900 seats and practically no obstructed views.
BAM uses it as a showcase for a variety of performing arts, including dance,
jazz and opera.

Tickets: Box office; Ticketmaster. **Credit cards:** All major. **Subway:** D, Q, 2, 3,
4, 5 to Atlantic Ave.; B, M, N, R to Pacific St.

Park Slope

At the turn of the century, Park Slope was one of the wealthiest neighborhoods in the country. But by the 1920's, mansions were being razed for apartment houses, and brownstones were going out of fashion. By the end of World War II, many had been carved up into rooming houses. Through the 50's, middle-class families moved to the suburbs and urban decay set in. In the early 60's, brownstone pioneers, recognizing bargains, arrived to renovate and restore fading brownstones and eventually reverse the area's precipitous decline. Park Slope has been on the rise ever since. Today, a stroll down 8th Avenue takes you past some of the finest brownstones in New York; start near **Grand Army Plaza** at the historic Montauk Club (at 8th Ave. and Lincoln Pl.), and follow Eighth Avenue south, exploring the homes on President Street, Carroll Street, and Montgomery Place.

In few other parts of Brooklyn does the past so enrich the present. The 526-acre **Prospect Park** on the neighborhood's eastern edge is thronged on weekends by parents and children. The Soldiers' and Sailors' Memorial at Grand Army Plaza, with its twin Doric columns, grand arch and crowning statute of Victory in her horse-drawn chariot, is modeled after the Arc de Triomphe. And every Labor Day weekend the massive West Indian American Day Parade rolls along nearby Eastern Parkway, the first six-lane parkway in the world.

With its exquisite churches, stellar brownstone row houses, thriving Seventh Avenue shops and restaurants and the eclectic spirit of both its people and its neo-Renaissance and neo-Classical architectural styles, Park Slope is one of Brooklyn's most popular neighborhoods. Its proximity to the park, the Brooklyn Public Library, the **Brooklyn Museum** and the **Brooklyn Botanic Garden** adds to its desirability, and subway links to Manhattan are numerous.

There are restaurants of many nationalities—Italian, Vietnamese, Chinese, Thai and Japanese—and cafes and coffeehouses along Seventh Avenue. Residents invariably speak of the small-town feeling and social cohesion of Park Slope, a tree-lined, nearly all-residential area especially attractive to families. It is a place where activities for children are unending, shopkeepers know their customers and people stop in the street to chat. The population mix is all-encompassing—whites, blacks, Hispanics and Asians, and a sizable lesbian and gay community as well.

Subway: D, F to 7th Ave.

HIGHLIGHTS OF THE NEIGHBORHOOD

Brooklyn Botanic Garden 1000 Washington Ave. (at Eastern Parkway) (718) 622-4433. A stunningly beautiful and tranquil place to help you forget you're anywhere near a city, the best time to visit the garden is from late March through mid-May. This is when the Oriental cherry trees flower in all their glory. And if you go on Tuesdays, you can even see them—and the roses and lilacs and daffodils, too—for free.

But there's plenty more to see year 'round. Wander through the famous collection of bonsai trees or steam yourself in a fern grotto in the Warm Temperate Pavilion. Admire a great reproduction of a Kyoto temple or visit the orchids in the Aquatic House.

In all, more than 12,000 kinds of plants from around the world fill the intricate, multi-level gardens and the insides of soaring greenhouses in the Steinhardt Conservatory. You could also end up seeing a wedding party spilling out of the glass-and-steel Palm House, the conservatory's Victorian centerpiece.

It's hard to imagine that the whole 52-acre spread was, in the late 1800's, mostly an ash dump. By the mid-1920's, the bonsai collection had already begun and the famous rose garden was being built. In the garden now, you can find a hybrid tea rose named for Audrey Hepburn and another variety called Elizabeth Taylors. In 1955, the Fragrance Garden was built, the first in the country to be designed for sight impaired people. And by the late 1970's, the garden was even granted its own patent—for developing the first yellow magnolia.

—Randy Kennedy

Admission: $3, adults; $1.50, seniors; $.50, children 6–16; children 5 and under free. **Hours:** Tues.–Fri., 8 A.M.–6 P.M.; Sat.–Sun., 10 A.M.–6 P.M.

Brooklyn Children's Museum *(See the section "New York for Children" for full description.).* There is a shuttle bus from the Brooklyn Museum and Grand Army Plaza subway station (#2 and #3 trains) on weekends.

Brooklyn Museum Of Art 200 Eastern Parkway (at Washington Ave.) (718) 638-5000 www.brooklynart.org. As Brooklyn's population skyrocketed in the 19th century, the Brooklyn Museum grew out of a library for apprentices into a full-fledged museum with an encyclopedic scope. Its monumental Beaux-Arts building, designed by McKim, Mead and White in 1893, is just one pavilion of a larger plan that was never completed. Having divested its science and natural history exhibits in the 1930's, the museum now concentrates upon the fine arts.

For most visitors, the major draw is the museum's far-reaching exhibition program, which in recent years has presented not only blockbusters (such as "Monet and the Mediterrenean"), but also smaller, highly innovative shows (on topics such as the relationship between hip-hop and fashion). From its inception, the museum has sought to serve as more than a repository of high culture. In fact, the monumental staircase that once faced Eastern Parkway was removed in the 1930's partly with the aim of making the museum more accessible to the public. In addition to its many educational activities, the museum also hosts thematic series of films.

Permanent Collection: The museum's more than 1,500,000 objects of art exemplify a comprehensive range of cultures—from classical antiquity to Asia to colonial America—and constitute the second-largest collection in the U.S. after the Metropolitan's. The museum's Egyptian art section, which is housed in ultramodern galleries designed by the Japanese architect Arata Isozaki, is considered to be one of the finest in the world. Other highlights include a Gilbert Stuart portrait of George Washington and an array of sculptures by Rodin.

Admission: Suggested admission: $4, general; $2, students and seniors, Children under 12. **Credit cards:** Cash only. **Hours:** Wed.–Fri., 10 A.M.–5 P.M.; Sat., 11 A.M.- 6 P.M.; Sun., 11 A.M.–6 P.M. First Saturday of each month, open until 11 P.M.; free admission from 5 P.M., drinks and live music available from 6 P.M. Closed Thanksgiving, Christmas, New Year's Day. **Programs for Children:** storytelling, studio classes and performances. Call for details. **Tours:** Docent-led tours for groups and special exhibitions. Groups, call: (718) 638-5000, ext. 234.

Grand Army Plaza Arch Intersection of Prospect Park West, Flatbush Ave., and Eastern Pkwy. This triumphal arch commemorates the soldiers and sailors who fought for the Union Army during the Civil War (which interrupted the construction of the park). The Arch was designed by John H. Duncan, the designer of Grant's Tomb, and sculpted by Frederick William MacMonnies. Art exhibits and tours are held in the spring and fall, and you can call: (718) 965-8999 for information on seeing the top of the arch. Nearby Bailey Fountain is the site of the second-largest Greenmarket in New York, after Union Square.

Prospect Park

As a destination in itself or as a starting point for exploring Brooklyn's artistic and cultural treasures, Prospect Park is well worth the trip. This 526-acre triangle is considered by many to be the crowning achievement of Olmsted and Vaux, who also designed Central Park a decade earlier. Unfortunately, many Brooklyn visitors never venture into the park, coming instead to explore the nearby Brooklyn Museum of Art, Brooklyn Botanic Garden and Brooklyn Public Library, or to visit Park Slope, one of Brooklyn's most beautiful neighborhoods, just outside the park across Prospect Park West.

But the park itself has many formal attractions, starting with its grand main entrance: the 72-foot-tall Memorial Arch in Grand Army Plaza with its bronze sculptures honoring the soldiers and sailors of the Union forces in the Civil War. The park offers a Wollman Rink for skating and Lefferts Homestead, a historic farmhouse with a children's museum. There's a zoo, a carousel and many fine examples of architecture from the late 19th and early 20th centuries: the whimsical Oriental Pavilion and neighboring formal garden and the elegant Italian-style boat house with its romantic setting along the Lullwater, a finger-like extension of Prospect Lake, and its view of the graceful arched Lullwater Bridge designed by McKim, Mead & White. At the lake, people feed ducks, fish for striped bass or pedal a boat into one of the many small inlets that make this body of water feel much larger than its 60 acres.

Twenty years ago the park was run down and could, at times, seem menacing: every building was closed and visitors had dwindled to 1.5 million annually. But with crime rates down and confidence in public safety improved, along with many restoration projects, the park is undergoing a renaissance. Bit by bit, the park has begun once again to serve as an urban oasis for its visitors.

Tours: The Prospect Park Alliance offers free tours of the park every Saturday and Sunday at 1 and 3 P.M. Visit *www.prospectpark.org* or call (718) 965-6988 for tour information.

Travel to and around Prospect Park

Subway: #2 or #3 to Grand Army Plaza; D or F to 7th Ave. The free *Heart of Brooklyn* Trolley leaves theWollman Center and Rink on the hour and makes a complete loop around the park, with stops near the Carousel, the Zoo, Grand Army Plaza (at about 15 and 40 minutes past the hour), Brooklyn Museum of Art, Brooklyn Botanic Garden, the Picnic House, Bandshell, and other locations on the park's perimeter.

Parking: Available at Wollman Rink, Bartel-Pritchard Circle, Litchfield Villa, and the Picnic House

Sites of Interest in Prospect Park

Lefferts Historic House Flatbush Ave. And Empire Blvd. (in Prospect Park) (718) 965-6505. Peter Lefferts was an affluent farmer, a delegate to the New York State Constitutional Convention in 1788 and head of the largest slave-holding family in Kings County. One of the few surviving Dutch-American farmhouses in Brooklyn, the homestead, which couples Dutch colonial architecture with Federal details, was built in 1783 to replace the earlier family home, destroyed by fire in the battle of Long Island in 1776. The period rooms reflect daily life in the 1820's, with changing exhibitions detailing the concerns of the day, including slave emancipation and the opening of the Erie Canal. The museum offers tours, demonstrations of early American crafts, family workshops and other educational events.

Hours: Mon.–Fri., 9 A.M.–5 P.M.; Reservations just for groups. **Price:** Free.

Litchfield Villa 95 Prospect Park West (between 4th and 5th Sts.) (718) 965-8951. Built in 1857 by prominent Brooklyn businessman Edwin Litchfield, this building is now the headquarters for City of New York/Parks & Recreation, as well as the office of the Prospect Park Administrator and the Prospect Park Alliance. It offers a dramatic hillside view of Park Slope.

The Long Meadow Prospect Park West from 15th to Union Sts. This 90-acre expanse of grass stretches nearly a mile down the west side of Prospect Park, and may be the most visited and familiar site in the park. Many of the park's six million annual visitors end up here at some point to play ball, fly kites, or just rest on the grass.

The Music Pagoda Lincoln Rd. and Ocean Blvd. This century-old structure, resembling a Chinese city gate, is the site of numerous concerts, religious ceremonies, and other activities throughout the year. Contact the Prospect Park Alliance for schedules.

The Nethermead Mid-park, on Center Drive. Somewhat smaller than the Long Meadow, this central, open field is nevertheless a popular spot for large group events.

Playgrounds The Prospect Park Alliance has directed extensive playground renovations over the last decade, making the park's major play areas safer and more entertaining for kids. In addition to the two areas highlighted below, there are renovated playgrounds near the Lincoln Rd., 3rd St. and Vanderbilt St. street park entrances.

Tot Spot, Garfield Pl. entrance. Designed specifically for the three-and-under set.
Imagination Playground, Ocean Ave. Entrance. In addition to safe, modern play equipment, the area features a storytelling area and an array of statues of characters from the books of Brooklyn-born author Ezra Jack Keats.

Prospect Lake SE Edge of Park. Swimming is prohibited in this 60-acre lake, but it hosts all kinds of other activities throughout the year. Visitors are welcome to fish on a catch-and-release basis, and each July kids 14 and under can compete in the annual Macy's Fishing Contest. Same-day registration is available, but groups of 10 or more should contact Urban Park Rangers at   (718) 438-0100. Fishing poles are provided or kids can bring their own. Pedal boats are also available for rental at the Wollman Center and Rink; for information, call (718) 282-7789.

Prospect Park Band Shell Ninth St. and Prospect Park W. (718) 855-7882. This amphitheater on the edge of Park Slope is one of the city's most pleasant venues for a summer afternoon or evening concert, particularly when it is part of the eclectic "Celebrate Brooklyn!" series. The world music concerts—from African to Brazilian to Asian—are some of the best in the city. Readings, children's shows, rock and folk music and occasional opera and classical performances round out the offerings. Most concerts are free to the public.
The Metropolitan Opera also performs in the park once each June, and the *New York Philharmonic Orchestra* plays one evening concert each July (generally on the Long Meadow), complete with fireworks.

Prospect Park Carousel Enter at Empire Boulevard and Flatbush Avenue. The Prospect Park Carousel is one of only twelve remaining carousels designed by renowned horse carver Charles Carmel. The carousel features fifty-one horses, as well as an assortment of other animals.
Admission: 50 cents. **Hours:** Open April through October, hours may vary.
Features: Party rentals. Call (718) 965-6512 for details.

Prospect Park Picnic House Enter at Prospect Park W. and 5th St. (718) 965-6512. The Picnic House pavilion can accommodate 175–200 guests for parties, concerts, or lectures. It offers excellent views of the Long Meadow, as well as a stage, fireplace, piano, and free tables and chairs for renters.

Prospect Park Tennis Center
(See the section "Sports and Recreation")

Prospect Park Wildlife Center
(See the section "New York for Children")

Wollman Center and Rink
(See the section "Sports and Recreation")

Activities in Prospect Park

Baseball Permits are required to play baseball or softball on the 9th Street ballfields at the southwest end of the Long Meadow. Call (718) 965-8943 for permits or (718) 965-8969 for more information on playing ball in Prospect Park.

Bicycling Cycling is only permitted on designated bicycle and runner lanes around the edge of the park. The Kissena Cycling Club (718-343-7343) and the Metropolitan Cycling Association (718-522-7390) can offer information on bicycle races.

Birding The Urban Park Rangers (718-438-0100) and the Brooklyn Bird Watchers Club (718-875-1151) run bird-watching tours in the park.

Festivals Prospect Park festival information is available at (718) 965-8999 and on the sandwich boards at Park entrances. One of the largest festivals is the Celebrate Brooklyn! Performing Arts Festival, running annually from June through August at the Bandshell. See **www.brooklynx.org/celebrate** or call (718) 855-7882 for details.

Horseback Riding Prospect Park's bridle path runs from Park Circle to the end of the Long Meadow. Kensington Stables offers horse rental information at: (718) 972-4588.

Nature Walks Park visitors can join the Prospect Park Alliance and the Urban Park Rangers (718-438-0100) from April through November to explore the Prospect Park Ravine, Brooklyn's last remaining forest. Guides and maps for self-guided walking tours are available at the Prospect Park Alliance office in Litchfield Villa and at the Wollman Rink

Picnics Permits are required for groups of more than 25; information is available at (718) 965-8969.

Running Running is only permitted on the 3.35-mile running lane along Park Drive, or on other sidewalks and paved surfaces in the park.

Williamsburg

Over the past several years, Williamsburg's well-established Hasidic, Puerto Rican, Dominican and Polish communities have made way for a newer group of residents—artists and other homesteaders seeking affordable space close to Manhattan.

In the mid-1800's, Williamsburg was a fashionable resort area, with hotels, clubs and beer gardens near the Brooklyn ferry attracting wealthy industrialists and professionals. The neighborhood's nature changed with the 1903 opening of the Williamsburg Bridge and the 1905 inauguration of trolley service over the bridge. Working-class Jews and other Eastern European immigrants flooded in from the crowded Lower East Side; they were followed by various groups of working-class immigrants, including Puerto Ricans working in the factories. In 1957, the Brooklyn-Queens Expressway opened, slicing through the neighborhood.

As recently as 1990, it was hard to find even basic services in Williamsburg. There is still a shortage of banks and ATM machines but the area now abounds with coin laundries and convenience stores; Bedford Avenue even features Sarkana Discount Art Supplies (the name means red in Latvian). So far, chain stores are nonexistent. But fresh food and well-regarded restaurants flourish including the landmark Peter Luger Steak House, in its original 1887 location.

Ground zero for the artistic renaissance of Williamsburg is Bedford Avenue and surrounding side streets, where Polish delicatessens are sandwiched in between galleries, shops, restaurants and bars. A day or night in this part of Williamsburg, can include everything from cinema to fusion food to avant-garde circus performances.

Subway: L train to Bedford Avenue.

HIGHLIGHTS OF THE NEIGHBORHOOD

McCarren Park Northern end of Bedford Ave. (between North 12th St. and Leonard Ave.). The park is a spiffier spot these days after the New York City Parks department gave it some long-overdue repairs. From spring through fall, this is a great place to take in the local scene. It's a conflagration of ethnic groups: older Polish men and women dance to live polka music; Latino families play fierce games of soccer and volleyball and stage huge festive barbecues; artist/hipster residents lie on the grass or play frisbee, and occasionally, Hasidic men toss baseballs in games of catch.

Metropolitan Pool and Bathhouse 261 Bedford Ave . (718) 965-6576. This historic site was reopened in the fall of 1997 after a $4.88 million renovation. The 1922 building, which includes a 30- by 75-foot swimming pool, two new locker rooms, a community room and a fitness area, was originally designed by Henry Bacon, architect of the Lincoln Memorial in Washington.

Williamsburg Bridge The Williamsburg Bridge was born of a dare. Could Leffert Lefferts Buck, the city's chief engineer, build a bridge that was longer than the Brooklyn Bridge, in half the time and with less money? He could, and did. When it opened in 1903, the Williamsburg was the world's longest suspension bridge, with a span of 1,600 feet, 5 feet more than the Brooklyn Bridge. At a cost of $24,188,090, it was $906,487 cheaper than its rival. And it was built in seven years, not the 13 required for the first East River crossing.

Art in Williamsburg

Galapagos 70 N. Sixth St. (Between Wythe and Kent Aves.) (718) 782-5188. This Williamsburg bar and arts center is hard to find, but worth the hunt for its expansive cathedral-like interior, brilliantly spotlit, with candles on the walls, bare I-beams, and a stark, minimal bar ringed with tables. Ocularis is Galapagos' screening room, run by Donal O'Ceille, a young Irishman who started showing old movies on the roof one summer and quickly attracted a local following. The space seats about 100 people.

Holland Tunnel 61 S. 3d St. (Between Berry St. and Wythe Ave.)   (718) 384-5738. One of the quirkiest art spaces in Williamsburg, Holland Tunnel is run by Pauline Lethen, an energetic Dutch woman who sees it partly as a conduit for Dutch art (hence the title). It occupies a small pre-fab gardener's shed set in a pretty little yard behind an old apartment building.

Art Moving 166 N. 12th St. (Between Berry St. and Bedford Ave.) (718) 486-8366. Art Moving is the accidental gallery of the artist Aaron Namenwirth, who in 1992 moved into a storefront that had been occupied by one of Williamsburg's first galleries. Passers-by regularly inquired about the next show, and the previous tenant's mail, including many artists' slides, continued unabated. Finally Mr. Namenwirth began holding sporadic shows of neighborhood artists.

Pierogi 2000 177 N. 9th St. (At Bedford Ave.) (718) 599-2144. Joe Amrhein decided to promote the work of Williamsburg artists by filling a flat file with their drawing portfolios, creating a remarkably efficient and mobile way to let interested parties see the work of hundreds of artists. Mr. Amrhein also mounts ambitious exhibitions in the space.

Hours: Mon.–Sat., noon–6 P.M.. **Price:** Free.

Recommended Restaurants

BROOKLYN HEIGHTS

Caffe Buon Gusto $25 & Under   ITALIAN
151 Montague St.   (718) 624-3838
Credit cards: All major   Meals: L, D

One of a chain of low-end mix-and-match pasta places, and not bad for the price. Stick with simple preparations and expect the usual economies, like tight seating and casual service, and enjoy the little surprises, like the basket of fluffy focaccia on every table. **Price range:** Entrees, $9.95–$17.95.

Gage & Tollner $ $ SEAFOOD/SOUTHERN
372 Fulton St.   (718) 875-5181
Credit cards: All major   Meals: L, D   Closed Sun.

Gage & Tollner opened in 1879 and moved to its current downtown Brooklyn
location in 1892. It is a wonderfully old-fashioned room. The beautiful old gas-
fired lights have been retrofitted and acoustic tiles have been removed, expos-
ing the original vaulted ceiling. Unlike the room, the menu has barely changed
in a century, with old favorites like soft clam bellies, lobster Newburg, she-crab
soup and "blooming onions," which are cunningly fried whole. **Price range:**
Entrees, $15–$27.

Grimaldi's $ $ PIZZA
19 Old Fulton St. (under Brooklyn Bridge)   (718) 858-4300
Credit cards: Cash only   Meals: L, D

This stellar pizzeria, overshadowed by the Brooklyn Bridge, makes classic, coal-
oven New York pizza. Crusts are thin and crisp in the center, blackened and
blistered around the dense and bready edges. The mozzarella is fresh, the tomato
sauce is fragrant and made at the restaurant, as are roasted peppers. Expect a
wait and expect to hear Sinatra playing in the background.

Park Slope Brewing Company   PUB
62 Henry St. (between Orange and Cranberry Sts.)   (718) 522-4801
Credit cards: All major   Meals: L, D

With homebrewed beer and a full menu, the Brewing Company serves as both a
pub and a family restaurant. At booths and at the bar, neighborhood locals
gather to sample the wide selection of homemade beer, socialize, and eat a meal.
The full menu includes burgers, chicken, catfish, and pastas. For Manhattanites,
this is a perfect spot to relax after a walk over the bridge and along the Brooklyn
Heights Promenade.

River Café ☆ ☆ $ $ $ $ NEW AMERICAN
1 Water St.   (718) 522-5200
Credit cards: All major   Meals: L, D

Is this New York City's most romantic restaurant? With waterside seating, a
spectacular view of downtown Manhattan, dim lighting, heaps of flowers and
live piano music, it certainly must be. Such a view might have made the food
irrelevant, but this has been a seminal restaurant in the annals of New American food. The food is excellent and innovative and brunch is a special pleasure. So too is the dessert made of chocolate and shaped like the Brooklyn
Bridge. **Price range:** Prix fixe, $70; tasting menu, $90.

CARROLL GARDENS

Banania Café $25 & Under FRENCH

241 Smith St. (between Butler and Douglas Sts.)   (718) 237-9100
Credit cards: Cash only   Meals: L, D

Banania, named for a French children's drink, has an enticing menu of reasonably priced bistro dishes. There are Asian and Middle Eastern touches, so that though it feels French, it falls into that catchall international category that might be called contemporary. Calamari rings, for example, are dusted with cumin, roasted and served with carrot purée, a happy match of power and pungency. Among main courses, braised lamb shank and moist roasted cod are delicious. **Price range:** Entrees, $12–$15.

Ferdinando's Focacceria $25 & Under ITALIAN

151 Union St.   (718) 855-1545
Credit cards: Cash only   Meals: L, D   Closed Sun.

They filmed *Moonstruck* on this street, and you can see why. This restaurant is a throwback to turn-of-the-century Brooklyn, before Ebbets Field had even been built. Ferdinando's serves old Sicilian dishes, like chickpea-flour fritters; vasteddi, a focaccia made with calf's spleen; and pasta topped with sardines canned by the owner. It's worth a visit. **Price range:** Entrees, $10–$13.

Mignon $25 & Under FRENCH

394 Court St.   (718) 222-8383
Credit cards: Cash only   Meals: L, D   Closed Mon.

Even when it's very busy, service in Mignon's lace-curtained dining room is friendly, courteous and efficient, food arrives at an acceptable pace, and best of all, it's delicious. Chilled seafood bisque, with the intense, rich flavors of shrimp and lobster reduced to their essences, is a great appetizer. Cod coated with ground almonds is terrifically moist and flavorful, while both sautéed monkfish and grilled red snapper are also perfectly cooked. Desserts include a wonderful fruit tart. **Price range:** Entrees, $13 to $18.50.

Patois $25 & Under BISTRO/FRENCH

255 Smith St.   (718) 855-1535
Credit cards: All major   Meals: Br, D   Closed Mon.

This small storefront restaurant offers rich, gutsy bistro fare that can range from authentically French tripe stew—a mellow, wonderful dish, if not destined for popularity—to juicy pork chops and satisfying casseroles. Dishes don't always work, but it's nice that Patois is trying. **Price range:** Entrees, $10–$17.

Saul $25 & Under   NEW AMERICAN
140 Smith St.   (718) 935-9844
Credit cards: MC/V   Meals: Br, D

The small menu in this sweet little brick storefront offers strong, clear flavors, bolstered by background harmonies that augment without overshadowing. The main courses seem familiar—salmon, chicken, pork loin—but they are beautifully handled and surprisingly good. Desserts are wonderful, like lush baked alaska with a chocolate cookie crust. **Price range:** Entrees, $15 to $20.

Sur $25 & Under   ARGENTINE
232 Smith St.   (718) 875-1716
Credit cards: All major   Meals: Br, D

This brick-walled, candlelit Argentine restaurant is warm and inviting without any of the usual gaucho clichés. The focus, naturally, is on beef, with top choices including the lean, almost grassy Argentine sirloin, served with a mound of crisp, salty french fries. Alternatives to beef include juicy and flavorful roast chicken and several pasta dishes. For dessert, try the crepes filled with dulce de leche, a sublime caramel-like confection of cream and sugar. **Price range:** Entrees, $12–$19.

COBBLE HILL

Harvest $25 & Under   AMERICAN
218 Court St.   (718) 624-9267
Credit cards: All major   Meals: Br, L, D, LN   Closed Mon.

A lively, appealing neighborhood restaurant that is plagued by inconsistency. Harvest feels like the best restaurant in a small college town, and the menu of American regional food like roasted beet salad, gumbo and meatloaf whets the appetite. **Price range:** Entrees, $9–$14.

CONEY ISLAND

Gargiulo's
2911 West 15th Street (between Surf and Mermaid Aves.)
(718) 266-4891

In business since 1907 and at this location since 1928, Gargiulo's is a longtime favorite, especially for the kind of subtle, freshly prepared Neapolitan specialties that are hard to find these days. You won't go wrong with roasted peppers; fried calamari with a delicate tomato sauce dip; baked clams; mussels in tomato broth; all of the southern pastas, like linguine with white clam sauce or with calamari, chicken scarpariello (better with bones in); lobster oreganato (here called racanati); simply prepared fish, and grilled veal chop. The cheesecake is good if it is not too cold.

Nathan's Famous
1310 Surf Ave. (between Stillwell Ave. and 16th St.)
(718) 946-2202

Famous is the word for this 1916 original, opened to compete with the long-gone Feltman's, where Charles Feltman, a German immigrant, is believed to have invented the hot dog, by slipping a frankfurter into a long heated roll. One of his waiters, Nathan Handwerker, spun off his own version, and the rest is hot-dog history. It is said that these sputtering, juicy all-beef franks are still made according to the meat and spice recipes developed by Nathan and his wife, Ida. In good weather, order and eat at the front windows.

Totonno's Pizzeria
1524 Neptune Ave. (between West 15th and West 16th Streets)
(718) 372-8606.

Just three blocks off the Boardwalk, in the heart of what's left of Coney Island's Little Italy, this is a highly touted 74-year-old pizzeria, more interesting for its history than for its pizzas, which can be fine or fair.

FORT GREENE

Cambodian Cuisine $25 & Under   CAMBODIAN
87 South Elliott Pl.   (718) 858-3262
Credit cards: MC/V   Meals: L, D

This may be the only Cambodian restaurant in New York City and is worth checking out for that reason alone. Most dishes are similar to Thai and Vietnamese foods but some of the preparations are unusual. In the signature dish, chicken ahmok, chicken breast is marinated in coconut milk, lemongrass, galangal and kaffir lime and steamed until it achieves a soft, pudding-like texture. The voluminous menu also includes quite a few dishes that seem more Chinese than Cambodian, and a list of interesting-sounding desserts. **Price range:** Entrees, $3.50–$14.95.

PARK SLOPE

Al di la $25 & Under   ITALIAN
248 5th Ave (at Carroll St.)   (718) 783-4555
Credit cards: Cash only.   Meals: D

The food at Al Di La is soulful and gutsy, with profound flavors. This neighborhood restaurant serves on bare wooden tables, but hints at a more sensual attitude with such luxurious touches as velvet drapes and chandeliers. The chef coaxes deep flavors out of simple dishes, and all the pastas are wonderful. **Price range:** Main courses, $8 to $16.

Coco Roco $25 & Under   LATIN AMERICAN

392 5th Ave. (near 6th St.)   (718) 965-3376
Credit cards: All major   Meals: L, D

This bright, pleasant restaurant offers some of the best Peruvian food in New York. The menu ranges from tender, delicious ceviches from Peru's coast to Andean dishes that have been enjoyed since the days of the Incan empire. Roast chicken is excellent, and desserts like rice pudding and lucuma ice cream, made with a Peruvian fruit, are wonderful. **Price range:** Main courses, $7 to $12.95.

PROSPECT HEIGHTS

Garden Café $25 & Under   NEW AMERICAN

620 Vanderbilt Ave.   (718) 857-8863
Credit cards: All major   Meals: D   Closed Sun., Mon.

This family-run operation, near the Brooklyn Academy, serves an ever-changing menu of artful American food that is always satisfying. Standards like grilled veal chops and steaks are superb, and the chef occasionally comes up with dishes like jambalaya with Middle Eastern spicing. It's the kind of place you wish was in your neighborhood. **Price range:** Entrees, $17.50–$20.

WILLIAMSBURG

Diner $25 & Under   DINER

85 Broadway   (718) 486-3077
Credit cards: Cash only   Meals: Br, L, D, LN

Diner brings the diner idea up to date, offering the sort of everyday food that appeals to the local art crowd. The basics are fine, and other dishes can be superb, like skirt steak, perfectly cooked whole trout, black bean soup and eggs scrambled with grilled trout. The atmosphere is bustling and smoky. **Price range:** Entrees, $6.50–$15.

Oznot's Dish $25 & Under   MEDITERRANEAN

79 Berry St.   (718) 599-6596
Credit cards: MC/V   Meals: Br, L, D, LN

Oznot's is truly unusual, a veritable flea market of mosaics, mismatched furniture and artwork set on a rickety, uneven wood floor. The blend of Mediterranean food is just as interesting, with dishes like grilled shrimp served over tabbouleh with fennel chutney. Main courses include fish and seafood stew served in a tomato-saffron broth and fennel-dusted tuna with hummus and tapenade. **Price range:** Entrees, $5–$9.

Peter Luger ☆ ☆ ☆ $ $ $ $ STEAKHOUSE

178 Broadway   (718) 387-7400
Credit cards: Cash only   Meals: L, D

Peter Luger serves no lobsters, takes no major credit cards and lacks a great wine list. Service, though professional and often humorous, can sometimes be brusque. So why is it packed night and day, seven days a week? Simple: Peter Luger has the best steak in New York City. The family that runs the restaurant buys fresh shortloins and dry-ages them on the premises. You know the steak is great from the fine, funky aroma that wafts across the table. An occasional diner will choose the thick and powerfully delicious lamb chops, or the fine salmon. And even side dishes have their moments. But the steak's the thing here, and they serve just one cut: an enormous porterhouse charred to perfection over intense heat. **Price range:** Avg. price for three courses, $60.

Plan-Eat Thailand   THAI
141 N. Seventh St. (Between Bedford and Berry Sts.)   (718) 599-5758
Credit cards: Cash only   Meals: L, D

This unusual, much-applauded Thai restaurant serving Williamsburg has its ups and downs, but more often than not serves spicy, meticulously prepared dishes like ground pork salad, sautéed bean curd and striped bass with crunchy greens. It is often crowded and loud. **Price range:** Entrees, $4.75–$12.95.

Brooklyn Nightlife

Go out in Brooklyn? On the weekend? For groovy New Yorkers, that was once an unbearably tepid proposition. Russian immigrants may drink vodka in Brighton Beach leisure palaces, and Trinidadians let loose to soca near Nostrand Avenue. But the students, artists and hipsters seeking the cultural edge started their evenings on the subway to the Village and beyond.

Now the Brooklyn-Manhattan power balance is changing. Exiled trendsetters eventually found themselves loving their neighborhoods and dressed them up with shops, restaurants and bars. Younger residents tried spots that no one else had yet declared chic. Hot spots multiplied, some as buzz-filled as Manhattan, others retaining an air of simplicity, messiness, home.

Brooklyn Heights, Cobble Hill, Boerum Hill, Carroll Gardens

Last Exit 136 Atlantic Ave. (between Henry and Clinton Sts.) (718) 222-9198. For a change of pace, try this welcome addition to Brooklyn's nightlife. With its brick walls, red track lighting, vintage couches and furniture, an art show on the walls and a full house of young, laid-back hipster types, you might think you're in the East Village, but—surprisingly—it's Cobble Hill.

Quench 282 Smith St. (at Sackett St.) (718) 875-1500. Behind its sleek, frosted-glass exterior, Quench—a new highlight on the Smith Street scene in Carroll Gardens—exudes an air of unpretentious sophistication. Illuminated orbs hang from the ceiling, while the rich-wood floor and bar gives the place a relaxed elegance.

Pete's Waterfront Ale House 155 Atlantic Ave. (between Clinton and Henry Sts.) (718) 522-3794. Pete's is the epitome of the friendly neighborhood bar. Not too divey or too classy, Pete's is really the neighborhood's anti-hip bar—it's all about decent beer in a nice, well-ventilated space that offers a kid- and dog-friendly environment.

Brooklyn Inn 138 Bergen St. (at Hoyt St.). Believed to have opened in 1868, the Brooklyn Inn is a regal, historic bar where the residents of Boerum Hill still gather over drafts of beer. There is no sign out front, adding to the bar's mysterious allure. Panels of stained glass with seemingly random letters on them dot the interior.

Fort Greene

Alibi 242 DeKalb Ave. (between Vanderbilt and Clermont Aves.) (718) 783-8519. Alibi is a dive bar in the great tradition of East Village. This one, though, lives across the East River in Fort Greene, and for what it offers, it doesn't have much local competition. Pratt students pack in, joining a decent-sized crowd.

Frank's Lounge 660 Fulton Street (at South Elliott Pl.). This old-school lounge is a Fort Greene gem. With Christmas lights, red vinyl seats and three-inch stucco spikes hanging from the ceiling over the bar, Frank's is a kitsch-lovers dream. Check local listings for DJs and other events both in the lounge and in the loft upstairs.

Park Slope, Prospect Heights

Freddy's Sixth Ave. (at Dean St.). With a neighborhood feel, cheap drinks and a backroom with a pool table, Freddy's is the ultimate dive. Everyone is welcome here where the crowd is a mix of older regulars, younger locals and everything in between.

The Gate 321 Fifth Ave. (at Third St.) (718) 768-4329. The Gate is a textbook example of low-key charm in every detail, from the attractive, distressed wood benches and tables to the amiable Irish bartender. This place provides a welcome antidote to the cutesiness of Park Slope.

Great Lakes 284 Fifth Ave. (at 1st St.) (718) 499-3710. Great Lakes on a busy Friday night would not surprise many Manhattanites. It is dimly lighted, smoky and filled with nicely dressed young professionals chatting about their day, sitting on couches and listening to the house DJ's funky sounds.

Loki 304 Fifth Ave. (at Second St.) (718) 965-9600. Dark and cavernous with something for everyone, Loki's front room is dominated by a long, dark-wood bar lined with candles—perfect for a quiet after-work read in the room's cafe-style ambiance. Loki's middle space is its rumpus room, with a pool table, jukebox and a dart board. And finally, tucked behind a cascade of heavy, red-velvet curtains, is a back room filled with a lavish, haphazard assortment of plush couches.

O'Connors 39 Fifth Ave. (between Bergen and Dean Sts.) (718) 783-9721. Although O'Connors might look scary from the outside, it's actually a delightful neighborhood bar where a mix of Park Slope residents socializes with ease. A second-generation Irish bar that was a speakeasy during Prohibition, O'Connors is a beer-and-smoke-worn watering hole with rickety old wooden booths.

Williamsburg, Greenpoint

The Abbey 536 Driggs Ave. (Between N. Seventh and N. Eighth Sts.) (718) 599-4400. Seeking a cozy cloister on a chilly night? Take refuge in the monastic intimacy of The Abbey. Exposed brick and a red felt pool table exude warmth, while torch-like wall candles dripping big blobs of wax enhance the medieval feel. Within, talkative, dressed-down 20-somethings cluster in booths, perch on stools, and circle the pinball machine.

Black Betty 366 Metropolitan Ave. (At Havemeyer St.) (718) 599-0243. Although Black Betty is popular with locals, it's easy to miss. The only sign out front says Don Diego's (a remnant from the previous tenant, a divey nightclub). The transition from divey club to divey bar seems to have been pretty smooth. The space's new décor is more sleazy than anything else, but not unpleasantly so.

Brooklyn Ale House 103 Berry St. (At N. Eighth St.) (718) 302-9811. The Brooklyn Ale House has a polished, interior-decorated look, from the mustard-colored walls to the purple pool table and the halogen track lighting. Enter through the multi-windowed storefront brimming with plants and stained glass and you'll find a clean, well-lighted place where Williamsburg social butterflies gather to sip and chat about their days slaving over mixed-media sculpture, typewriters, or, especially, city school kids.

Brooklyn Brewery 79 N 11th St (Between Berry St. and Wise Ave.) (718) 486-7422. You wouldn't spot the entrance to the Brooklyn Brewery's "tasting room" if it weren't for the dejected smokers pacing around after not being let in. Once inside the cavernous, brick-and-cinder-block-walled warehouse room, you'll feel like you're at the county fair: Brooklyn label brews are your only option here—unless you're interested in the Pepsi machine just inside the entrance.

Enid's 560 Manhattan Ave. (at Driggs Ave.) (718) 349-3859. This spot has struck the perfect formula for hipster caché. Once a raw loft space, Enid's has been transformed into a comfortable SoHo-style living room, complete with amber lighting and—with its plastic-covered couches and "Revenge from Mars" pinball machine—just the right touch of a suburban rec room.

Galapagos 70 N. 6th St. (between Wythe and Kent Aves.) (718) 782-5188. The species may be less varied here than on the original Galapagos islands—Williamsburg and Manhattan creative types, mostly—but the scenery is lush and the competition for mates is no less fierce. Better drown your dating sorrows in drink and take some Miyako sushi down with you. The music is international, but tends towards Electronica, intensifying as the night progresses.

Mug's Ale House 125 Bedford Ave. (Between North 10th and North 11th Sts.) (718) 384-8494. The name of this traditional bar and grill derives from the beer steins strung along the top of wall—they range from a simple glass to a monstrous, elaborate German tankard. Though it has a full bar, Mug's is, of course, all about beer, with over 20 varieties on tap for $3 to $5 a pint.

Pete's Candy Store 709 Lorimer St. (between Frost and Richardson Sts.) (718) 302-3770 As its name suggests, Pete's Candy Store is full of treats. The small, comfortable space is at once eclectic and traditional, a cross between a hip bar and a genuine sweets shop. Its appeal is in the details: tables covered in Japanese newspaper, a menu of various "toasted sandwiches," plastic chickens roosting in a bale of hay in the storefront window.

Sweet Water Tavern 105 N. Sixth St. (Between Berry and Wythe Sts.) (718) 963-0608. The steamed-up windows on the facade of this longtime Williamsburg joint seem to advertise a wanton world behind the glass. People hang out at the bar, mill around the pool table, or crowd into the small back room with its punk-and-metal jukebox, pinball machine and Sweet Water Tavern's take of local art, a wall full of playfully obnoxious graffiti.

QUEENS

There is more to Queens than two airports and Archie Bunker. Ethnically diverse and mostly residential, it is the second most populous borough (over 2 million residents) after Brooklyn, but far and away the largest , occupying one-third of the city's total area. Its neighborhoods are still identified by their names as villages before they were merged into New York City in 1898—Flushing, Jamaica, Astoria (named for John Jacob Astor), Little Neck (where the clams got their name), the Rockaways with their Atlantic Ocean beaches, and the upper-class enclaves of Forest Hills and Douglaston. Industry is concentrated in Long Island City on the East River facing Manhattan and in neighborhoods nearby—Steinway where William Steinway made pianos and his heirs still do, and Astoria where Gloria Swanson, Rudolph Valentino and the Marx Brothers made movies in the Kaufman Astoria studios, still the largest film and TV studios in the East.

Named in 1683 for Queen Catherine, wife of King Charles II of England, the borough was mostly farmland until the Queensboro Bridge to Manhattan was built in 1909—and there is still a working farm museum. But the population today is decidedly non-agrarian and increasingly foreign born or born of immigrants—more than 100,000 Chinese and Koreans in Flushing, Indian immigrants in Jackson Heights, Greeks in Astoria, Irish in Sunnyside and Latinos in Elmhurst. To see for yourself, take "the international express"—the No. 7 subway line from Times Square. That line is also how to get to a Mets game in Shea Stadium, the U.S. Open in the National Tennis Center, and the New York Hall of Science. (Take the "A" to get to Aqueduct racetrack near Jamaica Bay—or stay on the train for two more stops to the Jamaica Bay Wildlife Refuge, a renowned bird sanctuary.)

Astoria/Long Island City

Although Astoria has long been known as a Greek neighborhood, the area is extraordinarily diverse, with large numbers of Italians, Brazilians, Indians and Koreans making the Queens enclave their home. It's an anomaly, a wind-swept industrial district along the East River that is home—along with the waterfront section of nearby **Long Island City** —to some of the city's most exciting art institutions.

A visit to the **P.S. 1 Contemporary Art Center,** the **Isamu Noguchi Sculpture Museum,** the **American Museum of the Moving Image,** and the **Socrates Sculpture Park** are all worth the trip across the river. But while you're there, city sites ranging from the **Steinway Piano Factory** (built in the 1880's) to **Gantry Plaza park** (built in the 1990's) offer a glimpse of the area's past and future.

HIGHLIGHTS OF THE NEIGHBORHOOD

American Museum of the Moving Image 35 Ave. at 36 St. (718) 784-0077 Before Hollywood drew much of the film industry west, Long Island City was the heart of American film production. Now, appropriately, it is the location of this museum devoted to the art and history of film. The exhibits here skillfully demonstrate the science of moving images as well provide interesting collections of artifacts and set pieces from familiar movies and television shows. The museum also offers screenings of avant-garde films. Note: closed Monday.
Subway: R, G to Steinway St.; N to Broadway.

Gantry Plaza State Park 49th Ave. on the East River (718) 786-6385 The miracle of Gantry Park is that it takes risks in a city that has long been fright-

Gantry Plaza State Park

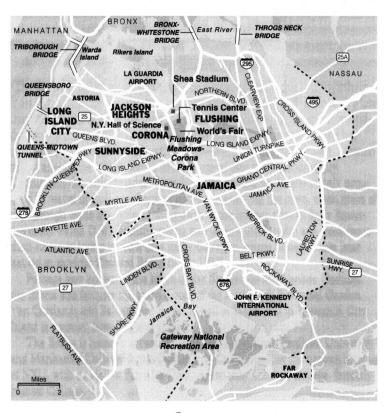

Queens

ened of them. The payoff is spectacular. With the Manhattan skyline as a
backdrop and gorgeous light bouncing off the river, the site itself is magnificent. The park takes its name from two giant, hulking structures of blackened
iron on the site, which used to lift freight trains onto river barges. The
gantries are as powerful as the triumphal arches and classical monuments built
by the City Beautiful Movement a century ago. So is the brick power station,
with its quartet of de Chirico stacks, that looms nearby. Visitors are greeted by
a circular area that encloses a fog fountain, a shallow cauldron of seething
mist that in summer cools the air. Beyond is a large, hemispherical plaza for
performances.

The plaza connects to two of four piers that project into the river. Each is
different in length, shape and furnishings. One has a circular lunch bar, with
stools and awning. Another, the Star Gazing Pier, is outfitted with overscaled
wooden chaises. On the Fishing Pier, there's a large, free-form table complete
with running water, for dressing the catch of the day. But the best thing about
the piers is the views they afford of each other and the people using them. Or
you can proceed along one of the paths that lead away from the plaza's southern
edge. The widest path, paved with stone, defines the water's edge in a series of

graceful, serpentine arcs. Along the way, it passes over a bridge that looks down on a small river inlet. From there, you can make your way down almost to the water. A second path, lined with gravel, takes you on an inland ramble, through vegetation and stone blocks clustered in crystalline formations. The blocks echo the Manhattan skyline and partly take the place of benches. The overall effect is of a Cubist rock garden.

—*Herbert Muschamp*

Isamu Noguchi Garden Museum 32–37 Vernon Blvd. (at 33d Rd.) (718) 721-1932 www.noguchi.org One of the most serene places in New York City, the Isamu Noguchi Garden Museum in Long Island City is a great spot for lovers of the Japanese-American sculptor, or anyone who just wants to get away from the city without ever leaving it. Noguchi is best known for melding Eastern and Western influences in his stark, beautiful abstract sculptures and for designing the world-famous "Akari" lamps, the multishaped paper lanterns that have become a staple of SoHo lofts and anyone with a taste for Japanese design. Visitors can stroll in the Japanese garden, buy Noguchi items in the gift shop or simply admire the haunting beauty of the artist's work. Designed by Shogi Shizao, the museum is steps away from the Socrates Sculpture Garden.

Permanent Collection: The museum houses a comprehensive collection of works by Noguchi (1904–1988) in 13 galleries and an outdoor sculpture garden. There are more than 250 works of stone, wood and clay, as well as the Akari light sculptures, dance sets and documentation of his gardens and playgrounds.

Admission: $4 adults, $2 students and seniors. Two-thirds of the collection is handicapped accessible. **Hours:** April-Oct.: Wed.–Fri., 10 A.M.–5 P.M.; Sat.–Sun., 11 A.M.–6 P.M. **Tours:** Free daily at 2 P.M.; group tours by appointment only, for school and university classes and other adult groups. Japanese tours and tours for groups with special needs are available. **Programs:** Documentary films on Noguchi, including interviews with the artist, are shown throughout the day in the 28-seat video room.

P.S. 1 Contemporary Art Center 22–25 Jackson Ave. (at 46th Ave. and 46th Rd.) (718) 784-2084 www.ps1.org Across the East River in Long Island City, the P.S. 1 Contemporary Art Center is far from SoHo and the Museum Mile. But its outer-borough location is an apt metaphor for the center's philosophy: it has always supported both artists who work on the margins and art that isn't usually exhibited in more traditional museums. P.S. 1 has presented over 2,000 exhibitions since 1976. It occupies a Romanesque Revival school building, built from 1893 to 1906 and renovated by Frederick Fisher with the addition of a 20,000-square-foot outdoor courtyard that serves as a sculpture garden, a dramatic front entry and a two-story project space. A branch, the Clocktower Gallery at 108 Leonard Street in the TriBeCa section of Manhattan, is open for special shows and events.

Permanent Collection: P.S.1 is a non-collecting institution but maintains many long-term, site-specific installations throughout its 125,000 square feet of gallery

space by artists including James Turrell, Pipilotti Rist, Richard Serra, Lucio Pozzi, Julian Schnabel and Richard Artschwager
Admission: $5 (suggested); $2, artists, students and seniors. **Credit cards:** All major. **Hours:** Wed.–Sun., noon–6 P.M.   Closed major holidays. **Services:** Food, tours, lectures, concerts. **Programs for Children:** "Art Camp" for elementary-school children throughout the year; "High School to Art School" preparation courses, and family events.
Tours: Docent-guided tours for groups and individuals, by appointment only. Prices vary.

The Queensboro Bridge (59th Street Bridge). Silhouetted against a darkening sky, this elaborate expanse looks like a work of crochet. Once known as the Blackwells Island Bridge, it is still known commonly as the 59th Street Bridge. Walking across on the south side, look through the lacy structure to appreciate the skyscraper panorama and the river opening wide. From the north walk, you will see river currents rushing over rocks, and get a good close-up of Roosevelt Island (formerly Blackwells Island, then Welfare Island) and the red Roosevelt Island tram mechanism that suggests a Calder mobile.

Socrates Sculpture Park Broadway and Vernon Blvd. (718) 956-1819. This 4.5-acre jewel on the banks of the East River in Long Island City was once a ship yard, then for 20 years an illegal dump site. Through the efforts of sculptor Mark di Suvero, the site was converted in the mid-1980's to an outdoor sculpture park. Leased from the New York City Department of Ports and Trade for $1 a year, the site features semi-annual exhibitions of public sculpture in a variety of media. Among the sculptures are subtle and pleasing artistic touches: winding paths, marble benches, and stones carved to resemble a child's letter blocks. The park hosts dance, film and video presentations.

Steinway and Sons Piano Factory 19th Ave. and 38th St. (718) 721-2600. Steinway's 440,000-square-foot factory in Astoria, built in the 1880's, still produces great pianos. A tour of the factory affords a close-up view of some 300 craftsmen who saw, bend and sand the wood, put on the strings and voice the instruments. Visitors are also allowed to enter the factory's "pounder" room, where a machine tests the integrity of each instrument by banging on all 88 keys at once, 10,000 times.

AREA RESTAURANTS

Christos Hasapo-Taverna   GREEK/STEAK
41–08 23rd Avenue at 41st Street   (718) 726-5195
Credit cards: All major   Meals: L, D, LN

Elias Corner   GREEK/SEAFOOD
24–02 31st St. at 24th Ave.   (718) 932-1510
Credit cards: Cash only   Meals: D, LN

This bright, raucous Greek seafood specialist offers no menus. Regulars know to check the glass display case in front to select the freshest looking fish. Elias is best in the off hours, before the crowd arrives. Otherwise the wait is interminable and the staff becomes harried. **Price range:** Entrees, $12–$17.

Syros $25 and Under GREEK/SEAFOOD
32–11 Broadway.   (718) 278-1877
Credit cards: All major   Meals: L, D, LN

Syros is named after the Greek island on which the owner grew up. It is attractive enough, in a conventional kind of way, and the Greek dips are particularly good. The grilled fish is superb—perfectly cooked, moist and delicious. Spanakopita, crisp layers of phyllo encasing spinach and feta cheese, is fresh and savory. Lemony fish soup is excellent, and even a T-bone steak is beefy and winning. **Price range:** Entrees, $9.25–$22.

Ubol's Kitchen THAI
24–42 Steinway St.   (718) 545-2874
Credit cards: All major   Meals: L, D

This simply decorated but authentic (there's a Buddhist shrine in the rear) Thai restaurant does not stint on its spicing or seasoning. Dishes marked on the menu as hot and spicy can be counted on to be searing, while dishes traditionally rich in fish sauce are suitably pungent. Top dishes include spicy salads and curries. **Price range:** Entrees, $5.95–$14.95.

Uncle George's GREEK
33–19 Broadway   (718) 626-0593
Credit cards: Cash only   Meals: B, L, D, LN

A cross between a giant diner that's always open and a boisterous family restaurant, Uncle George's is an Astoria Greek classic. Portions are big, service is speedy and the menu offers every kind of Greek dish, from great grilled fish to the ubiquitous spanakopita (spinach pie). You won't leave hungry. With bright lights, plastic table covers and seats crowded into every available spot, it's fair to say that Uncle George's doesn't attract people for the décor. **Price range:** Entrees, $6–$12.

Water's Edge ☆ ☆ NEW AMERICAN
44th Dr. at the East River   (718) 482-0033
Credit cards: All major   Meals: L, D

The best thing about the whole event is the free ferry ride from 34th Street and the East River in Manhattan. The restaurant sits on a barge in the East River with a ship captain's view of midtown Manhattan. The menu falls squarely in the mainstream, with all the trendy Asian touches and newly familiar ingredients. **Price range:** Prix-fixe dinner, $50–$80.

Flushing Meadows—Corona Park

Immortalized as the "Corona Dumps" in F. Scott Fitzgerald's *The Great Gatsby*, these former marshes were filled in long ago and became a park in 1939, when the site hosted the New York World's Fair. (It did so again in 1964). There's something for everyone at the park: You can catch a Mets game at **Shea Stadium** or watch the U.S. Open at the **U.S.T.A. National Tennis Center** (*see Sports & Recreation*). You can also marvel at the 12 story-high **Unisphere,** visit the **New York Hall of Science** collection of American spacecraft (*see New York for Children*) or walk around a scale model of New York at the **Queens Museum** —all of which were first built for the '64 fair.

HIGHLIGHTS OF THE NEIGHBORHOOD

Bowne House 37–01 Bowne St. (between 37th and 38th Aves.) (718) 359-0528. One of New York's oldest and most historic homes, this English-style farmhouse was built by John Bowne in 1661. He lived there and used it as New Amsterdam's first indoor Quaker meeting place, in defiance of the dominant Dutch Reformed Church. When Peter Stuyvesant expelled him from the colony, Bowne appealed to Stuyvesant's bosses—the West India Company in Holland—and won. His victory sowed the seeds of America's religious freedom. Nine generations of Bownes lived here while a bustling Flushing neighborhood grew up around them. The house features restored rooms and changing exhibits. Its grounds are in a smalll park that reflects the variety of flora for which the borough is noted, thanks to a colonial horticulturalist named William Prince. (George Washington mentioned visits to "Mr. Prince's gardens" in the diary he kept as President when New York was the new nation's capital.)
Admission: $4; $2, children and seniors.

Flushing Town Hall 137–35 Northern Blvd. at Linden Pl. (718) 463-7700. This two-story brick Romanesque Revival building served as Flushing's town hall until 1900, when the village was incorporated into New York City. Constructed in 1862 on what are believed to have been the Matinecock Indians' burial grounds, it is a veritable encyclopedia of American history. It served as a militia depot during the Civil War, a forum for speeches by Ulysses S. Grant and Teddy Roosevelt, a performance space for P. T. Barnum and Mark Twain, as well as a traffic court, jail, opera house, ballroom, police precinct and even a dinner theater. The Flushing Council on Culture and the Arts presents a variety of programs here now, including jazz on Friday nights, classical music on Sunday afternoons and student visits to its artist-in-residency program, in addition to art shows, lectures and special events.

Louis Armstrong's House 65–30 Kissina Blvd. between Horace Harding Pkwy. and Melbourne St. (718) 478-8274. Louis and his wife, Lucille, lived here from 1943 until they died. It was built in 1910, and is today just as Lucille left it when she died in 1983. As a museum now, it contains the Louis Armstrong Archives.

Queens Museum of Art New York City Bldg. (111th St. and 49th Ave.)
(718) 592-9700. www.queensmuse.org If you go to the Queens Museum only
to see the Panorama, an immense model of New York City, it would be well
worth the trip. Originally built for the 1964 World's Fair, the model repli-
cates in painstaking detail the geography, buildings, bridges and roads of all
five boroughs at a scale of 1,200 to 1. Tiny, glowing lights appear in the windows of the tiny skyscrapers when the overhead lighting dims to simulate
nightfall, while miniature airplanes take off and land at La Guardia Airport.
The model is at once immense and intimate. The world's largest scale model,
it fills a room the size of two basketball courts. But it also satisfies our longing
to see the unwieldy city brought down to a size where the Empire State
Building is only slightly taller than a ruler. Nonetheless, the museum has
more to offer than just the Panorama. The only art museum in Queens, it is
located in Flushing Meadows-Corona Park and is housed in one of the few
remaining buildings of the 1939 World's Fair. In addition to exhibiting contemporary art, the museum has an impressive collection of World's Fair
Memorabilia, an assortment of Tiffany lamps and a sculpture hall. The
museum's satellite exhibition space at Bulova Corporate Center in Jackson
Heights features a permanent sculpture exhibit as well as rotating shows of
work by emerging artists.

Admission: $4 (suggested); $2, students and seniors; children under 5, free.
Credit cards: Cash only. **Hours:** Wed.–Fri., 10 A.M.–5 P.M.;
Sat.–Sun., noon–5 P.M. **Services:** Gift shop, lectures.

AREA RESTAURANTS

Goody's ☆ $ CHINESE
94–03 63d Dr.   (718) 896-7159
Credit cards: All major   Meals: L, D

Goody's pride is the crab meat version of soup dumplings, xiao long bao,
tinted pink by the seafood that glows through the sheer, silky skin. But there
are other unusual dishes, like fabulous turnip pastries, yellowfish fingers in
seaweed batter, and braised pork shoulder, a kind of candied meat. This dish is
so rich that it must be eaten in small bites. Goody's kitchen also works magic
with bean curd, mixed with crab meat so it becomes rich and delicious. **Price
range:** $15–$20.

Joe's Shanghai CHINESE
136–21 37th Ave. (near Main St.)   (718) 539-3838
Credit cards: Cash only   Meals: L, D

Diners from all over the city line up night after night for a taste of the Chinese
cooking here. Joe's signature dish, "steamed buns," is alone worth the trip. The
buns are wonderful soup dumplings that hold a lusty blend of pork or crab meat
in a richly flavored broth. Among entrees, look for dishes like stewed mussels in
black bean sauce; beef shank with bean curd Sichuan style; crabs, steamed and

served over sweet sticky rice; tea-smoked duck; and braised pork shoulder in brown sauce. **Price range:** $9.50 and up.

Kazan Turkish Cuisine $25 & Under   TURKISH
95–36 Queens Boulevard   (718) 897-1509
Credit cards: All major   Meals: L, D

Kazan's stone oven produces exceptional pide, soft football-shape loaves of bread dotted with sesame seeds, which are just right with any of the superb cold appetizers. Eggplant is excellent, either charcoal grilled and puréed with garlic or left chunky and served with tomato and garlic. Kazan's short selection of main courses also includes some real winners like shish yogurtlu, juicy chunks of tender grilled lamb served over a sauce of yogurt blended with tomatoes. Kasarli kofte is another standout, made with chopped lamb blended with mild kasseri cheese, which gives the meat an unusual airiness. Desserts are good, but extremely sweet.**Price range:** Entrees, $8.50 to $13.95.

Master Grill   BRAZILIAN
34–09 College Point Blvd.   (718) 762-0300
Credit cards: All major   Meals: L, D

Possibly the most elaborate Brazilian rodizio in the city: Master Grill feels like an enormous banquet hall, with seating for 1,000 people and a samba band playing full tilt. It's all great fun if you're in the mood. The buffet itself is the size of a small restaurant, where you can fortify yourself with all manner of marinated vegetables, fruit, seafood, pasta, rolls, roasted potatoes and fried plantains. The parade of all-you-can-eat grilled meats, from chicken hearts to six kinds of beef, goes on as long as you can hold out. **Price range:** All you can eat for $18.95.

Pachas $25 & Under   LATIN AMERICAN
93–21 37th Avenue   (718) 397-0729
Credit cards: All major   Meals: B, L, D, LN

When a menu offers food from more than one land, the trick is knowing which way to go. Sometimes this is an easy call, but the Colombian-Venezuelan menu at Pachas presents problems. For one thing, the cuisines of Venezuela and Colombia have many dishes in common, yet items on the Venezuelan menu seem to lack sparkle. Order from the much bigger Colombian menu and the difference will be clear. A simple arepa con queso, fragrant with corn, is served steaming with a block of dense, salty cheese on top. Even better are the sublime arepa buche, a blend of tender tripe, tomato and onion, boiled down to a soulful essence; or the muchacho relleno, pork loin stuffed with chopped peppers, tomatoes, onions and peas and covered with a peppery Creole sauce. Pachas has no liquor license but makes excellent batidos, or fruit shakes, in tropical flavors. **Price range:** Entrees, $6–$13.

Pearson's Texas Barbecue $25 & Under   BARBECUE
71–04 35th Ave.   (718) 779-7715
Credit cards: Cash only   Meals: L, D

The only pit barbecue restaurant in New York City. The smoke outside may be gone, but once you enter Legends, a pleasant-enough brick-and-panel bar, you know you're in the right place. In the rear, burnished slabs of pork ribs glisten behind a counter next to piles of plump sausages and chickens turned almost chestnut by smoke. The glory of Pearson's is its brisket, superb, tender and fully imbued with smoke from the rosy-brown, almost crisp exterior through to the pink center. It is so good that it needs none of the tomato-based barbecue sauce, which is offered in mild, medium and hot gradations. Pork ribs are excellent, meaty, smoky and well-flavored. **Price range:** Sandwiches, $5.95; barbecue by the pound, $4–$14.

Penang   MALAYSIAN
38–04 Prince St.   (718) 321-2078
Credit cards: All major   Meals: L, D, LN

What started as a small Malaysian storefront in Flushing has turned into an institution serving surprisingly authentic Malaysian flavors. The dish not to miss is the roti canai, a seductive, savory crepe served with coconut milk sauce. **Price range:** Avg. entree, $13.95.

Ping's ☆☆ $$ CHINESE
83–02 Queens Blvd.(718) 396-1238
Credit cards: AE   Meals: B, Br, L, D, LN

Ping's looks like hundreds of other Chinese restaurants in New York City. Not until you approach the fish tanks do you appreciate how extraordinary the food is likely to be: in addition to the usual lobsters and sea bass, there may be several types of live shrimp, crab, both fresh-and salt-water eels and a number of fish rarely seen swimming around in restaurants. Fried giant prawns filled with roe and served with little sweet-potato dumplings are superb. Dungeness crab, topped with fried garlic, is irresistible, as is a home-style dish of greens with bits of pork and eggs. A perfect ending to the meal is steamed papayas wrapped in paper. For the best options, ask for the translation of the Chinese menu. **Price range:** Entrees, from $7.95 (all live seafood is market-priced).

Pio Pio $ PERUVIAN
84–13 Northern Blvd.   (718) 426-1010
Credit cards: All major   Meals: L, D, LN

With brick walls, a pressed tin ceiling and big windows, this is an attractive restaurant and a good place for a date. The menu is brief and the specialty is the moist and beautifully spiced roast chicken. Tostones are excellent, as are the pisco cocktails. Ceviche is served only on weekends. **Price range:** Combination dinner, $20 for two people.

Rumi-Huasi $25 & Under   LATIN AMERICAN
44-10 48th Ave.   (718) 784-5111
Credit cards: Cash only   Meals: L, D, LN   Closed Tues.

If you're having a bad day, owner Donny Salas has a prescription for you: sopa de pollo. The chicken soup speaks for itself, a rich, homey broth with a tender chicken thigh and white rice sprinkled with parsley and cilantro. Order k'jallu, a hominy salad, and she'll tell you not to worry, she'll serve it without the hot peppers. Protest that you love hot peppers, and she looks very happy. The rest of the menu is a carnivore's delight, particularly chicharrons, gnarled chunks of fried pork on the bone, basted with a garlic sauce and served with hominy. **Price range:** Entrees, $7.95-$9.95.

Shanghai Tang $25 & Under   CHINESE
135-20 40th Rd.   (718) 661-4234
77 W. Houston St. (at Wooster St.)   (212) 614-9550
Credit cards: MC/V   Meals: L, D

This bright, handsome restaurant, one of the best Chinese places in Flushing, serves many excellent Shanghai specialties. You know you're in for an unusual meal when you enter and see fish tanks full of lively eels. Service is unusually friendly and helpful. **Price range:** Entrees, $6.95-$13.95 (specials to $24.95).

Sweet 'n' Tart Café $25 & Under   CHINESE
136-11 38th Ave.   (718) 661-3380
Credit cards: Cash only   Meals: B, L, D, LN

The specialty here is tong shui, a range of sweet tonics intended to benefit specific parts of the body or to balance one's yin and yang. But Sweet 'n' Tart's more typical dishes are terrific as well, like Chinese sausage and taro with rice, served in a tall bamboo steamer, and congee with beef, pork and squid. Little English is spoken here, but waitresses describe dishes as well as they can. **Price range:** $5-$14.

OTHER ATTRACTIONS IN QUEENS

Gateway National Recreation Area—Jamaica Bay Wildlife Refuge Cross Bay Blvd., Broad Channel (718) 338-3338. The Jamaica Bay Wildlife Refuge near Kennedy Airport spans an area almost the size of Manhattan. Thousands of birds—including geese and ducks—stop here during their migration north and south along the Atlantic flyway. (The best time to visit is in the spring or fall, when birds fill the skies.) Over 300 species of birds and 65 species of butterflies have been found on the 9,000-acre preserve. Diverse habitats include salt marshland, upland fields, woods, ponds and an open expanse of bays and islands.

Queens County Farm Museum 73–50 Little Neck Pkwy. at Union Tpke., Floral Park (718) 347-3276. This 47-acre, 200-year-old farm became such an anomaly that the city decided to turn it into a museum. But it's not what you'd expect. To this day it continues as a working farm with planted fields, orchards and livestock. The historic 1770's home features period rooms and changing exhibitions on the history of agriculture. Special events include agricultural and craft fairs, apple festivals and antique car shows, as well as quilting, candle making and other craft demonstrations and courses.

STATEN ISLAND

With its 1960's-era duplexes, white-ethnic characters, conservative politics and gritty-suburban feel, Staten Island seems more New Jersey than New York City. And, in fact, a look at the map would farther that impression: tucked into a corner of Raritan Bay, at several points the island is only 500 feet across the Kill van Kill from the belching smokestacks of Linden, Perth Amboy and Port Elizabeth, while residents of the borough's south shore are about 20 miles from downtown Manhattan.

Well aware that they live in the city's least-populated and most-homogeneous borough, Staten Islanders take an almost perverse pleasure in referring to themselves as the forgotten New Yorkers. Long after the island was incorporated into greater New York in 1898, Staten Islanders still regard the other four boroughs with a mixture of suspicion, fear and fascination—like any other outsider. That sense of alienation has inspired a succession of secession movements, but when Rudolph Giuliani, a law-and-order, Italian-Catholic Republican, was elected Mayor in 1993, the secession frenzy came to a quick end. Staten Islanders considered Giuliani one of them, and Giuliani returned the favor with political patronage and special attention.

As recently as the mid-1960's, Staten Island was home to several working farms and vast tracts of undeveloped land. Its population in the 1960 census was just over 100,000. And, as if to confirm the borough's relationship with the larger city, the island quite literally had no connection to the other boroughs, save by ferryboat. Three bridges, however, connected Staten Island to New Jersey.

Everything changed with the opening of the Verrazano-Narrows Bridge in 1964. The bridge, which was master builder Robert Moses's last great public works project, made the island as accessible to the rest of New York as it already was to New Jersey. As the white middle class in New York, along with the rest of urban America, began to flee the inner city in the 1960's, the bridge to the open spaces of Staten Island became an escape route. Staten Island became one of the fastest-growing areas in the whole of New York State, and by 1990, the population had surpassed 400,000, and it continues to grow.

Staten Island's infrastructure has some of the unattractive qualities associated with boom towns. Yet for many middle-class New Yorkers, it remains a suburban refuge within the city's borders. And the exiles who call Staten Island home are not nearly as homogeneous as they were in the 1960's. The borough's minority and immigrant population, particularly on the more-urban North Shore, has grown considerably since the 1980's.

Getting There

By Boat: The Staten Island Ferry
The ferry is not just an excellent and free sightseeing cruise. Short of swimming, it's the only way to get to Staten Island directly from Manhattan.

By Bus or Car: Verrazano Narrows Bridge
The Verrazano Narrows Bridge runs from the Bay Ridge area of Brooklyn to Staten Island.

Getting Around

By Staten Island Railway: The Staten Island Railway, part of the Metropolitan Transit Authority, runs along one route between the St. George Ferry Terminal and Tottenville at the opposite end of the island. The fare system ($1.50 paid with token or Metrocard) is the same as on all MTA buses and subways.

By Bus: The bus service on Staten Island is extensive and fairly reliable. For routes, request a bus map at the Ferry Terminal Information Booth. The fare system ($1.50 paid with token or Metrocard) is the same as on all MTA buses and subways.

SIGHTS AND ATTRACTIONS

Alice Austen House Museum 2 Hylan Blvd. (between Bay St. and Harbor Rd.) (718) 816-4506. Turn-of-the-century photographer Alice Austen lived here for most of her life while documenting Staten Island in photographs. The house sits on the eastern edge of Staten Island, just north of the Verrazano-Narrows Bridge, and commands a breathtaking view of the both the Narrows and downtown Manhattan. The restored home has a gallery featuring Austen's work, in addition to a furnished period room.

Clay Pit Ponds State Park 83 Nelson Ave. (between Carlin St. and Sharrots Rd.) (718) 967-1976. Near the southwest shore of Staten Island, this oasis of mature woodlands, swamps, barrens and spring-fed streams seems much farther away than the 40-minute ferry and bus trip it takes to get there from lower Manhattan. The preserve offers guided nature walks, pond ecology, bird-watching, organic gardening and children's programs, as well as hiking paths and horseback riding trails year-round. The park takes its name from the shallow ponds that were left by a clay-mining business that once operated there.

Garibaldi Meucci Museum 420 Tompkins Ave. (at Chestnut St.), Staten Island (718) 442-1608. In 1956, the Order of the Sons of Italy opened a museum dedicated to Antonio Meucci, whom it credits with inventing the world's first telephone in his Staten Island home, and to his friend and house guest Giuseppe Garibaldi, the famed Italian freedom fighter. Inside Meucci's small two-story house is a room devoted to Garibaldi. Meucci filed a provisional patent for his invention in 1871, five years before Alexander Graham Bell filed his. On view are reproductions of the bell-shaped earpieces he designed in 1854 and 1867, as well as a copy of his preliminary patent.

Admission: $3, suggested donation. **Hours:** Tues.–Fri., 1 P.M.–5 P.M.; weekends by appointment. **Services:** Lectures, concerts.

Greenbelt Park 200 Nevada Ave. (at Rockland Ave.) (718) 667-2165. Nature and the city are not two things that usually go together. But one place they intersect—and with a vengeance—is the Greenbelt. A 2,800-acre swath of natural parkland preserved in the middle of Staten Island, the Greenbelt is crisscrossed by 32 miles of little-known hiking trails. Despite the nearness of city streets, it is possible, by sticking to the trails, to walk in the Greenbelt for hours without seeing another human being. The Greenbelt's extensive network of hiking trails are open for hiking year round, from dusk to dawn. Mountain biking is not permitted on the trails. Call for information on hikes and guided nature walks.

Historic Richmond Town 441 Clarke Ave. (at Richmond Rd.) (718) 351-1611. A picturesque restoration on Staten Island, historic Richmond Town includes more than 25 furnished buildings from the late 17th to the 19th centuries separated by dirt paths and spacious wooded lawns. The village and outdoor museum—including a general store, a tavern and one of the oldest schoolrooms in the United States—depict the history and life of Staten Island and the surrounding region. There is a Saturday-night concert series throughout the year.

Jacques Marchais Museum of Tibetan Art 338 Lighthouse Ave. (at Richmond Rd.) (718) 987-3500. The Jacques Marchais Museum is built in the style of a Tibetan temple, nestled on a steep wooded hillside on Staten Island and surrounded by terraced gardens, ponds, and views over Staten Island. The museum's founder, Jacques Marchais (born Edna Coblentz but also known by the name Jacqueline Klauber) was an avid collector of Tibetan and other Asian artifacts. She built the museum to house her extensive collection, which includes decorative objects, jewelry, masks and religious objects. She chose the site on **Lighthouse Hill**, all of 400 feet high, in an effort to simulate as best as she could, given the obvious constraints, a traditional Tibetan setting. The museum prides itself on being a "living museum," offering extensive educational programming, from concerts and lectures to the more unusual butter sculpture demonstrations and meditations.

Snug Harbor Cultural Center 1000 Richmond Terrace (between Tysen St. and Snug Harbor Rd.) (718) 448-2500. Set on 86 wooded acres, the Staten Island compound is the largest arts complex on the East Coast. Formerly a retirement home for sailors, the center has 28 historic buildings (including some of the city's finest examples of Greek Revival architecture), the magnificent **Staten Island Botanical Gardens** and the **Staten Island Children's Museum.** The **Newhouse Center for Contemporary Art** features changing exhibitions. Theater, music and dance events are held throughout the year in the **Veterans**

Barton Silverman/The New York Times

The Verrazano Bridge, at the start of the New York Marathon

Memorial Hall or on the lawn. A short bus ride from the ferry terminal, it's a great place to bring kids on a summer afternoon.

Staten Island Botanical Garden 1000 Richmond Terrace (at Snug Harbor Rd.) (718) 273-8200. Set within Snug Harbor's 86 acres, the Staten Island Botanical Garden maintains a collection of specimen trees and gardens, which are bordered by wetlands and woodlands. Inside the Conservatory, exotic blossoms change with the seasons. Displays include a White Garden, a Butterfly Garden, an Herb Garden, a Pond Garden and the new Chinese Scholar's Garden.

Staten Island Institute—Ferry Collection Richmond Terrace and Schuyler (off the St. George Ferry Terminal's waiting room). If the ride on the Staten Island Ferry leaves you with a burning curiosity about the ferry's inner workings and history, you'll be delighted to find this exhibit as you disembark at the St. George Ferry Terminal. This special collection of the nearby **Staten Island Institute of Arts and Sciences** includes an ongoing exhibit of ferry memorabilia from the past 90 years, including wheels, whistles and photos, as well as changing exhibits.

Verrazano-Narrows Bridge. With a main span of 4,260 feet, this is the longest suspension bridge in the United States and the second longest in the world. Even so, the Verrazano-Narrows seems doomed to forever play second fiddle to the Brooklyn Bridge. It lacks its elder sibling's pedestrian walkway, its close-up views of Manhattan and its rich, romantic history. But there's no denying the Verazzano's grandeur, with a total length (including the approaches) of over two and a half miles. The tops of the 693 foot high towers are 1 ⅝ inches farther apart than their bases, to compensate for the earth's curvature. And due to seasonal expansion and contraction of the bridge's cables, the roadway can be 12 feet lower in the summer than in the winter.

The Verrazano-Narrows opened to traffic in 1964, a project of Robert Moses and the Triborough Bridge and Tunnel Authority, which he headed. It is the youngest span in New York, but it is literally and figuratively linked to the past. The name comes from Giovanni da Verrazano, the first European to sail into New York Harbor, and the ends of the bridge lie in the historic guardians of the harbor: Brooklyn's Fort Hamilton and Staten Island's Fort Wadsworth. Today, the bridge is the only direct link between Brooklyn and Staten Island, and is an important part of the interstate highway system. It offers the shortest route between Long Island and the Middle Atlantic states, allowing drivers to circumvent the hassles of New York City driving.

Views from either end of the bridge are awe inspiring; you can only view the middle from the windows of a car or bus. Pedestrian and bicycle traffic are prohibited—except during the annual New York City Marathon and the 5-Borough Bike Tour, both of which run across the decks of the bridge.

RESTAURANTS ON STATEN ISLAND

Aesop's Tables
1233 Bay St. (near Hylan Blvd.) (718) 720-2005
Credit cards: All major Meals: L, D

From the bountiful garden at Aesop's Tables you can actually see stars. That's only one of the charms of this warm little country restaurant with such contemporary American appetizers as asparagus, fennel and grapefruit salad, and seared chicken glazed with lingonberries and balsamic vinegar. **Price range:** Entrees, $14–$20.

Denino's Pizzeria Tavern
524 Port Richmond Ave. (between Hooker Pl. and Walker St.)
(718) 442-9401
Credit cards: Cash only Meals: L, D

This off-the-beaten-path neighborhood spot serves some of the best pizza in the city. One slice of the white pizza would make the trip worthwhile. Grab a beer and a pie with a local crowd and chase it with an Italian ice at Ralph's across the street. **Price range:** Pizzas, $8.65 and up.

Killmeyer's Old Bavaria Inn
4254 Arthur Kill Rd. (at Sharrotts Rd.) (718) 984-1202
Credit cards: MC/V Meals: L, D

Bavarian food served in a charming 18th-century inn on Staten Island. Prices are moderate for cucumber and potato soup, roasted marinated beef, veal and pork sausages and goulash. **Price range:** Avg. entree, $18.

The Arts

If it is true, as many have observed, that the flesh and blood of New York are nourished by the financial and business communities, then surely its soul and spirit are sustained by the extraordinary art, music, theater and dance that pervade the entire city and lead so many people to spend their lives here. This has been so for over a century-and-a-half and in recent years an explosion of energy and talent, nourished by the city's great wealth, has made New York even more central to the nation's artistic well-being.

Like so many other aspects of New York, visitors can be slightly overwhelmed by the sheer depth of artistic possibilities available here. If you are bored in New York you've lost the desire for finding the finest experiences life has to offer. If you love painting there are not only five world-class museums featuring the work of every great artist, there are also literally hundreds of galleries spread throughout Manhattan, making available virtually every kind of work. For the devotee of music, where else can one find ten or more classical music events on a single evening? Or five or six dance performances? And of course the city has been home to the best in American theater for generations.

So whatever your artistic interests, we guarantee you will not be disappointed in New York. If the experience of many others proves true, most likely you will be planning another trip here on the journey back home.

ART MUSEUMS AND GALLERIES

New York City has dozens of museums and hundreds of art galleries, and even cutting those numbers down by eliminating everything except the important sites, you'd still be left with an impossible task if you tried to see all of what's going on at a given time. Art in the galleries changes more or less monthly and the endless rounds of exhibitions in the museums means aficionados must practice triage. Geography is a factor. The city being spread out across five boroughs, and art being concentrated in pockets separated by long subway rides and formidable taxi fares, a visitor with limited time who, say, makes the (highly recommended) trip to the Brooklyn Museum and the new galleries in Williamsburg, Brooklyn, may have to skip P.S. 1 in Long Island City, the contemporary art center now affiliated with the Museum of Modern Art as well as the Studio Museum in Harlem, and the conglomeration of galleries in the converted factories and garages in Chelsea, the neighborhood on the west side of Manhattan that has replaced SoHo as the most fashionable epicenter of new art.

How to make choices? Start with the basics. The Modern, more than any place else, defined the history of art in the 20th century through its permanent collection, which actually starts in the 19th century with Cezanne, Seurat, Gauguin and van Gogh. It's possible to list the greatest hits—van Gogh's

"Starry Night," Cezanne's "Male Bather," Picasso's "Demoiselles d'Avignon,"
Matisse's "Red Studio," Pollock's "One (Number 1, 1950)," Warhol's "Gold
Marilyn"—but suffice it to say that, having begun in 1929 in a few modest
rooms, the Modern has now grown to the point of occupying vast quarters on
the block between Fifth and Sixth Avenues and between 53rd and 54th Streets,
and like the Metropolitan Museum, it can, by itself, occupy an entire trip to
New York.

Museum Mile

The Met, being the country's, if not the world's, premier art museum, is naturally the locus of art in the city and, particularly, of Museum Mile, the city's
catchphrase for a stretch of Fifth Avenue on the Upper East Side of Manhattan
that also encompasses the Frick Collection, the Guggenheim Museum, the
National Academy of Design, the Jewish Museum, the International Center of
Photography and several other places that encapsulate the artistic diversity of
New York.

The smart visitor to the Met, having already checked out the European
paintings, Near Eastern and Egyptian rooms and the newly renovated Greek
and Roman galleries, which include the coffered, skylit, barrel-vaulted gallery
beside the Great Hall at the entrance to the museum (one of the city's most
splendid public spaces), avoids, if possible, the inevitable crowds at the special
exhibitions and in the Impressionist galleries and makes a beeline for less tram-
meled quarters. Examples include the Islamic galleries, with the burbling fountain in the Nur ad-Din Room; the Astor Court, a scholar's garden in the Chinese galleries, where you can approach Zen calm, the rooms of musical
instruments, of arms and armor and of American pioneer and Colonial-era furniture, which are so obscure that you almost feel like a pioneer yourself going to
see them.

Another must on Museum Mile, the Frick Collection, is almost everyone's
favorite small museum, the finest private collection put together in America,
even counting Isabella Stewart Gardner's collection in Boston. The Frick building, a mansion designed in 1913 by Thomas Hastings, the architect of the New
York Public Library, is one of the last of the great former private houses on Fifth
Avenue. Picture for picture (Bellini, Holbein, Rembrandt, Vermeer, Fragonard,
the list goes on) the quality of the collection is unsurpassed.

Farther up Museum Mile, tourists ogle Frank Lloyd Wright's spiral Guggenheim often without bothering about the art in it, although the permanent collection, which includes the Justin K. Thannhauser Collection, is, after the Modern's
collection, the top overview of art from the first half of the 20th century in the
city. The Jewish Museum is the best institution of its kind in the country, with not
only objects related to the history of Judaism but also a strong exhibition program
emphasizing modern and contemporary art. The Whitney Museum of American
Art, a block off Fifth, on Madison Avenue, isn't technically on Museum Mile but
should be on the itinerary, too. It has finally opened permanent galleries for visitors to see the Hoppers and Calders they expect to find there.

The savvy traveler along Museum Mile also makes sure to see the less-heralded stops at the north end of Fifth: the Museum of the City of New York, where paintings, sculptures, photographs and artifacts are devoted to the city's heritage, and El Museo del Barrio, a museum of the art and culture of Latin America and the city's expanding Latino community. Like the Studio Museum, El Museo del Barrio was founded during the late 1960's in a period of upheaval, when artists of many backgrounds clamored for places to show their work. The Museum of Modern Art, with its stress on high European modernism and big-name post-war Americans, wasn't paying them enough attention, they felt, and so they came up with the idea of community-based institutions, the result being a new breadth of collections and exhibitions—and renewed debate, as these young museums themselves turned into established institutions and faced criticism from within their own diversifying communities.

New York, they demonstrated, rejects the status quo, whatever it may be, which is of course the city's virtue. Its museums reflect this fact as well as anything else. To travel along Museum Mile from Frick's mansion to El Museo del Barrio is to see a fraction of what's going on in art, but it's to go a long distance toward understanding the essential nature of a place where culture, like the rest of life, remains a moving target.—*Michael Kimmelman*

Major Art Museums

Metropolitan Museum of Art
Fifth Ave. at 82nd St. (212) 535-7710

UPPER EAST SIDE
www.metmuseum.org

The Met is a national treasure, one of the world's great museums, right up there with the Louvre. Some of its art is the best anywhere and the collection as a whole is simply outstanding. From ancient cuneiforms, rare Greek vases and statuary to Monet, Jasper Johns and Ellsworth Kelly, its variety is breathtaking.

Altogether this magnificent museum has more than two million works of art—paintings, sculpture, decorative arts, artifacts from ancient cultures, arms and armor, elegant clothing and musical instruments. There are 53 (!) galleries devoted solely to European painters, and another maze devoted to Americans.

In fact, two American artists and a German were indirectly responsible for the creation of the Met in the 1880's—the majestic landscapes of Alfred Bierstadt and Frederic Church, and the dramatic "Washington Crossing the Delaware" by Emanuel Leutze, a German-American. Partly to establish a place to exhibit these huge pieces, the Met was born. You will find all three in the American Wing at the north end of the first and second floors, close to the massive Temple of Dendur, an actual Egyptian burial place that every visitor must see.

NAVIGATING THE MET

Of course there are so many highlights to see here, it is a good idea to plan ahead. Unfortunately, for all its grandeur, the Met does not make it easy to find your way around. There is a very general floor plan of the whole museum in English at both information desks as you enter the main lobby, and in several other languages if you ask. For detailed maps of where to find Rembrandt, Van Gogh et al. you must also ask. There are two detailed maps for the European paintings and sculpture; none for other collections.

Some galleries are numbered, but many aren't. As you enter a gallery, you may see numbers on your right and on your left; as a general rule, the one on your right is the one you are entering.

Finding the daily tour schedule is another challenge. It is posted on a obscured wall at the southern end of the lobby, to your left as you enter, just before the long corridor of Greek and Roman statuary. The children's gift shop is hidden, too. It is at the top of the main stairway, to the right, but you wouldn't know it until you are at the door. Inside are T-shirts, games, erasers in the shape of a sphinx, etc., etc. The escalator to the second floor isn't obvious either; look left as you approach the main stairs.

Best bet: Ask any uniformed guard where to find what you are looking for. They are walking, talking catalogs, and user friendly. If you hit upon one who doesn't have the answer, ask the next one.

Best bet beforehand: The Met's Web site—www.metmuseum.org—is excellent. Things that are hard to find in the museum itself are easy to find online, including daily schedules of tours and gallery talks, exact locations of the painting you're looking for, and everything else you might want to know before you mount the steps on Fifth Avenue.

Each of the Met's departments is a museum in itself. It would take more than an afternoon to fully explore the holdings of any one section. Wandering through gallery after gallery will impress you with the Met's vastness. You will also chance upon some wonderful surprises—a living room designed by Frank Lloyd Wright in the American Wing, a detailed scale model of the Parthenon at the street-level entrance to the museum, a tranquil Chinese scholar's garden in the Astor Court on the second floor and, in the music collection nearby, violins made by Nicolo Amati and his student Antonio Stradivari in the seventeenth century.

You may get more from your visit, however, by picking some objects or areas ahead of time, and searching them out. Or take a "highlights" tour to see what interests you and then go back and give it more time yourself.
Here is how the museum is laid out:

Main Floor

As you enter the main lobby, **Egyptian Art** collections and the **Temple of Dendur** are to your right, **Greek and Roman Art** to your left.

At the entrance to the Egyptian section is a tomb you can walk into—fun for kids. The Met's own archeological explorations are responsible for more than half of the collection, which extends chronologically through 40 galleries. The Temple of Dendur was a gift from Egypt in recognition of U.S. aid in saving ancient monuments from the rising waters of the Nile behind the Aswan Dam.

The Greek and Roman works explore the full range of classical art, from jewelry and pottery to sculpture and painting, with prize examples of Greek vases and Roman portrait busts.

Beyond these galleries you will find nourishment for the body in a pleasantly spacious **cafeteria** and a **restaurant.**

Straight through the main lobby from the entrance, passing to either side of the main stairway, you will find **Medieval Art** and a large spread of **European Sculpture and Decorative Arts.** This is one of the museum's largest collections. One of its gems is an ornate 15th-century "studiolo"—it means "little study"—with walls of inlaid woodwork that looks three-dimensional but is actually flat. There are only two such rooms in the world, this one and the one in the ducal palace in Urbino, Italy.

Continuing straight ahead to the back of the museum, don't miss the eclectic **Robert Lehman Collection** of Impressionists and Old Masters, paintings and drawings, and pieces of decorative arts. The gallery space, on two floors, is designed to evoke Lehman's own stately home on East 54th St. in Manhattan. Highlights include an Annunciation by Botticelli, a Rembrandt sketch of Leonardo's "Last Supper," a Leonardo sketch of "A Bear Walking," paintings by Rembrandt, El Greco, Goya, Renoir, Seurat, van Gogh and more, and impressive pieces of Renaissance earthenware and Venetian glass.

The southern flank of the first floor houses the **Arts of Africa, Oceania and the Americas** and a series of galleries of **20th Century Art.** The third-world collections are based on entire museum that Nelson Rockefeller gave to the Met—the Museum of Primitive Art, which he founded. Highlights include royal decorative art from the Court of Benin in Nigeria, and the world's most comprehensive collection of gold objects from the Americas.

The 20th Century collection, on two floors in the southwest corner of the building, is where to find Jasper Johns—and Picasso, Braque, Modigliani, O'Keeffe and Pollock.

In the northern flank of the first floor is the stunning **Arms and Armor** collection, as well as the Temple of Dendur. Another knockout at the same end of the museum is a grand wrap-around panorama of the palace and gardens at Versailles, from the early 1800's. Standing in the center of this large chamber you can imagine you are there on the palace steps. And while you are at the north end of the building, check out the Met's collection of classic baseball cards, exhibited in the hallway behind Dendur on the way to Versailles.

The Arms and Armor collection is unique among American museums, with elegantly etched armor and weaponry ranging from the 4th century B.C. to the 19th century A.D., and from ancient Egypt and Islam to the Americas. The Japanese pieces are generally regarded as the finest anywhere outside Japan.

The American Wing, on two floors, is a magnet for tourists and New Yorkers alike, sophisticated and otherwise. Everyone will recognize the epic "George Washington Crossing the Delaware," 21 feet wide, painted in Düsseldorf some 75 years after the fact by Emauel Leutze. Note also the surrounding display of that particular gallery (No. 223). It has been especially arranged to resemble the museums of a century ago, crammed full of art, with three, four or five paintings hung one above the other.

Elsewhere in this wing are familiar Washington portraits by Gilbert Stuart and Charles Wilson Peale, as well as John Singer Sargent's "Madame X," Frederic Church's "Heart of the Andes," Alfred Bierstadt's "Rocky Mountains: Lander's Peak," along with paintings by Winslow Homer, James McNeill Whistler and Mary Cassatt (whose brother, president of the Pennsylvania Railroad, told her she would never amount to anything as a painter), and sculptures by Frederic Remington and John Quincy Adams Ward.

Extraordinary features of the wing include 25 period rooms—furnished and decorated just as they were in years and centuries past—a renowned collection of stained glass, much of it by Louis Comfort Tiffany, and upstairs an "attic" of shelves where the museum displays things it doesn't have room to display out front. There you will see rows of antique chairs, Lincoln busts, crystal goblets and much, much more. This sort of display is especially useful to students and scholars, but made interesting for anyone by its sheer volume.

Second Floor

Straight ahead at the top of the central stairway from the lobby, push through a pair of glass doors and enter the wonderful world of **European Paintings.** This is one of the two collections for which there are detail maps if you ask for them at the information desk in the lobby. The works in this one are the Old Masters—starting with three enormous paintings by Tiepolo in the first gallery, past an remarkable diptych of "The Crucifixion" and "The Last Judgment" by Jan van Eyck, the most celebrated painter of 15th century Europe, to Bruegel, Rubens, El Greco, Raphael, Titian, Tintoretto, Vermeer, Rembrandt, Hals, Gainsborough, Velasquez, Fragonard, Goya and still more. The Met has more Vermeers than any other museum.

These galleries are not to be confused with **Nineteenth Century European Paintings and Sculpture**—the second collection for which there is a detailed map. Reach this area by turning left at the top of the central stairs and walking through a long gallery hall of etchings and photographs. Don't hurry. The etchings are the work of great artists; they illustrate how an artist sketches out ideas for later paintings—whole scenes, or a torso, or maybe just an elbow or a nose.

In the 19th century galleries you will find the popular works of the Impressionists, but first a large expanse of Rodin's sculptured marbles. Inside are the young Claude Monet's vibrantly colorful "Garden at Sainte-Adresse," daring for its time, a Cezanne still-life once owned by Monet, Edouard Manet's peaceful "Boating," van Gogh's "Cypresses," and room after room of Bonnard, Degas, Rousseau, Daumier, Toulouse-Lautrec, Renoir and more.

Adjacent to these galleries are, to the west, the second-floor space of the **20th Century Art** collection, and on the Fifth Avenue side to the east, **Islamic Art** and **Ancient Near Eastern Art.** The long Fifth Ave. side of the second floor proceeds geographically from the Near East at the southern end, through the balcony over the lobby to a half-dozen sectors of **Asian Art—Chinese, Japanese, Korean, South Asian** and **Southeast Asian**—at the northern end.

The Islamic collection may be the most comprehensive permanent Islamic art installation anywhere. Items of note include miniature paintings and huge 16th and 17th century carpets, as well as glass and metalwork from Egypt and Mesopotamia. Ancient and Near Eastern Art spans nearly 9,000 years, from Mesopotamia to the Indian subcontinent. The Asian collections are reputed to be the largest and most comprehensive in the West, best known for their Chinese calligraphy, folding screens and other decorative objects from Japan, sculpture from Southeast Asia and paintings from the Himalayan kingdoms. Here, too, is the restful **Chinese Scholar's Garden** called **Astor Court,** behind a wall with a round entryway symbolizing a full moon. Enter and sit a few minutes. You will be almost alone.

Close by are the upper floor of the **American Wing** and the **Musical Instruments** collection, where you will find a piano made by the instrument's inventor, Bartolomeo Cristofori, two guitars owned and used by Andres Segovia, and all sorts of rare horns, harps and other music makers from distant lands and other times.

Ground Floor

Entering the museum through the street-level door to the south of the outside steps, or through the parking garage, there is an information desk that will accept your "suggested donation," a splendid model of the Acropolis, and a coat check where the line moves faster than at the one upstairs in the main lobby. The museum library is down here, too.

The galleries of **The Costume Institute** are also on the ground floor, but they are entered from above, by stairs or an elevator from the main floor in the middle of **Egyptian Art.** A little hard to find, the institute is a small three-gallery treasure. Clothes dating back to the 18th century and up to the late 20th are exhibited on mannequins in glass showcases with informative descriptions, and shows are organized around themes and particular designers. It is more for women than men, but can be interesting for both.

Sculpture Garden

Last but not least, weather permiting, take yourself up to the **Sculpture Garden** on the roof, not only for the sculpture but for a treetop view of Central Park.

Admission: (These are suggested donations, but you will not be challenged if you give less. Many New Yorkers give $2 or $3.) Adults $10, students and seniors $5, children under 12 with an adult free.

Hours: Friday and Saturday, 9:30 A.M.–8:45 P.M.; Sunday, Tuesday, Wednesday, Thursday, 9:30 A.M.–5:15 P.M. Closed Monday, New Year's Day, Thanksgiving and Christmas.

Tours and gallery talks: Walking tours, gallery talks, lectures, films and workshops, call (212) 570-3930. Tourist groups call (212) 570-3711; school groups call (212) 288-7733.

There are daily escorted tours of "Museum Highlights" and "Old Masters," as well as tours that focus on specific collections. There are also audio tours in several languages. The basic tour is given by Philippe de Montebello, the museum's director, and the choice of what you see is his. It takes 2½ to 3 hours, depending on how long you choose to linger at each stop. The same equipment—daily rental charge

$5—includes tours of designated galleries and special exhibitions. On the "Musical Instruments" tour you will hear music played on the exhibited instruments.
Programs for Children: Gallery programs, lectures, films, workshops and printed gallery guides, call (212) 570-3932

Solomon R. Guggenheim Museum   UPPER EAST SIDE
1071 Fifth Ave. (at 89th St.) (212) 423-3500   www.guggenheim.org

Long before it was completed in 1959, the Guggenheim—the strange round building in a city full of square boxes—was already suffering darts from critics. It was called everything from a washtub to an indigestible hot-cross bun. Robert Moses, the city's irrascible master builder, said it looked like an inverted oatmeal dish.

But the museum's creator, Frank Lloyd Wright, called it nothing less than "the liberation of painting by architecture." And on the first Sunday it opened, 10,000 people lined up to get in for 50 cents a head. (Only 6,000 made it; bribes offered to guards did not work.)

Today, after a $24 million dollar renovation and the addition of a controversial 10-story annex in 1992, the landmarked museum, considered by some to be Wright's masterpiece, is celebrating its 40th anniversary. Along with one of the world's largest collections of Vasily Kandinsky, it has works by many major 20th Century artists—Constantin Brancusi, Alexander Calder, Marc Chagall, Robert Delaunay, Paul Klee, Joan Miro, and Pablo Picasso. The museum itself is, of course, a major attraction. And worth the trip, despite its admission charge, which is one of the highest in the city.

Instead of moving from room to room, as in other museums, you take the elevator to the top, 92 feet up, then soak up the art as you descend a gently sloping circular ramp, glancing across the sweeping rotunda at other art lovers winding their way around you.

—*Randy Kennedy*

Subway: 4, 5, 6, to 86th St.
Bus: 1, 2, 3, 4 (Madison Ave. to 89th St.)

Admission: $12; $7, students and seniors; children 12 and under, free. Credit cards: All major; checks. Hours: Fri.–Sat., 9 A.M.–8 P.M.; Sun.–Wed., 9 A.M.–6 P.M. Closed Thursday, New Year's Day and Christmas Day. Programs for Children: Films, tours and workshops throughout the year. Call for information. Tours: Daily; call for information. Services: Food, tours, gift shop, lectures, concerts.

The Guggenheim as Architecture
Frank Lloyd Wright's Guggenheim has always been like an explosion on Fifth Avenue. It is strident, it is loud, it defers not a whit to anything around it. It breaks every rule. It is so astonishing as a piece of architecture, of course, that it makes you feel that rules hardly matter. But the very way in which Wright's building breaks the rules of urban design becomes its own rule: the way it clashes with its surroundings is the way the Guggenheim communicates its architectural essence.

The Solomon R. Guggenheim Museum

It has been a commonplace since this building opened in 1959 to speak of it as inhospitable to paintings, to talk of the long spiral ramp and slanted walls as Wright's way of forcing painting to be subservient to architecture. While this complaint has always been exaggerated—Wright's space can work wonderfully for the display of large Color Field abstractions, Calder mobiles, Pop Art and other postwar works—there is no question that the architecture fights the art a lot of the time. The building usually ends up being in the foreground of one's consciousness, no matter what the paintings.

The rush of joy that Wright's great rotunda brings has always been worth its limitations as a gallery. There aren't a lot of cathedrals in New York—never mind that, there isn't a lot of architecture anywhere that is capable of making the heart beat faster, that so fills you with the sense that the making of enclosure can be an act of opening up, a discovery of noble possibilities. It is a wonderful paradox to find, in the act of enclosing, revelation. There is nowhere else in New York where the passion of architecture is more clearly there, set more directly in front of us for all to see and understand.

The north side addition (1992) contains double-height galleries, which give the Guggenheim the ability to display large contemporary canvases for the first time. While the galleries are not ideal display spaces—they are a bit narrow, and the elevator core intrudes partway into them—they are more versatile than anything the museum has had until now. This, then, is the great achievement: the building is now a better museum and a better work of architecture. If the Guggenheim's roles as a museum and as a piece of architecture have always been somewhat at odds, this renovation at least partly resolves them.

—*Paul Goldberger (1992)*

The Museum of Modern Art   MIDTOWN WEST
11 West 53rd St. (between Fifth and Sixth Aves.) (212) 708-9400;
(212) 247-1230 for the deaf   www.moma.org

It is hard to imagine that this museum started with eight prints and one drawing
in 1929, because it now houses one the largest collections of 20th-century
painting, drawings, photographs and sculpture in the world. Its permanent collection of Pablo Picasso, Frida Kahlo, Henri Matisse, Jackson Pollock and
Robert Rauschenberg alone draws the crowds, especially on Friday nights, when
there is a pay-what-you-wish admissions policy from 4:40 to 8:15 P.M. While
perhaps not the best time to get a peek at van Gogh's "Starry Night," Friday
nights offer their own pleasures, including jazz music in the garden cafe and
"Conversations with Contemporary Artists," during which artists talk about
their work in the galleries. Like most of New York's museums, there are places
in "MoMA"—as the museum is commonly called—to escape the headphone-
set crowd and contemplate the time you just passed with, say, Dali and
Duchamp. There is a nice comfy bench in front of Monet's "Water Lilies." The
sculpture garden on a quiet afternoon can be a pleasant respite. Indoors, the
architecture and design collection is rarely as crowded as are certain rooms filled
with important painters, and its fur coffee cup and silicon chips are an amusing
diversion. MoMA claims to be the first art museum to embrace motion pictures
as an art form. It has an extensive collection of significant films, including silent
films of D.W. Griffith and Charlie Chaplin, and contemporary works from
Scorcese to Kubrick. The museum is a regular host to film festivals and video
screenings.

—Jennifer Steinhauer

Architecture and Design Established in 1932, this was the first curatorial
department of its kind. The work of specific architects and general architectural
topics are illustrated through a variety of models, drawings and photographs.
The design collection includes everything from hockey masks to helicopters,
with substantial display space devoted to furniture and decorative and functional items for the home. There is also a highly-regarded collection of typogra-
phy, posters and other examples of graphic design.

Drawing This department holds over 6,000 drawings, including works in
watercolor and mixed media, making it one of the world's most comprehensive
collections of modern drawing. Highlights include works by Ernst, Schiele,
Degas and Cézanne.

Painting and Sculpture This is the heart of the museum: 3,200 works comprising the world's largest collection of modern art, from the late 19th century to
the present. Some of the most famous works of modern art are here, including
van Gogh's "Starry Night," Cezanne's "The Bather," Rodin's "Monument to
Balzac," Rousseau's "The Dream," and an impressive collection of Picassos.

Film and Video MoMA bills this as the strongest international film collection
in the United States, with over 14,000 films and 4 million film stills, ranging

from original Edison Company negatives to contemporary Hollywood movies, television documentaries and video art.

Photography The photography collection extends as far back as the 1840's, and reaches outside the art world to include photographs by journalists, scientists and amateurs. The collection includes important works by Walker Evans, Ansel Adams and Robert Frank.

Prints and Illustrated Books 40,000 prints and books chart the history of techniques like lithography, screenprinting, woodcut and more contemporary forms of printmaking. Famous works here include Edvard Munch's "The Kiss" and van Gogh's "Sorrow."

Admission: $9.50; $6.50 students and seniors; children under 16 accompanied by an adult, free. Friday, 4:30–8:15 P.M., donation requested. Handicapped accessible. **Credit cards:** Cash or checks only. **Hours:** Sat.–Tues. and Thur., 10:30 A.M.- 6:30 P.M.; Fri., 10:30 A.M.–8:30 P.M. Closed Wednesday. **Programs for Children:** Workshops and family programs. **Tours:** Daily; call for information. **Services:** Food, gift shop, lectures, concerts.
Subway: E, F to Fifth Ave. (one-half block from museum)
Bus: 1, 2, 3, 4 (Fifth and Madison Aves. To 53rd St.); 5, 6, 7 (Sixth Ave. to 55th St.)

Frick Collection   UPPER EAST SIDE

1 East 70th St. (between Fifth and Madison Aves.) (212) 288-0700
www.frick.org

As you walk through the rooms of this stately Upper East Side mansion, you almost expect to run into Henry Clay Frick himself. The house, completed in 1914, has been preserved much as it was when Frick (1849–1919), a steel magnate, lived there with the extraordinary art collection visitors see today. The experience is completely absorbing and transporting. The galleries are intimate and astoundingly quiet in every way, from the noise level to the lighting, allowing the unmatched collection to shine. The Frick hosts an excellent series of free concerts in the museum's music parlor and in the courtyard.

Permanent Collection: Highlights: Bellini, "Saint Francis in Ecstasy"; dell Francesca, "St. John the Evangelist"; van Eyck, "Virgin With Child, With Saints and Donor"; Vermeer, "Officer and Laughing Girl"; Holbein, "Sir Thomas More and Thomas Cromwell"; Rembrandt, "Self-Portrait"; Stuart, "George Washington."

Admission: $7; $5, senior and students; children under 10 not allowed, those under 16 must be accompanied by an adult. Handicapped accessible. **Credit cards:** All major credit cards. **Hours:** Tues.–Sat., 10 A.M.–6 P.M.; Sun., Lincoln's Birthday, Election Day, and Veterans Day., 1–6 P.M. Closed Monday, New Year's Day, Independence Day, Thanksgiving, December 24 and 25. **Programs for Children:** Free lectures and concerts. Call for information. **Tours:** Included in the price of admission is an audio tour of the permanent collection available in English, French, German, Italian, Japanese, and Spanish. School groups by reservation.

Whitney Museum of American Art   UPPER EAST SIDE
945 Madison Ave. (at 75th St.) (212) 877 WHITNEY www.whitney.org

Founded in 1914 by Gertrude Vanderbilt Whitney, the Whitney opened in 1931 in three adjoining brownstones on West Eighth Street—mostly as a response to a rebuff from the Metropolitan Museum, which refused the donation of the 500-work collection. The museum is now housed in a hulking building designed by a former Bauhaus teacher, Marcel Breuer. The Whitney includes among its programs the Biennial, a much-discussed and often controversial exhibition that surveys recent developments in American art. The museum's corporate-funded branches—including two in midtown and one in Stamford, Conn.—also have exhibitions.

Permanent Collection: The museum has an excellent permanent collection of 20th-century art, which can be seen in several new galleries opened in April 1998. Includes some 12,000 works of art representing more than 1,900 artists. Highlights: The entire artistic estate of Edward Hopper, as well as significant works by Marsh, Calder, Gorky, Hartley, O'Keeffe, Rauschenberg and Johns among other artists. The Whitney has plans to dedicate two floors in the museum to its Permanent Collection in 2000.

Admission: $12.50; $10.50, students and seniors; children under 12, free. First Thurs. each month, pay what you wish. **Credit cards:** Cash only. **Hours:** Tues., Wed., Fri.–Sun., 11 A.M.–6 P.M.; Thur., 1–8 P.M. Closed Monday. **Tours:** Call (212) 570-7722 for daily schedule; call (212) 570-7720 for group tours. **Services:** Food, tours, gift shop, lectures, concerts.

Other Art Museums

Alternative Museum of the Arts   TRIBECA/SOHO
594 Broadway (between Houston and Prince Sts.) (212) 966-4444

Operated by artists since its founding in 1975, the Alternative Museum sponsors work that is outside the mainstream. Its 3,200-square-foot space exhibits work in a variety of media and often presents shows that address social and political issues. The museum holds an Annual National Showcase Exhibition to benefit artists who are members of the museum. It also has a history of supporting new American music. Don Cherry, Kronos Quartet and Terry Riley have performed here. It also sponsors poetry readings, workshops and panel discussions. In 1996, the museum made a decision to focus on media-based arts: photography, video, film, and electronic and computer-generated art. In a project that explores the possibilities of the "virtual" museum, the "Alter-NET-ive" museum is developing interactive programming with online forums, debates and panels, as well as exhibitions of the "electronic" collection.

Admission: Suggested donation, $3. **Credit cards:** Cash only. **Hours:** Wed.–Sat., 11 A.M.–6 P.M. **Services:** Lectures.

American Craft Museum
MIDTOWN WEST

40 West 53d St. (between Fifth and Sixth Aves.) (212) 956-3535

Located directly across the street from the Museum of Modern Art, the American Craft Museum is the most significant museum in the country dedicated to exhibiting and supporting contemporary crafts. A visit will dispel anyone's notion that crafts aren't worthy of consideration as an art form. You'll see no macaroni necklaces or God's eyes on the museum's three floors of exhibition space. Instead, the work on display ranges from utilitarian objects with a strong aesthetic focus to sculptural pieces with a barely conceivable utilitarian purpose. The exhibits tend to be carefully designed and thematic, exploring a single craft or material or focused on the work of a single artist.

Admission: $5, adults; $2.50, seniors and students; free, children under 12; pay as you wish, Thurs. 6–8 P.M. **Credit cards:** All major. **Hours:** Tues.–Sun., 10 A.M.–6 P.M.; Thur., 10 A.M.–8 P.M.; closed Mon. **Services:** Gift shop, lectures.

Cooper-Hewitt National Design Museum

UPPER EAST SIDE

2 East 91st St. (at Fifth Ave.) (212) 849-8300 www.si.edu/ndm/

Peter Cooper would have been proud. The small museum he envisioned more than 100 years ago to support Cooper Union's instruction in the applied arts developed into what is now the country's best place to view and study design. In 1897 Sarah, Eleanor and Amy Hewitt, who were Cooper's granddaughters, opened a museum modeled after Paris's Musée des Arts Décoratifs in the Cooper Union Building.

The museum has amassed a collection encompassing objects as diverse as radiators, gloves and 18th-century French furniture. Part of the Smithsonian Institution since 1969, it later moved to Andrew Carnegie's Fifth Avenue mansion. Recent shows have focused on everything from Alexander Calder's designs for everyday objects to architects' plans for doghouses.

Permanent Collection: More than 250,000 objects; major holdings include drawings, prints, textiles, furniture, metalwork, ceramics, glass, wallcoverings and woodwork spanning 3,000 years and cultures from around the world. A 50,000-volume library includes 5,000 rare books.

Admission: $5, general; $3, students and seniors; Tuesday 5 P.M.–9 P.M., free. National Design Museum and Smithsonian Institution members, children under age 12, free. **Credit cards:** Cash only. **Hours:** Tues., 10 A.M.–9 P.M.; Wed.–Sat., 10 A.M.–5 P.M.; Sun., noon–5 P.M. Closed Federal Holidays. **Programs for Children:** Call (212) 849-8380 for information. **Tours:** Call (212) 849-8380 for information. **Services:** Tours, gift shop, lectures.

Dahesh Museum
MIDTOWN EAST

601 Fifth Ave. (between 48th and 49th Sts.) (212) 759-0606
www.daheshmuseum.org

The Dahesh Museum was opened in 1993 with the goal of collecting, preserving, exhibiting and interpreting 19th- and 20th-century European academic art.

Modern art was founded in opposition to academic art, which was subsequently dismissed for over a century. As the word "academic" became derogatory, once influential artists and teachers like William-Adolphe Bouguereau, Jean-Léon Gérome and Alexandre Cabanel were derided as reactionaries. More recent scholarship has taken a less ideological view. Drawing from its own collection as well as others, the Dahesh allows the most popular art of its time to be seen on its own terms.

Permanent Collection: More than 2,000 paintings, drawings, watercolors, sculptures and prints.

Admission: Free. Handicapped accessible. **Hours:** Tues.–Sat., 11 A.M.–6 P.M. Closed Monday, New Year's Day, July 4, Thanksgiving and Christmas Day. **Services:** Tours, gift shop. **Tours:** Participates in the "Insider's Hour" through the New York Convention and Visitors Bureau. Special tours can also be arranged through the Museum.

Dia Center for the Arts   CHELSEA

545 and 548 West 22d Street (212) 989-5566 www.diacenter.org

Once an isolated arts center on the edge of the West Side Highway, the Dia Center is now seen as a pioneer on the art world's latest frontier: West Chelsea. The original purpose of the Center over 20 years ago was to provide an exhibition space for large-scale works—particularly earth works and Minimalist sculpture—which conventional museums had trouble accommodating. Dia still supports long-term installations, including Walter De Maria's "Earth Room" and "Broken Kilometer." But since its move in 1987 to a 40,000-square-foot renovated warehouse on West 22d Street, it has focused on single-artist exhibitions that last anywhere from a few months to several years. There are also monthly readings of contemporary poetry, art lectures, artist's projects for the Web, music and art performances, and two bookstores: one at the West Chelsea space and another at Printed Matter, at 77 Wooster Street in SoHo. Dia also operates a space located directly across the street from the its main building which hosts long-term exhibits and installations. The Dia Center is also one of Chelsea's best hangouts, including a rooftop coffee bar overlooking the Hudson River. Plan to be there at sunset.

Permanent Collection: The collection is representative of the period that gave rise to pop, Minimalism, conceptual and land art, with works by Joseph Beuys, John Chamberlain, Walter De Maria, Dan Flavin, Donald Judd, Imi Knoebel, Blinky Palermo, Fred Sandback, Cy Twombly and Andy Warhol.

Admission: Adults, $6; students and seniors, $3; children under 10, free. **Hours:** Wednesday through Sunday, noon–6 P.M.

Drawing Center   TRIBECA/SOHO

35 Wooster St. (between Broome and Grand Sts.) (212) 219-2166

Housed in an airy ground-floor space on Wooster Street, the Drawing Center is a small nonprofit museum dedicated to drawings, loosely defined as original works on paper. Past exhibits have included wall drawings, monoprints and computer-generated drawings. In addition to its four or five annual group shows, usually featuring emerging artists, the center mounts historical and special exhibitions. Across the street is the Drawing Room, an annex dedicated to site-specific projects by individual artists. The gallery also runs the "Nightlight" reading series featuring prominent authors, as well as children's programs.

Admission: Free. **Hours:** Tues.–Fri., 10 A.M.–6 P.M.; Sat., 11 A.M.–6 P.M.

El Museo del Barrio   UPPER EAST SIDE
1230 Fifth Ave. (at 104th St.) (212) 831-7272 www.elmuseo.org

Located in the Heckscher Building across from the Conservatory Garden in Central Park, El Museo needs no introduction to art-savvy New Yorkers. Founded by a group of Puerto Rican educators, artists and activists in 1969, the museum was originally dedicated to serving the Puerto Rican community in Spanish Harlem. Its mission has since expanded in response to the growth of New York's Hispanic population—particularly the Mexican, Central and South American, and Caribbean communities. The museum's scope ranges from pre-Columbian to contemporary art. Two or more exhibitions are in progress here at any given time, along with a rotating installation of the splendid collection of Puerto Rican religious figures, or santos.

Admission: $4; $2, students and seniors; children under 12, free. Handicapped accessible. **Credit cards:** All major; checks. **Hours:** Wed.–Sun., 11 A.M.–5 P.M. Closed New Year's Day, Thanksgiving and Christmas Day. **Services:** Tours, gift shop, lectures, concerts, tours.

Guggenheim Museum SoHo
575 Broadway (at Prince Street), New York, 10012 (212) 423-3500

In 1992, the Guggenheim took another bold step, opening this contemporary art center on lower Broadway, with 30,000 square feet of exhibition space designed by Arata Isozaki.

Admission: Free. **Hours:** Thursday through Monday, 11 A.M.–6 P.M.

International Center Of Photography
1133 Sixth Ave. (between 43d and 44th Sts.) (212) 768-4680
1130 Fifth Ave. (at 94th St.) (212) 860-1777 www.icp.org

Established in 1974, the center mounts approximately 20 exhibitions per year, covering everything from photojournalism to fashion photography. In addition to its exhibition program, the center shows films and hosts a lecture series. ICP also accommodates those who want to get behind the camera by offering extensive continuing-education courses, as well as three certificate programs and an M.A. run jointly with New York University.

Permanent Collection: The Fifth Avenue center maintains a library with 8,000 books and 10,000 issues of periodicals. The Sixth Avenue facility houses collections and archives with over 45,000 photographs.

Admission: $6; $4, seniors and students. Pay as you wish Fri. 5 P.M.–8 P.M.
Credit cards: Cash only. **Hours:** Tues.–Thur., 10 A.M.–5 P.M.; Fri., 10 A.M.–8
P.M.; Sat.–Sun., 10 A.M.–6 P.M. Closed Monday. **Services:** Tours, gift shop,
lectures, classes. **Programs for Children:** Lectures, tours and workshops
throughout the year. **Tours:** For groups, call (212) 860-1777 ext. 154.

Jewish Museum   UPPER EAST SIDE

1109 5th Ave. (at 92d St.) (212) 423-3200 www.thejewishmuseum.org

Located on Museum Mile, the Jewish Museum is dedicated to showing work that
addresses issues related to Jewish identity and art by Jewish artists. The museum
is housed in the former Felix M. Warburg residence, a Gothic chateau built in
1908. In its exhibition program, the museum has shown work by individual
artists such as Camille Pisarro and Lasar Segall and has mounted thematic exhibitions, such as an exhibit of photographs taken during the Holocaust. The
museum also hosts film screenings, lectures and classical and klezmer concerts.

Permanent Collection: More than 27,000 objects that span 4,000 years, from
ancient artifacts to contemporary art. Highlights: Israeli archaeological artifacts;
textiles; ceremonial objects; paintings, drawings and prints by Louise Nevelson,
Marc Chagall, Ben Shahn, David Bomberg, Max Weber and Deborah Kass; and
George Segal's sculpture, "The Holocaust."

Admission: $8; $5.50, students and seniors; children under 12, free. Tues., 5–8
P.M., free. **Credit cards:** All major; checks. **Hours:** Sun.–Mon., Wed.–Thur.,
11 A.M.–5:45 P.M.; Tues., 11 A.M.–8 P.M. Closed Friday, Saturday, major legal
and Jewish holidays. **Programs for Children:** Art workshops, performances, film
and video screenings and family tours on Sundays from October through May
and on selected weekdays during school vacation times. **Tours:** Monday through
Thursday, 12:15 P.M. and 2:15 P.M.; Monday, Wednesday, Thursday, 4:15 P.M.;
Tuesday, 6:15 P.M. **Services:** Gift shop, food, tours, lectures, concerts.

Museum for African Art   TRIBECA/SOHO

593 Broadway (between Houston and Prince Sts.) (212) 966-1313
www.africanart.org

Until recently, you were more likely to encounter sub-Saharan African sculpture in anthropology textbooks than in art museums. Today, African art is considered one of the most inventive art forms of the past two centuries, and the
Museum for African Art can take much of the credit for this shift. Founded in
1984, the museum mounts provocative changing exhibitions, which include
historical surveys in addition to contemporary African art. Designed by Maya
Lin, the museum includes a bookstore where you can find basic introductions to
African art alongside advanced scholarship and reasonably priced art.

Admission: $5; $2.50, students, seniors and children (6–18). Handicapped
accessible. **Credit cards:** All major. **Hours:** Tues.–Fri., 10:30 A.M.–5:30 P.M.;
Sat.–Sun., noon–6 P.M. Closed Monday. **Services:** Tours, gift shop, lectures.
Tours: Groups of 10 or more may arrange tours by calling ext. 117 or 118 at
least two weeks in advance.

Museum of American Folk Art   MIDTOWN WEST
Columbus Ave. at 66th St. (212)977-7298

If the term "folk art" makes you think of craft shows and grandma's quilts, then you are overdue for a visit to the Museum of American Folk Art. Folk art is very hot among collectors and scholars intrigued by vernacular American culture, and the museum has contributed to this reinvigoration of the field. Shedding new light on folk art standbys like cigar store Indians, the museum also mounts provocative exhibitions of "outsider art," or "untrained art." The fact that folk art eludes simple classifications is an indication of its complexity. The museum houses temporary exhibitions as well as selections from its permanent collection. It is currently building a new home next to the Museum of Modern Art on West 53d Street, scheduled to open in 2000.

Admission: Free. **Hours:** Tues.–Sun, 11:30 A.M.–7:30 P.M.

National Museum of the American Indian
LOWER MANHATTAN
1 Bowling Green (between Whitehall and State Sts.) (212) 668-6624
www.si.edu/nmai

Housed in the former U.S. Custom House, a spectacular domed Beaux-Arts landmark at the foot of Broadway, this branch of the Smithsonian Institution is the model for a new national museum, which is scheduled to open in 2002 on the Mall in Washington, D.C.

Permanent Collection Wood, horn and stone carvings from the Northwest Coast of North America; Navajo weaving and blanket; archaeological objects from the Caribbean; textiles from Peru and Mexico; basketry from the Southwest; gold work from Colombia, Mexico and Peru; Aztec mosaics and painted hides and garments from the North American Plains Indians.

Admission: Free. Handicapped accessible. **Hours:** 10 A.M.–5 P.M; Thursday until 8 P.M.. **Services:** Lectures, tours, gift shop. **Programs for Children:** Offered throughout the year. **Tours:** For groups, call for information.

New Museum of Contemporary Art   TRIBECA/SOHO
583 Broadway (between Prince and Houston Sts.) (212) 219-1222
www.newmuseum.org

The New Museum celebrated the beginning of its third decade on art's cutting edge with a face lift that signaled other changes inside. Recent renovations expanded the museum's exhibition space, creating discrete galleries and a free public space with a bookstore, lounge and exhibits. Founded in 1977, the SoHo museum has a reputation for controversial exhibitions, edgy programs and a mixed critical reception. Yet by taking chances, the museum has given form to emergent art and created new standards for museums. The museum has long been focused on the international art scene and has often introduced new artists to New York audiences. Even as the museum moves toward less didactic exhibitions, you should expect it to continue to shake things up.

Admission: $6; $3, artists, students and seniors; children 18 and under, free. Thursday , 6 P.M.–8 P.M, free. **Credit cards:** All major. **Hours:** Wed. and Sun., noon–6 P.M.; Thur.–Sat., noon–8 P.M. Closed Monday and Tuesday. **Services:** Tours, lectures, concerts, gift shop. **Programs for Children:** Workshops. **Tours:** Group tours, call.

Nicholas Roerich Museum   UPPER WEST SIDE
319 West 107th St. (between Broadway and Riverside Dr.)
(212) 864-7752

Nicholas Roerich, the Russian-American star of this one-man museum, was a true Renaissance man, involved in a vast range of artistic, philosophical and spiritual pursuits. He worked with Stravinsky designing sets and costumes, studied Russian archaeology, and wrote, painted and traveled extensively. The museum features a permanent collection of Roerich's works and personal memorabilia, including numerous paintings inspired by his interest in Buddhism and the Tibetan highlands. The museum also hosts concerts and poetry readings.

Admission: Free. **Hours:** Tues.–Sun., 2 P.M.–5 P.M. **Services:** Concerts.

Studio Museum in Harlem   HARLEM
144 West 125th St. (between Lenox Ave. and Adam Clayton Powell Blvd.) (212) 864-4500 www.studiomuseuminharlem.org

Dedicated to African-American art, as well as work from Africa and throughout the diaspora, the Studio Museum was organized in 1967 for artists. Originally housed atop a liquor store on Fifth Avenue, the museum is now located on 125th Street in a building donated by the New York Bank for Savings. This Harlem museum organizes thematic and single-artist exhibitions. In addition, the building houses archives, studios, workshops and a museum shop.

Permanent Collection: The collection is divided into three main sections: 19th- and 20th-century African-American art, traditional and contemporary African art and artifacts, and 20th-century Caribbean art. Highlights include works by Romare Bearden, Elizabeth Catlett, Jacob Lawrence and Norman Lewis, and the James Van Der Zee photographic archives.

Admission: $5; $3, students and seniors; $1, children under 12; members, free. Free the first Saturday of each month. **Credit cards:** Cash and checks only. **Hours:** Wed.–Fri., 10 A.M.–5 P.M.; Sat.–Sun., 1–6 P.M. Closed Monday, Tuesday and major holidays. **Programs for Children:** Workshops, lectures, concerts, tours and outreach programs in local schools. **Tours:** Special tours with exhibition artists and curators; call for schedule. Group tours, call (212) 864-4500, extension 230. **Services:** Tours, gift shop.

Whitney Museum of American Art—
Philip Morris Branch   MIDTOWN EAST
120 Park Ave. (at 42d St.) (917) 663-2453

Philip Morris's headquarters building across the street from Grand Central Terminal houses a midtown exhibition space for the Whitney Museum. The Sculpture Court accommodates large sculptures that the museum cannot, while the gallery primarily shows contemporary painting and smaller sculptures.

Admission: Free. **Hours:** Gallery: Monday through Friday, 11 A.M.–6 P.M.; Thursday until 7:30 P.M. Sculpture Court: Monday through Saturday , 7:30 A.M.–9:30 P.M.; Sunday and Holidays, 11 A.M.–7 P.M. **Services:** Tours.

The Galleries

There are probably more art galleries with active exhibition schedules in New York than anywhere else—far too many to list them all here. But the names and brief descriptions of the dealers below represent a hearty sampling. From paintings to ceramics, from photography and film to Conceptual art, from small decorative objects to massive installations, their exhibitions make up an art menu unequalled in range and variety.

The criteria for the listed galleries are that they hold regular exhibitions and they are open to the public during normal viewing hours (generally from 10 A.M. to 6 P.M. five days a week, closed Sundays and Mondays). But it is always wise to call first, check *The New York Times* on Friday for art listings, or visit "Art and Museums" on nytoday.com. For the sake of convenience, the galleries are listed by neighborhood.

SOHO

ACE Gallery 275 Hudson St. (212) 255-5599. The menu in this large arena is Abstract Expressionist, Pop, Minimal and Conceptual art from 1960 to the present, along with established and emerging U.S. and international art going back to 1980. The exhibition schedule is full of surprises, from a huge suite of wall paintings by the Minimalist Sol LeWitt to an all-out show of creations by the fashion designer Issey Miyake. Behind it all is a sharp contemporary sensibility.

Howard Greenberg 120 Wooster St. (212) 334-0010. With one of the biggest inventories in the trade, this gallery focuses on classic 20th-century European and American photography. It handles the estates of such icons as Ruth Orkin, Roman Vishniac, James Van Der Zee, Andre Kertesz and Ralph Eugene Meatyard, and represents well-known contemporaries like William Klein, Sarah Moon, Bill Owens, Ralph Gibson, Gordon Parks and Mary Ellen Mark. Theme shows have dealt with American car culture, the New York subway and civil rights, among other topics.

Phyllis Kind Gallery 136 Greene St. (212) 925-1200. The quirky, the odd and the offbeat are to be found at this SoHo gallery, whose offerings run from far-out folk art like the garrulous paintings of the preacher Howard Finster to the wacky renderings of Chicago School painters like Jim Nutt. In fact, since it got its start in the Second City, a lively Chicago sensibility pervades the gallery.

Nolan/Eckman 560 Broadway (212) 925-6190. This small, intimate and easy gallery specializes in works on paper by contemporary American and German artists. Shows range from the outrageous, no-holds-barred polemics of the cartoony Peter Saul to the less scandalous musings of German stars like Gerhard Richter, Martin Kippenberger and Sigmar Polke.

Holly Solomon 172 Mercer St. (212) 941-5777. One of the earlier presences in SoHo, this sprightly gallery is seriously devoted to the witty, the decorative and the ingenious, like the inventions of TV wizard Nam June Paik. Other attractions include William Wegman's photographs of dogs dressed as people, the decorative paintings of Kim MacConnel and the witty visual scenarios of Izhar Patkin.

Yancey-Richardson 560 Broadway (212) 343-1255. Focusing on contemporary and vintage 20th century photography, this small gallery is known for excellent shows of the work of individual photographers, among them the Czech Josef Sudek, the Brazilians Sebastiao Selgado and Mario Cravo Netto, and from the U.S., Julius Shulman, Andrew Moore and Lynn Geesaman.

CHELSEA

Cheim and Read 521 West 23d St. (212) 242-7727. One of the more interesting galleries in Chelsea, this spacious, newish ground-floor showcase handles a wide range of contemporary painters, sculptors, photographers, video and installation artists of different generations. The gallery emphasizes art involved with strong psychological themes, like that of the sculptor Louise Bourgeois, as well as work devoted to the language of painting, like the abstractions of Richmond Burton. Other high-profile artists represented by the gallery are the sculptors Lynda Benglis and St. Clair Cemin, the photographers William Eggleston and Robert Mapplethorpe and the painters Pat Steir and Donald Baechler.

Paula Cooper 534 West 21st St. (212) 255-1105. Founded in 1968, this gallery was one of the very first to open in SoHo, establishing early on an agenda focused on (but not limited to) Conceptual and Minimalist sculpture. Sol LeWitt, Carl Andre, Donald Judd, Robert Grosvenor and Dan Flavin were among early exhibitors, but the gallery also has different breeds of artists in its stable, among them the painters Jennifer Bartlett and Michael Hurson, the sculptors Jonathan Borofsky and Jackie Winsor and the photographer Peter Campus.

Feigen Contemporary 535 West 20th St. (212) 929-0500. The newest branch of the veteran Richard L. Feigen Gallery, which in its uptown headquarters focuses on Old Masters, Feigen Contemporary moved from Chicago to Chelsea in 1997. It represents emerging, mid-career and established contemporary artists, ranging from James Rosenquist and the estate of Ray Johnson to the young video artist Jeremy Blake.

Matthew Marks Gallery 523 West 24th St. and 522 West 22d St. (212) 243-0200. It takes not one but two spacious galleries in Chelsea to display the work of the 20-odd artists on Matthew Marks' superstar roster, ranging from the English figure painter Lucian Freud and the estate of the Abstract Expressionist Willem deKooning to the less-is-more painters Brice Marden and Ellsworth Kelly and the hip "downtown" photographer Nan Goldin.

MetroPictures 519 West 24th St. (212) 206-7100. Receptive to the new and far-out when it opened in SoHo in 1980, this gallery—now occupying a vast space in Chelsea—represents an established group of contemporaries that includes the painter, sculptor and filmmaker Robert Longo, the video installation artist Tony Oursler and the photographer Cindy Sherman.

Ileana Sonnabend 536 West 22d St. (212) 627-1018. Noted for introducing '60's proto Pop pioneers like Rauschenberg and Johns to Europe, Sonnabend came to New York in 1970 and has assembled a stable of internationally known contemporary European and American painters, sculptors, photographers and installation artists. Some of its current stars are the English conceptualists Gilbert and George, kitsch-loving sculptor Jeff Koons, assemblagists Ashley Bickerton and Haim Steinbach from the East Village "Neo-Geo" movement of the mid-1980's, German photographers Bernd and Hilla Becher and site sculptors Anne and Patrick Poirier.

Leslie Tonkonow Artworks + Projects 601 West 26th St. (212) 255-8450. Offbeat photographers from the world over are the specialty of this young gallery, which occupies an intimate space high up in Chelsea's biggest building. A selective eye for quirky talent on the dealer's part makes this a don't-miss place for photography lookers.

Barbara Gladstone Gallery 515 West 24th St. (212) 206-0300. An émigré from SoHo (where it opened in the early 1980's) to Chelsea, this gallery is on the cutting edge of contemporary art, mounting eight exhibitions a year with the emphasis on Conceptual, installation, video and photographic work. The rhapsodic filmmaker Matthew Barney is one of its stars, along with the painters Anish Kapoor, Shirin Neshat and Lari Pittman, photographer Richard Prince, and Italian Conceptualists Mario and Marisa Merz.

UPTOWN

Mary Boone 745 Fifth Ave. at 58th St. (212) 752- 2929. Not so "cutting edge" as it once was, this trendy, highly publicized gallery, a launching pad for rockets like Julian Schnabel and David Salle, is still going strong. The gallery continues to represent some of the older talents from its roster in the 1970's and 80's, like Richard Artschwager, Ross Bleckner, Eric Fischl and Barbara Kruger, and it is still a showcase for younger artists like Leonardo Drew, Inka Essenigh, Damian

Loeb and Peter Wegner. In the fall of 2000 the gallery will open additional space in Chelsea for large-scale works and installations.

Garth Clark 24 West 57th St. (212) 246-2205. This small but serious showcase for 20th-century ceramics handles a mix of artists spanning the 20th century. Some come from the ceramics world, like George East Ohr, Beatrice Wood and Ron Nagle; others are better known in the fine arts field but turned their hands to ceramics, among them Lucio Fontana, Sir Anthony Caro, Joan Miro and Isamu Noguchi.

C & M Arts 45 East 78th St. (212) 861-0020. Distinguished presentations of European and American masters—from Impressionists through Matisse, Picasso, deKooning, Jackson Pollock and Joseph Cornell—are at home in this heavy-duty gallery, quartered in what was once a luxurious town house. The gallery, opened in 1992, does relatively few shows, but high standards prevail.

Barry Friedman, Ltd. 32 East 67th St. (212) 794- 8950. European decorative arts of the 20th century dominate this sumptuous townhouse, including French furniture and objects of the 1930's and '40's, Wiener Werkstatte and Bauhaus productions and avant-garde paintings from the '20's and '30's, works on paper, sculpture and contemporary vintage photography. The gallery is also moving into the field of contemporary decorative arts with shows of studio glass, art fur-niture, ceramics and wood objects by artists from all over the world. A keenly discriminating taste prevails.

Gagosian 980 Madison Ave. (212) 744-2313; 136 Wooster St. and 555 West 24th St. (212) 228-2828. Big-name contemporaries star in the big spaces of this triple-threat gallery, the only one with three locations in the city. Larger instal-lations appear in the SoHo and Chelsea branches; the Madison Avenue gallery is for relatively smaller paintings and drawings. The stable includes sculptors Damien Hirst, Maya Lin and Elyn Zimmerman and the painters Annette Mes-sager, Ed Ruscha and David Salle.

Galerie St. Etienne 24 West 57th St. (212) 245-6734. Austrian and German Expressionism from the turn of the century through the 1920's are the house specialties at this gallery, along with the work of American folk artists. Founded in 1939 by Dr. Otto Kallir, St. Etienne was the first to show Grandma Moses. The gallery introduced major Expressionists like Gustav Klimt, Oskar Kokoschka and Egon Schiele to the United States, and deals with other Aus-trian and German modernists, including Kaethe Kollwitz, Lovis Corinth and Paula Modersohn-Becker. Its stable of classic American folk painters includes John Kane, Morris Hirshfield and Horace Pippin.

Marian Goodman 24 West 57th St. (212) 977-7160. An international repertory distinguishes this long established gallery, a quiet but important pres-ence on the art scene that has recently added significantly to its space. To its schedule of shows by prominent European and American Conceptual artists like Jannis Kounellis, Rebecca Horn, members of the low-rent Italian Arte Povera group, Lawrence Weiner and Dan Graham, it has been adding the work of contemporary photographers, among them large-scale prints by Germany's Thomas Struth.

Hirschl & Adler from **Hirschl & Adler Modern** 21 East 70th St. (212) 535-8810. American and European paintings, watercolors, drawings and sculpture from the 18th through the early 20th centuries are the province of this active gallery, along with American prints of all periods and American decorative arts from 1810 to 1910. Established in 1952, it occupies a handsome landmark townhouse that is also home to a contemporary arm that deals with European and American art from post-World War II to the present.

Edwynn Houk 745 Fifth Ave. at 57th St. (212) 750-7070. Specializing in masters of 20th-century photography, with an emphasis on the 1920's and '30's as well as the work of contemporary Americans, this elegantly understated gallery has a cavernous space in which to show them. It represents the estates of Brassai and Dorothea Lange, among others, and is the exclusive representative for such American contemporaries as Elliott Erwitt, Sally Mann, Lynn Davis and Andrea Modica.

Kennedy Galleries 730 Fifth Ave. at 56th St. (212) 541-9600. Now celebrating its 125th year, Kennedy is one of the oldest dealers in American art. In its plush, carpeted quarters (unusual for a gallery) it shows paintings from an inventory that runs from the 18th to the 20th century, including the Hudson River School, American Impressionism, Social Realism and Modernism. On the 20th-century side, it handles exclusively the estates of Charles Burchfield and Rockwell Kent, and regularly exhibits the work of American classics like George Bellows, John Sloan, Stuart Davis, Charles Demuth, John Marin, and Walt Kuhn.

Knoedler & Company 19 East 70th St. (212) 794-0550. The oldest art gallery in New York, Knoedler goes back to 1846, when its French founder emigrated to America. It became a leading international dealer in European and American art and in 1930 scored a coup by buying 21 masterpieces from the Hermitage in St. Petersburg for the American acquisitor Andrew Mellon. Always a champion of contemporary artists as well, it shows works today by Helen Frankenthaler, Milton Avery, Adolph Gottlieb, Richard Pousette-Dart and other established talents.

Marlborough 40 West 57th St. (212) 541-4900 and **Marlborough Chelsea** 211 West 19th St. (212) 463- 8634. The emphasis in this spacious gallery is on contemporary artists with established reputations. Larry Rivers, Marisol, Alex Katz, Red Grooms and the Colombian sculptor-painter Fernando Botero are regular exhibitors at Marlborough's glossy uptown headquarters. A graphics division there shows 19th through 20th century work, with occasional historical shows; the roomy Chelsea branch specializes in the work of contemporary sculptors like Anthony Caro, Magdalena Abakanowicz and Kenneth Snelson.

McKee Gallery 745 Fifth Ave. at 58th St. (212) 688-5951. Established contemporaries and an outlook independent of fashions or trends are the strengths of this gallery, opened in 1974. Among its painters are Vija Celmins, Jake Berthot, Harvey Quaytman and the estate of Philip Guston; its sculptors include William Tucker, Martin Puryear and the young Spanish maestra Susanna Solano.

PaceWildenstein 32 East 57th St. (212) 421-3292 and 142 Greene St. (212) 431-9224; **PaceWildenstein MacGill** 32 East 57th St. Beautifully mounted shows in cool, elegant settings are the rule at PaceWildenstein, originally founded as the Pace Gallery in the 1960's. Not a hotbed of new talent, it's the place to see the work of contemporary "Old Masters," like Mark Rothko, Ad Reinhardt, Louise Nevelson and the satirist Saul Steinberg, as well as living icons like Julian Schnabel and Chuck Close. PaceWildenstein MacGill, in the same building, shows 20th-century American photography; the downtown branch of PaceWildenstein presents installation art and large-scale sculpture.

The Project 427 West 126th St. (212) 662-8610 This interesting new development in the Harlem contemporary art scene was started by the writer Christian Haye in 1999. The Project has brought an international roster of young artists from Europe, Asia, Africa and the United States to a cosmopolitan section of Manhattan. Recent exhibits have included work by Paul Pfeiffer, Tom Gidley, and Martín Weber.

Michael Rosenfeld 24 West 57th St. (212) 247-0082. Specializing in American art from 1910 to 1970, the gallery has mounted "movement" shows of early American abstraction and Abstract Expressionism; it also handles the estates of the Surrealist Alfonso Ossorio and the abstractionist Burgoyne Diller, and the work of contemporaries like Charles Seliger, Martha Madigan and Betye Saar. The gallery is particularly receptive to the work of minority artists, and has mounted a number of shows of African-American art.

Salander-O'Reilly Galleries 20 East 79th St. (212) 879-6606. With one of the most ambitious and far- flung rosters in the art world, this gallery in an impressive townhouse shows a broad range of American and European painting and sculpture from the 18th to the 20th centuries. It has mounted more than 300 exhibitions, from work by the 18th-century English painters John Constable and Joseph M.W. Turner to the American modernist Alfred Maurer and the contemporary abstractionist Stanley Boxer. It represents the estates of Stuart Davis, Gaston Lachaise, Gerald Murphy and Elaine deKooning, as well as the work of living artists like Paul Georges, Don Gummer, Graham Nickson, Larry Poons, Katherine Porter and Michael Steiner.

Joan T. Washburn 20 West 57th St. (212) 397-6780. American art from World War I to the present is the territory staked out by this long established gallery, which handles the estates of the painters Jackson Pollock and Myron Stout, Louise Nevelson's sculpture and drawings from the 1930's and '40's, and David Smith's paintings from the same period. Its contemporary stable includes the sculptors Jack Youngerman and Gwynn Murrill and the painter Richard Baker.

Zabriskie 41 East 57th St. (212) 752-1223. Opened in 1955, the Zabriskie

Gallery is known for its strong emphasis on American Modernism, Dada and Surrealism, showing works in all media. It is also a stronghold of modern and contemporary French and American photography, from the Frenchman Eugene Atget to the American Nicholas Nixon. The gallery represents the estates of the sculptors Richard Stankiewicz and William Zorach as well as the work of contemporary painters like Pat Adams and Katherine Schmidt. Group shows of important movements and periods are also part of the fare.

—*Grace Glueck*

PERFORMING ARTS
Theater in New York

Broadway, as a word, still has an enchanted sound to the stagestruck, summoning an impossibly glamorous neighborhood of palatial theaters, stars of incandescent wattage and plays and musicals of unmatchable wit and polish. That, anyway, is the myth. In reality, such a Broadway—and by Broadway, one means an area of roughly 40 square blocks around Times Square in midtown Manhattan—hasn't existed, if it ever did, for at least some 30 years and probably longer. Broadway more than ever is a state of mind, albeit a state within the city of New York. As a piece of nomenclature, it has never been exact, since most "Broadway" theaters are found on other streets. And if you can stretch your imagination—and your legs—to encompass at least a few hundred more blocks, you'll discover that something very much like the Broadway that was still exists. You just can't find it all in one place, anymore than all of the city's multistar restaurants are within an oyster shell's throw of one another.

Finding what meets your tastes may require a little more research that it might have in, say, the 1930's.

What is produced in the official Broadway area is still what gets the most attention nationally. The plays put on there have bigger budgets and usually bigger names, with ticket prices to match. What it seldom offers is much in the way of originality or daring. Investing in a Broadway production is a high-risk gamble and producers are accordingly cautious. That is why the neighborhood is dominated by revivals, shows based on successful movies and British imports perfumed with class and flowery reviews from abroad. With the cleaning up and slicking up of Times Square in the 1990's, there has also arisen a new crop of shows directly targeted at tourists, trading on brand-name familiarity, most notably those of Disney, whose "Lion King" (admittedly, a brilliantly rethought stage production of a cartoon movie) may well outlive us all.

There's still plenty to get excited about on Broadway. Revivals of dramas in recent seasons have been on an exceptionally high level. New musicals have tended to be either lost or leaden, with the blessed exception of Susan Stroman's multi-Tony-winning "Contact." But cutting edge, or even nicking edge, is definitely not an attribute of midtown Manhattan theater. When a production with a cool quotient shows up on Broadway ("Rent"), you can safely assume that it started life in some other neighborhood. Indeed, since 1970 the overwhelming majority of Pulitzer Prizes for drama have gone to non-Broadway productions.

Finding what's hot Off Broadway and in the increasingly less marginalized realm known as Off Off Broadway can take you as far from midtown as Brooklyn or as close as Theater Row—the stretch of 42nd Street west of Eighth Avenue. There's no strict rule of thumb for conducting your search: a theater, after all, is judged by what is on its stage, and that changes constantly.

In the glitzy block of 42nd Street between Seventh and Eighth Avenues, there is a most charming and innovative new theater for children, the restored little jewel box called the New Victory, right next door to the goliath Ford Performing Arts Center. If you're looking for literate, polished plays in thoroughly professional productions, there are several institutional theaters that have become bywords for just that: the Manhattan Theater Club, Lincoln Center, Playwrights Horizons and to a lesser extent, the Joseph Papp Public Theater. There are also younger, smaller and more vital companies that have already established a track record for putting on works that get people talking.

These include the Vineyard Theater, off Union Square (birthplace of Pulitzer winner Edward Albee's "Three Tall Women" and Paula Vogel's "How I Learned To Drive"), the New York Theater Workshop on 4th Street in the East Village (the cradle of the now fabled rock opera "Rent" and Claudia Shear's "Dirty Blonde") and MCC (the Manhattan Class Company) on West 23rd Street, which brought Margaret Edson's brave, surprisingly popular "Wit" to New York. The Drama Dept. on East 9th Street, filled with some of the most vital young theater talents in the city, has in five years established itself as a company whose imaginative reinventions of classic plays are essential viewing.

If your tastes lean more toward the truly experimental—that is, without such conventions as plot and easily understood characters—there remains a host of fertile outlets for such work, mostly located south of 14th Street, from the legendary LaMama on 4th Street in the East Village to the more recently created HERE performing arts complex on Sixth Avenue in SoHo, where an underwater puppet show became the talk of the town several seasons ago. Two mighty bastions of the avant-garde remain indomitably in place and abidingly influential: Richard Foreman's Ontological-Hysteric Theater and the Wooster Group, both of which have hardcore cult followings, making tickets to their productions tough to come by.

For theatergoers with an international palate, there is the annual Lincoln Center Festival, which in recent years has brought major works from Ireland, South Africa and Eastern Europe. And just across the river from Manhattan is the Brooklyn Academy of Music (*see entry in the "Brooklyn" section*), unquestionably the city's most ambitious and adventurous importer of theater, regularly bringing in productions from titanic directors like Peter Brook and Ingmar Bergman. Indeed, some of the most electric theater seen in New York of late has been at the Academy. Even those who consider Brooklyn a foreign country must concede that it's closer than Stockholm.

— Ben Brantley

Broadway

Broadway theater has become rather pricey—and the seats in the older theaters aren't terribly comfortable—but those things cease to matter when the lights go down and the curtain goes up. You are in the right place.

There are 32 "Broadway" theaters, and even more Off-Broadway and Off-Off-Broadway. Off- and Off-Off are less expensive than Broadway, and the theatrical quality can be superior, but the comfort level is no better. To find out what's playing and where, the fullest listings are in *Time Out* magazine, *The New Yorker* and *The New York Times* (listings every day, but more on Friday and Sunday); **nytoday.com** also has everything you need.

Getting Tickets

If you want to see "The Lion King" you should have written for tickets months ago. For everything else, there may be tickets available at the theater box office or through one of the telephone services that charge extra. Here are two: **Ticketmaster** at (212) 307-7171 and **Tele-Charge** at (212) 239-6200.

But many smart theatergoers don't pay full price: There are two ways to pay less. Best known are the half-price TKTS booths in Times Square and the World Trade Center. Also popular are the discount coupons distributed all over town by an organization that calls itself the Hit Show Club.

TKTS

The Times Square TKTS booth, on Broadway at 46th St., has tickets to dozens of Broadway and Off-Broadway shows for half-price on the day of the performance. The TKTS booth in the World Trade Center has shorter hours, shorter waiting lines and it's indoors—no problem with the weather. But note that this booth sells matinee tickets only on the previous day.

Tickets to a few shows are discounted 25 percent at the TKTS booths, but most are 50 percent. There is also a $2.50 charge per ticket, to support the TKTS operation. You can't buy the best seats but there are often very good ones. **NOTE:** Credit cards are not accepted. Cash and travelers checks only.

TKTS was established in 1973 by the Theater Development Fund to fill seats that weren't selling at full price. Hundreds of people line up for tickets at the two booths so the lines can be long, but the savings are real. At the Times Square booth, if the line is one block long, figure on waiting a half-hour; an hour in peak holiday seasons. At the Trade Center, a half-hour line runs the length of one side of the building. Remember, it's indoors.

TIP #1: The lines are longest when the booths open and for the next hour or so. They are dramatically shorter at the end of the day—as short as a 10-minute wait after 5 o'clock in Times Square, and even less after 7. Some tickets that were available when the booth opened may have been sold out if you go late, but the selection is usually good at any hour. Also, some shows that were not offering discount tickets earlier in the day may have released some as curtain time approached.

TIP #2: Tickets available at the Times Square booth are listed on the Internet every day after 4 P.M. at newyork.citysearch.com, which has a link to TKTS.

TIP #3: Do not buy tickets from hawkers along the waiting line. They offer deeper discounts, but you run the risk that they are counterfeit and the theater will turn you away.

Hours:

Times Square: (subway: N, R to 49th St. or any subway or bus to Times Square) The booth is technically in Duffy Square, an island between Broadway and 7th Ave. at 46th St. TKTS shares the island with statues of Father Francis Duffy, Roman Catholic chaplain of the Fighting 69th in the first World War and pastor of a church on 42nd St., and George M. ("I'm a Yankee Doodle Dandy") Cohan.

Hours: Monday through Saturday: 3 P.M.–8 P.M. for evening performances. Wednesday and Saturday: 10 A.M.–2 P.M. for matinees. Sunday: 11 A.M. to closing.

World Trade Center: (subway: C, E to World Trade Center, 1, 9, N, R to Cortlandt St.)

The booth is in #2 World Trade Center, the building with the observation deck. It is at the level of the plaza between the two towers, or up an escalator from the shopping mall.

Hours: Monday through Friday: 11 A.M. to 5:30 P.M. for same-day evening performances and next-day matinees. Saturday: 11 A.M. to 3:30 P.M. for Saturday evening and Sunday matinees.

Note: The World Trade Center booth sells tickets for matinees on the previous day only. It does not sell them on the day of the performance. It also sells full-price theater tickets in advance, including tickets for some special events like the U. S. Open tennis tournament.

Hit Show Club

Go to 630 Ninth Ave. between 44th and 45th Sts., Room 808, between 9 A.M. and 4 P.M. Walk in. You'll see a rack with discount coupons for maybe a dozen shows. The choice is smaller than same-day tickets at TKTS, but there is a big advantage: You can use these coupons to buy tickets in advance. Another advantage: You don't have to stand on a long line outside in foul weather. Take (or mail) the coupon to the theater, present the coupon, and if they have what you want they will sell you two tickets (or one) at the discount. Most Hit Show Club discounts are about 40 percent, with no extra charge, compared to 50 percent plus $2.50 for most TKTS shows. The dollar difference is minor.

There are smaller selections of Hit Show and other discount coupons beside the cash register in some restaurants. Not all discounts are the same, and not all shows offer discounts for all performances. Some long-run shows offer seats anywhere in the house. Others will not offer seats in the first 10 or 12 rows of the orchestra or the front balcony.

As an unexpected bonus, a leading architectural critic calls the landmarked lobby "one of the most beautiful Art Deco interiors in New York," with a glistening mosaic on one wall and a pleated gold ceiling. It is worth a visit.

Classical Music

Musical life in New York begins but by no means ends with two big institutions. **Carnegie Hall** (*see the section "Midtown West"*) and **Lincoln Center** (*see the section "Upper West Side"*) generate concerts of every size and description and have halls big and small to put them in. Next to these giants is a ring of smaller organizations; they organize chamber music, new music ensembles and recitals in series that stretch from September until well into June. Air-conditioning, moreover is blurring the idea of seasons altogether. It's now possible to find worthwhile events in August as well as November.

Surrounding these major islands of activity is an ocean of free enterprise, and it is this mass of self-generated events and cottage industries that give New York its energy. Experimental music groups, amateur choirs with big agendas, small opera companies doing new or esoteric repertory, self-financed and self-promoted debut performances fill downtown lofts and uptown churches in profusion. The quality will vary as much as the material, but the level of ambition is always high.

Carnegie Hall has no resident orchestras or ensembles; it is a presenter, gathering the best orchestras, singers and recitalists from this country and the world and fitting them into subscription series. Sign up for a season-long list, or choose individual events. In the main hall (seating 2,800) expect the Vienna and Berlin Philharmonics every year, as well as the orchestras of Cleveland, Philadelphia, Boston and Chicago. The Pittsburgh and Montreal Symphonies and many others will drop in, too, and there will be both familiar and exotic symphonic visitors from Europe and the East.

Lincoln Center's Avery Fisher Hall is Carnegie's equivalent in size and seating capacity, if not beauty. It produces series in the same way as well, but with a difference. For Fisher is also the home of the New York Philharmonic, and the smaller Alice Tully Hall next door houses the Chamber Music Society of Lincoln Center. The Philharmonic is at work steadily through the season, either under its music director Kurt Masur or guest conductors. Weekly programs are generally repeated three to four times, often with Friday morning performances for those less easy with nightlife in the city.

The Chamber Music Society is a permanent ensemble of 10 to 20 performers. They mix and match their instruments and skills to make all possible combinations. Sextets with bassoon are no problem, but conventional quartets and trios turn up as well. The Society's programs are usually repeated only once.

A major renovation a decade ago turned the dreary small theater at Carnegie Hall into a little gem called Weill Recital Hall. Formerly a rental operation for almost all comers, it is now the home of chamber music series, musical theater in concert, song recitals by good artists and, very important, debut recitals by beginning professionals. Deciding which new talent is worth a trip and the price of a ticket is a less haphazard procedure today. The performers are selected by Carnegie Hall in conjunction with several European concert halls, and the young people give their recitals in all of them.

Lincoln Center has several debut series as well, as does the **92d Street Y.**

Fred R. Conrad/The New York Times

Carnegie Hall

And then there is the Young Concert Artists which has been presenting and preparing young musicians and singers for a generation. The **Juilliard School** is eager to put its best students before the public and sponsors a number of in-house competitions with major public recitals as rewards. Go to the box office at the school in Lincoln Center for schedules and tickets. Most performances are free.

Indeed, the students of Juilliard and their companion schools, **Mannes** and **Manhattan,** often blur the distinction between amateur and professional. All three schools teem with concerts and operas at which the public is welcome, usually free. Opera productions at the Juilliard Theater (one of the city's best spaces) are often on a par if not superior to the professional efforts of companies in other cities. Manhattan regularly puts on skillful versions of out-of-the-way 20th-century operas, and Mannes is in the midst of an extensive Handel project.

Although New York is often criticized for having only one major orchestra, the accusation is deceptive. Floating groups like the estimable Orchestra of St. Luke's have their own seasons. The New York Chamber Symphony and the conductorless Orpheus are well-rated, and the American Symphony Orchestra is making strides as well. Under Robert Spano, the Brooklyn Philharmonic is giving some of the most interesting orchestra programs in town. The **Brooklyn Academy of Music** (*see "Brooklyn"*) where it performs is a quick and easy subway ride across (or underneath) the East River from Manhattan.

Smaller venues are remarkably active. The **Miller Theater** at Columbia University has become the hotbed of choice for the serious new-music crowd. **Merkin Concert Hall** is plain to look at but night after night provides a place for every kind of music, new and old, provocative and conservative. The **Florence Gould Theater** and the **Kaye Playhouse** join the **92d Street Y** as East Side presenters. **The Kitchen** downtown near the Hudson River is a clearinghouse for musical and theatrical experiment where electronic instruments and new sounds are the norm. The **World Music Institute** brings in ethnic performers from Tibet, darkest Africa or, for that matter, down the street.

Summer is becoming busy, although Carnegie Hall usually closes in August. In June and July the Lincoln Center Festival brings operas, orchestra concerts and interesting exotica. It uses its own halls and a few others nearby. There is also the vastly popular Mostly Mozart Festival which divides its frequent summer-long programs between Avery Fisher and Alice Tully Halls. The repertory is usually more comforting than challenging, and the air-conditioning is great.

A lot of summer entertainment is free: the Met giving concert versions of operas in the parks of the five boroughs, the New York Philharmonic doing much the same, and then Lincoln Center's Damrosch Park offering concert brass bands, choruses and mostly lighthearted fare.

—Bernard Holland

CLASSICAL MUSIC CENTERS

Below is a small list of places that offer concerts on a regular basis. The serious music lover should check listings every Sunday in *The New York Times* "Arts & Leisure" section (the next-to-last page) or online at nytoday.com.

Bargemusic
Fulton Ferry Landing (between Water and River Sts.), Brooklyn
(718) 624-4061

Olga Bloom, the driving force behind Bargemusic, deserves an award for creating a unique venue. "I wanted a place where musicians could escape the combat zone of the New York music scene," she said. So in 1974 Bloom, a violinist, purchased an old coffee barge, almost single-handedly refurbished it and turned it into a floating chamber music space where artists can perform in an informal atmosphere and actually enjoy making music.

Moored in the East River under the Brooklyn Bridge, with the Manhattan skyline providing a breathtaking backdrop, Bargemusic is a cozy, wood-paneled room which seats about 125 people on folding chairs. Year-round, the finest chamber music performers play concerts of the highest caliber. It's a magical spot, well worth the trip to Brooklyn Heights and the occasionally choppy waters. Advance reservations are necessary, as performances sell out.

Subway: A, C to High St.

CAMI Hall

165 West 57th St. (between Sixth and Seventh Aves.) (212) 841-9500

It may be one of the city's most nondescript concert halls, but no matter. It serves its purpose, which is to give performers a decent, affordable place to peddle their art in midtown. CAMI stands for Columbia Artists Management Inc., the prestigious firm that owns the pleasant 200-seat hall located directly across the street from Carnegie Hall (where Columbia's own artists are more likely to be appearing).

Credit cards: Cash and checks only. **Subway:** B, N, Q, R to 57th St.

Columbia University—Miller Theater

2960 Broadway (at 116th St.) (212) 854-7799

Thanks to a $3 million reconstruction, a third of which came from the Kathryn and Gilbert Miller Fund, Columbia now has a state-of-the-art theater that brings the finest opera, music and dance, as well as theater, poetry readings and lectures, to Morningside Heights. One extremely popular event is the sensational Sonic Boom Festival, a new-music series.

Credit cards: All major. **Subway:** 1, 9 to 116th St.

Juilliard School—Juilliard Theater

60 Lincoln Center Plaza (Broadway at 65th St.) (212) 799-5000

The Juilliard School enjoys a reputation as one of the world's leading music conservatories. Indeed, some of the world's best-known performers are graduates. The principal auditorium, the Juilliard Theater, is as impressive as the students who regularly appear on its stage. A steeply raked 933-seat hall with extremely comfortable seats, superior acoustics and excellent sightlines, it is most often used for opera and orchestral concerts, though chamber music, drama and dance are no strangers here.

Tickets: Many performances are free. Others have relatively modest ticket prices, available at the box office or, for a fee, through Ticketmaster. **Credit cards:** Cash and checks only at box office. **Subway:** 1 to 66th St.

Kosciuszko Foundation

15 East 65th St. (between Madison and Fifth Aves.) (212) 734-2130

On the second floor of the Kosciuszko Foundation's splendid three-story limestone town house, just off Central Park, is one of the loveliest recital spaces in town. An elegant wood-paneled parlor at the top of a red-carpeted spiral staircase, the room doubles as a gallery for 19th- and 20th-century Polish art and is dominated by a large portrait of Tadeusz Kosciuszko, a Polish-born military engineer who fought with colonial American forces, designed the fortress at West Point and achieved the rank of major general in the Polish army. The Foundation, founded in 1925, is a center for Polish culture and education, so naturally the focus of its excellent concert series is on Polish music and musicians.

Tickets: Purchase at office during office hours. **Credit cards:** MC/V. **Subway:** 6 to 68th St.; N, R to Fifth Ave,

Manhattan School of Music
122 Claremont Ave. (at Broadway and 122d St.) (212) 749-2802

One of the country's premier conservatories, the Manhattan School of Music is located just a few blocks from Grant's Tomb and Riverside Church in the less-than-glamorous building that was the Juilliard School before it moved to posher digs at Lincoln Center. The Manhattan School is bustling with all sorts of music, from student, faculty and professional recitals and chamber music to opera, orchestral and jazz presentations. The quality is usually high and the price of admission often free. There are several auditoriums at the school. The two principal spaces are Borden Auditorium, a long, narrow 1,000-seat hall with decent if not wonderful sound, and upstairs, the intimate, 380-seat Hubbard Recital Hall.

Tickets: Call for prices (often free). **Subway:** 1, 9 to 125th St.

Mannes College of Music
150 West 85th St. (between Amsterdam and Columbus Aves.)
(212) 580-0210

When Mannes moved in 1984 from the Upper East Side into new quarters on West 85th Street—a six-story, red-brick, Federal-style building that once belonged to the United Order of True Sisters—it became the third big-name music school, along with Juilliard and the Manhattan School of Music, on Manhattan's West Side. Like other conservatories, Mannes has an impressive student body and faculty and presents a wide array of high-quality events, from early music consorts to grand opera and beyond. Its two auditoriums—the 200-seat Concert Hall and the 60-seat Goldmark Auditorium, used mainly for recitals—are adequate if not luxurious. (For larger-scale events, Mannes often uses the nearby Symphony Space.)

Tickets: Free. **Subway:** 1, 9, B, C to 86th St.

Merkin Concert Hall
129 West 67th St. (between Broadway and Amsterdam Ave.)
(212) 362-8719

"Intimate" is a word that gets its share of use, or misuse, in describing mid-size concert venues. But in the case of Merkin, it applies. The 457-seat hall is an attractive space with superior acoustics, making it a favorite for chamber ensembles, recitalists and even mid-size orchestras and choral groups. A number of popular series are held here, including "Interpretations" and "New Sounds Live," both of which focus on avant-garde, jazz or ethnic music. Merkin is part of the Elaine Kaufman Cultural Center, which means that many programs here highlight Jewish roots and culture. It also means that the hall is dark on Friday nights, Saturdays and all Jewish holidays.

Credit cards: All major; checks. **Subway:** 1, 9 to 66th St.

Metropolitan Museum of Art—Grace Rainey Rogers Auditorium

1000 Fifth Ave. (between 81st and 82d Sts.) (212) 570-3949

An excellent 708-seat hall, acoustically one of the best in town, it is particularly well suited for recitals and chamber music. One of its secrets is the warm-toned African korina wood paneling, a highly reflective material that helps magnify sound. Many of the world's prominent performers appreciate the merits of this hall, which is why you'll find the Juilliard and Guarneri String Quartets, the Beaux Arts Trio and other big-name artists gracing the stage. There's also a sporadic jazz concert, and many of the museum's popular lectures take place here. One of the best things about Grace Rainey Rogers is that to enter the auditorium you have to walk through the museum's spectacular Egyptian collection, which is always a thrill. Concerts are also regularly presented in other locations around the museum—call ahead for times and locations.

Credit cards: All major. **Subway:** 4, 5, 6 to 86th St.

New School University

66 West 12th St. (between Fifth and Sixth Aves.) (800) 709-4321

A rich array of lectures and concerts take place at the New School University's varied venues: in the Orozco Room, at the Parsons School of Design (66 Fifth Avenue), at the Mannes College Jazz Performance Space and in the Tishman Auditorium. The Tishman is a cozy Art Deco auditorium designed by the architect Joseph Urban in 1930 and named an interior landmark in 1993. Urban's rounded ceiling of concentric rings inspired a similar design at Radio City Music Hall a few years later. Raked seating makes for clear views all around.

Credit cards: All major. **Subway:** F to 14th St.

Opera

Opera in New York means, first and foremost, the **Metropolitan Opera** at Lincoln Center. Sometimes it seems that opera in the whole world means, first and foremost, the Metropolitan Opera. The company essentially deserves its iconic status. Leading international singers regularly perform there; indeed, a Metropolitan Opera debut is still a benchmark of a singer's career. In over 25 years as artistic director, James Levine has built the Met orchestra into one of the finest anywhere. The musicians know they are good and play with palpable pride and confidence. The 3,900-seat opera house, which opened its doors in 1966, is looking a bit tattered these days, but the sound in the auditorium remains marvelous, and, if anything, the sound up in the cheaper balcony and family circle seats is better than the pricey orchestra section.

Which brings up price. The Met is expensive. But putting on international-level opera is an expensive enterprise. It's mostly worth it. Yes, there are off-nights at the Met, and ill-conceived productions, and automatic-pilot performances of the most popular bread-and-butter operas. And sometimes second-string casts fall too far below the level of the name singers who open a run of an opera and garner the reviews. Still, company officials assert that, night for night, the Met presents opera on a more consistently high level than any other company, and they are right.

A newcomer to opera or a visitor from out of town will be tempted to go to the crowd-pleasers, like *La Boheme, Tosca,* and *Aida.* These are good shows. But it would be wise to check out reviews and select something that is special, for the Met at its best is exhilarating. In recent seasons, for example, the presentations of Tchaikovsky's *Queen of Spades,* Mozart's *Marriage of Figaro,* Strauss's *Ariadne auf Naxos,* Wagner's *Meistersinger* and Berg's *Wozzeck* have been exceptionally produced and splendidly sung.

By the way, the Met's official guided tour is one of the best kept secrets in New York. It's fascinating to go back stage and see the rotating stage, the set shops, the rehearsal spaces. The costume builders are happy to demonstrate how they must adapt outfits to singers with enormously varying sizes and shapes.

Across the plaza from the Met, in the New York State Theater, is the **New York City Opera,** and the biggest frustration of this enterprising company is its location. The mission of the company under its current leader, Paul Kellogg, is to create an identity that is distinct from its neighbor's. Why do what the Met can do better? So City Opera may not offer world-famous singers in the standard repertory, but it can offer young, eager artists who look and act like the characters they portray. Moreover, the City Opera tends to be more daring about repertory than the Met. The company regularly offers Baroque operas by Handel, neglected 20th century works like Strauss' *Intermezzo,* Britten's *Paul Bunyan* (an entrancing production), and Carlisle Floyd's *Of Mice and Men* (a riveting musical and dramatic experience).

Ticket prices there are much more affordable than at the Met, as well. All this has made the company attractive to younger, hipper audiences.

The company's goal of distinguishing itself from the Met would be easier, however, if it performed in a different facility in a different neighborhood. With over 2,700 seats, the New York State Theater is somewhat too big for the type of involving musical theater experience the City Opera works have to offer. And the acoustics of the auditorium are far from ideal, though the company is currently experimenting with an electronic sound-enhancement system for the space, a move that has agitated many traditionalists but been largely unnoticed by most attendees. All in all, the City Opera is not just a cheaper alternative to the Met, but an interesting company in its own right.

There are many other smaller opera companies in the city, organizations that typically present two or three productions per season.

DiCapo Opera is a scrappy company that performs in an appealing modest-sized theater on East 76th Street, and presents classics and occasionally contemporary works in effective productions with, by and large, talented young casts.

Amato Opera is a mom-and-pop outfit which for 50 years, on a tight budget, has offered popular operas in a theater on the Bowery that gives new meaning to the term "intimate" drama.

The **Brown Opera** usually presents just two productions a years (check local listings), in English translation, on two consecutive weekends, first at the Lehman Center in the Bronx, then at John Jay College Theater in Manhattan.

The **Juilliard Opera Center** is not, as its name implies, a company of students from the Juilliard School, but a training institute that offers singers in leading roles who are on the brink of, or already engaged in, professional careers. Students fill out the smaller roles and provide the orchestra and chorus. But Juilliard students are more accomplished than many professionals, and the Opera Center productions are often excellent. The **Manhattan School of Music** also presents some worthwhile productions in its commodious theater on Broadway and 122nd Street, for example, an important recent revival of Ned Rorem's stirring operatic adaptation of Strindberg's *Miss Julie*. Opera at the **Mannes College of Music** on West 85th Street is also worth checking out.

The estimable **L'Opera Francais de New York** presents stylish, semi-staged performances of French operas, often rarities, at Alice Tully Hall in Lincoln Center, though just two a year (check local listings). They are always first-rate.

If you can do without sets and costumes entirely the **Opera Orchestra of New York,** directed by the conductor Eve Queler, is a must. Ms. Queler seeks out inexplicably neglected operas and presents them in concert performances at Carnegie Hall with strong casts, sometimes including major singers. In recent seasons Renee Fleming, Ruth Ann Swenson, and Vesselina Kasarova, to cite just some illustrious artists, have scored triumphs with the Opera Orchestra. Ms. Queler's work reminds us that opera is, at its core, music, and can work quite effectively without its theatrical trimmings.

—*Anthony Tommasini*

Amato Opera Theater

319 Bowery (between 2d and Bleecker Sts.) (212) 228-8200

Tickets: Avg. $20. **Credit cards:** MC/V. **Subway:** F to Second Ave.; 6 to Bleecker St.; B, D, F, Q to Broadway-Lafayette St.

DiCapo Opera Theater

184 East 76th St. (between Lexington and Third Aves.)
(212) 288-9438

Tickets: $33. **Credit cards:** MC/V. **Subway:** 6 to 77th St.

Juilliard Opera Center—Juilliard Theater

60 Lincoln Center Plaza (Columbus Ave. and 64th St.) (212) 799-5000

Tickets: Avg. $20. **Credit cards:** Cash only. **Subway:** 1, 9 to 66th St.-Lincoln Center; N to57th St.; A, B, C, D to Columbus Circle.

Metropolitan Opera House—Lincoln Center

Columbus Ave. and 64th St. (212) 362-6000

Tickets: $23–$200. Standing room tickets are usually $12–$16, on sale at the Box Office Saturday mornings at 10:00 A.M., for Saturday through Friday per-

formances. Lines start early. **Credit cards:** All major. **Subway:** 1, 9 to 66th St.-
Lincoln Center; N to57th St.; A, B, C, D to Columbus Circle.

New York State Theater—Lincoln Center

20 Lincoln Center Plaza (Columbus Ave. and 63d St.) (212) 870-5570

Tickets: $20–$85. **Credit cards:** All major. **Subway:** 1, 9 to 66th St.-Lincoln
Center; N to57th St.; A, B, C, D to Columbus Circle.

Dance

Ballet, modern dance, jazz dance, tap dance and folk groups: As the dance capital of the world, New York plays host to all. Troupes from abroad and resident
companies perform throughout the year.

The New York City Ballet and American Ballet Theater, the country's top
classical troupes, have regular seasons. Founded in 1948 by the Russian-born
choreographer George Balanchine and his American patron, Lincoln Kirstein,
New York City Ballet remains faithful to Balanchine's view of dance for
dance's sake. One-act plotless works, not story ballets, are the norm. The focus
on the company's two late resident geniuses, Balanchine and Jerome Robbins,
makes for high art. New works by Peter Martins, the current director, continue
the emphasis on distinguished composers. The company has a winter season
(including five weeks of *The Nutcracker*) and a spring season at the **New York
State Theater** at Lincoln Center (*see "Upper West Side"*).

American Ballet Theater, founded in 1939, is more eclectic and its reputation stems from its ballets in different styles and an ability to attract great
dancers. Male virtuosity has been dazzling. The company favors 19th-century
classics and other three-act story ballets in May and June at the **Metropolitan
Opera House** at Lincoln Center. In the fall, a brief season at **City Center** concentrates on one-act works, including premieres by contemporary choreographers like Twyla Tharp.

New York has a variety of theaters and performing spaces that are hospitable
to dance. For raw cutting edge, the loftlike spaces of **The Kitchen, Dance Theater Workshop, P.S. 122** and **St. Mark's Church** are a must (*see listings below*).
Many a newcomer, including Mark Morris, had a start in these well-attended
nonproscenium theaters.

City Center of Music and Drama

131 West 55th St. (between Sixth and Seventh Aves.) (212) 581-1212.

The Paul Taylor Dance Company performs in the spring and the Alvin Ailey
American Dance Theater is here in December. Both are highly popular modern-
dance companies with brilliant dancers. Taylor's choreography ranges in mood
from light to dark and his mastery is unquestioned. Ailey died in 1989 but his
troupe, inspired by African-American heritage, is directed now by Judith Jami-
son, who has brought the dancing to an even more exciting level. The company's signature work is "Revelations," a masterpiece that Ailey set to spirituals.

Dance Theater of Harlem performs here and in other venues. It is an internationally known ballet troupe with a strong neo-Classical style. Arthur Mitchell, once a star at New York City Ballet, used the Balanchine esthetic as a springboard for the company he founded in 1969 as an outlet for black ballet dancers.

The Martha Graham Dance Company appears at City Center when not at the Joyce Theater. Often compared to Picasso and Stravinsky as one of the 20th-century's groundbreaking artists, Graham died in 1991 but left extraordinary works that are powerfully danced by a dedicated company. Highly dramatic pieces inspired by Greek myth share the stage with the striking spare pieces of Graham's early years. (Recent financial problems have put the company's future in doubt.)

As a different icon of American modern dance, Merce Cunningham changed the way audiences look at choreography. The Merce Cunningham Dance Company's works often resemble collages. When composing dances, Cunningham uses coin tossing or other chance procedures to decide which movement follows which and his experiments make him the pope of the avant-garde. Once a City Center regular, the company has recently appeared at Lincoln Center.

Joyce Theater
175 Eighth Ave. (between 18th and 19th Sts.) (212) 242-0800.

The choreographer Eliot Feld created the Joyce, a former movie house, as a theater for dance and a home for his ballet company, now called Ballet Tech. Feld's quirky ballets for young dancers have a loyal following and can be seen in the spring and in August, with a brief season in December. In January, the intimate 500-seat theater produces the "Altogether Different" series that features small experimental troupes. Modern dance predominates during the year with a range wide enough to keep the viewer abreast of what is happening in more than one precinct of dance. The popular Pilobolus troupe appears in July.

Brooklyn Academy of Music
651 Fulton St. (between Rockwell and Ashland Places)
(718) 636-4100.

The Next Wave Festival in the fall makes the Academy the mecca of trendy and serious audiences (sometimes the two overlap). Experimental dance is at the heart of the festival. Pina Bausch, Germany's iconoclastic choreographer, and Sankai Juku, a group working in Japan's post-Hiroshima Butoh style, are staples of the series. Leading American experimental choreographers associated with the Next Wave and the Academy are more unpredictable and include Trisha Brown, Bill T. Jones, Meredith Monk, Lucinda Childs and Mark Morris.

Metropolitan Opera House
Lincoln Center, Columbus Ave. and 64th St. (212) 362-6000.

The Met is the way station for major ballet companies from abroad in July. You might see Russia's Kirov Ballet and Bolshoi Ballet, the Royal Ballet from England or the Paris Opera Ballet. Lincoln Center Festival uses the Met, the New

York State Theater and the Center's smaller theaters for dance attractions in July. *(See "Upper West Side" for full listing)*

Sylvia And Danny Kaye Playhouse At Hunter College

Hunter College, East 68th St. (between Park and Lexington Aves.)
(212) 772-4448.
Modern-dance companies like the joint troupe of Alwin Nikolais and Murray Louis, mixed- media pioneers, have performed here as has the great French mime Marcel Marceau.

—Anna Kisselgoff

OTHER DANCE THEATERS AND STUDIOS

Dance Theater Workshop—Bessie Schonberg Theater 219 W. 19th St. (between Seventh and Eighth Aves.) (212) 924-0077. A couple of flights of stairs and a few twists and turns get you to the Bessie Schonberg Theater, one of the city's best dance venues. The theater packs a lot of performances into its season, with an array of artists from the dance and the music worlds generally performing for one to three nights. Best of all, tickets tend to range from $8 to $15.

Dixon Place at Vineyard 26 309 East26th St. (at Second Ave.) (212) 532-1546. Choreographers, actors, writers, performance artists and musicians can present works in progress here. It remains a playground for starry-eyed wannabes and a refuge for the already established. Tickets prices range from nothing to $12, depending on the event.

Fiorello H. LaGuardia High School for the Performing Arts 108 Amsterdam Ave. (at 64th St.) (212) 496-0700. This high school theater presents mostly student performances, but occasionally offers dance festivals and opportunities for master classes with visiting choreographers. The level of talent is extraordinary, as displayed in the movie "Fame."

Free Range Arts 250 W. 26th St. Fl. 3 (between Seventh and Eighth Aves.) (212) 691-4551. Free Range showcases the works of a wide variety of performers and choreographers at their spacious studio and at other locations around New York.

Isadora Duncan Foundation Studio 141 W. 26th St., 3rd Fl. (between Sixth and Seventh Aves.) (212) 691-5040. This small, attractive studio seats about fifty for its occasional shows of classic Duncan works and dances from contemporary choreographers.

Joyce Soho 155 Mercer St. (between Houston and Prince St.) (212) 431-9233. The Joyce SoHo provides a place for experimental and new choreographers to showcase their work before they venture on to larger performance spaces like the Joyce itself in Chelsea. With 75 freestanding seats, the comfortable loft-like space has a very open feel. Thanks to the lack of columns, every seat in the house is a good one.

The Kitchen 512 West 19th St. (between 10th and 11th Ave.) (212) 255-5793. The careers of avant-garde luminaries such as the composer Philip Glass and the performance artist Laurie Anderson began at The Kitchen. Today the theater continues to present unknown artists in dance, theater, film and everything in between in innovative ways.

La MaMa ETC 74A East 4th St. (between Second Ave. and Bowery) (212) 254-6468. La MaMa's four stages showcase a diverse and sometimes bizarre program of avant-garde dance and performance from American and international troupes.

Merce Cunningham Studio 55 Bethune St. (between Washington and West Sts.) (212) 255-8240. Save yourself some embarrassment and wear socks with no holes. No one—not even Michael Flatley, Mr. Lord of the Dance himself—is allowed to wear shoes at the Merce Cunningham Studio; they have to be left in the lobby to preserve the floor for the dancers. The studio is large and can easily accommodate 200 people.

Movement Research at the Judson Church 55 Washington Square South (212) 477-0351. Since the 1960's, this former house of worship has hosted performances of bold and eclectic new work by experimental dance and performance artists. Movement Research continues the tradition with a free Monday-night series.

Mulberry Street Theater 70 Mulberry St. (between Mulberry and Mott Streets.) (212) 349-0126. Once a public school, this theater space has been transformed effectively into two dance studios and a black-box theater. It is home to H.T. Chen and Dancers, a company that infuses technically vigorous American modern dance with Chinese inflections. In addition to forging ahead with Chen's aesthetic imperative, Mulberry hosts programs that feature the work of unknown and mid-career artists, including "Moving Word," a series devoted to choreography inspired by poetry.

St. Mark's Church in the Bowery 131 East 10th St. (at Second Ave.) (212) 674-6377. Following a devastating fire in 1978, the interior of the city's second-oldest church was restructured into a versatile open space that hosts performing arts, especially dance, as well as religious services.

Squid Dance Performance Space 127 Fulton St. (between Nassau and Williams Sts.) (212) 566-8041. The Squid Dance group presents its own work and rents out this large studio for classes, rehearsals and performances.

Warren Street Performance Loft 46 Warren St. (212) 732-3149. This is an intimate space in which to view the improvisational work of Richard Bull Dance Theatre and other visiting groups.

Film

Whether New York is watching movies or making them, there is no question that this city is in love with film. No American city can account for more cinemas consistently screening independent and foreign movies or showing revivals of old classics. A walk through Manhattan inevitably leads you to a block crowded with a film crew and actors, or a cluster of New York University film students fine tuning their craft on a downtown street corner with an old camera. With New York hosting so many up and coming auteurs it comes as no surprise that several Greats in the movie industry—Martin Scorsese, Woody Allen and Spike Lee—not only call New York home but also feature it prominently in their films, including *Goodfellas, Taxi Driver, Annie Hall, Manhattan* and *Malcolm X.*

So many movies show throughout the city in a single evening that it's important to learn a few basic essentials if you want to find what you're looking for. For starters, tickets to most standard theaters are now nearly $10, and if you buy your tickets in advance through Moviefone at (212) 777-3456, an additional $1.50 will be charged to your credit card. There is *no* surcharge for online orders at **www.moviefone.com.** Moviefone services every major movie house, and it's well worth the price hike if you're hoping to see a popular movie or a recent release. Local papers, including *The New York Times* and the *Village Voice* print times and locations.

NOTE: The serious moviegoer will want to hop on the subway and visit The American Museum of the Moving Image *(see "Queens")*.

MOVIE THEATERS OF NOTE

Angelika Film Center 18 West Houston St. (at Mercer St.) (212) 995-2000. One of New York's favorite cinemas for independent and foreign films, this six screen theater on the border of SoHo and Greenwich Village, offers the extra bonus of midnight screenings on weekends. In addition to the concession stand, the theater's lobby cafe serves higher than standard fare to match its higher prices. It is advisable to buy tickets in advance as shows can sell out quickly.
Subway: B, D, F, Q to Broadway-Laffayette St.

Anthology Film Archives 32 Second Ave. (at Second St.) (212) 505-5181. It's no surprise that this theater has a wealth of unusual material to offer. In 1970 it began as a museum dedicated to avant-garde cinema; true to its history the films shown here are often unknown, but in spite of their obscurity you're likely to find the best of the genre. Check listings for early works from better known directors as well as the chance to catch a loved classic on the big screen. Tickets are only available at the box office.
Subway: F to Second Ave.

Film Forum 209 West Houston St. (between Sixth Ave. and Varick St.) (212) 727-8110. Film buffs throughout the city know this charming three screen theater consistently provides some of the best cinema New York offers, ranging from recent documentaries to silent films. The concession stand offers the best movie theater popcorn in the city. Tickets are *only* sold at the box office and sell out quickly, especially on weekends.
Subway: 1, 9 to Houston St.; C, E to Spring St.

Lincoln Plaza Cinemas 1886 Broadway (at 62d St.) (212) 757-2280. This modest looking, six screen theater tucked away on the cusp of the Upper West Side may be the best place to see foreign and independent movies uptown; but don't expect to find Snow Caps at the concession stand—instead you're more likely to overpay for a smoked salmon sandwich. Still, its devotees steadily show up for new independent releases and events such as the occasional Fellini or Bergman retrospective.
Subway: 1, 9, A, B, C, D to 59th St.-Columbus Circle.

The Quad
34 West 13th Street (between Fifth and Sixth Aves.) (212) 225-8800
If the movies at this four theater cinema were not some of the best independent and foreign shows in town nobody would put up with watching movies on such tiny screens. However its charm as well as its selection of films keep people coming back to this Village standby.
Subway: 4, 5, 6, L, N, R to 14th St.

The Screening Room 54 Varick St. (at Canal St.) (212) 334-2100. Found near the industrial entrance to the Holland Tunnel, this little theater redefines dinner and a movie. One part restaurant and one part cinema, the independent, foreign and classic material found in the theater beats the fare found on the dinner menu. Though the schedule changes, you can count on a regular offering of Sunday brunch followed by a showing of "Breakfast At Tiffany's."
Subway: 1, 9, A, C, E to Canal St.

Sony IMAX at Lincoln Center 1992 Broadway at 68th St. (212) 336-5000.At the top of the four story monolithic movie theater on the Upper West Side is New York's only IMAX theater. The size and scope of the screen is tremendous, the seats on an alarmingly steep angle and the schedule of films range from enhanced Discovery Channel material to animation and science fiction. Some of the features require goggles in order to catch every 3-D effect while others presentations keep to the standard IMAX format, though even those might upset viewers prone to motion sickness.
Subway: 1, 9 to 66th St.

Walter Reade Theater 70 Lincoln Center Plaza (at Columbus Avenue) (212) 875-5600. The clientele at this spacious, state-of-the-art theater located at the heart of the Lincoln Center complex is as varied and diverse as the films that are shown here. Recent festival themes have included Jewish cinema, films celebrating human rights, Iranian cinema and a "dance on camera" series. Also common are retrospectives of particular actors and directors, films by up-and-coming Independent American directors and silent movies accompanied by a live orchestra.
The best ways to keep up with what is going on are via the Film Society of Lin-

coln Center Web site or by phoning the box office. Alternatively, each month's schedule is available outside the theater. Inside, the atmosphere is spacious and the single screen is large. The 268 plush, comfortable seats are set on a sloping floor, which ensures that there is not a bad seat in the house. Tickets (which sell out quickly) are only available at the box office.

Subway: 1, 9 to 66th St.

The Ziegfeld 141 West 54th St. (at Sixth Ave.) (212) 765-7600. One of the few old fashioned movie palaces left in New York that hasn't been renovated into a multiplex, this midtown classic with a bright red decor boasts an enormous screen, seating for nearly 1,200 people, and is the perfect place for a revival of *Gone With the Wind* or the viewing of a modern epic.

Subway: B, D, E to Seventh Ave.; N, R to 57th St.

FILM FESTIVALS

Name any type of film it seems that New York has a festival for it—in fact, it's difficult to find a time of the year when a film festival is *not* occurring somewhere in the city. The **New York Film Festival,** now in it's 38th year, is easily the biggest and most famous of the group. Held annually the end of September or the beginning of October, approximately 20 independent, foreign and big studio films are screened in a two-week run at Lincoln Center's Alice Tully Hall (*see "Upper West Side"*). Tickets go on sale at the box office the first Sunday after Labor Day and they sell quickly so it's advisable to buy tickets early—especially for the much anticipated film that opens the event. Call (212) 875-5600 for details.

Another festival of note, **The New Directors/New Films** held at the Museum of Modern Art is one of the most celebrated cinematic events in the city. The Film Society of Lincoln Center and the Museum of Modern Art co-sponsor this March affair that hosts a series of diverse and daring projects. For the past 28 years the New Directors/New Films festival has offered first glimpses at the work of directors as talented and varied as John Sayles, Steven Spielberg, Peter Greenaway and Whit Stillman. Tickets are sold at the Museum of Modern Art box office, and due to the popularity of the event it is a good idea to buy tickets well in advance.

Among the city's other film festivals is the **Margaret Meade Film Festival** held each November at the Museum of Natural History, which presents anthropological documentaries (212-769-5650). The **Independent Feature Film Market** at the Angelika Film Center in September shows films looking for distribution—but note that tickets for this event are particularly pricey (212-995-2000). The **Lesbian And Gay Film Festival** occurs each June at the Public Theater in the East Village (212-924-3363). And the **First Run Festival** gives New York University's best and brightest students a chance to show off their efforts at this April event (212-924-3363).

Institutes of World Culture

Asia Society   UPPER EAST SIDE
725 Park Ave. (between 70th and 71st Sts.) (212) 517-ASIA
www.asiasociety.org

The Asia Society was founded by John D. Rockefeller III to encourage better relations between the U.S. and Asia by introducing Americans to the cultures of Asia
and the Pacific. Scholarly symposia, films, public programs and publications have
long been central to its mission, with an emphasis on the arts. Today, its elegant
galleries feature changing exhibitions for connoisseurs as well as the general public.

Admission: $4; $2, students and seniors; free, Thur., 6–8 P.M. **Credit cards:** All
major. **Hours:** Tues.–Sat., 11 A.M.–6 P.M.; Thur., 11 A.M.–8 P.M.; Sun.,
noon–5 P.M. **Services:** Tours, gift shop, lectures.

China Institute In America   UPPER EAST SIDE
125 East 65th St. (between Park and Lexington Aves.) (212) 744-818

Housed in an elegant red-brick building on the Upper East Side, the China
Institute offers Chinese language classes and hosts lectures, films and discussions. If you're fascinated by Chinese culture, but don't feel up to the daunting
task of learning Mandarin, you can also sign up for calligraphy and Chinese art
classes. Courses for children are also available. The institute's gallery hosts periodic shows of Chinese art.

Admission: $3, suggested donation; $2, suggested for students and seniors;
Free Tues. and Thurs. 6–8 P.M. **Credit cards:** Cash only. **Hours:** Mon., Wed.,
Fri.–Sat., 10 A.M.–5 P.M.; Tues. and Thurs., 10 A.M.–8 P.M.; Sun., 1 P.M.–5
P.M. **Services:** Gift shop.

French Institute and Florence Gould Hall MIDTOWN EAST
55 East 59th St. (between Park and Madison Aves.) (212) 355-6100

A cultural institute for Francophile New Yorkers and the city's French community, the French Institute/Alliance Française offers language courses as well as a
variety of cultural events with French themes. Florence Gould Hall features
films, concerts and dance, while the smaller Tinker Auditorium holds lectures,
receptions and cabaret performances. In 1996 the organization opened a downtown branch at 95 Wall Street.

Credit cards: All major. **Hours:** Mon.–Thur., 9 A.M.–8 P.M.; Fri., 9 A.M.–6
P.M.; Sat., 9 A.M.–1:30 P.M. **Services:** Theater, library.

Goethe-Institut/German Cultural Center UPPER EAST SIDE
1014 Fifth Ave. (between 82d and 83d Sts.) (212) 439-8700

A cultural institute funded by the German government, the Goethe-Institut
promotes German language and culture abroad. The New York center, one of
roughly 150 branches in some 60 countries, organizes cultural events, including

lectures, art exhibitions and concerts of contemporary classical music. Occupying a Beaux-Arts limestone townhouse that was formerly the residence of a U.S. Ambassador to Germany, the institute also collaborates with other organizations around the city in presenting events such as the annual "Recent Films from Germany" series at the Museum of Modern Art. The organization operates a lending and reference library at its Fifth Avenue headquarters, and offers language courses through New York University's Deutsches Haus.

Admission: Free. **Hours:** Tues. and Thur., 10 A.M.–7 P.M.; Wed. and Fri., 10 A.M.–5 P.M.; Sat. noon–5 P.M.; closed Sun. **Services:** Lectures, concerts.

Japan Society   MIDTOWN EAST
333 East 47th St. (between First and Second Aves.) (212) 832-1155

Founded in 1907, the Japan Society made its permanent home on East 47th Street in 1971. The society's mission is to promote relations between the U.S. and Japan and to bring New Yorkers a wonderful blend of the traditional and the contemporary in Japanese culture. Events include regular film series, art exhibits and live theater. If you want to learn the ins and outs of Japanese conversation, the society also offers language lessons of all levels.

Hours: Tues.–Sun., 11:00 A.M.–6:00 P.M. **Services:** Lectures.

Museum of Jewish Heritage—
A Living Memorial to the Holocaust
18 First Pl., Battery Pk. City (at West St.) (212) 968-1800
www.mjhnyc.org

Many people wondered if it was really necessary: Why build a museum dedicated to Jewish heritage in a city that boasted, just for starters, the Jewish Museum and the Eldridge Street Synagogue? Did the nation need another Holocaust memorial in addition to the Holocaust Museum in Washington, D.C.? Since opening in 1997, the Museum of Jewish Heritage—A Living Memorial to the Holocaust, has quieted most of the skeptics. Strongest on the social history of European Jews and Israel, the museum is dedicated to living history, and to recording and preserving the memories of Holocaust survivors, rescuers and witnesses. On the Hudson River, with a view of the Statue of Liberty setting off the Star of David formed by the six sides of its impressive granite structure, the institution is a dignified reminder of New York's important place in Jewish history.

Admission: $7, general; $5, students and seniors; children under 5, free.
Hours: Sun.–Wed., 9 A.M.–5 P.M.; Thur.,9 A.M.–8 P.M.; Friday, 9 A.M.–3 P.M.; eve of Jewish holidays 9 A.M.–3 P.M.last admission one hour before closing.

Ukrainian Museum   EAST VILLAGE
203 Second Ave. (between 12th and 13th Sts.) (212) 228-0110
www.brama.com/ukrainian_museum.

The Ukrainian Museum is in the East Village, a neighborhood that is home to a small but thriving Ukrainian population. The museum houses permanent and changing exhibitions of Ukrainian arts and crafts, including photos, documents, coins, stamps, textiles, costumes, Easter eggs and rare books.

Admission: $3; $2, seniors and students; children under 12 free. **Credit cards:** Cash or checks only. **Hours:** Wed.–Sun., 1 P.M.–5 P.M. **Services:** Food, gift shop, lectures, tours.

Yeshiva University Museum   WASHINGTON HEIGHTS
2520 Amsterdam Ave. (between 185th and 186th Sts.) (212) 960-5390

Begun in 1886 as an elementary yeshiva for Orthodox Jewish boys, the school expanded during the early 1900's to include a theological seminary and the first Orthodox Jewish high school in the United States. Yeshiva College, with its campus in Washington Heights, was formed in 1929, and in 1946 it was incorporated as a university. The museum features exhibits and cultural artifacts relating to Jewish history as well as some secular art.

Admission: $3; $2, seniors and children. **Credit cards:** Cash only.
Hours: Tues.–Thur., 10:30 A.M.–5 P.M.; Sun., noon–6 P.M.
Services: Gift shop, lectures, tours.

For the latest information on restaurants, hotels, concerts, nightlife, sporting events and more, check online at New York Today, the *New York Times* website devoted entirely to life in New York City: www.nytoday.com.

Shopping in New York

What appeals most to out-of-towners about a shopping spree in New York is the myriad number of possibilities the city affords. From the world famous department stores to the seemingly infinite variety of hundreds of little shops, the New York experience has no equal. Even the relatively brief number of pages below reveals that this is not more New York hype but a mere statement of fact. Everything you've heard is true: you can buy anything here (and it's a lot more fun than surfing the Internet!).

UPTOWN SHOPPING

Shopping in Manhattan above 34th Street is a little like ascending a Himalayan peak. The foot of the mountain is dense and rich with store growth, but there is a lot of undesirable vegetation. Ascend to the lofty heights of the peak and the views are spectacular, but the expenses are so steep that it might make your blood thin.

The trail head for the expedition is **Herald Square,** home, of course, to **Macy's,** made famous by Thanksgiving parades. Navigating this department store, which takes up an entire city block, is neither easy nor particularly satisfying. Best to stick to the subterranean floors where bargains are most abundant.

Move up Broadway from 34th and come smack into the heart of the **garment district.** The claustrophobic emporia that crowd the streets between Broadway and 9th Avenue are a paradise for do-it-yourself *fashionistas*. Every fabric, button, feather, or bit of leather trim ever imagined is available here. Shops tend to specialize in one niche or another, so if you do not see what you want ask the proprietor to direct you to a store that will.

Continue walking north up Broadway and emerge at the recently cleansed and sanitized **Times Square.** The goods news is that most of the triple X pornography is gone, the bad news is that there is mostly schlock in its place. But for those who cannot leave the city without a Yankees baseball cap or a Statue of Liberty headpiece made of green Styrofoam—this is the place. Beside the innumerable trinket vendors, **Disney, Warner Brothers** and the **World Wrestling Federation** all have stores here.

Style mavens with something a little classier in mind should make a quick break east and start strolling up Fifth Avenue. As the famous sites of St. Patrick's Cathedral and Rockefeller Center loom ahead, **Saks Fifth Avenue,** the venerable clothier to the ladies who lunch, will appear on the right. The store has undergone extensive remodeling on the upper floors and is almost up to its plush reputation.

The first floor is home to a vast array of upscale accessories and cosmetics. Grab a Prada handbag or snag a $75 lipstick from the house makeup brand By Terry. The second floor is home to established designers like Max Mara, Bill

Terry. The second floor is home to established designers like Max Mara, Bill Blass, and Zoran. The 3rd and 5th floors are for those who want to sample the latest concoctions from the emerging and lesser known designers like Australian Collette Dinnigan or Alexander McQueen.

Fifth Avenue from 50th Street to Central Park is one of the richest shopping corridors in the world. As you parade up the Avenue, be sure not to miss two of the more unique offerings. Whatever you think of the clothes, the **Versace** store at 52nd Street is worth a quick stop. Remodeled to look like an 18th century palazzo, it comes complete with a marble facade, a sweeping serpentine staircase, and elaborate mosaics.

The first floor of **Takashimaya,** the New York entry of the Japanese Department Store chain, is an art gallery. Instead of being spritzed with perfume or peddled lipsticks, customers are treated to traditional wares like ink drawings on fine linen papers and artistic gardening items—think delicate pearl-handled scissors for trimming miniature bonsai trees instead of clunky bush pruners.

Downstairs, the Tea Box is a restful oasis to stop for lunch. The menu features fusion Nippon-American cuisine like roast chicken sandwiches with wasabi mustard and smoked salmon served on pressed rice cakes, as well as a large selection of teas.

As Fifth Avenue meets Central Park at 60th Street, it suddenly morphs from a commercial hub into a fancy residential boulevard. But right at the corner of 59th is a landmark institution for children of all ages: **F.A.O. Schwartz.** For better or for worse, every outlandish toy your child has ever dreamed of is here in a huge city-block long building. The bad news are the prices (you know, if you have to ask . . .), but the good news is that small people are free to mount the life-sized stuffed elephants or drive the pint-sized Porsches as they please.

Go east one block and yet another Gold Coast emerges. It seems that every upscale merchant on the planet has a store front on Madison Avenue between 57th Street and 72nd. There are names you would expect, like **Calvin Klein** and **Ralph Lauren,** and names that baffle like **Mount Blanc**—why a pen manufacturer needs a fancy retail showcase is a bit mysterious.

Almost any store offers a wide variety of sumptuous merchandise, but a few are particularly entertaining. Both **Nicole Farhi** and **Donna Karan** have recently opened stores (a step away from each other on 60th) that offer very personal statement s about their vision of style. Farhi's showcase is wide open with clean lines and a muted palette. The clothes range from simple cotton separates to orange leather shirt coats. The main floor is suspended above a lower level, which houses Nicole's, a restaurant that serves Mediterranean food and is a good place to see and be seen.

Donna's opus is infused with the color and energy that have been the designer's hallmark. Patrons here can browse not only for the newest fashion collections, but also shop for antiques and bric-a-brac that Donna herself has collected from European flea markets.

The other must stop on Madison is **Barneys.** Since emerging from bankruptcy, the once infamously snooty retailer has a kinder, gentler persona—even women who no longer fit a size 6 can expect service. The prices remain as high-handed as ever—Pashmina shawls, for example, hundreds of dollars at most stores, start at $3,000.

Before getting lost up Madison, it is worth a quick detour to Lexington to visit the ultimate capital of American consumer consumption: **Bloomingdale's.** In *Moscow on the Hudson,* Robin Williams' Russian character is lured into defecting by the overwhelming material plenty on display here. Now, as then, it is a dizzying display of overabundance and a fitting conclusion to a shopping spree, Manhattan style.

—Leslie Kaufman

DEPARTMENT STORES

Barneys New York
660 Madison Ave. (at 61st St.) (212) 826-8900
2 World Financial Center

Once known for their controversial and whimsical store windows, Barneys continues to be the purveyor of what is hip and fashion chic. The store provides cutting-edge designer fashions, accessories and cosmetics, and showcases up-and-coming visionaries, both international and homegrown. Fashionistas usually go straight to the shoe section first to do some serious business. What may vie for more attention than the store itself are the warehouse sales. Here native and tourist hipsters compete to find the perfect black Italian suit, and other huge savings. Call ahead to learn about upcoming warehouse sales, held at 255 West 17th Street (between Seventh and Eighth Aves.).

Bergdorf Goodman
754 Fifth Ave. (at 58th St.) (212) 753-7300

Shopping for a tiara? Bergdorf is the suitable shopping mecca for royalty, or those who live like they are. For all others, if you find the place intimidating, it should be. The posh and refined atmosphere complements the high-end and exclusive fashions of Badgley Mischka, Yohji Yamamoto, Givenchy, and Dolce and Gabbana. A worthy neighbor of Tiffany's and the Plaza, Bergdorf maintains an air of privilege as provider of luxe goods for the Park Avenue circuit. The elegant emporium is particularly excellent in housewares, haute couture, jewelry and shoes. Bergdorf was the first to sell London-based Jo Malone's skincare in New York, to the delight of weary Concorde jet-setters.

Bloomingdale's
1000 Third Ave. (at 59th St.) (212) 355-5900

More upscale than Macy's though still crowded, Bloomingdale's is a place full of surprises if you go at the right time. Great for shoes, coats, cosmetics and home furnishings, the store boasts a huge men's department for the fashion-conscious who demand a certain cut and design. Excellent selections of high-end men's and women's apparel include American classic designers Ralph Lauren, Calvin

Klein and Donna Karan plus the sexy international threads of Helmut Lang, Jean Paul Gaultier and Gucci. Salespeople are young, friendly and accessible.

Felissimo
10 West 56th St. (at Fifth Ave.) (212) 956-4438

Remodeled for the new 21st century, this Japanese-based store is dedicated to providing beautifully designed goods for the home. Felissimo embraces an eastern influence with products such as amulets, hand-made journals, bath oils and soaps, aromatherapy incense, and organic cotton sheets. While designing a calm and meditative home atmosphere, Felissimo also provides alternatives to the hard edge and high-tech toys of the digital age with multifunctional furniture that is user and spirit-friendly. With new purchases in hand, sit for a cup in the tearoom to take pause and collect your thoughts amidst a busy shopping day.

Henri Bendel
712 Fifth Ave. (at 56th St.) (212) 247-1100

Bendel provides an excellent selection of designer dresses, cashmere sweaters, shoes and bags. On the first floor take a look at the first-rate selection of make-up. Then pick up the signature brown and white striped Bendel bags in a variety of sizes and shapes. Your eye will be drawn to the large circular staircase that winds up the entire store, enabling you to spot the silk scarf on the third floor that will go perfectly with the cashmere twin set you are holding on the second.

Lord & Taylor
424 Fifth Ave. (between 38th and 39th St.) (212) 391-3344

This venerable store offers stock with reasonable prices, regular sales, and some big name established designers. Shoppers browse mostly for dresses, bags, and work suits. Although not competitive in terms of high-end or trendy fashion, the store holds a certain modest charm of shopping days past with the signature red rose logo and hand painted glass elevators. Think quiet, conservative and tasteful. One may browse quickly around for what's on sale such as summer floral dresses or strappy sandals, but what many women buy on their lunch breaks here is hosiery. There is also a charming restaurant here, and like Saks, Lord & Taylor is famous for its Christmas windows.

Macy's
151 West 34th St. (between Broadway and Seventh Ave.)
(212) 695-4400

Macy's is the shopper's common denominator. The largest department store in the world is also one of the most crowded because you can find everything for everyone. Macy's bridal registry is one of the most popular and practical in town. Known for one-day sales and great Cellar bargains, you can find essentials for the home from Calvin Klein sheets to Calphalon pans to Henckel knives. Or you can simply browse the massive perfume and cosmetic department on the first floor. The coat, bathing suit and shoe sections are exceptionally large. The junior department packs a dense array of trendy gear over the din of pop music.

Saks Fifth Avenue
611 Fifth Ave. (between 49th and 50th Sts.) (212) 753-4000

Saks can be described in three words: sophistication, style and selection. In a coveted spot across from Rockefeller Center, Saks has been part of New York for almost a century, selling to an upscale crowd. Saks provides most high-end labels for both women and men. The store's private label, SFA, offers more affordable yet similar styles as current designer fashions. Browse through each well-organized section for apparel, accessories, and cosmetics. If you visit during the holidays, be sure to check out the famous Christmas windows before sweeping in to pick up an early present of Ferragamo cashmere shoes for yourself.

Takashimaya
693 Fifth Ave. (bet 54th and 55th Sts.) (212) 350-0100

Exquisite and spare, this is Zen shopping. Enjoy the beautifully arranged flowers and garden essentials on the first floor. Other floors present home, bath, and fashion accessories both luxe and minimalist. Takashimaya seduces customers into browsing with a new sense of peace after the sensory overload of Fifth Avenue. Candles, lamps, pajamas and robes of the finest quality will urge you to ponder why one should bother ever leaving home again. From a perfect presentation of soaps to charming beaded floral barrettes, high-end household gifts are for people with an eye for design.

DOWNTOWN SHOPPING

The premiere shopping district of downtown Manhattan is a square mile known as SoHo, or South of Houston (New York pronounces it "How-stun"). A jumble of cobblestone streets and industrial-era loft buildings that once served as factories, SoHo grew to prominence two decades ago as an artists' paradise—a place where an aspiring painter or sculptor could grab 6,000 square feet of raw space in crowded Manhattan. That's no longer true, of course. The artists created cachet, which in turn attracted rock stars, fashion models and then anyone with loads of cash, and prices soared.

The creative community has largely been driven out, but the cavernous spaces they once inhabited have been converted to galleries and lots and lots of fabulous stores. Everything from vinyl platform boots to minimalist beige bed linens is available in this richly varied shopping district, but (fair warning) everything costs top dollar.

To start indulging simply stroll the main drag on **West Broadway.** Plenty of big-name fashion designers have large flagship stores here including **Rene Lazard, Eileen Fisher,** and **Ralph Lauren,** who has devoted an immense space entirely to his new sports line. **D&G,** the downtown flagship for those fashion runway bad boys Dolce & Gabbanna, wins the award for most neon.

Other better than garden-variety merchants include **Otto Tootsie Plohound,** which offers the latest in platform and wedged footwear in a setting that is more like a dance club than a store. **Dom,** a state-of-the art inflatable furniture and home decorations emporium, is ideal for new homeowners or parents with college-age children. **Anthropologie** has a whimsical selection of velvet slip dresses, antiqued candlesticks, and wicker furniture to go with its mod-attic decor. The elegant **Rizzoli** bookstore is a nice stop for those in this post-Internet era who still like to smooth the pages of a new text instead of just clicking on them. And **Kate's Paperie** on Spring Street is a veritable wonderland of textured and swirled papers.

Prices for clothing drop precipitously as you move east from West Broadway to **Broadway,** where a much grittier but just as lively apparel scene emerges. Storefront after storefront here displays sportswear, jeans, and workman's boots at prices you can haggle over. Teens clued to the hip-hop culture use **Transit** as the bellwether for what brand of active-wear will be cool on the street in the upcoming season.

Those individuals who are eager for something eclectic or unique should continue east off the beaten track and be rewarded with **NoLIta,** meaning North of Little Italy. This neighborhood still clings to its turn-of-the century immigrant neighborhood feel. The streets are small and cluttered, and locals still hang from the fire escapes of the tenements to have conversations or yell at wayward children. And it was here, at the Ravenite Social Club on Mulberry Street that mob boss John Gotti Sr. directed the notorious Gambino family.

Now the byways of this colorful area teem with tiny boutiques and stores offering little gems like vintage Pucci girdles or hand-blown glass bowls. The best bet is to meander among streets such as **Mulberry** and **Elizabeth** and look into whatever catches your fancy. If you have a passion for headwear, do not miss hat designer **Kelly Christy,** who can frequently be found outside her shop sipping coffee with friends. Or if you want something with a slinky fit, drop by **About Time** to order a made to measure slip dress in bedroom peach silk. **Just Shades** has lamp covers in every conceivable shape and material. Need a leopard print number for the living room? Just ask!

Native New Yorkers do their heavy duty shopping to the north of SoHo in the far less rarified atmosphere of Lower Chelsea and Union Square. Neither of these areas are much for the eyes, but they have become a kind of urban mall for the locals, which is both good and bad. **Fifth Avenue** right above 14th Street is awash with the same ubiquitous chains that clog suburbia: **Gap, Banana Republic, J. Crew, Body Works,** etc. But the avenue is also home to some more colorful alternatives in chain shopping. There is **Bebe,** which specializes in a kind of sophisticated slut look, **Zara, Ann Taylor,** which has career clothing with a very Continental feel, and **Club Monaco,** the Canadian chain recently bought by Polo Ralph Lauren that specializes in Gucci and Prada knockoffs.

Armani has an appropriately sleek and silvered showplace in this district—the seductive minimalist café in the back is an ideal quiet place to stop for an in-between-purchases cappuccino. Prices here are steep, so if you want Armani or any designer for less head west, where the triumvirate of off-price designer labels—**T J Maxx, Filene's Basement** and **Loehmann's**—have made homes a block apart from each other on Sixth Avenue. Really committed bargain hunters take the train to the end of the island for **Century 21,** four floors of designer madness housed at the foot of the World Trade Center. *(See "Bargain Shopping" below)*.

If you leave Fifth by heading east instead of west, you run into upper Union Square, which has become a corridor of home decorating stores. The essential stop here is **ABC Carpet & Home,** an eclectic, expensive bazaar of furnishing and linens. The store is housed in two pieces on either side of Broadway at 17th street. On one side, customers wade through nothing but piles upon piles of rugs—everything from knotted Persians to hand-loomed Italians. The main building is full of luxuriant clutter, where one can spot everything from hand-painted raw silk pillows to wrought iron tables with mosaic tile tops. Also, be sure to drop by the restaurant where everything—yep, even the painted sun-flower bowl that your Cream of Cauliflower soup came in—is for sale.

One last stop on the downtown tour that fashionistas will not want to skip is **Jeffrey's.** Located, unlikely enough, at the far west end of 14th Street in the Meat Packing District, Jeffrey's is a palace of excess (think pony skin belts and fur-lined stiletto heels), but what better way to sum up a trip of shopping in New York?

—*Leslie Kaufman*

BARGAIN SHOPPING

Bargains, bargains come and get your bargains! Manhattan, even these days, is full of hawkers. Try the **Diamond District,** 47th Street between Fifth and Sixth Avenues. You can get an emerald ring for one-fifth the price of a similar ring at Tiffany's, but you have to know what you're doing. Take a course. Bring a jeweler. Or go by yourself, if you dare, but ask for a gemological certificate.

It's not as tough to find real bargains in clothes, but you still have to know where to go. Generally speaking, stay off Madison Avenue, or, if you must go there, go at night and window shop. During the daylight hours, try **Daffy's** ("Clothing Bargains for Millionaires"). It's a badly organized, slightly neurotic atmosphere, but persevere.

And without doubt, take a subway (F Train to Delancey) to **Orchard Street.** This is one of the most unchanged neighborhoods in Manhattan, and it's easy to imagine the hustle and bustle of this place around the turn of the century. The street has a tarnished reputation. People say the bargains are only pseudo-bargains, but check out **Ben Freedman,** an old-world cheapie paradise with sidewalk racks that feature $5 leather belts and $6 ties. And don't miss the string of leather shops, and **Joe's Fabrics** (102 Orchard St. at Delancey St.), a kaleidoscope of linens, velvets, silks and damasks. The secret on Orchard Street is haggling: Don't be afraid. You don't have to be a pro. Just try walking out. . . . and see what happens. Think of what you want to pay, and just keep repeating it on your way to the door. It's fun, and you'll probably get what you want. But don't play the game if you're not serious or you'll end up with some angry merchants! In New York City, the greatest bargains are in jewelry and men's and women's clothes. (For kids, try a local thrift shop, or, if you just want to dream, look at the smocked dresses in Bonpoint on Madison Avenue—they'll only set you back a couple of hundred dollars.)

If you arrive just before or even better just after Christmas, or in mid-summer, check out the sales in the world's best stores. As you as you hit the pavement, open the daily paper and start researching; the sales in the finest stores usually appear in the first couple of pages. If you see advertisements for sales at Fratelli Rossetti, Etro, Hermes, Tanino Crisci or Henri Bendel, do not delay. Even on sale, the prices won't be cheap, but you won't find merchandise of this quality anywhere else, including the so-called premium outlet malls.

The other secret of New York City bargains is the sample sale, in which the last season's designer merchandise is offered at a fraction of the price. These sales go on all year, and many appear in *Time Out New York,* a weekly magazine that can be purchased at any news stand. To give you an idea, take the Echo Scarf sample sale: silk scarves that normally sell for between $60 and $90 can be found in cardboard boxes labeled $5, $10 and $15. Portolano, an Italian leather glove manufacturer, holds sample sales for three days every month. Here the merchandise is overruns, rather than samples, so you can buy more than one of each. Delicious kid gloves come in all the regular colors, with tangerine and deep purple and canary yellow thrown in, for between $35 and $45, about half what they might be in an uptown shop, if you could find them.

And remember, New York is full of young and older designers, men and women who might sell to the fancy stores but, if you know where they are, run sales of their own merchandise, at significant savings, on a by-appointment basis. Take Gabrielle Carlson, a charming middle-aged woman with a cherubic grin, who runs a business on one of the seedier blocks of the Lower East Side. Just when you think you were out of your mind to come looking for designer clothes in a walk-up tenement, she opens her door and unveils her luminous up-to-the-minute ladies' clothes, at near give-away prices. (But note: it's alright to bargain here, too, within limits, and only after you've established a certain rapport.)

For men's clothes, there are dozens of places to shop. If you're ready to splurge on a custom-made suit or jacket (don't gasp, it's almost affordable), try **Saint Laurie Merchant Tailors,** a company that used to sell racks of inexpensive knock-offs downtown but now has moved to Park Avenue. The shop is fun to visit; there are tables full of bolts of wonderful fine wools and heathery tweeds lying around with fascinating descriptions of "Scottish Saxony" and "Whiskey and Camel Glen Plaid," along with the price tags for suit or sportscoat. You can also choose your style: fitted like an Italian count or baggy like a Boston Brahmin. All this for only $899, more or less. Jackets run about $699. (They will also make suits for women, in a few, highly traditional styles, for roughly the same price.)

There is a raft of men's discount clothing stores downtown in what is called the **Flatiron District,** named after the neighborhood's well-known skyscraper.

Moe Ginsburg is the most famous, but the prices aren't much different from those you'd find in a suburban discount mall. Instead, try the **Gilcrest Clothing Inc.**

And while you're there, pop over to the landmark **Ladies' Mile,** along Sixth Avenue below 21st Street. There, you'll see some familiar names: **T.J. Maxx, Bed, Bath and Beyond,** and **Filene's Basement.** But you've never seen them in more magnificent quarters: these are buildings that once housed the city's finest stores, and whose wedding-cake columns have recently been restored. Some say that the merchandise in these stores is picked especially for chic Manhattan shoppers, and is better than what comes to the suburbs. See what you think. While you're in the neighborhood, check out the thrift shops just around the corner. The **Housing Works Thrift Shop** on West 17th Street (between Sixth and Seventh Aves.) is a gem, for men's and women's clothes, shoes and best of all, for furniture, with items like a great-looking oval Biedermyer center table for $200. Also try the **Out of Our Closet Thrift Shop** a block away on West 18th Street (*see also "Vintage & Thrift Shops"*). They specialize in the glamorous, for both men's and women's clothes.

That's just a quick survey. New York City is awash with bargains in clothes, jewelry, furniture and fabrics. And if you're in town on a weekend, don't forget the indoor and outdoor flea markets that operate all year round on and near the corner of Sixth Avenue and West 26th Street. Recently, some developers announced plans to build yet another multi-story mega-building on the site of several of the flea markets. But, like any true New Yorkers, the entrepreneurs were undaunted. They just moved next door.

—*Tracie Rozhon*

Diamond District:

M Khordipour Enterprises 10 West 47th St. (at Fifth Ave.) (212) 869-2198

Peachtree Jewelers Inc. 580 Fifth Ave. (at 47th St.) (212) 398-1758

Orchard Street:

Arivel Fashions Corp. 150 Orchard St. (between Rivington and Stanton Sts.) (212) 673-8992

Ben Freedman 137 Orchard St. (at Delancey St.) (212) 674-0854

Joe's Fabrics 102 Orchard St. (near Delancey St.) (212) 674-7089

Klein's of Monticello 105 Orchard St. (at Delancey St.) (212) 966-1453

Rita's Leather Fair 176 Orchard St. (between Stanton and East Houston Sts.) (212) 533-2756

Soha's Leather 132 Orchard St. (at Delancey St.) (212) 674-8868

Discount Clothing Stores:

Century 21 22 Cortlandt St. (between Broadway and Church St.) (212) 227-9092

Daffy's 111 Fifth Ave. (at 18th St.) (212) 529-4477. (Other locations: 335 Madison Ave. at 44th St., 135 East 57th St. between Park and Lexington Aves.)

Filene's Basement 620 Sixth Ave. (at 18th St.) (212) 620-3100. (Other location: 2222 Broadway at 79th St.)

Gilcrest Clothing Inc. 900 Broadway, 3d Floor (at 20th St.) (212) 254-8933

Loehmann's 101 Seventh Ave. (at 16th St.) (212) 352-0856

Moe Ginsburg 162 Fifth Ave. (at 21st St.) (212) 242-3482

Saint Laurie Merchant Tailors 350 Park Ave. (between 51st and 52d St.) (212) 473-0100

T J Maxx 620 Sixth Ave. (at 18th St.) (212) 229-0875

Syms 400 Park Ave. (at 54th St.) (212) 317-8200. (Other location: 42 Trinity Pl. at Rector St.)

ANTIQUES

New York is the largest center for antiques and collectibles in the world, a giant bazaar stocked with period furniture, china, glassware, textiles, books, coins, jewelry, rugs and toys from—you name it—just about anywhere on earth. Collectors who shop in New York are either ecstatic or frustrated by the sheer abundance and the difficulty of finding exactly what they seek—an American 19th century trotting-horse weathervane, a Ming vase, an 18th century desk from Versailles, a Mickey Mouse toy or a baseball bat signed by Babe Ruth.

Since the 1980's, antiques dealers have followed art dealers out of storefront galleries and into new quarters in town houses, art-gallery buildings, converted factories, warehouses and their own apartments. Rents are lower and spaces larger and more secure. Many dealers now see clients by appointment only.

Antiquing in Manhattan today differs dramatically from that of yesteryear, when pursuing silver teapots, paperweights and tapestries meant browsing in neatly clustered and dimly-lighted curio shops along Third Avenue, 57th Streeet and University Place. Collectors with limited time plan ahead: they put together an itinerary, often letting the dealer know beforehand about the type of pieces they wish to see. Dealers are busy too, especially world-class dealers like James J. Lally, a specialist in Chinese art and Michael Ward, a dealer in antiquities and medieval art. To present scholarly exhibitions with catalogues in their museum-style galleries, they travel as much as some of their clients.

For the people who prefer a hands-on experience, New York is host to about 60 antiques fairs each year, 10 times as many as were held in the mid-1960's. Dealers come from throughout the world to participate in fairs, the most notable of which take place in the Park Avenue and Lexington Avenue armories. The Asian Art Fair, a Spring event, is often described as the best of the art and antiques shows in Manhattan. The preeminent dealer in Asian art, Robert H. Ellsworth, explained its success, saying, "Even if you spent a year going around the world, you would never be able to see all the fine Asian art exhibited here."

So hot are the fairs and auctions that foreign dealers like Giuseppe Eskenazi,

London's leading dealer in Chinese art, rent galleries to present private exhibitions. And some dealers go farther: they open an annex in New York. In 1978, Didier Aaron, a prominent Parisian dealer in French 18th century palace-quality furniture, opened a gallery in a town house on East 67th Street. Then in late 1999, after exhibiting at the International Fine Art and Antique Dealers Fair each fall the last four years, the Art Deco dealers Robert and Cheska Valois of Paris opened a New York version of Galerie Valois, also on East 67th Street. The Valois gallery in New York operates in partnership with Barry Friedman, another Art Deco dealer, specializing in furniture and decorations by masters like Jean-Michel Frank, Eileen Gray, Jacques-Emile Ruhlmann and Jean Dunand.

Antiques and collectibles are also sold year round at the Pier shows on the Hudson River and at flea markets, the most enduring of which is held on weekends at a parking lot on the Avenue of the Americas at 26th Street.

As fast as antiques and collectibles turn over these days in shops, fairs and at flea markets, they move even more swiftly at auctions. The largest gatherings of antiques enthusiasts take place at the auctions, especially at the celebrity auctions organized by New York's largest auction houses—Sotheby's and Christie's, both of which dramatically expanded in 1999. Sotheby's doubled the size of its 20-year-old house at York Avenue and 72d Street, and Christie's moved into much larger quarters on 49th Street in Rockefeller Center.

Now antiquing is changing again, said William West Stahl Jr., an executive vice president at Sotheby's: "We've added thousands of new clients since we started auctioning on the Web."

—*Rita Reif*

Barry Friedman 32 East 67th St. (between Park and Madison Aves.) (212) 794-8950

Didier Aaron 32 East 67th St. (between Park and Madison Aves.) (212) 988-5248

J. J. Lally & Co. 41 East 57th St. (at Madison Ave.) (212) 371-3380

Michael Ward Antiques 10 Greene St. (between Canal and Grand Sts.) (212) 966-5759

WaterMoon Gallery 211 West Broadway (near Franklin St.) (212) 925-5556 Specializes in fine Chinese antique softwood furniture, Tibetan antique furniture. Tibetan carpets and a selection of Chinese porcelain and ceramics from the Neolithic era up to the Ming Dynasty. Along with a unique and changing collection of decorative items, WaterMoon has an extensive selection of Chinese and Miao textiles. To complement the collection of antiques, WaterMoon carries contemporary artwork by young Chinese artists, most of whose work has not previously been shown outside of China.

AUCTIONS

Manhattan has always attracted art lovers and collectors, and the local auction houses are among the world's most renowned. They have long provided lavish forums for those who can afford to indulge their passions and find those must-have items to add to their personal collections. If you are interested in buying, be sure to attend the sale preview and study the catalogue for price estimates before you raise your paddle and bid. For those who are not in the market to buy, simply watching the ceremonious sale of items pulled from the canon of art history or even the homes of pop culture's greatest icons can be a delight. Check local newspapers and magazines such as *The New York Times* and *Time Out New York* for dates and events.

Christie's
20 Rockefeller Plz. (49th St. between Fifth and Sixth Aves.) (212)636-2000.

This British institution boasts a history that dates more than two centuries back. Items that have graced the block here include everything from Henri Matisse canvases to an Academy Award won by Clark Gable. Although this house is best known for sales that make headlines, it also has departments for items such as wine, cars, coins and sports memorabilia. The sister branch, Christie's East (219 East 67th St. between Second and Third Aves., (212) 606-0400) is relatively modest.

Sotheby's
1334 York Ave. (at 72nd St.) (212) 606-7000

From its humble beginnings in 1744 as a London book dealer, this house has grown to include branches all over the world. Sotheby's now handles the sale of great masters such as Renoir as well as rare books like a first edition copy of Dickens' "A Christmas Carol." Arcade, a separate house at the same location handles more moderately priced sales.

Guernsey's
108 East 73rd St. (between Park and Lexington Aves.) (212) 794-2280

One of New York's smaller auction houses, this institution is an esteemed source for modern collections. One 2000 auction focused entirely on graffiti art.

Swann Galleries
104 East 25th St. (between Park and Lexington Aves.) (212) 243-5343

This specialized house devotes itself to the printed word and items such as photographs, autographs, antique maps and atlases.

Tepper Galleries
110 East 25th St. (between Park and Lexington Aves.) (212) 677-5300

To simply say that estates are sold off here would not do justice to the fine pieces that pass through this house. Items such as antique furniture, fine silver, jewelry, carpets and fine works of art can all be purchased.

SPECIALTY STORES
Beauty & Spa

Aveda Salon & Spa 456 West Broadway (212) 473-0280 Known for their plant-derived hair products, Aveda has branched out to provide more scents and sensibility. The Aveda spa offers a truly satisfying aromatherapy massage. Through consultation, the super-friendly staff will know to work out the kinks in your mouse hand or your shoulder that carries too much in the kate spade tote. But don't forget to check out Aveda's skin care and makeup as well. And pick up a bottle of conditioner from Black Malva to Madder Root.

Bliss 568 Broadway, 2nd Fl. (between Prince and Spring Sts.) (212) 219-8970. Bliss is a heavenly favorite for all media darlings. Book yourself an Oxygen Blast or the infamous Ginger Rub. Since this is *the* spa of the moment schedule an appointment way in advance. If there is no time for the white bathrobe wait, simply stop by the bright main area and browse for souvenirs like a Diptych candle, Chantecaille lipstick, or Bliss Foot Patrol.

5S 98 Prince Street (between Broadway and Mercer) 1–877-phone-5S. 5S promotes five senses for the soul and body that will make anyone smile: purifying, calming, energizing, adoring and nurturing. Skincare and makeup are organized by these principles and displayed on island counters for testing and playing. Pick up a Rebirth body powder of ginseng extract and chamomile for that second shopping wind.

Fresh 57 Spring St. (between Lafayette and Mulberry Sts.) (212) 925-0099. The Boston-based Fresh presents delicious treats for the bath and body. Their popular Sugar line comes in perfume, shower gel and lotion. Cocoa, Lychee, Lemon, Milk, Honey, Soy and Rose are other irresistible flowers and sweets to test. With an exotic touch, soaps are individually wrapped and tied with wire and stone, perfect gifts to go.

Kiehl's 109 Third Ave. (at 13th St.) (212) 677-3171. The line is always dotted with models and extreme sports athletes devoted to the skin and hair products that have made Kiehl's a venerable New York landmark. Test the Coriander body lotion, the ultra facial moisturizer with SPF, or the deluxe Creme de Corps. Check out the sporty photos and vintage motorcycles in the nineteenth century parlor. And try to stay calm as knowledgeable staff reward you for your wait with samples of other exceptional products.

L'Occitane 109 Third Ave. (at 13th St) (212) 677-3171. Who knew that triple-milled French soap would be so coveted? This is a bath lover's dream, so enjoy and prepare for lots of sniffing. Soaps from Provence come in all shapes and sizes, some gift-wrapped to go. For an extra splurge, pick up a tin of shea butter that works wonders on skin, lips and even hair.

M·A·C 113 Spring St. (between Mercer and Greene) (212) 334-4641. With spokesdivas as cool as RuPaul and K.D. Lang, M·A·C is makeup with an attitude. It is impossible not to buy a lipstick with a name like Wuss or Rocker. If eyes are your thing, there is a great array of eyeshadows from muted to amplified. For the drama queen in all of us, a stop at M·A·C is essential.

Sephora 555 Broadway (between Prince and Spring Sts.) (212) 625-1309. Like a duty-free superstore, Sephora's black and white striped columns hold up an impressive emporium of high-end cosmetics and skin and hair care products including Stila, Hard Candy, Clarins, and Phytologie. Shelves, literally from A-Z, stock every perfume imaginable. Sephora's own label includes a perfume bar where customers can create their own scent.

Shu Uemura 121 Greene St. (between Prince and Houston) (212) 979-5500. A well-lit workstation encourages customers to experiment. You will have success here finding the complexion-perfect face powder or a blush for that natural glow. With a selection of over one hundred brushes, Shu Uemura is a great place to pick up basic makeup tools including sponges, makeup palettes, pads, and clear containers for everything.

Bookstores

New York is Book City. Major publishers publish from here. Minor publishers, too. Writers write here. Booklovers browse and buy here. On a Sunday in September eight blocks of Fifth Ave. in the vicinity of Rockefeller Center are blocked off for a giant open-air book fair. While the big book chains with discount prices and huge inventories have driven some favorite independents out of business, there are still more good neighborhood stores here and many more specialized niche stores than you'll ever find back home.

MAJOR CHAINS

Barnes & Noble

Barnes & Noble has been selling books at its main store on Fifth Ave. since 1932. There is nothing fancy about that store, just an expanse of shelves with books on every imaginable specialty, as well as popular fiction and non-fiction. For fancy, try any number of their newer "superstores" with chairs and tables where you can sit and read all day and much of the night. Stores are generally open from 9 A.M. to 11 P.M. Most have cafes for Starbucks coffee, tea and pastry. You can, of course, get Starbucks coffee all over America, but there aren't many bookstores where you can hear best-selling authors read from, talk about their latest. Schedules of author appearances -are posted in the stores, advertised weekly in *The New York Times* and *Time Out* magazine, and listed on the chain's Manhattan Events Line: (212) 727-4810. Orders placed on www.bn.com by 11 A.M. get same-day delivery in Manhattan.

Main store: 105 Fifth Ave. at West 18th St. (Annex is across 5th Ave.)

Superstores:
675 Sixth Ave. at West 22nd St.
Citicorp Bldg., East 54th St. at Third Ave. (strong on business books)
4 Astor Place, between Broadway and Lafayette (Greenwich Village)
1280 Lexington Ave. at 86th St.
600 Fifth Ave. at West 48th St. (near Rockefeller Center)
1960 Broadway at 66th St. (Lincoln Center: strong on theater, performing arts)
33 East 17 between Broadway and Park Ave. South
2289 Broadway at West 82nd St.

Smaller stores:
Manhattan Mall on Sixth Ave. at West 33rd St.
385 Fifth Ave. and East 36th St.
750 Third Ave. and East 47th St.

Children's bookstore: 120 East 86th St. at Lexington Ave.
College bookstore: 33 East 17th St. between Broadway and Park Ave. South

Borders Books and Music

There are three big stores in Manhattan—one downtown at the World Trade Center, and two midtown on theEast Side, all open every day. They average 150,000 book, music and video/DVD titles per store. The Park Ave. and World Trade Center stores are almost twice as large as the one on Second Ave. For online shoppers, the company's website—www.borders.com—has access to nearly 700,000 titles in stock and ready to ship. The www.bordersstores.com site lists author appearances and other events.

5 World Trade Center (Church and Vesey Sts.) (212) 839-8049
Open: 7 A.M.–8:30 P.M. weekdays, 10–8:30 Sat., 11–8:30 Sun.

576 Second Ave. and 32nd St. (212) 685-3938
Open: 9 A.M.–11 P.M. Mon.–Sat., 9–9 Sun.

461 Park Ave. at 57th St. (212) 6785
Open: 9 A.M.–10 P.M. weekdays, 10–8 Sat., 11–8 Sun.

INDEPENDENT BOOKSTORES

Bookberries 983 Lexington Ave. at East 71st St. (212) 794-9400

Coliseum Books 1771 Broadway (at 57th St.) (212) 757-8381. Consistently ranked as one of the city's most popular independent bookstores, this sprawling space located just below Columbus Circle offers both an extensive collection of books as well a knowledgeable staff willing to help you in your search.

The Corner Bookstore 1313 Madison Ave. at 93rd St. (212) 831-3554

Gotham Book Mart 41 West 47th St. (between Fifth and Sixth Aves.) (212) 719-4448. This has been a mecca for serious readers since it was founded in 1920 by the late Frances Steloff, book-loving daughter of a dry goods peddler and itinerant rabbi. Steloff championed the works of Henry Miller, Gertude Stein, Ezra Pound and other luminaries. She sold forbidden copies of James Joyce's *Ulysses*, and once hired Tennessee Williams as a clerk, then fired him for tardiness. Gotham is smack dab in the middle of the wholesale diamond district. *The New York Times* has described it as "both keystone and touchstone of the literary life of New York City . . . an honest-to-goodness shrine."

Rizzoli World Financial Center (212) 385-1400; 454 West Broadway (between Houston and Prince Sts.) 212) 674–1616; 31 West 57th St. (between Fifth and Sixth Aves.) (212) 759-2424; 1334 York Ave. (at 72nd St.) (212) 606-7434. The West Broadway branch of this bookstore has long been regarded as a New York institution, with its sweeping entrance of marble, oak and crystal chandeliers. The specialty here is books and magazines devoted to the fine arts as well as architecture, design, photography and travel. Three additional branches now exist, all of them providing excellent collections. The store on 57th St. specializes in high-end coffee table books; the two-level shop is charming and staffed by knowledgeable people eager to help their customers.

Shakespeare & Co. 939 Lexington Ave. (between 68th and 69th Sts.) (212) 570-0201; 137 East 23rd St. (at Lexington Ave.) (212) 220-5199; 716 Broadway (at Washington Pl.) (212) 529-1330; 1 Whitehall St. (at Beaver St.) (212) 742-7025. Native New Yorkers mourned the loss of the Upper West Side branch of this charming bookstore with a remarkably local feel, but four locations remain, all of them still providing the same diverse selection of books and periodicals—everything from literature's greats to celebrity tributes.

St.Marks Bookshop 31 Third Ave. (between St. Marks Pl. and 9th St.) (212) 260-7853. This small, East Village book shop has flourished in the shadow of the monolithic local Barnes & Noble because it offers such a thorough and unusual selection. Especially of note are its film and literature sections.

Three Lives 154 West 10th St. (at Waverly Pl.) (212) 741-2069

Twelfth St. Books 11 East 12th St. (212) 645-4340

OUT OF PRINT, USED AND RARE BOOKS

Academy 10 West 18th St. (near Fifth Ave.) (212) 242-4848

Gotham Book Mart 41 West 47th St. (between Fifth and Sixth Aves.) (212) 719-4448. (See above)

Gryphon 2246 Broadway (between 80th and 81st Sts.) (212) 362-0706. Piled on the floor and reaching as high as the ceiling are nothing but books, books and more books stuffed into this cramped Upper West Side store. If you spend the time and look carefully you'll see that the shelves house a wide array of new, used and rare editions making this unusual collection a bibliophile's dream.

Mercer St. Books 206 Mercer St. (212) 505-8615

Skyline 13 West 18th St. (across the street from Academy) (212) 759-5463

The Strand 828 Broadway (at 12th St.) (212) 473-1452; 95 Fulton St. (between William and Gold Sts.) (212) 732-6070. Browse through the overstuffed shelves packed onto three floors at this monolithic used bookstore and you'll see why the Strand's claim that they have "eight miles of books" probably isn't an exaggeration. With patience and a little time spent looking through the wares you are guaranteed to turn up some rare gems that will confirm why this bookstore is one of New York's favorites. There are lots of new books at greatly reduced prices, supplied by book reviewers or drawn from publishers' overstocks

Ursus Books Ltd.
375 West Broadway (near Spring), 3rd floor (212) 226-7858
981 Madison Ave. at 76th St. (in the Carlyle Hotel) (212) 772-8787

SPECIALTY BOOKSTORES

New York has dozens of specialty bookstores for every specialized interest—the arts, comics, yoga—you name it. The following list is just a sampling of stores in Manhattan. Many carry a full range of non-specialty titles as well. The Yellow Pages of the telephone book list many more, including stores that concentrate on titles in French, German, Spanish, Russian and other languages.

Academic

Postman Books 1 University Pl. (between Washington Sq. North and 8th St.) (212) 533-2665; 70 Fifth Ave. (at 12th St.) (212) 633-2525. The two branches of this bookstore both have an scholastic slant, though the strengths of each one differ. The one near NYU offers a range of philosophy and various cultural studies books while the store located near the New School is an excellent resource for art and design books. However both offer a fantastic selection of new and used academic books.

Art and Architecture

Hacker Art Books 45 West 57th St. (near Fifth Ave.) (212) 688-7600

Urban Center Books
457 Madison Ave. (behind St. Patrick's Cathedral) (212) 935-3595

Biography

Biography Bookshop 400 Bleecker St. (at 11th St.) (212) 807-8655. This store is the ideal place for the voyeur, fan or scholar looking to delve into the personal history of their favorite celebrity. Aside from the assortment of biographies, look for collections of letters, diaries, a small section offering fiction, and guide books as well as a notable gay and lesbian section.

Boating

New York Nautical 140 West Broadway (212) 962-4522

Business, Financial, Management, Computers

McGraw-Hill Bookstore
1221 Ave. of the Americas
(Rockefeller Center) (212) 512–4100

Children

Bank St. College Bookstore 610 West 112th St at Broadway (212) 678-1654

Books of Wonder 132 Seventh Ave. at 17th St. (212) 989-3270

Teachers College Bookstore 1224 Amersterdam Ave. (212) 678-3920

Comics

Cosmic Comics 36 East 23rd St. at Madison Ave. (212) 460-5322

St. Marks Comics 11 St. Marks Pl. (212) 598-9439

Cooking and Gourmet

Kitchen Arts & Letters 1435 Lexington Ave. (between 93rd and 94th Sts.)
(212) 876-5550. Both the professional chef and the at-home gourmet will relish
the vast collection of more than 10,000 cookbooks in this Upper East Side
store. It's all here—everything from recipes for Algerian couscous to Viet-
namese-style grilled crab.

Joanne Hendricks Cookbooks 488 Greenwich St. (212) 226-5731

Fine Bindings

Bartfield Fine Books 30 West 57th St. (212) 245-8890

Gay and Lesbian

A Different Light 151 West 19th St. (between Sixth and Seventh Aves.)
(212) 989-4850. One of the city's largest gay and lesbian bookstores, this popular space features a huge collection of fiction, nonfiction, periodicals and an
assortment of cards, posters and odds and ends. Be sure to stop in at the cafe
located downstairs; also a gallery space hosting nightly events including readings and films.

Oscar Wilde Memorial Bookshop 15 Christopher St. (212) 255-5756

Government

U. S. Government Bookstore 26 Federal Plaza (near City Hall)
(212) 264-3825

History

Argosy Bookstore 116 East 59th St. (between Park and Lexington Aves.)
(212) 753-4455. There are few bargains to be found at this midtown shop specializing in rare books, but it's the best place to look if you're in the market for a
first edition, an antique map, or just want to browse through the six cluttered
stories to see what unusual finds turn up.

The Liberation Bookstore Lenox Ave. at 131st St. (212) 281-46

Military

The Military Bookman 29 East 93rd St. at Madison Ave. (212) 348-1280

Mystery

Murder Ink 2486 Broadway (between 92nd and 93rd Sts.) (212) 362-8905.
1467 Second Ave. (between 76th and 77th Sts.) (212) 517-3222. The armchair
detective will love this store stocked with both new and used mysteries—from
the classics to the modern novels. It's also worth checking the schedule for one
of the store's frequent book signings by local authors.

Partners and Crime
44 Greenwich Ave. (212) 243-0440

Photography

A Photographer's Place
133 Mercer St. near Prince St.
(212) 431-9358

Chartwell Booksellers, 55 East 52nd St. at Madison Ave.
(212) 308-0643

Religious

Christian Publications Inc.
315 West 43rd St. (212) 582-4311

Levine Books and Judaica
5 West 30th St. at Fifth Ave.
(212) 695-6888

Logos Bookstore
1575 York Ave. at 83rd St. (212) 517-7292

Theater

Drama Book Shop 723 Seventh Ave. (between 48th and 49th Sts.) (212)
944-0595
In a city full of aspiring artists it's necessary to have a store that specializes in
the performing arts, and whether it's modern screenplays, Oscar Wilde scripts or
biographies of the legends of the silver screen, this store is bound to have it.

Richard Stoddard Performing Arts Books 18 East 16th St. (212) 645-9576

Travel

Complete Traveller 199 Madison Ave. (212) 685-9007

Traveler's Choice 111 Greene St. (212) 941-1535

Yoga

East-West Books 78 Fifth Ave. (between 13th and 14th Sts.) (212) 243-5994
If you're interested in learning some more about Taoism or the history of Confu-
cianism then head to this Greenwich Village store where the name says it all;
the specialty here is books that bring Eastern philosophy, religion and literature
to the West.

Quest 240 East 53rd St. (212) 758-5521

Cameras & Electronics

Stroll through Manhattan and you are bound to encounter a dizzying amount
of electronics stores, but within the bunch a few retailers can be found who
offer both top-of-the-line equipment as well as sales people willing to help you
select the product that best suits your needs. If it's bargains that you are after
it's worth walking along Canal Street near East Broadway and looking through
the several storefronts hawking their wares, but bear in mind that while you
are likely to find a deal you also might find a dud so it's always a good policy to
test a product before you buy it. If you prefer guarantees and informed service
then we recommend looking through some of New York's better-known electronics retailers.

B&H Photo 420 Ninth Ave. (between 33rd and 34th Sts.) (212) 444-6600.
Many professional photographers wouldn't consider going to any other store for
their equipment. This cavernous store sells everything one could want ranging
from an impressive selection of cameras to the dark room equipment needed to
develop the final print. Additionally, you can find audio and video items as well
as a decent selection of used merchandise.

Harvey Electronics 2 West 45th St. (between Fifth and Sixth Ave.) (212) 575-5000; 888 Broadway (at 19th St., inside ABC Carpet & Home) (212) 982-7191; 927 Broadway (at 21st St.) (212) 388-9792. If you are looking for audio-visual equipment and have money to spend, Harvey's is the place to go. The store has been highly regarded since it opened 75 years ago, and the remarkably informed staff here can help you find anything from a standard video camera to high-end home theater components. They will also help with home installation. A third branch recently opened on Broadway at 21st street that specializes exclusively in products from the high-end Danish company Bang & Olufsen.

J&R Music/Computer World 31 Park Row (between Beekman and Ann Sts.) (212) 238-9000. J&R stands out both for its reasonable prices as well as its extensive range of merchandise. Anything needing a battery can be found here, including stereo equipment, video and manual cameras and of course the latest in computer hardware.

Olden Camera & Lens Co. Inc 1265 Broadway (between 31st and 32nd Sts.) (212) 725-1234 Hidden behind a huge, faded sign in Herald Square, this store contains a wealth of photography equipment, from the most technologically advanced to used Super 8s. Both new and used equipment is offered and the prices range just as drastically as the selection of products.

The Wiz 2577 Broadway (at 97th St.) (212) 663-8000, check Yellow-Pages for other locations   With several locations around Manhattan, this stands out as one of the best electronics stores for one-stop shopping. The products span from low- to high-end, and the merchandise is priced to matched, but you're likely to find what you are looking for here.

Children's Clothing

The world of children's clothing is a varied one, ranging from durable overalls that can withstand the hazards of life on the playground to precious lace and linen party dresses. **Baby Gap** and **Gap Kids** are good bets for fairly priced casual children's apparel in the latest styles. **Lester's** (1522 Second Ave., 212-734-9292) also sells items for children at reasonable rates. The shoe department is especially reliable, with several different brands and styles, but don't neglect the clothing department where you can often find a deal on imported designers that go for twice the price on Madison Avenue. **Oshkosh B'Gosh** (586 Fifth Ave., (212) 827-0098) also sells relatively inexpensive, multi-purpose items. However if you are searching for something special, perhaps a navy cotton sailor suit, an adorable straw hat with a delicate ribbon or even trendy school wear, then New York has loads of charming boutiques.

Bebe Thompson 1216 Lexington Ave. (between 82nd and 83rd Sts.) (212) 249-4740. A sign used to hang in the window of this upscale shop stating that they take customers by appointment only. Although the rules have changed, the atmosphere here remains exclusive and the prices are high. But it's worth it to those who know that this store is among the very best for delightful, well-crafted French and German imports for infants and children, selling up to size 16.

Bu and the Duck 106 Franklin St. (between Church St. and West Broadway) (212) 431-9226. It is apparent from the inviting atmosphere and quality merchandise that Susan Lang, the owner and designer, really likes kids—and she understands them. Gone are pastels and the cuddly farm animals that adorn many children's designs; instead, the items here are bold and interesting, using adult practicality while leaving the playful touches of youth firmly intact.

CO2 284 Columbus Ave. (at 74th St.) (212) 721-4966. Among the hippest pre-teen and teen places to shop, this Upper West Side store with sizes 6 to 16 has everything, including accessories, a girl needs to sport the week's most urban styles in school.

Greenstones & Cie 442 Columbus Ave. (between 82nd and 83rd Sts.) (212) 580-4322; 1184 Madison Ave. (between 86th and 87th Sts.) (212) 427-1665. Not your traditional smock dresses, the garments here are punctuated with bright colors and daring designs, all with a European edge. The imported labels come from France, Italy, Spain, Britain and the sizes range from infants through 12. Be prepared to pay top dollar.

Jacadi 1281 Madison Ave. (at 91st St.) (212) 369-1616; 787 Madison Ave. (at 67th St.) (212) 535-3200. For beautiful, French-designed clothing for infants and children and all the accessories to match including shoes, tights, hats and even some furniture, this charming store is ideal. Although the prices are high it's a pleasure to shop here where you will be blissfully free of the off-putting attitude of several Madison Avenue children's boutiques. Look for the sales, often in January and June.

Lilliput 265 Lafayette St. (between Spring and Prince Sts.) (212) 965-9567. With an eclectic combination of apparel for infants and young children that spans darling to utilitarian, this store warrants a trip downtown. Although the price tags on the several imported labels stocked here are as high as they are elsewhere the range is wider and includes shoes, accessories and a fine selection of collectable toys.

Peanutbutter & Jane 617 Hudson St. (at 12th St.) (212) 620-7952. A store for teenagers as well as younger kids and remarkably enough appealing to both, this West Village store stocks clothes and accessories with the imagination of youth and the funky style traditional to the Village. Brightly colored shoes, leather skirts and charming, girlish party outfits are hang together on these racks.

Z'baby Company 100 West 72nd (at Columbus Ave.) (212) 579-2229; 996 Lexington Ave. (at 72nd St.) (212) 472-2229. Located on streets lined with clothing retailers selling urban styles and upscale brands, these stores fit right in. Boys and girls through age 16 can be outfitted into these popular, bold styles that are as suited for playtime as they are for the ceremonious first day of school.

Flea Markets

Manhattan's flea markets offer wonderful opportunities for the bargain hunter in search of finds as valuable as antique dishware or as sentimental as an old copy of David Cassidy on vinyl. **The Annex Antiques Fair and Flea Market** (212-243-5343) on Sixth Avenue between 24th and 27th Streets is the city's biggest outdoor flea market, and is open Saturdays and Sundays. Here's a great spot for high-end items such as oil paintings and antique furniture. **Green Flea** (212-721-0900) runs the bustling Sunday bazaar located on Columbus Avenue off of 77th Street where everything from 1920s magazine advertisements to house plants to piles of junk go for bargain basement prices. For endless racks of trendy clothing check out **The Daily Market** on the corner of Spring and Wooster Street in SoHo (open, yes, daily), or in the small corner lot found every Saturday and Sunday on Broadway at 4th Street. At 23,000 square feet, **The Garage** on West 25th Street between Sixth and Seventh Avenues (212-647-0707) is the city's largest indoor market, brought to life every Saturday and Sunday in a former parking garage.

Food Markets

Agata and Valentina 1505 First Ave. (at 79th St.) (212) 452-0690. This shop is worth visiting almost as much for the sense of discovery it provides as for its wonderful food. With its focus on Sicily (the shop was built with Sicilian materials) there are many products—olives, oils, cheeses, meats, prepared foods—you are not likely to find anywhere else. Pricey? Yes, but the quality and service are peerless.

Barney Greengrass 541 Amsterdam Ave. (between 86th and 87th St.) (212) 724-4707. Barney Greengrass, the self-proclaimed "Sturgeon King,"has been a fixture on the Upper West Side since 1929—but the family, now in its third generation, has been selling caviar, smoked fish, and herring since 1908. Sturgeon here is exquisitely moist and thin, as is the smoked salmon. Everything, including the excellent whitefish salad, borscht, blintzes and chopped liver can be carried home or eaten in a variety of dishes at the lively next door restaurant.

Chelsea Market 88 10th Ave. (between 15th and 16th Sts.) (212) 243-6005. Surreal and dreamlike, with a waterfall streaming from a deliberately broken pipe, this black-floored brick-walled ex-cracker factory is in the heart of the city's old meat-packing district. Wonderful food purveyors line the cavernous concourse where you can buy bread, caviar, lobster, professional kitchenware, or Italian specialties like chestnut flour and salted capers. You can lunch at several small restaurants both inside the concourse and outside in the factory building.

Citarella 2135 Broadway (at 75th St.) (212) 874-0383; 1313 Third Ave. (at 75th St.) (212) 874-0383. Citarella packs everything—a wide variety of breads, cheeses, specialty oils, condiments and sauces, prepared foods, house-made pastries, pasta, and produce into a relatively small space. Produce is usually so good you don't have to spend time picking it over. Add one of the city's finest and friendliest fish and seafood counters, obliging butchers with specialties like ostrich steak and demi-glace, and you've got dinner in no time flat. Such choice and service comes at a price, but Citarella offers good value and service.

Dean and Deluca 560 Broadway (at Prince St.) (212) 431-1691. With stratospheric prices, picture-perfect produce and handsomely displayed hard-to-find food items, this stylish SoHo shop is a mecca for well-heeled foodies. The city's finest bakeries are the source of its superb pies, cakes, and breads, and the impeccably fresh cheeses include unusual French and Italian varieties. There is also a small selection of fine cookware and the latest cookbooks.

E.A.T. 1064 Madison Ave. (between 80th and 81st Sts.) (212) 772-0022. Founded by Eli Zabar, nephew of the owners of the original Zabar's on Broadway, E.A.T. is a restaurant that offers catering services, takeout food, fabulous bread, cheese and smoked fish. Its commitment to quality is obvious, but it decisively eschews bargains and revels in its high prices. Sandwiches here are served on mouth-watering breads baked by Eli and filled with the finest meats, cheeses and smoked fish. Salads are good, too, and desserts, sublime.

Fairway 2127 Broadway (at 74th St.) (212) 595-1888; 132nd St. (at the Hudson River) (212) 234-3883. You can't beat Fairway's two uptown stores for low prices, no-frills shopping and a huge selection of everything—olive oils, sauces, condiments, meat, fresh fish, bread and groceries. Both feature enormous produce sections with some of the best organic fruits and vegetables in the city, as well as hard-to-find tropical specialties; the choice and quality of cheeses surpasses that of much fancier shops. There is something for everyone and everyone is here. Service is spotty (and can be rude) at both stores, fish bears watching, and produce is sometimes not as good as it looks—but the crowds are cheerful, the variety astonishing and the price is definitely right.

Grace's Marketplace 1237 Third Ave. (between 71st and 72nd Sts.) (212) 737-0600. Grace Balducci and her husband, Joe Doria, created the Marketplace a dozen years ago. Like her family's downtown shop, it offers fine service, stunning displays of produce, wonderful baked goods and cheeses, quality smoked and fresh meats and fish, fresh pastas, coffee, teas and everything you hope for in a gourmet market. Sandwiches are excellent and fairly priced.

International Groceries and Meat Market 543 9th Ave. (at 40th St.) (212) 279-1000. If you like fresh spices sold in bulk, this market is hard to beat for price and variety. They're sold alongside such original Greek specialties as fresh feta cheese, taramosalata (an ethereal fish spread), a selection of Greek olives and oils, dried fruits and nuts, as well as some of the best halvah around. Thick, sour Greek yogurt as well as limited quantities of lamb and goat meat are also available here.

Kam Man Food Products 200 Canal St. (between Mott and Mulberry Sts.) (212) 571-0330

Kam Kuo Foods 7 Mott St. (at Park Row) (212) 349-3097. Kam Man is the largest Asian food market on the East Coast, selling shark fins, fresh water chestnuts, dried fish, pickled vegetables, soy sauces, hoisin, dried mushrooms and a broad selection of fresh vegetables as well as the woks and steamers to cook them. It also sells barbecued duck, sausages and pork dumplings, as well as specialties from Vietnam and Thailand. Smaller, with fewer cooked foods and less produce, Kam Kuo carries frozen Chinese foods, a large selection of teas and cooking utensils. The staff is generally friendly in both crowded stores; prices are low, but the language barrier can be formidable.

The Market at Grand Central Terminal Lexington Ave. (between 43rd and 44th Sts.) Don't miss the newest and spiffiest food mart in New York City at Grand Central Station, with everything from chocolate to cheese from some of the city's finest shops. You'll find stores offering exotic seafood like oysters, live sea urchins and scallops in pale pink and purple shells; patês, rillettes and fresh foie gras; German cold cuts; and exotic spices and seasonings.

Russ and Daughters 178 East Houston St. (212) 475-4800. If you don't mind crowds, Sunday morning is when Jewish customers observe their post-sabbath ritual—buying smoked fish, cream cheese and old-fashioned, sturdy, hand-made bagels made in nearby Kossar's bakery. Schmooze with the countermen who will tell you how to prepare the excellent herrings. Prices are lower—even for the excellent caviar—than in most uptown stores.

The Vinegar Factory 431 East 91st St. (near York Ave.) (212) 987-0885 **Eli's Manhattan** 1411 Third Ave. (between 80th and 81st Sts.) (212) 717-8100. To rival his uncles on Broadway, Eli Zabar purchased an old vinegar factory and turned it into a market selling produce, cheese, meat, fish, deli prepared foods, excellent salads, fresh flowers, baked goods and Eli's tasty breads as well as wines, liquors, housewares and books. Prices for excellent produce—even the tomatoes grown in the factory roof greenhouse—are not unreasonably high, and there are new products every day. Eli's Manhattan offers virtually the same products and services (some at higher prices) as well as home shopping, an oyster and sushi bar and an on-site café and restaurant.

Zabar's 2245 Broadway (between 80th and 81st Sts.) (212) 787-2000. Zabar's is a West Side institution—known for its smoked fish and herring counter where you can taste before your smoked salmon is sliced paper-thin, or order caviar at bargain prices. Other delights (all available through a catalogue) include hundreds of kinds of cheeses, breads, condiments, candy, produce, kosher foods, a large variety of cold cuts and patês and an array of prepared foods. Housewares are bargain-priced on the second floor. Service is fast and efficient.

GREENMARKETS

More than 20 years ago, the Council on the Environment of New York City invited a few farmers to offer their products from stands set up on a city lot on 59th Street and Second Avenue. Today there are 32 weekly markets in all five boroughs—17 open year-round—and the original seven purveyors have grown to number more than 130. These include traditional family farmers, recent hippies, Amish dairy farmers, aqua and fish farmers, meat and game farmers, as well as mom and pop stands selling jams, jellies, flavored vinegars, smoked fish, and freshly baked pies and cakes.

On a visit to the **Union Square Greenmarket,** you might discover crosnes (tiny snail-like vegetables that taste like Jerusalem artichokes but don't require peeling), a wide variety of potatoes including heirloom blues, diminutive Japanese turnips and baby Chinese cabbages. Everything is fresh, there are lots of organics and prices tend to be low. You'll have fun discovering different suppliers, finding old friends each time you visit, and watching—everyone from moms with strollers and dads with kids on their shoulders, to well-dressed professionals, kids with green hair, and occasional chefs in uniform. This is the real New York: diverse, friendly and enthusiastic. The Union Square market, on East 17th St. and Broadway, is open Monday, Wednesday, Friday and Saturday from 8 A.M. to 6 P.M.—with the biggest markets on Saturday and Wednesday when 50 to 70 producers from New York, New Jersey and Pennsylvania jam the attractive park.

The **World Trade Center Market** is open from 8 A.M.–5 P.M. every Thursday year-round, and on Tuesday from June to September. There's a lively neighborhood market every Sunday at **Intermediate School 44** on Columbus Avenue and 77th Street from 10 A.M.–5 P.M. For times and locations of other greenmarkets, telephone (212) 477-3220.

ETHNIC MARKETS

With people from virtually every country and region of the world living in New York, it is possible to find ingredients from virtually every cuisine in specialty markets set up by immigrants determined to maintain their own cuisines. Shopping in most of these markets is relatively simple as owners and clerks are happy to share their knowledge with you. Be aware that some smaller markets will not take credit cards or checks. Call ahead to find out. Asian markets are usually crowded and their harried staffs lack sufficient command of English. To get the most out of your visit to Chinatown, pick up a copy of Linda Bladholm's *The Asian Grocery Demystified* (Renaissance Books, 1999; $14.95). Its clear description of the principles which order these markets can help you find what you want. The author names the vegetables and dried foods, tell you how they look, what they taste like and how they are used.

Chinese: Chinese American Trading Co., 91 Mulberry St. (at Canal St.) (212) 267-5224

English: Myers of Keswick, 634 Hudson St. (between Jane and Horatio Sts.) (212) 691-4194

German: Schaller and Weber, 1654 Second Ave. (between 85th and 86th Sts.) (212) 879-3047

Indian: Foods of India, 121 Lexington Ave. (bet 28th and 29th Sts.) (212) 683-4419

Italian: Di Palo Fine Foods, 206 Grand St. (at Mott St.) (212) 226-1033. Todaro Brothers, 555 Second Ave. (between 30th and 31st Sts.) (212) 532-0633

Japanese: Katagiri, 224 East 59th St. (between Second and Third Aves.) (212) 755-3566

Korean: Han Arum Market, 25 West 32nd St. (between Broadway and Fifth Ave.) (212) 695-3283

Latin American: Mosaico: 135 Madison Ave. (between 33rd and 34th Sts.) (212) 213-4700

Mexican: Azteca Deli Grocery, 698 Amsterdam Ave. (between 93rd and 94th Sts.), no phone. Kitchen Market, 218 Eighth Ave. (between 21st and 22nd Sts.) (212) 243-4433

Middle Eastern: Kalustyans, 123 Lexington Ave. (between 28th and 29th Sts.) (212) 685-3451. Melange, 1277 First Ave. (bet 68th and 69th Sts.) (212) 535-7773

Polish: East Village Meat Market, 132 Second Ave. (between 9th St. and St. Mark's Pl.) (212) 228-5590. Kurowycky's Meat Products, 124 First Ave. (between 7th St. and St. Mark's Pl.) (212) 477-0344

Thai: Bangkok Center Market, 104 Mosco St. (near Mott St.) (212) 349-1979

Vietnamese: Thuan Nguyen Market, 84 Mulberry St. (212) 964-6296

West African: West African Grocery, 535 Ninth Ave. (between 39th and 40th Sts.) (212) 695-6215

Jewelry

Everything from costume jewelry to the world's most renowned designers can be found in New York. If it is diamonds you're after then head over to the **Diamond District** on 47th Street between Fifth and Sixth Avenues, but be sure to research cuts and prices in advance so you know how to bargain. Broadway between 25th and 30th Streets hosts the **Costume Jewelry District** which offers fantastic items for the bargain hunter. Although many of these stores only sell wholesale, the minimum order is often low enough for the solo shopper. However, if you are in the market for a delicate designer watch with a jewel encrusted clasp or a pair of emerald earrings to wear to a black tie affair then New York has numerous stores that can cater to you.

Bulgari 730 Fifth Ave. (at 57th St.) (212) 315-9000; 783 Madison Ave. (between 56th and 57th Sts.) (212) 717-2300. These designs are as high caliber as they are bold, often combining different materials such as fine gems, 24K gold and even stainless steel. This collection includes everything from silk neckties with stunning Italian prints to lighters designed from precious metals.

Cartier 653 Fifth Ave. (at 52nd St.) (212) 446-3400; Trump Tower, 725 Fifth Ave. (at 56th St.) (212) 308-0840. The stunning, traditional designs of Pierre

Cartier are widely admired, and a viewing of the stately pieces leaves no question why. The selection ranges from the every day to the very dressy.

Fortunoff 681 Fifth Ave. (at 54th St.) (212) 758-6660. Known for fine merchandise and competitive prices, this store boasts one of the city's largest selections of fine jewelry including many designer pieces and an especially impressive selection of antique silver. Crystal and clocks can also be found here, though the range is less extensive.

H. Stern 645 Fifth Ave. (between 51st and 52nd St.) (212) 688-0300. This company originating in Brazil and specializing in modern, high-end designs makes a visit feel like a trip to an art museum. Perhaps it is the polished, modern setting of the store. Some of the pieces are also crafted with unusual semiprecious stones.

Harry Winston 718 Fifth Ave. (at 56th St.) (212) 245-2000. For an outstanding diamond set beautifully on a platinum band or a sapphire bracelet destined to become a family heirloom, this is the store to find it. The items here are for the most special of occasions, but you are unlikely to find a better place to search those pieces out. The quality here simply cannot be surpassed, especially for precious stones.

Me & Ro 239 Elizabeth St. (between Prince and Houston Sts.) (917) 237-9215. Beautiful, contemporary designs in silver and gold have steadily emerged from this tiny Nolita shop for a few years now, adorning both the fashionable downtown set and well known celebrities in blockbuster films. It's a wonder that the prices haven't inflated to match the store's popularity.

Mikimoto 730 Fifth Ave. (between 56th and 57th Sts.) (212) 664-1800. This store is known exclusively for it's diverse range of quality, high-luster pearls. While countless perfect strands of cultured pearls come from Mikimoto's own farms, you can also find some of New York's most respectable South Sea and fresh water varieties.

Tiffany & Co. 727 Fifth Ave. (at 57th St.) (212) 755-8000. Long before Audrey Hepburn gazed into the window of this store in "Breakfast at Tiffany's" it was firmly established as one of the world's premier jewelers. Everything from affordable silver necklaces to jewel studded bracelets costing thousands of dollars are found in the elegant display cases. The fine china, sterling silver and crystal also make up a magnificent collection.

Tourneau 500 Madison Ave. (at 52nd St.) (212) 758-6098; 12 East 57th St. (between Fifth and Madison Aves.) (212) 758-7300; 200 West 34th St. (at Seventh Ave.) (212) 563-6880. You'll find mostly watches at this store, but it's easily among the world's better collections of fine time pieces—over 70 brands are represented including Rolex, Patek, Philippe, and also more affordable ones such as Seiko. With its futuristic interior, TimeMachine, the three story 57th Street location is the most modern of the branches, but all of them offer the same range and quality.

Leather & Luggage

Altman Luggage 135 Orchard St. (between Delancey and Rivington Sts.) (212) 254-7275. For fairly priced utilitarian bags and luggage, this downtown, discount store offers an extensive selection including reliable brand names such as Timberland, Samsonite and Jansport.

Botega Veneta 635 Madison Ave. (between 59th and 60th Sts.) (212) 371-5511. The name is known for fine woven leather products including handbags suitable for every day use, backpacks, shoes and smaller items. The smaller selection of coats and accessories is equally high quality.

Coach 342 Madison Ave. (at 44th Street) (212) 599-4777, check Yellow Pages for other locations. Known for their butter soft leather and classic designs, this designer's every day leather goods include bags, backpacks, briefcases, wallets and accessories. Recently shoes and more contemporary colors have been added to their line of merchandise.

Jutta Neuman 317 East 9th St. (between First and Second Aves.) (212) 982-7048. The German-born owner of this charming East Village store has developed a recognizable line of bags, back packs, wallets and sandals. All items are crafted in beautiful, contemporary designs from supple skins died in bold colors. The items are fairly expensive but worth the price.

Louis Vuitton 116 Greene St. (between Spring and Prince) (212) 274-9090; 49 East 57th St. (between Park and Madison Aves.) (212) 371-6111. Long regarded for their bags and luggage decorated with the unmistakable mono-grammed logo, these high-fashion bags range from enormous, stately pieces suit-able for a trip on the Orient Express to tiny, everyday purses. The newer line has, in some cases, discarded the logo, instead incorporating brave, modern col-ors and a stylish line of clothing and shoes designed by Marc Jacobs.

Manhattan Portage 333 East 9th St. (between First and Second Aves.) (212) 995-5490. First loved for their durable bike messenger bags finished off with the recognizable red patch bearing the company's logo, this store has now expanded to include both larger bags suitable for weekends away and smaller, trendier bags coming in every vivid color imaginable. Blessedly the bargain basement price has remained the same.

Music

Bleecker Bob's Golden Oldie's Record Shop 118 West 3rd St. (between McDougal St. and Sixth Ave.) (212) 475-9677. Okay, so it's not located on Bleecker Street, but don't be put off by this store's quirks—it has the definitive collection for the genuine rock fan, fairly boasting that it carries almost every rock album ever cut. Add to that impressive claim a host of jazz records and hours that allow for impulse shopping until 3 A.M. on weekends.

HMV U.S.A. 57 West 34th St. (at Herald Square) (212) 629-0900, call for other locations. From the contemporary selection of music, DVDs and videos you might never guess that this store has been around for over one hundred years. Music for any taste has its own department, including rock, pop, classical, dance and country, and if you are not sure what you are in the mood for stop by one of the many in-store listening stations for a taste of some new releases.

Jazz Record Center 236 West 26th St., Rm. 804 (between Seventh and Eighth Aves.) (212) 675-4480. Frederick Cohen, the owner of this specialty store is world famous for his extensive knowledge of jazz, and a trip to his shop proves that he really knows his stuff; collected within is hands down the best selection of jazz music in New York. Posters, videos and CDs are part of the assortment, but what most everyone really comes in for is the wide selection of records including an phenomenal choice of out-of-print records.

Joseph Patelson Music House 160 West 56th St. (212) 582-5840. For the concert violinist to the enthusiastic student, this store has everything to satisfy anyone serious about music. Selling both common and unusual scores, sheet music, music books, even metronomes and pitch pipes, the true music lover will feel at home here.

Tower Records 692 Broadway (at 4th St.) (212) 505-1500, call for other locations. It's no wonder the crowds pack in, a department for almost every variety of musical tastes can be found inside—rock, classical, alternative, country, folk, blues and more. Many locations also offer videos, books and rentals, and the selection in each department is broad. If you have difficulty finding what you want in the racks then the staff here is quick to lend a hand.

Venus Records 13 St. Marks Pl. (between Second and Third Aves.) (212) 598-4459. For the true rock consoler, this East Village find offers an extraordinary choice of early rock including some original editions. Hard-to-find imported and independent releases also have their place here, as do alternative and punk. As it sells both new and used recordings, you can knock down the price of your sale by exchanging your old LPs, tapes and CDs for trade-ins or cash.

Virgin Megastore
1540 Broadway (at 45th St.) 921–1020
Richard Branson didn't create a veritable empire based on nothing, and the overwhelming sights and sounds of his $15 million Time Square entertainment complex redefine the "mega" in "megastore." The more than one million CDs in stock here make it a solid bet, and the stock of videos, DVDs, CD-ROMS, and laser discs is also vast.

Shoes

Known for its cutting edge fashion sense, New York has an endless supply of shoe retailers selling everything from sturdy work boots to stiletto heels that just walked off the runway. Several clothing stores carry their own line of shoes, or for discounts on trendy footwear or, in some cases, designer knockoffs look in the stores lining 8th Street between Fifth and Sixth Avenues. If you are willing to pay top dollar for fine labels then Madison Avenue is sure to have what you are looking for, and for a sampling of those same labels several department stores provide everything from the casual to the very dressy in their shoe departments.

Billy Martin 810 Madison Ave. (at 68th St.) (212) 861-3100. Known for their western wear including jackets, hats and all manner of accessories, this store is most loved for its fantastic range of cowboy boots for both men and women in a range of colors and skins.

Church English Shoes 428 Madison Ave. (at 49th St.) (212) 755-4313. Those who know Church's well maintain that it's been a standard in men's shoes since 1873 as a result of its top quality leather, craftsmanship and unwavering devotion to traditional styles. Moreover, the store itself provides a delightful trip into the tasteful world of manners that does not yield to the whimsical winds of change.

Jimmy Choo 645 Fifth Ave. (at 51st St.) (212) 593-0800. These designs beautifully pull together bold, alluring finishes with the very best materials and workmanship. The women's line of sexy, narrow heels is its staple, but a small selection of footwear for men is found here, too.

Kenneth Cole 107 East 42nd St. (between Vanderbilt and Park Aves.) (212) 949-8079, call for other locations. For the most updated styles in shoes this store has everything, from sandals for both men and women to laced boots perfect to complete the look of a three-button suit. Wallets, belts and other well-crafted accessories can also be bought here. Though the quality is high the prices are not.

Manolo Blahnik 31 West 54th St. (between Fifth and Sixth Aves.) 582–3007. Devotees of these shoes will grow misty-eyed as they tenderly describe the captivating beauty of this designer's footwear, so it's no wonder that people pay hundreds of dollars for a single pair. Not for the every day, these sultry styles are marked by their pointy toes and narrow heels, which in some cases are even thinner than a stiletto.

Otto Tootsi Plohound 137 Fifth Ave. (between 20th and 21st Sts.) (212) 460-8650, call for other locations. Many of the designs found on the shelves lining this store are as whimsical as the store's name, but the trendy, cutting edge style here never means skimping on quality. Both men and women can choose from an extensive selection of boots, shoes and sandals, but the price is often as high as the style.

Salvatore Ferragamo *Men:* Trump Tower, 725 Fifth Ave. (212) 759-7990; 661 Fifth Ave. (at 34th St.) (212) 759-3822. For those devoted to both high style and tradition Ferragamo is the place to go. This Italian designer has long been admired for the selection of fine leather and tasteful, classic designs.

Stuart Weitzman 625 Madison Ave. (between 58th and 59th Sts.) (212) 750-2555. The materials and craftsmanship here are among the best in women's shoes, and this store caters to those looking for difficult-to-fit sizes in a variety of styles.

Sporting Goods

Bicycle Renaissance 430 Columbus Ave. (at 81st St.) (212) 724-2350. Selling everything from the newest models of mountain bikes to the sleeker racing variety, this shop also offers repair services and biking accessories. Depending on how serious you are about the sport you might want to take advantage of the custom bikes built by in-house professionals. For all the expertise found here the prices are still moderate.

Eastern Mountain Sports 611 Broadway (at Houston St.) (212) 505-9860; 21 West 61st St. (between Broadway and Columbus Ave.) (212) 397-4860. If you are planning a camping trip, learning to kayak, or just want the best insect repellent for your afternoon picnic in the park, EMS is sure to have everything you need. They sell several top brands such as North Face as well as their own sturdy label that caters to almost every outdoor activity.

Modell's 200 Broadway (between Fulton and John Sts.) (212) 964-4007, call for other locations. Founded in 1889, this store is still family owned and operated. Its good reputation is fairly bestowed—for one-stop athletic wear shopping this place cannot be beat. A variety of labels such as Nike, Reebok, New Balance, Wilson, Fila and more are found in the racks here.

Niketown 6 East 57th St. (between Fifth and Madison Aves.) (212) 891-6453. In this five-story building with a flashy decor inspired by school gymnasiums, nothing but Nike clothing and shoes (1,200 varieties) are sold. The prices soar, but the experience of shopping here is considered by many to be well worth it.

Paragon Sports 867 Broadway (at 18th St.) (212) 255-8036. Manhattan's definitive sporting goods store, this sprawling shop has separate departments for racquet sports, ice skating, in-line skating, skiing, biking, sailing, golf, camping and so much more—all top-of-the-line equipment. Whatever you want for athletics, chances are good that you'll find it here. Be warned, though, the prices can be steep.

Toys

Big City Kite Company 1210 Lexington Ave. (at 82nd St.) (212) 472-2623. This entire store is a loving ode to kites, stocking everything that can be caught on a breeze from delicate tissue paper creations that double as art to utilitarian plastic varieties that can be yanked from trees and remain intact. The staff is wonderfully attentive and provides repair services. Prices vary.

Children's General Store 2473 Broadway (at 92nd St.) (212) 580-2723; Grand Central Station (near Lexington Ave. entrance) (212) 628-0004. These stores sell well-constructed, beautiful and creative pieces; however they are not well-stocked with the latest in high-tech toys and games.

Classic Toys 218 Sullivan St. (between Bleecker and 3rd Sts.) (212) 674-4434. Both kids and collectors love this toy store for the wide choices of both old and new toys—diecast vehicles and Matchbox cars to the most modern selection of this year's line. Be sure to examine the toy soldiers—over one hundred years of them all collected and on display. Also of note are the antique toys.

Dinosaur Hill 306 East 9th St. (between Second and Third Aves.) (212) 473-5850. Toys from around the world can be found in this tiny, fanciful, East Village space—old-fashioned American wooden blocks, Latin American masks, beautiful marbles from across the Atlantic, as well as a good selection of children's
literature.

Disney Store 711 Fifth Ave. (at 55th St.) (212) 702-0702, call for other locations. You'll be well acquainted with the characters you encounter in this enormous megastore—Cinderella on watches, Mickey on t-shirts, figurines of the dancing tea cups from "Sleeping Beauty," back packs shaped like Winnie the Pooh. Every Disney-related item that you can think of and several more that you couldn't imagine are all packed into this popular, bustling store.

Enchanted Forest 85 Mercer St. (between Spring and Broome Sts.) (212) 925-6677. As loved for its collection of toys as much as for its fantastical gallery backdrop created by the theater set designer Matthew Jacobs. It's a child's dream world actualized, including a crystal cave and a Victorian room that seems straight from the Narnia tales. Though the selection of toys is a fine one, this store's selection of children's books really shines.

F.A.O. Schwarz 767 Fifth Ave. (at 59th St.) (212) 644-9400. Long before Tom Hanks danced down a set of piano keys here in the movie *Big*, this three-level mega toy store was the number one destination of choice for any kid visiting New York—and with good reason. The enormous space literally buzzes with the zaps and beeps of toys in motion, and everywhere you look is a stuffed bear, or a train that's bigger, softer, or faster than any you've seen before. You'll find everything here but a bargain.

Wynken, Blynken & Nod's 306 East 55th St. (between First and Second Aves.) (212) 308-9299. Deborah Kleman quit her job at a law practice to open this treasure chest of toys, and her charming store proves that she's found her calling. Much of the stock here has been crafted by local artists. You can also find unusual and, in some cases, antique furniture, games, puppets, and a small stock of clothing. Prices range from moderate to steep.

Vintage Clothing/Thrift

The Antique Boutique 712–714 Broadway (at Washington Pl.) (212) 460-8830. With new, used and vintage apparel this place is a wealth of one-of-a-kind finds, though you'd never know it from the reasonable price tags you can find in certain sections. Fringed 20s style dresses, used Levis that somehow fit so much better than the newer versions and a choice of perfectly worn leather jackets are typical finds.

Domsey's Warehouse Outlet And Annex 431 Kent Ave. (at Broadway), Brooklyn (718) 384-6000. The eclectic mix of items in this store is an enticing combination of clutter and gems. As advertised they offer 26 feet of nothing but fancy dresses, each sold for under $10. You may have to hunt but chances are what you want—be it housewares, shoes, clothing or knickknacks—is in here . . . somewhere.

Housing Works Thrift Shop 143 West 17th St. (between Sixth and Seventh Aves.) (212) 366-0820; 202 East 77th St. (at Third Ave.) (212) 772-8461; 306 Columbus Ave. (between 74th and 75th Sts.) (212) 579-7566. Selling items that include fashionable clothing, accessories, books, housewares and a wide selection of furniture, this store caters to almost all your living needs. The wares are almost exclusively "uptown" and the proceeds benefit people living with AIDS.

Salvation Army Thrift Store 536 West 46th St. (between 10th and 11th Aves.) (212) 664-8563. If shopping by the pound appeals to you, then this two level resale emporium will be ideal. An entire floor here is devoted exclusively to furniture and major appliances, and the clothing department is a sprawling maze stocked with prizes for the patient bargain hunter.

Screaming Mimi's 382 Lafayette St. (between 4th and Great Jones Sts.) (212) 677-6464. Laura Wills, the owner of this downtown spot has rigorous standards. The clothing here all has something special, whether it's a vividly colored floral design stamped onto an A-line mini dress or a perfectly preserved vintage dress from the 40s. Housewares, bags, shoes and even lingerie can be found here. Be sure to spend some time in the gift department loaded with outrageous items promoting New York.

Tatiana 860 Lexington Ave., 2nd Fl. (between 64th and 65th Sts.) (212) 717-7684. If you thought that resale had to mean musty or eccentric this store will change your mind. Top designer outfits in mint condition mostly bearing labels like Chanel, Gucci and Armani are sold on consignment for incredibly fair prices. The stock here includes jewelry, bags and shoes.

Tokyo 7 64 East 7th St. (between First and Second Aves.) (212) 353-8443. You are as likely to find a pointelle knit dress that's perfect for a garden party as you are to walk away with bright yellow leather pants at this East Village thrift shop. But whatever you find, it will be one of a kind.

Wine Shops

New York has the best selection of wine shops in the world; no other city comes close. There are the old standards like **Sherry-Lehmann** (679 Madison Ave. at

61st St.); **Morrell and Co.** which just moved to sumptuous new quarters in Rockefeller Center, **67 Wines & Spirits** (179 Columbus Ave.) and **Acker, Merrall & Condit** (160 West 72d St.).

These are full service shops where the clerks are knowledgeable and always ready to rescue the clueless—provided it's not during a busy Saturday morning or in the middle of the frantic holiday season.

Bargain hunters often head to **Garnet Wines & Liquors** (929 Lexington Ave.) or **Crossroads** (55 West 14th St.). The atmosphere in these shops, particularly Garnet, can be hectic and savvy customers try to know what they want before they push open the doors. If business is slow, which it rarely is, the staff can be most helpful. And prices can be appealingly low.

New York has its specialists, too. When they run short on Romanee-Conti, Burgundy lovers head for **The Burgundy Wine Company** (323 West 11th St.) in the West Village, where you usually have to ring the bell and wines are often selected from an order book rather than samples on the very tiny floor.

Italian wine fans now have their own store, too. Looking for a special Barolo or a little-known Chianti? Take a trip to the new shop called **Italian Wine Merchants** (108 East 16th St.). Some of New York's best-known Italian restaurateurs, like Lydia Bastinich, of Felidia's are involved in Italian Wine Merchants.

Devotees of rare old Bordeaux know they are likely to find what they want at **Royal Wine Merchants Ltd.** (215 Waterside Plaza), far over on the East Side near 32d Street.

The more adventurous will strike out for Long Island City in Queens where they can poke through the offerings, usually at very attractive prices, at the **New York Wine Warehouse** (805 43d Ave.).

New Yorkers have many complaints. Being short of good wine is not one of them.

—Frank Prial

New York for Children

Adults tend to think of New York as a less-than-hospitable place for children: all concrete and steel, with high culture appreciated mainly by the sophisticated. But real New Yorkers know that the city could not be more welcoming to the young. The parks system more than makes up for the lack of street-side greenery, and the Urban Park Rangers' free weekend programs demonstrate that peregrine falcons and raccoons are as likely as Wall Street moguls to reside here. Central Park, which all Manhattan children regard as their personal backyard, offers playgrounds, a Swedish marionette theater and a recently refurbished children's zoo, as well as Belvedere Castle which presents free nature workshops. And in the Bronx, there's the Everett Children's Adventure Garden at the New York Botanical Garden, a paradise of plants and interactive exhibits that invites children to learn about the flowers as well as smell them.

In addition to the Central Park Zoo, several other wildlife centers compete with the world-class Bronx Zoo: the Queens Zoo specializes in American species (this is where the buffalo still roam), while the Staten Island Zoo offers a prodigious reptile collection and a "Breakfast With the Beasts" program for children several times a year. Brooklyn is home to the alluring New York Aquarium, where children can observe dolphin and orca shows, get nose to nose with sharks and handle crabs and starfish in a "touch tank" (the aquatic equivalent of a petting zoo).

Indoor New York also provides a wealth of fun and learning. Almost all of the major cultural institutions have young people's programs, from the Museum of Modern Art to the American Museum of Natural History, which is New York's answer to Jurassic Park, with its magnificently redone hall of dinosaurs. In the outer boroughs, young people's attractions range from the BAM Family series at the Brooklyn Academy of Music to the enormous insect collection at the Staten Island Institute of Arts and Sciences.

But while most of New York's famous places welcome children, there are some locations that were built with them especially in mind. The following are a few of the best places and programs to visit if you're 12 or under—or love someone who is.

Six Great Places for Kids

New Victory Theater   MIDTOWN WEST
209 West 42d St. (between Seventh and Eighth Aves.) (212) 564-4222

If you think of children's theater as marionettes, fairy tales and clowns, you have obviously never visited the New Victory. This is not to say that its productions never use these elements, but if they do, the marionettes are likely to be life-size, the fairy tales sometimes grim (as well as Grimm), and the clowns more like Bill Irwin than the Three Stooges. Opened in December 1995 as part of the redevelopment of Times Square, the New Victory is Broadway's first theater for families, and it is determined never to condescend to its audiences. Its season (October to May) includes the best productions worldwide, from extravaganzas like the Shanghai Circus and Circus Oz (Australia) to small, intimate productions like "Old Man River," a one-woman play. Generally geared to children 6 and older, the season also includes "Step Lively: Dance at the New Victory," a series that exposes young people to different forms of dance. Participants in the one-hour programs, which include a question-and-answer session with the audience, have ranged from Suzanne Farrell's ballet troupe to the Peter Pucci Plus Dancers. This is thinking children's theater, with family-friendly prices ($10–$25; $6–$15 for members) and a location that can't be missed: right across from *The Lion King* on 42nd Street.

Subway: 1, 2, 3, 9, A, C, E, N, R to 42d St.

Theaterworks/USA   CHELSEA
151 West 26th St. (between Sixth and Seventh Aves.) (212) 647-1100
www1.playbill.com/twusa/html/home.html

You don't have to spend money on Disney to take your children to a memorable musical that will send them (and you) home humming. Theaterworks/USA, founded in 1961, produces both musicals and drama that not only introduce children ages 5 and above to the theater, but also provide them with insights into history that are so entertaining that they may not realize how much they're learning. In the last several years, Theaterworks has illustrated a number of important chapters in the growth of the United States, with plays like "Gold Rush," "Young Tom Edison," "The Color of Justice" (about Thurgood Marshall and *Brown v. Topeka*) and "Paul Robeson, All-American." It has also brought literary favorites to the stage, with productions like "Swiss Family Robinson," "Ramona Quimby" (based on Beverly Cleary's novels) and "A Christmas Carol." The 17-show season of hourlong plays runs October to April, with special free productions over the summer. The best works are repeated season to season, but somehow they never get old.

Subway: 1, 9, F to 23d St.

Children's Museum of Manhattan   UPPER WEST SIDE
212 West 83d St. (between Amsterdam Ave. and Broadway)
(212) 721-1223
www.CMOM.org

Children are often consumed by fascinating exhibitions, but the Children's Museum of Manhattan is one of the few places where this can be literally true. At "Body Odyssey," they can enter a huge mouth, wander down a human digestive tract (it even pulsates) and shoot blasts of mock digestive juices. This combination of fun and learning is typical of the museum, which is unusual for both the breadth of its offerings and the wide age range it serves. One of its exhibitions, "Wordplay," includes places for infants to crawl, gaze at mobiles and push buttons as their parents learn about the role of language in their babies' lives. Literacy, in fact, is one of the museum's passions. Having just closed its "Seuss!" exhibition, the museum is about to open (fall 2000) "Good Grief!," on the humor of Charles Schulz and "Peanuts."

Conveniently located on the Upper West Side, the museum also offers the Time-Warner Media Center, an actual television studio where visitors 6 and over can produce their own versions of a newscast or a talk show, and the Sussman Environmental Center, an outdoor oasis for learning about urban ecology. Currently in the midst of a major expansion, the museum will only offer more as the millennium progresses, from a renovated performance theater to a glass-enclosed rooftop garden.

Admission: $5; $2.50, seniors; children under 1, free. **Credit cards:** All major. **Hours:** Wed.–Sun., 10 A.M.–5 P.M. **Services:** Gift shop. **Subway:** 1, 9 to 86th St.

Brooklyn Children's Museum   BROOKLYN
145 Brooklyn Ave. (at St. Mark's Ave.) (718) 735-4400

City chauvinists wouldn't be surprised to learn that the world's first children's museum is in New York. They might be shocked, however, to learn that it's in Crown Heights, Brooklyn. This museum, which celebrated its centennial in 1999, pioneered the hands-on approach characteristic of contemporary children's exhibitions as early as 1904, when it began taking the objects on display out of their glass cases. That's still the philosophy at the museum, which invites children to pluck at musical instruments, handle insect models or try on shoes. Distinctive because it has a permanent collection (very few children's museums do), the Brooklyn Children's Museum has more than 27,000 objects, ranging from an elephant skeleton to Queen Elizabeth II coronation dolls. Early in 2000, the museum opened its Learning Early Gallery, an exhibition space devoted to toddlers. The museum also has a greenhouse, where children can "adopt a plant" and handle earthworms, and a live animal collection whose residents range from furry to scaly. After all, how many museums invite you to pet a snake?

Admission: $3. **Credit cards:** Cash and checks only. **Hours:** Wed.–Fri., 2–5 P.M.; Sat.–Sun., 10 A.M.–5 P.M. **Services:** Gift shop, tours. On weekends the museum holds a series of special events and performances ranging from circus arts presentations to film festivals. **Subway:** 3 to Kingston Ave.; shuttle bus from Brooklyn Museum and Grand Army Plaza subway station (2, 3) on weekends.

Staten Island Children's Museum   STATEN ISLAND
1000 Richmond Terrace (between Tysen St. and Snug Harbor Rd.) (718) 273-2060

Staten Island has become notorious for its landfill, but that's not all that's remarkable about the borough. Consider the Snug Harbor Cultural Center, home to the Staten Island Children's Museum. Nestled in one of the most bucolic settings a New York institution can boast, the museum has a huge front lawn that is turned into a festival site every spring when the museum hosts its Meadowfair, an indoor-outdoor carnival. (The lawn also has a large praying mantis—or, as the museum puts it, playing mantis—sculpture that children climb on.) Indoors, it's just as enticing, with Block Harbor, an area for preschoolers that includes a pirate ship; Portia's Playhouse, which offers children costumes, props and a stage to act out their fantasies; and permanent exhibitions on irresistible subjects like water and bugs (there's an Arthropod Zoo), as well as traveling displays. Now 20,000 square feet, the museum is expanding into an adjacent turn-of-the-century barn (yes, a barn).

Admission: $4; children under 2, free. **Hours:** Sept.-June: Tue.–Sun., noon–5 P.M. **Directions:** Staten Island Ferry to S40 bus.

New York Hall of Science   QUEENS
47–01 111th St. (At 47th Ave.) Flushing (718) 699-0005
www.nyhallsci.org

Any playground is potentially a lesson in physics. But only one playground in New York is especially designed to teach children the scientific concepts that are behind every sway of the seesaw and zoom down the slide. That is the Science Playground at the New York Hall of Science in Queens, the largest (30,000 square feet) playground of its kind in the Western Hemisphere and winner of several awards since it opened in 1997. In 1999, the Hall of Science opened a companion area, the Sound Playground, which is understandably— and educationally—noisy.

Although these special playgrounds are open only to children over 6, the Hall of Science, which began as a pavilion for the 1964–65 World's Fair, offers attractions for younger adventurers, too. The Preschool Discovery Place allows them to explore sound, color, light and simple principles of construction, while permanent displays in the Exhibition Hall offer their older siblings forays into the physical world, from the atomic level on up. Major recent additions include "Marvelous Molecules," an in-depth look at the building blocks of all life, with a biochemistry laboratory that invites young visitors to isolate their own DNA. The city's only hands-on science and technology museum, the Hall is best summed up by its own slogan: "Where Minds Play."

Admission: $7.50; $5, children (4–16) and seniors; Thur.–Fri., 2–5 P.M., free. **Credit cards:** MC/V; checks. **Hours:** Mon.–Wed., 9:30 A.M.–2 P.M.; Thur.–Sun., 9:30 A.M.–5 P.M. **Services:** Gift shop, lectures. **Subway:** 7 to 111th St. in Queens.

—Laurel Graeber

MORE ACTIVITIES FOR KIDS
Zoos and Wildlife Centers

Bronx Zoo (Wildlife Conservation Park)   BRONX
2300 Southern Blvd. at Bronx Park South (718) 367-1010
(See "The Bronx" for full description.)

Admission: Thur.-Tue., adults, $7.75; children 2–12 and seniors, $4; children
under 2, free. (less in the off-season). Wed. daytime, free, except for Holiday
Lights. **Credit cards:** Cash only. **Hours:** Mon.–Fri., 10 A.M.–5 P.M.; Sat.–Sun.
and holidays, 10 A.M.–5:30 P.M. Children's Zoo and all rides closed during winter. Tickets sold until 4 P.M., Mon.–Fri.; until 4:30 P.M., weekends and holidays,
Children's Theater, 11 A.M.–4 P.M. (adults, $2; children $1.50). **Services:** Gift
shop, cafeteria, stroller rental, handicapped accessible. **Subway:** 2, 5 to Bronx
Park East.

Central Park Zoo   UPPER EAST SIDE
Fifth Ave. and 64th St. (212) 861-6030

*(See **Central Park** for full listing.)*
Generations of New Yorkers have grown up with the Central Park Zoo. Divided
into three zones—Arctic, rain forest and temperate—the center features animals in naturalistic settings. Its emphasis on public education is evident in the
newly remodeled Tisch Children's Zoo, in which interactive nature exhibits
have replaced kitschy storybook characters. Admission to the children's zoo is
included in the general admission price, but make sure you bring along an extra
pocketful of quarters for the feed dispensers near the goat and cow pens. Parents
will also want to check on sea lion, polar bear, and penguin feeding times—all
of which provide a fascinating spectacle for kids and adults.

Admission: $3.50, adults; $1.25, seniors; $.50, children 3–12; under 3, free. (No
group rates.) **Hours:** Open 365 days a year, 10 A.M.–5 P.M. weekdays and 10:30
A.M.–5:30 P.M weekends and holidays April-Oct; 10 A.M.–4:30 P.M. daily
Nov.-Mar. **Services:** Cafeteria, gift shop, handicapped accessible. **Subway:** N, R
to Fifth Ave.; 4, 5, 6 to 59th St.

New York Aquarium for Wildlife Conservation
BROOKLYN
Surf Ave. and West 8th St., Brooklyn (718) 265-3400

Located on a strip of coastline between Coney Island and Brighton Beach, the
aquarium may at first seem prohibitively remote. But it's out there for a reason,
and worth the trip. With more than 300 species of marine life and an impressive
collection of marine mammals, the aquarium has narrated feedings, underwater
viewing areas, and up-close animal encounters. Check out the sea lion and dolphin performances in the Aquatheater, as well as the hands-on Discovery Cen-

ter. The aquarium also offer special seasonal events, like the Halloween "Sea Monsters" weekend.

Admission: $8.75, adults; $4.50, children 2–12 and seniors; children under 2, free. Children under 16 must be accompanied by an adult. Special group rates are available by reservation only, call (718) 220-5198. **Credit cards:** Cash only. **Hours:** Mon.–Fri., 10 A.M.–5 P.M.; Sat.- Sun., 10 A.M.–6 P.M. **Services:** Tours, lectures, handicapped accessible. **Subway:** F, D to West 8th St.; take pedestrian bridge to aquarium.

Prospect Park Zoo   BROOKLYN
450 Flatbush Ave. (718) 399-7339

It isn't as comprehensive as the Bronx Zoo, but this 19-acre park is still worth a trip out of Manhattan. It's extremely kid-friendly, featuring giant lily pads and kid-size goose eggs to play with, plus a "barnyard" with assorted touchable animals. Kids will also enjoy the interactive Wildlife Center, home to numerous lectures and special workshops throughout the year.

Admission: $2.50, adults; $.50, children 3–12; $1.25, seniors; children under 3, free. No group rates. **Hours:** Open 365 days at 10 A.M.; close, 5 P.M., weekdays, and 5:30 P.M. weekends and holidays, (4:30 P.M. Nov.-Mar.). **Services:** Gift shop, café, handicapped accessible. **Subway:** D, Q to Prospect Park.

Queens Wildlife Conservation Center   QUEENS
111th St. (at 54th Ave.), Flushing, Queens (718) 886-3800

This 11-acre park was renovated in 1992, making it more child-oriented and interactive. Kids will enjoy the aviary, the herd of American bison, and a variety of domesticated animals in the petting zoo. The zoo runs special seasonal programs, too, including an elaborate Groundhog's Day "celebration of prognosticating rodents."

Admission: $2.50 Adults; $1.25 Seniors; $.50 Children, over 3–12; free under 3 yrs. **Hours:** Open 365 days at 10 A.M.; close, 5 P.M., weekdays and 5:30 P.M., weekends and holidays April-Oct (4:30 P.M. Nov.-Mar.) **Services:** Gift shop, café, handicapped accessible. **Subway:** 7 to 111th St.

Staten Island Zoo   STATEN ISLAND
614 Broadway(at Glenwood Pl.) (718) 442-3100

Opened in 1936, the Staten Island Zoo is smaller than the zoos in the other four boroughs, but it holds its own as an educational institution by offering extensive outreach programs. The zoo houses a menagerie of more than 400 animals on its eight acres. There is also an aquarium, a children's zoo where youngsters can feed the animals, a noteworthy display of reptiles, a tropical forest exhibit and a simulation of the African savannah at twilight. The zoo is closed only three days of the year.

Admission: $3, adults; $2, children, 3–11; children under 3, free. Wed. after 2 P.M., free. **Hours:** Daily, 10 A.M.–4:45 P.M.

Museums and Programs for Children

Brooklyn Children's Museum
See introduction for description.

Children's Museum of Manhattan
See introduction for description.

Children's Museum of the Arts   SOHO
182 Lafayette St. (between Broome and Grand Sts.) (212) 941-9198

The museum's new home on Lafayette Street in SoHo includes interactive installations like the ever-popular Ball Pond, a room filled with oversized rubber balls that children can crawl through, and two floors of art studios for children to participate in hands-on projects. There is also gallery space exhibiting work by children and adults.

Admission: $5; seniors and children under 1 year free. **Credit cards:** MC/V. **Hours:** Wed., noon–7 P.M.; Thur.–Sun., noon–5 P.M. **Subway:** N, R to Prince St.

South Street Seaport Museum   LOWER MANHATTAN
207 Front St. (between South and Water Sts.) (212) 425-3737

There is a special children's center here, but all of the nautical galleries, shops, and ships are meant to be family-friendly.

Admission: $6, general; $5, seniors; $4, students. **Hours:** Daily, 10 A.M.–6 P.M. **Services:** Tours, gift shop, lectures. **Subway:** 2, 3, 4, 5, to Fulton St.

Staten Island Children's Museum
See introduction for listing.

Special Children's Tours at NYC's Top Museums
Phone numbers in this section are hotlines for child and family programs, when available.

American Museum of Natural History Central Park West (at 79th St.) (212) 769-5100. This is a can't-go-wrong trip for families. Kids and adults will find much here to enjoy together, from the Dinosaur Halls to the enormous IMAX theater to the Hall of Ocean Life, with its giant blue whale hanging from the ceiling. On the last weekend of each month, families can also visit the Discovery Room (with children over 5, closed holidays, weekdays, and Sept.) noon to 4:30 P.M. Free with museum admission, this learning center offers touchable specimens and "discovery boxes" that teach the kids about science. The Leonhardt People Center (open 1–5 P.M. Oct.-May, every weekend) presents a wide range of cross-cultural learning opportunities in music, dance, lectures, and films meant for all ages.

Prices: (Suggested admission) $9.50, adults; $6, children; $7.50, students and seniors. **Hours:** Sun.–Thur., 10 A.M.–5:45 P.M.; Fri.–Sat., 10 A.M.–8:45 P.M. Closed Thanksgiving and Christmas.

Brooklyn Museum 200 Eastern Parkway, Prospect Park
(718) 638-5000. Kids will enjoy the largest collection of mummies outside Egypt, as well as an excellent children's workshop. Visit *www.brooklynexpedition.org* to pick up a free online pass for one adult and one child to this museum or to the Brooklyn Children's Museum.

Guggenheim Museum 1071 Fifth Ave. (at 88th St.) (212) 423-3587
www.guggenheim.org If nothing else, kids will enjoy the fun, spiraling space (but remember, no strollers). Make time for the café, too, and consider coming in for one of the Friday or Saturday night Jazz sessions. Call ahead to find out about special family programs, like the Family Tour and Art Workshops: tours of current exhibits folloWed. by a hands-on workshop for the whole family.

The Jewish Museum 1109 Fifth Ave. (at 92d St.) (212) 423-3200.
The museum offers a diverse series of family programs every Sunday, from sing-a-longs to storytimes to art activities to theater performances.

Metropolitan Museum of Art 1000 Fifth Ave. (at 82d St.) (212) 535-7710
www.metmuseum.org Children and adults alike will find the Met overwhelming, so come here with a game plan. The "Museum Hunt" guides, available at information desks, are a good place to start: they present special and permanent collections to kids through fun activities. There are a number of family tours and workshops, like A First Look, offered Saturdays at 11 A.M. and 2:30 P.M., and Sunday at 11 A.M. These hour-and-a-half sessions introduce adults and kids age 6–12 to art via discussions and assorted art projects. The museum also offers family films on Saturday from 12:30–1:00 P.M. and 2:00–2:30 P.M.

Museum of Modern Art (MoMA) 11 West 53d St. (between Fifth and Sixth Aves.) (212) 708-9400 www.moma.org MoMA offers some of the most extensive and varied family programs around. The museum is unique in offering Tours for Tots—introductions to painting and sculpture for kids as young as four. You can also try the One-at-a-Time drop-in guided walks for kids 5–10, or the Two-in-a-Row tours (held on two consecutive mornings) for the entire family. Or take a break from walking, and enjoy MoMA's family films, generally strong in live action, animation, documentary, and fantasy. Films are introduced by a museum educator who encourages discussion and suggests related activities to pursue in the galleries. Don't forget the Donnell Public Library across the street, which houses the original Winnie the Pooh collection.
Prices: Gallery Talks: One-at-a-Time, $5 per family, $3 members; Two-in-a-Row, $15 per family, $10 members. Family Films: $5 per family, members free.
Hours: Most family programs are held Saturday mornings, and advance reservations are necessary for most talks and tours.

The Whitney Museum 945 Madison Ave. (at 75thSt.) (212) 570-7710
www.whitney.org The Whitney offers programs and activities in conjunction
with current exhibitions, encouraging adults and children to learn about American
art and culture together. In addition, families can attend a free guided tour
every Saturday at 1 P.M. No reservations are required.

Science for Children

Liberty Science Center   NEW JERSEY
251 Phillip St. (at Communipaw Ave.), Jersey City (201) 200-1000

The Liberty Science Center in Jersey City is an institution that uses interactive
exploration to teach visitors about science and technology. Each of the
center's three floors is devoted to a specific theme: environment, health and
invention. Visitors of all ages can touch starfish or giant insects at the center's
many hands-on exhibits, crawl through a 100-foot "touch tunnel," play virtual
basketball or see movies on the domed Imax screen. At Roach World,
renowned entomologist Betty Faber will teach you everything there is to
know about your unwelcome kitchen guests. There are also many temporary
exhibitions.

Admission: $9.50; $7.50, children and seniors. **Credit cards:** All major. **Hours:**
Daily, 9:30 A.M.–5:30 P.M. **Services:** IMAX films. **Directions:** Free shuttle
buses from the Grove Street PATH train station and the Colgate Center, which
is linked by ferry to the World Financial Center in Manhattan.

New York Hall of Science
See introduction for description.

Sony Wonder Technology Lab   MIDTOWN EAST
550 East 56th St. (between Madison and Fifth Aves.) (212) 833-8100

No doubt about it: Sony Wonder Technology Lab is one of the city's coolest
destinations for kids, and it's free. Greeted by a talking robot, kids get bar-
coded cards that make them part of the lab's attractions. They can produce
their own TV shows or remix a song by Celine Dion. At a command center,
they can analyze weather data to avert disasters, cruise the Net or watch
HDTV. But, keep in mind, this free public space dedicated to technology education is more specifically dedicated to Sony technology education. It just happens to be operated by Sony's retail division, and, not surprisingly, showcases
only Sony products.

Admission: Free. **Hours:** Tue.–Wed., Fri.–Sat., 10 A.M.–6 P.M.; Sun., noon–6
P.M.; Thur., 10 A.M.–8 P.M. **Services:** Tours, gift shop. **Subway:** E, F to Fifth
Ave.; 4, 5, 6 to 59th St.

Music for Children

Amato Opera-in-Brief   EAST VILLAGE
319 Bowery (at 2d St.) (212) 228-8200

In addition to its standard performances, this company has been doing opera for
children for over 50 years. The "Brief" performances are fully-costumed, abbre-
viated versions of classic operas, featuring interwoven narration so everyone can
follow the story. All performances are only 90 minutes long (including intermission) and should be appropriate for children 5 and up.

Prices: $15 all seats. **Schedule:** Usually six shows per year, all start at 11:30
A.M., days vary.

Carnegie Hall Family Concerts   MIDTOWN
152 West 57th St. (at Seventh Ave.) (212) 903-9670

At these hour-long Saturday afternoon concerts, families get an introduction to
music and musical instruments and concepts through a variety of demonstrations and activities led by well-known performers and groups. Kids also get a
special "KidsBill," filled with musical activities and information.

Prices: $5. **Schedule:** Held throughout the season.

Lincoln Center Children's Programs
Broadway and 64th Street. (See individual programs for phone numbers.)

Many people don't know about the special kids' concerts available at Lincoln
Center, most of which feature the same performers as the regular season concerts. Unfortunately, there are only a few of these concerts each year, and
schedules can vary from season to season; parents should call well in advance to
find out when these shows will be available.

Growing Up With Opera (212) 769-7008 The Metropolitan Opera sponsors
two different shows each year for kids aged 4–6 and 6–12, often featuring question-and-answer sessions and "cast parties" with the artists afterwards.
Prices: Avg. $10.

Jazz for Young People Alice Tully Hall (212) 721-6500. Wynton Marsalis
hosts and performs at these educational concerts, delving into themes like
"What is Swing Dancing?" and "What is Afro Cuban Jazz?" Concerts are usually
held three Saturdays a year.
Prices: $15, adults; $10, children 18 and under.

Little Orchestra Society Avery Fisher Hall (212) 704-2100. Each season, the
New York Philharmonic plays four concerts geared toward 5–12 year old children, and three concerts for 3–5 year olds. Shows often sell out, but sometimes
same-day tickets do become available.

Meet the Music Alice Tully Hall (212) 875-5000. The Chamber Music Society of Lincoln Center sponsors four concerts each year, introducing children to chamber music.

New York City Opera Family Workshops New York State Theater (212) 870-5600. These hour-long workshops are held before select City Opera weekend matinee performances. Children ages 6–12 can participate in musical numbers and dances with opera performers, as well as other educational activities.

New York Philharmonic Young People's Concerts (212) 721-6500 www.nyphilharmon.org The Philharmonic offers four of these Saturday afternoon concerts each year, providing a fun introduction to symphonic music for 6–12 year olds. Ticket holders can also attend the one-hour "Children's Promenades" before each concert, where children can participate in music-making activities and meet members of the orchestra.
Prices: $6–$21.

Theater for Children

Arts Connection   MIDTOWN WEST
120 West 46th St. (bet. Sixth Ave. and Broadway) (212) 302-7433

Ask about the "Saturdays Alive" series of affordable performances and workshops.

Subway: 1, 2, 3, 9, B, D, F, Q, N, R to 42d St.; 7 or Times Sq.-Grand Central Shuttle to Times Square.

Grove Street Playhouse   WEST VILLAGE
39 Grove St. (Seventh Ave. and Bleecker St.) (212) 741-6436

This group adapts classics for children with humor for adults, and presents shows in a participatory manner: kids are encouraged to talk, move, and even shout.

Subway: 1, 9 to Christopher St.

Henry Street Settlement Abrons Arts Theater
LOWER EAST SIDE
466 Grand St. (at Pitt St.) (212) 598-0400

Weekly Arts for Family series, from puppetry to magic to theater.

Subway: B, D, Q to Grand St.

Here   SOHO
145 Sixth Ave. (near Spring St.) (212) 647-0202

Productions for kids every Saturday.

Subway: C, E to Spring St.

Lunt-Fontanne Theater   MIDTOWN WEST
205 West 46th St. (between Eighth Ave. and Broadway)

The current home of Disney's ever-popular production of *Beauty and the Beast*.

New Amsterdam Theater   MIDTOWN WEST
214 West 42d St. (between Seventh and Eighth Aves.) (212) 282-2900

Tickets for the theater's current and seemingly permanent attraction, *The Lion King*, are hard to come by, but Disney does offer tours of the theater. But if you can get your hands on them, when Julie Taymor's life-size animal puppets and costumes lumber down the aisles, pandemonium erupts.

Subway: 1, 2 , 3, 9, N, R to 42d St.

New York Youth Theater   UPPER EAST SIDE
593 Park Ave. (at 64th St.) (212) 242-2822

Saturday and Sunday performances of kids' productions.

Subway: 6 to 68th St.

New Victory Theater
See introduction for description.

TADA! Youth Ensemble   CHELSEA
120 West 28th St. (between Sixth and Seventh Aves.) (212) 243-6736

They sell out quickly, but most kids will appreciate these one-hour original shows performed by 6–17 year old actors. The schedule runs throughout the year, and frequently includes weekday and Friday night performances.

Subway: 1, 9, to 28th St.

Theaterworks/USA
See introduction for description.

13th Street Repertory Theater   WEST VILLAGE
50 West 13th St. (between Fifth and Sixth Aves.) (212) 675-6677

Located in a Greenwich Village brownstone, this theater's lobby is cozy, with lots of worn but comfortable chairs and sofas. A few steps farther and a short hallway away is the actual theater, with 72 cushioned seats and a slightly elevated and modestly wide and deep stage. On weekend afternoons there are children's shows.

Subway: F to 14th St.

West End Café Children's Theater   UPPER WEST SIDE
2911 Broadway (at 113th St.) (212) 877-6115

A wide variety of shows for family audiences are offered at this location near Columbia University. This is actually a restaurant, too, so it's best to arrive a half-hour or so before the 1 P.M. showtimes to order food.

Subway: 1, 9 to 110th St.

Puppets

Crowtations CENTRAL PARK
Bethesda Fountain (mid-park and 72d St.)

In good weather, this group performs between 1 and 6 P.M. on weekends.

Subway: 1, 2, 3, 9 to 72d St.

The Lenny Suib Puppet Playhouse UPPER EAST SIDE
555 East 90th St. (between York and East End Ave.) (212) 369-8890 ext. 159

This large theater offers puppet shows, magicians, clowns, ventriloquists, and storytellers.

Subway: 4, 5, 6 to 86th St.

Swedish Cottage Marionette Theater CENTRAL PARK
Central Park West Drive (at 81st St.) (212) 988-9093

*See **Central Park** for details.*

Puppetworks BROOKLYN
338 Sixth Ave. (at 4th St.), Park Slope (718) 965-3391

This group has been performing with their hand-crafted marionettes since 1938. They generally offer three or four stories per year, with performances Saturdays and Sundays.

Subway: F to Seventh Ave.

Circuses

Big Apple Circus
(800) 922-3772
www.bigapplecircus.org

With its local roots, intimate one-ring big top and kid-friendly mission, the Big Apple Circus has staked out its own ground between the glitz of Ringling Brothers and the artistry of Cirque du Soleil. Performances are held in the circus's quaint big top in Damrosch Park at Lincoln Center, from late October to early January. Performance times and ticket prices vary, and there are a number of weekend and weekday matinees.

Cirque du Soleil

Battery Park (near World Financial Center) (800) 678-5440
www.cirquedusoleil.com

This French-Canadian troupe reaches New York with one of its touring shows
about every other year. No animals here, but kids and adults won't miss them—
each of Cirque du Soleil's several themed shows includes an incredible variety
of performers from clowns to trapeze artists to other talents you never knew
existed. The surreal humor of most of these shows may be over the heads of
young children, but they'll still be entranced by the spectacle.

Ringling Brothers and Barnum and Bailey Circus

Madison Square Garden, Seventh Ave. (at 33d St.) (800) 755-4000
www.ringling.com

The classic American three-ring circus—trapeze artists, lion tamers, and all—
descends on Madison Square Garden every spring, running shows in March and
April.

Play Spaces

Chelsea Piers   CHELSEA

Pier 62 (West Side Hwy. and 23d St.) (212) 336-6500

Two gyms for kids with some designated free hours. There's also an area for
younger kids that is completely supervised at times.

Subway: C, E to 23d St.

Lazer Park   MIDTOWN WEST

163 West 46th St. (between Sixth and Seventh Aves.) (212) 398-3060

A 5,000-square-foot laser tag arena, meant solely for older kids.

Subway: 1, 2, 3, 9, B, D, F, Q, N, R to 42d St.

My Favorite Place   UPPER WEST SIDE

265 West 87th St. (at Broadway) (212) 362-5320

One room with lots of toys, right under a toy store. They offer all sorts of arts
and crafts activities, as well as special Friday night programs.

Subway: 1, 9 to 86th St.

Playspace   UPPER WEST SIDE

2473 Broadway (at 92d St.) (212) 769-2300

This is a bright and clean operation, with a good café for parents. It will be
crowded on rainy weekends. It also offers birthday parties and classes.

Subway: 1, 2, 3, 9 to 96th St.

Rain or Shine   MURRAY HILL
115 East 29th St. (Park and Madison) (212) 532-4420

Everything under one roof: a sandbox, tree house, playhouse, art center, and baby center. They sometimes offer puppet shows and free playtime.

Subway: 6 to 28th St.

X S New York   MIDTOWN WEST
1457 Broadway (at 41st St.) (212) 398-5467

Laser tag, video games, virtual reality simulations, and a café.

Subway: 1, 2, 3, 9, N, R to 42d St.

Outdoor Attractions and Activities for Children

See also "Prospect Park" and "Sports and Recreation" sections.

Central Park
(See the entry "Central Park" in Exploring New York *for more detailed information on the park)*

Central Park's Children's District (mid-park, 64th-65th St.) offers a wealth of activities, from the **Carousel** and **Wollman Skating Rink** to the **Heschker Playground.** A good place to start is **The Dairy** (mid-park at 64th St.)—originally a real dairy, now an information center with a variety of activities for children. It also offers an excellent map of the park. Perhaps the most popular children's attraction in the park lies to the east, along Fifth Avenue: the **Children's Zoo,** part of the Central Park Wildlife Conservation Center, has interesting exhibits, a petting zoo and structures (like a giant spider's web) for kids to climb.

Around 74th Street, also on the east side of the park, lies **Conservatory Water,** a popular pond where kids and adults can rent remote controlled boats in the afternoon. Nearby are the well-known statues of **Alice in Wonderland** and **Hans Christian Andersen** (story readings Wed. and Sat., 11 A.M., at this statue during the summer). Towards the center of the park, around 79th Street, is **Belvedere Castle;** kids will love this miniature storybook castle and the **Nature Observatory** inside. You can also see a show at the **Swedish Cottage Marionette Theater,** located just to the west of the Castle.

If you find yourself above the 97th Street Transverse, you'll want to stop at the **North Meadow Recreation Center** (mid-park, around 98th Street) to borrow one of their great "field kits" for kids, packed with assorted toys and activities to try in the park. And if you're at the very top of the park, plan to spend some time around the body of water known as **Harlem Meer.** From the **Charles A. Dana Discovery Center,** to **Conservatory Garden** with its charming Secret Garden statue, to **Lasker Rink and Pool,** families will easily find a fun way to while away the afternoon.

New York Botanical Garden   BRONX
200th St. (at Southern Blvd.) (718) 817-8705

A 25-minute tram tour gives an excellent overview of the gardens. The Everett Children's Adventure Garden provides eight acres and hours of entertainment. There's a three-foot high hedge maze that will delight small children, and the Gardens' numerous workshops and activities give kids a good introduction to botany and gardening. *See the entry in "The Bronx" for complete description.*

Admission: $10, adults; $7.50, seniors and students; $4, children 2–12; children under 2 free. **Hours:** Tue.–Sun., 10 A.M.–6 P.M.

OTHER SELECTED PLAYGROUNDS AND PARKS

Upper West Side

Riverside Park playgrounds (72d-129th Sts. and Riverside Dr.), a number of distinctive playgrounds with good views of the Hudson River.

Riverbank State Park (137th-145th Sts. and Hudson River)

Sakura Park (122d St. and Riverside Church/Int'l House)

Cathedral of St. John the Divine (110th-113th Sts. and Amsterdam Ave.), Biblical garden with hens and peacocks, plus a small playground.

Sol Bloom Playground (93d St. between Columbus and Central Park West)

Saint Gregory the Great Playground (W. 90th St. between Columbus and Amsterdam Aves.)

77th St. Park (Wood Park) (Amsterdam Ave and 77th St.), featured on Sesame Street

Upper East Side

Twenty-four Sycamores (Gateway Park) (61st St. and York Ave.)

St. Catherine's Playground (First Ave. between 67th and 68th Sts.)

John Jay Park (76th St. and York Ave.), quiet and well-renovated with a public pool nearby.

Carl Schurz Playground (East End Ave. and 84th St.), safe and clean with family-friendly shops nearby.

Ruppert Park Playground (Second Ave. between 90th and 91st St.)

Asphalt Green Playground (York Ave. between 91st and 92d Sts.), next to a swimming center.

Hunter School Playground (Madison Ave. between 94th and 95th Sts.), open to the public after school hours.

Lexington Avenue Playground (96th St. and Third Ave.)

Midtown

Sutton Place Park (Sutton Place and 57th St.), only for toddlers.

Tudor City Playground (42d St. between First and Second Aves.)

Bryant Park (Sixth Ave between 40th and 42d St.), good fountain.

Robert Moses Playground (FDR Dr. between 41st and 42 St.), good playground, handball and basketball courts.

Chelsea/Flatiron

Madison Square (Broadway bet 23d and 26 Sts.)

Clement Clarke Moore Playground (22d St. and 10th Ave.), tiny, but near Chelsea Piers.

Augustus St. Clemen Gaudens Playground (Second Ave. and 18th St.)

Union Square (16th-19th St. and Broadway), two playgrounds and a dog run.

East Village

Tompkins Square Park (Ave. A and 9 St.)

Greenwich Village

Abingdon Square Park (Eighth Ave. and 12th St.)

32 Carmine Street Playground (Sixth Ave and Bleecker)

Bleecker Street Playground (at Bleecker and Hudson Sts.)

Washington Square Park (Fifth Ave between Waverly Pl. and West 4th St), two playgrounds, a big fountain, and near-constant shows by assorted street musicians, magicians, and other performers.

SoHo

Mercer Street Playground (Mercer St. between (Bleecker and West 3d Sts.), special area for kids 8–12 and an in-line skate path.

Thompson St. Playground (Thompson St. between Prince and Spring Sts.)

Chinatown

Columbus Park (Worth St. between Baxter and Mulberry Sts.)

Wall Street

Pearl St. Playground (Fulton St. between Water and Pearl Sts.), very modern.

Little Italy

De Salvio Playground (at Mulberry and Spring Sts.), lots of shade and a multicultural crowd.

TriBeCa

Rockefeller Playground (Chambers St. at Hudson River), consistently voted best in city, with award-winning architecture, a carousel, and all sorts of water and climbing equipment for different ages.

Pier 25 Children's Park (N. Moore St. and Hudson River), features a "beach" with lots of activities, and a great café for parents.

Washington Market Park (Greenwich St. between Chambers and Duane St.), three acres of grass and a tiny playground.

Battery Park Esplanade (World Financial Center, Rector St. at Hudson River)

Robert F. Wagner Park (next to Battery Park City), good view and a café.

Battery Park City (South tip of Manhattan), two playgrounds—the best is by the yacht basin.

Brooklyn Heights
Pierrepont Playground (Promenade South, Brooklyn Heights), beautiful public space from the designer of the Rockefeller Playground in TriBeCa).

Kid-Friendly Restaurants

Too often taking children out to eat is more about endurance than enjoyment. But these restaurants are welcoming to families, relaxing for parents and adept at putting children at ease, making them less conscious of being on their best behavior.

Upper West Side

Avenue 520 Columbus Ave. (at 85th St.) (212) 579-3194. This informal French restaurant features a baby-food menu, including carrots with a soft but slightly chunky texture, a tasty organic pear purée and a vanilla custard that parents will finish if the baby does not.

Upper East Side

Barking Dog Luncheonette 1678 Third Avenue (at 94th St.)
(212) 831-1800. If the children fidget while waiting for the All-American menu items or rich, bountiful desserts, distract them with the restaurant's dog tchotchkes. For families that can't get going in the morning, breakfast is served until 4 P.M.

Pig Heaven 1540 Second Ave. (near 80th St.) (212) 744-4333. The staff at this terrific Chinese restaurant is friendly, efficient and especially receptive to children, who love the new collection of pig decorations. They will also love the exotic desserts, like frozen praline mousse or the Peking snowball.

Saigon Grill 1700 Second Ave. (at 88th St.) (212) 996-4600. This plain, bright Vietnamese restaurant is usually packed with families. Despite the volume, it manages to serve delicious, meticulously prepared dishes like green papaya salad, topped with grilled beef; cool rice noodles; and summer rolls wrapped in rice paper.

East Village

Cyclo 203 First Avenue (near 12th St.) (212) 673-3957. Many children love Vietnamese restaurants for chao tom, the ubiquitous appetizer of grilled shrimp paste wrapped around a stalk of sugar cane. Cyclo offers other kid-pleasing dishes like greaseless spring rolls, or chicken roasted with lemongrass and lime juice.

Midtown West

John's Pizzeria 260 West 44th Street (between Seventh and Eighth Aves.) (212) 391-7560. Housed in what used to be the Christian Alliance Gospel Tabernacle Church, this is both the largest pizzeria in New York and the most beautiful. For families, there are two important distinctions: the service is friendly, and you are likely to get a seat without waiting.

Virgil's 152 West 44th St. (between Broadway and Sixth Ave.) (212) 921-9494. How could parents not appreciate a restaurant that offers towels in place of napkins? Virgil's also offers uncanny reproductions of barbecue styles from North Carolina to Texas. Family favorites like pork ribs and pulled Carolina pork are top-notch.

Little Italy

Lombardi's 32 Spring Street (near Mott St.) (212) 941-7994. The chefs at historic Lombardi's love to show off their pizza oven. If it's not too busy, they shepherd children to the rear, explain how the oven works and even allow them to toss in a chunk of coal.

TriBeCa

Odeon 145 West Broadway (at Thomas St.) (212) 233-0507. The dining room here is unpretentious, comfortable and friendly to children. Entrees stretch from hamburgers to risotto, roast chicken and the usual pastas. A children's menu is available at all times, even 2 A.M.

Sosa Borella 460 Greenwich St. (near Desbrosses St.) (212) 431-5093. With its open-arms policy toward children, this quiet, out-of-the-way restaurant is a natural choice for a family weekend brunch. There is an extensive list of delicious sandwiches at midday and an Argentine dinner menu. Desserts and cookies are delectable.

SoHo

Penang 109 Spring St. (between Mercer and Greene Sts.) (212) 274-8883. This wonderfully authentic Malaysian restaurant is popular with children for the rocky waterfall in back and for the delicious roti canai, a thin crepe served with mild coconut curry sauce. Children also like the pork ribs and the sweet, crunchy peanut pancake.

Popular Theme Restaurants for Families

Hard Rock Café
221 West 57th St. (at Broadway) (212) 459-9320
Credit cards: All major;   Meals: L, D, LN

Don't be deterred when you see a busload of kids waiting outside. If you are on your own, they'll give you a pager that calls you from the Hard Rock souvenir store next door when your time has come. Service inside is quick and friendly. The walls are covered with "memorabilia"—rock stars' guitars, platinum platters, more guitars, photos, posters.

Price range: Avg. kids meal, $6.99; adult entrees, $8–$18.

Jekyll & Hyde Club
1409 Ave. of the Americas (at 57th St.) (212) 541-9505
Credit cards: All major;   Meals: L, D, LN

Spooky, bizarre and famously camp, with generous helpings of food. Jekyll & Hyde packs hair-raising hourly entertainment, animated skeletons, roving actors and a conversational sphinx into a dark old four-story mansion. The best tables for seeing and interacting are on the first two floors. A voice from nowhere wishes "Happy Birthday!" to all who admit it. Waits can be long, but children are usually enchanted. Reservations are required for groups of 15 or more.

Price range: Avg. kids meal, $7.95; adult entrees, $7.95–$19.50.

Mars 2112
1633 Broadway (at 51st St.) (212) 582-2112
Credit cards: All major;   Meals: L, D

It doesn't get any stranger than this. Mars 2112, the multimillion-dollar theme restaurant, features a mock flight to Mars, where steaming lava pools greet your arrival. At the Mars Bar, you'll find everything from planetary news and weather reports to scenic views of the planet, not to mention fancifully named drinks and locally brewed "Martian" beers. Sit-down dining in one of the three dining areas in the Martian colony offers much of the same visual experience, with options ranging from Big Bang bruschetta to Ziggy Stardust spaghetti. Souvenirs, of course, are available for sale at the Martian shopping complex.

Price range: Avg. kids meal, $8.95; adult entrees, $10–$20.

Official All Star Café

Broadway and 45th St. (212) 840-8326

Credit cards: All major;   Meals: L, D, LN

In a big round room with a sky high ceiling, the Official All Star Café is all stars—Tiger Woods, Monica Seles, Wayne Gretzky and more. Their photos line the walls, from childhood to superstardom, surrounded by golf balls, tennis balls, hockey sticks, etc. There is so much going on, in so many media, that it is easy to forget that this is a restaurant. But yes, there's plenty of food—a sort of greatest hits of American fast food; it includes appetizers like egg rolls and quesadillas, salads of all sorts and burgers with a dizzying array of toppings.

Price range: Avg. kids meal, $4.95; adult entrees, $7.50–$19.

For the latest information on restaurants, hotels, concerts, nightlife, sporting events and more, check online at New York Today, the *New York Times* website devoted entirely to life in New York City: www.nytoday.com.

Nightlife

By now, most visitors (as well as the majority of residents) have grown tired of song lyrics about "the city that never sleeps"; where you "can do a half a million things, all at a quarter to three." Well, like most clichés, these are entirely true. With the possible exception of New Orleans during Mardi Gras, New York reigns as—get ready for another cliché—the nightlife capital of the world.

All platitudes aside, bar closing time *is* at 4 A.M. Dance clubs often stay open until well into the morning, but stop serving at the bar. Music venues may close after the last set or keep jumping with a DJ or jukebox until the last customer has gone home. Whichever nighttime activities are on the agenda, chances are you will be exhausted before your options are.

The distinctions among bars, lounges, clubs and music venues are blurry at best. Expect live music at bars and clubs, dancing at lounges and music venues and DJ's everywhere.

Because so many establishments feature a variety of activities, it is always important to check local listings. *The New York Times* (Friday), *www.nytoday.com* (*The New York Times'* city guide on the Web), *Time Out New York,* the *Village Voice, New York* magazine, *The New Yorker* and the *New York Press* all run weekly listings.

BARS & LOUNGES BY NEIGHBORHOOD

Many tourists concentrate on dance clubs and other places with music (*discussed later in this section*) when planning their evenings in the city. And while New York's clubs are essential to the city's nightlife, it's often in the pubs and lounges, the neighborhood watering holes and swank hot spots, that New York after dark can really be appreciated. From the most elegant hotel bars to the deepest of dives, New York has something for everyone—often all on one block.

The difference between bars and lounges is subtle and usually lies in the attitude—and maybe a few couches. Lounges also often have DJ's, but not the cabaret license required to host legal dancing. Although the Giuliani administration has conducted frequent raids in recent years, the requisite signs reading, "No dancing by order of law," are often disregarded by patrons and displayed with a wink from the management.

The following listings cover only a small fraction of the more than 1,000 bars in Manhattan. They were chosen for their historical significance, current popularity, location or other particular points of interest. For more complete listings go to *www.nytoday.com.*

Lower Manhattan/TriBeCa

Bridge Café 279 Water St. (at Dover St.) (212) 227-3344. The Bridge Café, located in a three-story wood-framed building dating from 1794, may be the oldest continually operated eating and drinking establishment in the city. Neighborhood residents and employees of the nearby courthouses, financial district and City Hall crowd the cafe's bar stools and petite burgundy cloth-covered tables. The drink list includes more than 60 domestic wines and 30 varieties of single malt scotch.

Credit cards: All major. **Subway:** J, M, Z, 2, 3, 4, 5 to Fulton St.; A, C to Broadway-Nassau St.

Bubble Lounge 228 West Broadway (between White and Franklin Sts.) (212) 431-3433. This sophisticated bar is a great place to take a date if you're trying to look classier than you really are. With over 290 types of champagne and sparkling wines, expensive cigars, caviar and clams on the half shell, there's no shortage of opportunities to splurge. With plush red couches, seductive lounge music and dim lighting, the Bubble Lounge is highly conducive to flirting.

Credit cards: All major. **Subway:** 1, 9 to Franklin St.; A, C, E to Canal St.

El Teddy's 219 West Broadway (Between Franklin and White Sts.) (212) 941-7070. Finding decent Mexican food and drink in this city is harder than finding a good apartment. It's no wonder, then, that El Teddy's is constantly packed to the gills, combining a schmaltzy 1980's wonderland decor with solid cocktails and dining. Its TriBeCa location means the bar is packed with after-work Wall Streeters slamming back the fruits of the bull market over some seriously tasty guacamole and chips.

Credit cards: All major. **Subway:** 1, 9 to Franklin St.

Liquor Store 235 West Broadway (at White St.) (212) 226-7121. The laid-back locals who frequent this undersized corner bar blend congenially with the more upscale crowd that takes over on the weekend. Big windows and little attitude tempt you to kick back and watch the goings-on across the street at the Bubble Lounge, where there is a lot more upholstered seating. Summertime means a happy clutter of plastic chairs—many without tables—scattered outside, just waiting for you to plop down and have a cool margarita al fresco.

Credit cards: Cash only. **Subway:** 1, 9 to Franklin St.

North Star Pub 93 South St. (between South and Fulton Sts.) (212) 509-6757. Just a stone's throw from the South Street Seaport and all of its maritime glory is this quaint English-style pub. It's about as real as Epcot's European pavilion, but for Anglophiles and Wall Streeters it does the trick. There are more than 75 types of single-malt Scotch, a good selection of British ales and a menu of hearty pub fare.

Credit cards: All major. **Subway:** J, M, Z, 2, 3, 4, 5 to Fulton St.; A, C to Broadway-Nassau St.

Puffy's Tavern 81 Hudson St. (between Harrison and Jay Sts.) (212) 766-9159. On one of those sleepy corners in TriBeCa, Puffy's offers something that is getting harder to come by these days: A low-key, scene-free, classic neighborhood bar. And it may actually stay that way because it's the kind of exceptionally unexceptional place that most people won't go out of their way to get to. If they did, they'd find a beautiful, welcoming, old-fashioned place with dark wood, sultry fans and a darts alcove, frequented by a mix of locals, old-timers and folks from the nearby financial district.

Credit cards: All major. **Subway:** 1, 9 to Franklin St..

Walkers Restaurant 16 N. Moore St. (at Varick St.) (212) 941-0142. Walkers is TriBeCa's version of Cheers: The staff and the regulars might not necessarily know your name, but they'll be decent to you anyway. An enormous mahogany bar, high tin ceilings and good, uncomplicated cuisine recall old New York—right down to the red-and-white-checked tablecloths. There's plenty of history in the walls, or you can write your own in Crayolas on the white paper table covers. This is a down-to-earth holdout in a neighborhood where prices—and attitude—snake steadily heavenward.

Credit cards: Cash only. **Subway:** 1, 9 to Franklin St.

Lower East Side

Baby Jupiter 170 Orchard St. (at Ludlow St.) (212) 982-2229. This bar and restaurant is devoted to the graffiti art of André Charles, who did the Houston Street obituary wall featuring Tupac, Princess Diana and Joe Camel, among others. The bar serves Cajun food during the day and into the night, when it opens as a full-functioning funk parlor. Bands play or DJ's spin funk, soul and hip-hop in a room next to the restaurant.

Credit cards: All major. **Subway:** F to Second Ave.

bOb 235 Eldridge St. (between Houston and Stanton Sts.) (212) 777-0588. This living room-sized bar attracts a gaggle of Lower East Side hipsters who'd love to groove along to bOb's numerous house, hip-hop and reggae DJ's, if only they could. Once a popular (and cramped) place to dirty dance, bOb has been forced to reduce its debauchery quotient since it hasn't got a cabaret license. But it's still a great place to have a drink.

Credit cards: All major. **Subway:** F to Second Ave.

Idlewild 145 East Houston St. (between First and Second Aves.) (212) 477-5005. It's a bar, it's a plane, it's Idlewild. This lounge takes the theme bar concept to another dimension, or at least another elevation. Meticulously designed, Idlewild's front room is done up like the first-class section of a jetliner, complete with real airplane seats, and the back room resembles a sleek 1960's airport lounge. The barmen don ground-crew jumpsuits and the waitresses dress like vintage stewardesses. Drinks are pricey, but it's worth seeing.

Credit cards: All major. **Subway:** F to Second Ave.

Lansky Lounge 104 Norfolk St. (between Delancey and Rivington Sts.)
(212) 677-9489. From its subterranean alleyway entrance to its art deco bar
lamps, Lansky Lounge goes all out in its attempt to conjure the atmosphere of a
speakeasy-style swinger joint. The music is mostly non-stop Frank, with a few
other swingin' tunes thrown in. It's attached to the restaurant Ratner's (they
even share a coat check), but one enters Lansky through the stairway on Norfolk. On weekends, when the $5 cover kicks in, the place is bursting with
downtown types—weekdays can be virtually empty.
Credit cards: All major. **Subway:** F to Delancey; J, M, Z to Essex St.

Ludlow Bar 165 Ludlow St. (between Houston and Stanton Sts.) (212) 353-
0536. The epicenter of Ludlow hip, this dimly lit, low-ceilinged, drinking den
features cheap pours and a pool table in the back; its grubby neighborhood
clientele seems to suggest that grunge never ended. There are a number of great
weekly events that attract some of the best DJ's in the city.
Credit cards: All major. **Subway:** F to Second Ave.

Max Fish 178 Ludlow St. (between Houston and Stanton Sts.)
(212) 529-3959. One of the first venues to attract bar-goers to the burgeoning
Lower East Side scene, Max Fish still draws its fair share of hipsters. Brightly lit
and without downtown attitude, Max Fish is both hip and casual at the same
time. Never lacking in interesting artwork, this spot also offers plenty of other
attractions, including pinball, video games, a pool table and cheap beer.
Credit cards: Cash only. **Subway:** F to Second Ave.

Swim 146 Orchard St. (between Stanton and Rivington Sts.) (212) 673-0799.
This swank new arrival could convince you that Orchard Street has finally
become too hip for its own good, but don't let it! Nice touches and friendly DJ's
belie its cooler-than-thou façade, which comes complete with an imposing
doorman and heavy curtains. Swim's décor includes funky lighting, exposed
brick walls, wooden beams and air ducts, resulting in a fine mixture of grunge
and slick.
Credit cards: Subway: F to Second Ave.

Welcome to the Johnsons 123 Rivington St. (between Norfolk and Essex
Sts.) (212) 420-9911. Welcome to the Johnsons is a nostalgic visit to some
cool kid's 70's-style basement—and, here's the good part, the parents are
away! Everything about this bar is designed to make you feel at home (that is,
someone else's retro home). The orange-and-brown furniture is covered in
plastic and the place is snazzed-up with giant wooden spoons and forks,
macramé curtains, trophies and houseplants. Strong mixed drinks are whipped
up behind a sizable bar, and bottles are served from a vintage, avocado-green
refrigerator.
Credit cards: Cash only. **Subway:** F to Delancey St.; J, M, Z to Essex St.

Chinatown/Little Italy to Houston

Botanica 47 East Houston St. (between Mott and Mulberry Sts.) (212) 343-7251. An evening in this subterranean dive is like a house party in someone's basement. The furniture motif is Thrift Shop Eclectic: Naugahyde couches, 70's easy chairs, Formica tables, old theater seats and red lighting from Holiday Inn table lamps. The front door opens into the faintly lit bar area and past the two unisex bathrooms, is a back room with a mishmash of seating choices and an elevated lounge area.

Credit cards: Cash only. **Subway:** B, D, F, Q to Broadway-Lafayette St.

Double Happiness 173 Mott St. (at Broome St.) (212) 941-1282. It's easy to miss this Chinatown lounge: only the long line outside gives its existence away. But Double Happiness is worth the wait. Once inside, you will be surrounded by the young and fashionable nestled comfortably into various softly lit nooks. Settle into your own corner and sip the bar's delectable martinis (including the house speciality, which adds a dash of green tea to the concoction).

Credit cards: MC/V. **Subway:** B, D, Q to Grand St.; N, R to Prince St.

M & R Bar 264 Elizabeth St. (between Houston and Prince Sts.) (212) 226-0559. Any evening is a good one at M & R, where the marble bar, tin ceilings and brick wall beckon. Polished and professional, the bar staff is never too stuffy to chat or too busy to keep you filled up. Friday nights the DJ sets up in one corner of the bar looking happy while spinning Latin jazz and funk. M & R's bar area fills up fast and, unless you're eating dinner, it can be tough to get a seat.

Credit cards: All major. **Subway:** B, D, F, Q to Broadway-Lafayette St.

Mare Chiaro 176 1/2 Mulberry St. (between Broome and Grand Sts.) (212) 226-9345. At first glance, Mare Chiaro seems like the ultimate in Little Italy authenticity: obese Italian men smoking cigars, a jukebox that's about 85 percent Sinatra and photos of the owner alongside the Chairman of the Board himself. Look more closely and you'll notice that the crowd is largely hipsters and slumming Ivy League kids. It's this crazy mix that makes Mare Chiaro such a good time: it's a place where you can as easily trade recipes for manicotti as discuss post-structuralism with a date.

Credit cards: Cash only. **Subway:** B, D, Q to Grand St.; N, R to Prince St.

Milano's 51 East Houston St. (between Mulberry and Mott Sts.) (212) 226-8632. Sitting down at Milano's smoothly worn wooden bar with a cold pint is like taking a step back in time. Long, narrow and dark, this hole-in-the-wall on Houston is a familiar, no-frills pub that stands out in an era of theme bars and gimmicks. For more than 90 years, things have stayed simple here: a jukebox stocked with old favorites, faded Frank Sinatra posters and New York-themed detritus above the bar. During the day (or morning—Milano's opens for business at 8 A.M.), older patrons tell stories over pints of perhaps the freshest Guinness in town, while a younger crowd mixes with the barflies at night.

Credit cards: Cash only. **Subway:** B, D, F, Q to Broadway-Lafayette St.

SoHo

Ear Inn 326 Spring St. (between Greenwich and Washington Sts.) (212) 226-9060. Longevity is rare for the city's bars and restaurants; many are regularly washed away. But the Ear Inn has withstood even the shifting of the Hudson River. Built in the 1830's, this landmark Federal-style house once stood on the river's edge and was a favorite spot for sailors. Although landfill has pushed the shoreline a few blocks westward, the bar still sports remnants of its nautical past. In this friendly neighborhood atmosphere, you're likely to find men in pinstripe suits sharing the bar with tattooed bikers. The bar also presents live weekly acoustic music and poetry readings.

Credit cards: All major. **Subway:** C, E, to Spring St.; 1, 9 to Houston St.

Fanelli 94 Prince St. (at Mercer St.) (212) 226-9412. Fanelli's, an unfussy place with tiled floors, tin ceilings and a great deal of old New York atmosphere (it opened in 1872), is incongruously nestled among Soho's glitzier restaurants and stores. The bar draws a mixed clientele and can be crowded on weekends, but during the week the place caters to locals, and is always laid-back. Basic but tasty bar food is available, and there is a back room intended for those more interested in eating than imbibing. The bartenders are friendly and jocular, and the old-fashioned mugs are perfect for a frosty beer.

Credit cards: All major. **Subway:** B, D, F. Q to Broadway-Lafayette St.; N, R to Prince St.

Lush 110 Duane St. (between Church St. and Broadway) (212) 766-1275. After picking out Lush's unmarked door on Duane Street, cozy up to the invit- ing couches in the window or hold court from the high banquette across from the bar. Down a hallway lined with flickering votive candles lies the requisite, mysteriously alluring "reserved" lounge. Around 11 P.M., a "Bright Lights Big City" set filters in. The good-looking crowd is an indication of the secret of Lush's success: mirrors. Installed all around, some tilted for optimal viewing— Lush is a scene for being seen.

Credit cards: All major. **Subway:** A, C, E to Canal St.

Merc Bar 151 Mercer St. (between Houston and Prince Sts.) (212) 966-2727. The beautiful people may have moved on from this SoHo hot spot, but the Merc Bar still offers softly lit, lounge-like surroundings, great tunes on a great sound system and bartenders who mix a good stiff drink. So if you're kicking back on the comfortable couches out front or mingling in the red room in back, drinking an $8 martini, remember that this place used to be standing room only and enjoy the fact that the crowds have gone elsewhere.

Credit cards: All major. **Subway:** B, D, F, Q to Broadway-Lafayette St.; N, R to Prince St.

Pravda 281 Lafayette St. (between Prince and Houston Sts.) (212) 226-4944. Pravda has succumbed to the inevitable condition that afflicts all hip SoHo nightspots. Word of the lounge's appeal has spread to the Wall Street crowd, who now flock here, driving out the beautiful people who once actually stood in line to get in. Stockbrokers may be the only people willing to pay these outrageous prices now that the spot is no longer the latest place to be seen. However, the downstairs room maintains its allure, with arched, cavelike ceilings that create a feeling of intimacy.

Credit cards: All major. Food. **Subway:** B, D, F, Q to Broadway-Lafayette St.; N, R to Prince St.

Void 16 Mercer St. (at Howard St.) (212) 941-6492. Like a Czech rock club in the days of Communism, Void prides itself on being difficult to locate. No obvious façade greets visitors; only a tiny sign directs patrons into an industrial loft building, down a hallway and past a heavy door. Of course, Void's clandestine overtures now seem quaint, as news of the club has spread far beyond SoHo. Opened when downtown was becoming a hive of new-technology activity, Void was one of the first bars to embrace electronic interactivity as a nightlife concept. Early visitors scrambled to commandeer the club's Web-browsing terminals which are now most often used as cocktail tables.

Credit cards: Cash only. **Subway:** N, R to Canal St.

Wax Bar 113 Mercer St. (between Prince and Spring Sts.) (212) 226-6082. A former "It" bar, this boîte remains a major player in the downtown, velvet-rope scene. Wax's lounge caters to a beautiful and wealthy mixed crowd (cell phones and Tocca abound). Its Paisley Park meets Addams Family interior—gargoyles, candelabras and haunted-house murals compete with oceans of purple chintz— makes for a hot setting to cool your heels after a day of shopping. Drinks are pricey, but the service is friendlier than it needs to be.

Credit cards: All major. **Subway:** N, R to Prince St.

East Village

(See also "Dive Bars in the East Village," below.)

Angel Share 8 Stuyvesant St. (between Second and Third Aves.) (212) 777-5415. This tiny hot spot is both hard to find and hard to get into. Hidden behind a door in a bustling Korean barbecue restaurant, Yoko Cho, Angel Share diligently sticks to four rigid guidelines: no standing, no smoking cigars or pipes, only groups of four or less and only 40 are allowed in at a time altogether, making it a tough place to grab a drink Friday nights. At any other time it's perfect for relaxing to the royal treatment of waiters who make drinks like works of art with great fanfare and finesse. The plush, cozy and dimly lit room is ideal for a romantic rendezvous or after-work drink

Credit cards: All major. **Subway:** 6 to Astor Pl.

Baraza 133 Ave. C (between 8th and 9th Sts.) (212) 539-0811. From the chil-

dren's letter blocks that spell the bar's name on the blue front door to the cadre
of DJ's that spin Brazilian-tinged records and the tropical drink menu, Baraza has
the perfect tone for a hip Alphabet City lounge. Inside, there's dim lighting over
small tables and an enticing back corner with sofas and a metal-plated fish tank.
Be sure to visit the bathroom, which is "wallpapered" with pennies. Baraza fills
up on weekend nights, but it's enough out of the way to remain comfortable.
Credit cards: Cash only. **Subway:** L to First Ave.; N, R, 4, 5, 6 to 14th St.

Beauty Bar 231 East 14th St. (between Second and Third Aves.) (212) 539-
1389. A beauty salon for decades, it's now a bar. From the people who brought
you Barmacy—a mom-and-pop pharmacy reinvented as a hipster watering
hole—comes this popular spot. You can sit beneath antique hair dryers and swill
Rolling Rocks, or go whole hog and get your nails done at the bar—just don't
soak 'em in your Jack Daniel's. Is it mere coincidence that many of Beauty Bar's
female clientele resemble 50's pinup icon Bettie Page?
Credit cards: All major. **Subway:** N, R, 4, 5, 6 to 14th St; L to Third Ave.

Bond Street 6 Bond St. (between Broadway and Lafayette St.) (212) 777-
2500. This hip hangout (from the same folks who brought you Republic, Indo-
chine and Bar d'O) caters to a consciously upscale crowd. The space is designed
in sparse Japanese fashion, with lots of dark wooden beams separating several
cubicle-like areas that offer a pleasant seating arrangement for large groups. The
lounge can get rather crowded on busy evenings, so if cell-phone users (or
abusers) bother you, stay away.
Credit cards: All major. **Subway:** B, D, F, Q to Broadway-Lafayette St.; 6 to
Bleecker St.

B Bar 40 East 4th St. (at Bowery) (212) 475-2220. Though it's past its peak of
popularity, the B Bar (formerly known as the Bowery Bar) still has two major
attractions: its weekly DJ events and the garden area. The L.A.-style front room
consists of a long, sleek bar, a handful of table and couches, and a large dining
area. There are two more rooms in the back, both on the plush side decorated
with a hodge-podge of contemporary photos. During the spring and summer,
however, the crowd empties into the inviting garden area, which allows for
more mingling than the East Village usually provides.
Credit cards: All major. **Subway:** B, D, F, Q to Broadway-Lafayette St.; 6 to
Bleecker St.

Global 33 93 Second Ave. (between 5th and 6th Sts.) (212) 477-8427. The
original jet-age throwback lounge, Global 33 serves some of the best cosmopolitans in the city. The other drinks are equally refreshing, and the conscientious
use of fresh citrus—like a healthy juice bar—diminishes neither the alcohol
content nor the bar's ironic sophistication. Along with Latin music that varies
from soothing to mildly pulsating, Global 33 also serves up tapas. This trendy
nightspot not only attracts well-off East Village locals, but it also draws in West
Siders and uptown yuppies.
Credit cards: All major. **Subway:** F to Second Ave.

McSorley's Old Ale House 15 East 7th St. (between Second and Third Aves.) (212) 473-9148. Anybody who has ever read a book by Joseph Mitchell owes himself a visit to this historic bar, though it's not as old as it pretends. Have a drink and forget the food.

Credit cards: Cash only. **Subway:** 6 to Astor Pl.; N, R to 8th St; F to Second Ave.

Niagara 112 Ave. A (at 7th St.) (212) 420-9517. The primary draw of Niagara is its downstairs "Lei Lounge," a bamboo and palm frond-filled room, which offers regularly changing tropical drinks for those who like to vary the flavor of their daquiris. Upstairs, red leather diner-style booths, the neon and chrome bar, along with the bartenders and their pompadourish do's, are reminiscent of a 40's scene, and the tunes are similarly retro.

Credit cards: All major **Subway:** 6 to Astor Pl.; F to Second Ave.

St. Dymphna's 118 St. Marks Pl. (between First Ave. and Ave. A) (212) 254-6636. As legend has it, pilgrims to the tomb of St. Dymphna in the Belgian town of Gheel might find solace from all manner of insanity. A considerably more jolly crowd can be found making their way to the saint's namesake in the East Village, a genuine Hibernian tavern in a city filles with Blarney Stones and their imitators. Simple wooden tables, strong Guinness and the genuine Irish accents of the staff make St. Dymphna's feel like a real pub. There is also a little-used but immensely pleasant back garden, which stays open till midnight.

Credit cards: All major. **Subway:** 6 to Astor Pl.

288 Bar (also called Tom and Jerry's) 288 Elizabeth St. (at Houston St.). This friendly neighborhood bar offers a relaxed atmosphere and more space than can normally be found in an East Village venue. There are several large, round wooden tables that allow groups to sit together, and a cavernous area in the back of the bar where you can actually talk to a group of people without the feeling that you're blocking traffic. 288 features average prices for drinks (including a decent Scotch selection) and a jukebox heavy on classic-rock tunes.

Credit cards: Cash only. **Subway:** B, D, F, Q to Broadway-Lafayette St.; 6 to Bleecker St.

Temple Bar 332 Lafayette St. (between Houston and Bleecker Sts.) (212) 925-4242. The crowd inside this softly lit, wood-paneled lounge is just as refined as the drinks served—Temple Bar has 42 different varieties of vodka from 15 different countries. Bankers in expensive suits and models with expensive hair gather at the green marble-topped bar and in a second room of octagonal tables and plush banquettes. But as popular as the Temple Bar is it's been around too long to be considered hot, so you don't have to worry about too much attitude.

Credit cards: All major. **Subway:** B, D, F, Q to Broadway-Lafayette St.; 6 to Bleecker.

Dive Bars in the East Village

Neighborhood bars and local holes-in-the-wall are some of the best places in the city to see the real New York. This is particularly true in the East Village where dives are equivalent to the town hall. Hipsters, artists and colorful residents retreat to chat over cheap drinks, shoot pool or melt into a bar stool. If you find the smell of stale beer, a surly bartender and air thick with smoke and character appealing, an East Village dive crawl is highly recommended.

Ace Bar 531 East 5th St. (between Aves. A and B) (212) 979-8476
Ace is perfect for people with limited attention spans—pool, darts, pinball, and video games are all provided for your enjoyment, as well as a virtual museum of over 100 children's lunchboxes.

Blue and Gold Tavern 79 East 7th St. (between First and Second Aves.) (212) 473-8918
This is a no-nonsense beer and whisky kind of a place, where many a cigarette has been smoked over a Bud at the ancient wooden booths. On weekends the pool table can see some heated action.

Cherry Tavern 441 East 6th St. (between First Ave. and Ave. A) (212) 777-1448
One of the hippest of the East Village dives, Cherry Tavern has seen a model or two in the crowd. Though there's a pool table and a good jukebox, the drink special—a shot of tequila and a can of Tecate beer for $4—may be Cherry's biggest attraction.

Coyote Ugly Saloon 153 First Ave. (between 9th and 10th Sts.) (212) 477-4431
It's ugly, all right, but there's something truthful—even pure—about this place, with its bending, squeaking floorboards, lopsided bar stools, country jukebox and buxom bartender in her half-shirt and tight jeans.

Holiday Cocktail Lounge 75 St. Marks Pl. (between First and Second Aves.) (212) 777-9637
This classic East Village hangout is famous for its never-changing aesthetic; quilted faux-leather booths, a cigarette machine, a jukebox and video games are worn and sprinkled with a palpable seediness. Be prepared for the bar to close at any time, according to the bartender's whim.

International Bar 120 First Ave. (between 7th St. and St. Marks Pl.) (212) 777-9244
Much like Johnny's S&P in the West Village, International is very local, very casual and very cheap. Though this tiny bar can get crowded on the weekends, it remains unaffected.

Joe's Place 20 East 6th St. (between Aves. A and B) (212) 473-9093
The jury's still out on whether this hole-in-the-wall is a dive or a honky-tonk bar. On the dive side, it's unpretentious, homey and on the honky -tonk side, it's known for its mostly country jukebox. It attracts a neighborhood mix of old-timers and young locals.

Marz Bar 25 East 1st St. (at Second Ave.)
This punk-art bar on the corner of Second Avenue and First Street has been around for well over a decade, and continues to revel in its downhill slide. We're talking hardcore—yet harmless. This unpretentious little dive is a breath of fresh air for those who don't associate spending money with being cool.

Vazac's (7B) 108 Ave. B (at 7th St.) (212) 473-8840
Alphabet City's population of musicians, writers and actors congregates at Vazac's (a.k.a. 7B or the Horseshoe bar) to pick from the decent selection of beers on tap and to enjoy the red light-tinged, grunge-punk ambience and the loud, high-energy music.

Greenwich Village/West Village

Art Bar 52 Eighth Ave. (between Jane and Horatio Sts.) (212) 727-0244. Certainly more bar than gallery, the Art Bar consists of two spaces: a front barroom with large, curvy booths and a cozy back room with a working fireplace. Candles provide intimate lighting and a jukebox plays rock music, but not so loudly as to drown out conversation. The womblike back room, with its antique couches and armchairs, is a particularly good spot for couples and small groups.
Credit cards: All major **Subway:** A, C, E to 14th St.; L to Eighth Ave.; 1, 2, 3, 9 to 14th St.

Automatic Slims 733 Washington St. (between 11th and 12th Sts.) (212) 645-8660. Though Exteriors can be deceiving at the isolated bars in the way-West Village, you can usually get a take on things once you walk in the door. No so with Automatic Slims; this tiny place could keep you guessing all night. The crowd consists of old barflies flanked by a couple of investment banker types, pockets of gay men and yuppie girls. The décor is classic, modern and cozy all at once.
Credit cards: All major. **Subway:** A, C, E to 14th St.; L to Eighth Ave.; 1, 2, 3, 9 to 14th St.

Cedar Tavern 82 University Pl. (between 11th and 12th Sts.) (212) 741-9754. The spacious, two-story Cedar Tavern is a bohemian landmark. In the 1950's, Jackson Pollock, Willem de Kooning and other artists came here to drink and talk. More recently, the Cedar has hosted Sunday evening poetry readings upstairs in its glass-enclosed roof garden. There are plenty of booths for sitting, vintage New York drawings and photos on the walls, a beautiful bar, a classic-rock-tinged jukebox and a bar-food menu.
Credit cards: All major. **Subway:** L, N, R, 4, 5, 6 to 14th St.

Chumley's Restaurant 86 Bedford St. (between Bleecker St. and Seventh Ave. South) (212) 675-4449. The story of Chumley's heyday as a former speakeasy is as worn as its old wood tables, but it seems to keep people coming to the place in droves, especially on weekends. The pub's three rooms are rustic, with a fireplace, sawdust on the floors and walls hung with book jackets by famous authors who used to be regulars. F. Scott Fitzgerald allegedly wrote part of *The Great Gatsby* in a corner booth, Robert Kennedy wrote a speech here, and the place is said to be haunted by the ghost of the woman who owned it in the 30's. All lore aside though, today Chumley's resembles an upscale frat house for a clientele of young professionals swilling pints of the impressively varied beers on tap.

Credit cards: Cash only. **Subway:**

Corner Bistro 331 West 4th St. (at Jane St.) (212) 242-9502. If a simple, straightforward place to drink a beer (or something stiffer) and chomp on a top-notch burger is what you're after, then the Corner Bistro is a godsend. The front room has a worn, wooden bar and worn, wooden tables all on top of a worn, wooden floor. In back is more worn seating, and if you arrive after 7 P.M. any night of the week, be prepared to wait for a table. The bartenders are no-non-sense neighborhood types and the beer menu is simple as are the food offerings.

Credit cards: Cash only. **Subway:** A, C, E to 14th St.; L to Eighth Ave.; 1, 2, 3, 9 to 14th St.

Hogs n' Heifers 859 Washington St. (at 13th St.) (212) 929-0655. Tucked away in Manhattan's meat packing district, Hogs n' Heifers offers a taste of Haz-ard County for anyone with a hankering for Budweiser and debauchery. Here brawny bikers and yuppies ogle female bartenders dancing on the bar. If nothing else, this place is a testament to the effectiveness of hard liquor and peer pres-sure in convincing women to abandon their inhibitions as well as their bras.

Credit cards: Cash only. **Subway:** A, C, E to 14th St.; L to Eighth Ave.; 1, 2, 3, 9 to 14th St.

Johnny's S&P 90 Greenwich Ave. (between West 12th and Jane Sts.) (212) 741-5279. One of the few neighborhood bars in the increasingly touristy West Village, Johnny's S&P keeps a low profile. A nondescript red neon "BAR" sign dangles out front and Johnny's front window, weather permitting, is open to the street so passers-by can peek in at the barflies, teetering on the red vinyl bar stools and gulping beers served by the tattooed barmaid. Johnny's S&P is a clas-sic, hole-in-the-wall, perfect for either drinking yourself silly or crying in your beer.

Credit cards: Cash only. **Subway:** 1, 2, 3, 9 to 14th St.

White Horse Tavern 567 Hudson St. (at 11th St.) (212) 989-3956. Located in one of the few remaining wood-framed buildings in Manhattan, the White Horse Tavern opened in 1880. The tavern was a speakeasy during Prohibition, and poet Dylan Thomas was a regular in the late 1940's. Legend has it that, in 1953, Thomas drank 18 shots of whisky, stepped outside onto the sidewalk and dropped dead. (The truth is it was about seven whiskies, and what really killed him was a misdiagnosis of his diabetes.) Though once considered a "writer's bar," the three darkly paneled sections are now populated with more former frat boys than literary types.

Credit cards: Cash only. **Subway:** A, C, E to 14th St.; L to Eighth Ave.; 1, 2, 3, 9 to 14th St.

WXOU Radio 558 Hudson St. (between Perry and 11th Sts.) (212) 206-0381. While there's nothing remarkable about this neighborhood bar, there's nothing offensive either. In this simple rectangular room with white walls darkly paneled halfway down, a twenty-something crowd in jeans and baseball caps sits at small, wood tables lining one wall, and orders drinks from the bar lining the other.

Credit cards: Cash only. **Subway:** A, C, E to 14th St.; L to Eighth Ave.; 1, 2, 3, 9 to 14th St.

Flatiron/Union Square/Murray Hill

Belmont Lounge 117 East 15th St. (between Park Ave. and Irving Pl.) (212) 533-0009. Dark, discreet, and dripping with attitude, the Belmont Lounge has secured a permanent place in the pantheon of downtown hipster hangouts. The bar has all the requisites for downtown cool: candlelight, velvet curtains and a smattering of deep, comfy couches. The crowd is usually young and gawking, though an occasional posse of suits can be found at the bar. Most nights feature a DJ, usually spinning trip-hop or other moody, lyric-less compositions.

Credit cards: All major. **Subway:** L, N, R, 4, 5, 6 to 14th St.

Heartland Brewery and Restaurant 35 Union Square West (between 16th and 17th Sts.) (212) 645-3400. With the music of the Grateful Dead or the All-man Brothers wafting through its unpretentious, spacious confines, this Union Square address feels more Colorado than Manhattan. An all-American, khaki-clad crowd lines the bar, lounges on the terrace or perches at the high pub tables to linger over the award-winning brews. A two-time laureate of New York magazine's "Best Brew Pub" award, Heartland also won the gold medal at the 1997 Great American Beer Festival for its Farmer Jon's Oatmeal Stout.

Credit cards: All major. **Subway:** L, N, R, 4, 5, 6 to 14th St.

Molly's 287 Third Ave. (between 22d and 23d Sts.) (212) 889-3361. A blazing fireplace, photos of Irish writers and the quintessential green-and-white checked tablecloths add to the special flavor of this dark (but not dingy) Hibernian pub. So do the uneven floors, which are camouflaged by layers of sawdust. The crowd ranges from twentysomethings clutching Guinnesses at the bar to older couples dining on the excellent traditional fare. The strong and reasonably priced drinks are served up by boisterous bartenders and motherly waitresses.

Credit cards: All major. **Subway:** 6 to 23d St.

Old Town Bar and Restaurant 45 East 18th St. (between Broadway and Park Ave. S.) (212) 529-6732. There are no gas-lit lamps or horse-drawn carriages on the streets outside this tavern. But inside, you feel as though you have entered a bygone era from New York's history. Built in 1892, the Old Town Bar and

Restaurant is one of the city's oldest taverns. From the 14-foot pressed-tin ceiling to the mahogany bar and huge beveled mirrors, it's filled with details from another time. Even the booths tell a story: they were specially built during Prohibition with a hidden compartment in for stowing liquor. Although the Old Town was almost turned into a museum, it doesn't feel like a tourist attraction.
Credit cards: All major. **Subway:** L, N, R, 4, 5, 6 to 14th St.

119 Bar 119 East 15th St. (between Irving Pl. and Union Square) (212) 777-6158. There isn't a time of night when 119's sound system isn't cranked up to ground-shaking levels. But if you can get past the idea of shouting all night to be heard, you'll have a good time in this relatively inexpensive divey bar. 119 is split into three rooms: the first houses a pool table and a few distressed velvet sofas; in the main room are the bar and a few booths; and the final room is all about darts. 119 Bar gets extremely busy on weekends and even weeknights attract a healthy crowd of grungy downtowners and slumming interlopers.
Credit cards: Cash only. **Subway:** L, N, R, 4, 5, 6 to 14th St.

Chelsea

Lot 61 550 West 21st St. (between 10th and 11th Aves.) (212) 243-6555. Every hot neighborhood has one incredibly popular bar, and in the case of West Chelsea this restaurant-cum-lounge is it. Lot 61 is housed in a vast, converted warehouse space, cleverly divided by sliding panels and bursting with furniture straight out of Elle Decor (don't miss the rubber sofas salvaged from insane asylums). In keeping with the area's burgeoning art scene, Lot's walls are adorned by all the right painters' works (Hirst, Landers and Salle, to name a few). And if that weren't enough eye candy, there's always the drop-dead gorgeous staff to gawk at. Keep your eye out for celebrities.
Credit cards: All major. **Subway:** C, E to 23d St.

Triple Crown Ale House 330 Seventh Ave. (between 28th and 29th Sts.) (212) 736-1575. A perfect mix of Irish pub and American sports bar, the Triple Crown caters to a mostly young professional crowd during the week and post-event crowds from Madison Square Garden on the weekends. Spacious with elegant, dark-wood paneled walls, the bar goes on red alert for sporting events. Eight TVs (one of them a very, very big-screen) broadcast the action for those who care. For those who don't, there's plenty of mingling room away from the roar of the crowd. The full menu features excellent pub fare.
Credit cards: All major. **Subway:** 1, 9 to 28th St.

Midtown East and Murray Hill

British Open 320 East 59th St. (between First and Second Aves.) (212) 355-8467. Although a round of golf requires a trip over a bridge or tunnel, Manhattan boasts a golf pub with warmth and conviviality. The bar draws a well-heeled clientele who, even if they've never picked up a golf club, appreciate the civilized tenor of the game and its associated lifestyle. An unexpected oasis, the mood here is set by easy swing music and twinkling lights tied to trees. The patrons, though not particularly aged, seem like throwbacks to another era. Imagine bachelors in their late 40's wearing ascots and ordering Brandy Alexanders for their dates.

Credit cards: All major. **Subway:** 4, 5, 6 to 59th St.; N, R to Lexington Ave.

Ginger Man 11 East 36th St. (between Fifth and Madison Aves.) (212) 532-3740. Combining old-world charm with new-world overkill, the Ginger Man has the feel of a British pub—just on a larger scale, with 100 bottled beers and 66 beers on tap from around the world. A 45-foot-long oak bar dominates the spacious high-ceilinged area in the front. In the back room the atmosphere is more intimate, with comfortable couches and chairs ideal for the end-of-day unwind. The menu contains all kinds of bar food with an upscale twist.

Credit cards: All major. **Subway:** 6 to 33d St.

P.J. Clarke's 915 Third Ave. (at 55th St.) (212) 759-1650. P.J. Clarke's, in a two-story brick building with a frosted glass façade, feels like a remnant from an older New York. There are dark wood walls, a tile floor, a bar with an altar-like, wood-carved back and hand-painted, brown-lettered signs listing the draft prices. It has the look of a Hollywood set created for a serious movie about drinking, and, in fact, scenes from the 1945 classic "The Lost Weekend," about an alcoholic writer, were shot here.

Credit cards: All major. **Subway:** 4, 5, 6 to 59th St.; N, R to Lexington Ave.

Midtown West

Jimmy's Corner 140 West 44th St. (between Sixth Ave. and Broadway) (212) 944-7819. Tucked away among big Midtown hotels, is this New York gem. Covering almost every inch of wall space at this narrow spot are posters, photos and newspaper clippings about boxing. The space at front is so small that you can barely squeeze past the regulars holding court at the bar, but that's not a problem, because everyone is friendly. The crowd is happily diverse: there are scruffy slacker types and men and women in suits, construction workers and, of course, boxing enthusiasts, all clearly glad to have found this slice of authenticity in touristy Midtown.

Credit cards: All major. **Subway:** B, D, F, N, Q, R, 1, 2, 3, 7, 9 to 42d St.

Landmark Tavern 626 11th Ave. (at 46th St.) (212) 757-8595. When it first opened in 1868, the view from the Landmark's three-story brick building was of bustling piers and a neighborhood full of longshoremen. Since then, the river's edge has moved westward, pushed back by landfill and 12th Avenue, and the docks have gone quiet. But unlike the streets around it, the Landmark Tavern has hardly changed. Not that it still serves nickel beers, but the enormous bar—turned from a single mahogany tree—and the potbellied stove in the rear dining room remain.

Credit cards: All major. **Subway:** A, C, E, N, R, 1, 2, 3, 7, 9 to 42d St.

P G Kings 18 West 33d St. (between Fifth and Sixth Aves.) (212) 290-0080.
This most authentic of pubs is one of New York's untapped treasures. It's hard to
imagine why New Yorkers would ignore the gorgeous wood-paneled front room
with its tiled floor and vintage oak bar. Or the hearty pub fare served in the
back room dominated by a Tiffany stained glass window. Or the excellent selection of tap beers, the genial and professional bartenders and the shelf full of
paperbacks available for solo drinkers who forgot to bring a book. Go, discover a
masterpiece, and make it yours—before everyone else does.

Credit cards: All major. **Features:** Food. **Subway:** B, D, F, N, Q, R to 34th St.

Siberia 50th St. 1/9 Subway Station (at Broadway) (212) 333-4141. The tiny
bar Siberia, located on the downtown side of the 50th Street 1/9 subway station, attracts pre-commuters by the dozen as well as midtown regulars who
descend into the bowels of the subway system for drinks served in little plastic
cups. The site is said to be a former drop-off point for KGB spy documents—
hence its name. The cracked walls are papered with pictures of Lenin and other
Soviet politicos and the lighting fixtures are falling out of the ceiling.

Credit cards: Cash only. **Subway:** Guess.

Credit cards: All major. **Subway:** B, D, F, Q to 47–50 Sts.-Rockefeller Center.

Upper East Side

Dorrian's Red Hand Restaurant 1616 Second Ave. (at 84th St.)
(212) 772-6660. This bar may never live down its association with Robert
Chambers, who met Jennifer Levin here in 1986 and then murdered her the
same night in Central Park. Despite the bad publicity, Dorrian's is recovering
from the heady days of the late 80's and remains a respectable neighborhood bar
and restaurant with an eclectic menu and window seating at red checkered
tables. The CD jukebox offers a mix of classic tunes and contemporary hits. Ask
the bartender about the gory legend of the "red hand."

Credit cards: All major. **Subway:** 4, 5, 6 to 86th St.

Elaine's 1703 Second Ave. (between 88th and 89th Sts.) (212) 534-8103. A
meeting place for the older guard of New York's celebrity elite (think Joan
Collins and Ivana Trump). A collage of literati memorabilia covers the walls,
and *Entertainment Weekly* has been throwing its Oscar party here for years. In
addition to the famous frequenters, watch for Elaine herself, who opened these
doors almost 40 years ago and routinely table-hops to schmooze with her guests.
But you won't received the royal treatment if they don't know you.

Credit cards: All major. **Subway:** 4, 5, 6 to 86th St.

Subway Inn 143 East 60th St. (at Lexington Ave.) (212) 223-8929. The Subway Inn has a lengthy bar, jukebox, cracked red-and-white tile floor and a row
of high-backed booths against a mirrored wall. A few small orange globes cast a
faint glow about the room, revealing a hard-drinking crowd at the bar. The real
surprise here is the occasional handful of marquee-pretty, stylishly outfitted

young people found mixing with workers from the nearby hotels and stores, and students from Hunter College. Yet there's no threat of the place being overrun by Beautiful People: It's still a place where they serve dollar draft beers, though only during the day.

Credit cards: Cash only. **Subway:** N, R to Lexington Ave; 4, 5, 6 to 59th St.

Upper West Side

Alligator Alley 485 Amsterdam Ave. (between 83d and 84th Sts.) (212) 873-5810. If you long to crawl back into the undergraduate womb, you'll find a reasonable approximation at Alligator Alley. This Upper West Side watering hole provides school-sick twenty-somethings a haven from the cold reality of the working world, faithfully recreating the décor and ambiance of a frat-house basement lounge. The jukebox offers a selection of classic rock, alternative and top 40, and the reasonably priced bar has a comforting selection of beers on tap.

Credit cards: All major. **Subway:** 1, 9 to 86th St; B to 81st St.

All State Cafe 250 West 72d St. (between Broadway and West End Ave.) (212) 874-1883. Inside this narrow, cozy, basement-level dive there's a brief stretch of bar, a jukebox and postage-stamp sized color TV, a well-trod floor and to the rear, a patch of little wooden tables where fine pub fare is served.

Credit cards: Cash only. **Subway:** 1, 2, 3, 9 to 72d St.

Dive 75 101 West 75th St. (at Columbus Ave.) (212) 362-7518. Tucked away on a side street, Dive 75 merges the friendliness of a neighborhood bar with the atmosphere of a living room. A large blue aquarium separates the bar area from a small collection of tables; wooden bookshelves house a selection of board games. The bar attracts a local twenty-something crowd seeking an alternative to the neighborhood's array of swanky lounges and raucous frat bars.

Credit cards: All major. **Subway:** 1, 2, 3, 9 to 72d St.

Hi-Life Bar and Grill 477 Amsterdam Ave. (at 83d St.) (212) 787-7199. The management of Hi-Life proclaims that their mission is to recreate the great restaurant-lounges of the 1930's and 40's. With its dark wood furnishings, padded black Naugahyde walls and matching banquettes, large round mirrors and curved wooden bar, it comes awfully close. The crowd is mostly professional, late 20's and up. Hi-Life offers a full-New American menu and prides itself on cocktails, like the innovative Sake-tini Martini.

Credit cards: All major. **Subway:** 2, 3 to 72d St.; 1, 9 to 79th St.

A Grand Oasis: New York's Hotel Bars

New York City is filled with unappreciated treasures. But in the world of food and drink, none are so neglected as hotel bars. They have been here for ages, planted like pillars around the city. Many are elegantly decorated, like miniatures of the grand hotels that engulf them. Perhaps that is why they tend to be overlooked by New Yorkers. But beyond the barrier of the hotel lobbies lie some of the city's most secluded oases, where you can relax over a well-mixed drink, be treated like a king or simply be as anonymous as the bars themselves.

—*Amanda Hesser*

(See hotel listings for addresses and phone numbers; see also Cabarets and Supper Clubs for more listings)

Cafe Pierre—Hotel Pierre
The dark and often empty Cafe Pierre could be a French Embassy tearoom. There is piano music every evening at 8:30 P.M.

Fifty-Seven Fifty-Seven—Four Seasons Hotel
At the top of a short set of polished stone stairs on the main floor of the Four Seasons Hotel, is in an icy space with 30-foot ceilings, enormous mirrors, limestone walls and hard-wood floors. It attracts mainly executives with a yen for heavily made-up companions and pricey drinks. You can also order off the famous Fifty-Seven Fifty-Seven restaurant menu.

44 Bar—Royalton Hotel
A sleek, austere corridor lobby filled with chic women. If you're really ambitious, try to snag a seat in the tiny Round Bar.

Grand Bar—SoHo Grand Hotel
The polyglot crowd at this striking, plush and expensive hotel bar creates an energetic buzz that makes you feel like you're at the center of things—much like New York itself.

Journeys Bar—Essex House Hotel
This tiny bar in the Essex House hotel has an opulent, old-money feel to it, though it has only occupied the space since 1989.

King Cole Bar—St. Regis Hotel
The very essence of swank, where even the chips are served in silver-plated dishes. The King Cole Bar also claims to have invented the Bloody Mary—though they call it the Red Snapper. Whatever you order, it's bound to be well made, because the friendly bartenders know a thing or two about mixing drinks.

Mark's Bar—The Mark Hotel
The Mark Hotel is known for its relaxed elegance, a reputation that rightly extends to its gem-like bar, which draws in European tourists and Upper East Side matrons-in-training.

Mercer Kitchen—Mercer Hotel
Cool lighting and clean lines make the bar at Mercer Kitchen feel like the set for a fashion shoot. Identification is probably not necessary, but something with a Prada tag may be.

Morgans Bar—Morgans
At the cavelike bar, calling ahead for a table is a good idea. The place can get quite crowded on weekends—or, during the summer, on Thursday, when the pre-Hamptons crowd congregates.

Oak Room and Bar—Plaza Hotel
A beer hall for men in suits. The Oak Room features live cabaret nightly.

Oasis Bar—W New York Hotel
The ambiance at the Oasis Bar at the W New York Hotel is California and casual. One day it is calm and Zen-like, the next it is filled with "Friends" cast look-alikes.

Serena—Chelsea Hotel
Though almost antithetical to the Chelsea Hotel spirit, this swank lounge which opened in 1999 has quickly become a major hot spot. (Think very thin people lining up in very expensive dresses to push through Serena's heavy wrought-iron door to sip cosmopolitans under tin palm trees and lounge on plush couches).

Whiskey Bar—Paramount Hotel
235 West 46th St. (between Seventh and Eighth Ave.) (212) 819-0404
Adjacent to the hyper-swanky Paramount (a hotel so exclusive it lacks a marquee), the Whiskey is smaller than one might expect, but just as dark and well appointed as the Paramount's lobby. The bar attracts an odd mix of business types, tourists and hipsters.

GAY & LESBIAN

The following listings are a selection of bars that cater the gay and lesbian communities of New York. See also **Dance Clubs** and **Cabarets & Supper Clubs** later in this section. Many of the city's premier dance and cabaret venues are predominately gay or gay-friendly; several have gay or lesbian parties at least one night per week. Also check *Homo Xtra (HX)*, *Next magazine*, *HX for Her*, or *Time Out New York* for weekly events.

Men

Barracuda CHELSEA 275 West 22d St. (between Seventh and Eighth Aves.) (212) 645-8613. This popular gay bar is often described as an oasis of East Village-style nightlife in the heart of tan-and-taut Chelsea. Barracuda's decor is decidedly low-key, effecting an Alphabet City aesthetic of kitschy squalor. But don't be fooled. Despite the assumed atmosphere, aging disco-bunny muscle-queens in tank tops and skin-tight Diesel gear still abound.
Credit cards: Cash only. **Subway:** C, E, 1, 9 to 23d St.

Boiler Room EAST VILLAGE 86 East Fourth St. (between First and Second Aves.) (212) 254-7536. The Boiler Room has the magnetic charm of a black hole: its dim lighting and powerful gravity draws in and compresses ever-increasing masses of darkly-clothed gay East Village guys in their 20's and early 30's. Though the crowd can approach gridlock proportions on Friday and Saturday nights, the Boiler Room retains the feel of a neighborhood bar.
Credit cards: Cash only. **Subway:** F to Second Ave.

Chase Midtown WEST 255 West 55th St. (between Eighth Ave. and Broadway) (212) 333-3400. This attractive bar, located on the northern border of Hell's Kitchen, is a welcome addition to the neighborhood and a comfortable spot for locals and out-of-towners. While the actual bar can only accommodate six or seven people, there's room up front for a modest crowd, and a cozy lounge in the back. The atmosphere is best described as serene, with a tasteful array of flowers and candles, and a subdued level of background music.

Credit cards: All major. **Subway:** A, B, C, D, 1, 9 to 59th St.

Cleo's Ninth Ave. Saloon MIDTOWN WEST 656 Ninth Ave. (between 45th and 46th Sts.) (212) 307-1503. About the only dead giveaway to the gay and lesbian nature of this friendly, laid-back bar is the large rainbow flag that hangs on the back wall. Otherwise, distinguishing Cleo's from any other local dive would take a discerning eye, perhaps noticing that the large number of men may be hugging instead of high-fiving. The beer is cheap (Budweiser is actually served in a can), the jukebox has a good selection and they serve popcorn in a basket. There isn't much more you could ask for.

Credit cards: Cash and checks only. **Subway:** A, C, E to 42d St.

East of Eighth CHELSEA 254 West 23d St. (at Eighth Ave.) (212) 352-0075. Join the fun at this small but spirited Chelsea bar, where a mostly gay crowd mingles to the sounds of 80's favorites. The lighting here is superb; the red bulbs and candles will make you look as though you've been on a long, restful vacation even if you haven't left the confines of the city in a great while. The staff at East of Eighth is as gracious as the lighting and the service is swift.

Credit cards: All major. **Subway:** C, E to 23d St.

G Lounge CHELSEA 223 West 19th St. (between Seventh and Eighth Aves.) (212) 929-1085

Smart-dressed Chelsea gay guys line up on the weekends to get into this den of chic, with a juice bar in the back and a bar in the middle of the main room to encourage smooth cruising. G also features some of the best DJ's in the city. A hot spot from the day it opened.

Credit cards: Cash only. **Subway:** C, E, 1, 9 to 23d St.

Hell WEST VILLAGE 59 Gansevoort St. (between Washington and Greenwich Sts.) (212) 727-1666. A nice, dimly lit lounge up the street from the popular late-night diner Florent, Hell attracts a mostly gay clientele (and a classy, not overtly cruisey one at that). It's a swell place to have a Cosmopolitan as long as there's a DJ spinning. Otherwise it's those same old Erasure and Everything But the Girl songs on the jukebox—always something there to remind you of an ex-boyfriend or two.

Credit cards: All major. **Subway:** A, C, E to 14th St.; L to Eighth Ave.

Monster WEST VILLAGE 80 Grove St. (between West 4th St. and Waverly Place) (212) 924-3557. Located on Sheridan Square (with a view of Stonewall), the Monster is one of New York's oldest gay establishments. On the main floor, there's a huge, attractive wooden bar with plenty of seating for everyone. Moving further in, you'll hear various patrons by the piano belting out a favorite show tune (or 10). Venture downstairs and there's another large bar and a fairly spacious dance floor.

Credit cards: Cash only. **Subway:** 1, 9 to Christopher St.

Saints UPPER WEST SIDE 992 Amsterdam Ave. (between 109th and 110th Sts.) (212) 222-2431. This is not your typical gay bar. For one thing, its location is far from the city's other gay watering holes. For another, the patrons of this neighborhood hangout are much more diverse—and far less cruisey—than one might find in Chelsea. Saints is a stone's throw from Columbia, so students often pack the bar.

Credit cards: Cash only. **Subway:** 1, 9 to 110th St.

Starlight Bar & Lounge EAST VILLAGE 167 Avenue A (between 10th and 11th Sts.) (212) 475-2172. This elegant, congenial bar with a sizable gay clientele smack dab in the center of the East Village reflects the local penchant for dive-to-diva makeovers. The clean décor and dark, muted color scheme seem to be appreciated by the buff, clean-cut male (and the occasional female) crowd that frequents the place from early evening into the wee hours. Wednesday nights feature cabaret performances; Thursdays feature Raven-O singing smoky ballads for a $5 cover.

Credit cards: Cash only. **Subway:** L to First Ave.

Stonewall WEST VILLAGE 53 Christopher St. (between Sixth and Seventh Aves.) (212) 463-0950. Get out your gay history books: Stonewall is the little hole in the wall where the famous riots started. (The brief version: The police raided the bar, a drag queen threw a bottle, purses flew and, over the course of a couple of days in the summer of 1969, the gay rights movement was born.) These days, the bar is a quieter, more open, less tumultuous neighborhood hangout.

Credit cards: Cash only. **Subway:** 1, 9 to Christopher St.

Townhouse MIDTOWN EAST 206 East 58th St. (between Second and Third Aves.) (212) 826-6241. A "gentleman's club" in the truest sense of the term, this classy gay bar has the old boys' atmosphere down pat. A dress code ensures that the clientele maintains the proper image at all times. Dark wood, tapestry carpeting, and paintings of hunting scenes provide the perfect backdrop for the civilized meeting and greeting that goes on here. The crowd consists of older, well-polished men in suits lounging on couches or leaning suavely against walls.

Credit cards: All major. **Subway:** 4, 5, 6 to 59th St.; N, R to Lexington Ave.

Wonder Bar EAST VILLAGE 505 East Sixth St. (between Aves. A and B) (212) 777-9105. Formerly one of the cheesiest gay bars in the city, this spot is quickly surpassing the Boiler Room as the coolest place to meet the man of your dreams. Having gotten rid of the black-light decor and a seedy back room, the owners have created a warm, Wallpaper-style lounge complete with low couches and an elevated DJ booth. The young, mixed crowd is fashionable without being pretentious, cruisey without being seedy and cute without being intimidating.

Credit cards: Cash only. **Subway:** F to Second Ave.; L to First Ave.

The Works UPPER WEST SIDE 428 Columbus Ave. (between 80th and 81st Sts.) (212) 799-7365. An ad for The Works proclaims: "89% have jobs, 73% own their own apartments, the odds are in your favor. Find your new husband here." A hint, ladies: this ad isn't aimed at you. This bar is a neighborhood fixture, and—as the ad might indicate—attracts guppies of all ages. As gay bars go, the crowd is friendly, and the bartender swears that the chocolate martinis are delicious.

Credit cards: Cash only. **Subway:** B, C to 81st St.

Lesbian

Cubby Hole WEST VILLAGE. 281 West 12th St. (at West 4th St.) (212) 243-9041 A lack of pretension characterizes this narrow room, which lives up to its matchbook's claim of being "the friendly neighborhood bar." Although it caters predominantly to casually dressed, 30- and 40-something local lesbians, this West Village bar welcomes all. A miscellaneous collection of genders, races, ages and styles makes up the usual crowd.

Credit cards: Cash only. **Subway:** 1, 2, 3, 9 to 14th St.

Dumba Café BROOKLYN 57 Jay St. (between Front and Water Sts.), Brooklyn (212) 726-2686. A raw loft space in Dumbo (Down Under Manhattan Bridge Overpass), an artists' enclave in Brooklyn, Dumba has a riot-grrl and lesbian bent, but welcomes all types and ages into its makeshift, artsy environs. Exceptional punk bands on the riot-grrl circuit often play semi-secret concerts here.

Credit cards: Cash only. **Subway:** F to York St.

Henrietta Hudson WEST VILLAGE 438 Hudson St. (between Morton and Barrow Sts.) (212) 924-3347. A younger, less high-powered crowd than at Rubyfruit. Some nights are packed, others are dead, but the service is always pleasant and friendly. The crowd ranges from locals to bridge-and-tunnel girls, seductively (they think) grinding their hips to Madonna.

Credit cards: All major. **Subway:** 1, 9 to Christopher St.

Meow Mix LOWER EAST SIDE 269 East Houston St. (between Aves. A and B) (212) 254-0688. The epicenter of the lesbian queercore scene, Meow Mix has been immortalized in several films including *All Over Me* and *Chasing Amy*. It's a tiny place with a rec-room-type basement where young lesbians can go and shoot pool, flirt and drop quarters in the Ms. Pac Man machine. There's a small stage upstairs where local bands perform and the bar's restrooms feature the most exciting graffiti in town. Although primarily lesbian there's almost always a handful of men in attendance, with no hostility toward them.

Credit cards: Cash only. **Subway:** F to Second Ave.

Rubyfruit Bar and Grill WEST VILLAGE 531 Hudson St. (between West 10th and Charles Sts.) (212) 929-3343. A mature, friendly lesbian crowd gathers here to relax at the bar or on one of the richly upholstered settees, and tables are made of such artifacts as old-fashioned sewing machines, with pedals that still work. For added privacy, there is a step-up seating area at the back of the bar area, partially enclosed by lush draperies.

Credit cards: All major. **Subway:** 1, 9 to Christopher St.

DANCE CLUBS

More than any other nightlife activity in New York, dancing requires some research. Most of the city's dance clubs host several different parties each week. There is usually a cover charge that differs with each event and an occasional dress code. In addition, thanks to the Giuliani administration's periodic "crackdowns," there's always a chance that a venue will be closed. It is in any clubgoers best interest to call first and check local listings for details (see **Nightlife** Introduction for resources). Note: Clubs usually do not accept credit cards for the cover charge.

Also very popular are roving parties that change location at will, but are worth finding. **Organic Grooves** is one of the best; call (212) 439-1147 for location and information. Other events can be found by calling record store **Liquid Sky,** (212) 226-0657, **Urban Works,** (212) 629-1786, or **Giant Step,** (212) 714-8001.

Cheetah FLATIRON/UNION SQUARE 12 West 21st St. (between Fifth and Sixth Aves.) (212) 206-7770. The former Sound Factory Bar space has changed clientele entirely; the gay crowd stays away, while the champagne-swilling European set flocks here on weekends and the hip-hop crowd packs the place on Mondays for the popular Purr party. The venue's tacky décor leaves a lot to be desired, but Cheetah's a good space as far as midsized clubs go. There is also a downstairs lounge that is mellower, both in atmosphere and sound.

Credit cards: All major. **Subway:** F, N, R, 1, 9 to 23d St.

China Club MIDTOWN WEST 268 West 47th St. (between Broadway and Eighth Ave.) (212) 398-3800. This glitzy dance spot in the theater district attracts a fair number of movie, theater and music people. Just don't ogle—the club has a reputation as a safe haven for celebrities. The massive upstairs space has three full bars, a dance floor and stage. Wednesday nights feature live music ($10 cover) and sets often turn into jam sessions with unexpected celebrity guests. Weekends, when the cover jumps to $20, feature DJ house and top-40.

Credit cards: D/MC/V. **Subway:** A, C, E, N, R, 1, 2, 3, 7, 9 to 42d St.

Club New York MIDTOWN WEST 252 West 43d St. (between Broadway and Eighth Ave.) (212) 997-9510. If you're looking for a comfortably mainstream crowd in a comfortably mainstream setting, you could hardly do better than Club New York. Located in the heart of the "new" Times Square, Club New York targets the hotel and international tourist crowd. Most of the club's DJs spin a dance-friendly mix of accessible house and hip-hop spiced with a bit of Brazilian beat. Be prepared to part with $15 at the door, $3 at the coat-check and obscene sums at the bar.

Credit cards: MC/V. **Subway:** A, C, E, N, R, 1, 2, 3, 7, 9 to 42d St.

Don Hill's TRIBECA/SOHO 511 Greenwich St. (at Spring St.) (212) 219-2850. A small bar on the fringes of SoHo that has played host to Squeezebox, Michael Schmidt's raucous party, for several years now. As popular as ever, though somewhat straighter than it once was, Squeezebox still features renegade drag queen hostesses, live acts of a proudly dubious quality and a familiar sleazy 1970's and 80's soundtrack spun by the extraordinary Bowie-obsessed drag queen Miss Guy. BeavHer is a more behaved night of disco and 80's classics for a decidedly vanilla crowd.
Credit cards: All major. **Subway:** 1, 9 to Houston St.; C, E to Spring St.

Flamingo East EAST VILLAGE 219 Second Ave. (between 13th and 14th Sts.) (212) 533-2860. Though at its height a couple of years ago, a hip clientele still turns out at Flamingo East, particularly on Fridays for Lasia Alexine's frenetic, fabulous Honey Rider disco extravaganza. Saturday's Breakfast Club party fills the room with bland borough people who never got over 80's new wave and Gant Johnson's five-year-old Salon party for sharp-dressed gay guys who don't go for East Village grunge is on Wednesday nights; lunatic drag queen Justin Bond does his much-loved Kiki persona here on Thursdays.
Credit cards: All major. **Subway:** N, R, 4, 5, 6 to 14th St.; L to Third Ave.

Kit Kat Klub MIDTOWN WEST 124 West 43d St. (between Sixth Ave. and Broadway) (212) 819-0377. If this former Club Expo spot looks like a decadent theater in Weimar-era Berlin, that's because the revival of "Cabaret" performed here (at the Henry Miller Theater) before the Kit Kat opened its doors to the club crowd. Events include Go, Cafe Con Leche and Prestige.
Credit cards: All major. **Subway:** A, B, C, D, E, F, N, Q, R, 1, 2, 3, 7, 9 to 42d St.

La Nueva Escuelita MIDTOWN WEST 301 West 39th St. (at Eighth Ave.) (212) 631-0588. Transsexuals, drag queens, gay men and the women who love them and a progressive straight crowd mix it up on the dance floor. No doubt it's one of the cheapest dance venues in town—patrons pay no more than three dollars on most nights and when you add the free condoms you can score in the back from Nora Molina, a buxom brunette, it's clearly worth the price.
Credit cards: Cash only. **Subway:** A, C, E, N, R, 1, 2, 3, 7, 9 to 42d St.

Life/The Ki Club WEST VILLAGE 158 Bleecker St. (between Sullivan and Thompson Sts.) (212) 420-1999. Life is still hot—quite an accomplishment considering the transitory nature of New York nightlife. Erich Conrad's bitchy Thursday night affair, Get a Life!, is more or less an offshoot of his bitchy Beige party at B Bar, though at Life the people-watching is better. Wednesday belongs to Michael Schmidt's glammy Lust for Life, an extension of his Friday night Squeezebox at Don Hill's. Most other nights at the former Village Gate space feature private parties.
Credit cards: All major. **Subway:** A, B, C, D, E, F, Q to West 4th St.

Limelight CHELSEA 660 Sixth Ave. (at 20th St.) (212) 807-7850. With its exterior bathed in red floodlights, this church turned nightclub looks as sacrilegious as ever. But after a drug-addled past that shut its doors for nearly two years, the new Limelight is projecting a fresh, angelic face. Limelight's promoters really don't have much of a choice (the club is still under heavy scrutiny), but they are making a sincere attempt at infusing the place with culture. Go-go girls and boys have been replaced by modern-dance troupes, and amateur theater and poetry readings will be regular features.

Credit cards: All major. **Subway:** F to 23d St.

Nell's WEST VILLAGE 246 West 14th St. (between Seventh and Eighth Aves.) (212) 675-1567. The old mainstay from the 80's is still kicking along, but you won't see any of the big names that made the scene—they've all had children and moved to Westchester. Nell's has gone hip-hop, mostly, but there's still the long-running and much beloved Wild Seed party on Sunday nights, with disco spun by Jonny Sender.

Credit cards: All major. **Subway:** A, C, E, 1, 9 to 14th St.; L to Eighth Ave.

NV TRIBECA/SOHO 304 Hudson St. (between Spring and Vandam Sts.) (212) 929-6868. This hot spot on the western bounds of SoHo is a lounge palace. Heavy scarlet curtains cloak the main parlor and a brown-marble and copper bar curves along the length of the mezzanine. On Wednesday evenings live jazz hums from a small elevated stage. NV puts on its club face every night at 10 P.M., when the $20 cover charge kicks in and DJ's meld dance tracks with hip-hop and R&B. A favorite among New York's professional athletes, NV has also seen Mariah Carey do some impromptu time in the DJ booth.

Credit cards: All major. **Subway:** 1, 9 to Houston St.; C, E to Spring St.

Ohm FLATIRON/UNION SQUARE 16 West 22d St. (at Sixth Ave.) (212) 229-2000. An ultra-swank dance and supper club that features an eclectic array of expensive food, a lounge area and a dance floor upstairs. A second lounge and DJ-driven dance area are downstairs. Patrons can dance up an appetite, then hit the prix-fixe breakfast starting at 2 A.M.

Credit cards: All major. **Subway:** F to 23d St.

Polly Esther's WEST VILLAGE 186 West 4th St. (between Sixth and Seventh Aves.) (212) 924-5707. All dressed up in flammable synthetics and no place to go? Then consider Polly Esther's: With a floor-to-ceiling "fresco" of Travolta in his "Saturday Night Fever" prime, Charlie's Angels collages, and, of course, ABBA blaring from the speakers, the theme of this franchise (yes, this is a chain of nightclubs) is unmistakable. And that people pay the $8 cover on weekends to pack the place proves that the 70's just will not die.

Credit cards: All major. **Subway:** A, B, C, D, E, F, Q to West 4th St.

Roxy CHELSEA 515 West 18th St. (between 10th and 11th Aves.) (212) 645-5156. A cavernous Chelsea club that takes its weekend parties deep into the night (and early morning). The club draws a mixed crowd and music ranging from hip-hop to house to salsa depending on the night. Saturdays are mostly gay and on Wednesdays the place turns into a roller disco as it was originally.

Credit cards: Cash only. **Subway:** A, C, E to 14th St.

Sapphire Lounge LOWER EAST SIDE 249 Eldridge St. (between Houston and Stanton Sts.) (212) 777-5153. On weekends, the $5 cover, velvet rope, hulking bouncers, pounding dance music and young, rowdy crowd spilling onto the grubby street outside the Sapphire Lounge suggest a large, exclusive club. In truth, Sapphire is a small, overstuffed bar, decorated in cheap, haphazard lounge style. DJ's spin a range of house, funk and jazz, making Sapphire a good place for some weeknight dancing.

Credit cards: Cash only. **Subway:** F to Second Ave.

XVI EAST VILLAGE 16 First Ave. (between 1st and 2d Sts.) (212) 260-1549. Whether the evening's theme is Blaxploitation films or French strip-pop, XVI has the unique ability to adopt the character of any party—and not because it lacks its own. Long and narrow with a wall of exposed brick, XVI's main floor features a go-go cage, retractable film screen and, in the rear, a decently-stocked bar. Downstairs, congestion decreases and a Persian motif prevails. Intricately-cut glass mirrors, tile work tables and tapestry wall hangings dominate the room.

Credit cards: All major. **Subway:** F to Second Ave.

Sound Factory MIDTOWN WEST 618 West 46th St. (between 11th and 12th Aves.) (212) 489-0001. Closed for a short time by federal prosecutors the Sound Factory re-emerged, bloodied but unbowed. It's still a hopping late-night weekend destination that keeps the deep house pumpin' until well beyond dawn. Not quite as enthralling as the original Sound Factory, its latest incarnation nevertheless boasts an impressive sound system in addition to one of the more workable dance floors in town.

Credit cards: Cash only. **Subway:** A, C, E to 42d St.

Speeed MIDTOWN WEST 20 West 39th St. (between Fifth and Sixth Aves.) (212) 719-9867. Speeed (a.k.a. Creation) can't help feeling like a multi-level mall. There's the VIP room on the third floor, the Moroccan Room on the first floor, the main dance floor in the basement and the Vinyl Room on the second floor (featuring a DJ spinning vinyl, as well as vinyl furniture and padded vinyl walls). Also like a mall, Speeed (which is an 18-and-over club) is filled with wide-eyed and trendy youngsters trying to look more experienced than their parents hope they are.

Credit cards: All major. **Subway:** B, D, F, Q to 42d St.

13 EAST VILLAGE 35 East 13th St. (between University Pl. and Broadway) (212) 979-6677. This cozy second-story boite below Union Square hosts a number of weekly parties, most notably Sunday night's long-running "Shout!," a glamorous but young gathering of immaculately turned-out mods, skins, soulies and ska babies, all frugging away to an eclectic 60's soundtrack. It's an Anglophile's dream. Cheap drinks, comfy seating and a small dance floor help to make 13 an off-the-beaten-path downtown gem.

Credit cards: All major. **Subway:** L, N, R, 4, 5, 6 to 14th St.

Tunnel CHELSEA 220 12th Ave. (between 27th and 28th Sts.) (212) 695-4682. One of the biggest, most labyrinthine discos in town, the Tunnel has seen its share of license revocations. Though the scene is not as hip as it once was, this mammoth club is worth seeing.

Credit cards: Cash only. **Subway:** C, E to 23d St.

Twilo CHELSEA 530 West 27th St. (between 10th and 11th Aves.) (212) 268-1600. Yes, it's still got the best sound system in town, and yes, they still come to worship at DJ Junior Vasquez's altar on Saturday nights. But something about Twilo just isn't the same. Every other song sounds like hip French techno of the Daft Punk variety; every other patron looks like Antonio Sabato Jr., but with acne; the same old drag queens and trannies shake it loose on the podiums. The last Friday of every month features beloved U.K. DJ's Sasha and John Digweed.

Credit cards: All major. **Subway:** C, E to 23d St.

205 Club LOWER EAST SIDE 205 Chrystie St. (at Stanton St.) (212) 473-5816. This corner bar on the easternmost fringe of red-hot NoLIta attracts mostly a not-very-NoLIta crowd. Several local house and techno DJ's spin here on the weekends, when the bar becomes a bass-lover's banquet of throb. Kick back on the cruddy thrift-shop sofas and chairs in the back room and let the beat invade you.

Credit cards: Cash only. **Subway:** F to Second Ave.

Vanity FLATIRON/UNION SQUARE 28 East 23d St. (at Madison Ave.) (212) 254-6117.Blessed with a refreshingly attitude-free door and non-industrial location, Vanity is fast becoming one of Manhattan's best mid-size clubs—despite its unfortunate name. The dance floor is a sexy little space tucked into the rear of the club and in the basement, you'll find all the homey trappings of a suburban rec room (including a stain-proof rug of indeterminate color). With entire nights dedicated to funk, dub, British house or blaxploitation tunes, Vanity's crowd is largely determined by the evening's party.

Credit cards: MC/V. **Subway:** N, R, 6 to 23d St.

Vinyl TRIBECA/SOHO 6 Hubert St. (between Hudson and Collister Sts.) (212) 343-1379. Once a rave hall for New Jersey teens, now the home to uber-DJ Danny Tenaglia, as well as several popular parties. Vinyl's Body and Soul may be the hippest place to be on a Sunday afternoon. At Tsunami, a psychedelic trance party, dancers wear neo-hippy clothing in a hallucinogenic ambiance. No alcohol is served.

Credit cards: Cash only. **Subway:** A, C, E to Canal St.; 1, 9 to Franklin St.

Webster Hall EAST VILLAGE 125 East 11th St. (between Third and Fourth Aves.) (212) 353-1600. A cavernous, multi-level East Village club. On weekends you can't get near the place, which may be just as well; 11th Street is closed to all through-traffic. Thursday is Girls Night Out, with free admission and a complimentary drink for the ladies. Various DJ's spin various sounds in various rooms.

Credit cards: All major. **Subway:** L, N, R, 4, 5, 6 to 14th St.

POPULAR MUSIC VENUES
Rock, Folk and Country

Acme Underground EAST VILLAGE 9 Great Jones St. (between Lafyette St. and Broadway) (212) 659-2461. Located beneath Acme Bar and Grill, Acme Underground presents live rock and eclectic music most nights. (Weekend shows tend to be strictly 21 and over, while weekday age limits fluctuate.) There's room for a standing crowd of 225 and performers often mingle with the crowd as they walk to the stage, giving the place an intimate atmosphere.

Credit cards: D/MC/V. **Subway:** B, D, F, Q to Broadway-Lafayette St.; 6 to Bleecker St.

Arlene Grocery LOWER EAST SIDE 95 Stanton St. (between Ludlow and Orchard Sts.) (212) 358-1633. With its stellar sound system, relaxed atmosphere, willingness to book unknown acts and free admission, Arlene Grocery (housed in an old bodega) has quickly become an integral part of the rapidly expanding Lower East Side bar circuit. Emerging stars such as Beth Orton and Ron Sexsmith, as well as older performers like Marianne Faithful, have used the club for special intimate engagements. The club has the feel of a musicians' hangout, much like CBGB in its 1970's heyday. The few tables in the small, 150-person-capacity room quickly fill up, so most patrons stand for performances.

Credit cards: Cash only. **Subway:** F to Second Ave.

Baggot Inn WEST VILLAGE 82 West 3d St. (between Thompson and Sullivan Sts.) (212) 477-0622. Formerly the Sun Mountain Cafe, the Baggot Inn continues the folk music tradition of long-gone 1960's coffeehouses on Bleecker Street. Occasionally, performers go electric among the flock of aspiring singer-songwriters. For the most part, however, the stage at the back of the club offers acoustic sounds. Poetry, comedy, open-mike nights and DJ events also take place.

Credit cards: All major. **Subway:** A, B, C, D, E, F, Q to West 4th St.

Bitter End WEST VILLAGE 147 Bleecker St. (between Thompson St. and LaGuardia Place) (212) 673-7030. Bob Dylan, Joan Baez, Harry Chapin, Paul Simon and Patti Smith have graced this rickety wooden stage on their way to larger fame, and the promotional posters that line the walls give a sense of the venue's history. Opened in 1961 as an ice cream shop, the Bitter End has maintained its informal feel and continues to present aspiring folk and rock acts for a mix of curious tourists, N.Y.U. students and each band's contingent of fans. A decent sound system works for the usual lineup of mellow folk and folk-rock, as well as occasional jazz, blues, funk and poetry.

Credit cards: Cash only. **Subway:** A, B, C, D, E, F, Q to West 4th St.

The Bottom Line WEST VILLAGE 15 West 4th St. (at Mercer St.) (212) 228-6300. Since 1974, the Bottom Line has presented singer-songwriters—a young Bruce Springsteen, an older Elvis Costello, among others—in its spacious room. Patrons sit cabaret-style at tables, and though the seating arrangement is a bit cramped, it is more pleasant than standing, especially when the main musical fare is meant for listening more than for dancing. The crowd varies according to the performer, but audiences tend to be slightly older than those at typical New York concerts. One of the best things about the Bottom Line is its willingness to book rarely heard country and bluegrass performers.

Credit cards: Cash only. **Subway:** B, D, F, Q to Broadway-Lafayette St.; N, R to 8th St.

Brownies EAST VILLAGE 169 Ave. A (between 10th and 11th Sts.) (212) 420-8392. Transformed in the early 90's from a neighborhood bar to one of the best indie-rock clubs on the downtown circuit, Brownies continues to present punk-inspired, guitar-driven bands in a no-frills, music-first bar environment. Not the most comfortable of spaces, especially when the rectangular room gets crowded, Brownies redeems itself by putting together thoughtful bills of local bands with potential and touring acts that have garnered a buzz in the college-rock world.

Credit cards: Cash only. **Subway:** L to First. Ave.

Cafe Wha? WEST VILLAGE 115 Macdougal St. (between Bleecker and 3d Sts.) (212) 254-3706. Decorated with hanging lights and wooden booths packed tightly together, this cozy basement club has been a Greenwich Village institution for more than 30 years. Cafe Wha? once hosted performances by young artists like Bob Dylan and Jimi Hendrix. The standout night nowadays is Brazilian night on Mondays—a festive, Carnaval-like party that combines the hip-shaking sounds of bossa nova, samba and Brazilian rock and jazz. Tuesday nights features the funky Slam Clinic with Mike Davis; various rock and pop musicians play on the weekends.

Credit cards: All major. **Subway:** A, B, C, D, E, F, Q to West 4th St.

CBGB LOWER EAST SIDE 315 Bowery (at Bleecker St.) (212) 982-4052. The famed CBGB's is still an ideal place to try out unknown rock bands and catch the occasional bigger name playing an intimate show.

Since its heyday (The Ramones, the Talking Heads and Blondie are some of the bands that got their start here), CB's has lost some of its hold on the rock scene, but only because other similar venues have arisen. Patrons are allowed to enter and leave the club at will, giving CB's a neighborhood-hangout feel. The club's infamous bathrooms, which patrons used to destroy on a regular basis, have acquired a modicum of decorum.

Credit cards: Cash only. **Subway:** 6 to Bleecker St.; B, D, F, Q to Broadway-Lafayette St.

CB's 313 Gallery EAST VILLAGE 313 Bowery (at Bleecker St.) (212) 677-0455. By presenting mellow, acoustic-based sounds and monthly art exhibits in a cafe setting, CB's Gallery offers an entirely different experience from its legendary progenitor, CBGB. Here you'll find tables and candles instead of a mosh pit, spoken word and poetry instead of guitar distortion and sonic shriek. Like the original CBGB, however, the gallery makes an effort to present new and unknown talent.

Credit cards: All major. **Subway:** 6 to Bleecker St.; B, D, F, Q to Broadway-Lafayette St.

Continental EAST VILLAGE 25 Third Ave. (between St. Marks Place and 9th St.) (212) 529-6924. With a dive-bar feel, four to five aspiring rock bands nightly and a blaring sound system, the sublimely sleazy Continental is the tongue-pierced stud at the mouth of St. Marks Place. Formerly known as the Continental Divide, the bar has launched many a career—from jam-band success Blues Traveler to garage-rock renovators the Pristeens. Punk legends such as Iggy Pop, Patti Smith and Joey Ramone have been known to perform unannounced sets.

Credit cards: Cash only. **Subway:** 6 to Astor Pl.

Fez Under Time Cafe EAST VILLAGE 380 Lafayette St. (at Great Jones St.) (212) 533-2680. Two floors below the trendy Time Cafe, Fez presents indie-rockers, weekly jazz band "workshops," comedy acts and cabaret shows—all in a swank clubhouse atmosphere. It's equal parts Moroccan hashish den (hence the name), Village Vanguard-like basement jazz club and gangster hideaway. Patrons, generally a bit older than your average rock club crowd, sit at tables or in the plush leather booths that line the back wall of the room, which accommodates about 150.

Credit cards: All major. **Subway:** 6 to Bleecker St.; B, D, F, Q to Broadway-Lafayette St.

Lakeside Lounge EAST VILLAGE 162 Ave. B (Between 10th and 11th Sts.) (212) 529-8463. Enter the Lakeside Lounge and you could be in a shack on the edge of a pond deep in the country—it's trout fishing in Alphabet City. At first glance, East Village hipsters appear to dominate the front-room bar, but all are welcome. Excellent rockabilly, country and "cowpunk" bands that appear most nights.

Credit cards: Cash only. **Subway:** L to First Ave.

The Living Room LOWER EAST SIDE 84 Stanton St. (at Allen St.) (212) 533-7235. With its affordable but scrumptious vegetarian-leaning menu and its intimate folk music, the Living Room lives up to its name. The decor is makeshift but elegant. There are games and puzzles for playing with friends or for breaking the ice. Rows of tables take up most of the floor space leading up to the stage. Fans of singer/songwriter folk music will enjoy the relaxed atmosphere, the sincere performances, and the casual, parlor-room feel.

Credit cards: All major. **Subway:** F to Second Ave.

Luna Lounge LOWER EAST SIDE 171 Ludlow St. (between Houston and Stanton Sts.) (212) 260-2323. Luna Lounge is half bar hangout, half free-music venue. Décor is minimal, but the wood bar adds a touch of elegance. The back room is an intimate space where alternative pop acts play for free each night. At the infamous Monday night comedy sessions, local pros try out their more edgy material. After the bands, a good jukebox makes Luna Lounge a quality last stop on the Ludlow Street bar circuit.

Credit cards: Cash only. **Subway:** F to Second Ave.

Mercury Lounge LOWER EAST SIDE 217 East Houston St. (between Essex and Ludlow Sts.) (212) 260-4700. The Mercury Lounge attracts a varied crowd that comes to listen to everything from singer-songwriters and alterna-rockers to the latest experimental electronic music practitioners. Since the back room only holds 200 people, buying tickets at the bar ahead of time is recommended when bigger names are on the bill. Inside the performance space, there are a few highly-coveted tables, but most patrons stand. Be sure to bring ID; most shows are strictly 21 and over.

Credit cards: All major. **Subway:** F to Second Ave.

Nightingale Music Bar EAST VILLAGE 213 Second Ave. (at 13th St.) (212) 473-9398. A neighborhood dive that looks like a tomb from the outside but is warm and festive inside, Nightingale's is a prime spot for sipping a Budweiser and taking in a groovy jam. Loud and passionate live rock and funk (with occasional jazz) are presented nightly. Performers like Blues Traveler, the Spin Doctors and Joan Osborne got their start playing on the miniature stage, barely 10 feet from the bar in this small, almost windowless room.

Credit cards: Cash only. **Subway:** L to Third Ave.; N, R, 4, 5, 6 to 14th St.

Paddy Reilly's Music Bar MURRAY HILL 519 Second Ave. (at 29th St.) (212) 686-1210. Over the last few years, this bar has become a prime spot for all things Irish. The Irish expatriate community gathers here to catch up on gossip and news and to drink and dance, but all are welcome. The decor of the long bar, the small stage, and the adjoining billiard room strike a balance between dive-bar sublimity and aged-wood elegance. Of particular interest are the "sessiuns," traditional Irish jam sessions where participants sit in a circle and play Celtic songs on guitar, hand drum and sometimes the uilleann pipes.

Credit cards: Cash only. **Subway:** 6 to 28th St.

Rodeo Bar MURRAY HILL 375 Third Ave. (at 27th St.) (212) 683-6500. When it opened in 1987, the Rodeo Bar was one of the first places in New York to feature roots-rock made for and by local performers. Since then, it has expanded its booking policy to include touring roots-rockers as well. Long wooden railings and peanut shells on the floor add to the honky-tonk atmosphere. There is no music cover, making the Rodeo Bar a prime spot for savoring the flavor of longtime New York bar bands.

Credit cards: All major. **Subway:** 6 to 28th St.

Sidewalk EAST VILLAGE 94 Ave. A (at Sixth St.) (212) 473-7373. The back of the Sidewalk Cafe is home to the Fort, where a musician who calls himself Lach books like-minded "anti-folk" singer/songwriters eager to rescue folk music from cloying sentimentality by adding a dose of punk sass. Most shows at the Fort have no cover and a one-drink minimum at tables. Performers pass the hat for donations. Pinball machines are in the front room, and a pool table is located in the basement.

Credit cards: All major. **Subway:** 6 to Astor Pl.; F to Second Ave.

The West End UPPER WEST SIDE 2911 Broadway (between 113th and 114th Sts.) (212) 662-8830. Jack Kerouac and Allen Ginsberg spent much of their college years as burgeoning beatniks eating and drinking at this Columbia University hangout, just as many a Columbian does today. Jazz (as well as rock and folk by student bands) still plays in the back room. But what was a dive is now a pleasant restaurant. The brick and wood décor, tall ceilings and overhead fans give it an airy roominess and maybe at one of the booths in the back, some young Columbians are creating more great American literature.

Credit cards: All major; checks. **Subway:** 1, 9 to 116th St.

Jazz, Blues & Experimental

Birdland MIDTOWN WEST 315 West 44th St. (between Eighth and Ninth Aves.) (212) 581-3080. Birdland features some of the most thoughtfully booked jazz in the city. The club pays direct homage to its namesake, the legendary original Birdland at Broadway and 52d Street. (The only thing missing are the caged parakeets that used to slowly asphyxiate on cigarette smoke during bebop's heyday in the 1940's and 50's.) Though it's a fully functional restaurant with a Southern-tinged menu, Birdland's main attraction is music. Reservations are recommended for the music sets ($10–$15 and a one-drink minimum).

Credit cards: All major. **Subway:** A, C, E to 42d St.

Blue Note WEST VILLAGE 131 West 3d St. (between Sixth Ave. and Macdougal St.) (212) 475-0049. Performances by jazz heavyweights such as Tony Bennett, Oscar Peterson and Chick Corea, and exhilarating double bills are the main attractions at the Blue Note. A night at the Blue Note can easily cost you $100. Because the club's seating sometimes makes rush-hour subway trains seem cozy, reservations and early arrival are essential. Record labels use Monday nights, when it's considerably less expensive, to break in new acts—a real bargain when established musicians join in.

Credit cards: All major. **Subway:** A, B, C, D, E, F, Q to West 4th St.

Chicago Blues WEST VILLAGE 73 Eighth Ave. (between 13th and 14th Sts.) (212) 924-9755. There's nothing fancy here. It's just a bar and a plain, brick-walled music room with a robust sound system. But the club is an outpost of the Chicago-centered Midwestern blues circuit, which yields some of the most subtle and big-hearted American music. Unlike the run of New York blues clubs, Chicago Blues books not only the headliner but the whole band, which provides qualitatively different music.

Credit cards: All major. **Subway:** A, C, E to 14th St.; L to Eighth Ave.

Cooler WEST VILLAGE 418 West 14th St. (between Ninth Ave. and Washington St.) (212) 645-5189. Once a meat market—literally—this former basement butchery offers some of the best edgy experimental music around. Much like the Knitting Factory, the Cooler has become a center for strange, new sounds with its booking policy based on a "downtown" aesthetic rather than a particular genre of music: everything from DJ's to ska to noise-rock can be heard, sometimes all at once. The Cooler is a great place to expand one's appreciation of the sonic boundaries where music meets chaos, and dance while doing so.

Credit cards: Cash only. **Subway:** A, C, E to 14th St.; L to Eighth Ave.

Iridium Jazz Club UPPER WEST SIDE 44 West 63d St. (at Columbus Ave.) (212) 582-2121. Since opening in 1993 below the Merlot Bar and Grill, this tony club has become one of the top jazz venues in the city. Success has led to three renovations and a series of "Live at the Iridium" recordings on various labels. In addition to presenting legendary guitarist Les Paul every Monday night, Iridium features both established and up-and-coming jazz stars.

Credit cards: All major. **Subway:** 1, 9 to 66th St.

Izzy Bar EAST VILLAGE 166 First Ave. (between 10th and 11th Sts.) (212) 228-0444. Upstairs there's a bar with fashionable club music on the speakers and fashionable young Manhattanites on the comfy chairs. The bottom floor, unexpectedly, has a music space for fairly experimental jazz and dance music; center stage seats are almost right in the bandleader's face. The bookings are a mixed lot and the cover charge is usually $10 or less.

Credit cards: All major. **Subway:** L to First Ave.

The Jazz Standard FLATIRON/UNION SQUARE 116 East 27th St. (between Park and Lexington Aves.) (212) 576-2232. Some of the best food to be had while listening to live jazz in New York is at the Jazz Standard, beneath the restaurant 27 Standard. For a time, the food was the main draw. Bookings started with double-A farm team musicians (a risk for a 150-capacity room), but the club has already worked up to some of the best younger musicians out there, including Eric Reed and Steve Wilson.

Credit cards: All major. **Subway:** 6 to 28th St.

Knitting Factory TRIBECA/SOHO 74 Leonard St. (between Broadway and Church St.) (212) 219-3055. With four spaces for live music, the Knitting Factory is host to not only the avant-garde jazz that first earned this place its reputation, but also rock, spoken word, theater, film and even children's shows. So much is going on in the Knitting Factory on any given night that there's often a bottleneck at the front door. The Main Space holds 350 patrons and can get quite crowded. The Alterknit Theater presents lesser-known acts as well as spoken word, theater and films in a space that holds 90. Free performances occur in the downstairs Tap Room, which has over 15 microbrews on tap. And the newest space, the Old Office, presents up-and-coming jazz artists in a more traditional jazz-club setting.

Credit cards: All major. **Subway:** 1, 9 to Franklin St.; A, C, E to Canal St.

Lenox Lounge HARLEM 288 Lenox Ave. (between 124th and 125th Sts.) (212) 722-9566. The odds are good that Mickey Bass, the bassist who now books the weekend jazz at this Harlem art-deco bar, will get on stage between sets and point out the corner banquette where Billie Holiday liked to claim a regular table. Bandleaders are mostly drawn from New York jazz's middle-aged netherworld: Musicians like Chico Freeman and James Spaulding—too old to be lions, too young to be legends. And the management doesn't rustle you out between sets; you can settle in for the evening. That's the type of peace of mind you can't buy downtown.

Credit cards: All major. **Subway:** 2, 3 to 125th St.

Manny's Car Wash UPPER EAST SIDE 1558 Third Ave. (between 87th and 88th Sts.) (212) 369-2583. There's nothing but the blues, fierce and unadulterated, at Manny's Car Wash, a narrow, smoky bar on the Upper East Side. Most nights, it's standing room only with limited seating available at just a few long bench tables near the stage. With its serious sound system, well-known acts like Bo Diddley and John Lee Hooker and local favorites, Manny's Car Wash is still a prime stop for hearing the blues in New York. For the adventurous, an incendiary open jam takes place most Sunday nights.

Credit cards: All major. **Subway:** 4, 5, 6 to 86th St.

Roulette TRIBECA/SOHO 222 West Broadway (between Franklin and N. Moore Sts.) (212) 219-8242. Above boisterous young professionals drinking champagne in the Bubble Lounge, serious avant-garde music takes place in Roulette. This nonprofit performance space has a mix of elegant informality and concentrated audacity, with musicians trying all sorts of new, experimental ideas. Avant-garde saxophonist John Zorn performed some of his first "game piece" compositions at Roulette, and everyone from Oliver Lake, the esteemed jazz composer, to Thurston Moore, guitarist for the noise-rock band Sonic Youth, has appeared as part of Roulette's concert programs.

Credit cards: Cash only. **Subway:** 1, 9 to Franklin St.

Smoke UPPER WEST SIDE 2751 Broadway (between 105th and 106th Sts.) (212) 316-3737. Smoke (formerly known as Augie's Pub) captures the spirit of legendary jazz jam joints like Minton's—where bebop was born in the 1940's. Up-and-coming jazz musicians blow and wail in the small, cozy storefront room. It can get quite packed, but the atmosphere is friendly and the music is almost always exciting. Jazz aficionados such as the authors Stanley Crouch and Albert Murray regularly show up, crowding in alongside Columbia University students.

Credit cards: Cash only. **Subway:** 1, 9 to 103d St.

St. Nick's Pub HARLEM 773 St. Nicholas Blvd. (at 149th St.) (212) 283-9728. St. Nick's Pub, a legendary Harlem jazz bar, still serves up live jazz six nights a week, Wednesday to Monday. Saxophonist Patience Higgins and the Sugar Hill Jazz Quartet lead a popular jam session every Monday, with musicians playing well past 1 A.M. When the band takes a booze break, the jukebox cranks up, blaring both classic jazz and R&B, as well as contemporary hip-hop. Even on a Monday, seats are difficult to come by in this tiny shoebox of a bar.

Credit cards: Cash only. **Subway:** A, B, C, D to 145th St.

Sweet Basil WEST VILLAGE 88 Seventh Ave. South (between Bleecker and Grove Sts.) (212) 242-1785. New York's underdog jazz joint, Sweet Basil usually doesn't get weeklong engagements with the latest big-label, critics' rave. But the club has taken chances on such excellent musicians as Andy Bey, Michele Rosewoman and Marc Cary, and occasionally presents A-list room-fillers like Kenny Garrett.
Credit cards: All major. **Subway:** 1, 9 to Christopher St.

Terra Blues WEST VILLAGE 149 Bleecker St. (between Thompson St. and LaGuardia Pl.) (212) 777-7776. In the heart of the Village, a flight above Bleecker Street, Terra Blues is home to both local and national blues acts. Though it's named after an obscure, rural Mississippi blues genre, Terra Blues is a modern-day urban saloon with surreal sculpture and blowzy curtains framing the small stage. Musicians like playing the club and the same performers are likely to return throughout the month.
Credit cards: All major. **Subway:** A, B, C, D, E, F, Q to West 4th St.

Tonic LOWER EAST SIDE 107 Norfolk St. (between Delancey and Rivington Sts.) (212) 358-7501. Downtown nightlife goes synergistic in a former kosher wine market next to the parking lot for Ratners Restaurant. Tonic, which opened in early 1998, used to be a hair salon, but is. now a nightspot with experimental jazz, comedy nights, spoken words and occasional movie screenings.
Credit cards: Cash only. **Subway:** F to Delancey St.; J, M, Z to Essex St.

Village Vanguard WEST VILLAGE 178 Seventh Ave. S. (between West 11th St. and Waverly Pl.) (212) 255-4037. Known for its intimacy, pristine acoustics and lack of pretense, the Village Vanguard is the one of the world's finest jazz venues. Since 1935, this basement hideaway has hosted a staggering lineup— from Barbra Streisand and Woody Allen to John Coltrane and Thelonious Monk. Over 100 albums bear the imprimatur "Recorded Live at the Village Vanguard." In 1965, the Mel Lewis-Thad Jones Orchestra began a Monday night big band tradition that endures under the moniker Vanguard Jazz Orchestra. Reservations are recommended.
Credit cards: Cash only. **Subway:** 1, 2, 3, 9 to 14th St.

Zinno WEST VILLAGE 126 West 13th St. (between Sixth and Seventh Aves.) (212) 924-5182. Zinno, an intimate jazz supper club, is spread between two brownstones where piano and bass duos dominate the nightly festivities. The high ceilings, peach brick walls, mahogany bar and dining room make for an elegant atmosphere. During the consistently superb Sunday brunch shows, the polished wood floors often gets a workout from a largely improvised jazz-tap dance extravaganza.
Credit cards: All major. **Subway:** F, 1, 2, 3, 9 to 14th St.

World & Latin

Bistro Latino MIDTOWN WEST 1711 Broadway (at 54th St.) (212) 956-1000. Most of the friendly, all-aged Latino crowd at the upscale Bistro Latino come for dinner and stay to tango on Wednesdays, mambo on Thursdays and salsa on Fridays and Saturdays. You can also pay a small cover to skip dinner and go straight for the music and dancing and sip one of the Bistro's delicious, fruity cocktails made with mangoes, passion fruit, and South American specialty liquors like Chilean Muscat brandy or Brazilian sugar cane rum.

Credit cards: All major. **Subway:** A, B, C, D, 1, 9 to 59th St.

Copacabana MIDTOWN WEST 617 West 57th St. (between 11th and 12th Aves.) (212) 582-2672. Copacabana is both a Latin American club where the most respected salsa and merengue musicians perform and a disco where house music thunders. The crowd is predominantly Latino, but New Yorkers of all stripes mix together along with tourists from Europe, South America and Japan. Most wear formal attire and come to dance. Seasoned veterans and hot newcomers, from Eddie Palmieri to La India, play Tuesday, Friday and Saturday evenings.

Credit cards: All major. **Subway:** A, B, C, D, 1, 9 to 59th St.

El Flamingo CHELSEA 547 West 21st St. (between 10th and 11th Aves.) (212) 243-2121. A snazzy venue on the far West Side that plays up the Art Deco supper-club theme to the hilt. The main room has a good-sized dance floor that splits in half when the club hosts live music performances; the non-rhythmically inclined can watch from above. Various promoters use El Flamingo for shows, so keep an eye out for upcoming gigs. There are also "regular" nights: Saturday hosts live Greek performances for a late-night crowd, and Sunday is a popular Latin music party.

Credit cards: MC/V. **Subway:** C, E to 23d St.

Gonzalez y Gonzalez EAST VILLAGE 625 Broadway (between Bleecker and Houston Sts.) (212) 473-8787. On Friday or Saturday nights bands play salsa, mambo and merengue and DJ's spin the latest Latin-tinged records in this bar's back room, the Blue Lounge. Outside, there's often a line of stylishly dressed patrons (semi-formal attire is the norm but not required) who come from far and wide for the mango or guava margaritas, scorching sounds and moderately priced Mexican food.

Credit cards: All major. **Subway:** B, D, F, Q to Broadway-Lafayette; 6 to Bleecker St.

Latin Quarter UPPER WEST SIDE 2551 Broadway (between 95th and 96th Sts.) (212) 864-7600. Even on Sunday at 2 A.M., the atmosphere at the Latin Quarter is electrifying. As the second-floor dance club pulsates to the sound of a salsa band, several hundred nattily attired people are on the dance floor—from grooving 20-somethings to white-haired couples executing precision dance routines. Hundreds more are at tables, with still more at the bars at either end of the enormous room. Speaking Spanish helps at the Latin Quarter, but it isn't required.

Credit cards: MC/V. **Subway:** 1, 2, 3, 9 to 96th St.

S.O.B.'s TRIBECA/SOHO 200 Varick St. (at Houston St.) (212) 243-4940. The audience sways more than the palm fronds on the faux-tree, making S.O.B.'s one of the city's best clubs for Latin, Caribbean and Afropop music. Decorated in a copacabana-hut style, but with disco lights, S.O.B.'s is a dancer's heaven. The club even offers salsa and tango lessons before most weekend shows. In the best New York manner, ethnic groups mix at S.O.B.'s to produce a culture greater than that of any individual subgroup. Make reservations or purchase advance tickets for popular shows.

Credit cards: All major. **Subway:** 1, 9 to Houston St.; C, E to Spring St.

Zinc Bar WEST VILLAGE 90 West Houston St. (between Thompson St. and LaGuardia Place) (212) 477-8337. The Zinc Bar is a downtown venue that manages to be sophisticated yet retain an informal atmosphere. Opened in 1993, the Zinc presents some of the best up-and-coming jazz and world sounds—especially Brazilian music—in the city. The Zinc Bar can get quite crowded, so arrive early if you want to sit. Be on the lookout for two kinds of cats at the Zinc Bar: famous jazz musicians kicking back after a gig and the two felines who fearlessly roam through the crowd.

Credit cards: All major. **Subway:** B, D, F, Q to Broadway-Lafayette St.

CABARET

One of the singular attractions of New York City is its busy cabaret scene. The term "cabaret" applies to high-end supper clubs featuring singers who perform popular standards from the pre-rock era on. Cabaret flourishes in New York because of its proximity to Broadway. Theater stars often moonlight as cabaret performers, and a nightclub act can also be a stepping stone to Broadway. Cabaret also intersects with the world of jazz, although these two worlds are quite distinct

An evening of cabaret with an entertainment charge and food and drink minimum can cost quite a bit more than a Broadway show. But the kind of magical intimacy that the best cabaret has to offer is something that can only be experienced in a nightclub where the lights are low and the champagne flowing.

The city's three leading cabarets are the chic **Café Carlyle,** in the Carlyle Hotel, the **Oak Room** at the Algonquin Hotel, and the **Firebird Café,** an adjunct of the Firebird Restaurant which serves Russian haute cuisine. In late 1999, **Feinstein's at the Regency** (named after the popular singer and pianist Michael Feinstein who helps book the club and who has performed there) opened at the Regency Hotel. Whether or not it will feature acts regularly or function only on a sporadic basis remains to be seen. **Arci's,** a new club on Park Avenue South (at 30th St.) also opened in 1999 with a month-long engagement of the Broadway singer Karen Mason.

Café Carlyle

Carlyle Hotel, 35 East 76th St. (at Madison Ave.) (212) 744-1600

The Café Carlyle, the Rolls Royce of the city's cabarets, books the same performers every year for extended engagements. Ruling the roost in the late spring and late fall is the singer and pianist Bobby Short who has appeared there every year for more than three decades. Now in his 70s, Mr. Short is an effervescent musical bon vivant with exquisite taste in songs who brings the urbane music of Cole Porter, Cy Coleman and others thrillingly to life in performances that have the feel of nightly parties.

The onetime Broadway ingenue Barbara Cook also appears at the Café twice a year interpreting Broadway and popular standards in an ageless lyric soprano that conveys equal measures of sweetness and wisdom. Eartha Kitt, the ranking comic femme fatale of American pop also appears there each winter.

Oak Room
The Algonquin, 59 West 44th St. (between Fifth and Sixth Aves.) (212) 840-6800

The Oak Room of the Algonquin (the site of the famous literary Round Table in the 1920's and 30's) is the regular home of the brilliant pop-jazz singer Mary Cleere Haran whose witty musical shows conjure up the worlds of the Gershwins, Irving Berlin and Rodgers and Hart. The room's other top draw is the singer and actress Andrea Marcovicci, who appears in the late fall resurrecting the same past but in a more romantic style.

Firebird Café
365 West 46th St. (between Eighth and Ninth Aves.) (212) 586-0244

The Firebird Café is the regular fall hangout for Steve Ross, the sophisticated singer and pianist who specializes in Cole Porter, Noel Coward and Fred Astaire.
—*by Stephen Holden*

Other Cabarets and Supper Clubs
(See also "A Grand Oasis: New York's Hotel Bars,"above)

Bemelmans Bar Carlyle Hotel, 981 Madison Ave. (between 76th and 77th Sts.) (212) 744-1600. At Bemelman's, for only a $10 cover, you can hear Barbara Carroll, one of the great jazz pianists, who's in residence half the year and attracts a celebrity audience. (Tony Bennett has been known to drop in and join her for a song or two.) Peter Mintun provides the music the rest of the year. Enjoy the private, romantic booths or reserve one of the small tables for two right by the piano.
Credit cards: All major, checks. **Subway:** 6 to 77th St.

Danny's Skylight Room 346 West 46th St. (between Eighth and Ninth Aves.) (212) 265-8133. There is a skylight in Danny's Skylight Room, but don't expect to see too much sky—or too much light, for that matter. But that's O.K., because your focus should be on the front of this rather unadorned, crowded room in the back of Danny's Grand Sea Palace, a good Thai restaurant on Restaurant Row. That's where you'll find some of the city's finest cabaret performers, from fresh upstarts to great old-timers like Blossom Dearie. As you enter Danny's, there's also a narrow piano bar, a cramped but festive spot decked out with strings of Christmas lights, where you can sing along with the theater types who've made the stools around the piano their second home.

Credit cards: All major. **Features:** Food. **Subway:** A, C, E to 42d St.

Delmonico Lounge Hotel Delmonico, 502 Park Ave. (at 59th St.) (212) 355-2500. A remarkably small room (seating just 38), the D Lounge is the only bar at the Hotel Delmonico, so patrons are not necessarily here for the music. But the room itself is very comfortable; especially if you can ease back into one of the cushy banquettes. The performers (usually a singer accompanied by trio or piano) are practically at one with the patrons. Shows are presented only on weekends, and the music goes on hiatus in the summer, when the D Lounge becomes a hotel bar again.

Credit cards: All major. **Features:** Food. **Subway:** 4, 5, 6 to 59th St; N, R to Lexington Ave.

Don't Tell Mama 343 West 46th St. (between Eighth and Ninth) (212) 757-0788. This enterprising theater district perennial is really three venues in one: two cabaret rooms and a piano bar under the same management. On weekdays, there are up to four shows a night, and on weekends, up to eight— and that's in addition to the virtually nonstop show in the bar, which features singing waiters after 9 P.M. Cover charges and minimums vary, but the piano bar has no cover.

Credit cards: AE. **Features:** Food. **Subway:** A, C, E to 42d St.

The Duplex 61 Christopher St. (at Seventh Ave. S.) (212) 255-5438. Village bar and cabaret ought to be called Camp Duplex, given the nature of the crowd and many of the shows. It's the oldest continually running cabaret in the city, where many a career was launched. With three levels—a lively piano bar on the first, a lounge/game room on the second and, tucked away off to the side between the two, a small cabaret/theater—the Duplex always seems to be hopping. The cabaret has a tiny proscenium stage (an unusual feature for a cabaret) with rows of crowded cocktail tables providing the seating. Besides the standard music, there's comedy, improv, theater and drag.

Credit cards: Cash only. **Subway:** 1, 9 to Christopher St.

Greatest Bar On Earth 1 World Trade Center, 107th Fl. (between Liberty and Vesey Sts.) (212) 524-7000. While no place could possibly live up to this moniker (there's just too much competition in New York), The Greatest Bar on Earth sometimes comes close. It's worth the trip, even if you don't live near the World Trade Center. Of course, this spot boasts a great view, with a wall of windows spanning the back of the room. Everything here is sleek and sexy, from the huge circular bar, to the long, thin table against the back wall, where the even longer and thinner patrons congregate. The bar features live music Monday through Saturday; the weekend swing nights, in particular, should not be missed.

Credit cards: All major. **Features:** Dancing, food. **Subway:** N, R to Cortlandt St.; C, E, to World Trade Center.

Joe's Pub 425 Lafayette St.(between Astor Pl. and 4th St.) (212) 539-8777. A portrait of the legendary producer Joseph Papp watches over the plush banquettes, red votives and zinc ballustrades at what is already one of the latest buzz-heavy nightspots. Depending on the time and the scheduled act, Joe's Pub will be a swank cabaret, a pre-theater watering hole, a place to slam poetry or a late-night drop-in center for hip, downtown laze-abouts. You'll usually find top-quality performers in this friendly, laid back setting.

Credit cards: All major. **Subway:** 6 to Astor Pl.; N, R to 8th St.

Judy's 169 Eighth Ave.(between 18th and 19th Sts.) (212) 929-5410. Judy Kreston, a singer, and her husband, David Lahm, a pianist, run this Chelsea cabaret and restaurant that attracts interesting lounge acts. Kreston and Lahm frequently perform on Saturday nights.

Credit cards: Cash only. **Services:** Food. **Subway:** A, C, E to 14th St.

Michael's Pub at Bill's Gay 90's 57 East 54th St. (between Park and Madison Aves.) (212) 355-0243. Time seems frozen in the Roaring Twenties at this former East Side speakeasy. Open since 1925, it's the kind of place where you almost expect Dutch Schultz to step out of the shadows. The upstairs dining room and cabaret is covered from floor to ceiling with old theater programs and posters. The dark wood paneling, floral carpet and deep red velvet curtains behind the singers' platform give Bill's Gay Nineties a certain patina. It's not posh, but at the same time, there's an air of class.

Credit cards: All major. **Subway:** 4, 5, 6 to 59th St.; N, R to Lexington Ave.

Roseland Ballroom 239 West 52d St. (between Broadway and Eighth Ave.) (212) 247-0200. Arena-like rock shows, retro-big band jazz nights, occasional salsa dancing and rhythm and blues "Rhythm Revues" are all on the program in this legendary palace. Opened by Louis Brecker in 1951, the Ballroom moved to its current location on 52nd Street, once occupied by the Gay Blades ice-skating rink, in 1956. Inside, the gigantic dance floor (it can hold 3,200 people) fills up for rock concerts. Arrive early, since the line to get in, complete with friskers and multiple ticket checks, can wrap around the block. The swing and salsa nights usually require formal or semi-formal attire.

Credit cards: MC/V. **Subway:** C, 1, 9 to 50th St.

Rose's Turn 55 Grove St. (between Bleecker St. and Seventh Ave. South) (212) 366-5438. One of the friendliest cabaret and piano bars in the West Village, Rose's Turn attracts a mixed crowd—gay, straight, locals and tourists who hear the music and laughter and wander in off the street. Upstairs there are singers, comedy acts and musical revues (usually for a cover charge and a two-drink minimum). Downstairs you can just hang out at the bar or sit by the piano. The in-house talent varies from night to night, but none can hold a candle to the team on Saturday nights: a piano player who takes requests (anything except Barry Manilow's "Mandy") and three warbling bartenders who sing and tell jokes.

Credit cards: MC/V. **Subway:** 1, 9 to Christopher St.

Supper Club 240 West 47th St. (between Broadway and Eighth Ave.) (212) 921-1940. A historic ballroom that once served as the theater of the Edison Hotel, the Supper Club holds rock shows during the week. But the club's heart lies in swanky ballroom dinner dances and late-night jump-swing parties, which it presents Friday and Saturday nights. Although some rockers play the club cabaret-style to listeners seated at tables, most perform to a standing-only audience. Top-notch musicians play at the big-band and jump-swing shows, and a full restaurant menu is available. The Blue Room, which is a separate upstairs space with velvet couches, periodically features cabaret acts.
Credit cards: All major. **Subway:** A, C, E to 42d St.

Torch 137 Ludlow St. (between Rivington and Stanton Sts.) (212) 228-5151. There's no name on the facade of this addition to the Lower East Side's burgeoning scene, but it would be hard to walk by or mistake it for one of its worn-looking neighbors. The front of 137 Ludlow is an appealing mix of brushed steel, birch-colored wood grain and frosted glass. Inside the atmosphere recalls a 40's or 50's lounge, with a long narrow bar area at the front, semicircular booths at the back and cabaret seating in front of a small stage. Expect fabulous torch singers, all glammed up, filling the air with newfangled renditions of vocal jazz classics.
Credit cards: All major. **Subway:** F to Second Ave.

Triad Theater 158 West 72d St. (between Columbus Ave. and Broadway) (212) 362-2590. The Triad Theater is usually home to a show with an open-ended run, and after 10 P.M. becomes a cabaret space. What it lacks in atmosphere it makes up in sightlines and proximity to the performers. Downstairs, in the Dark Star Lounge, an average of four performers a night keep customers satisfied. Food is served in both rooms, and downstairs, in addition to the comfortable tables near the stage, there's a friendly bar that attracts neighborhood regulars.
Credit cards: All major. **Subway:** 1, 2, 3, 9 to 72d St.

Wilson's Grill 201 West 79th St. (at Amsterdam Ave.) (212) 769-0100. Occupying what used to be the ballroom of the Lucerne Hotel next door, this Upper West Side find is a sophisticated change of pace from the yuppified beer joints lining Columbus and Amsterdam Avenues. High ceilings and a deep, rich, wood interior create a regal ambiance, enjoyed by a clientele of mainly young professionals. There's live music seven nights a week with no cover. The schedule is jazz heavy, but classical, Motown and R&B groups are frequent performers.
Credit cards: All major. **Subway:** 1, 9 to 79th St.

COMEDY CLUBS

Boston Comedy Club GREENWICH VILLAGE 82 West 3d St. (between Sullivan and Thompson Sts.) (212) 477-1000. This lesser-known basement club features comedy nightly, often with several acts on the bill. Monday is open-mike.

Price: Sun.–Thur., $5, two-drink minimum; Fri.–Sat., $10, two-drink minimum. **Credit cards:** All major. **Subway:** A, B, C, D, E, F, Q to West 4th St.

Caroline's Comedy Club MIDTOWN WEST 1626 Broadway (at 49th St.) (212) 757-4100. Just when you were afraid fun had been banished from Times Square, Caroline's comes to the rescue. In 15 years, Caroline Hirsch's club has gone from a comedy fledgling to a block-long complex where many TV stars perform, often testing new material. Save some dollars and ask about the dinner-and-show packages.

Price: $20–$27, two-drink minimum. **Credit cards:** All major. **Services:** Food. **Subway:** N, R to 49th St.; C, E, 1, 9 to 50th St.

Comedy Cellar WEST VILLAGE 117 Macdougal St. (between 3d and Bleecker Sts.) (212) 254-3480. In the more than 20 years that it has been open, Robin Williams, Stephen Wright and Jerry Seinfeld have made surprise appearances at this intimate Greenwich Village club. Thursday nights are free.

Price: Sun.–Thur., $5; Fri.–Sat., $10, two-drink minimum. **Credit cards:** All major. **Subway:** A, B, C, D, E, F, Q to West 4th St.

Comic Strip UPPER EAST SIDE 1568 Second Ave. (between 81st and 82d Sts.) (212) 861-9386. You'll find 24 years' worth of autographed photos on the wall of alums such as Eddie Murphy (one of the club's discoveries), Paul Reiser and Chris Rock. New comics are so eager to perform in the no-cover "Monday Talent Spotlite" that twice a year they line the streets to get a lottery number. Drinks are top-dollar, but usually so are the headliners.

Price: Credit cards: All major. **Subway:** 4, 5, 6 to 86th St.

Dangerfield's Comedy Club MIDTOWN EAST 1118 First Ave. (between 61st and 62d Sts.) (212) 593-1650. Rodney Dangerfield's 30-year-old club feels like it's in a 1960's time warp with its swingin' red velvet and wood paneling. There's no drink minimum (a rarity in New York), affordable $5 parking and a large menu. The featured acts are pros from the circuit, and Rodney himself performs when in town.

Price: Sun.–Thur., $12.50; Fri.–Sat., $15. **Credit cards:** All major. **Subway:** N, R to Lexington Ave.; 4, 5, 6 to 59th St.

Gotham Comedy Club FLATIRON/UNION SQUARE 34 West 22d St. (between Fifth and Sixth Aves.) (212) 367-9000. With its comfortably upscale atmosphere this Flatiron oasis beckons audiences tired of divey or over-crowded clubs. Top-notch comics who regularly emcee jokingly complain that the bathrooms here are nicer than their apartments. The room is only a few years old, but name stars and TV comics all perform here and there are also frequent new talent nights.

Price: $8–$12, two-drink minimum. **Credit cards:** All major. **Subway:** F, N, R, 1, 9 to 23d St.

New York Comedy Club FLATIRON/UNION SQUARE 241 East 24th St. (between Second and Third Aves.) (212) 696-5233. It's a small, divey joint that many comedians have played at least once. Despite its size, the club does pull in pros, and on a regular night, expect truly funny performances from younger comedians.

Price: Sun.–Thur., $5, two-drink minimum; Fri.–Sat., $10, two-drink minimum. **Credit cards:** All major. **Subway:** 6 to 23d St.

Stand-Up New York UPPER WEST SIDE 236 West 78th St. (between Broadway and Amsterdam Ave.) (212) 595-0850. What do Denis Leary, Jon Stewart and Comedy Central's Dr. Katz have in common? They all started at this 10-year-old club. While short on atmosphere, it's full of comedy history. There have been surprise visits from stars like Drew Carey, Robin Williams, Dennis Miller and Al Franken.

Price: Sun.–Thur., $7; Fri.–Sat., $12, two-drink minimum. **Credit cards:** All major. **Subway:** 1, 9 to 79th St.

Upright Citizens Brigade Theater CHELSEA 161 West 22d St. (between Sixth and Seventh Aves.) (212) 366-9176. The Upright Citizens Brigade, now with their own series on Comedy Central and their own 74-seat theater in Chelsea, are some of the most talented performers around. They supplement their comedic arsenal with equally talented guests, like David Cross of "Mr. Show" and Janeane Garofalo. The Sunday 9:30 show is free.

Price: $5. **Credit cards: Subway:** F, 1, 9 to 23d St.

For the latest information on restaurants, hotels, concerts, nightlife, sporting events and more, check online at New York Today, the *New York Times* website devoted entirely to life in New York City: www.nytoday.com.

Sports & Recreation

Whether the bleachers are your milieu or you like to get your hands dirty, New York City can satisfy the most avid sports enthusiast. There are countless professional and amateur sporting events for spectators, though some tickets are easier to come by than others. And for those who want to be part of the action there are venues throughout the city, both private and public, that offer virtually every kind of activity. According to the Parks Department, the municipal park system has more than 28,000 acres including 854 playgrounds, 700 playing fields, 500 tennis courts, 33 outdoor swimming pools, 10 indoor swimming pools, 33 recreation and senior centers, 15 miles of beaches, 13 golf courses, six ice rinks, four major stadiums and four zoos. The department's Web site, *www.ci.nyc.ny.us/html/dpr,* is extremely useful with information on area parks, facilities and activities throughout the year.

PARTICIPANT SPORTS & ACTIVITIES

Since 1995, New Yorkers have enjoyed the benefits of the 40-acre **Chelsea Piers** sport complex (17th St. to 23rd St., on the Hudson River), offering everything from basketball and batting cages to golf and gymnastics. Once the city's premier passenger terminal, it is a site steeped in history; here many immigrants first set foot on American soil, and it was the intended destination of the *Titanic* (instead, the *Carpathia* arrived with the "unsinkable" ship's 675 survivors on April 20, 1912). There may be more scenic or historic playing fields in New York, but nowhere else will you find so many activities in one convenient location. Call (212) 336-6666 for general information, or see below for specific sports and prices.

Baseball/Softball Field House, (212) 336-6500. There are four batting cages, two for righties, one for lefties, and another that serves both. Try hitting major league heat in the fast-pitch cage, where the speed is set to about 90 mph. 10 pitches for $1.

Basketball Field House, (212) 336-6500. There are two hardwood courts in the Field House. Walk-ons are welcome, but call ahead for available hours. The cost is $7per hour.

Bowling Chelsea Piers Bowl, (212) 835-BOWL. The avid bowler will appreciate the 40 new lanes and automatic scoring. $6.25 per person per game, $4 shoe rental charge; 9 A.M.–2 A.M. (to 4 A.M. Fri., Sat.).

Dance Field House, (212) 336-6500. The 1,400-square-foot air-conditioned dance studio features Gerstung sprung flooring and can be divided into three separate studios. Jazz, tap, and modern dance classes are offered.

Golf Golf Club at Chelsea Piers, (212) 336-6400. This multi-tiered, year-round facility must be seen to be believed. Offering 52 heated stalls and an automatic tee-up system, the driving range is a net-enclosed, artificial turf fairway stretching 200 yards out into the Hudson River. There is also a 1,000-square-foot putting area, or call ahead to rent a sand bunker for practice. Lessons are available at the Golf Academy, where PGA professionals offer video analysis of your swing.

Rates: $15 minimum, (for 94 or 65 balls, depending on time of day); indoor sand bunker, $15/half hour; club rentals, $5 (one club).

Gymnastics Field House, (212) 336-6500. With 23,000-square feet of floor space, Chelsea Piers Gymnastics is New York City's largest and best-equipped gymnastics training center and the only one sanctioned by USA Gymnastics for local, state, and regional competitions. Call for class schedule and walk-on hours.

Health Club Sports Center, (212) 336-6000. The 150,000-square-foot Sports Center at Chelsea Piers offers two fitness studios with over 150 sports and fitness classes a week; the world's longest indoor running track (1/4 mile); a 200-meter banked competition track; three wood basketball/volleyball courts; Manhattan's only indoor sand volleyball court; one of the largest and most challenging rock climbing walls in the world; a six-lane, 25-yard swimming pool; a separate Spinning Room; two outdoor sun decks overlooking the Hudson River; Manhattan's largest and most extensive cardio and strength-training areas; a boxing ring and equipment circuit; and personal and sport-specific training. And once you're spent from all that activity, relax in the club café. You deserve it. Non-member rate is a hefty $36.00 per day.

Ice Hockey Sky Rink (212) 336-6100. Open ice hockey time is available daily, and follows this schedule: Mon.–Thur., Noon–1:20 P.M.; Fri., Noon–1:20 P.M. and 1 A.M.–2:20 A.M.; Sat. and Sun. 11:30 A.M.–12:50 P.M. If you're a goalie you can play for free. Otherwise it's $20 for 80 minutes.

Ice Skating Sky Rink (212) 336-6100. Sky Rink, which has been one of New York's favorite places to ice skate for more than a quarter of a century, moved to Chelsea Piers in 1995. The new twin-rink facility on Pier 61 operates 24 hours a day, seven days a week, year-round, welcoming skaters of all ages and ability levels for general skating sessions, figure skating, hockey training and league play.

Admission: Adult, $11 (Ten Pass, $95); youth/senior, $8 (Ten Pass, $72); Skate Rental, $5; Helmet Rental, $3.

In-line Skating Roller Rink, (212) 336-6200. Open skating time is available on both the outdoor (weather permitting) and indoor roller rinks. There is also an outdoor skate park offering challenging ramps, rails, and launch boxes that are sure to thrill the extreme athlete.

Skate Park Mon.–Sun., 10 A.M.–6 P.M. (admission $8). **Rink rates:** $5, adults;

$4, kids. **Rentals:** $13.50, adults; $8, kids. Rentals require credit card or $150/per pair for security deposit.

Soccer and Lacrosse Field House, (212) 336-6500. The Field House is the only facility in New York City with two state-of-the-art indoor playing fields built specifically for indoor soccer and lacrosse. Measuring 55' by 110', the climate-controlled, artificial turf fields are surrounded by Plexiglass boards, and equipped with goals, nets and electronic scoreboards.

Rock Climbing Field House, (212) 336-6500. The 30-foot high artificial rock surface offers a variety of routes that challenge climbers of all skill levels. Cost is $17 per person. As the schedule is seasonal, call for available times.

Roller Hockey Roller Rink, (212) 336-6200. Chelsea Piers, in addition to numerous leagues and clinics, also offers open roller hockey on the weekends. Cost is $15 for one and a half hours of pick-up play.

General Information Dining: Chelsea Brewing Company, (212) 336-6440; Famous Famiglia at Sky Rink, (212) 803-5552 (pizza); Chelsea Piers Bowl Snack Bar, (212) 835-2695; Rita's Burgers, (212) 604-0441.
Parking: Available at Pier 62 (212) 336-6840. **Subway:** 1, 6, 9, C, F to 23rd St.; crosstown bus to west end of route.

Basketball

Pick-up, playground basketball is one of New York's great traditions. Players of NBA caliber such as Connie Hawkins and Stephon Marbury have all honed their game on the city's blacktop courts, as have legends of more local renown such as The Goat of Amsterdam Avenue, Joe "The Destroyer" Hammond, and Pee Wee Kirkwood to name but a few.

Many of the top games are hard to join if you're not a regular, so the best places for a quick run are usually inside city gyms. The **Westside YMCA** (5 West 63d St. off Central Park West, $15 day pass) has one of the nicest, full-length floors, and the **Vanderbilt YMCA** offers a smaller court (47th St. between Second and Third Aves., $20 day pass). The **Harlem YMCA** (180 West 135th St.) also offers basketball, and a day pass is only $10. The relatively new **Basketball City,** offering six hardwood courts at 24th Street and the Westside Highway also allows walk-ons ($10, 9 A.M.–3 P.M, M-F; weekends, $15 for half-hour sessions), as does the **Field House at Chelsea Piers** ($7 per hour; call 212-336–6666 for available hours). The **Carmine Street Recreation Center** also offers basketball, though it can be crowded, and you must purchase a year membership for $25 (which you can do on-site).

If you're determined to play outside, playgrounds where one is likely to get into a full-court game include **Riverside Park** (courts can be found at 79th, 96th, and 110th Sts.), **Central Park** (just north of the Great Lawn), **Asphalt Green** (York Ave. between 91st and 92d Sts.), **96th Street Playground** (96th St. between First Ave. and the FDR Dr.), and the courts at 37th Street and Second Avenue.

But no trip to New York is complete for the basketball enthusiast without a visit to the West Fourth Street courts (at Sixth Ave.) where many tournaments featuring some of the best talent in the city are played in the warmer months. Despite his departure for the Charlotte Hornets a few years back, Queens-born Anthony Mason is still known to post-up hapless opponents during the off-season on this hallowed ground.

Biking

Organizations and Tours

Bike New York 891 Amsterdam Ave. (at 103d St.) (212) 932-2300. Sponsored by the Hostelling International American Youth Hostels and the New York City Department of Transportation, Bike New York is a 42-mile, five-borough tour of New York City that takes place each year in early May. This unique cycling tour begins at Battery Park in Lower Manhattan, follows Sixth Avenue to Central Park, and then winds its way over five bridges and through the many ethnic neighborhoods of the Bronx, Queens, and Brooklyn before it ends in Staten Island. The pace is comfortable, there are plenty of rest stops, and the route is entirely traffic-free. At the Tour-ending Festival at Fort Wadsworth in Gateway National Recreation Area on Staten Island you can relax, dance to live music, purchase lunch and eventually return to Manhattan on a free Staten Island Ferry ride.

The Fast and Fabulous Cycling Club Fast and Fab, as it is more widely known, a lesbian and gay bike club, was formed in 1994 when triathletes needed to train for Gay Games IV. Recognizing that not everyone would be able to cycle together, founder Bob Nelson drew up ride lists, one column marked "Fast" and the other—avoiding the word "slow" so as not to discourage anyone from participating—"Fabulous." Rides for both levels begin at the Boathouse in Central Park at 9 A.M. Sunday morning. For more information on joining these fun and free rides call Bob Nelson (212-567-7160) or Paulette Meggoe (718-293-0885).

Time's Up! (212) 802-8222 www.times-up.org Activist in spirit, Time's Up! sponsors a number of free bicycle and in-line skate tours that challenge the traffic-centered nature of New York City. The monthly "Critical Mass" ride is an attempt to defy the dominance of motor vehicles by bringing together many bikers to "raise the profile of cyclists" in the city, and assert equal rights to the road. On the other hand, many of the club-sponsored rides have no political aim at all: they're simply fun and even educational. The "Historical Ride" looks at important urban sites in Lower Manhattan and compares them to archival photographs, while the "Socrates Sculpture Ride" takes cyclists along the shores of Manhattan, Wards and Randalls Islands, and Queens to the Socrates Sculpture Park in Long Island City. There cyclists can relax and enjoy its many large-scale works set against the backdrop of the East River and the Manhattan skyline.

Bicycle Rentals

Larry and Jeff's Bicycles Plus 1690 Second Avenue (between 87th and 88th Sts.), (212) 794-2929, rents bikes for $7.50/hour. or $25/day. Credit card necessary for deposit.

Loeb Boathouse in Central Park (74th St. and East Drive) (212) 861-4137, rents a variety of bicycles. Three-speed bikes are $8 the first hour, $4 for each additional half hour; 10-speed bikes, $10 first hour, $5 each additional half hour; tandem bikes, $14 first hour, $7 each additional half hour.

Metro Bicycle Stores with six locations in Manhattan, is one of the more convenient places to go for a bike rental. All stores offer bicycles at $7/hour. and $35/day. 332 East 14th St. (between First and Second Aves.) (212) 228-4344; 546 Sixth Ave. (at 15th St.) (212) 255-5100; 417 Canal St. (212) 334-8000; 231 West 96th St. (between Broadway and Amsterdam Ave.) (212) 663-7531; 360 West 47th St. (at Ninth Ave.) (212) 581-4500; 1311 Lexington Ave. (at 88th St.) (212) 427-4450.

Pedal Pusher Bicycle Shop 1306 Second Ave. (at 68th St.) (212) 228-5592 has the best rental deal in the city, offering hybrids and mountain bikes for just $5.77/hour and $17.32/day. They require that a credit card, driver's license, or passport be left at the store as security.

Toga Bike Shop 110 West End Ave. (65th Street) (212) 799-9625, will rent you a bicycle for $25/day. They do not offer hourly rates. It's convenient for exploring Manhattan's Upper West Side, or Central Park only blocks away.

Sizzling Bicycle Inc. 3100 Ocean Pkwy, Brooklyn (718) 372-8985), has a limited number of bikes available for $6/hour or $49.95/day, if you'd like to explore the Brooklyn waterfront or the bustling Russian community of Brighton Beach.

Billiards/Pool

Amsterdam Billiard Club West Side Club, 344 Amsterdam Ave. (at 77th St.) (212) 496-8180. East Side Club, 210 East 86th St. (between Second and Third Aves.) (212) 570-4545
Up-scale venues with plentiful, well-kept tables, full bars, and amiable table-to-table waitress service.
Price: $4–$7.50/hour per person. **Credit cards:** All major. **Subway:** Westside: 1, 9 to 79th St. Eastside: 4, 5, 6 to 86th St.

Billiard Club 220 West 19th St. (between Seventh and Eighth Aves.) (212) 206-7665. This is the place to go for an intimate game of pool in a somewhat clubby environment, with its uncarpeted floor made of polished pine, low-key atmosphere, and dark wood paneling. The 42 tables are spread out over two levels.
Price: $7/hour per table, 11 A.M.–7 P.M.; $12/hour per table after 7 P.M.
Credit cards: All major. **Subway:** 1, 9 to 18th St.

Chelsea Billiards 54 West 21st St. (between Fifth and Sixth Aves.) (212) 989-0096. With its high ceilings and large windows, the atmosphere inside is more sedate than seedy. There are 43 generously spaced green baize-covered pool tables, two billiard tables, and eight snooker tables.

Price: $4–$5/hour per person or $8–$10/hour per table. **Credit cards:** All major. **Subway:** 1, 9, F to 23d St.

Corner Billiards 85 Fourth Ave. (at 11th St.) (212) 995-1314. Corner Billiards is your only option is you want to shoot a rack in the Village (excluding the numerous bars with smaller-sized pool tables that proliferate in the area). The 28 Brunswick Gold Crown Tables, a café, a microbrewery, and waitress service all conspire to make this a much more civilized experience than one might expect.

Price: $9/hour for one player; $2/hour for each additional player. **Credit Cards:** D. **Subway:** 4, 5, 6, L, N, R to 14th St.

SoHo Billiard Sport Center 56 East Houston St. (between Mulberry and Mott Sts.) (212) 925-3753. Brightly lit and pleasantly spacious, this street level pool hall has a young downtown crowd. Players shoot pool on 28 tables spread out on multiple levels.

Price: $7–$10/hour for one player, $2/hour each additional player. **Credit cards:** Cash only. **Subway:** B, D, F, Q to Broadway-Lafayette St.; 6 to Bleecker St.

Boating

Downtown Boathouse West St. (between Chambers and Canal Sts.) (212) 966-1852. From May through October, the Downtown Boathouse offers free kayaking in between two piers on the Hudson River. A staff of volunteers will outfit you with a flotation jacket and a boat and give you some brief basic instructions about kayaking. Once you have gained some experience, you can join them for longer kayaking trips. They don't take reservations for the free kayaking; it's strictly on a first-come, first-served basis.

Hours: May 15-Oct. 15; Sat., Sun and holidays, 9 A.M.–6 P.M. **Price:** Free. **Subway:** 1, 9 to Canal St.

Floating the Apple Hudson River (at 44th St.) (212)564–5412. The aim of this club is to make the waters of New York City more accessible to boating enthusiasts. How do they do it? By offering a series of weekly events in Manhattan, Brooklyn, and the Bronx that encourage use of the area's waterways and harbor by water-sports aficionados. The Manhattan activities originate at Pier 40 (Hudson River at Houston St.) and include youth and adult rowing programs. The Club also sponsors various sailing and swimming events, including The Great Hudson River Swim from the Marina at 79th Street to Chelsea Piers at 23rd Street.

Loeb Boathouse Central Park Lake (74th St. and East Drive) (212) 517-2233. For one of the most relaxing (and romantic) summer afternoons you'll ever experience, rent a rowboat at Central Park's Loeb Boathouse and ply the waters of one of the Park's most scenic areas. Explore the western marsh area, visit one of the gazebos, or enjoy a picnic lunch. Or simply watch as other landlubbers try to tame their oars and proceed on a relatively straight course.

Season: Year-round, weather permitting. **Price:** $10/hr, $30 cash deposit required. **Subway:** 6 to 77th St.

Prospect Park Brooklyn, (718) 282-7789. Get some exercise and a different view of the Park by touring the Lullwater and the Lake on a pedal boat. A great way to spend a lazy summer afternoon, pedal boats may be rented from the Wollman Center and Rink on weekends and holidays from May 15 through September.

Price: $10/hour. **Subway:** D, Q to Prospect Park or Parkside Ave.

Bowling

Bowlmor Lanes 110 University Pl. (between 12th and 13th Sts.) (212) 255-8188. Weekend nights at Bowlmor Lanes rival some of the neighboring bars and clubs for popularity—and noise. Two floors of lanes and a large bar area, complemented by a dance music soundtrack, make for a vibrant evening. Monday nights feature Nightstrike, the only DJ party with a mixture of house and techno tracks, pitchers of beer and bowling shoes. Expect to wait for a lane.

Hours: Sun., Tues.–Wed., 10 A.M.–1 A.M.; Mon., 10 A.M.–4 A.M.; Thur., 10 A.M.–2 A.M.; Fri.–Sat., 11 A.M.–4 A.M. **Price:** $5.95 per person per game (slightly more or less at times); $3 shoe rental. **Credit cards:** All major. **Subway:** 4, 5, 6, L, N, R to 14th St.

Chelsea Piers (see above)

Leisure Time Bowling 625 Eighth Ave., 2d Fl. (at Port Authority Bus Terminal) (212) 268-6909. When Leisure Time Bowling opened its modern 30 lanes a few years ago on the second floor of the Port Authority Bus Terminal, it seemed curiously out of place. Now the alley is more popular than ever, with people of all ages trying to knock down a few on the lanes. Waits for a lane can be over two hours on weekends and days with bad weather.

Hours: Mon.–Thur., 10 A.M.–11 P.M.; Fri.–Sat., 10 A.M.–1 A.M.; Sun., 10 A.M.–11 P.M. **Price:** $4.25 per person per game; $15 /hour or 2.5 hours for $25; $2.50 shoe rental. **Credit cards:** All major. **Subway:** A, C, E to 42d St.—Port Authority.

Golf

Perhaps surprisingly, New York City offers a number of excellent golf courses, in addition to other golf resources such as driving ranges and instruction. Listed below are some of the most noteworthy and accessible of the area links.

Douglaston Golf Course 63-20 Marathon Pkwy, Queens (718) 224-6566. This short course will challenge you with narrow fairways, and its hilly nature will often result in uneven lies. While there is only one water hazard on the course, the many blind shots required make Douglaston relatively difficult. The course's signature hole is #18, a 550-yard, par 5, requiring an approach shot to a large, well-bunkered green.

Green Fees: Weekdays, $24/18 holes and $13/9 holes; weekends, $26/18 holes and $13/9 holes. **Reservations:** 10 days in advance. Call (718) 225-GOLF. **Directions by car:** Long Island Expy. east to Douglaston Pkwy; turn left, continue to 61st Ave. and make a left; turn right on Marathon; drive 2 blocks and course will be on the right.

Dyker Beach 7th Ave and 86th St., Brooklyn (718) 836-9722. This is perhaps the ultimate inner-city golfing experience. Because of the streets adjacent to the course, the sounds of the city usually follow golfers along the fairway. The course has undergone a dramatic renaissance, and is now considered one of the best maintained in the city, despite the over 80,000 rounds played here each year.

Green Fees: Weekdays, $23/18 holes; weekends, $26/18 holes. **Reservations:** Seven days in advance. Call (718) 225-GOLF. **Subway:** R to 86th St.; walk along 86th Street to course or take B64 bus or cab.

Kissena Park Golf Course 164–15 Booth Memorial Ave., Flushing, Queens (718) 939-4594. This is a short course (the back tees play only 4,727 yards), but the hilly terrain makes it a rather difficult one. Built in 1934 and redesigned in 1986, the course requires a variety of shots. According to the course pro, it will require every club in your bag.

Green Fees: Weekday $18/18 holes and $9/9 holes; weekends, $23/18 holes. **Reservations:** Seven days in advance. Call (718) 225-GOLF. **Subway:** 7 to Main St., Flushing; cab from station (about 3 miles). **By car:** Long Island Expy. east to Exit 24 (Kissena Blvd.); proceed on the service road to 164th St, turn left, go to the traffic light (Booth Memorial Ave.); turn right, you'll see the course from there.

La Tourette Golf Course 1001 Richmond Hill Rd., Staten Island (718) 351-1889. Once a private course, this verdant oasis from the city offers open, rolling fairways, plenty of bunkers, and countless trees. The 1836 Greek-revival clubhouse is a landmark itself, and this venerable course is home to the annual New York City Amateur tournament. It is the only city course that offers a driving range on the property.

Green Fees: Weekdays, $16/18 holes and $9/9 holes. **Reservations:** Ten days in advance. Call (718) 225-GOLF. **Directions by car:** Brooklyn-Queens Expy. (BQE) to Verrazano Bridge to the Bradley Ave exit; at second traffic signal (Wooley Ave), turn left and proceed past the next 5 traffic signals; left on Richmond Hill Rd.

Marine Park Golf Course 2880 Flatbush Ave., Brooklyn (718) 338-7113.

Built in 1964, Marine Park was designed by the legendary Robert Trent Jones, Sr. and its large and undulating greens are, according to regulars, the finest in the city. The signature hole is #15, a 467-yard, par 4, featuring a well-bunkered fairway and requiring a downhill approach shot to a sloping green.

Green Fees: Weekdays $24/18 holes and $24/9 holes. Weekends, $26/18 holes and $24/9 holes. **Reservations:** Seven days in advance. Call (718) 225-GOLF. **Subway:** D, Q to Kings Highway; #100 bus to course. **Directions by car:** Long Island Expy. to Brooklyn-Queen Expy. (BQE) to Belt Pkwy east; take exit 11N (Flatbush Ave), drive down to the second traffic signal and you will see the course entrance on the left.

Mosholu Golf Course 3700 Jerome Ave., Bronx (718) 655-9164. This is another classic inner city course, with tenements rising above the many trees to provide a uniquely urban backdrop. Built in 1904, it is one of the oldest in the city. Nine holes were lost some years ago to the addition of parkways to the area, but it is a difficult course nonetheless: the tree-lined fairways are narrow, the medium-sized greens are fast, and there are several blind fairways in the design. Easy to get to via public transportation.

Green Fees: $16/9 holes. **Reservations:** Two days in advance. Call (718) 225-GOLF. **Subway:** 4 to Woodlawn (last stop); course is across the street on the left.

Pelham Bay/Split Rock 870 Shore Rd., Bronx (718) 885-1258. Pelham Bay Park offers two excellent eighteen-hole courses in a particularly bucolic setting: it is not unusual to have pheasant, wild turkey, and deer cross your path as you traverse either of these courses. The Pelham Bay Course offers a links-style design, and it the easier of the two. Its signature hole is #9, a 433-yard, par 4, requiring a shot to an extremely undulating green that is well bunkered. The Split Rock Course is more difficult because it is very wooded and has tight fairways. A creek comes into play on four holes, and the terrain is rolling. The signature hole on the Split Rock Course is #18, a 392-yard, par 4, requiring a tee shot around what may be America's oldest living White Oak tree.

Green Fees: Weekdays, $24/18 holes and $24/9 holes; weekends, $26/18 holes and $24/9 holes. **Reservations:** Ten days in advance. Call (718) 225-GOLF. **Subway:** 6 train to Pelham Bay Park (last stop); W45 or M45 bus or cab to course (as this is quite a long trip, driving is preferable). **By car:** FDR Dr. to Triboro Bridge, exit toward Bronx; take 95 going North (New England Thruway); get off at Exit 8B; the course is one mile away, look for the course entrance off Shore Rd.

Silver Lake Park 915 Victory Blvd., Staten Island (718) 447-5686. This course is well manicured and located within a tight wooded area. The design includes several sloping, tight fairways, two water hazards, and many trees lining the fairways.

Green Fees: Weekdays, weekends, $17/18 holes and $9/9 holes. **Reservations:** Eleven days in advance. Call (718) 225-GOLF. **Directions by car:** Brooklyn-Queen Expy. (BQE) to Verrazano Bridge; stay on the Staten Island Expy., get off at the Clove Rd./Victory Blvd. exit, turn right on Clove Rd.; proceed on to Victory Blvd., travel one mile, the course is on the left.

South Shore Golf Course 200 Huguenot Ave., Staten Island (718) 984-0101. This very scenic and picturesque course was built on hilly terrain and seems to have been cut out of very forest itself. Designed by Alfred H. Tull in 1927, the course challenges golfers with narrow fairways, and large, fast greens.
Green Fees: Weekdays, $24/18 holes and $15/9 holes; weekends, $26/18 holes and $15/9 holes. **Reservations:** Eleven days in advance. Call (718) 225-GOLF. **Directions by car:** Brooklyn-Queen Expy. (BQE) to Verrazano Bridge; stay on the Staten Island Expy., get off at the Clove Rd./Victory Blvd. exit; turn right on Clove Rd.; proceed on to Victory Blvd., travel one mile, the course is on the left.

Van Cortlandt Golf Course Van Cortlandt Park S. and Bailey Ave., Bronx (718)543-4595. The granddaddy of New York City courses and the nation's oldest public course, designed by Tom Bendelow and built in 1885. Van Cortlandt is well maintained, and there is a nice mix of long par 5s and short par 4s, with a few difficult par 3s thrown in for good measure. While you might drive the green on #6, a 292-yard par 4, watch out for #2, the signature 620 yard par 5, and the par 3 #13 that requires a shot over water to a large, undulating green. The final four holes are extremely hilly and offer a challenging end to this scenic course. Easy to reach via public transportation.
Green Fees: Weekdays, $26.00 for 18 holes and $26.00 for 9 holes. Weekends, $28.00 for 18 holes and $26.00 for 9 holes. **Reservations:** 10 days in advance. Call (718) 225-GOLF. **Public Transportation:** 1, 9 to Van Cortlandt Park (last Stop); exit from El to the right; turn left across park above the stadium oval; follow path beneath underpass; course is to the left.

Gyms & Health Clubs

Most of the hundreds of health clubs around the city offer one-day passes. You'll save time and money if your bring your own lock, though most will rent you one and nearly all (even the Ys) will provide a towel. Make sure to bring a picture ID with you too, as most require one for their records.

Private Gyms

Asphalt Green 555 East 90th St. (between York Ave. and 91st St.) (212) 369-8890. A wave-shaped building constructed in 1993 on the site of the city's former asphalt plant. What really separates this from other gyms are the full-size Astroturf soccer field and Olympic-sized pool with a hydraulic floor that adjusts the water depth for children and those learning to swim. Day passes are $15.
Subway: 4, 5, 6 to 86th St.

Crunch Fitness www.crunchfitness.com, or check Yellow Pages for nearest location. This self-styled alternative gym offers seven locations in Manhattan. A day pass at any of Crunch's gyms is $22.00.

New York Sports Club (800) 796-NYSC, for nearest location www.nysc.com
The New York Sports Clubs, with their 28 Manhattan locations, are about as
common a sight on the New York streets as pizzerias and Chinese restaurants.
Day passes are $25.00 at all locations.

World Gym 232 Mercer St. (between Bleecker and Third Sts.)
(212) 780-7407 www.worldgym.com; 1926 Broadway (between 64th and 65th
Sts.) (212) 874-0942. These gyms are subdued, with a peaceful atmosphere conveyed through natural light flowing through large windows, natural wood surfaces and warm lighting. They are rarely crowded, and music is isolated to certain areas of the facilities.
Day membership is $20.

YMCAs

New York City's YMCAs offer an affordable alternative to the health club
scene, though the gyms can often be quite crowded.

Harlem YMCA 180 West 135th St. (at Seventh Ave.) (212) 281-4100
Day pass: $10. **Subway:** 2,3 to 135th St.

Vanderbilt YMCA 224 East 47th St. (between Second and Third Aves.)
(212) 756-9600
Day pass: $20. **Subway:** 6 to 51st St.

West Side YMCA 5 West 63d St. (between Broadway and Central Park West)
(212) 875-4100
Day pass: $15. **Subway:** 1, 9, A, B, C, D, F to 59th St.; 1, 9 to 66th St.

Horseback Riding

Claremont Riding Academy 175 West 89th St. (between Amsterdam and
Columbus Aves.) (212) 724-5100. Built in 1892, Claremont is the oldest stable
in the country. Experienced equestrians can hire horses by the hour to ride on
the six miles of bridle paths in nearby Central Park. Lessons are available and
there is an indoor arena for beginners.
Price: $35/hour. **Credit cards:** MC/V. **Subway:** 1, 9 to 86th St.

Kensington Stables 51 Caton Pl., Brooklyn (718) 972-4588. Horses can be
hired here for leisurely guided rides on Prospect Park's trails. Lessons are also
available.
Price: $20/hour. **Subway:** F to Ft. Hamilton Pkwy.

Ice Skating

Chelsea Piers (see above)

Central Park—Wollman Memorial Rink Enter park at Sixth Ave. and

Central Park South (212) 396-1010. To appreciate the beauty and calm of Central Park, head to the 33,000-square-foot Wollman Rink. Wollman offers a spacious skating area and an unparalleled view of the Duck Pond framed by landmark buildings like the Plaza Hotel.

Hours: Open seasonally Sun.–Thur., 10 A.M.–9:30 P.M.; Fri. and Sat. 10 A.M.–11:30 P.M. (hours vary). **Admission:** Adults, $7; children and seniors, $3.50. **Skate Rental:** $3.50 **Subway:** N, R to 5th Ave.

Central Park—Lasker Rink Central Park at 106th Street (212) 396-0388. Located just below the scenic Harlem Meer, the Lasker Rink is open for ice skating during the winter season (it serves as Central Park's only swimming pool in the summer months).

Subway: 6 to East 103d St.; B, C to West 103rd St.

Rink at Rockefeller Plaza 601 Fifth Ave. (between 49th and 50th Streets) (212) 332-7654. Throughout the holiday season, music plays as skaters waltz around the rink under the glow of the awe-inspiring Rockefeller Center Christmas tree. While the rink is cramped and often crowded, the thrill of skating at the epicenter of the city's holiday spirit is unrivaled. Visit earlier or later in the season for a less crowded (but no less enjoyable) experience. Call ahead for available dates and times.

Admission: Adults, $14; children under 12, $10.00 (admission varies, so call ahead). **Skate rental:** (figure skates only) $6. **Credit cards:** Cash only. **Subway:** B, D, F, Q to 47th-50th St.—Rockefeller Center.

Prospect Park—Wollman Rink (718) 287-6431. Kate Wollman Center and Rink is located near the Lincoln Road entrance of the Park and is open for ice skating from November until March. An especially nice feature of this rink is the "early bird" session from 8:30–10:30 A.M. on weekdays. If you're an avid skater who hates the crowds at most public rinks, this is the place for you.

Hours: Various. **Admission:** $4. **Skate rental:** $3.50. **Subway:** F to Prospect Park.

In-Line Skating

Popular street skating spots include "the cube" at **Astor Place** in the East Village, "the banks" under the **Brooklyn Bridge** (Manhattan side) and Union Square. **Central Park** is full of great places to skate outside the Wollman Rink (listed below), especially the main drives throughout the park, the open plaza at the north end of the Mall and the closed driveway west of the Mall. Skating in the **Riverside Park** grounds near 108th Street, which is permitted in the warmer months, requires a helmet, signing of a waiver and a $3 fee. Wrist and kneepads are essential, and elbow pads are recommended (212-408-0239 for info). See also **Chelsea Piers.**

Central Park—Wollman Memorial Rink Enter park at Sixth Ave. and Central Park South (212) 396-1010. During the summer months, Rollerblades replace ice skates at Wollman Rink. The rink also offers classes and guided skating tours around the park. Compared to the skating lanes in the park, the rink is fairly uncrowded, leaving plenty of room for New Yorkers to strut their stuff.

Admission: Adults, $7; children and seniors, $3.50. **Rental:** Rollerblades and safety equipment (State law requires children 14 and under to wear helmets and pads) can be rented for rink use ($6) or for park use ($15 with a $100 deposit). **Subway:** N, R to 5th Ave.

Empire Skate Club of New York (212) 774-1774 www.empireskate.org
The Empire Skate Club of New York is a non-profit organization of in-line skaters dedicated to having fun and improving the skating environment in New York. The Club organizes social skates and get-togethers in the city, trips around the eastern seaboard and farther afield, clinics, seminars, parties and skate advocacy. A year's membership is $25.00.

Time's Up (see "*Biking*" entry) Other places to rent skates: **Blades,** 160 East 86th St. (between Third and Lexington Aves.) (212) 996-1644, or 120 West 72d St. (between Amsterdam and Columbus Aves.) (212) 787-3911. **Peck & Goodie,** 919 Eighth Ave. (at 55th St.) (212) 246-6123

Running

While out-of-towners may think of NYC as a concrete jungle with few safe places to run, there are actually many excellent—even tree-lined and relatively bucolic— routes right in Manhattan. **East River Park** is a favorite of those living downtown, offering a scenic course that stretches along the river just across from downtown Brooklyn. The **Battery Park Promenade** is also well suited for those who enjoy sightseeing as they work out: the Statue of Liberty is visible from this route, as is Ellis Island. Farther north, **Riverside Park**—which stretches with some interruptions from 72d Street to the George Washington Bridge on Manhattan's Upper Westside—offers some excellent courses, both on pavement and dirt.

But the crown jewel of the NY runner's kingdom is **Central Park,** unofficial home of the **New York Road Runners Club** (212-860-4455). The club sponsors many races throughout the year, usually along the Park's main Loop, the most famous of which is the **New York City Marathon**, finishing at Tavern on the Green on the west side. You don't have to be a member to run in club-sponsored events (though there's usually a small fee), and an excellent place to find out about upcoming races in the Road Runners Club Web site (www.nyrrc.org).

The length of the entire Central Park Loop—the road that follows a circular route through the interior of the park—is 6.1 miles. This road is closed to cars 10 A.M.–4 P.M., and then again 7 P.M.–dusk. During the hours when vehicular traffic is permitted, there is a runner's lane that is open for use, though it is unprotected. Good short courses include the 3.5 mile route used by Chase's Corporate Challenge races, which begins at the Puppet Theater (roughly West 70th St.), follows the Loop to the 102d Street transverse, rejoins the Loop on the Eastside, and ends at the Rumsey Playground (where Summerstage events are held) at about East 70th Street. A popular 5K course (3.1 miles) begins at the East Drive (Loop) and 86th Street, proceeds north and across the 102d

Street transverse, back onto the Drive and finishes at the Engineer's Gate (90th St. and Fifth Ave.). The Reservoir run is one of the most popular courses in the city. The cinder track offers a level run of 1.6 miles and offers great views of the Manhattan skyline at virtually every step. In spring it is especially pleasant as flowering tree line the eastern side of the course. Enter the park at 86th St. on the east or west side. **Don't run in the park at night.**

The Bronx, **Van Cortlandt Park** (242d St. and Broadway). As well as regular roads there are hilly 2.5-mile, 5-kilometer (3.1-mile) and 5-mile trails. Van Cortlandt Park Track Club stages weekly runs. No parking within the park. Nonmembers are welcome. Call (718) 796-0736 for information.

Brooklyn, **Prospect Park.** Take the Manhattan Bridge to Flatbush Avenue. There is dirt path, roughly three miles, on inside of the roadway (3.5 miles) circling the park grounds, along with other isolated trails. Prospect Park Track Club has Sunday morning runs at 8 A.M. Meet at the Park Circle, Railroad Avenue and Prospect Park South West. Nonmembers are welcome. Call (718) 224-5814 for information.

Swimming

(See also *"Gyms and Health Clubs"* for YMCAs and private gyms with pools).

Public Pools

Asphalt Green 555 East 90th St. (between York Ave. and 91st St.) (212) 369-8890. Asphalt Green has one of the biggest and newest public pools in the city. The 50-by-20-meter indoor pool is heated to an even 80 degrees. While nonmembers can purchase a day-pass to swim, some lap swimming lanes are always reserved for members only.
Hours: Mon.–Fri.,5.30 A.M.–10 P.M.; Sat.–Sun., 8 A.M.–8 P.M. **Rates:** Day passes, $15 for adults, $7 for children. **Credit Cards:** All major. **Subway:** 4, 5, 6 to 86th St.

Lasker Pool Central Park, East Drive and 106th St. Swimming in Lasker Pool is by far one of the favorite activities for kids visiting Central Park. During the summer months, Lasker is open for community swimming, racing and lessons. At 3'8" deep, the pool is ideal for kids. You can't beat the cost either: swimming here is free of charge. Swimmers must wear a swimsuit (no denim shorts or t-shirts), and while lockers are available, swimmers must bring their own lock.
Hours: Open daily 11–3 and 4–7. **Subway:** 6 to East 103d St.; B, C to West 103d St.

Riverbank State Park Pool 679 Riverside Dr. (at 145th St.) (212) 694-3666. This is one of the most recently built pools in Manhattan, located in Riverbank State Park, built atop a sewage treatment center on the Hudson. It's not as grim as it sounds: the park is very attractive, and offers many other sports in addition to swimming. And the view along the Hudson on a clear day is quite spectacular.

Sheraton Manhattan Hotel 790 7th Avenue (between 51st and 52nd Streets) (212) 581-3300. This midtown hotel offers an indoor swimming pool and an adjacent outdoor sundeck, and non-guests are allowed to use the facilities for a fee.

Municipal Pools

New York City's municipal pools require a year's membership, but it's only $25 and can be paid on the spot. If you're planning on returning to the Big Apple in the next 12 months, this might be your best option.

East 54th St. Recreation Center 348 East 54th St. (212) 397-3154 Midtown

59th Street Recreation Center 533 West 59th St. (212) 397-3159 West Side

Asser Levy Park 23d St. and Asser Levy Place (212) 447-2020 Gramercy Park

Carmine Street Recreation Center 1 Clarkson St. (212) 242-5228 Greenwich Village

Dry Dock Swimming Pool 408 East 10th St (212) 677-4481 East Village

Hamilton Fish Recreation Center Pool 128 Pitt St. (212) 387-7687 Downtown

John Jay Swimming Pool 77th St. and Cherokee Pl. (212) 794-6566 Upper East Side

Lenox Hill Neighborhood House 331 East 70th St. (212) 744-5022 Upper East Side

Tennis

Public Courts

The Har-tru public courts at Central Park's venerable **Tennis Center** (mid-park, 94th-96th Sts.) are among the nicest in the city, but half of the 24 courts are booked in advance, and the rest are usually reserved on a first-come, first-served basis early each morning. Plus, you have to put up with a lot of attitude on the part of regulars who treat the Center as their own private club. But if you can handle these obstacles, playing amidst the trees of the park is a real treat. The Center also offers a pro shop, a locker room with showers, and a snack bar. Call (212) 360-8133 for information

Other less crowded courts include those at **Riverside Park,** which boasts beautiful red-clay courts at the western end of 96th Street (no reservations) and recently restored hard-surface courts at 118th Street. **East River Park** (East River at Broome St.) also offers 12 hard-surface courts, and these are perhaps the least crowded in Manhattan. If you can make it to Brooklyn, **Prospect Park Tennis Center** provides ten Har-tru courts, located at the southwest corner of the Park, near the park circle. From mid-October through the end of April, a bubble structure covers these courts, and a private company rents them by the hour (call one day ahead to make reservations). Also in Brooklyn are the six excellent hard-surface courts at **Fort Greene Park.** These are among the least-used in the city, and, while there is a core group of regulars, it's relatively easy to walk on and play. Use of all city tennis courts requires either a season pass ($50) or a day pass ($5) which can be purchased either at the Tennis Center or Paragon Sporting Goods (867 Broadway at 18th Street). Permits are less apt to be checked at the courts at Riverside and 118th and Fort Greene Park. The season is Apr.-Nov., 7 A.M.–8 P.M. (light permitting). Call for information on individual courts.

Private Courts

Crosstown Tennis Club 14 West 31st St. (212) 947-5780. The Crosstown facility just steps from the Empire State Building offers four Championship DecoTurf tennis courts, each with an 18-foot back-court area and a 40-foot ceiling height.

Price: Weekdays, (all rates hourly), $49–$57; weekends, $49–$88. **Credit cards:** All major. **Subway:** 1, 2, 3, 9, B, D, E, F, Q, N, R to 34th St.

New York Health and Racquet Club (HRC) Tennis Piers 13 and 14 (at Wall St.) (212-422-9300); 110 University Pl. (at 13th St.) (212-989-2300). HRC offers two climate-controlled facilities in the city, offering members a total of eight Har-Tru courts and two Supreme courts. Non-members can reserve courts too, though the price might make you seek out a municipal alternative.

Price: Various, $50–$120 per hour. **Credit cards:** All major.

Midtown Tennis Club 341 Eighth Ave. (27th street) (212) 989-8572. When it opened in 1965, the Midtown Tennis Club was the first indoor club in Manhattan, and it's still one of the largest and most accessible tennis sites in the city. Air-conditioned, with eight tournament Har-Tru courts, and full locker room facilities, the Club offers tennis in a comfortable and relaxed, club-like atmosphere at low rates.

Price: Various, $35–$68 per hour. **Credit cards:** All major. **Subway:** 1, 9 to 28th St.; 2, 3 A, C, E to 34th St.

USTA National Tennis Center (718) 760-6200 Ext. 6213 and ask for the program office. The USTA National Tennis Center, site of the US Open Tennis Championships, is the largest public tennis facility in the world, offering 9 indoor courts, 18 practice courts, and 18 tournament courts. All courts are open to the public year round except for August and September, during the US Open itself. They reopen for public play one week after the last day of the US Open.

Court Information: Various, $14–$40 per hour. **Credit cards:** All major. **Subway:** 7 to Willets Point—Shea Stadium.

The Urban Jungle Gym, All Within a Metrocard Ride

Who needs Boulder, Colorado when you can boulder in Central Park, parasail by the Statue of Liberty or surf the Rockaways? New York, with its diverse geographical terrain, tidal channels, deep harbor and rocky outcrops can compete recreationally with any city on the planet. Outdoor enthusiasts and extreme athletes may want to try one of these activities.

Canoeing At Pier 63 (23d St. and 12th Ave.) **New York Outrigger** (212-684-0812) offers canoe clinics and half-day excursions for $50/hour per person. The **Parks Department** also has six sites where the public can launch canoes and kayaks throughout the city. Call (212) 360-8134 for locations and information. (*See also "Boating"*).

Mountain Biking Trail biking is allowed on the abandoned Old Putnam railroad track bed in **Van Cortlandt Park** (Bronx). Elsewhere in city parks, mountain bikes are allowed on paved roads and paths only.

Parasail New York The ride with views of Wall Street and the Statue of Liberty cost $55 for 10 minutes in the air; or reserve the entire six-seat boat at a discount. Clients take off and land from a small platform on the boat, the *Airgasm*, and don't get wet unless they ask to be "dipped." The boat leaves from Liberty State Park in New Jersey and water taxis are available from the World Financial Center. (212) 691-0055

Rock Climbing To find **Rat Rock,** a popular boulder in Central Park enter at 63d Street and Central Park West. Walk east toward the Heckscher Playground. The boulder is to the right of the ballfields. You'll know it by the chalk marks left by climbers who powder their fingers for a good grip. Other small outcrops are scattered throughout the park. The **Parks Department** offers rock climbing at other locations. Call (212) 348-4867 for information on classes. There are also artificial climbing walls at **Chelsea Piers** (*see "Chelsea Piers" entry*) and **Extravertical Climbing Center,** (212) 586-5718, where day passes and equipment rental are available.

BEACHES

From the heart of Manhattan, it's easy to forget that New York is actually a coastal town. But believe it or not, beyond the wall of skyscrapers, are the Atlantic Ocean and miles and miles of beach. There are city beaches in Brooklyn, Queens and the Bronx, as well as some very accessible spots on Long Island. If the temperature hits 90 degrees on a summer weekend, expect crowds. For millions of New Yorkers, the Atlantic provides the only hope for relief from the heat.

Brooklyn

Coney Island Surf and Stillwell Aves. (718) 946-1350. (*See "Brooklyn" for full entry*). Though this is by far the most famous of the Brooklyn beaches, you may also want to try **Brighton Beach** right next door or **Manhattan Beach** next to that. **Subway:** B, D, F, N to Coney Island—Stillwell Ave.

Bronx

Orchard Beach Long Island Sound (between Park Dr. and Bartow Circle)
(718) 885-2275. At the turn of the century, this was a popular bathing spot for
the affluent residents of Pelham Manor. A large, luxurious stand of trees skirts
the beach, giving the place a feeling of anti-urban festivity. From the vantage
point of a patio between the two halves of the old bathhouse, one can gaze over
the entire expanse of sand at the people, umbrellas and bathers dotting the
shore, as idyllic as a picture postcard.

Subway: 6 to Pelham Bay Park; BX12 bus to Orchard Beach.

Queens

Rockaway Beach Beach First St. and Beach 149th St. (718) 318-4000.
Unlike most of the city's other public beaches, Rockaway has no distinctive
New York flavor; its plain plank boardwalk, pale arc of sand and high-rise con-
dos are welcoming enough, but they could just as easily belong to Long Island,
Virginia or any other point on the East Coast. That's not to say it's without
character. The beautiful old buildings, nearby hotels and ornate subway station
have a kind of windswept, sunburned grandeur, and the fact that it's accessible
only by bridge gives it the aura of adventure and isolation.

Subway: A to Rockaway Park.

Long Island

Fire Island For info call (516) 852-5200. Fire Island is a barefoot society, car-
free and carefree. A barrier island, it stretches across 32 miles between the end
of **Robert Moses State Park** (best bet for day-trippers) and Moriches Inlet,
where the Hamptons begin. Despite an influx of tourist attention, the island has
changed little in the last century. The concrete walks (rustically wooden in
some communities) are still lined with cedar-shingled cottages hemmed in by
pines and bayberry, and bicycle and walking paths are still the transportation
arteries of choice.

Directions: From Penn Station, take the Long Island Rail Road to Babylon.
Take Suffolk Buses, or taxi to ferries (total price, $10–$15 one way).

Jones Beach (516) 785-1600. Jones Beach is the single most popular site in
the entire state park system averaging nearly seven million visitors a year—
more than Niagara Falls. The swimming and sunbathing crowds for which Jones
Beach is famous are only a part of the action. Elsewhere in the 2,413-acre park,
people fly kites and determined joggers, bikers and skaters swoosh along their
designated paths. In the bushes birdwatchers and other nature lovers stalk their
prey. Surf-casters think bluefish, while anglers on the four-bay piers are after
fluke. The park is open 365 days a year. The truly faithful visit even in winter,
by the thousands.

Directions: From Penn Station, take the Long Island Railroad to Freeport.

Yankee Stadium

Buses run every half hour from the train station to the beach ($11, includes shuttle bus). If you go by car, go early because parking lots fill quickly.

Long Beach In recent years, this seaside city—once the playground of the wealthy, then a dumping ground for the elderly poor and the mentally ill—has made a remarkable comeback. Smart new high-rise oceanfront buildings have emerged, and young families, attracted by the Atlantic Ocean beaches and the 53-minute commute by train to Manhattan, are moving here in droves.

For the weekend visitor, the best reason to trek to Long Beach is its boardwalk. At a little more than two miles in length, it is Long Island's longest, and its 60-foot width is double that of Jones Beach's. Open 24 hours a day, the boardwalk features a block of stores and eateries.

Directions: From Penn Station, take the Long Island Railroad to Long Beach ($11 round-trip package).

SPECTATOR SPORTS
Baseball

New York Yankees—Yankee Stadium
161st St. (at River Ave.), Bronx (718) 293-4300

Like Fenway Park in Boston and Wrigley Field in Chicago, Yankee Stadium is steeped in history, a place where it's easy to remember that, once upon a time, baseball truly was America's favorite pastime. While the 75-year-old park was remodeled in the mid-70's, the reminders of a bygone era are everywhere: the decorative white colonnade above the outfield (Mickey Mantle hit the one above right field with a monster blast in 1965), the plaques in Monument Park, the "Bronx cheers" that still greet hapless opponents. This is, after all, home to some of the game's most legendary ballplayers: Babe Ruth, Lou Gehrig, Joe DiMaggio, Roger Maris and Reggie Jackson to name a few. And now the Bronx Bombers boast one of the best lineups in the contemporary game, with Derek Jeter, Bernie Williams, Roger Clemens, and David Cone making up the roster of new legends. **Price:** $8–$29. **Credit cards:** All major; checks. **Subway:** 4, B, D to 161st St.— Yankee Stadium.

New York Mets—Shea Stadium

123–01 Roosevelt Ave. (between Grand Central Pkwy. and Van Wyck Expwy.), Flushing, Queens (718) 507-6387

While the Mets can't compete with the Yankees in terms of history—or World Series Championships (the Yankees have appeared in the Fall Classic almost as many years as the Mets have been in existence)—the team has certainly had its share of colorful moments. The Amazins' first season was in 1962 when the likes of Marvelous Marv Throneberry made them the most inept team in the history of the game: 40 wins and a whopping 120 losses. Shea Stadium opened amidst the bustle of the adjacent World's Fair in 1964, and things finally got better when the Mets completed an improbable championship run in 1969, defeating the Orioles four games to one. They appeared in the series again in 1973 (losing to the A's in seven games) and won their second championship in 1986 (who can forget their game six come-from-behind, 10th-inning victory over the Boston Red Sox?). After a decade of mediocrity the Mets are again a force to be reckoned with in the National League East, with All-Star catcher Mike Piazza leading the way.

Price: $10–$30. **Credit cards:** All major. **Subway:** 7 to Willets Point—Shea Stadium. **Long Island Railroad:** Stops at stadium on game days (from Penn Station, peak $5.50, off-peak $3.75, one way).

Basketball

New York Knicks—Madison Square Garden

2 Penn Plaza (at 33d St. and Seventh Ave.) (212) 465-6727

Madison Square Garden is the world's most famous arena—according to the public address system that welcomes the crowd to Knicks games. It is true that the Garden has more than its share of memories, from prize fights to championship basketball and hockey. Few basketball fans will forget Willis Reed's heroic, limping entrance onto the court for game seven of the 1970 finals, in which the Knicks defeated Wilt Chamberlain's L.A. Lakers for their first NBA title. More recently it's been Patrick Ewing holding court, though some of the most vivid memories in recent years have been of defeat rather than victory: Reggie Miller's astounding 25 points in the fourth quarter of a 1994 semi-finals game, Michael Jordan lighting up the Knicks for 55 points soon after his return from minor league baseball, Charles Smith missing four put-backs in the final seconds, any one of which would have advanced the Knicks to the 1993 finals. But the Knicks made it to the championship series in 1999 with the new, up-tempo game of Latrell Sprewell, Allan Houston , and Marcus Camby. Though tickets are hard, if not impossible, to come by and often obscenely expensive, a night at the Garden with the Knicks is a must for any die-hard hoops fan.

Price: $20–$1,500. **Tickets:** Ticketmaster; for ticket info call (212) 465-JUMP. **Credit cards:** All major. **Subway:** 1, 2 , 3, 9, A, B, C, D, E, F to 34th St.

New Jersey Nets—Continental Airlines Arena (Meadowlands)

50 Rte. 120 (at Rte. 3), East Rutherford, NJ (201) 935-3900

When the Nets played on Long Island with Julius Erving running the show, they were the best in the old ABA. Alas, things haven't gone quite so well since their admission into the NBA in 1977. Since moving to New Jersey the following year, the Nets have only made it past the first round of the playoffs once. But they currently boast one of the best young squads in the league, and it's much easier to get tickets to see Stephon Marbury, Keith Van Horn, Jayson Williams, and Kerry Kittles than it is to see their cross-river rivals.

Tickets: Ticketmaster. **Credit cards:** MC/V. **Directions:** Bus service for all events at the Meadowlands Sports Complex from Port Authority ($6.50 round trip). **By car:** New Jersey Turnpike to exit 16W to Complex. Or Garden State Pkwy south to exit 153 (153N if you're northbound), Rte. 3 east to the Complex.

New York Liberty—Madison Square Garden

The Liberty squad is a power in the new WNBA, having appeared in the finals twice in the league's first three years. And they've built quite a fan base, one that Liberty die-hards proudly describe as non-corporate, unlike the clientele of their male counterparts. Also unlike Knicks games, it's easy to get good seats to watch the Liberty, and it won't cost you a second mortgage.

Price: $8–$55. **Credit cards:** All major. **Subway:** See NY Knicks entry.

Boxing

Madison Square Garden

Madison Square Garden has a long and storied history of boxing, a tradition that began inside its first, 19th-century building in Madison Square at 23rd Street (built in 1879, this roofless arena was also the site of chariot races) and continuing through to its present and fourth location. On March 8, 1971, one of the most anticipated sporting events of the 20th Century took place when Joe Frazier defeated Muhammad Ali in a 15-round decision for the heavyweight title. In a pale imitation of that bout in March, 1999, Evander Holyfield battled Lennox Lewis to a draw in a 15-round fight. Your best hope for exciting (and affordable) boxing is the annual **Golden Gloves tournament** (April) where kids from around the city battle for top honors in all weight divisions.

Price: Depends on event. **Credit cards:** All major. **Subway:** See NY Knicks entry.

Church Street Boxing Gym

25 Park Pl. (between Church St. and Broadway) (212) 571-1333

This is New York City's premiere boxing training facility, with over 10,000 square feet of gym space located in the heart of downtown Manhattan. The well-known gym has showcased many up-and-coming professional boxers, kick-boxers, and Thai-boxers and has worked on site with such marquee names as Evander Holyfield, Larry Holmes, and Mike Tyson. Call for a fight schedule.

Subway: 4, 5, 6 to Brooklyn Bridge; 2, 3 to Park Pl.

Cricket

Because of the concentration of recent immigrants from cricket-playing countries (mainly from India, Pakistan, and the West Indies), it's not surprising that the New York metropolitan area is considered the mecca of cricket in North America. There are twelve leagues comprising over 200 clubs, and play can be watched in a number of area parks. **Bronx:** Van Cortlandt Park, Ferry Point Park, Randall's Island, Soundview. **Queens:** Flushing Meadow Park, Baisley Park, Kissena Park, Edgemere. **Brooklyn:** Marine Park, Seaview.

Football

New York Giants—Giants Stadium (Meadowlands)

59 Rte 120 (at Rte. 3), East Rutherford, NJ (201) 935-3900

The Giants moved to their 77,716-seat home in 1976, having played throughout most of their history in Yankee Stadium. And good luck getting tickets: the waiting list for season tickets goes all the way back to their first year in the Meadowlands stadium. The Giants have won two championships since moving across the Hudson, years when Lawrence Taylor struck fear in the hearts of visiting quarterbacks. While LT has moved to the Hall of Fame, the tailgate parties are still in high gear: during the season, a hoard of die-hard tailgaters sporting kielbasa, burgers, and Budweiser claim the stadium's 25,000 parking spots.

Price: $40–$45, if available. **Credit cards:** All major. **Directions:** See NJ Nets entry.

New York Jets—Giants Stadium

The Jets were lured to the Meadowlands after the 1983 season, so both metro-politan-area NFL franchises are actually New Jersey teams, despite what it says on their helmets. While the Jets won the Super Bowl in 1969 under the flashy guidance of Joe Namath (an event that directly led to the merging of the AFL with the NFL), wins have been hard to come by since. But Bill Parcells—so familiar with the confines of the Meadowlands after his long stint as head coach of the Giants—is now working his magic, and the Jets are contenders again. It's almost as hard to get a ticket for a Jets game as it is for those of their co-tenants: the waiting list for season tickets is currently twelve years.

Price: From $35, if available. **Credit cards:** All major. **Directions:** See NJ Nets entry.

Hockey

New York Rangers—Madison Square Garden

One of the "Original Six" NHL teams, the Rangers have a long tradition, yet only two championships. Until their successful Stanley Cup run in 1994—led by captain Mark Messier—the last time the Cup had been held aloft on Garden ice was fifty-four years and two buildings before. But win or lose, the Rangers have some of the most loyal—and vociferous—fans in the league, and games at the Garden, if you can find tickets, are not for the faint of heart.

Price: $22–$675. **Credit cards:** All major. **Subway:** See NY Knicks entry.

New York Islanders—Nassau Veterans Memorial Coliseum

1255 Hempstead Tpke., Uniondale, Long Island (516) 794-9300

When the Islanders came back in the 1975 playoffs to defeat the Pittsburgh Penguins in seven games after falling behind 3–0 in the series, the fortunes of the franchise were on a meteoric rise. They won four successive Stanley Cups in the first years of the 80s and were the team to beat until the advent of Wayne Gretsky and his Edmonton Oilers. Islanders fans think back fondly on those years: the team hasn't qualified for the playoffs since the Rangers made quick work of them in a series sweep en route to the 1994 title.

Price: $15–$115. **Tickets:** Ticketmaster. **Credit cards:** All major **Directions:** Long Island Railroad to Hempstead (peak $6.25, off-peak $4.25); walk one block to the Hempstead Bus Terminal and take N70, N71 or N72 bus to Coliseum. **By car:** Midtown Tunnel to Long Island Expwy. (495) east to exit 38; Northern State Pkwy. to exit 31A; Meadowbrook Pkwy. south to exit M4, Nassau Coliseum. Parking is $6.00.

New Jersey Devils—Continental Airlines Arena

50 Rte. 120 (at Rte. 3), East Rutherford, NJ (201) 935-3900

Transplanted from Colorado in 1982, the New Jersey Devils have risen from depths of the Patrick Division to become one of the better teams in the NHL and a perennial playoff contender. While rabid Rangers fans had to wait over five decades for the return of the Stanley Cup to New York, the wait in Jersey was only thirteen years: in 1995, a year after their cross-river rivals won hockey's ultimate honor, the Devils captured their first league championship.

Tickets: Ticketmaster. **Credit cards:** MC/V. **Directions:** See NJ Nets entry.

Horse Racing

Aqueduct Racetrack

110th St. (at Rockaway Blvd.), Ozone Park, Queens (718) 641-4700

The old Aqueduct, which opened in 1894, was replaced by the new "Big A" in 1959. In 1975 the inner track was constructed, allowing for winter racing. Aqueduct was the scene on July 4, 1972 of Secretariat's first event, a 5½ furlong maiden race.

Hours: Gates open at 11 A.M.. **Admission:** Grandstand, $1; Clubhouse, $3; Skyline Club, $4; children under 12, free. **Subway:** A to Aqueduct Racetrack; courtesy bus service to admission gate. **By car:** Midtown Tunnel to Long Island Expwy east, to Van Wyck Expwy south to exit 3, Linden Blvd.; right on Linden to track. General parking $1.00.

Belmont Park

2150 Hempstead Tpke. (at Plainfield Ave), Elmont, Long Island (718) 641-4700

In addition to hosting the Belmont Stakes each year, the final leg of the Triple Crown, Belmont Park has been the scene of many other historic events. One of America's oldest and most beautiful tracks, Belmont opened on May 4, 1905, and it was here that the Wright brothers supervised an international aerial tournament before 150,000 in 1910. It was also the site of the first American airmail service (1918) between New York and Washington, D.C. But most important, of course, is its glorious racing past. It was here in 1973 that Secretariat won the Triple Crown, engaging Sham out of the gate in a six-furlong duel, which at 1:09 4/5 was the fastest in Belmont history (and a speed that finished Sham, who never raced again). Secretariat cruised to a 1:59 flat finish, winning the race by an astonishing 31 lengths.

Hours: Doors open at 11 A.M.; races are 1 P.M.–5 P.M. Closed Mon., Tue except holiday weekends (closed Wed.). Season is May-Jul., and Sept.- mid-Oct. **Admission** Grandstand, $2; Clubhouse, $4. **Directions:** Long Island Rail Road, round-trip package from Penn Station that includes $1 off racetrack admission. **By car:** Cross Island Pkwy. to exit 26D. General parking is $2.00.

Meadowlands Racetrack

Rte. 3, East Rutherford, NJ (201) 935-8500

Harness and thoroughbred horse racing are the staples at this one-mile oval track next to Giants Stadium. The 40,000-person-capacity racetrack was built in 1976 and christened in high style when horseman Anthony Abbatiello rode across the George Washington Bridge to the Meadowlands.

Hours: Gates open at 6 P.M. **Price:** Grandstand,$1; Clubhouse, $3; Pegasus (Dining Floor), $5. **Credit cards:** Cash only. **Directions:** See NJ Nets entry.

Yonkers Raceway

Central Ave., Yonkers (718) 562-9500

Although the history of the modern Yonkers Raceway dates from only 1950, the Westchester oval's impressive past actually dates back to the 19th century, when it was founded as a replacement for Fleetwood Park, a Grand Circuit stop in the Bronx. The facility reopened as Yonkers Raceway and had its inaugural meet on April 27, 1950.

Hours: 8 P.M. with 12:30 P.M. matinees. **Price:** Grandstand, $2.25; Empire Terrace Floor, $4.25. **Credit cards:** Cash only. **Subway:** 4 to Woodlawn; B, D to Bedford Park Blvd.; 5 to 238th St.; 1, 9 to 242d St. Take express buses from stations to track. **By car:** New York Thruway I-87 to exit 2 North, exit 4 South; Bronx River Pkwy. to Oak St., Mt Vernon exit; Saw Mill River Pkwy. to Cross County Pkwy. to Yonkers or Central Ave. exit).

Soccer

New York/New Jersey MetroStars— Continental Airlines Arena

Major League Soccer began in 1996 A.M.idst the enthusiasm generated by the World Cup, held in this country for the first time in its long history. And now the MetroStars have German superstar Lothar Matthäus playing for the team in 2000. Certainly the best soccer in America is being played in MLS venues, and with the recent ban of the game-deciding shootout in favor of overtime, league officials are trying to make this a more exciting game for purists. Europe, take note.

Tickets: For info call 1-888-4METROTIX. **Credit cards:** MC/V. **Directions:** See NJ Nets entry.

Tennis

Chase Championships—Madison Square Garden

Taking place in Madison Square Garden every November, the Chase Championships is one of the last events on the Women's Tennis Association Tour. It is also one of the most prestigious tournaments, featuring a singles field limited to the top sixteen point-earners on the Tour, and a similar field of eight doubles teams. The tennis is top-notch, and the Garden ambiance is, as always, electric.

Price: $10–$125. **Tickets:** Ticketmaster. **Credit cards:** All major. **Subway:** See NY Knicks entry.

U.S. Open—USTA National Tennis Center

Flushing Meadows—Corona Park, Queens (718)760–6200

The oldest American tournament moved to the National Tennis Center, built on the former site of the 1939 and 1964 World's Fairs. Now the best in tennis players converge on NYC each September hoping to play at center court for the championship in the new and spacious Arthur Ashe Stadium. Fans can pay top dollar to see the showcased matches, or purchase admission to the grounds, which entitles them to wander from one early-round match to another for a more intimate tennis experience.

Tickets: Call Tele-charge at 1–888-OPEN-TIX. **Grounds Admission:** Aug. 30-Sept. 3, $25; Sept. 4-Sept. 6, $35. **Credit cards:** All major. **Subway:** 7 to Willets Point—Shea Stadium. **Long Island Railroad:** Stops at stadium during the Open (from Penn Station, peak $5.50, off-peak $3.75, one way).

For the latest information on restaurants, hotels, concerts, nightlife, sporting events and more, check online at New York Today, the *New York Times* website devoted entirely to life in New York City: www.nytoday.com.

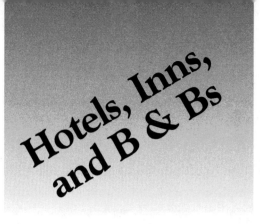

Hotels, Inns, and B & Bs

New York's good fortune at the close of the century means it welcomes millions of visitors every year, touching off a scramble to offer fresh accommodations. Every hotel, it seems, is redecorating. There are more and better hotels in New York than there have ever been.

Following the usual high-demand, limited space pattern of the city, though, New York has its own unwritten rules about hospitality. Room size is almost invariably smaller here than in most other places, including bathrooms and closets. New York is more expensive than most other places. Paying more for less space is a familiar New York routine.

It is easy to spend hundreds of dollars a night to sleep in Manhattan, but it's not necessary to do so. In this section there are many places to stay for (relatively) reasonable rates—inns, guest houses, bed and breakfasts—that can offer a special way of experiencing New York.

New hotels are opening with regularity, and older ones are renovating feverishly. Ask when you reserve if the hotel is renovating when you plan to visit. Even if the renovation isn't taking place on the floor you're staying on, it can be disruptive.

For updated information on hotels, as well as reviews and directions by car or mass transit, check online at New York Today (*www.nytoday.com/hotels*)

Getting the Best Rate

Many hotels have their published "rack rates," which they then discount six ways (or more) from Sunday. Don't accept the first rate you're quoted. It used to be the case that New York hotels offered serious discounts on the weekends, but you'll find less of that than there used to be. The hotel tax has been reduced to a somewhat more reasonable 13.25 percent (plus a $2 per night room charge)— keep it in mind when you're calculating the real cost of a visit. In all of the listings in this section, we have provided both specific prices and a broad range that encompasses the average daily rate for a double room:

$ under $150
$$ $150–$249
$$$ $250–$350
$$$$ 350 and over

It is wise to try the following hotel reservation agencies before booking a room.

These agencies buy up blocks of rooms in advance and offer them at discount rates with no additional charge:

Accommodations Express (800) 444-7666
Central Reservations Service (800) 950-0232
Hotel Reservations Network (800) 964-6835
Express Reservations (800) 356-1123
Quickbook (800) 789-9887
Room Exchange (800) 846-7000

DOWNTOWN

Best Western Seaport Inn   GOOD **$$**

33 Peck Slip (at Front St.), Lower Manhattan
www.bestwestern.com/seaportinn
Phone: (212) 766-6600, (800) 468-3569   Fax: (212) 766-6615

Although this hotel is a stone's throw from the South Street Seaport, it still feels out of the way. The traditional rooms, done in green and beige, don't deviate much from designs at other Best Western hotels. Rooms with a terrace are especially desirable. You can lounge and soak in views of the Seaport, the Fulton Fish Market and, best of all, the Brooklyn Bridge.

Rooms: 72; 7 floors; designated nonsmoking rooms. **Hotel amenities:** None. **Food services:** None. **Cancellation:** 4 P.M. day of arrival. **Wheelchair access:** Fully accessible; ADA compliant.

The Chelsea Hotel   GOOD **$$**

222 West 23d St. (between Seventh and Eighth Aves.), Chelsea
www.chelseahotel.com
Phone: (212) 243-3700   Fax: (212) 675-5531

A stay at the Chelsea may not be an indulgence in creature comforts, but it is a window into a remarkable artistic heritage. Dozens of authors, artists, actors and other creative types have stayed at or lived in the Chelsea Hotel, built in 1884. As a building, as a crucible of creative forces, as an idea, the Chelsea is unique. In the lobby, artwork from tenants covers the walls and hangs from the ceiling, enlivening every available space. The Chelsea is largely residential today, but has about 70 hotel rooms as well. Although well-kept, the ghosts hovering in every corner of this landmark see to it that nothing is obsessively clean. Still, you get more space than in most New York hotels; most rooms have good light and walls are famously thick. Some have nonworking fireplaces made of hand-carved marble.

Rooms: 400; 12 floors; all smoking rooms. **Hotel amenities:** Laundry and dry cleaning, valet parking. **Food services:** Restaurant, bar (Serena), room service. **Cancellation:** 3 days prior to arrival. **Wheelchair access:** Fully accessible; ADA compliant.

Chelsea Inn   GOOD **$$**

46 West 17th St. (between Fifth and Sixth Aves.), Flatiron
www.chelseainn.com
Phone: (212) 645-8989, (800) 640-6469   Fax: (212) 645-1903

A hotel with a lot of heart and a lot of stairs, the Chelsea Inn offers friendly,
simple and spotlessly clean lodging. The ceilings are remarkably high, which
adds to the ambience, but fluorescent lights in the hallways and bathrooms
detract. The front desk isn't staffed 24 hours—guests are given keys to the front
door, and callers can leave a voice mail message for a guest at all times.

Rooms: 25 (includes 16 suites); 5 floors; all smoking rooms. **Hotel amenities:**
Business services, some shared baths. **Food services:** None. **Cancellation:** 2 days
prior to arrival. **Wheelchair access:** Not accessible.

Gramercy Park Hotel   GOOD **$$**

2 Lexington Ave. (at 21st St.), Gramercy Park
Phone: (212) 475-4320, (800) 221-4083   Fax: (212) 505-0535

The Gramercy has changed hands over the years, but nothing seems to affect its
character. Babe Ruth and Humphrey Bogart stayed here, but guest rooms now
have more history to them than design sense, and the old bathrooms have no
amenities except soap. One of the perks of the hotel is that guests get a key to
the idyllic Gramercy Park, a privilege otherwise given only to residents of buildings that face the park. The hotel also has a terrific outdoor space on the roof
with great views of the city to the north and south.

Rooms: 356 (includes 157 suites); 17 floors; designated nonsmoking rooms.
Hotel amenities: Laundry and dry cleaning, meeting and function rooms, valet
parking. **Food services:** Restaurant, bar, room service. **Cancellation:** 6 P.M. 3
days prior to arrival. **Wheelchair access:** Fully accessible; ADA compliant.

Holiday Inn Downtown   BASIC **$$**

138 Lafayette St. (between Canal and Howard Sts.), Chinatown
www.holiday-inn.com
Phone: (212) 966-8898, (800) 465-4329 (HOLIDAY)
Fax: (212) 966-3933

Visitors not used to this bustling neighborhood might find its littered streets and
noisy main arteries off-putting. If noise is an important consideration for you, be
sure to ask for a room at the back of the hotel. Visitors from Asia make up about
25 percent of the hotel's guests, the rest being government employees (visiting
the nearby government offices) and tourists. Some accommodations are
extremely small.

Rooms: 227 (includes12 suites); 14 floors; designated nonsmoking floors. **Hotel
amenities:** Concierge, valet dry cleaning, valet parking. **Food services:** Restaurant, bar, room service. **Cancellation:** 6 P.M. day of arrival. **Wheelchair access:**
Fully accessible.

The Inn at Irving Place   VERY GOOD $$$$

56 Irving Pl. (between 17th and 18th Sts.), Gramercy Park
www.innatirving.com
Phone: (212) 533-4600, (800) 685-1447   Fax: (212) 533-4611

There are hotels in the city with more amenities, but not many with more charm.
The Inn at Irving Place is unconventional, without even a sign out front to distinguish it from the other town houses in the fashionable, historic Gramercy Park
neighborhood. Each guest room has a different layout and design, and the antique
or antique-style furniture, queen-size beds, nonworking fireplaces, wood floors
and oriental rugs make it feel like a hideaway-away-from-home. The adjacent
two-star restaurant, Verbena, supplies room service, which is certainly an added
value. But some rooms are right over the restaurant's uncovered and sometimes
noisy back garden and the three-story inn doesn't have elevators.

Rooms: 12 (includes 6 suites); 3 floors; all smoking rooms. **Hotel amenities:**
Business services, function rooms, laundry and dry cleaning, valet parking. **Food
services:** Restaurant, bar, room service. **Cancellation:** 2 days prior to arrival.
Wheelchair access: Not accessible.
*Note: no children under 12

The Mercer Hotel   EXCELLENT $$$$

The Mercer Hotel, 147 Mercer St., (at Prince St.), SoHo
www.themercer.com
Phone: (212) 966-6060, (888) 918-6060   Fax: (212) 965-3838

The hotel reflects the neighborhood's mix of classic and cutting-edge, but isn't
insistent that you pay attention to it at every turn. With owner Andre Balazs,
designer Christian Liaigre has created an environment with a cool, modern,
downtown ambience—clean, elegant, comfortable, unshowy and secure enough
for flowers on the windowsills. The rooms have ample space, the bathrooms
especially. There is 24-hour room service from the Mercer Kitchen (overseen by
Jean-Georges Vongerichten, of the four-star restaurant Jean-Georges).

Rooms: 75 (includes 5 suites); 6 floors; all smoking rooms. **Hotel amenities:**
Business services, laundry and dry cleaning. **Food services:** Restaurant (The
Mercer Kitchen), bar, room service. **Cancellation:** 2 days prior to arrival.
Wheelchair access: Fully accessible.

Millenium Hilton   VERY GOOD $$$

55 Church St. (between Fulton and Dey Streets), Lower Manhattan
                          www.newyorkmillenium.hilton.com
Phone: (212) 693-2001, (800) 752-0014   Fax: (212) 571-2316

You feel the Millenium's corporate focus when you enter the double-story lobby,
which has the modern, dark-wood ambience of a boardroom, albeit on a large
scale. Hallways are modern and bright, with delightful views overlooking
Brooklyn. Guest rooms rise up 55 floors, and few Manhattan hotels can compete with their thrilling views of downtown Manhattan and the Hudson. The

rooms are contemporary in design and tend to be on the small side, though prints of old New York offer a nice contrast to the modern feel of the hotel.

Rooms: 561 (includes 98 suites); floors 55; designated nonsmoking rooms. **Hotel amenities:** Business center, concierge, health club, laundry and dry cleaning, meeting and function rooms, swimming pool, valet parking. **Food services:** Two restaurants, two bars, room service. **Cancellation:** 4 P.M. day prior to arrival. **Wheelchair access:** Fully accessible; ADA compliant.

New York Marriott Financial Center   VERY GOOD $$$

85 West St. (between Carlisle and Albany Sts.), Lower Manhattan
www.marriott.com
Phone: (212) 385-4900, (800) 242-8685   Fax: (212) 227-8414

For the business traveler who wants to be in the center of the action but at a peaceful remove, the Marriott Financial Center would be a good choice. The rooms here are traditional in design though a bit drab with low ceilings and armoires instead of closets. Some rooms have appealing views of the southern tip of the island. The hotel also houses Roy's New York, one of the growing chain of chef Roy Yamaguchi's Hawaiian-fusion restaurants. The hotel also has a business center with two computers, a copy machine and a fax machine, as well as a modest fitness room and a 50-foot by 20-foot pool.

Rooms: 504 (includes 13 suites); 38 floors; designated nonsmoking rooms. **Hotel amenities:** Concierge, health club, laundry and dry cleaning, meeting rooms, swimming pool, valet parking. **Food services:** Restaurant (Roy's New York), bar, room service. **Cancellation:** 6 P.M. day of arrival. **Wheelchair access:** Fully accessible; ADA compliant.

New York Marriott World Trade Center

VERY GOOD $$$

3 World Trade Center (between Liberty and Barclay Sts.),
Lower Manhattan   www.marriott.com
Phone: (212) 938-9100, (800) 550-2344   Fax: (212) 444-4094

The business traveler should be well served here and the tourist can take advantage of the hotel's proximity to neighborhoods like TriBeCa and SoHo. The hotel connects to one of the World Trade Center concourses, offering guests easy access to things like airline ticket desks, car rental counters, a discount theater ticket booth, the WTC observation deck and an indoor shopping mall. One of the most attractive amenities is the full-service health club near the top of the building. Besides a range of machines, there is a running track and lap pool, all with views over the Hudson into New Jersey. The hotel also has a small but nicely designed business center.

Rooms: 818 (includes 17 suites); 21 floors; designated nonsmoking rooms. **Hotel amenities:** Business center, concierge, health club, laundry and dry cleaning, meeting rooms, swimming pool, valet parking. **Food services:** Two restaurants, bar, 24-hour room service. **Cancellation:** 6 P.M. day prior to arrival. **Wheelchair access:** Fully accessible; ADA compliant.

SoHo Grand Hotel   VERY GOOD $$$$

310 West Broadway (between Grand and Canal Sts.), SoHo
www.sohogrand.com
Phone: (212) 965-3000, (800) 965-3000   Fax: (212) 965-3244

You can't beat the sheer effect of ascending the staircase from the ground floor
to this hotel's lobby, in which bold, industrial, urban elements give way to 24-
foot ceilings and two-story windows. The SoHo Grand is full of allusions to
SoHo present (cool, understated design), to SoHo past (cast-iron architectural
elements) and even to the Colonial era (the lanterns outside guests' doors). In
the rooms there are saddle stitch leather headboards, pedestal sinks and honey-
comb-pattern tile floors. Many rooms boast entrancing views, including one
north to midtown that is worth the price of admission. There are some drawbacks, however: rooms, bathrooms and closets are spatially challenged, and
there are no in-room fax machines, CD or video players, irons or ironing boards,
no business center and no night turndown service.

Rooms: 369 (includes 4 suites); 17 floors; designated nonsmoking rooms. **Hotel
amenities:** Concierge, fitness equipment, laundry and dry cleaning, meeting and
function rooms, valet parking. **Food services:** Restaurant, bar, room service.
Cancellation: 4 P.M. day of arrival. **Wheelchair access:** Fully accessible.

Wall St. Inn   VERY GOOD $$

9 S. William St., (between Broad and Beaver Sts.), Lower Manhattan
www.wallstinn.com
Phone: (212) 747-1500   Fax: (212) 747-1900

The best deal downtown and a very nice place to stay. Located on a historic
site, they have done everything right at this hotel, paying close attention to the
fundamentals and staying away from showier but less useful gimmicks. The
basics start with bedding—high-quality mattresses and 200-thread count sheets.
Windows are not only double-paned, they are filled with argon gas and the
panes are of different thicknesses—another noise baffler. Rooms are not large,
but don't feel cramped relative to the rest of the city's rooms.

Rooms: 46 (includes 10 suites); 7 floors; designated nonsmoking floor. **Hotel
amenities:** Business center, concierge, health club, laundry and dry cleaning,
meeting and function rooms. **Food services:** Room service. **Cancellation:** 4
P.M. day prior to arrival. **Wheelchair access:** Fully accessible; ADA compliant.

Washington Square Hotel   GOOD $$

103 Waverly Pl. (between MacDougal and Waverly Sts.), West Village
www.wshotel.com
Phone: (212) 777-9515, (800) 222-0418   Fax: (212) 979-8373

The hotel has been in the Paul family for more than two decades. This must
account for some of the hotel's character, which, along with modest prices and
downtown location, keeps it full year round. Rooms are attractive, featuring sea-
green sponged walls and new furniture. The mostly leisure travelers who come

to the Washington Square appreciate the clean rooms, firm mattresses, double-glazed windows and high ceilings. On the down side, many rooms have extremely limited closet space, and the lighting throughout could do with some softening. If you want a room with good natural light, ask for one facing the front. There is a small fitness room, a restaurant, C3, and a lounge featuring jazz on Tuesday nights and during Sunday brunch.

Rooms: 170; 3 floors and 9 floors in two connecting buildings; all smoking rooms. **Hotel amenities:** Fitness equipment, meeting and function room. **Food services:** Restaurant. **Cancellation:** Noon day prior to arrival. **Wheelchair access:** Not accessible.

Cheap

Carlton Arms Hotel   BASIC $
160 East 25th St. (between Third and Lexington Aves.),
Gramercy Park   www.carltonarms.com
Phone: (212) 679-0680   Fax: none

This is a bohemian crash pad in a non-bohemian neighborhood. What makes the Carlton Arms far from ordinary are the leaps and swoops of various artists' imaginations; they have transformed the rooms into three-dimensional art installations. There's no elevator or AC and most bathrooms are shared.

Rooms: 54; 4 floors; all smoking rooms. **Hotel amenities:** Some shared baths. **Food services:** None. **Cancellation:** "It's nice if they cancel." **Wheelchair access:** Not accessible.

Chelsea Pines Inn   GOOD $
317 West 14th St. (between Eighth and Ninth Aves.), Chelsea
www.q-net.com/chelseapines
Phone: (212) 929-1023   Fax: (212) 620-5646

Chelsea Pines offers modest accommodations, mostly to the gay and lesbian community. The rooms here have been decorated with a sense of humor—each is named for a film star, from Susan Hayward to Rock Hudson. There are five floors and no elevator, and some rooms share a bath.

Rooms: 23; 5 floors; all smoking rooms. **Hotel amenities:** Some shared baths. **Food services:** None. **Cancellation:** $50–$100 cancellation fee. **Wheelchair access:** Not accessible.

Hotel 17   BASIC $
225 East 17th St. (between Second and Third Aves.), Flatiron
hotel17.citysearch.com
Phone: (212) 475-2845   Fax: (212) 677-8178

The Hotel 17 offers basic accommodations with few amenities. The rooms are bare bones and most do not have a private bath, but the hall bathrooms are reasonably clean. Not all rooms have AC, and those that do fetch a higher rate. The Hotel 17 has something of a hip reputation, as it is used for magazine shoots, among other things.

Rooms: 130; 8 floors; all smoking rooms. **Hotel amenities:** Laundry. **Food services:** None. **Cancellation:** 1 P.M. day prior to arrival. **Wheelchair access:** Not accessible.

Larchmont Hotel   GOOD **$**

27 West 11th St.(between Fifth and Sixth Aves.), West Village
www.larchmonthotel.citysearch.com
Phone: (212) 989-9333   Fax: (212) 989-9496

Downtown could use a dozen more Larchmonts. The West Village is short on hotels and the Larchmont is not only a cheerful, small lodging, it's a value. The rooms come equipped with many amenities as well as slippers and a robe for getting back and forth to the all-shared bathrooms. Complimentary breakfast is offered in the basement breakfast room.

Rooms: 57; 6 floors; all smoking rooms. **Hotel amenities:** Business services, shared kitchens. **Food services:** None. **Cancellation:** 2 days prior to arrival. **Wheelchair access:** Not accessible.

MIDTOWN EAST AND MURRAY HILL

Beekman Tower Hotel   VERY GOOD **$$$**

3 Mitchell Pl. (49th St. and First Ave)   www.mesuite.com
Phone: (212) 355-7300, (800) 637-8483   Fax: (212) 753-9366

What's best about the Beekman, one of ten hotels in the Manhattan East Suite Hotels chain, is the amount of space you get. The suites have full kitchens with essential appliances, cookware and silverware. The hotel also offers a grocery shopping service. There is a fitness center as well as his and hers saunas, and the Top of the Tower restaurant and bar offers drinks, dinner and views. It has never been particularly elegant up there, nor is the food top drawer, but it is user friendly. That could be said of the entire hotel.

Rooms: 174 (all suites); 26 floors; designated nonsmoking rooms. **Hotel amenities:** Business services, concierge, health club, laundry and dry cleaning, meeting and function rooms, valet parking. **Food services:** Two restaurants, two bars, room service. **Cancellation:** 3 P.M. day of arrival. **Wheelchair access:** Fully accessible.

The Benjamin   EXCELLENT **$$$**

125 East 50th St. (at Lexington Ave.)   www.thebenjamin.com
Phone: (212) 715-2500, (800) 637-8483   Fax: (212) 715-2525

Geared to the executive business traveler, this hotel has been wired like an office building, so that the hotel is as ready as it can be for whatever technology throws its way. The look of the rooms is contemporary, in a soft and pleasing way, as if someone took the family living room and made improvements. The Serta mattresses are especially comfortable, and the hotel had a wonderful idea with its "pillow menu." There are eleven types, including down, foam, hypoallergenic gel-filled, and a five-foot body cushion pregnant women often find helpful. Given the noisy Lexington Avenue address, the rooms are quiet because the windows are double-paned and injected with argon gas. Suites with terraces are also pleasant.

Amenities include a fax/scanner/printer/copier, a safe large enough for a laptop, Frette bed linen and bathrobe, Bose radio, movies on command, TV Web browser, individual temperature control, video checkout, fresh flowers, and CD and tape player (the latter in the one-bedroom suites). The white marble bathrooms are also well stocked. Visitors who are in town on business will not only appreciate the high-speed Internet access but also the large desk on wheels which doubles as a dining room table.

Rooms: 209 (includes 97 suites); 26 floors; nonsmoking rooms. **Hotel amenities:** Concierge, health club, laundry and dry cleaning, meeting rooms. **Food services:** Restaurant (An American Place), bar, room service. **Cancellation:** 3 P.M. day of arrival. **Wheelchair access:** Fully accessible.

Crowne Plaza Hotel at the United Nations

VERY GOOD **$$$**

304 East 42d St., (between First and Second Aves.)
www.crowneplaza-un.com
Phone: (212) 986-8800, (800) 227-6963   Fax: (212) 297-3440

This hotel's location on the far eastern side of midtown makes the Crowne Plaza convenient to the United Nations. It also makes sense for visitors who want to be near midtown, but not in the thick of it. New windows were installed in 1999, giving guests triple-paned protection from city noise. Guest rooms have traditional decor and an array of amenities.

Rooms: 300 (including 14 suites); 20 floors; nonsmoking rooms. **Hotel amenities:** Business center, concierge, fitness equipment, laundry and dry cleaning, meeting and function rooms, valet parking. **Food services:** Restaurant, bar, room service. **Cancellation:** 6 P.M. day of arrival. **Wheelchair access:** Fully accessible.

Dumont Plaza

VERY GOOD **$$$**

150 East 34th St. (between Lexington and Third Aves.)
www.mesuite.com
Phone: (212) 481-7600   Fax: (212) 889-8856

The Dumont Plaza is one of ten all-suite hotels in the Manhattan East Suite Hotels chain. The Dumont has a modern tilt, with a cool, all-marble lobby and room designs that fall between traditional and contemporary. The fluorescent lighting in the hallways is the least appealing feature, but inside the rooms guests will find restful olive green and beige colors, as well as a kitchen or kitchenette. Some have a dishwasher, though the housekeeping staff will do your dishes for you as well as your grocery shopping. On the "D" line of rooms, the studio suites get views of the Empire State Building. Those on the "E" line are corner rooms and get lots of light plus views east to the East River. On the "F" line, the studio suites have wonderful southern exposures. There is a fitness room with men and women's saunas, and the Sonia Rose restaurant has a lovely terrace for outdoor dining.

Rooms: 248 (all suites); 37 floors; designated nonsmoking rooms. **Hotel amenities:** Business center, health club, laundry and dry cleaning, meeting and function rooms, valet parking. **Food services:** Restaurant (Sonia Rose), bar, room service. **Cancellation:** 3 P.M. day of arrival. **Wheelchair access:** Fully accessible; ADA compliant.

Eastgate Tower   VERY GOOD $$$

222 East 39th Street (between Second and Third Aves.)
www.mesuite.com
Phone: (212) 687-8000, (800) 637-8483   Fax: (212) 490-2634

The Eastgate Tower is one of 10 all-suite hotels in the Manhattan East Suite Hotels chain. The lobby here isn't unpleasant, but it is totally nondescript—more like an anonymous office building than a hotel. The hallways are cast in depressing fluorescent light, but the rooms have a much more cheerful look: a contemporary design with purple and beige figuring prominently.

All accommodations have a kitchen or kitchenette that is fully stocked (down to the dishes and silverware). The housekeeping staff will do the dishes for you as well as your grocery shopping.

Rooms: 188 (all suites); 25 floors; designated nonsmoking rooms. **Hotel amenities:** Grocery shopping, health club, laundry and dry cleaning, meeting and function rooms, valet parking. **Food services:** Restaurant, bar, room service. **Cancellation:** 3 P.M. day of arrival. **Wheelchair access:** Fully accessible; ADA compliant.

The Fitzpatrick Grand Central Hotel   VERY GOOD $$$

141 East 44th St. (bet Lexington and Third Aves.)
www.fitzpatrickhotels.com
Phone: (212) 351-6800, (800) 367-7701   Fax: (212) 308-5166

The Fitzpatrick Grand Central may have more polish than the Fitzpatrick Manhattan (its sister property) but both are notable for their warm hospitality. The emerald-aisled hallways are bright and pleasant, as are the rooms. Most are king- and queen-bedded, the mattress quality is good, and many have canopies. There are two-line phones with dataport and voice mail, fax, clock radio, bathrobe, iron and ironing board, hair dryer, coffee maker, and makeup mirror. VCRs are available on request along with complimentary Irish and kids movies. Night turndown service is standard. Other hotel amenities

center and no room service per se, though the hotel supplies menus from neighborhood restaurants that will deliver. For visitors who don't need a wide array of services, the Helmsley Middletowne offers an unassuming place to rest your head.

Rooms: 192 (includes 42 suites); 16 floors; designated nonsmoking floors. **Hotel amenities:** Laundry and dry cleaning, meeting room, valet parking. **Food services:** None. **Cancellation:** 4 P.M. day of arrival. **Wheelchair access:** Fully accessible.

Hotel Bedford   GOOD $$

118 East 40th St. (between Park and Lexington Aves.)
www.bedfordhotelbox.com
Phone: (212) 697-4800, (800) 221-6881   Fax: (212) 697-1093

In a city where some hoteliers think nothing of charging a lot and offering little, it's nice to visit a hotel where the equation is reversed. As with its sister property, the San Carlos, the Bedford offers comfortable, low-to-no-style lodging at modest prices. If the blah, old-fashioned design doesn't matter to you, you may be pleasantly surprised by the rest. There are spacious rooms with standard amenities and a complimentary continental buffet breakfast. Other features include room service and both laundry and dry cleaning. The doubles and suites have an equipped kitchen. Rooms facing south get plenty of light and some suites have balconies.

Rooms: 136 (includes 60 suites); 17 floors; designated nonsmoking rooms. **Hotel amenities:** Laundry and dry cleaning. **Food services:** Restaurant, bar, room service. **Cancellation:** Day prior to arrival. **Wheelchair access:** Not accessible.

Hotel Delmonico   VERY GOOD $$$$

502 Park Ave. (at 59th St.)   www.srs-worldhotels.com
Phone: (212) 355-2500, (800) 821-3842   Fax: (212) 755-3779

Given the hotel's prime location, the large guest rooms and the relatively moderate rates, the Delmonico is a hotel that can be recommended with enthusiasm. These traditionally designed suites give you a fair amount of room and the feel of an apartment as much as a hotel. Each suite has a kitchen with a refrigerator (some small, some full-size), microwave, dishwasher, cookware and some even have ovens. Rooms come with fax machines, voice mail, thick, old walls (some of which are a bit scuffed) and large-to-very-large closets. Fifteen guest rooms have terraces. Guests have complimentary use of the adjacent New York Sports Club, an excellent facility. One notable feature is the Lighthouse Suite, designed for the needs of a blind or partially sighted visitor.

Rooms: 157 (all suites); 30 floors; designated nonsmoking rooms. **Hotel amenities:** Business center, concierge, laundry and dry cleaning, valet parking. **Food services:** Bar. **Cancellation:** Day prior to arrival. **Wheelchair access:** Rooms not accessible.

Hotel Elysée   GOOD $$$

60 East 54th St. (between Park and Madison Aves.)
members.aol.com/elysee99
Phone: (212) 753-1066, (800) 535-9733   Fax: (212) 980-9278

The Elysée is a small, few-frills boutique hotel with charm but not pretension.
The traditional rooms are done in pale gray and blue tones. A few rooms have sun-
room sitting areas, while others have terraces. Amenities include a complimentary
breakfast as well as tea, coffee and cookies served in the afternoon and hors d'oeuvres in the evening. While the Elysée has an appealing, cosmopolitan New York
feel, noise can be a problem; request a quieter, but darker, room at the back.

Rooms: 99 (includes 11 suites); 15 floors; designated nonsmoking rooms. **Hotel
amenities:** Laundry and dry cleaning, meeting room, valet parking. **Food services:** Restaurant/bar (Monkey Bar), room service. **Cancellation:** Day prior to
arrival. **Wheelchair access:** Fully accessible.

Hotel Inter-Continental   VERY GOOD $$$

111 East 48th St. (between Lexington and Park Aves.)
www.new-york.interconti.com
Phone: (212) 755-5900, (800) 327-0200   Fax: (212) 644-0079

The Inter-Continental has much potential, but much of it is unrealized. The
once-moribund lobby has been redesigned, making it livelier than before. Renovation of the meeting rooms and guest room suites is continuing with a major
overhaul of the hotel scheduled for 2001. These changes are needed. The neo-
Federalist look of the guest rooms seems to be left over from Zachary Taylor's
administration and gives the accommodations a decidedly dowdy atmosphere.
Amenities include two-line phones with dataport, voice mail and in-room
video checkout. The bedding is adequate, and windows are double-paned. The
Inter-Continental is proud of its international staff, and of Abby Newman, an
award-winning concierge. There are meeting and function rooms and a well-
equipped fitness center.

Rooms: 686 (includes 86 suites); 14 floors; designated nonsmoking rooms.
Hotel amenities: Business services, concierge, fitness equipment, laundry and
dry cleaning, meeting and function rooms, valet parking. **Food services:**
Restaurant, bar, room service. **Cancellation:** 4 P.M. day prior to arrival. **Wheelchair access:** Fully accessible; ADA compliant.

Jolly Madison Towers Hotel   GOOD $$

22 East 38th Street (at Madison Ave.)
Phone: (212) 802-0600   Fax: (212) 447-0747

This hotel's "good" rating is on the borderline of "very good," and may improve
after the ongoing renovations are done. The biggest downside of the hotel is the
size of the rooms—most are fairly small. Even so, the Italian company that owns
it (it's a well-known chain in Europe) has brought in Italian fabrics for the bedspreads, Italian marble for the bathrooms and Italian flair in general. Guests can

control heat and air conditioning in the room. Bedding is very good, there are double-paned windows and fair water pressure. Room service is available for breakfast only. The hotel connects to Cinque Terre, an admirable Italian restaurant. The Jolly Madison Towers also has a concierge, and everyone at the front desk speaks at least two languages, English and Italian.

Rooms: 252 (includes 6 suites); 18 floors; designated nonsmoking rooms. **Hotel amenities:** Concierge, laundry and dry cleaning, valet parking. **Food services:** Restaurant, bar, room service. **Cancellation:** Day prior to arrival. **Wheelchair access:** Fully accessible.

Kimberly Hotel   VERY GOOD $$$

145 East 50th St. (between Lexington and Third Aves.)
www.kimberlyhotel.com
Phone: (212) 755-0400, (800) 683-0400   Fax: (212) 486-6915

The Kimberly was conceived in the mid-1980's as an apartment building but, during construction, was reconceived as a hotel. The practical effect of this is plenty of room for guests. One-bedroom suites run about 600 square feet, two-bedroom suites about 1200 square feet. The style throughout the hotel is consistent—tasteful enough, but standard issue. In addition to plenty of space in each room, suites (which make up most of the rooms) include full kitchens and a pull-out couch in addition to the beds. When you reserve, you can request a firmer or softer mattress. Most rooms have balconies, some with views of the Chrysler Building. Two of the three concierges have the Clefs d'Or designation. Guests get a free pass to any of the New York Health and Racquet Clubs, and 151, a nightclub, is on the hotel premises.

Rooms: 186 (includes 154 suites); 31 floors; designated nonsmoking rooms. **Hotel amenities:** Concierge, laundry and dry cleaning, meeting room, valet parking. **Food services:** Two restaurants, two bars, room service. **Cancellation:** Day prior to arrival. **Wheelchair access:** Fully accessible.

The Kitano New York   EXCELLENT $$$$

66 Park Ave. (at 38th St.)   www.kitano.com
Phone: (212) 885-7000   Fax: (212) 885-7100

In the middle of the Kitano's lobby sits a bronze dog by the sculptor Botero. He seems to be listening to the lobby's classical music, among the rich woods, green suede couches and Japanese flourishes. It's a peaceful tableau and a fitting one, given this Japanese-owned hotel's general feeling of repose. The hotel was built in 1995 and the most notable feature of its modern, understated guest rooms is an absence of noise—though the windows do open, they seem to hermetically seal each room. You're on Park Avenue, a few blocks from Grand Central, but a good night's sleep is practically guaranteed. The beds have duvets instead of blankets and there are plenty of amenities that should keep you relaxed. Many rooms have appealing views, which could be of Grand Central, the Empire State Building or of Park Avenue.

The hotel has a concierge and a restaurant, Nadaman Hakubai, which is an exceptional excursion into haute Japanese cooking. A business center is in the works. Guests receive complimentary passes to a New York Sports Club three blocks away.

Rooms: 150 (includes 18 suites); 18 floors; designated nonsmoking rooms. **Hotel amenities:** Concierge, laundry and dry cleaning, meeting and function rooms, valet parking. **Food services:** Restaurant (Nadaman Hakubai), bar, room service. **Cancellation:** 4 P.M. day prior to arrival. **Wheelchair access:** Fully accessible; ADA compliant.

Loews New York Hotel   GOOD $$$

569 Lexington Ave. (at. East 51st St.)   www.loewshotels.com
Phone: (212) 752-7000, (800) 836-6471   Fax: (212) 752-3817

There are no city buses in this hotel's lobby, but otherwise it does a fair impression of congested Lexington Avenue outside its door. Long check-in lines can form in this hectic space filled with airline flight crews on their way in and out, and people entering and leaving a bar that is so close to the check-in area that it seems the bartender could take your order while you're waiting for your room key. Rooms are small, done in tones of brown, beige and rust. Windows are also small so there isn't a great deal of light. Since some of these windows are single-paned, you are almost certain to get noise from the street. Loews has a full fitness center and a business center, as well as upgraded rooms on their "VIP floors" that include use of a lounge.

Rooms: 722 (includes 38 suites); 20 floors; designated nonsmoking rooms. **Hotel amenities:** Business center, concierge, fitness equipment, laundry and dry cleaning, meeting and function rooms. **Food services:** Restaurant, bar, room service. **Cancellation:** 4 P.M. day of arrival. **Wheelchair access:** Fully accessible.

The Lombardy   EXCELLENT $$$

111 East 56th St. (between Park and Lexington Aves.)
www.lombardyhotel.com
Phone: (212) 753-8600, (800) 223-5254   Fax: (212) 754-5683

William Randolph Hearst built the hotel in 1926, and one has the sense that old West R. would like what he found here, not least the solicitous staff. But the rating here is really a split decision—"excellent" for the one and two bedrooms, "very good" for the rest. The better rooms are beautifully done, but since each of the guest quarters is privately and separately owned decor varies considerably, though the standards throughout are high. The one- and two-bedrooms are beauties, more attractive by far than the singles. The marble bathrooms are pleasant but, as always, not large. Closets, on the other hand, are roomy and have plenty of shelves and hangers. In most cases, there are fully equipped kitchens. The fitness room isn't much—some inexpensive-looking treadmills, bike, stairstepper and free weights. A much more exciting hotel perk is Soma Park restaurant, with chef Gary Robins at the helm. Soma Park provides room service as well.

Rooms: 125 (includes 70 suites); 14 floors; all smoking rooms. **Hotel amenities:** Concierge, fitness equipment, function rooms, laundry and dry cleaning, valet parking. **Food services:** Restaurant (Soma Park), bar, room service. **Cancellation:** 2 P.M. day of arrival. **Wheelchair access:** Fully accessible; ADA compliant.

Lyden House   VERY GOOD $$

320 East 53rd St. (between First and Second Aves.)   www.mesuite.com
Phone: (212) 888-6070, (800) 637-8483   Fax: (212) 935-7690

In the Manhattan East Suite Hotels chain, this is one of the nicest properties. One-bedroom suites are the most common accommodation here, but all come complete with kitchen, two-line phones and dataport and voice mail. Also standard are a clock radio, iron and ironing board, hair dryer and movies on command. There are some distinctive suites here, too—one on the ground floor has a Jacuzzi, a small patio and a circular, glass-enclosed dining room. The four penthouse suites have terraces to enjoy the views of the Empire State Building, the Chrysler Building and a sliver of the East River. There is a laundromat in the basement, particularly helpful for longer stays. The Lyden House has no food and beverage service, but they will do grocery shopping for you to stock up the kitchen.

Rooms: 80 (all suites); 11 floors; designated nonsmoking rooms. **Hotel amenities:** Laundry and dry cleaning. **Food services:** none. **Cancellation:** 3 P.M. day prior to arrival. **Wheelchair access:** Fully accessible; ADA compliant.

Midtown East Courtyard by Marriott   VERY GOOD $$

866 Third Ave. (at 53d St.)
Phone: (212) 644-9600, (800) 321-2211   Fax: (212) 813-1945

This new Courtyard by Marriott midtown offers an alternative to the other midtown Courtyard, located just south of Times Square. The two hotels are roughly comparable, although this location has larger rooms. The lobby, however, looks like the office building it was. Fortunately, the rooms are much better, if you can find yours. The hallways zigzag, and there are few directional signs. The majority of rooms, done in green and purple tones, have ample space (by New York standards) and very large windows. This keeps the slightly sterile accommodations from any kind of gloominess. Since the guest rooms start at the 14th floor, you're likely to get light and a feeling of openness, not to mention, in some cases, a bird's-eye view of the wonderful Lipstick Building, so-called because of its similarity to a lipstick tube. In spite of the large windows and busy Third Avenue, the rooms are quiet, and the ones on the 04 line have wonderful East River views.

Rooms: 306 (includes 8 suites); 18 floors; designated nonsmoking rooms. **Hotel amenities:** Concierge, fitness equipment, laundry and dry cleaning, meeting rooms, valet parking. **Food services:** Restaurant, bar, room service. **Cancellation:** 6 P.M. day of arrival. **Wheelchair access:** Fully accessible; ADA compliant.

Morgans   VERY GOOD $$$

237 Madison Ave. (between 37th and 38th Sts.)
Phone: (212) 686-0300, (800) 334-3408   Fax: (212) 779-8352

When they were installing new televisions in the rooms at Morgans, hotelier Ian
Schrager lay on a guest room bed while his staff adjusted the TV until finally Mr.
Schrager said, "That's the perfect angle." This attention to detail is a primary
reason why Schrager is a successful hotelier. In the case of Morgans, designer
Andrée Putman's stylish rooms don't hurt, either. Rooms aren't spacious, but
everything in them is low—18 inches off the ground. This trick of the eye makes
the rooms feel larger than they are. Fabrics are not typical of other hotel rooms,
and most hotels don't have signed Mapplethorpe prints on the walls, either. The
bathrooms are quite small, but well designed. Amenities are excellent.

Rooms: 113 (includes 27 suites); 15 floors; designated nonsmoking rooms.
Hotel amenities: Business services, valet parking. **Food services:** Restaurant
(Asia de Cuba), bar, room service. **Cancellation:** 3 P.M. day prior to arrival.
Wheelchair access: Rooms not accessible.

New York Helmsley   VERY GOOD $$$$

212 East 42d St. (between Second and Third Aves.)
www.helmsleyhotel.com
Phone: (212) 490-8900   Fax: (212) 490-8909

Wide hallways with mellow lighting lead to the sort of ornate French designs
that Mrs. Helmsley favors, here emphasizing beige and cream colors. Black-and-
white photos of old New York add a bit of atmosphere. The hotel's restaurant is
Mindy's, which provides room service. There are three people on the concierge
staff, one of whom has the Clefs d'Or designation. A tiny business center offers
a full range of services.

Rooms: 788 (including 10 suites); floors 41; designated nonsmoking rooms.
Hotel amenities: Business services, concierge, laundry and dry cleaning, meeting and function rooms, valet parking. **Food services:** Restaurant, bar, room service. **Cancellation:** 4 P.M. day of arrival. **Wheelchair access:** Fully accessible;
ADA compliant.

New York Marriott East Side   VERY GOOD $$$

525 Lexington Ave. (at 49th St.)
Phone: (212) 755-4000, (800) 242-8684   Fax: (212) 980-7625

The guest rooms are distinctive. They tend not to be large, but are snappily
contemporary, with beige and camel colors predominating. The hotel is on the
uncommon "four-pipe system" which means you can have heat or air-conditioning at any time of the year and guests have their own climate control. Water
pressure, though, isn't strong. The Marriott offers a "concierge" level, which
means you get use of a special lounge, upgraded amenities, a room on a higher
floor, continental breakfast and an honor bar. All guests have access to the
hotel's concierge. There is a business center and a fitness center.

Rooms: 643 (includes 5 suites); 33 floors; designated nonsmoking rooms. **Hotel amenities:** Business center, concierge, fitness center, laundry and dry cleaning, meeting and function rooms, valet parking. **Food services:** Restaurant, bar, room service. **Cancellation:** 6 P.M. day of arrival. **Wheelchair access:** Fully accessible; ADA compliant.

The New York Palace Hotel   EXCELLENT $$$$
455 Madison Ave. (between 50th and 51st Sts.)
www.newyorkpalace.com
Phone: (212) 888-7000, (800) 697-2522   Fax: (212) 303-6000

Two hundred and twenty-seven staff members—close to 25 percent of the Palace's employees—have been with the hotel for 15 years or more. That's one of the best indicators of the quality of service in this well-run, near-the-top-of-the-market hotel. Built by the Helmsleys over the beautiful and historic Villard Houses, the Palace is now owned by the Sultan of Brunei, who has done a mostly superior job with renovations that were completed in 1997. The four-star restaurant, Le Cirque 2000, is on the grounds, giving the compound enormous cachet.

There are essentially three levels of service and amenities. There are the standard rooms, nine executive floors geared to the business traveler, and the Towers, virtually a boutique hotel in its own right. The rooms in the Towers are done in either classic or modern design (the modern is really modern Deco), room service is available from Le Cirque, and amenities, such as customized business cards and stationery, are provided for every Towers guest. You don't have to be in the Towers, though, to benefit from spectacular views (if views are important, avoid floors nine through the mid-teens facing east). The Palace has a complimentary, well-outfitted health club where you can gaze at St. Patrick's Cathedral while you're on the Stairmaster.

Rooms: 900 (includes 110 suites); 54 floors; designated nonsmoking rooms. **Hotel amenities:** Concierge, business center, meeting and function rooms, health club, laundry and dry cleaning, valet parking. **Food services:** Restaurant (Le Cirque 2000), two bars, 24-hour room service. **Cancellation:** 2 P.M. day of arrival. **Wheelchair access:** Fully accessible; ADA compliant.

Omni Berkshire Place   EXCELLENT $$$
21 East 52d St. (between Madison and Fifth Aves.)
www.omnihotels.com
Phone: (212) 753-5800, (800) 843-6664 (THE OMNI)
Fax: (212) 754-5020

Omni may not have as high a profile as some hotels in the city, but it does have comfortable, quiet rooms with plenty of amenities. The building was built in 1926 by the well-known architectural firm Warren and Wetmore. More than 70 years, many owners, and a $70 million renovation later, you won't find much of the roaring '20's left. Rooms are done in classic contemporary style with pale yellows and greens. Next to the exceptionally comfortable bedding is a super-phone—besides two lines, dataport and voice mail, it also controls the light, temperature, TV, music and gives you the time around the world. The rooms are reasonably quiet and the marble bathrooms have good water pressure, though, as usual, it's weaker on the upper floors. There is night turndown service and 24-hour room service from the restaurant Kokachin, which serves contemporary continental and American food.

Rooms: 396 (includes 47 suites); 21 floors; designated nonsmoking rooms. **Hotel amenities:** Business center, concierge, fitness center, laundry and dry cleaning, meeting and function rooms, valet parking. **Food services:** Restaurant, bar, 24-hour room service. **Cancellation:** 4 P.M. day prior to arrival. **Wheelchair access:** Fully accessible; ADA compliant.

The Pierre   EXCELLENT $$$$
2 East 61st St. (between Fifth and Madison Aves.) www.fourseasons.com
Phone: (212) 838-8000, (800) 332-3442   Fax: (212) 758-1615

The Pierre not only has elevator operators, but they wear white gloves. The hotel is old-world, well-mannered and enormously appealing. After a night at this hotel, stepping out onto the hurly-burly of New York's streets can be a difficult adjustment. The style of the rooms is traditional—dark woods, chintzes and prints—and everything is done in good taste. Ceilings are high, which means that even the smaller rooms feel airy. The amenities do not include a large number of electronics and gadgets (things like VCRs and fax machines are mostly on request), but you can leave your shoes outside your door for an overnight shine and there are superb mattresses, a tie rack in the closet and even a small humidifier. While the water pressure is good, many of the bathrooms we visited were not especially spacious. The most memorable rooms are the ones with views west over Central Park and north over Manhattan.

This is not a business-oriented hotel, so the business facility is one desk with a computer, but most of the business services you need can be arranged by the concierge staff, several of whom have the Clefs d'Or designation. There is a fitness facility (open to hotel guests only) and you can take tea in the distinctive Rotunda room, with its trompe l'oeil murals by artist Edward Melcarth.

Rooms: 202 (includes 52 suites); 39 floors; designated nonsmoking rooms. **Hotel amenities:** Business services, concierge, fitness equipment, laundry and dry cleaning, meeting and function rooms, valet parking. **Food services:** Two restaurants, bar, 24-hour room service. **Cancellation:** 6 P.M. day of arrival. **Wheelchair access:** Fully accessible; ADA compliant.

Plaza Fifty   VERY GOOD $$$
155 East 50th St. (between Lexington and Third Aves.)
www.mesuite.com
Phone: (212) 751-5710, (800) 637-8483   Fax: (212) 753-1468

The Plaza Fifty is one of ten hotels in the Manhattan East Suite Hotels chain. It isn't a design award-winner, but it is a quality hotel at a fair price. There are twelve deluxe one-bedrooms, and all but one have balconies as well as a more contemporary look, larger size and plenty of light. The Plaza Fifty may not have much of a lobby, but you could always stay here and hang out at the Waldorf.

Rooms: 129 (all suites); 22 floors; designated nonsmoking rooms. **Hotel amenities:** Business services, health club, laundry and dry cleaning, meeting and function rooms, valet parking. **Food services:** Room service. **Cancellation:** 3 P.M. day prior to arrival. **Wheelchair access:** Fully accessible.

Regal United Nations Plaza   EXCELLENT $$$

1 United Nations Plaza at East 44th St. (between First and Second Aves.)
www.regal-hotels.com
Phone: (212) 758-1234, (800) 222-8888   Fax: (212) 702-5051

What is now the Regal U.N. Plaza was built in 1977 to house diplomats. In its current state, the hotel rooms are quite pleasant and comfortable, boasting views of the east side of Manhattan and of Queens.

Rooms are particularly quiet and the bedding is good. One of the most distinctive features of the hotel is its collection of tapestries, batiks, silks and brocades, which adorn hallways and some guest rooms. They are donations of United Nations members (the U.N. is across the street). The beige, handwoven bedspreads from India are a pleasant change from the usual floral prints. Tennis players will love the single court at the top of the building—it feels very secluded up there, a rare commodity in Manhattan. The health club is small but adequate. Its views, though, to the north and east, are dazzling. The heated swimming pool, with views east and south, is equally arresting.

Rooms: 427 (includes 45 suites); 13 floors; designated nonsmoking rooms. **Hotel amenities:** Concierge, health club, indoor tennis court, laundry and dry cleaning, meeting and function rooms, swimming pool, valet parking. **Food services:** Restaurant, bar, 24-hour room service. **Cancellation:** 4 P.M. 2 days prior to arrival. **Wheelchair access:** Fully accessible; ADA compliant.

The Roger Smith Hotel   GOOD $$$

501 Lexington Ave. (between 47th and 48th Sts.) www.rogersmith.com
Phone: (212) 755-1400, (800) 445-0277   Fax: (212) 319-9130

Frumpy, eccentric and hip, pretty much at the same time. The hotel attracts a sizeable number of rock performers and groups (Barenaked Ladies, Jewel, Sheryl Crow) as guests, who take in stride that the rooms have more character than charm. In some rooms the smell test has competing claims from mildew, room deodorant and smoke. Windows are single-paned, and the hotel is on Lexington Avenue, so you're bound to get street noise. There are, however, a fair number of amenities for the price range: voice mail, iron and ironing board, hair dryer, coffee maker, unstocked mini-fridge and continental breakfast.

The hotel is run by artist/sculptor James Knowles, which helps explain the hotel's adjacent art gallery, the art exhibits throughout the property and the col-

orful, abstract murals in the restaurant. They were painted, the hotel says, by
Mr. Knowles in the course of one frenzied day.

Rooms: 136 (includes 26 suites); 16 floors; designated nonsmoking rooms.
Hotel amenities: Business services, laundry and dry cleaning, meeting rooms,
valet parking. **Food services:** Restaurant, bar. **Cancellation:** 4 P.M. day prior to
arrival. **Wheelchair access:** Rooms not accessible.

The Roger Williams   VERY GOOD **$$$**
131 Madison Ave. (at 31st St.)   www.uniquehotels.com
Phone: (212) 448-7000, (888) 448-7788, (877) 847-4444
Fax: (212) 448-7007

A mid-priced hotel that has been enhanced with a lot of style and a fair number
of amenities. The rooms are on the small side, but Rafael Viñoly, the architect,
has wrangled use out of every bit of space. The layout is as interlocking as an
ocean liner cabin. The style is sleek and contemporary but not cold: beige and
taupe colors soothe and there are interesting touches, such as shoji screens, covering some windows, with far more interesting prints on the wall than the usual.
On the penthouse level, rooms have semi-private terraces with memorable
views of midtown.

Room service is provided by the restaurant Mad 28, the hotel serves a complimentary European breakfast and a dessert buffet, and there's a 24-hour coffee
and tea service on the mezzanine.

Rooms: 185 (includes 2 suites); 16 floors; designated nonsmoking rooms. **Hotel
amenities:** Concierge, laundry and dry cleaning, spa services, valet parking.
Food services: Room service. **Cancellation:** Day prior to arrival. **Wheelchair
access:** Fully accessible; ADA compliant.

Roosevelt Hotel   GOOD **$$$**
45 East 45th St. (at. Madison Ave.)   www.theroosevelthotel.com
Phone: (212) 661-9600, (888) 833-3969 (TEDDYNY)
Fax: (212) 885-6168

The Roosevelt is a large hotel near Grand Central Terminal, offering straightforward, reliable lodging, perfectly in keeping with its namesake. After a top-to-
bottom 1997 renovation, it is possible to imagine Teddy Roosevelt striding
through the bustling, old-fashioned lobby, nodding approval and shouting
"Bully!" The traditionally-styled rooms are spotless, if not overflowing with personality. Mattresses are good and windows are double-glazed, though you may
get some traffic noise on the lower floors over Madison Avenue. Closets and
bathrooms can be small, but water pressure and cleanliness are fine. All rooms
have a full run of amenities. Hallways are roomy and pleasant even if the lighting is harsh. The business center and fitness center are both adequate, if small.

Rooms: 1,013 (includes 34 suites); 18 floors; designated nonsmoking rooms.
Hotel amenities: Business center, concierge, fitness equipment, laundry and dry

cleaning, meeting and function rooms, valet parking. **Food services:** Restaurant, bar, room service. **Cancellation:** 4 P.M. day prior to arrival. **Wheelchair access:** Fully accessible; ADA compliant.

The St. Regis EXTRAORDINARY $$$$

2 East 55th St. (between Fifth and Madison Aves.)
www.luxurycollection.com
Phone: (212) 753-4500, (800) 759-7550   Fax: (212) 350-6900

There may be hotels in town with more gadgets and better views, but none match the St. Regis for grace and civility. The industrialist John Jacob Astor commissioned the St. Regis Hotel, purchasing the land in 1891 (the hotel was completed in 1904). A major renovation in 1991 insured thoroughly modern conveniences, but in terms of style, it's old world all the way. After checking in, guests are escorted to their floor, where they are greeted by a butler. If you don't have a butler in your everyday life, you will get used to it easily. The rooms are little laps of luxury: high ceilings, silk wall coverings, perfect beds, 300-thread count Egyptian cotton sheets, a console on the telephone that controls the lights, temperature and television. There's also a portable phone. Most bathrooms have two sinks, bathrobes, a scale, a makeup mirror and a hair dryer. It has a number of other noteworthy features: concierges who have the Clef d'Or designation; a small, comfortable fitness center; the King Cole Bar with its Maxfield Parrish mural, and the St. Regis Rooftop, one of the most sought-after spaces in the city for weddings and other events.

Rooms: 314 (includes 91 suites); 20 floors; designated nonsmoking rooms. **Hotel amenities:** Business center, concierge, health club, laundry and dry cleaning, meeting and function rooms, valet parking. **Food services:** Restaurant (Lespinasse), bar, 24-hour room service. **Cancellation:** 3 P.M. day prior to arrival. **Wheelchair access:** Fully accessible; ADA compliant.

San Carlos Hotel GOOD $$

150 East 50th St. (between Lexington and Third Aves.)
www.sancarloshotel.com
Phone: (212) 755-1800, (800) 722-2012   Fax: (212) 688-9778

The San Carlos hasn't got the latest whiz-bang technology or sleek lines, but it's as appealing as a pair of fluffy slippers on a winter night. Many of the staff have been with the hotel for many years; Gabriel, the front desk manager, has been there for 22 years and he's a favorite of kids, for whom he does magic tricks. Many of the hotel's guests have themselves been coming back to the San Carlos for a long time, attracted by the reasonable prices and the spacious rooms.

The lobby is attractively old-fashioned in a wood-paneled way, consisting of the front desk and a small sitting area. Two vases of fresh flowers cheer up the proceedings. As befits its 1950's aura, many of the hallways and guest-room walls are beige, though some of the recently repainted hallways have made it up to yellow. Accommodations aren't chic, but what you give up in style you gain in space; for the money, it's one of the roomiest hotels in the city. This is one hotel where you will almost certainly have more closet space than you can use.

Rooms: 146 (including 75 suites); 18 floors; designated nonsmoking rooms. **Hotel amenities:** Concierge, laundry and dry cleaning, valet parking. **Food services:** Room service. **Cancellation:** 11 A.M. day prior to arrival. **Wheelchair access:** Not accessible.

Shelburne Murray Hill   VERY GOOD $$$

303 Lexington Ave. (between 37th and 38th Sts.)   www.mesuite.com
Phone: (212) 689-5200, (800) 637-8483   Fax: (212) 779-7068

The Shelburne, now part of the Manhattan East Suite Hotels chain, was built in 1926. The lobby maintains an old-world aura with chandeliers, wallpaper, and oriental rugs. Unlike some of the other Manhattan East hotels, the hallways here are quite pleasant in a traditional hotel way, with the addition of atmospheric black-and-white photos of New York. Guest rooms are traditionally designed with plenty of dark, hardwood furniture. There is a fully stocked kitchen or kitchenette, and housekeeping will do the dishes for you as well as your grocery shopping.

Floors twelve and above are considered "deluxe" suites—which means they are a bit larger, have bathrobes, and night turndown. In addition, rooms on floors 12, 13 and 15 have terraces. One unusual feature of the hotel is the five suites that are accessed only by going outside on the roof. When you're on the roof, you get great views of the Empire State Building, the Chrysler Building and the East River. In the morning, there couldn't be a more delightfully New York place to have your coffee.

Rooms: 270 (all suites); 16 floors; designated nonsmoking rooms. **Hotel amenities:** Fitness room, laundry and dry cleaning, meeting and function room, valet parking. **Food services:** Restaurant, bar, room service. **Cancellation:** 3 P.M. day prior to arrival. **Wheelchair access:** Fully accessible; ADA compliant.

Sheraton Russell Hotel   VERY GOOD $$$$

45 Park Ave. (between 36th and 37th Sts.)   www.sheraton.com
Phone: (212) 685-7676, (800) 325-3535   Fax: (212) 315-4265

This hotel hums: it is pleasant in the extreme and very well run. The lounge in the lobby, which they call the "living room," does look more like a living room than a lounge, with comfortable couches set in a room with bookshelves and a gas fireplace. Two concierges have the Clefs d'Or designation. Upon entering your room, you first hear music coming from a Bose Wave Radio. You find a traditionally designed room in many respects, but the tones are light and the atmosphere inviting. Desk chairs are ergonomically designed swivel chairs and an under-desk pulls out for more workspace. There is also a Hewlett Packard fax/printer/copier in each room.

Rooms: 146 (includes 26 suites); 10 floors; designated nonsmoking rooms. **Hotel amenities:** Concierge, fitness room, laundry and dry cleaning, meeting and function room, valet parking. **Food services:** Restaurant, bar, room service. **Cancellation:** 6 P.M. day prior to arrival. **Wheelchair access:** Fully accessible; ADA compliant.

Swissotel New York—The Drake EXCELLENT $$$

440 Park Ave. (at. 56th St.) www.swissotel.com
Phone: (212) 421-0900, (888) 737-9477 Fax: (312) 565-9930

The room amenities and hotel facilities are certainly impressive. Guests walk into handsome, classic contemporary-styled rooms that are most pleasing to the eye. The furniture is modern and elegant, windows are triple-paned, and they open. There are three phones per room with two lines, dataport and voice mail. A fax/copier/printer, clock radio, coffeepot and coffee, mini-bar and movies on command are all standard. In the closets you'll find wood hangers, an umbrella, bathrobe, iron and ironing board. Room service is 24 hours, and there is night turndown, individual climate control, and a personal wakeup call.

The Drake has three levels of accommodations—superior (standard to you), deluxe, which is larger than a superior, and executive deluxe, which is both larger and has a better location in the building. Many of the Park Avenue Suites have terraces. Other rooms, too, may have terraces but it's the luck of the draw when you check in. The fitness center has not only the requisite aerobics and weight resistance machines, as well as free weights, but a spa center with a variety treatments (facials, hydrotherapy, massage, hand and foot paraffin treatments and aromatherapy.) Steam and sauna use comes with any treatment.

Rooms: 495 (includes 108 suites); 21 floors; designated nonsmoking floors. **Hotel amenities:** Business center, concierge, fitness equipment, laundry and dry cleaning, meeting and function rooms, valet parking. **Food services:** Restaurant (Quantum bar), 24-hour room service. **Cancellation:** 4 P.M. day prior to arrival. **Wheelchair access:** Fully accessible; ADA compliant.

W New York GOOD $$$

541 Lexington Ave. (at. 49th St.) www.whotels.com
Phone: (212) 755-1200, (877) 946-8357 Fax: (212) 644-0951

There is a great deal to like about the exciting W New York but there is one mistake so serious that it is hard to believe. New York, it should not come as news, is a noisy place, and busy Lexington Avenue, which has its share of traffic and frequent sirens, is especially so. Unfortunately, this spa hotel, designed throughout every cubic inch to reflect nature and inspire mind and body relaxation, does not have double-paned windows in every guest room. The guest rooms from the third through twelfth floors do, but the ones from the twelfth through eighteenth floors do not.

Still, designer David Rockwell has had a field day with this property. His nature theme is played out in many ways, including a repeating pressed leaf motif and rooms with a decorative box of grass. The rooms, closets and bathrooms tend to be on the small side; space may be at a premium, but amenities are plentiful. Much attention has been given to the beds, which include feather bedding, 200-thread-count sheets and a down comforter. On the border of the sheets, there are sayings such as "Dance with Abandon" and "Sleep with Angels." A button on the telephone marked "Whatever, whenever" connects you to hotel staffers who provide additional concierge services. The spa called Away offers massage, facials, wraps and other kinds of treatments in addition to a full range of health-club equipment. The restaurant, Heartbeat, has a menu oriented toward fresh and healthy eating.

Rooms: 720 (includes 50 suites); 18 floors; designated nonsmoking floors. **Hotel amenities:** Business services, concierge, health club, laundry and dry cleaning, meeting and function rooms, spa, valet parking. **Food services:** Restaurants (Heartbeat), two bars, 24-hour room service. **Cancellation:** 4 P.M. day of arrival. **Wheelchair access:** Fully accessible; ADA compliant.

W New York, The Court   VERY GOOD $$$

130 East 39th St. (at Lexington Ave.)   www.whotels.com
Phone: (212) 685-1100, (877) 946-8357 (W HOTELS)
Fax: (212) 770-0148

W New York, The Tuscany   VERY GOOD $$$

120 East 39th St. (between Lexington and Park Aves.)
www.whotels.com
Phone: (212) 686-1600, (877) 946-8357 (W HOTELS)
Fax: (212) 779-0148

The modern, understated rooms are mostly black, white, brown and gray, with red accents. The rooms are quiet—the double-paned windows keep most of the city noise out. Bedding is exceptionally comfortable—including quality mattresses, feather bedding, chenille throws. Bathrooms aren't generously spaced as many of the rooms are. On the walls, black framed black-and-white photos of New York. In virtually all of the suites, there is a desk, making it possible and comfortable to do some work in your room. The differences between the Court and the Tuscany are that the Tuscany is smaller, but the rooms are a bit larger, and there is a bit less activity at the Tuscany.

W New York, The Court

Rooms: 199 (includes 49 suites); 16 floors; designated nonsmoking rooms. **Hotel amenities:** Concierge, health club, laundry, meeting and function rooms. **Food services:** Restaurant, bar. **Cancellation:** 4 P.M. day prior to arrival. **Wheelchair access:** Fully accessible; ADA compliant.

W New York, The Tuscany

Rooms: 122 (includes 12 suites); 16 floors; designated nonsmoking floors. **Hotel amenities:** Health club, laundry, spa. **Food services:** None. **Cancellation:** 4 P.M. day prior to arrival. **Wheelchair access:** Fully accessible; ADA compliant.

Cheap

Habitat Hotel   BASIC $

130 East 57th St. (at Lexington Ave.) stayinny.com
Phone: (212) 753-8841, (800) 255-0482   Fax: (212) 829-9605

The Habitat, formerly a women's residence offers the bare necessities at low prices in a swanky neighborhood. Bathrooms are shared. The plain but tidy bedrooms are small, with enough space for a trundle bed.

Price range: Rooms: 207; 17 floors; designated nonsmoking rooms. **Hotel amenities:** Some shared baths. **Food services:** None. **Cancellation:** Day prior to arrival. **Wheelchair access:** Not accessible.

Murray Hill Inn   BASIC $

143 East 30th St. (between Lexington and Third Aves.)

www.murrayhillinn.com

Phone: (212) 683-6900   Fax: (212) 545-0103

While there are some inconveniences here, you won't pay a lot of money for safe and clean, if basic, accommodations. Most of the rooms share bathrooms, in which everything is clean and well kept. Hallways are extremely narrow and it is a walk-up (there are five floors).

Rooms: 50; 5 floors; designated nonsmoking rooms. **Hotel amenities:** None. **Food services:** None. **Cancellation:** 2 days prior to arrival. **Wheelchair access:** Not accessible.
*Note: accepts payment in cash and traveler's check only

Pickwick Arms Hotel   BASIC $

230 East 51st St. (between Second and Third Aves.)
Phone: (212) 355-0300, (800) 742-594   Fax: (212) 755-5029

No one, it's safe to say, is staying at the Pickwick because the rooms are so beautiful. They're tiny and plain as can be. Most of the rooms here are singles; about one-third of the accommodations do not have a private bath. Every room has a sink. There are two terrific dining spots on the ground floor.

Rooms: 330; 13 floors; all smoking rooms. **Hotel amenities:** Some shared baths. **Food services:** Restaurant, bar. **Cancellation:** Day prior to arrival. **Wheelchair access:** Rooms not accessible.

MIDTOWN WEST

The Algonquin   VERY GOOD $$$
59 West 44th St. (between Fifth and Sixth Ave.)
www.camberleyhotels.com
Phone: (212) 840-6800, (800) 555-8000   Fax: (212) 944-1618

A stay at this hotel feels like a cultural immersion. The Algonquin is closely identified with the regular gathering of 1920's literary luminaries known as the Round
Table, and as the setting for the birth of *The New Yorker* magazine. It's also where
Lerner and Lowe wrote *My Fair Lady*, and it continues to book top singing talent in
the Oak Room cabaret. It is, not surprisingly, an official New York City landmark.

Today, the hotel is looking refreshed from a 1998 overhaul. The lobby is inviting, and the guest floor hallways have new wallpaper composed of *New Yorker* car-
toons. The hotel cat, (there have been a number of them) is always named Hamlet,
except when it's named Matilda. Guest rooms are small and all traditionally furnished. The rooms with window seats set into bay windows are especially charming.
Since space is at a premium, many rooms forgo mini-bars, fax machines and VCRs.
The hotel does have some themed suites focused around Algonquin legends.

Rooms: 165 (includes 23 suites); 12 floors; designated nonsmoking floors.
Hotel amenities: Business center, health club, laundry and dry cleaning, meeting and function rooms, valet parking. **Food services:** Two restaurants, bar,
room service. **Cancellation:** Day prior to arrival, September-December 3 days
prior to arrival. **Wheelchair access:** Fully accessible; ADA compliant.

Ameritania   GOOD $$
230 West 54th St. (at Broadway)   www.nycityhotels.net
Phone: (212) 247-5000, (800) 922-0330   Fax: (212) 247-3316

This hotel offers reasonably priced lodging with some flair. The newly redeco-
rated rooms feature bold, checkerboard-pattern carpets and solid armoires.
There aren't many amenities, but mattresses are good, hangers are real wood
and windows are double-glazed. Given the location in the busy theater district,
however, ask for a room on a higher floor if you're sensitive to noise. Room
1105 is a two-bedroom suite with a Jacuzzi. It typically goes for $350 and is a
nice way for four adults to have a little bit of style and a good soak.

Rooms: 207 (includes 13 suites); 12 floors; designated nonsmoking rooms. **Hotel
amenities:** Laundry and dry cleaning. **Food services:** Restaurant, bar, room service. **Cancellation:** 3 P.M. day prior to arrival. **Wheelchair access:** Not accessible.

Best Western Manhattan   GOOD $$
17 West 32d St. (between Fifth Ave. and Broadway)
www.applecorehotels.com
Phone: (212) 736-1600, (800) 567-7720   Fax: (212) 790-2760

For many years this was a down-on-its-luck lodging with a Beaux Arts façade.
But it has a new lease on life as part of the Best Western chain. The lobby is dis-

tinctive: black and white with contemporary, clean lines. The rooms, though, are far more predictable: traditional decor without much finesse. There's a "concierge," but she also runs the gift shop, and a business center. Rooms are generally adequate, certainly for the price range, which means things are clean and in good working order. Drawbacks: limited drawer and closet space, and small bathrooms with few amenities. On the plus side there are a fair number of extras, especially for a budget-conscious hotel. The Sky Bar is an open-air rooftop bar that operates during the warmer months under the looming Empire State Building.

Rooms: 176 (includes 35 suites); 13 floors; designated nonsmoking rooms. **Food services:** Restaurant, bars, room service. **Hotel amenities:** Business center, fitness equipment, laundry and dry cleaning, valet parking. **Cancellation:** 3 P.M. day prior to arrival. **Wheelchair access:** Fully accessible.

Carnegie Hotel   GOOD $$$

229 West 58th St. (between Broadway and Seventh Ave.)
www.newyorkhotel.com
Phone: (212) 245-4000, (888) 468-3558 (HOTEL 58)
Fax: (212) 245-6199

If the Carnegie keeps the prices low and you keep your expectations low too, all should be well. For about $200 a night, visitors to the city get a reasonably comfortable, if not especially charming, hotel near Central Park and many prime tourist spots. The pattern-on-pattern lobby has large, low candles on the tables in the seating areas. Befitting the name, classical music is playing. The semblance of atmosphere created in the lobby is dispensed with in the guest rooms. The usual dark furniture prevails, along with green carpet and pink and green bedspreads. Some rooms have an armoire instead of a closet; there are three clothes drawers and each room has a kitchen

Rooms: 20 (all suites); 5 floors; all smoking rooms. **Hotel amenities:** None. **Food services:** None. **Cancellation:** 5 P.M. day prior to arrival. **Wheelchair access:** Rooms not accessible.

Central Park Inter-Continental New York

EXCELLENT $$$$

112 Central Park South (between Sixth and Seventh Aves.)
www.new-york.interconti.com
Phone: (212) 757-1900, (800) 327-0200   Fax: (212) 757-9620

This hotel has changed owners almost as frequently as bed linen. Since none of the owners could improve the views over Central Park, they have instead insured that everything within the place is gleaming. The elegant old-world atmosphere will come closer to most guests' image of a New York hotel than many of the newer kids on this and other blocks. This impression continues through the hallways and into the tastefully appointed rooms. Rooms with a view are the jewels (some even have terraces), but view or not, there's plenty of creature comfort. Room service is available 24 hours, night turndown is standard and the hotel's fitness room has views of the park.

Rooms: 208 (includes 16 suites); 25 floors; designated nonsmoking floors.
Hotel amenities: Business center, concierge, fitness equipment, laundry and dry cleaning, meeting and function rooms, valet parking. **Food services:** Restaurant, bar, 24-hour room service. **Cancellation:** 4 P.M. day prior to arrival.
Wheelchair access: Fully accessible; ADA compliant.

Crowne Plaza Manhattan   VERY GOOD $$$
1605 Broadway (between 48th and 49th Sts.)   www.crowneplaza.com
Phone: (212) 977-4000, (800) 243-6969 (NYNY)
Fax: (212) 315-6164

The Crowne Plaza is quite a pleasant hotel as things stand, although they have begun a multimillion-dollar renovation featuring an Adam Tihany design. Mr. Tihany is best known for his work on the restaurants Le Cirque 2000 and Jean Georges, and he will likely add a more dramatic luster to this mainstream-style hotel. Some of the more winning assets will remain the same. The views, for example, start in the hallways, where single, square windows are cut out at various points, giving guests a connection to the city below. There are no hotel rooms below the 16th floor, and the panoramas from many guest rooms are energizing.

Each room has a generous number of amenities. "Club" level rooms are not significantly different from other rooms in the hotel but guests in these rooms get private check-in and the use of a special lounge on the 46th floor for $30 more per night. The hotel also has an excellent, 29,000-square-foot New York Sports Club that boasts a 50-foot swimming pool.

Rooms: 770 (includes 19 suites); 46 floors; designated nonsmoking rooms.
Hotel amenities: Business center, concierge, health club, laundry and dry cleaning, meeting and function rooms, swimming pool, valet parking. **Food services:** Three restaurants, two bars, 24-hour room service. **Cancellation:** 6 P.M. day of arrival. **Wheelchair access:** Fully accessible; ADA compliant.

Doubletree Guest Suites   VERY GOOD $$$
1568 Broadway (at 47th St.)   www.nyc.doubltreehotels.com
Phone: (212) 719-1600, (800) 325-9033   Fax: (212) 403-6340

Doubletree's location and amenities make it a good choice for families, people on business and theater lovers alike. Everyone should be comfortable in the attractive, contemporary suites. The ceilings are low but you don't feel cramped. There are armoires in lieu of closets and a separate chest of drawers. The rooms are remarkably quiet, given the location, and there is 23-hour room service. Theater-lovers will appreciate the concierge in the lobby to help with tickets, as well as the million-dollar views of Times Square. There are 28 rooms that look out over 1 Times Square, where the New Year's ball drops. Business people will appreciate the meeting rooms and the "conference suite" guest rooms. Each of these contains a conference table that can seat up to eight instead of a more traditional sitting area. Families will like the attention paid to kids. The hotel offers them a welcome pack and a "club"—it's a room (unsupervised) with Nintendo, stuffed animals, toys and books. Parents will appreciate that children 17 and under are free. It's one more surprising touch in a hotel that has many of them.

Rooms: 460 (all suites); 44 floors; designated nonsmoking rooms. **Hotel amenities:** Business center, concierge, health club, laundry and dry cleaning, meeting and function rooms, valet parking. **Food services:** Restaurant, bar, room service. **Cancellation:** 6 P.M. day of arrival. **Wheelchair access:** Fully accessible; ADA compliant.

Essex House, A Westin Hotel   EXCELLENT $$$$
160 Central Park South (between Sixth and Seventh Aves.)
www.essexhouse.com
Phone: (212) 247-0300, (800) 937-8461 (WESTIN1)
Fax: (212) 484-4602

The Essex House, over 60 years old, got a makeover in 1990 and now reflects a glamorous, romanticized version of the city's past. The gorgeous Art Deco lobby is instantly transporting to a time when the hotel hosted celebrity-filled parties, Hollywood premieres and big bands broadcasting over the radio. Rooms from the eighth floor and up on the front side of the hotel get views of Central Park. It's hard to say exactly what style of room you will get because the Essex House has 28 different types, but you can expect traditional design, high-quality mattresses and decent-sized bathrooms. However, you may also get some street noise and a room of modest if not downright small proportions. There are four concierges employed by the hotel, three of whom have the designation Clefs d'Or. The hotel has a pleasant and well-equipped business center, a fitness center that features ten or so machines along with a sauna, tanning bed and spa services. You can get a massage, facial and many other treatments.

Rooms: 597 (includes 79 suites); 39 floors; designated nonsmoking floors. **Hotel amenities:** business center, concierge, health center, laundry and dry cleaning, meeting and function rooms, valet parking. **Food services:** Restaurant, bar, 24-hour room service. **Cancellation:** 3 P.M. day prior to arrival. **Wheelchair access:** Fully accessible; ADA compliant.
*Note: pets permitted with advance approval

Flatotel   VERY GOOD $$$$
135 West 52d St. (between Sixth and Seventh Aves.)
www.flathotel-intl.com
Phone: (212) 887-9400, (800) 352-8683 (FLATOTE)   Fax: (212) 887-9838
Flatotel started out as a condo development but became a hotel in 1994 when not enough units were sold. That explains why its rooms are so big and why each one comes with a fully equipped kitchen. The smallest rooms are 750 square feet with more closet space than you might find in an entire brownstone. Bathrooms are roomy. "Executive Level" rooms also come with VCR, CD player and bathrobe. This spot give you an awful lot—especially space.

Rooms: 169 (all suites); 46 floors; designated nonsmoking rooms. **Hotel amenities:** Business center, 24-hour fitness center, valet parking. **Food services:** None. **Cancellation:** 6 P.M. day prior to arrival. **Wheelchair access:** Fully accessible.

Helmsley Park Lane   VERY GOOD $$$$

36 Central Park South (between Fifth and Sixth Aves.)
www.helmsleyhotels.com
Phone: (212) 371-4000, (800) 221-4982   Fax: (212) 682-6299

Nothing about the Helmsley Park Lane is as memorable as its park views, but everything about the hotel seems to run smoothly. The hallways have low ceilings but are brightly lit and have a cheerful enough aspect. Rooms have the old French style you expect, are good-sized and have two or three closets per room. There is 24-hour room service. You should be able to get a good night's sleep here—beds are firm and the rooms are quiet. The hotel has a concierge staff, two of whom have the Clefs d'Or designation. There is a small business center with computers, a color copier, Internet access, and cell phone rental. On the second floor, Harry's Bar leads into the dining room called Room with a View, featuring double-height windows overlooking Central Park.

Rooms: 630 (includes 39 suites); 46 floors; designated nonsmoking rooms. **Hotel amenities:** Business center, fitness center, laundry and dry cleaning, meeting and function rooms, valet parking. **Food services:** Restaurant, bar, room service. **Cancellation:** 4 P.M. day of arrival. **Wheelchair access:** Fully accessible.

Hotel Casablanca   VERY GOOD $$$

147 West 43rd St. (between Broadway and Sixth Ave.)
www.casablancahotel.com
Phone: (212) 869-1212, (888) 922-7225   Fax: (212) 391-7585

This Moroccan-spiced hotel avoids the kitsch pitfall—the theme is done with a light hand. You may not expect to find such a welcoming, charming, peaceful spot in the eye of the Times Square storm. The rooms are more comfortable and solid than luxurious. There is not extensive closet space and bathtubs are undersized. What distinguishes the hotel are the thoughtful touches—and there are many of them—and the service. In the rooms, you'll find bathrobes, complimentary bottled water, Ghirardelli chocolate and a bottle of wine. Over 150 movies are available at no charge for your VCR. Design flourishes include modern Murano glass sconces and framed Berber pillowcases in the hallways. On the second floor there is an extremely inviting lounge with books, newspapers, coffee, leather chairs and laptops with free Internet access. Classical music plays softly in the background. In warm weather months, the lounge opens out onto a small outdoor space where you can have breakfast. You also won't encounter many warmer hotel staffs.

Rooms: 48 (includes 5 suites); 6 floors; designated nonsmoking floors. **Hotel amenities:** Business services, laundry and dry cleaning, meeting and function rooms. **Food services:** Restaurant, bar, room service. **Cancellation:** 3 P.M. day prior to arrival. **Wheelchair access:** Fully accessible; ADA compliant.

Hotel Metro   GOOD $$
45 West 35th St. (between Fifth and Sixth Aves.)
www.hotelmetronyc.com
Phone: (212) 947-2500, (800) 356-3870   Fax: (212) 279-1310

The Metro has a bright and jaunty Art Deco ambience. The lobby lounge is especially comfortable and roomy for a small hotel. The back room, called the library, could give you the illusion of having your own living room in the city. Guest rooms all have the same Deco design, and up on the roof there is a public area where you can relax and soak in the Empire State Building, which looms dramatically. The hotel makes especially good sense for people in the fashion and garment industries—this isn't a high luxe property, but coming back here after a long day would be cheering: the Metro is spotless, peaceful, and well designed.

Rooms: 175 (includes 21 suites); 14 floors; designated nonsmoking rooms. **Hotel amenities:** Business services, health club, laundry and dry cleaning, meeting room. **Food services:** Restaurant, bar, room service. **Cancellation:** 4 P.M. 1 day prior to arrival. **Wheelchair access:** Rooms not accessible.

The Iroquois New York   VERY GOOD $$$
49 West 44th St. (between Fifth and Sixth Aves.)   www.iroquoisny.com
Phone: (212) 840-3080, (800) 332-7220   Fax: (212) 398-1754

The Iroquois—right next door to the Algonquin—was built in 1923, and, except for the fact that James Dean lived here from 1951 to 1953, it faded into the landscape without much notice. A young new owner had other ideas, remodeling it from top to bottom. Guest rooms, while not large, have been redone attractively in traditional style with light olive-green tones and a fair number of amenities. They include a bathroom phone, a clock radio with a CD player, a VCR (the hotel has a complimentary video library) and Frette linens. Suites have whirlpool tubs.

Rooms: 114 (includes 9 suites); 12 floors; designated nonsmoking floors. **Hotel amenities:** Business center, concierge, laundry and dry cleaning, meeting and function rooms, valet parking. **Food services:** Restaurant, bar, 24-hour room service. **Cancellation:** 6 P.M. day prior to arrival. **Wheelchair access:** Fully accessible; ADA compliant.

The Mansfield   GOOD $$$
12 West 44th St. (between Fifth and Sixth Aves.)
www.uniquehotels.com
Phone: (212) 944-6050, (877) 847-4444   Fax: (212) 764-4477

Even if the rooms are small, the Mansfield exemplifies how distinctive a small hotel can be. Located just east of the theater district, you can get great style at relatively affordable rates. The original terrazzo floors and mahogany balustrades in the hallways are the link to old New York. Once you're in one of the small rooms the look is mostly modern, although the walls have appealing framed prints with a nostalgic cast. Each room has a sleigh bed with a black mesh headboard, Belgian bed linen, VCR, CD player, (there's a free video and CD library in the lobby) and a copy of *Time Out*. There is a complimentary continental breakfast.

Rooms: 124 (includes 20 suites); floors 12; designated nonsmoking floors. **Hotel amenities:** Business services, concierge, laundry and dry cleaning, meeting and function rooms, parking. **Food services:** Bar, room service. **Cancellation:** Day prior to arrival. **Wheelchair access:** Fully accessible; ADA compliant.

Mayfair New York   GOOD $$
242 West 49th St. (between Eighth Ave. and Broadway)
www.mayfairnewyork.com
Phone: (212) 586-0300, (800) 556-2932   Fax: (212) 307-5226

The Mayfair is one of the nicest budget hotels in the theater district. Rooms here are small, but stylish. Continuing a theme from the lobby, the rooms have black-and-white historic photos of New York and other subjects. The hotel has focused on the basics. The bedding is exceptionally comfortable, with good mattresses and Irish linen. Note that all rooms are one-bedded king or queen, and all are nonsmoking. Deluxe rooms, which don't cost much more than standard rooms, are somewhat larger, have marble baths and glassed-in showers. There is a complimentary continental buffet breakfast served in the hotel's restaurant—The Garrick, an inexpensive favorite of *New York Times* critic Eric Asimov.

Rooms: 77; 7 floors; all rooms are nonsmoking. **Hotel amenities:** Laundry and dry cleaning. **Food services:** Restaurant. **Cancellation:** 3 P.M. day prior to arrival. **Wheelchair access:** Fully accessible.

The Michelangelo   VERY GOOD $$$$
152 West 51st St. (at Seventh Ave.)   www.michelangelohotel.com
Phone: (212) 765-1900, (800)237-0990   Fax: (212) 541-6604

The Michelangelo may not live up to its namesake in terms of beauty, but the hotel makes up for it by being surprisingly peaceful given its high-traffic location. There are four styles of rooms—contemporary, neo-Classic, Art Deco and French country—with French country the most popular. Nice touches include a dressing area in "Executive" rooms, large bathtubs, a mini-TV in every bathroom and Frette terrycloth bathrobes. The fitness room is fairly basic, but for $15 guests can use the excellent Equitable Fitness Center around the corner. On the downside, you do get some street noise in the rooms, and ceilings can be low.

Rooms: 178 (includes 52 suites); 7 floors; designated nonsmoking floors. **Hotel amenities:** Concierge, fitness room, laundry and dry cleaning, meeting and

function rooms, valet parking. **Food services:** Two restaurants, bar, 24-hour
room service. **Cancellation:** 6 P.M. day prior to arrival. **Wheelchair access:**
Fully accessible; ADA compliant.

Millennium Broadway   VERY GOOD $$$
145 West 44th St. (between Broadway and Sixth Ave.)
www.millbdwy.com
Phone: (212) 768-4400, (800) 622-5569   Fax: (212) 789-7688

Millennium Premier   VERY GOOD $$$$
133 West 44th St. (between Broadway and Sixth Ave.)
www.millbdwy.com
Phone: (212) 768-4400, (800) 622-5569   Fax: (212) 789-7688

The Millennium is built for business, but suitable for any visitor wanting a sleek
hotel in the theater district. There are three levels of accommodations here.
The basic Millennium hotel rooms are contemporary in design and many have
views to the south and the west. The fundamentals are good: mattresses, double-glazed windows, water pressure and room amenities. Guests on the ten
"Club" floors have use of an appealing lounge with sweeping views west over
midtown. There are some additional amenities to the Club rooms, including a
fax machine and complimentary bottled water. These rooms run $50 over the
standard rate. For $100 more than the standard rate, you can stay at The Pre-
mier, an annex to the Millennium, which opened in November, 1998. There is
no lobby here to speak of, which give a more residential, if somewhat sterile,
feel. The rooms here are, in most ways, handsome and inviting. White sycamore
veneer predominates, making the rooms feel cool and light. The Premier is not
as tall as the Millennium, so the views are not as good, and some of the closets
are simply too small. The Millennium has 33 meeting rooms spread out over
several floors, and they are well equipped and good-looking. For visitors on business, the Millennium offers a flexible range of options for meetings. For everybody else, it's an attractive place to stay.

Millennium Broadway
Rooms: 627 (includes 10 suites); 52 floors; designated nonsmoking floors.
Hotel amenities: Business center, concierge, health club, laundry and dry clean-
ing, meeting and function rooms, valet parking. **Food services:** Restaurant, bar,
24-hour room service. **Cancellation:** 4 P.M. day of arrival. **Wheelchair access:**
Fully accessible; ADA compliant.

Millennium Premier
Rooms: 125; 21 floors; designated nonsmoking floors. **Hotel amenities:** Business center, concierge, health club, laundry and dry cleaning, meeting rooms,
valet parking. **Food services:** 24-hour room service. **Cancellation:** 6 P.M. day
prior to arrival. **Wheelchair access:** Fully accessible; ADA compliant.

New York Hilton and Towers   GOOD $$$

1335 Sixth Ave. (between 53d and 54th Sts.)

www.newyorktowers.hilton.com

Phone: (212) 586-7000, (800) 445-8667 (HILTONS)

Fax: (570) 450-1590

The largest hotel in New York is a virtual city, with huge amounts of traffic in the lobby, guests from all over the planet, a staff that speaks 30 languages and a 24-hour foreign currency exchange office. Visitors come for the Hilton name, which guarantees a certain level of quality. Rooms are small, as are bathrooms. The design isn't at all distinguished, but most of the things Hilton guests want are here.

The Towers section of the hotel is a slightly upscale hotel-within-a-hotel. These rooms have a more handsome, contemporary style and a few (but only a few) more amenities. You also get the Tower Lounge, with complimentary breakfast, tea, nice views of midtown and a place to work or meet with people. The Towers have their own manager, staff and private check-in on the 39th floor. The hotel's hallways are incredibly long—*amazingly* long—and it can be a hike from your room to the nearest elevator. The hotel plays host to countless conferences, meetings, charity events and weddings in a number of function rooms, including the largest grand ballroom in New York.

Rooms: 2,041 (includes 95 suites); 46 floors; designated nonsmoking rooms. **Hotel amenities:** Business center, concierge, health club, laundry and dry cleaning, meeting and function rooms, valet parking. **Food Services:** Three restaurants, Two bars, room service. **Cancellation:** 2 days prior to arrival. **Wheelchair access:** Fully accessible; ADA compliant.

New York Marriott Marquis   VERY GOOD $$$

1535 Broadway (between 45th and 46th Sts.)   www.marriot.com

Phone: (212) 398-1900, (800) 843-4898   Fax: (212) 704-8966

When construction on this hotel began in the 1980's, even the thought of a renaissance in Times Square seemed fantastical. The hotel put eight floors between the pavement and its lobby (which may have helped improve security) and did everything else it could to make you forget you were in Times Square. The look is somewhere between a convention hall and a parking garage.

Still the Marriott Marquis is a reliable place to stay. The reasonably-sized rooms are completely tolerable, done in greens and rusts with cherry wood accents, and include a rolling desk with wheels and useful workspace. Although the ceilings are low, you get a sense of space in those rooms with views over Broadway or the Hudson River. You get a lot of extras, including a small business center and a basic fitness room as well as a number of bars and restaurants. The Encore is the busiest restaurant in Marriott's chain worldwide; there is Katen, a sushi bar with a chef formerly of the three-star Nobu, and the revolving restaurant called The View on the 47th through 49th floors.

Rooms: 1,919 (includes 57 suites); 35 floors; designated nonsmoking floors.
Hotel amenities: Business center, concierge, health club, laundry and dry clean-
ing, meeting and function rooms, valet parking. **Food services:** Three restau-
rants, two bars, 24-hour room service. **Cancellation:** 6 P.M. day of arrival.
Wheelchair access: Fully accessible; ADA compliant.
*Note: small pets permitted with advance approval.

Novotel New York   GOOD $$$

226 West 52d St. (between Broadway and Eighth Ave.) www.accor.com
Phone: (212) 315-0100, (800) 221-3185   Fax: (212) 765-5365

The Novotel is acceptable lodging in the theater district, though not an especially good value in high season. The hallways are carpeted in bright orange and
blue with pale orange walls; they are jaunty enough that guest rooms are a bit of
a letdown. The rooms have low ceilings and are furnished in a simple, contemporary design with orange and blue (and some beige thrown in), but the furniture, bedspreads and curtains look like they're from the bargain basement.
Guests may get a good view from their room of the Hudson River or down
Broadway to Times Square, but this is a theater district hotel without any of the
Great White Way's razzle-dazzle.

Rooms: 479; 33 floors; designated nonsmoking floors. **Hotel amenities:**
Concierge, fitness equipment, laundry and dry cleaning, meeting and function
rooms. **Food services:** Restaurant, bar, room service. **Cancellation:** 4 P.M. day
prior to arrival. **Wheelchair access:** Fully accessible; ADA compliant.

Paramount   GOOD $$$

235 West 46th St. (between Broadway and Eighth Ave.)
Phone: (212) 764-5500, (800) 225-7474   Fax: (212) 575-4892

Style over square footage—that's what this Ian Schrager-owned and Philippe
Starck-designed hotel offers, and there are plenty of takers. Much of the appeal
of the Paramount is outside of the rooms: a newly redone lobby that's still great
for people-watching; the Whiskey Bar; the newer, loungey Library Bar off the
second floor balcony; the Italian restaurant Coco Pazzo Teatro, and a Dean and
Deluca gourmet snack shop. The fitness room has also had a makeover and
there is a small, whimsical playroom for young children, created by the designer
of the television show *Peewee's Playhouse*. The hallways leading to guest rooms
are narrow but Zen-like, thanks to pale walls, chocolate brown carpet and soft,
low-wattage lighting. Your blood pressure will stay low if you know what to
expect, which means very small, very white rooms.

Rooms: 602 (includes 12 suites); 19 floors; designated nonsmoking floors.
Hotel amenities: Business services, concierge, fitness equipment, laundry and
dry cleaning, meeting room. **Food services:** Two restaurants, two bars, 24-hour
room service. **Cancellation:** 4 P.M. day of arrival. **Wheelchair access:** Fully
accessible.

The Park Central Hotel   VERY GOOD $$$
870 Seventh Ave. (between 55th and 56th Sts.)
Phone: (212) 247-8000, (800) 346-1359   Fax: (212) 707-4500

A $60 million overhaul by Image Design of Atlanta has put the spring back in this hotel's step. An attractive palette of browns, blacks and golds gives the rooms a handsome look. The Executive Club level rooms on the upper floors, more than one fourth of the hotel, costs $25 over the regular rate. These include additional amenities; a fax machine, desk and ergonomic chair and mini-bar, as well as access to the Executive Club lounge. In that lounge, complimentary continental buffet breakfast is available as are evening hors d'oeuvres. An especially attractive feature of the lounge is its three terraces—so you can grab some coffee, walk outside and soak in the city.

Rooms: 935 (includes 21 suites); 25 floors; designated nonsmoking floors.
Hotel amenities: Fitness equipment, laundry and dry cleaning, meeting rooms, valet parking. **Food services:** Restaurant, bar, room service. **Cancellation:** 4 P.M. day of arrival. **Wheelchair access:** Fully accessible; ADA compliant.

Le Parker Meridien   EXCELLENT $$$$
118 West 57th St. (between Sixth and Seventh Aves.)
www.parkermeridien.com
Phone: (212) 245-5000, (800) 543-4300   Fax: 212 708–7471

Le Parker Meridien is emerging from a slump and has an unmistakable new energy and look. Guests have use of the first-class, 15,000-square-foot health club, which includes two racquetball courts, a squash court and a spa. Up at the top of the building, there is a glass-enclosed swimming pool, an outdoor jogging track and a sundeck. Le Parker Meridien has a basic business center (one IBM computer, one Mac, a printer and fax) as well as a concierge staff. One of the concierges holds the Clefs d'Or designation. The look of guest rooms is classic contemporary, making elegant use of ivory, beige and black. Most suites have kitchens or kitchenettes. Rooms with a north view look toward Central Park.

Rooms: 700 (includes 100 suites); 42 floors; designated nonsmoking floors.
Hotel amenities: Business center, concierge, health club, laundry and dry cleaning, meeting and function rooms, swimming pool, valet parking. **Food services:** Two restaurants, bar, 24-hour room service. **Cancellation:** 4 P.M. day of arrival. **Wheelchair access:** Fully accessible; ADA compliant.

The Peninsula New York   EXCELLENT $$$$
700 Fifth Ave. (at 55th St.)   www.peninsula.com
Phone: (212) 956-2888, (800) 262-9467   Fax: (212) 903-3943

A $45 million renovation has turned the Peninsula into one of the city's top hotels. Not a great deal of the money spent refurbishing the Peninsula was earmarked for the lobby, but the guest rooms have had a total structural and cosmetic makeover. They are exquisitely done in a classic contemporary style. Every possible high- and low-tech amenity seems to have been included. There are mini-bars and TVs built in behind doors, along with a bedside electronics console that controls the lights, room temperature and does everything but tuck you in. There are flowers in every room, Art Nouveau wooden headboards and attractive paintings and prints on the walls.

The hotel's spa is a big asset, offering a full range of services, a complete health club and a swimming pool with lovely views.

Rooms: 241 (includes 55 suites); 23 floors; designated nonsmoking rooms. **Hotel amenities:** Business center, concierge, health club, laundry and dry cleaning, meeting and function rooms, swimming pool, valet parking. **Food services:** Two restaurants, two bars, room service. **Cancellation:** 6 P.M. day prior to arrival, 2–3 days during peak seasons. **Wheelchair access:** Fully accessible; ADA compliant.
*Note: small pets permitted with advance approval

The Plaza   VERY GOOD $$$
Fifth Ave. (at Central Park South and 59th St.)   www.fairmont.com
Phone: (212) 759-3000, (800) 759-3000   Fax: (212) 546-5324

If ever a hotel has earned the right to be called a landmark, it is The Plaza. At the 1907 French Renaissance building, designed by famed architect Henry J. Hardenbergh, people from all worlds have crossed paths. The first guest book was signed by Alfred G. Vanderbilt, Mark Twain and "Diamond" Jim Brady, and it has been ever thus at The Plaza. Kings and movie stars have been frequent guests, and the hotel itself has starred in many movies. The 19-story building was declared a New York City landmark in 1969 and a National Historic Landmark in 1986. The Palm Court, where brunch and afternoon tea are served, the Oak Bar, various movie and television crews, and 805 guest rooms keep The Plaza on its toes. The guest rooms got a $60 million sprucing up in 1998 and look good, though there is a wide variety of rooms here both in terms of size and design. Inevitably, some are better than others. The design reflects an amalgam of periods, emphasizing its Edwardian heritage. Some rooms get a view as well—especially coveted are the ones facing north over Central Park. The Plaza has a wealth of services, including 24-hour room service, a concierge staff that includes a member with the Clefs d'Or designation, and a business center with computers, copiers and fax machines. A small fitness room would suffice for the basics, but guests have use of the nearby NY Health and Racquet Club for $25 a day. As in hotels of old, there are many shops on site.

You may be familiar with The Plaza from movies where it is featured, such as *Plaza Suite, North by Northwest, Funny Girl and Crocodile Dundee*. All this fame has its down side—The Plaza can be unpleasantly overcrowded, and so many people can cause service to be uneven. So, too, the rooms, which run rather too large a gamut.

Rooms: 805 (includes 96 suites); 18 floors; designated nonsmoking rooms. **Hotel amenities:** Business services, concierge, fitness equipment, laundry and dry cleaning, meeting and function rooms, valet parking. **Food services:** Three restaurants, bar, 24-hour room service. **Cancellation:** 4 P.M. day prior to arrival. **Wheelchair access:** Fully accessible; ADA compliant

Renaissance New York Hotel   VERY GOOD $$$$
714 Seventh Ave. (between 47th and 48th Sts.)
www.renaissancehotels.com
Phone: (212) 765-7676, (800) 468-3571 (HOTELS1)
Fax: (212) 261-5167

The lobby proper of this trapezoidal-shaped hotel, straddling the break between Broadway and 7th Avenue in the theater district, is on the third floor. This separation makes the hotel feel disconnected from the city, but it also enhances security. In the lobby is the Clefs d'Or concierge Christine Spencer, who was voted (along with a concierge from the Waldorf) Chief Concierge of the Year for New York. The classic contemporary-styled rooms feature wonderful beds, double-paned windows and a host of amenities. The biggest drawback is the low ceilings. There is no business center, but the hotel does offer a few business services. The restaurant, Foley's Fish House, is glass-enclosed and perched over 47th Street facing south to Times Square. In 1998, Marriott took over the management of the hotel, but you won't find their name embossed on much of anything here. The Renaissance impresses quietly.

Rooms: 305 (includes 10 suites); 26 floors; designated nonsmoking rooms. **Hotel amenities:** Business services, fitness center, laundry and dry cleaning, meeting rooms, valet parking. **Food services:** Restaurant, two bars, 24-hour room service. **Cancellation:** 4 P.M. day prior to arrival. **Wheelchair access:** Fully accessible.

RIHGA Royal   EXCELLENT $$$$
151 West 54th St. (between Sixth and Seventh Aves.)   www.rihga.com
Phone: (212) 307-5000, (800) 937-5454   Fax: (212) 765-6530

The RIHGA Royal caters to plenty of celebrities, tycoons, and movers and shakers who need comfort, luxury, privacy and security. Each of the 500 rooms is a suite, done in classic contemporary style; the most demanding should be at least content with the amenities of the standard accommodations, delighted with their "Pinnacle," top-of-the-line suites. It's the Pinnacle Suites that are the hotel's pride. These are on the hotel's highest floors (better views) and include a full range of business accessories and services. Some suites have small kitchenettes, and the top suites also have sauna and whirlpool. The 24-hour, guests-only fitness center has men's and women's saunas and an instructor during peak hours. The 24-hour business center has Internet access, fax, copier, typing and other services. Two of the five concierges at the hotel have the Clefs d'Or designation. Guests concerned about security should note that the RIHGA has a small lobby, which helps keep an eye on who's coming and going.

Rooms: 500 (all suites); 54 floors; designated nonsmoking rooms. **Hotel amenities:** Business center, concierge, health club, laundry and dry cleaning, meeting and function rooms. **Food services:** Restaurant, bar, 24-hour room service. **Cancellation:** 3 P.M. day prior to arrival. **Wheelchair access:** Fully accessible.; ADA compliant

Royalton
EXCELLENT **$$$$**

44 West 44th St. (between Fifth and Sixth Aves.)
Phone: (212) 869-4400, (800) 635-9013   Fax: (212) 869-8965

The Royalton is the city's most strikingly designed hotel and, not incidentally, the sexiest. The sensual aesthetic permeates every aspect of this Ian Schrager-owned, Philippe Starck-designed hotel. Look at the long runner carpet in the lobby, somewhere between azure and sapphire blue, the bow-legged tables and the white, slip-covered chairs, the tusk-like sconces, the deftly flattering lighting. In the guest-room hallways, it is always midnight. Behind the closed doors, ultra-modern guest rooms are not spatially endowed, but compensate in a number of ways. The most noticeable is that the furniture is low to the ground. Grays and whites predominate with contrast from dark wood; the effect is cool and unclut-tered. The beds and the bedding are exceptionally comfortable, closets adequate, and room amenities include an iron and ironing board, two-line phones, a VCR and a flower. Many rooms have an "under desk" on which you can eat or work. Forty suites have working fireplaces. Guests have use of a small fitness room, a concierge, the restaurant 44 and the hidden Round Bar just to the right after you enter the hotel. Guests may have to share space with New Yorkers; this is one of the few lobbies where natives like to spend time.

Rooms: 169 (includes 24 suites); 12 floors; designated nonsmoking rooms.
Hotel amenities: Business services, concierge, fitness equipment, valet parking.
Food services: Restaurant, bar, room service. **Cancellation:** 3 P.M. day prior to arrival. **Wheelchair access:** Not accessible.

Salisbury Hotel
GOOD **$$**

123 West 57th St. (between Sixth and Seventh Aves.)
www.nycsalisbury.com
Phone: (212) 246-1300, (888) 692-5757   Fax: (212) 977-7752

The 57th Street location of the Salisbury, the large rooms and the moderate rates make it an attractive hotel on many counts. Bright hallways lead to guest rooms with steel-blue doors and traditional American design, with olive green carpets, dark woods and floral print bedspreads. Phones in standard rooms have not been brought up to millennial standards—there is voice mail but only one line and no dataport. Most rooms have a small pantry area with an unstocked mini-fridge, microwave, coffeepot and coffee. Closet space is generous. About 40 percent of the Salisbury is made up of suites. These have large desks, data-port, and two-line phones. Sofabeds are in each suite as well, and bathrooms in this category of room are larger. The hotel doesn't have a fitness room, but guests can work out for $10 a day at the nearby NY Health and Racquet Club or NY Sports Club. There is a concierge desk.

Rooms: 196 (includes 80 suites); 17 floors; designated nonsmoking rooms.
Hotel amenities: Business services, concierge, laundry and dry cleaning. **Food services:** None. **Cancellation:** 6 P.M. day prior to arrival. **Wheelchair access:** Fully accessible.

Sheraton Manhattan   VERY GOOD $$
790 Seventh Ave. (at West 51st St.)   www.sheraton.com
Phone: (212) 581-3300, (800) 325-3535   Fax: (212) 315-4265

Sheraton New York Hotel and Towers VERY GOOD $$$
811 Seventh Ave. (between West 52d and 53d Sts.)
www.sheratonnyc.com
Phone: (212) 581-1000, (800) 325-3535   Fax: (212) 841-6491

The Sheraton Manhattan and the Sheraton New York are located catty-corner across the street from each other. Even so, it makes sense to think of them as one mega property. The Sheraton Manhattan is big, the New York bigger. Rooms, however, are tight squeezes. The look is standard—mostly light goldish walls, browns, greens and rusts—earth tones, attractive even if ceilings are low. The Manhattan has standard and club levels. The New York has three level of rooms: standard, club and towers. Room size and decor remain essentially the same. Club-level rooms, located on higher floors, are more oriented to the business traveler. Additional amenities include a fax/printer/copier (this actually crowds the room somewhat), two-line phones, bathroom scale, Bose radio and separate check-in. This takes place in the club lounge, which boasts views over Times Square, the Hudson and north to Central Park. Complimentary continental breakfast is served here as well as hors d'oeuvres in the evening. Club guests also have access to their own business center, a small room with two PCs, printer and typewriter. At this level, there is no charge for access to the health club. These rooms cost $25–$35 above standard rack. The tower-level is available only at the New York property. It has its own check-in, a more elegant and smaller version of the club lounge on a still higher floor. Rooms include all of the concierge-level amenities, plus more luxurious bedding, slippers and chocolate with the automatic night turndown. You can have breakfast in either of the lounges, in your room or in any of the hotel's restaurants. They'll do a complimentary press of two clothing items and shoeshine. Service is emphasized on the tower-level, and rates are $20–$45 above the club-level average.

The pleasant, 24-hour health club is available at no charge to concierge- and tower-level guests, at a fee to guests in standard rooms. There is a full range of equipment, steam and sauna, and personal trainers are available. At the Manhattan, there is a pleasant pool with a sundeck. The general business center is full service: copying, faxing, secretarial services, overhead transparencies, cell phone rental and customized name tags and business cards. The meeting facility at the New York, located below ground, is as handsome as they come, with state-of-the-art meeting rooms.

Sheraton Manhattan
Rooms: 650 (includes 8 suites); 22 floors; designated nonsmoking floors. **Hotel amenities:** Business services, concierge, fitness equipment, laundry and dry cleaning, parking, swimming pool. **Food services:** Restaurant, bar, 24-hour room service. **Cancellation:** 4 P.M. day of arrival. **Wheelchair access:** Fully accessible; ADA compliant.

Sheraton New York Hotel and Towers

Rooms: 1,750 (includes 51 suites); 50 floors; designated nonsmoking rooms.
Hotel amenities: Business center, concierge, health club, laundry and dry cleaning, meeting and function rooms, parking. **Food services:** Two restaurants, two
bars, 24-hour room service. **Cancellation:** 4 P.M. day of arrival. **Wheelchair
access:** Fully accessible; ADA compliant.

The Shoreham   VERY GOOD $$$

33 West 55th St. (between Fifth and Sixth Aves.)
www.uniquehotels.com
Phone: (212) 247-6700, (800) 553-3347, (877) 847-4444
Fax: (212) 765-9741

Media and fashion people are particularly attracted to The Shoreham, and it's
easy to see why. It is good-looking and has most of what you need for a pleasant
night's sleep in Manhattan. The style is contemporary—modern torch sconces
in the hallways, lots of taupe, grays and beige in the rooms, velveteen sofabeds,
steel headboards, not much on the walls. The closets are lined with cedar, and
the bed linens are Belgian cotton. The only serious drawbacks are bathrooms
that are small and have sluggish water pressure, and some rooms that have far
more atmosphere than actual light. A real plus is room-service dinner, provided
by the adjacent, three-star restaurant La Caravelle, one of the city's top French
restaurants.

Rooms: 176 (**CHK**) (includes 34 suites); 11 floors; designated nonsmoking
floors. **Hotel amenities:** Business services, laundry and dry cleaning, valet parking. **Food services:** Restaurant, bar, room service (**CHK**). **Cancellation:** Day
prior to arrival. **Wheelchair access:** Fully accessible; ADA compliant.

Southgate Tower   GOOD $$$

371 Seventh Ave. (at 31st St.)   www.mesuite.com
Phone: (212) 563-1800, (800) 637-8483 (MESUITE)
Fax: (212) 643-8028

The Southgate, one of the ten in the Manhattan East Suite Hotels chain, was
renovated in 1999. For those seeking lodging near Penn Station or Madison
Square Garden, the renovated rooms make this an especially good choice. The
lobby area has been extensively redone, and you are likely to experience a pleasant surprise when you come off the street into the attractive lobby. There are six
passenger elevators so you aren't likely to wait for a ride. Guest room hallways
are wide, if not exactly cheery. Rooms are pleasing in a quiet way, with red
drapes and olive carpets and they have individually controlled AC and heat.
Each room has a fully functional kitchen. One other note: The building was
built in 1929, and there are wonderful period details—be sure to note the lobby
ceiling, the elevator doors and the beautiful old clock.

Rooms: 523 (all suites); floors 28; designated nonsmoking floors. **Hotel amenities:** Business services, concierge, fitness equipment, laundry and dry cleaning,

meeting and function rooms, valet parking. **Food services:** Two restaurants, bar, room service. **Cancellation:** 3 P.M. day of arrival. **Wheelchair access:** Fully accessible; ADA compliant.

The Time   VERY GOOD $$$

224 West 49th St. (between Broadway and Eighth Ave.)
www.thetimeny.com
Phone: (212) 246-5252, (877) 846-3692 (TIMENYC)
Fax: (212) 245-2305

At The Time, you take a glass elevator to the second floor, where the check-in desks have laptops, not big, unaesthetic computer monitors. That sort of attention to detail is evident throughout. Nothing about the Time is plush—it is all clean lines and stripped down. Most of the colors are black, beige and gray, accented by primary colors. But the hotel has laid the amenities on thick. Each guest room has three phones (two-line, dataport and voice mail), a desk, fax, TV Internet browser and Bose radio. VCR and mobile phones are available on request. The suites have Jacuzzis. The hotel has focused on fundamentals such as plumbing, so the water pressure is good, as are mattresses. While the windows are double-paned, they don't fully eliminate noise from the street. Closets are something of a drawback, small and sometimes simply an area separated by a drape. There is night turndown. The Time has a concierge and an exercise room. It also has the highly-rated restaurant Palladin, run by Jean-Louis Palladin, a well-known chef.

Rooms: 193 (includes 30 suites); 16 floors; designated nonsmoking rooms. **Hotel amenities:** Concierge, exercise room, meeting rooms, valet parking. **Food services:** Restaurant, two bars, room service. **Cancellation:** 4 P.M. day prior to arrival. **Wheelchair access:** Fully accessible; ADA compliant.

The Warwick   VERY GOOD $$$

65 West 54th St. (at Sixth Ave.)   www.warwickhotels.com
Phone: (212) 247-2700, (800) 223-4099   Fax: (212) 713-1751

The formerly dowdy and inexpensive Warwick has gone all fussy, with renovated rooms, marble and palms in the lobby (though the chandeliers are unsparkly, a nod to the Warwick of old). That said, there's no denying that this hotel has good bones. It was built in 1927 by William Randolph Hearst for his mistress Marion Davies, which may account for the liberally-sized rooms. There are marble bathrooms with slightly under-pressured water, windows are double-glazed and some rooms have fax machines. The decor is traditional, and the roomy, old-style hallways give the impression of an intimate hotel. Some suites and regular rooms have balconies, though the hotel management doesn't advertise it.

Rooms: 422 (includes 70 suites); 33 floors; designated nonsmoking rooms. **Hotel amenities:** Business services, laundry and dry cleaning, meeting and function rooms. **Food services:** Restaurant, bar, room service. **Cancellation:** 4 P.M. day of arrival. **Wheelchair access:** Fully accessible.

Wyndham
VERY GOOD **$$**

42 West 58th St. (between Fifth and Sixth Aves.)
Phone: (212) 753-3500, (800) 257-1111   Fax: (212) 754-5638

A stay at the Wyndham is like submitting to the charms and ministrations of a beloved, if slightly dotty, aunt. The rooms are oversized and underpriced, which means they are a favorite of, among others, theater and film people in town for a Broadway run or a film shoot. A bit over $200 gets you a suite with enough room to rehearse your lines, reasonably good bedding, double-paned windows and a small pantry with a fridge and sink. The rooms have a feminine touch, with pink or soft blue carpets and many floral motifs. Most hotels have far more amenities, but many people can't help loving the Wyndham. Guests who demand standardization won't like it—all the rooms are different, and the place is full of quirks. Most hotels in the city with comparable room sizes, though, would be charging twice the rates.

Rooms: 212 (includes 60 suites); 17 floors; all smoking rooms. **Hotel amenities:** Laundry and dry cleaning. **Food services:** None. **Cancellation:** 2 days prior to arrival. **Wheelchair access:** Fully accessible; ADA compliant.

Cheap

Broadway Inn
GOOD **$**

264 West 46th St. (between Broadway and Eighth Ave.)
www.broadwayinn.com
Phone: (212) 997-9200, (800) 826-6300   Fax: (212) 768-2807

The stocked bookshelves in the lobby, newspapers and magazines strewn around, geraniums in the windowsill and classical music in the background create a casual, peaceful and homey impression. The rooms are far from the most glamorous in the city, but they're impeccably clean and the prices are certainly fair, given the location.

Rooms: 41 (includes 12 suites); 3 floors; designated nonsmoking rooms. **Hotel amenities:** None. **Food services:** None. **Cancellation:** 3 P.M. day prior to arrival. **Wheelchair access:** Not accessible.

Herald Square Hotel
BASIC **$**

19 West 31st St. (between Fifth Ave. and Broadway)
www.heraldsquarehotel.com
Phone: (212) 279-4017, (800) 727-1888   Fax: (212) 643-9208

This hotel has been regularly cited in guidebooks as one of Manhattan's better value hotels. The plain, clean rooms are in fairly good shape but are fairly low on amenities. It's an option for budget-minded travelers for whom price is of far more interest than charm.

Rooms: 120; 9 floors; all smoking rooms. **Room amenities:** AC. **Hotel amenities:** Some shared baths. **Food services:** None. **Cancellation:** Day prior to arrival. **Wheelchair access:** Fully accessible.

Hotel Edison   BASIC $

228 West 47th St. (between Broadway and Eighth Ave.)
www.edisonhotelnyc.com
Phone: (212) 840-5000, (800) 637-7070   Fax: (212) 596-6850

The Edison, located in the heart of the theater district since it opened in 1931,
has been through good times and bum times. The popular Cafe Edison is a de
facto canteen for people in the theater, and it's a good place to eavesdrop on
showbiz gossip. The Supper Club is also located here, a popular nightclub that
books many types of musical artists. Given what's happened to the neighborhood, the Edison is a hotel that has seen better days but one that could yet stage
its own revival.

Rooms: 900 (includes 30 suites); 22 floors; designated nonsmoking rooms.
Hotel amenities: Laundry and dry cleaning, parking. **Food services:** Two
restaurants, bar. **Cancellation:** 2 P.M. day prior to arrival. **Wheelchair access:**
Fully accessible.

UPTOWN HOTELS

Barbizon   VERY GOOD $$$

140 East 63d St. (at Lexington Ave.)
Phone: (212) 838-5700, (800) 223-1020   Fax: (212) 223-3287

The Barbizon opened in 1927 as a hotel for women. With the Barbizon's purchase by hotelier Ian Schrager and the presence of the stylish gym Equinox on
the ground floor, the Barbizon seems to have relinquished its past for a leap into
the future. Its location, at the southern end of the Upper East Side, remains a
prime asset. There is a substantial "but." Over one-third of the hotel has rooms
that are 10 feet by 12 feet. A queen-sized bed, which most of these rooms have,
means you have just enough room to sleep but no room to gather your thoughts.
Among the amenities is a CD player—if you haven't brought any, housekeeping
will bring one to your room. Bathrooms are slightly larger than average in town,
but they're still likely to seem small to visitors. Guests get complimentary use of
the Equinox health club on the ground floor. This large, full-service club has
everything you could want in the way of machines as well as a pool, Jacuzzi,
steam, sauna and spa.

The top-of-the-line tower suites are worth a special note. Located from the
18th to the 22nd floors, the Moorish influence of the hotel's design is in evidence, particularly the arched forms of the terraces. The penthouse suite is also
a knockout. In it, there is a loft area library and writing desk. From that desk,
you can look out the large windows and get a view of Central Park.

Rooms: 306 (includes 27 suites); 22 floors; designated nonsmoking rooms.
Hotel amenities: Concierge, laundry and dry cleaning, valet parking. **Food ser-
vices:** Room service. **Cancellation:** 4 P.M. day of arrival. **Wheelchair access:**
Fully accessible; ADA compliant.

The Bentley
VERY GOOD **$$$**

500 East 62d St. (at York Ave.) www.nychotel.com

Phone: (212) 644-6000, (800) 664-6835 (66HOTEL)

Fax: (212) 751-7868

The Bentley, in an unlikely location for a hotel, looks like an office building; in fact, it was once the NAACP headquarters. Once you're inside, though, the Bentley reveals itself to be a very pleasant surprise. The lobby is strikingly stylish and the rooms are clean and comfortable, if somewhat spare-looking, including amenities such as Nintendo and a phone in the bathroom. Given the hotel's offbeat location, it has some unusual city views. There are invigorating views facing west to the East Side, and an up-close look at the 59th Street Bridge. The Bentley offers a complimentary continental breakfast in its rooftop restaurant.

Rooms: 197 (includes 21 suites); 21 floors; designated nonsmoking rooms. **Hotel amenities:** Laundry and dry cleaning, meeting and function room, parking. **Food services:** Restaurant, bar, room service. **Cancellation:** 3 P.M. day prior to arrival. **Wheelchair access:** Not accessible.

The Carlyle
EXTRAORDINARY **$$$$**

35 East 76th St. (at Madison Ave.)

Phone: (212) 744-1600, (800) 227-5737   Fax: (212) 717-4682

The Carlyle is discreet and glamorous. About half of the Carlyle is comprised of permanent residents and that is reflected in its distinctly un-public, subdued lobby with its soft light and an unmistakable aura of glamour. The Carlyle is about continuity. Fifty years ago you would have seen the delightful bell captain, Michael O'Connell, and the same was true at a recent visit. It is also about discretion, and it is that discretion which draws the moneyed, the power brokers and the well-known. Understated, traditional elegance and little frippery gives the rooms a timeless feel. You'll find chintz coverlets and satin-covered chairs; most have wooden floors with a large area rug, imparting a character that wall-to-wall does not. There is a full roster of standard amenities, plus many that you won't find other places: several types of hangers (skirts, pants), a tie rack and bed tray. Many prefer the rooms on the higher floors, in the tower. They're not large, but the light and the views, particularly those overlooking Central Park, are enthralling. The fully-equipped gym, open only to hotel guests, is especially attractive. For the more sedentary, Bobby Short and Barbara Cook perform regularly in Cafe Carlyle while Barbara Carroll entertains in Bemelman's Bar with its famously charming murals.

Rooms: 190 (including 52 suites); 34 floors; all smoking rooms. **Hotel amenities:** Business services, concierge, health club, laundry and dry cleaning, meeting and function rooms, valet parking. **Food services:** Two restaurants, two bars, 24-hour room service. **Cancellation:** 6 P.M. day prior to arrival. **Wheelchair access:** Fully accessible.

Empire   GOOD **$$**

44 West 63d (between Broadway and Columbus Ave.)
www.empirehotel.com
Phone: (212) 265-7400, (888) 822-3555   Fax: (212) 245-3382

You would never know the Empire, a former Radisson, is owned by high-style
hotelier Ian Schrager. Situated across from Lincoln Center, this hotel is still
Radisson through and through, with pink-striped hallways, apron-plaid curtains
and furniture with no sharp edges. The standard rooms are quite small, suitable
for one person or two people who are very well acquainted, but with plenty of
amenities. The bathrooms can also require some shuffling—doors open
inward—but once in the shower, you'll appreciate the strong water pressure.
The rooms facing Lincoln Center have the most interesting views. On the second floor of the hotel is the West 63d St. Steakhouse, which also has some
prime seats facing Lincoln Center. Iridium, the popular jazz club and bar, is just
outside the hotel's front door.

Rooms: 381 (includes 28 suites); 11 floors; designated nonsmoking rooms.
Hotel amenities: Laundry and dry cleaning, meeting rooms, concierge, valet
parking. **Food services:** Restaurant, bar, room service. **Cancellation:** September-December, 14 days prior to arrival; January-August, 3 P.M. day prior to
arrival. **Wheelchair access:** Fully accessible; ADA compliant.

Excelsior Hotel   GOOD **$$**

45 West 81st St. (between Columbus Ave. and Central Park West)
www.excelsiorhotel.com
Phone: (212) 362-9200, (800) 368-4575   Fax: (212) 580-3872

Located across the street from the American Museum of Natural History and
just a 10-minute walk from Lincoln Center, the Excelsior has grown in popularity over the past few years. A total renovation has helped to upgrade its image
as well as its prices, but it's still a bargain compared to midtown. The new second floor dining room provides a quiet setting for breakfast before you have to
set off on a day of hectic activity.

Rooms: 197 (includes 80 suites); 16 floors; designated nonsmoking rooms. **Hotel
amenities:** Concierge, laundry and dry cleaning. **Food services:** None. **Cancellation:** 4 P.M. day prior to arrival. **Wheelchair access:** Rooms not accessible.

The Franklin   GOOD **$$**

164 East 87th St. (between Lexington and Third Aves.)
www.uniquehotels.com
Phone: (212) 369-1000, (877) 847-4444   Fax: (212) 369-8000

The look is modern: blacks, whites, beiges, with white swag canopies and bright
white sheets with no bedspread. If you like that look, it's inviting. But everything is mini here. Mini-rooms, mini-bathrooms, mini closets. The in-room safe
is mini—too small for a laptop. Standard rooms have full-size beds and a sink in
the room instead of in the bathroom. These rooms face the back. Superior

rooms have queen-size beds, are somewhat more spacious, and face the front. The "one" line of superior rooms are especially popular—the closets are cedar, they're the largest in the hotel and the room configuration may also be the most comfortable. Amenities include a CD player and a VCR (there's a complimentary CD and video library downstairs), but there are no restaurants or concierge services.

Rooms: 53; 9 floors; designated nonsmoking floors. **Hotel amenities:** Dry cleaning, valet parking. **Food services:** None. **Cancellation:** Day prior to arrival. **Wheelchair access:** Not accessible.

Hotel Beacon   GOOD $$
2130 Broadway (between 74th and 75th Sts.)   www.beaconhotel.com
Phone: (212) 787-1100, (800) 572-4969   Fax: (212) 787-8119

The focus at the Beacon isn't on hotel amenities or service but rather on room size and value—on those counts, it scores well. The Beacon was built in 1929 as an apartment hotel and for many years was primarily residential. Since 1990 it has moved toward becoming a full-fledged hotel. In addition to a lot of space, most of the traditionally designed rooms have two comfortable, full-size beds and fold-out couches. All rooms have a small kitchen that includes a mini-fridge, range top, coffee maker, a few pots and pans, dishes and silverware. Fairway and Citarella, two excellent markets, are across the street. On the down side, some bathrooms are so small you almost have to side step in and even though the windows are double-glazed, the noise from Broadway is still noticeable.

Rooms: 230 (includes 105 suites); 25 floors; designated nonsmoking rooms. **Hotel amenities:** Concierge, laundry and dry cleaning. **Food services:** Restaurant. **Cancellation:** 6 P.M. day of arrival. **Wheelchair access:** Fully accessible; ADA compliant.

Hotel Wales   VERY GOOD $$
1295 Madison Ave. (between 92d and 93d Sts.) www.uniquehotels.com
Phone: (212) 876-6000, (877) 847-4444   Fax: (212) 860-7000

Carnegie Hill is a civilized neighborhood and this is a civilized hotel. The design mixes contemporary lines and colors with warm details such as wood door moldings. Guest rooms aren't large, but they're outfitted with ample amenities. Breakfast, at which a harpist plays, is included in the rate. It consists of muffins, rolls, cereal, and hard-boiled eggs. Guests can work off the muffins in the fitness room, where there are a couple of treadmills, a bike and free weights. Room service is available from Sarabeth's—a popular restaurant best known for its brunch.

Rooms: 87 (includes 40 suites); 10 floors; designated nonsmoking floor. **Hotel amenities:** Laundry and dry cleaning, valet parking. **Food services:** Restaurant (Sarabeth's). **Cancellation:** Day prior to arrival. **Wheelchair access:** Not accessible.

The Lowell   EXCELLENT $$$$

28 East 63d St. (between Madison and Park Aves.)
www.preferredhotels.com
Phone: (212) 838-1400, (800) 221-4444   Fax: (212) 605-6808

The Lowell is among the very best "boutique" hotels in New York. Small, quiet, private, elegant, and service-oriented, it feels like a hideaway even though it's well located at the midtown end of the Upper East Side. The front desk is right by the elevators, which helps insure privacy and security, and warmth is the order of the day from the staff. Staying at the Lowell in a standard room would be very nice. Staying in one of the suites would be a joy. There are 46 of them and 33 have wood-burning fireplaces (wood is included); all the suites have small kitchens. The Lowell Suites, chintzed to the max, are just right for honeymoons and special occasions (they're also used for interviews by Barbara Walters and Dateline NBC). The Gym Suite came about because Madonna was staying for a longer period at the hotel, ordered gym equipment and it stayed. It's the only hotel room in town with a ballet barre. The Hollywood Suite has a 41-inch TV, a stack of videos of Hollywood classics and movie paraphernalia. The Garden Suite, with two terraces, is an absolute delight. The hotel has a snappy fitness room and the Pembroke Room is lovely for breakfast or tea; the Post House, a steak house, does room service.

Rooms: 67 (includes 46 suites); 17 floors; designated nonsmoking rooms. **Hotel amenities:** Concierge, fitness center, laundry and dry cleaning, meeting and function rooms, valet parking. **Food services:** Restaurant (Post House), two bars, room service. **Cancellation:** 2 days prior to arrival. **Wheelchair access:** Fully accessible.

The Mark   EXCELLENT $$$$

25 East 77th St. (at Madison Ave.)   www.themarkhotel.com
Phone: (212) 744-4300, (800) 843-6275 (THE MARK)
Fax: (212) 472-5714

At this exceptional hotel, the doormen are white-gloved. The lobby is bright with an old-fashioned front desk—trim, elegant, understated. The head concierge holds the Clefs d'Or designation. Guest rooms are a comfortable mix of traditional and contemporary design. The king-size beds, with a phone on each side, are luxurious—Frette bed linens on top of cushiony mattresses. Kitchens or kitchenettes are in three-quarters of the guest rooms and those that do not have either have a mini-bar. Bathrooms at the Mark tend to be larger than in other New York hotels. Most have separate tub and shower. Cell phones are available at no charge, and the hotel offers a shuttle to Wall Street and the theater district at certain hours.

Rooms: 180 (includes 60 suites); 15 floors; designated nonsmoking floors. **Hotel amenities:** Complimentary shuttles, concierge, fitness equipment, laundry and dry cleaning, meeting and function rooms, valet parking. **Food services:** Restaurant, bar, 24-hour room service. **Cancellation:** 4 P.M. day of arrival. **Wheelchair access:** Fully accessible; ADA compliant.

The Mayflower Hotel on the Park GOOD $$
15 Central Park West (between 61st and 62d Sts.)
www.mayflowerhotel.com
Phone: (212) 265-0060, (800) 223-4164   Fax: (212) 265-0227

A Central Park view is one of the compelling reasons to stay at the Mayflower. The thrill of the park's beauty and the satisfaction of a bargain could be considered a quintessential New York moment. The hotel has a lived-in feel to it, rooms with room to breathe, large closets and not-overcrowded bathrooms. While most have pantries and mini-fridges, no cooking is allowed. Amenities are limited. The fitness room has a few machines—treadmill, bike, Stairmaster—but no multifunction machine or free weights. The Mayflower hasn't been cutting edge in over 70 years—but it's got that front row seat on the park that has a timeless appeal.

Rooms: 365 (includes 180 suites); 17 floors; designated nonsmoking rooms. **Hotel amenities:** Fitness equipment, laundry and dry cleaning, meeting and function rooms, valet parking. **Food services:** Restaurant, bar, room service. **Cancellation:** 4 P.M. day of arrival. **Wheelchair access:** Rooms not accessible.

On The Ave VERY GOOD $$
2178 Broadway (at 77th St.)   www.stayinny.com
Phone: (212) 362-1100   Fax: (212) 787-9521

What was once an extremely unattractive hotel is now the most stylish place to stay in the area. Rooms come in three sizes: standard, then the larger superior, then deluxe. For $175, even a standard feels roomy. One of the more distinctive features is the "floating bed" intended to "create a clean, almost a Zen, environment," according to the designer. The earth tones are even extended to the ecru-colored sheets. You know when a hotel is paying this much attention to the beds that they're on the right track. The bathrooms are marble with slate floors and custom-designed stainless sinks. Some of them have a window from which you have Upper West Side views. Not all have tub and shower—some are shower only, so specify if you have a preference.

Rooms: 250 (includes 15 suites); 15 floors; designated nonsmoking floors. **Hotel amenities:** Laundry and dry cleaning. **Food services:** 24-hour room service. **Cancellation:** 4 P.M. day prior to arrival. **Wheelchair access:** Fully accessible.

Plaza Athénée VERY GOOD $$$$
37 East 64th St. (between Park and Madison Aves.)
www.plaza-athenee.com
Phone: (212) 734-9100, (800) 447-8800   Fax: (212) 772-0958

The decor is French, all right, but there is no longer any connection between this hotel and the Paris hotel of the same name. The Plaza Athénée is regularly cited in magazine articles and travel books as a top New York hotel, but it has some formidable competition at this price level. Windows are not double-paned, and you may find flaccid mattresses, small, dark rooms, low ceilings and tiny bathtubs. Some rooms have considerably more charm than others, certainly, and there is a fair roster of room amenities. The larger rooms and suites are richly and attractively furnished, but the fitness room has fewer than a dozen machines and there is no business center.

Rooms: 152 (includes 36 suites); 17 floors; designated nonsmoking floors. **Hotel amenities:** Business services, concierge, fitness equipment, laundry and dry cleaning, meeting and function rooms, valet parking. **Food services:** Restaurant, bar, 24-hour room service. **Cancellation:** 1–3 days prior to arrival depending on season. **Wheelchair access:** Fully accessible; ADA compliant.

The Regency, A Loews Hotel   EXCELLENT $$$$
540 Park Ave. (at East 61st St.)   www.loewshotels.com
Phone: (212) 759-4100, (800) 233-2356   Fax: (212) 688-2898

The Regency has new polish, grace and flair following a major renovation. Connie Beale was the designer, and she has done fine work enriching the rooms with silks, velvets, leather and mahogany. The newly redone lobby and the lovely hallways, too, now live up to the Park Avenue address. It is all seductively plush. The guest rooms have a strong lineup of amenities. Bathrooms, though well-equipped, are something of a drawback—many of them are quite small. The hotel has a well-outfitted fitness center that includes a full range of equipment. The hotel has concierge services, and overnight shoeshine, and guests can observe one of the city's most serious "power breakfasts" in the hotel's restaurant.

Rooms: 351 (includes 86 suites); 21 floors; designated nonsmoking floors. **Hotel amenities:** Fitness center, concierge, laundry and dry cleaning, business center, meeting and function rooms, valet parking. **Food services:** Restaurant, bar, 24-hour room service. **Cancellation:** Day prior to arrival. **Wheelchair access:** Fully accessible; ADA compliant.

The Sherry-Netherland   EXCELLENT $$$$
781 Fifth Ave. (between 59th and 60th Sts.) www.sherrynetherland.com
Phone: (212) 355-2800, (800) 247-4377   Fax: (212) 319-4306

The Sherry has successfully created a world of its own, with comfortable but understated rooms and allusions to grandeur. The Sherry has never been a part of any chain, and its distinctiveness shows. Guest rooms vary considerably in decor, but all are traditional, and you won't feel the walls are closing in on you. There is a copy of every Academy Award-winning movie downstairs as well as a stock of *New York Times* bestsellers. The staff-to-guest ratio is 2:1. The Sherry is also permanent home to many New Yorkers and they obviously prefer a quiet lobby over an array of amenities. There is a fitness room with a multifunction machine, bike, stairstepper, treadmill and a few free weights. Breakfast and room service are provided by Cipriani's restaurant. The Sherry has great views over Central Park (and also of the Plaza).

Rooms: 150 (including 75 suites); 37 floors; designated nonsmoking rooms.

Hotel amenities: Fitness equipment, laundry and dry cleaning, meeting and function room, valet parking. **Food services:** Restaurant, bar, 24-hour room service. **Cancellation:** 3 P.M. day prior to arrival. **Wheelchair access:** Fully accessible; ADA compliant.

The Stanhope   EXCELLENT $$$$

995 Fifth Ave. (at 81st St.)   www.thestanhope.com
Phone: (212) 288-5800, (800) 828-1123   Fax: (212) 650-4705

Guests of the Stanhope have the Metropolitan Museum of Art across the street, the Frick, the Guggenheim, and the Whitney in easy walking distance, as well as the elegant charms of the Upper East Side at hand. That might be enough reason to stay at the Stanhope, but the hotel offers many additional incentives. Primary among these might be privacy and security. Another attraction is the room design, done in peach and gold French Empire, accented with Chinoiserie. The list of room amenities is impressive, and bathrooms can be small but are well-stocked. Many rooms get a lot of light. The oatmeal cookie the hotel gives you at night turndown should help get you off to sleep. Hotel amenities include a concierge staff, one of whom has the Clefs d'Or designation. There is a workout room with aerobics machines, free weights and a sauna. Guests can enjoy the restaurant Mayrose. There is a nice little bar just off the lobby but, when weather permits, most guests sit at the outdoor cafe called The Terrace. It is a quintessential New York view.

Rooms: 187 (includes 61 suites); 16 floors; designated nonsmoking floors.
Hotel amenities: Business services, concierge, fitness equipment, laundry and dry cleaning, meeting and function rooms, valet parking. **Food services:** Restaurant (Mayrose), bar, room service. **Cancellation:** 6 P.M. day prior to arrival. **Wheelchair access:** Fully accessible; ADA compliant.
*Note: small pets allowed with advance approval.

Surrey Hotel   VERY GOOD $$$$

20 East 76th St. (between Fifth and Madison Aves.)   www.mesuite.com
Phone: (212) 288-3700, (800) 637-8483   Fax: (212) 465-3697

Room service from Daniel Boulud's three-star Café Boulud isn't the only good reason to stay at the Surrey, but what could be better than that? The lobby has a slightly faded air, and the hallways upstairs could do with some gentler lighting. But the studio and one-bedroom suites are solid, old-fashioned New York hotel rooms. They have thick walls, roomy bedrooms and closets, and black and white tiled bathrooms. All rooms have fully-eqiupped kitchens and the hotel will do grocery shopping for you. The Upper East Side location is attractive to many leisure travelers, and the hotel's rates, while not exactly bargain, aren't staggering either.

Rooms: 131 (all suites); 16 floors; designated nonsmoking floors. **Hotel amenities:** Business services, concierge, fitness equipment, laundry and dry cleaning, meeting and function rooms, valet parking. **Food services:** Restaurant, bar, room service. **Cancellation:** 4 P.M. day of arrival. **Wheelchair access:** Fully accessible; ADA compliant.

Trump International Hotel and Tower

EXTRAORDINARY $$$$

1 Central Park West (between Columbus Circle and 61st St.)
www.trumpintl.com
Phone: (212) 299-1000, (888) 448-7867   Fax: (212) 299-1150

The Trump International may be considered a diamond with a curse—controversial Donald Trump is, we think it's fair to say, not universally beloved by New Yorkers. Even so, it is hard to imagine any New Yorker (or, more to the point, any visitor), finding fault with the diamond-of-a-hotel that bears his name. It is simply beautiful. Rooms with a view over Central Park are the most prized. You can gaze at the panorama of the park or, as each room comes with a small telescope, focus on a single leaf. Those rooms with a "city view" over Broadway lose some of the magic but retain their luxuriousness. The rooms are restrained sumptuousness, contemporary but timeless-looking, with warm, soft beiges and honey colors predominating. The hotel is located at a busy crossroads of New York, yet the rooms are quiet enough for meditation and roomy.

The bathrooms are Italian marble and come with a Jacuzzi. The majority of the rooms have kitchens—range top, dishwasher, Limoges china. The four-star restaurant Jean Georges is part of the hotel, and if you don't feel like eating in the dining room, one of the sous-chefs of the restaurant will come up to your room and prepare a meal for you. No hotel in town has a similar perk. The impressive health club is open to hotel guests and condo residents only. In addition to all the machines you want, there is a lap pool, steam and sauna.

Rooms: 167 (includes 128 suites); building has 52 floors, hotel rooms are on floors 3 through 17; designated nonsmoking rooms. **Hotel amenities:** Business services, concierge, health club, laundry and dry cleaning, meeting and function rooms, swimming pool, valet parking. **Food services:** Restaurant (Jean Georges), bar, 24-hour room service. **Cancellation:** 4 P.M. day prior to arrival. **Wheelchair access:** Fully accessible; ADA compliant.

Cheap

The Comfort Inn at Central Park West   GOOD $

31 West 71st St. (between Columbus Ave. and Central Park West)
Phone: (212) 721-4770, (877)-727–5236 (PARKCEN)
Fax: (212) 579-8544

All the rooms here are small, so if limited space is a deal-breaker, look elsewhere. But otherwise, the Comfort is a good value for the neighborhood. Rooms have ample amenities and a relatively extensive complimentary breakfast.

Rooms: 102; 14 floors; designated nonsmoking floors. **Hotel amenities:** Business center, laundry and dry cleaning, meeting room. **Food services:** Room service. **Cancellation:** 4 P.M. day prior to arrival. **Wheelchair access:** Fully accessible; ADA compliant.

Hotel Olcott   GOOD $

27 West 72d St. (between Central Park West and Columbus Ave.)
Phone: (212) 877-4200   Fax: (212) 580-0511

While you can't talk about glamour in the same sentence with the Olcott, it is generous in terms of space and gentle on your wallet. The rooms are clean, mattresses are firm, windows are double-paned, but amenities are generally low-tech. Instead, roomy closets and kitchens.

Rooms: 150 (includes 110 suites); 16 floors; all smoking rooms. **Hotel amenities:** None. **Food services:** Restaurant, bar. **Cancellation:** One week prior to arrival. **Wheelchair access:** Fully accessible.

BED AND BREAKFASTS AND GUEST HOUSES

There are many alternatives in New York to standard hotel accommodations, including some charming bed and breakfasts. Some are hosted in the traditional way, and some are unhosted and therefore more like renting an apartment. As well as the following specific suggestions, there are several agencies that represent hundreds of B&Bs throughout the city:

At Home in New York (212) 956-3125, (800) 692-4262

Bed and Breakfast (and Books) (212) 865-8740

Bed and Breakfast in Manhattan (212) 472-2528

City Lights Bed and Breakfast (212) 737-7049

Manhattan Home Stays (212) 737-3868

Manhattan Lodgings (212) 475-2090

New World Bed and Breakfast (212) 675-5600, (800) 443-3800

New York Bed and Breakfast Reservation Center (212) 977-3512, (800) 747-0868

Urban Ventures (212) 594-5650

West Village Reservations (212) 614-3034

Abingdon Guest House   GOOD $$

13 Eighth Ave. (between West 12th and Jane Sts.), West Village
www.abingdonguesthouse.com
Phone: (212) 243-5384   Fax: (212) 807-7473

The two West Village townhouses that make up the Abingdon Guest House are over 140 years old. They have wonderfully creaky staircases, and many rooms have wood floors, brick walls and tin ceilings. Much care has been take to create an inviting, residential feel that is authentically "Village." Staying here is like staying with a friend—one with a good eye for detail.

Other things you should know about the Abingdon: Two rooms share a bath, there is no elevator (there are as many as four flights of stairs), and while the windows are double-paned, Eighth Avenue has its noisy moments. This is a gay-friendly guest house, though by no means exclusively gay.

Rooms: 9; 4 floors; all nonsmoking rooms. **Hotel amenities:** None. **Food services:** None. **Cancellation:** 2 P.M. 4 days prior to arrival. **Wheelchair access:** Not in public areas.
*Note: no children.

Country Inn the City   VERY GOOD $$
W. 77th St. (between Broadway and West End Ave.), Upper West Side
www.countryinnthecity.com
Phone: (212) 580-4183   Fax: (212) 874-3981

A charmer. You enter a small, limestone building (built in 1891) on a residential side street, and walk up the stairs (as many as three flights) to one of the four thoughtfully and attractively outfitted guest rooms. Guests enjoy creaking wood floors, four-poster beds, (nonworking) fireplaces, ceiling fans, and, in one room, a delightful terrace. Each comes with a fully equipped kitchen that the owners stock with coffee, milk, jam and cereal. Nice touches include free local calls, the flagon of brandy (very English country house), the bed tray and the moose head in the hallway.

Note well: there is a three-day minimum, they accept no credit cards, smoking is not permitted, no children under 12 years of age are allowed and a there is a maximum of 2 people per apartment. It is a small price to pay for the small price you pay. Every neighborhood should have a Country Inn.

Rooms: 4 apartments; 5 floors; all nonsmoking. **Hotel amenities:** None. **Food services:** None. **Cancellation:** 30 days prior to arrival. **Wheelchair access:** Not accessible.

Incentra Village House   GOOD $
32 Eighth Ave. (between West 12th and Jane Sts.), West Village
Phone: (212) 206-0007   Fax: (212) 604-0625

The Incentra is an inviting guest house geared towards gay and lesbian visitors but welcoming all. Two adjacent 1841 townhouses have twelve rooms. In one of the houses, the Victorian double parlor is the common room, and it has two fireplaces, a piano (which guests can play) and daily papers. Each room is named for a place or thing that figured prominently in the life of Gaylord Hoftiezer, the man who started the Incentra. When he passed away, he left the house as a trust. It is popular with Europeans. One room has access to a small garden, ten have working fireplaces. The Incentra wins you over with its West Village ambience and friendly staff.

Rooms: 12 (includes 1 suite); 3 floors; all smoking rooms. **Hotel amenities:** None. **Food services:** None. **Cancellation:** 3 days prior to arrival. **Wheelchair access:** Not accessible.
*Note: no children under 10; 3 night minimum stay for weekends; for holidays, 4 night minimum stay with a nonrefundable one night charge.

Inn New York City EXCELLENT $$$$

W. 71st St. (between Broadway and West End Ave.),
Upper West Side www.innnewyorkcity.com
Phone: (212) 580-1900   Fax: (212) 580-4437

Everything about this four-room inn is immensely charming and special. It is
the very antithesis of cookie-cutter, corporate lodging and the Manhattan
apotheosis of individual hospitality. As such, it isn't for everybody—places this
distinctive never are.

On a quiet block just east of West End Avenue lies a brownstone with virtually no marking. On entering, you find a small hallway and a staircase—
there is no front desk, no concierge, no lobby. There's no common area to
speak of, all the space goes into the rooms. It's pure lodging. And what lodging! Everything you can think of has been thought of and then some; each
suite has a unique flavor and features. There is the Opera, the Library, the Spa,
and the Vermont suites.

Before you arrive, your kitchen is stocked with wine, gourmet breads, cakes
and staple foods. After that, they keep an eye on what guests are eating—not to
bill you, only to replenish the supply. Inn New York City is expensive, but
sometimes the best things in life are.

Rooms: 4 (all suites); 4 floors; all nonsmoking. **Hotel amenities:** Business services, laundry room. **Food services:** None. **Cancellation:** 14 days prior to
arrival, forfeit $50 for cancellation. **Wheelchair access:** Not accessible.
*Notes: two-night minimum stay (Vermont Suite, one month); no children
under 12 years of age; no smoking.

The Inn on 23rd St. VERY GOOD $$

131 West 23rd St. (between Sixth and Seventh Ave.), Chelsea
Phone: (212) 463-0330, (877) 387-2323   Fax: (212) 463-0302

The Inn on 23rd Street is a marvelous bed and breakfast at modest prices in a
neighborhood that has few choices for lodging. This new inn is the right place
at the right time.

Each room is themed. There is the Victorian Room with a canopy bed and
the '40's room with a genuine Haywood-Wakefield furniture set. In the Rosewood room, the furniture hangs from rosewood panels (you have to see it . . .).
There are 11 rooms in all on five floors (with an elevator).

While the bathrooms may be small, the rooms are quite large by New York
standards. There is much exposed brick throughout, adding to the charm, and
rooms on the top floor have large skylights. The Loft Room has the bed on a
loft at the skylight level. You climb up via a ship's ladder. On the second floor of
the Inn is a library where guests can relax, read a book or play cards. On the
ground floor, there is a front parlor, kitchen and dining room table.

Rooms: 11 (includes 1 suite); 5 floors; all nonsmoking rooms. **Hotel amenities:**
Function room, library. **Food services:** None. **Cancellation:** One week prior to
arrival or forfeit one night's rent. **Wheelchair access:** Fully accessible.

Second Home on Second Ave.   GOOD $

221 Second Ave. (between 13th and 14th Sts.), East Village
www.citysearch.com/nyc/secondhome
Phone: (212) 677-3161   Fax: (212) 677-3161

This small, attractive lodging has the same owner as East Village Bed and Coffee on Avenue C. As with that property, the exterior promises little. But after
you walk up the flight of stairs to the first level of guest rooms, it's immediately
obvious that you have stumbled onto a nifty secret.

The seven large bedrooms are done in different themes (tribal, modern and
Caribbean, for instance), and they are tastefully, if not luxuriously, executed.
Most of the bathrooms are shared.

It wouldn't be a second home without a kitchen, and this one is stocked
with the basic pots, pans, dishes and silverware. It's a four-flight climb from the
ground level to the top guest floor room, with no elevator. But even with its
drawbacks, Second Home is well done.

Rooms: 7 (includes 1 suite); 4 floors; all smoking rooms. **Hotel amenities:**
Common kitchen. **Food services:** None. **Cancellation:** 3 days prior to arrival.
Wheelchair access: Not accessible.

SoHo Bed and Breakfast   VERY GOOD $

167 Crosby St., (at Bleecker St.), East Village
Phone: (212) 925-1034   Fax: (212) 226-9081

You could pass this B and B a thousand times and never know it's there. The
building, on a back street just north of Houston Street, dates from 1792. Rent
one of the two available spaces, though, and you could get hooked. The first is
the large loft over a live-in studio of the artist/owner. It's a genuine SoHo loft
(though not quite in SoHo) and the bedroom is separate. Artifacts collected
from Africa, the South Seas and Mexico adorn the brick walls. A large (full)
kitchen area is next to a large dining room table. There's also a living room
area, with TV, VCR, couches. The bedroom is comfortable but note it's the only
area with an air conditioner. Ceiling fans do a good job on all days but New
York's worst. This loft is considered a "hosted" accommodation, which means
the owner will be a discreet part of your vacation. It will only enhance your stay.

The adjoining carriage house, considered "unhosted." It's much smaller than
the loft, but it has its own charms and some history, as well. Billie Holiday lived
here for a time. The three skylights add plenty of light.

Rooms: 2 apartments; 2 floors; all smoking rooms. **Hotel amenities:** Bike
rental. **Food services:** None. **Cancellation:** forfeit 20% deposit. **Wheelchair
access:** Not accessible.
*Note: does not accept credit cards

Wyman House   VERY GOOD $$

Riverside Dr. (at 75th St.), Upper West Side   www.abodenyc.com
Phone: (212) 472-2000, (800) 835-8880

This 1886 house on Riverside Drive has been tenderly cared for, so you get rooms with character and some remarkable details—the carved alabaster fireplace comes to mind. There's a Victorian feel to some of the rooms, but it's not overdone—there's a light touch at work. Modern amenities come in the form of AC (except in one room), clock radio, hair dryer, iron and ironing board, answering machine and a full kitchen. Guests receive a start-up basket consisting of muffins, jam, yogurt, orange juice and coffee. There are wonderful views of the Hudson from the penthouse terrace.

A lovely way to experience the Upper West Side and New York.

Rooms: 6; 4 floors; all nonsmoking rooms. **Hotel amenities:** Kitchen (equipped). **Food services:** None. **Cancellation:** 14 days prior to arrival. **Wheelchair access:** Not accessible.
*notes: three-night minimum stay; no children under 10; no pets; no smoking.

THE OUTER BOROUGHS
Bronx

Le Refuge Inn Bed and Breakfast   VERY GOOD $
620 City Island Ave. (between Sutherland and Cross Sts.)
www.cityisland.com/lerefuge
Phone: (718) 885-2478   Fax: (718) 885-1519

The warmth of the welcome, the pleasant old sea captain's house on the main strip of City Island, and the chamber concerts on Sundays are the best reasons to visit Pierre Saint-Denis' inn in the far reaches of the Bronx. M. Saint-Denis is also the proprietor of the delightful Le Refuge restaurant on the Upper East Side. For us, City Island allows you to feel far removed from many aspects of city life, yet you can stand at the water's edge and see the twin towers on the far horizon.

Rooms: 9 (includes 2 suites); 3 floors; designated nonsmoking rooms. **Hotel amenities:** Some shared baths, parking. **Food services:** Restaurant, room service. **Cancellation:** Noon 2 days prior to arrival. **Wheelchair access:** Not accessible.

Brooklyn

Bed and Breakfast on the Park   VERY GOOD $$
113 Prospect Park West (between 6th and 7th Sts.), Brooklyn
www.bbnyc.com
Phone: (718) 499-6115   Fax: (718) 499-1385

A lovely building built in 1895, right across from Prospect Park. The house is enchantingly outfitted out with antiques, oriental rugs, oil painting and stained glass. Pity the fireplace doesn't work. Breakfast is vast and satisfying.

Rooms: 7; 4 floors; all nonsmoking rooms. **Hotel amenities:** None. **Food services:** None. **Cancellation:** 10 days prior to arrival; $25 cancellation fee. **Wheelchair access:** Not accessible.

New York Marriott VERY GOOD $$

333 Adams St. (between Tillary and Willoughby Sts.), Brooklyn
www.marriotthotels.com
Phone: (718) 246-7000, (888) 436-3759   Fax: (718) 246-0563

This hotel, which opened in 1998, is seven floors of a big office tower. It's the first full-service hotel the borough has had in over 50 years. Brooklyn feels part of it. As you ride up the escalator, your eye is drawn upward to a trompe l'oeil cupola on the ceiling imitating the conservatory dome at the Brooklyn Botanic Garden. A mural of the Brooklyn Bridge is behind the front desk, throughout the hotel artwork and photos of Brooklyn or by Brooklyn artists adorn the walls. Books by or about its famous natives or about the city itself line the walls of the lounge. The Brooklyn Historical Society has filled several glass showcases with Brooklyn memorabilia and artifacts. Park Slope pilsner is on tap in the bar.

When you've reached your room, it's strictly Marriott. All the basics are well covered. Each room has individually controlled heat and air-conditioning. *USA Today* gets delivered to every guest. One thing you notice right away: even though the hotel is built over busy Adams Street, the rooms are tranquil.

In the lobby, you'll find a concierge desk, an ATM, and a small business center. Many of the guests of the hotel are from Washington D.C., making it a home base to the nearby government offices in downtown Brooklyn. Quite a few subway lines converge in this area, so access citywide is easy.

Rooms: 376 (includes 21 suites); 7 floors; designated nonsmoking rooms. **Hotel amenities:** Business center, concierge, health club, lap pool, laundry and dry cleaning, meeting and function rooms, valet parking. **Food services:** Restaurant, bar, room service. **Cancellation:** 6 P.M. day of arrival. **Wheelchair access:** Fully accessible; ADA compliant.

Staten Island

Harbor House Bed and Breakfast GOOD $

1 Hylan Blvd.(at Edgewater St.)   www.nyharborhouse.com
Phone: (718) 876-0056, (800) 626-8096   Fax: (718) 983-7768

Next door to the charming Alice Austin House is the Harbor House, built in 1890, which has its own charms. It's not luxurious in any way, but it does have views over the harbor to Manhattan. One smart man rented the whole place for the fourth of July and had his family there to watch the fireworks. The Harbor House feels more like a beach house than anything else, and you can lie in bed and look out to the water. Rooms tend to be large, with a TV, dresser, armoire, ceiling fan, but no phone. A good-size continental breakfast is offered. The house is far enough east that you don't see the less attractive parts of Staten Island—it's the water, the Verrazano Bridge, the Statue of Liberty, Manhattan, and it feels like it's all yours.

Rooms: 11 (includes 3 suites); 3 floors; all nonsmoking rooms. **Hotel amenities:** Some shared baths, free parking. **Food services:** None. **Cancellation:** 10 days prior to arrival. **Wheelchair access:** Not accessible.

Staten Island Hotel GOOD $

1415 Richmond Ave. (between Christopher Lane and Akron St.)
(off I-278 expressway)
www.statenislandhotel.com
Phone: (718) 698-5000, (800) 532-3532   Fax: (718) 354-7071

This comfortable, full-service hotel is a quick car ride from the Staten Island Ferry. Traditional guest rooms, Americana-style, have ample amenities and in spite of its proximity to a highway, it's reasonably quiet. Some guest rooms have a balcony. The hotel has a restaurant, lounge and room service. If you want some exercise, there are free guest passes to a Bally gym about half a mile away. There is a coin-op laundry and guests are offered a number of freebies for people who have forgotten to pack something—left your toothbrush at home? They'll give you one at no charge. That's the kind of hospitality that seems par for the course here.

Rooms: 187 (includes 3 suites); 9 floors; designated nonsmoking floors. **Hotel amenities:** Business services, free parking, laundry and dry cleaning, meeting rooms. **Food services:** Restaurant, bar, room service. **Cancellation:** 6 P.M. day prior to arrival. **Wheelchair access:** Fully accessible.

Queens

LA GUARDIA AIRPORT

Crowne Plaza Hotel La Guardia VERY GOOD $$

104–04 Ditmars Blvd. (at 23d Ave.)
www.crowneplazalaguardia.citysearch.com
Phone: (718) 457-6300, (800) 692-5429   Fax: (718) 899-9768

A renovation in 1998 has left the Crowne Plaza in fighting form. Classic contemporary rooms have ample amenities. Closets aren't large, and ceilings are low but, crucially, the soundproofing is very good. For $20 over the rack rate, guests get access to the executive level lounge which has a full American breakfast buffet, hors d'oeuvres in the evening and enhanced rooms. A pleasant indoor pool with a sun deck, Jacuzzi, sauna, and a room with free weights and aerobics equipment are pluses here. There is an airline screen with up-to-date flight information as you'd expect, and a chef who makes amazing chocolate sculptures—you probably weren't expecting that.

Rooms: 358 (includes 23 suites); 7 floors; designated nonsmoking rooms. **Hotel amenities:** Business services, concierge, free parking, health club, laundry and dry cleaning, meeting rooms, swimming pool. **Food services:** Restaurant, bar,

24-hour room service. **Cancellation:** 6 P.M. day of arrival. **Wheelchair access:** Fully accessible; ADA compliant.

La Guardia Marriott

VERY GOOD   **$$**

102–05 Ditmars Blvd. (at 23d Ave.)   www.marriott.com

Phone: (718) 565-8900, (800) 228-9290   Fax: (718) 533-3001

Competent, comfortable, if not colorful lodging near to La Guardia's terminal. That it's positioned near the terminal, rather than a runway, helps keep the noise down in the room. Familiar Marriott trappings. Ask for one of the "rooms that work" and you'll get, at the same rate as a room that doesn't, a pull-out under desk, swivel chair, and a dataport located in the desk lamp base. For $20 over the rack rate, guests are upgraded to the Concierge level—which entitles you to use of a lounge with a concierge, continental breakfast, checkout service. This lounge is closed weekends. The hotel has a whirlpool, a 50-foot pool, sauna, 24-hour gym and an airline monitor.

Rooms: 436 (includes 3 suites); 9 floors; designated nonsmoking floors. **Hotel amenities:** Business center, dry cleaning, free parking, health club, meeting and function rooms, swimming pool. **Food services:** Restaurant, bar, room service. **Cancellation:** 6 P.M. day of arrival. **Wheelchair access:** Fully accessible; ADA compliant.

J. F. K. AIRPORT

Holiday Inn J. F. K. Airport

VERY GOOD   **$$**

144–02 135th Ave. (off exit 2 of the Van Wyck Expressway)
www.holidayinnjfk.com

Phone: (718) 659-0200, (800) 692-5350   Fax: (718) 322-5769

The Holiday Inn, on the airport's periphery, offers some serenity. It has quiet rooms, a pleasant pool and even a Japanese garden. In fact, if you have a room facing away from the airport, it would be possible not to know you were there. The rooms aren't bursts of charm, but they are clean, comfortable and decently-sized. Bedding is quite comfortable, closets are small, bathrooms are plain but adequate.

The Holiday Inn offers some other helpful and popular amenities: the up-to-date airline schedules available at a kiosk in the lobby; a selection of fairly new movies (while you're watching, you can order up a pint of ice cream); the pool that, in warm weather, has a roof that retracts. There is also a substantial exercise room, sauna and whirlpool.

The hotel offers a complimentary shuttle every half hour to J. F. K., and three morning shuttles to La Guardia as well as one to the Green Acres mall. The Park and Fly package is one night's stay plus you can leave your car for up to 14 days, for $199.

Rooms: 360 (includes 11 suites); 12 floors; designated nonsmoking rooms. **Hotel amenities:** Business center, health club, laundry and dry cleaning, meeting and function rooms, parking, swimming pool. **Food services:** Two restaurants, bar, room service. **Cancellation:** 6 P.M. day of arrival. **Wheelchair access:** Fully accessible.

Radisson Hotel J. F. K. Airport   GOOD $$

135–30 140th St. (at 140th St.)   www.radisson.com
Phone: (718) 322-2300, (800) 333-3333   Fax: (718) 322-6894

The newest of the airport hotels, this Radisson opened in 1998—there was an abandoned hotel on this site when Radisson bought it and renovated to the tune of $30 million.

Greens and rust are used heavily in the traditionally designed rooms. Mattresses are good, but your sleep may be undermined by noise from the Belt Parkway just outside. Closets are large, bathrooms small and ceilings quite low.

The Radisson is the only one of the four hotels in the area to have a 24-hour restaurant and room service. The hotel offers complimentary shuttle service to J. F. K. and the Green Acres mall. The lobby has an ATM, a flight information kiosk, a business room with fax machine, Internet access, copier and printer. The fitness room is spacious, with bike, stairsteppers, treadmills, free weights, lockers and showers. It's the only place we know of in New York where you can work out while watching planes land.

Rooms: 386; 12 floors; designated nonsmoking floors. **Hotel amenities:** Business center, fitness equipment, laundry and dry cleaning, meeting and function rooms, parking. **Food services:** Restaurant, bar, 24-hour room service. **Cancellation:** 4 P.M. day of arrival. **Wheelchair access:** Fully accessible.

NEWARK INTERNATIONAL AIRPORT, NEWARK NJ

Newark Airport Marriott   VERY GOOD $$

Newark International Airport (center of airport)
www.marriotthotels.com/ewrap
Phone: (973) 623-0006, (800) 882-1037   Fax: (973) 623-7618

The only hotel on Newark Airport property, this Marriott, which opened in 1985, has the company's familiar combination of comforts and corporate traveler amenities. They got a key ingredient right, too. The windows offer virtually complete soundproofing against airplane noise. Rooms aren't particularly spacious, but they're adequate, done in the familiar Marriott pinks, greens and floral prints. Concierge level rooms, $20 over the standard rack rate, have additional amenities and use of a separate lounge. It serves continental breakfast, evening hors d'oeuvres, and there are views over the airport. A telescope helps you keep track of the air traffic, and an airline monitor in the lobby helps you keep track of flight schedules.

The pool gets a lot of natural light, and there is also a whirlpool and sauna. There are several dining options, including 24-hour room service and a bar with a pool table and outdoor patio. You can take a hotel van directly to your airline at no charge.

Rooms: 610 (includes 6 suites); 10 floors; designated nonsmoking floors. **Hotel amenities:** Business center, concierge, health club, laundry and dry cleaning, meeting and function rooms, parking, swimming pool, 24-hour shuttle to all terminals. **Food services:** Two restaurants, bar, 24-hour room service. **Cancellation:** 6 P.M. day prior to arrival. **Wheelchair access:** Fully accessible.

HOTELS BY PRICE

$$$$ Very Expensive

The Carlyle	Upper East Side	Extraordinary
Central Park Inter-Continental NY	Midtown West	Excellent
Essex House, A Westin Hotel	Midtown West	Excellent
Flatotel	Midtown West	Very Good
The Four Seasons	Midtown East	Extraordinary
Helmsley Park Lane	Midtown West	Very Good
Hotel Delmonico	Midtown East	Very Good
The Inn at Irving Place	Gramercy Park	Very Good
Kitano New York	Murray Hill	Excellent
Le Parker Meridien	Midtown West	Excellent
The Lowell	Upper East Side	Excellent
The Mark	Upper East Side	Excellent
Mercer Hotel	SoHo	Excellent
The Michelangelo	Midtown West	Very Good
Millennium Premier	Midtown West	Very Good
The New York Palace Hotel	Midtown East	Excellent
The Pierre	Midtown East	Excellent
The Peninsula	Midtown West	Excellent
The Regency	Upper East Side	Excellent
Renaissance New York Hotel	Midtown West	Very Good
RIHGA Royal	Midtown West	Excellent
Royalton	Midtown West	Excellent
The St. Regis	Midtown East	Extraordinary
Sheraton Russell Hotel	Murray Hill	Very Good
The Sherry-Netherland	Upper East Side	Excellent
SoHo Grand Hotel	SoHo	Very Good
The Stanhope	Upper East Side	Excellent
The Surrey Hotel	Upper East Side	Very Good
Trump International Hotel and Tower	Upper West Side	Extraordinary

$$$ Expensive

The Algonquin	Midtown West	Very Good
Barbizon	Upper East Side	Very Good
Beekman Tower Hotel	Midtown East	Very Good
The Benjamin	Midtown East	Excellent
The Bentley	Upper East Side	Very Good

Carnegie Hotel	Midtown West	Good
Crowne Plaza Hotel at the U.N.	Midtown East	Very Good
Crowne Plaza Manhattan	Midtown West	Very Good
Doubletree Guest Suites	Midtown West	Very Good
Dumont Plaza	Murray Hill	Very Good
Eastgate Tower	Murray Hill	Very Good
The Fitzpatrick Grand Central Hotel	Midtown East	Very Good
The Fitzpatrick Manhattan Hotel	Midtown East	Good
Grand Hyatt New York	Midtown East	Very Good
The Helmsley Middletowne	Midtown East	Good
The Iroquois New York	Midtown West	Very Good
Hotel Casablanca	Midtown West	Very Good
Hotel Elysée	Midtown East	Good
Hotel Inter-Continental	Midtown East	Very Good
Kimberly Hotel	Midtown East	Very Good
Loews New York Hotel	Midtown East	Good
The Lombardy	Midtown East	Excellent
Lyden House	Midtown East	Very Good
The Mansfield	Midtown West	Good
Millenium Hilton	Lower Manhattan	Very Good
Millennium Broadway	Midtown West	Very Good
Morgans	Murray Hill	Very Good
New York Helmsley	Murray Hill	Very Good
New York Hilton and Towers	Midtown West	Good
New York Marriott East Side	Midtown East	Very Good
New York Marriott Marquis	Midtown West	Very Good
Novotel New York	Midtown West	Good
NY Marriott Financial Center	Lower Manhattan	Very Good
NY Marriott World Trade Center	Lower Manhattan	Very Good
Omni Berkshire Place	Midtown East	Excellent
Paramount	Midtown West	Good
The Park Central	Midtown West	Very Good
The Plaza	Midtown West	Very Good
Plaza Athénée	Upper East Side	Very Good
Plaza Fifty	Midtown East	Very Good
Regal United Nations Plaza	Midtown East	Excellent
The Roger Smith Hotel	Midtown East	Good
The Roger Williams	Murray Hill	Very Good
Roosevelt Hotel	Midtown East	Good
Shelburne	Murray Hill	Very Good
Sheraton New York Hotel and Towers	Midtown West	Very Good
Southgate Tower	Midtown West	Good
The Shoreham	Midtown West	Very Good
Swissotel New York—The Drake	Midtown East	Excellent
The Time	Midtown West	Very Good
The Warwick	Midtown West	Very Good

W New York	Midtown East	Good
W New York, The Court	Murray Hill	Very Good
W New York, The Tuscany	Murray Hill	Very Good

$$ Moderate

Ameritania	Midtown West	Good
Best Western Manhattan	Midtown West	Good
Best Western Seaport Inn	Lower Manhattan	Good
The Chelsea Hotel	Chelsea	Good
Chelsea Inn	Flatiron	Good
Empire	Upper West Side	Good
Excelsior Hotel	Upper West Side	Good
The Franklin	Upper East Side	Good
Gramercy Park Hotel	Gramercy Park	Good
Holiday Inn Downtown	Chinatown	Basic
Hotel Beacon	Upper West Side	Good
Hotel Bedford	Murray Hill	Good
Hotel Metro	Midtown West	Good
Hotel Wales	Upper East Side	Very Good
Jolly Madison Towers Hotel	Murray Hill	Good
Mayfair New York	Midtown West	Good
The Mayflower Hotel on the Park	Upper West Side	Good
Midtown East Courtyard by Marriott	Midtown East	Very Good
On the Ave	Upper West Side	Very Good
Salisbury Hotel	Midtown West	Good
San Carlos Hotel	Midtown East	Good
Sheraton Manhattan	Midtown West	Very Good
Wall Street Inn	Lower Manhattan	Very Good
Washington Square Hotel	West Village	Good
Wyndham	Midtown West	Very Good

$ Inexpensive

Broadway Inn	Midtown West	Good
Carlton Arms Hotel	Gramercy Park	Basic
Chelsea Pines Inn	Chelsea	Good
Comfort Inn at Central Park West	Upper West Side	Good
Habitat Hotel	Midtown East	Basic
Herald Square Hotel	Midtown West	Basic
Hotel Edison	Midtown West	Basic
Hotel Olcott	Upper West Side	Good
Hotel 17	Flatiron	Basic
Larchmont Hotel	West Village	Good
Murray Hill Inn	Murray Hill	Basic
Pickwick Arms Hotel	Midtown East	Basic

It is not uncommon for people to visit New York just to sample some of its fine restaurants. And why not? According to *New York Times* food critic, William Grimes, "The quality, range and sheer number of the city's restaurants has made New York the world's most exciting place to eat. Paris may have more French restaurants, and Rome more trattorias, but no city on earth offers the adventurous eater more variety and depth than New York at the present moment."

For more than thirty years, New Yorkers have been relying on restaurant reviews in the *Times* for the most trustworthy advice about where to eat in their hometown. The 300 or so restaurants included here have all been reviewed by the three major food critics of the *Times* in recent years: William Grimes, Eric Asimov and Ruth Reichl. Since 1992 Mr. Asimov has been responsible for finding those quintessential New York restaurants that serve high quality food at reasonable prices (his reviews are clearly identified by the term **"$25 & Under"** which appears at the top of the review). Restaurants with stars have been reviewed by Mr. Grimes since 1999 and by Ms. Reichl before then. Many of the original reviews were updated in the "Eating Out" and "Good Eating" columns that appear weekly in the newspaper and those changes are reflected here.

(Note: The best restaurants in Brooklyn, Queens and the other boroughs can be found in the appropriate sections.)

Using This Guide

What the Stars Mean:

 Extraordinary

☆ ☆ ☆ Excellent

☆ ☆ Very Good

☆ Good

Price Range: The dollar signs that appear at the top of each review are based on the cost of a three-course dinner and a 15 percent tip (but not drinks).

$ $25 and under
$$ $25 to $40
$$$ $40 to $55
$$$$ $55 and over

$25 & Under: A restaurant where you can get a complete meal, exclusive of drinks and tip, for $25 or less; recently, as a concession to inflation, some restaurants have been included where only an appetizer and main course total $25.

Abbreviations: Meals: B = Breakfast, Br = Brunch, L = Lunch, D = Dinner. LN = Late Night (restaurants open till midnight or later). Credit cards: AE = American Express; DC = Diner's Club; D = Discover; MC = Master Card; V = Visa; "All major" means at least three of these cards are accepted.

The Best Restaurants in New York City

Selected by Ruth Reichl and William Grimes

☆ ☆ ☆ ☆—EXTRAORDINARY

Bouley Bakery	Le Cirque 2000	Lespinasse
Jean Georges	Le Bernardin	

☆ ☆ ☆—EXCELLENT

Aquavit	Honmura An	Patria
AZ	JoJo	Patroon
Babbo	Judson Grill	Peacock Alley
Baldoria	Kuruma Zushi	Periyali
Café Boulud	La Caravelle	Peter Luger
Cello	La Côte Basque	Picholine
Chanterelle	La Grenouille	San Domenico
Daniel	Lutèce	Sugiyama
Danube	March	Sushi Hatsu
Felidia	Molyvos	Sushi Yasuda
Fifty Seven Fifty	Montrachet	Tabla
Seven	Next Door Nobu	Union Pacific
The Four Seasons	Nobu	Veritas
Gotham Bar and Grill	Oceana	
Gramercy Tavern	Park Bistro	

☆ ☆—VERY GOOD

Alison on Dominick	Blue Ribbon Sushi	Chola
An American Place	Blue Hill	Christer's
Aquagrill	Brasserie	Churrascaria
Arqua	Campagna	Plataforma
Aureole	Chelsea Bistro & Bar	Circus
Balthazar	Chez Josephine	City Hall
Bambou	Chez Louis	Clementine
Bayard's	Chianti	Deniz à La Turk
Beacon	Chicama	Destinée
Bice	Cho Dang Gol	Eight Mile Creek

Eleven Madison Park
EQ
Estiatorio Milos
Etats-Unis
Filli Ponte
Firebird
Follonico
Fresco By Scotto
Gabriel's
Grill Room
Guastavino's
Hangawi
Hatsuhana
Heartbeat
Hudson River Club
Icon
I Trulli
Il Valentino
Joe's Shanghai
Kang Suh
L'Actuel
Layla
Le Colonial
Lenox Room
Little Dove
Lobster Club
Local
Manhattan Ocean Club

Mark's
Match Uptown
Matthew's
Maya
Meigas
Mercer Kitchen
Mesa Grill
Mi Cocina
Michael Jordan's
Michael's
Moomba
Nadaman Hakubai
New York Noodle
    Town
Nick & Toni's Cafe
Nicole's
Odeon
Osteria Del Circo
Otabe
Palio
Palladin
Paola's
Parioli Romanissimo
Park View at the
    Boathouse
Payard Patisserie
Petrossian
Quilty's

Quince
Remi
Rosa Mexicano
Ruby Foo's
Salaam Bombay
Savoy
Screening Room
Sea Grill
Shun Lee Palace
Smith & Wollensky
Solera
Sono
Surya
Tapika
Thalia
Tocqueville
The Tonic
Tribeca Grill
21 Club
27 Standard
Union Square Café
Verbena
Water Club
Windows on the
    World
Zarela

☆ —GOOD

Asia de Cuba
Atlantic Grill
Avra
Baldoria
Blue Water Grill
Bouterin
Calle Ocho
Commune
Coup
Dawat

Della Femina
Delmonico's
Dock's Oyster Bar
Frank's
Goody's
La Nonna
Maritime
One If By Land, Two
    If By Sea
Pastis

Pop
Provence
The Red Cat
Redeye Grill
Scalini Fedeli
Tavern on the Green
Viceversa
West 63rd Street
    Steak House
Wild Blue

Quick Guide to the
Best Inexpensive Restaurants

Selected by Eric Asimov

Acquario
Al Di La
Alley's End
Alouette
Amy Ruth's
Avenue
Bali Nusah Indah
Bandol
Bar Pitti
Bayou
Bistro le Steak
Boca Chica
Brawta Caribbean
    Cafe
Bright Food Shop
Café Fès
Cambodian Cuisine
Carnegie Deli
Chimichurri Grill
Christos Hasapo-
    Taverna
Cyclo
Diner
El Fogon
El Pollo
Emily's
Evergreen Shanghai
Gus's Figs Bistro & Bar
First

Flor's Kitchen
Frank
Gabriela's
Garden Cafe
Goody's
Grand Sichuan
Grange Hall
Habib's
Han Sung Garden
Holy Basil
Home
'ino
Island Spice
Isola
Jean Claude
Joe's Shanghai
Josie's
Jubilee
Katsu-Hama
Komodo
Kori
L'Ardoise
Lavagna
Le Gigot
Le Tableau
Little Basil
Los Dos Rancheros
    Mexicanos
Lupa

Luzia's
Marumi
Mavalli Palace
Max
Meltemi
Metisse
Moustache
Nha Trang
Oznot's Dish
Pão
Pepe Verde
Pepolino
Pio Pio
Pongal
Prune
Puttanesca
Rafina
Rinconcito Peruano
Rocking Horse Cafe
Shanghai Tang
SoHo Steak
Sushi Masa
Sweet n' Tart
Tiffin
Ubol's Kitchen
Velli
Wu Liang Ye

MANHATTAN RESTAURANTS, A-Z

Acquario   **$25 & Under**   MEDITERRANEAN
5 Bleecker St. (near Bowery)   (212) 260-4666
Credit cards: Cash only   Meals: D   Closed Sun.

With its candles, brick walls and casual service, Acquario is a small, warm place straight out of the Village's bohemian past. A couple of Acquario's large appetizers can easily make a light meal. Try the fresh sardines, which have a strong, briny aroma but a mild, wonderfully nutty flavor and are served with a small green salad. Fennel salad is also wonderful, though it's hard to find a more alluring dish than the Portuguese fish stew. **Price range:** Entrees, $12–$18.

Alison on Dominick ☆☆ **$$$$**   FRENCH
38 Dominick St. (between Varick and Hudson Sts.)   (212) 727-1188
Credit cards: All major   Meals: D

One of New York City's most surprisingly romantic restaurants is hidden away on an obscure SoHo side street. The light here is perfect: so soft and dim that everybody looks good. The music is perfect, too: loud enough to hear and low enough not to intrude. The design is so simple it seems unplanned, but it has an easy, offhand elegance. The food and wine list are primarily French and overwhelmingly wonderful. **Price range:** Entrees, $27–$33.

Alley's End   **$25 & Under**   BISTRO/NEW AMERICAN
311 West 17th St. (between Eighth and Ninth Aves.)   (212) 627-8899
Credit cards: D/MC/V   Meals: D

Enter a portal and traverse a passageway, and you leave the workaday Chelsea world for Alley's End, a lovely network of dining rooms and gardens that feels as pastoral and isolated as an oasis. The brief American menu (with some international notes) manages to match the romantic draw of the interior. **Price range:** Entrees, $14–$22.

Alouette   **$25 & Under**   BISTRO/FRENCH
2588 Broadway (near 97th St.)   (212) 222-6808
Credit cards: All major   Meals: Br, D

Dishes at Alouette are cleverly conceived, beautifully presented and moderately priced; each item promises excitement. Service has its ups and downs, however, and the second-floor dining room is rather warm and stuffy. **Price range:** Entrees, $15–$18.50.

Amy Ruth's   **$25 & Under**   SOUTHERN
113 West 116th St. (between Lenox and Seventh Aves.)   (212) 280-8779
Credit cards: All major   Meals: B, L, D

Amy Ruth's presents Southern food that is up-to-date without sacrificing time-honored traditions. Chicken is served with crisp yet fluffy waffles, a common pairing, but you can also order whole-grain waffles, and they're all served with real maple syrup. The real stars of the menu include short ribs that are falling-off-the-bone tender in an earthy, oniony brown gravy, and deliciously spicy shrimp, perfect over fluffy white rice, and baked spareribs served in a sweet barbecue sauce. Many of Amy Ruth's side dishes shine, like buttery string beans and eggy potato salad. Deep-dish sweet potato pie and pineapple-coconut cake are terrific. **Price range:** Dinner, $7.95–$17.95.

An American Place ☆☆ $$$$ NEW AMERICAN
565 Lexington Ave. (between 50th and 51st Sts.)   (212) 888-5650
Credit cards: All major   Meals: L, D

The name is as simple as Main Street, and like Main Street it has been around long enough that it seems almost timeless, expressing a vision of American cuisine as an infinitely renewable resource. Now located in a dressy-casual hotel dining room, the food has the right blend of boldness and subtlety. The pot-roasted short ribs do not require a lot of fuss and bother; this signature dish is served with whipped potatoes that cut the richness of the meat with a sharp horseradish edge and fresh herbs. The cedar-planked salmon has a nice, crisp char, and the rich, pillow-soft dollop of corn pudding on the side cannot be beat. The wisest course for dessert is to order the double chocolate pudding, a satisfyingly regressive treat served with Schrafft's sugar cookies. **Price range:** Entrees, $26–$32.

Aquagrill ☆☆ $$$ SEAFOOD
210 Spring St. (at Sixth Ave.)   (212) 274-0505
Credit cards: All major   Meals: Br, L, D   Closed Mon.

Aquagrill has the comfortable air of a neighborhood place, the sort of restaurant that ought to be serving burgers and beer. Instead there's an oyster bar in front and the menu is refreshingly original. Devoted almost entirely to fish, it offers unusual dishes like "snail-snaps" (bite-size popovers holding a single snail) and salmon in falafel crust. Soups are also satisfying. All the fish is well prepared and some with imagination, but the kitchen also has a way with plain fish as well. Yellow potato hash is excellent, and the best dessert is the apple tart with cinnamon ice cream and caramel sauce. **Price range:** Entrees, $18.50–$24.

Aquavit ☆☆☆ $$$$ SCANDINAVIAN
13 West 54th St. (between Fifth and Sixth Aves.)   (212) 307-7311
Credit cards: All major   Meals: Br, L, D

Surrounded by glass and sky, Aquavit occupies a magical space; this is one of the city's most beautiful restaurants. Walking a tightrope between Swedish tradition and modern taste, the chef makes delicate and beautiful food. Even the cheese plate is decorative: wedges of cheese have long, crisp crackers stuck in them so they look like chess pieces. Desserts are pretty too. Arctic Circle turns out to be a sort of ice cream sandwich of meringue, vanilla ice cream and cloudberry sorbet nestled against a puree of salmon-colored cloudberries. The staff is generally helpful and will offer enthusiastic recommendations about the list of aquavits, which are like flavored vodkas. **Price range:** Pre-theater menu, $39; 3-course prix-fixe, $55; 5-course tasting menu, $75

Arqua ☆☆ $$ ITALIAN
281 Church St. (at White St.)   (212) 334-1888
Credit cards: All major   Meals: L, D

The setting of this restaurant named for a village in northern Italy, is alluring, but the noise can be deafening when all the chairs are occupied at night. Lunch is a more tranquil time, and the rustic fare is unfailingly good. Starters include grilled chicken and mushroom sausage on a warm lentil salad; fresh pickled sardines with sweet and sour onions; a soup of the day, and several homemade pastas. Some recommended main dishes are pan-seared tuna loin with ginger sauce; baked duck breast with a sauce of black currant and cassis, and braised rabbit with white wine and herbs. Before the espresso, try a ricotta cheesecake or a poached pear with caramel sauce and ice cream. **Price range:** Entrees, $16–$20.

Artie's New York Delicatessen $25 & Under   DELI
2290 Broadway (Between 82nd and 83rd Sts.)   (212) 579-5959
Credit cards: All major   Meals: L, D

Artie's may not be ready to take its place among the deli elite, but it shows promise. And it already makes a fine egg cream. Artie's pastrami has potential, and the hot dogs are excellent, slender, garlicky and crisp around the edges, arriving already spread with mustard and sauerkraut. Potato pancakes are exceptionally crisp, with a solid center trailing crunchy slivers of potato. The dining room is bright and functional, and it's clear that Artie's has also been working on the deli atmosphere. **Price range:** Entrees, $7.95–$17.95.

Asia de Cuba ☆ $$$ ASIAN/LATIN AMERICAN
237 Madison Ave. (near 37th St.)   (212) 726-7755
Credit cards: All major   Meals: L, D, LN

You won't eat very well at Asia de Cuba. But you will have so much fun being there that you may not notice. The manic energy of the place makes every night feel like a party. The most successful invention is the oxtail spring roll, a wonderful combination of rich, fatty meat with crisp pastry and forceful flavors. A black bean, cucumber and tomato relish is the perfect foil. Aside from the tamarind-and-rum-glazed pork and the Chinese five-spice sirloin, there aren't many main dishes to recommend. But who can think about all that when desserts are exploding all over the room? Guava Dynamite is the life of this party; it is just guava mousse wrapped in a chocolate tuille, but the sparkler on top is seductive. **Price range:** Entrees, $16–$29.

Atlantic Grill ☆ $ $ SEAFOOD
1341 Third Ave. (near 77th St.)   (212) 988-9200
Credit cards: All major   Meals: Br, L, D

This appealing, affordable restaurant with its bustling but surprisingly quiet dining room and attentive service will rarely let you down. The cold seafood platter
with four sauces, which costs $48 and serves four, is fresh and tasty; a better
appetizer is the sweet, smoky, hickory-roasted sea bass with cucumber and ginger
salsa. Simplicity is the key to the best main dishes: fish served with rice and vegetables is perfectly grilled to order, and makes a satisfying meal. And the red
Thai curry is an absolute delight. Desserts are not a strong point. **Price range:**
Entrees, $14.50–$19.95.

Aureole ☆ ☆ $$$$ FRENCH/NEW AMERICAN
34 East 61st Street (between Madison and Park Aves.)   (212) 319-1660.
Credit cards: All major   Meals: L, D

Aureole is one of the city's most popular and revered restaurants. The reasons
are perfectly understandable. Aureole serves appealing food in stylish surroundings, with polished service and a warm atmosphere. When chef Charlie Palmer
pulls it all together, his food has an unfussy, direct appeal that makes other chefs
seem neurotic. The best entrees, like pan-seared quail with sautéed foie gras,
cornbread and chanterelles, have a winning simplicity to them. The flavors are
direct and concentrated, and there's an imaginative twist that adds intrigue to
what otherwise might be a plodder. The intelligently selected wine list does not
have the category "monster reds," but it might be a good idea. This is one occasion when you want a bottle that's led snarling from a cage. **Price range:** three-
course prix fixe, $65; tasting menu, $85.

Avenue $25 & Under   BISTRO/FRENCH
520 Columbus Ave. (at 85th St.)   (212) 579-3194
Credit cards: All major   Meals: B, Br, L, D, LN

This informal corner restaurant (with an unexpectedly French atmosphere and
efficient service) serves breakfasts and light meals by day and full dinners at
night. Smoked pork loin, sliced lamb and sliced steak are excellent. At brunch,
try the hot chocolate, which is thick as pudding and rich as a chocolate truffle.
From the terrific food to the daylong service and the good values, Avenue is a
formula that works. **Price range:** Entrees, $13.95–$16.95.

Avra ☆ $$$ GREEK/SEAFOOD
141 East 48th St. (between Third and Lexington Aves.)   (212) 759-8550
Credit cards: All major   Meals: L, D

Greek cuisine is a modest thing, a fairly limited catalog of simple pleasures, and
Avra gives it honest, honorable representation. Fresh fish, barely touched, is the
selling point here. In the open kitchen, a ball of fire blasts each side of a sea bass

or red snapper imprisoned in a grilling basket; the fish gets a squirt of lemon, a drizzling of olive oil and a sprinkling of herbs, then heads to the table. The seafood counter offers about a dozen fish listed on the menu and perhaps an extra two picked up at the market unexpectedly. Lamb loin chops, served with lemon potatoes and okra, are tender and flavorful, and grilled chicken is served with string beans, in a zesty stewed tomato sauce. Avra's spanakopita is a flawless layering of good feta cheese, firm spinach and leeks, with crackling-fresh leaves of phyllo dough. **Price range:** Entrees, $18.50–$26.

AZ ☆☆☆ $$$$ FUSION
21 W. 17th St. (bet. Fifth & Sixth Aves.) (212) 691-8888
Credit cards: All major   Meals: Br, L, D

AZ is gorgeous, an improbable but enchanting blend of strict Asian geometry, Western Art Nouveau and turn-of-the century Viennese craft influences. The decor, in other words, matches the menu. In the third-floor dining room, tilted glass panels open up to the sky in clear weather, and a thin sheet of water flows down a stone slab near the entrance. A flagstone floor and exposed brick walls cool the room, but the color scheme is warm and opulent. It's a room to dream in, and a threat to steal the show. When the food arrives, however, the stargazing stops. After that, Patricia Yeo's highly inventive, extroverted and wildly successful brand of fusion cooking holds center stage.

Duck schnitzel sounds like a joke. The laughter stops after one bite, when the rich duck meat, wrapped in a paper-thin crunchy layer of breading, makes contact with brown butter, specks of hazelnut and a well-judged intervention of sweet and bitter flavors provided by sliced golden beets. Ms. Yeo also works wonders with Asian teas. Chicken smoked in Lapsang souchong leaves absorbs the dusky perfume of the tea, which is nicely offset by a scallion pancake and a thick fig chutney. Two non-Asian desserts make the strongest impression, a fig tarte Tatin with fromage blanc ice cream, and a small coconut financier, almost a cross between cake and macaroon, topped with a ball of very rich vanilla ice cream and sweetened just a bit with chips of buttery macadamia brittle. **Price range:** Three-course prix fixe, $52; six-course tasting menu, $75.

Babbo ☆☆☆ $$$$ ITALIAN
110 Waverly Pl. (at Ave. of the Americas)   (212) 777-0303
Credit cards: All major   Meals: D

The upstairs room is small, spare and intimate with warm golden light. Downstairs the bar is crowded and lively but the tables are uncomfortable. The menu is loaded with dishes Americans are not supposed to like: fresh anchovies and warm testa (head cheese) are among the appetizers, and pastas include bucatini with octopus, and ravioli filled with beef cheeks and topped with crushed squab livers. I like the pastas so much—my favorite is made with calf's brains wrapped in tender sheets and sprinkled with fragrant sage and thyme flowers—that I am always tempted by the pasta tasting menu: five different pastas followed by two desserts. But I cannot imagine a meal at Babbo that did not include spicy, robust calamari. Wine is served by quartinos (250 milliliters, or a third of a bottle). Try one; if you don't like it, the kitchen will take it back. The best ending to a meal here is saffron panna cotta with poached peaches. Like the restaurant itself, it is an unusual combination of ingredients that seem destined to be together. **Price range:** entrees, $15–$35; 7-course pasta tasting menu, $43; 7-course traditional tasting menu, $49.

Baldoria ☆ $$$ ITALIAN
249 W. 49th St. (bet. Seventh & Eighth Aves.) (212) 582-0460
Credit cards: All major Meals: D Closed Sun.

Baldoria (pronounced bal-DOR-ia, meaning "rollicking good time") is a big slice of neighborhood Italian, New York style, transferred, in a slicker format, to the theater district. It is the offshoot of Rao's, the cult restaurant in East Harlem. It's a prime specimen of a special genre, the Italian-American restaurant. They serve feel-good food in a feel-good atmosphere that inclines diners to overlook short-comings. In restaurants like these, Frank Sinatra is more important than the chef. When it's good, Baldoria is quite good. The greens and the tomatoes are always fresh and flavorful, and they do a lot to regain lost ground in dishes like the tough, overbreaded veal Milanese, topped with wonderfully pungent arugula. Pastas, too, perform strongly, especially trenette with prosciutto, peas and onions in a light cream sauce. Standard appetizers like vitello tonnato and clams sautéed in white wine are respectable, as are main courses like sweet sausages with pepper and onions. Get the costata di manzo, a thuggish-looking hunk of charred rib chop, weighing in at 54 ounces; it's an incredibly flavorful piece of beef, juicy, tender and perfectly cooked. **Price range:** Entrees, $18$32.

Bali Nusa Indah $25 & Under   INDONESIAN
651 Ninth Ave. (near 45th St.)   (212) 765-6500
Credit cards: All major   Meals: L, D

Bali Nusa Indah offers fresh and lively Indonesian dishes in a tranquil and pretty setting. Most of the food is forcefully spiced, yet respectful of the flavors of each dish. Among the dishes worth trying are Javanese fisherman's soup; corn fritters gently flavored with shrimp; nasi goreng, the wonderful Indonesian ver-sion of fried rice, and sea bass broiled in a banana leaf. There are exceptional desserts as well. **Price range:** Entrees, $6–$13.50.

Balthazar ☆☆ $$ BISTRO, FRENCH
80 Spring St. (between Lafayette St. and Broadway)   (212) 965-1785
Credit cards: All major   Meals: B, L, D, LN

Dinner at midnight? If you don't have the private number for this oh-so-trendy SoHo French brasserie, that is probably what you'll be offered, so book weeks in advance. Try going for breakfast or lunch; the room is still beautiful, the afford-able food still delicious. The Balthazar salad is a fine mix of asparagus, haricots verts, fennel and ricotta salata in a truffle vinaigrette. Sautéed foie gras is excellent, as is an appetizer of grilled mackerel with a warm potato salad. The short ribs are awesome: rich and meaty, they are accompanied by fat-soaked carrots and buttery mashed potatoes. Lighter dishes are also attractive, like seared salmon served over soft polenta. **Price range:** Entrees, $9.50–$16.

Bambou ☆☆ $$$ CARIBBEAN
243 East 14th St. (between Second and Third Aves.)   (212) 505-1180
Credit cards: All major   Meals: D

The best Caribbean food in New York City is served in a room with such cozy elegance, it feels as if a warm breeze is blowing through it. The tables are filled with the beautiful and the famous. There is no better way to begin a meal here than with the eggplant soup, a thick dark liquid with the scent of curry and the deep, intoxicating taste of coconut. Bambou shrimp, each encrusted in coconut, are sweet and tasty, an appetizer that could almost be a dessert. Grilled marlin, a dense, meaty fish steak, comes on a buttery bed of mashed plantain that is the perfect foil for the subtle flavor of the fish. The tropical fruit plate glows with color and the coconut crème brûlée is fabulous. **Price range:** Entrees, $17–$26.

Bandol $25 & Under FRENCH
181 East 78th St. (between Third and Lexington Aves.)   (212) 744-1800
Credit cards: AE   Meals: D   Closed Sun.

Bandol, named for a fine Provençal wine, offers dreamy Mediterranean flavors that are especially transporting in a cold spell. The food is very good, the atmosphere warm and neighborly. Even the overly familiar dishes like lamb shank, salmon and scallops have clear, direct flavors that convey their appeal rather than their popularity. Among the appetizers, the pissaladiére, a tart of onions, olives and anchovies served with a green salad, is so good that you could eat two and call it a meal. While the main courses don't have the consistency of the appetizers, they are still satisfying. Coq au vin is lighter than usual, grilled steak is juicy and flavorful, and the tender lamb shank offers primal enjoyment. The mostly French wine list is long but not very exciting, and while it's not expensive, it is hard to find many good values. **Price range:** Entrees, $14–$18.

Barking Dog Luncheonette $25 & Under DINER
1678 Third Ave. (at 94th St.)   (212) 831-1800
1453 York Ave. (between East 77th and 78th Sts.)   (212) 861-3600
Credit cards: Cash only   Meals: B, Br, L, D, LN

With its dark wood paneling, comfortable booths, bookshelves and low-key lighting, the Barking Dog looks more like a library than a luncheonette. That, in part, explains its appeal to adults, along with its up-to-date American menu, which ranges from hamburgers, fried chicken and meatloaf to leg of lamb and roasted trout. If the children begin to fidget while waiting for the rich, bountiful desserts, distract them with the restaurant's dog tchotchkes, which can be a parent's best friend. **Price range:** Entrees, $11.

Bar Pitti $25 & Under   ITALIAN
268 Sixth Ave. (near Houston St.)   (212) 982-3300
Credit cards: Cash only   Meals: L, D, LN

This casual cafe offers superbly simple Tuscan fare and draws an arty, fashion-conscious crowd. Bar Pitti's ease with people and with food is what makes it seem so Italian; its atmosphere of jangly controlled frenzy makes it a wonderful New York experience. Outdoor seating on Sixth Avenue is remarkably pleasant. The menu is small and familiar, and almost all the main courses are superb. Peak hours are not times for a quiet meal here, but even just before closing time, you will receive the same beautifully cooked food and offhand service. **Price range:** Entrees, $10.50–$19.

Bayard's ☆ ☆ $$$ NEW AMERICAN
1 Hanover Sq. (between Pearl and Stone Sts.)   (212) 514-9454
Credit cards: All major   Meals: D   Closed Sun.

The former Cotton Exchange, now India House, a businessmen's club, has been beautifully restored to create one of New York's most gracious dining rooms. The service is decorous too, and the mostly French food is elegant and good. The terrine of foie gras is pure, classic excellence, served with peppered brioche. Salmon is also impressive, slowly poached so that it is almost translucent. And the côte de boeuf for two is just the sort of dish you want to eat in a historic restaurant. There is also a fun assortment of crème brûlées in silly flavors—licorice, strawberry, espresso. **Price range:** Entrees, $22–$35.

Bayou $25 & Under   CAJUN/SOUTHERN
308 Lenox Ave. (between 125th and 126th Sts.)   (212) 426-3800
Credit cards: All major   Meals: L, D

Bayou, a handsome new Creole restaurant in Harlem, would do any New Orleans native proud. With its brick walls, retro brass lamps and woody touches, Bayou looks like countless other neighborhood bars and grills, but its big picture windows and second-floor setting offer an unusual New York panorama, unimpeded by tall buildings. The menu is short, but includes standout appetizers like earthy chicken livers in a rich port wine sauce, and shrimp rémoulade, piquant with mustard and hot pepper and served with deviled eggs. The rich turtle soup is thick with bits of turtle meat and smoky andouille sausage, spiked with sherry and lemon. The sautéed snapper Alexandria, sprinkled with roasted pecans and drenched with lemon butter, is moist and altogether delicious. For dessert, both a bread pudding with a vanilla-whiskey sauce and a fudgy, wedge-shaped pecan brownie topped with peppermint ice cream and chocolate sauce are excellent. **Price range:** Entrees, $12.95–$21.95.

Beacon ☆☆ $$$ NEW AMERICAN
25 West 56th St. (between Fifth and Sixth Aves.)   (212) 332-0500
Credit cards: All major   Meals: L, D   Closed Sun.

This classy looking new midtown restaurant knows exactly what it's about. It offers civilized dining in a beautiful setting. Organized around an open kitchen and a huge wood-burning oven, it delivers uncomplicated big-flavored food emphasizing fresh, seasonal ingredients. Meat and fish pick up a smoky tang from the oven, roasted vegetables are served with entrees and even desserts feature roasted fruits. Two of the best entrees are triple lamb chops, rubbed with cumin and pureed picholine olives, and a plain trout roasted over high heat with a bright vinaigrette of chervil, parsley, cilantro and shallots. For dessert soufflés are a point of pride but it's the carmelized apple pancake that grabs the brass ring. **Price range:** Entrees, $19–$29.

Bice ☆☆ $$$ ITALIAN
E. 54th St. (between Fifth and Madison Aves.)   (212) 688-1999
Credit cards: All major   Meals: L, D, LN

With a main dining room done in beige and wood with brass sconces and indirect lighting, Bice is the handsomest Italian restaurant in town. If you have lots of money, good ears and a desire to see the fast and the fashionable, this offshoot of a Milanese restaurant is for you. The food is predictable but good. Fresh pastas, risotto, and the essentially uncomplicated main courses—veal chop, chicken paillard and duck breast with mango—are all recommended. The mostly Italian wine list is well chosen. Desserts include a napoleon with strawberry sorbet, ricotta cheesecake, hazelnut parfait, and caramelized banana tart with apricot compote. **Price range:** Entree, $24.

Big Wong $ CHINESE
67 Mott St., Chinatown   (212) 964-0540
Credit cards: Cash only   Meals: B, Br, L, D

This bright, bare-bones Chinatown restaurant serves excellent barbecued meats and congee. At lunch, it is packed with jurors on lunch break from the courthouse nearby and local residents drinking tea from water glasses. **Price range:** Entrees, $5–$10.

Bistro le Steak $25 & Under BISTRO/STEAK
1309 Third Ave. (at 75th St.)   (212) 517-3800
Credit cards: All major   Meals: L, D

Bistro le Steak hardly strikes a false note. It does look Parisian. The friendly staff conveys warmth and informality, and the food is both good and an excellent value. Steak is the specialty, but other simple bistro specialties are consistently satisfying and desserts are terrific. **Price range:** Entrees, $15–$30.

Blue Hill ☆☆ $$ FRENCH

75 Washington Place (at Avenue of the Americas)   (212) 539-1776.
Credit cards: All major   Meals: D   Closed Sun.

A few steps below sidewalk level in an old Greenwich Village town house, Blue
Hill almost shrinks from notice. The décor barely exists, just enough to give off
a vaguely pleasant impression. This quiet, adult setting admirably suits a style of
cooking that is both inventive and highly assured. There are dull spots on the
menu, but the overall standard is high enough to make up for the excruciating
banquette seating, where diners are pressed close to one another. Poached duck
deserves to be the restaurant's signature: a skinned duck breast, poached in
beurre blanc and duck stock, is paired with leg meat done as a confit, then
crisped at the last minute and placed over pureéd artichokes. For dessert, chocolate bread pudding, a sizable cube of brioche, undergoes a miraculous transformation after marinating overnight in a loose chocolate ganache. It is a conver-
sation-stopper. **Price range:** Entrees, $18–$23.

Blue Ribbon Sushi ☆☆ $$$ JAPANESE/SUSHI

119 Sullivan St. (between Prince and Spring Sts.)   (212) 343-0404
Credit cards: All major   Meals: D, LN   Closed Mon.

Blue Ribbon Sushi has good fish and an awesome list of sakes, but beyond that
it has very little in common with a classic Japanese sushi bar. If you have ever
felt like a clumsy foreigner and worried about doing the wrong thing, this is the
sushi bar for you. The menu is enormous, and almost everything is good, from a
pretty seaweed salad to broiled yellowtail collar. But the high point of the meal
is always sushi and sashimi. The sushi chefs are at their best when inventing
interesting specials like an appealing roll filled with fried oysters. And unfet-
tered by tradition, they create unusual special platters filled with whatever happens to be best that day. Just name the price you are willing to pay and let them
amaze you. **Price range:** Entrees, $11.50–$27.

Blue Water Grill ☆ $$ SEAFOOD

31 Union Sq. West (at 16th St.)   (212) 675-9500
Credit cards: All major   Meals: Br, L, D, LN

Built as a bank in 1904, this is a big, breezy room with a sidewalk cafe and a
casual air. Along with pleasant service, large portions and reasonable prices
can come large crowds and long waits. Shrimp and oysters are good choices; so
is the grilled fish. The most successful dish was grilled wild sea bass, which
arrived perfectly cooked and beautifully served. Desserts are not among Blue
Water Grill's happy surprises, but the brownie sundae would make most people
very happy. **Price range:** Entrees, $12.95–$19.95.

Boca Chica Restaurant $25 & Under   LATIN AMERICAN
13 First Ave. (at 1st St.)   (212) 473-0108
Credit cards: All major   Meals: L, D

Many cuisines are juxtaposed on the enticing menu of this little pan-Latin restaurant. Top choices include camarones chipotle, shrimp in a tomato, chili and cilantro sauce; crisp, tangy chicharrones de pollo, the classic Dominican dish of chicken pieces marinated in lime, soy and spices; and pinones, sweet plantains stuffed with ground beef and pork. **Price range:** Entrees, $6.50–$15.95.

Bongo $25 & Under   SEAFOOD
299 10th Ave. (near 28th St.)   (212) 947-3654.
Credit cards: MC/V   Meals: D, LN

On any given day, Bongo serves half a dozen kinds of oysters, from Fanny Bays, which have a flavor shockingly like cucumbers, to Pemaquids, which are impressively salty, to Wellfleets, which have a pronounced mineral tang. With no more than a squirt of lemon, and they are always impeccably fresh and gloriously sensual. The decadent allure of the oysters makes an amusing contrast to the style of the room, a quirky replica of 1950's living rooms. The limited menu has a few other highlights, like wonderful, meaty lobster rolls and an excellent smoked trout salad **Price range:** Oysters, $1.50 to $2.25 each.

Bouley Bakery ☆ ☆ ☆ ☆ $$$$ FRENCH
120 West Broadway (at Duane St.)   (212) 964-2525
Credit cards: All major   Meals: L, D

After an expansion and a slick renovation Bouley Bakery has quietly re-emerged as a resplendent, reinvented, finer version of its former self. The restaurant crackles with a new energy, and Mr. Bouley, as though responding to his new jewel box of a theater, is turning out food that is nothing less than inspired. It is stunningly good, and consistently ascends to the highest level. As a chef, Mr. Bouley has it all—elegance, finesse and flair. His flavors are extraordinarily clear and exquisitely balanced; his use of seasoning is so deft as to be insidious. Even his most complex creations have a classical simplicity to them. Mr. Bouley cooks the way Racine wrote and Descartes thought. Mr. Bouley has found his match in Bill Yosses, the pastry chef, whose creations are unfailingly elegant, restrained and imaginative.

Despite its expansion and the fireworks in the kitchen, Bouley Bakery retains the feel of a small neighborhood restaurant. Diners feel comfortable showing up in shirtsleeves, and the staff shrewdly maintains a delicate balance between informality and the more disciplined level of service implicit in the food and décor. The intensity of the service at Bouley Bakery is remarkable in

New York. The waiters seem passionate about the food and deeply concerned that diners enjoy it to the full. **Price range:** Entrees, $26–$32

Bouterin ☆ $$$$ FRENCH
420 East 59th St. (between First Ave. and Sutton Pl.)   (212) 758-0323
Credit cards: All major   Meals: D

Serving Provençal food in a Provençal atmosphere, this restaurant can be charming. The best dishes are the chef's old family recipes, like the hearty vegetable soupe au pistou, which tastes the way it might if had been made on a wood-burning oven on a Provençal farm, the tarte a la Provençale, the rack of lamb wrapped in a herbal crust, and sea bass in a bold bouillabaisse sauce. The daube of beef, too, is delicious, the beef slowly stewed in red wine and garlic. **Price range:** Entrees, $19–$28.

Brasserie ☆ ☆ $$$ BISTRO/FRENCH
100 East 53rd St. (at Lexington Ave.)   (212) 751-4840
Credit cards: All major   Meals: B, Br, L, D, LN

The old Brasserie (which closed in 1995 after a kitchen fire) was a part of the city's fabric. When patrons enter the newly-renovated restaurant, their jaws drop. The staircase down to the dining room has been transformed into a gentle slope of translucent steps. In futuristic booths along the side of the room, the tables are slabs of translucent lime-green acrylic. The Brasserie is ready for a new life, and Chef Luc Dimnet delivers sensible, well-executed food with up-to-date touches but not too many neurotic kinks. For dessert try the chocolate beignets: each powdered morsel, oozing with a perfectly measured mouthful of molten chocolate, reaffirms the genius of the doughnut concept. **Price range:** Entrees, $14–$28.

Bright Food Shop $25 & Under   NEW AMERICAN
216 Eighth Ave. (at 21st St.)   (212) 243-4433
Credit cards: Cash only   Meals: Br, D

This spare, minimalist former luncheonette serves an exciting blend of Asian and Southwestern ingredients. Scallop ceviche—chopped, marinated shellfish served on a crisp tostada—is a terrific appetizer. Green chili pozole is tart, vinegary and thick with chorizo and hominy, while the smoked trout and red peppers, wrapped in rice and seaweed, is a post-modern sushi roll. Bluefish salpicon, in which the fish is chopped and pickled with vinegar and chilies and served in corn tortillas, stands out among the main courses. **Price range:** Entrees, $11.75–$17.25.

Café Boulud ☆ ☆ ☆ $$$$ FRENCH
20 East 76th St. (near Madison Ave.)   (212) 772-2600
Credit card: All major   Meals: L, D

Café Boulud is sleek and easy; this is your opportunity to find out what happens when a great chef at the top of his form stretches out and takes chances. The menu, which changes frequently, is divided into four sections: La Tradition (classic country cooking), La Saison (seasonal dishes), Le Potager (vegetarian choices), and Le Voyage (world cuisine). What that really means is, anything goes. Most days there are 30 or more dishes, and none are ordinary. The most satisfying sections are La Saison and La Tradition: in the latter, you may find pig's feet laces with truffles, or salads scattered with skate or chicken livers. Equally inspired by the passing of the seasons, Mr. Boulud roasts fat sea scallops and serves them with crosnes, a crisp little white root vegetable. His scallion risotto is lavish with white truffles. Soup is another sure thing. The Potager and Voyage sections are less successful, but never dull. The same willingness to take risks can be found on the wine list, which explores little-known vineyards. **Price range:** Entrees, $24–$32.

Café de Bruxelles $ $ BELGIAN
118 Greenwich Ave. (between Seventh and Eighth Aves.)
(212) 206-1830
Credit cards: All major   Meals: Br, L, D

The little zinc-topped bar at this cozy Belgian cafe is a warm and welcoming stop. The frites, served in silver cones with dishes of mayonnaise, go beautifully with the unusual Belgian beers, while mussel dishes and heartier Belgian stews are all very good. The small tables near the battered zinc bar are good for solo diners. **Price range:** $13.75–$19.50.

Café des Artistes $$$ CONTINENTAL
1 West 67th St. (between Central Park West and Columbus Ave.)
(212) 877-3500
Credit cards: All major   Meals: Br, L, D

Its signature murals, leaded-glass windows and paneled wood walls contribute to the genteel impression at this grand cafe. The main room is more neighborly and louder than the intimate tables that ring the bar on the second level. The continental food, however, is surprisingly old-fashioned. Best for grazing before or after a concert. **Price range:** Entrees, $22–$40.

Café Fès $25 & Under MEDITERRANEAN
246 West 4th St. (at Charles St.)   (212) 924-7653
Credit cards: All major   Meals: D

One of the city's top Moroccan restaurants owes as much to France as it does to North Africa. A delicious smell permeates this pretty little corner restaurant, and the food is meticulously prepared. The small dining room has a wonderful Left Bank feel to it, though at times it can feel cramped and uncomfortable as well. **Price range:** $18–25.

Café Loup $ $ BISTRO
105 West 13th St. (between Sixth and Seventh Aves.)   (212) 255-4746
Credit cards: All major   Meals: Br, L, D
Every neighborhood should have a place like easy, comfortable Café Loup,
where you can effortlessly feel like a regular. The menu of traditional bistro
favorites doesn't challenge, but the restaurant does well by the standards, and
that's really the point. **Price range:** Entrees, $13.50.

Calle Ocho ☆ $ $ SPANISH/DINER
446 Columbus Ave. (between 81st and 82d Sts.)   (212) 873-5025
Credit cards: All major   Meals: D

At this homage to South American cooking, the kitchen makes food with
authority, like complicated ceviches and seductive shrimp chowders. It is hard
to resist the beauty of camarones, big shrimp brushed with rum and beautifully
arranged around a heap of fried seaweed, or crisp chicken cooked in lime. The
dining room is handsomely decorated, and the big, separate bar in front has
turned into a singles scene where people sip rum, lime juice and mint mojitos
while they listen to soft mambo music. **Price range:** Entrees, $16–$22.

Campagna ☆ ☆ $ $ $ ITALIAN
24 East 21st St. (between Broadway and Park Ave. S.)   (212) 460-0900
Credit cards: All major   Meals: L, D

The rustic charm of the setting befits the bold, alluring cooking at this popular
restaurant. It's an unbeatable combination: big portions and a big scene. To begin
there is grilled sausage (made on premises) set over broccoli rabe, and grilled calamari adorned with arugula and marinated tomatoes. Pastas include spaghetti in
white baby clam sauce and goat cheese tortellini mixed with fava beans, asparagus, peas and prosciutto. For main courses, try pan-roasted chicken breast in a balsamic reduction; grilled pork chop, aromatic of lemon and thyme, served with
roasted fennel; and salmon baked with olives, capers and sun-dried tomatoes.
Price range: Entrees, $17–$31.

Carnegie Deli $ $ DELI
854 Seventh Ave. (at 55th St.)   (212) 757-2245
Credit cards: Cash only   Meals: B, L, D, LN

A raucous, quintessential New York City experience, from pickles to pastrami.
Carnegie's sandwiches are legendarily enormous, big enough to feed you and a
friend and still provide lunch for tomorrow. That doesn't stop people from trying to eat the whole thing, a sight that must gratify the deli's notoriously crabby
waiters. The pastrami is wonderful, of course, but so are the cheese blintzes with
sour cream, which are only slightly more modest. **Price range:** Entrees,
$10–$20.

Casa Mexicana $25 & Under   MEXICAN
133 Ludlow Street at Rivington Street, Lower East Side
(212) 473-4100.
Credit cards: All major   Meals: L, D, LN

The most surprising thing about the menu here is how little it resembles the
usual array of Mexican street foods. The main courses include four steak dishes,
duck breast, sea bass, halibut and scallops, along with a couple of chicken dishes
and a single pork dish. Either this is typical of an upscale Mexican establishment or it is meant to cater to New Yorkers who expect such luxuries. Either
way, the Azteca steak and the sirloin Tampiquena are both fine pieces of beef.
Pellizcadas, little disks of fried cornmeal with toppings like chorizo, chicken or
crisp bits of pork, are always lively, as are tiny half-moon quesadillas, made with
paper-thin, crisp tortillas. The best dessert is a warm chocolate cake with a liquid center, topped with raspberry sauce and vanilla ice cream and surrounded by
raspberries. **Price range:** Entrees, $13–$21.

Cello ☆☆☆ $$$ FRENCH
53 East 77th St. (At Madison Ave.)   (212) 517-1200
Credit cards: All major   Meals: L, D

Cello's minuscule, cocoonlike dining room provides a neutral backdrop for
thrilling food. The owner and chef have conspired brilliantly to create a top-
class French fish restaurant. Entrees show remarkable refinement. Grilled
Alaskan black cod, a monumental chunk of ideally moist fish, floats serenely in
a lightweight but intense morel bouillon that diners can thicken with the gar-
lic-parsley purée that's served on the side. In a special menu, the chef does variations on a single theme, a two-and-a-half-pound lobster. For the grand finale,
he slow-roasts the tail, douses it in an emulsion made from the pan drippings
and serves it with basil, fava beans, morels and gnocchi. Desserts are top-notch.
Price range: three-course prix-fixe, $62; three-course lobster prix-fixe, $74.

Chanterelle ☆☆☆ $$$$ FRENCH
2 Harrison St. (At Hudson St.)   (212) 966-6960
Credit cards: All major   Meals: L, D   Closed Sun.

It's not hard to understand why New Yorkers keep a warm spot in their hearts
for Chanterelle. Few restaurants are as welcoming or comfortable to enter.
There's a soft, casual edge to the atmosphere and the service. Chef David Waltuck favors an opulent style. His strong suits are depth and intensity of flavor,
and he doesn't shy away from thick, rich sauces in his quest to ravish the palate.
The menu changes every four weeks and includes splendid dishes like a simple,
pristine beef fillet, drenched in a red wine and shallot sauce with more layers of
flavor than a complex Burgundy. Mr. Waltuck pulls off some dazzling effects,
especially with a sushi-size piece of salmon marinated overnight in mirin, soy
and sake, and then dry-cured for two days, and a delectable slice of salmon pick-

led in sweet ginger brine. There are always some thrilling desserts like a coura-
geously bitter chocolate tart, served with a pastry ice-cream cone filled with
banana malt ice cream.

The room itself looks as though it should be serene and hushed, but in fact
the acoustics are poor, and when the place fills up, it takes some real lung power
to carry on a conversation. Chanterelle and its owners have shown admirable
single-mindedness, consistency and immunity to fashion. In a city of neighborhoods, they created a neighborhood restaurant almost without equal—a warm,
welcoming haven dedicated to cooking at a very high level. **Price range:**
Three-course prix-fixe, $75; five-course tasting menu, $89 or $139 with match-
ing wines.

Chat 'n Chew $25 & Under   NEW AMERICAN
10 East 16th St. (between Fifth Ave. and Union Sq. West)   (212)
243-1616
Credit cards: All major   Meals: Br, L, D

Middle American farm dishes and homespun décor set the tone at this restaurant, which could lead you to believe it was off a small-town courthouse square
rather than off Union Square. Portions are huge, desserts are luscious and the
place is particularly appealing to children. **Price range:** Entrees, $7–$14.

Chelsea Bistro & Bar ☆☆ $$$ BISTRO/FRENCH
358 West 23d St. (between Eighth and Ninth Aves.)   (212) 727-2026
Credit cards: All major   Meals: D, LN

With a cozy fireplace, a great wine list and really good French bistro food, this is
a find in the neighborhood. Some of the dishes are superb; most of the food is
the satisfying fare you expect in a bistro. If the first thing you eat here is the fabulous mussel and clam soup, you will be hooked forever. The fricassee of lobster
and sea scallops is almost as good. The hanger steak is fine and rare, with a
dense red-wine sauce. The restaurant serves predictable and good classic New
York bistro desserts. The bread pudding is slightly less conventional, if only
because it is enlivened with a shot of rum. **Price range:** entrees, $17.95–$24;
pre-theater prix-fixe, $28.50.

Chez Josephine ☆☆ $$$ BISTRO/FRENCH
414 West 42d St. (between Ninth and Tenth Aves.)   (212) 594-1925
Credit cards: All major   Meals: D, LN   Closed Sun.

This Theater Row pioneer has been entertaining us with its colorful parade of
musicians, singers and dancers for more than a decade and is still going strong.
Its reliably pleasing bistro fare and attentive service add to the charm. Highlights among starters include the crunchy endive salad topped with crumbled
Roquefort and crushed walnuts and the subtle goat-cheese ravioli in a delicate
veal broth scented with fresh dill. Favorite entrees include lobster cassoulet
replete with scallops, shrimp, lobster, seafood sausage and black beans; sautéed

calf's liver with honey mustard sauce and grilled onions, and grilled salmon with a coulis of fine herbs. **Price range:** Entree, $18.

Chez Louis ☆☆ $$$ BISTRO/FRENCH
74 West 50th St. (at Sixth Ave.)   (212) 333-3388
Credit cards: All major   Meals: L, D   Closed Sun.

Although the interior needs a little work Chez Louis may be just what jaded New Yorkers are looking for today: food they can recognize. Who isn't seduced by the promise of an expertly roasted chicken suffused with rosemary and thyme and strewn with cloves of roasted garlic, or impeccably crisp pommes frites? For once an aged sirloin steak tasted like a piece of beef. But for something a tad less rich, try the seared sea scallops coated with porcini mushroom dust and served with black truffle vinaigrette, or a quickly seared tuna on a bed of buttery vegetables, which was a special one evening. This is a bistro that cares not a whit about wasp-waisted women—cream and butter are used with abandon, and many doggie bags make it out the door. The tender, perfectly cooked veal chop, deliciously glazed with a demiglace thinned with foie gras fat, weighs a pound.

There are seven wines by the glass all fairly priced, and desserts are well-executed. **Price range:** Entrees, $18.50–$34.

Chianti ☆☆ $$ ITALIAN
1043 Second Ave. (at 55th St.)   (212) 980-8686
Credit cards: All major   Meals: L, D

This small, cozy East Side restaurant has been transformed into a satisfyingly upscale eating experience, though it can feel cramped and modest. Chianti serves some extremely impressive dishes at very reasonable prices, like extraordinary diced, marinated salmon tossed with shavings of bottarga (a pressed fish roe) and topped with caviar. The braised boneless short ribs set on a bed of farro (a barley-like grain) is a masterful dish with robust flavors. The kitchen uses its wood-fired grill to good effect. A piece of tuna is beautifully seared and rare in the center. Chicken is moist and crisp; the veal chop is excellent. For dessert, try the delicious sesame cannoli with orange-mascarpone filling. **Price range:** entrees, $13.75–$27.50.

Chicama ☆☆ $$$ LATIN AMERICAN
35 East 18th St. (At Broadway)   (212) 505-2233
Credit cards: All major   Meals: L, D, LN

Hung with Peruvian rugs and decorated with Peruvian religious statues, this restaurant has a eucalyptus-burning wood oven and a big ceviche bar. The chef generates a special brand of excitement that somehow becomes part of the food, cooking in an exuberant, often flashy style that can be overwhelming, with plate-filling dishes that seem like the culinary equivalent of a carnival float. Alio chicken, a house specialty, deserves its star billing on the lunch menu. It's a half chicken, smoky tasting after roasting over eucalyptus wood, served on a hash made from malanga root and suffused with a truffle mushroom mojo. Supporting the ceviche menu is a long list of serious beers, including some unusual South and Central American beers. The dessert list is short and almost chaste. Vanilla flan infused with bay leaf may be, in a mild way, the most striking dessert on the menu, delicately herbal with a nicely paired accompaniment of carpaccio-thin pineapple slices decorated with a little goat cheese and accented with cracked pepper. **Price range:** Entrees, $19–$39

Chimichurri Grill $$ LATIN AMERICAN/ARGENTINE
606 Ninth Ave. (between 43d and 44th St.)   (212) 586-8655
Credit cards: All major   Meals: L, D   Closed Mon.

This is a good, casual place for dinner before or after the theater. Simultaneously sophisticated and homelike, it combines all the elements that make the food of Argentina so appealing: great grilled beef, a few Italian pasta dishes and some pure home cooking, like the tortilla, a frittata filled with potatoes, chorizo and onions. The empanadas are excellent, crisp little turnovers filled with a mixture of ground beef and olives. **Price range:** Entrees, $14–$24.

Cho Dang Gol ☆☆ $$ KOREAN
55 West 35th St. (between Fifth and Sixth Aves.)   (212) 695-8222.
Credit cards: All major   Meals: L, D, LN

Cho Dang Gol serves uniquely rustic food that is very different from what is available at other Korean restaurants in the surrounding blocks. The specialty here is fresh soybean curd, made daily at the restaurant. The kitchen makes each dish with extreme care, but for the uninitiated, searching out the best dishes is not easy. Try cho-dang-gol jung-sik. It arrives in three bowls: one with rice dotted with beans, another with "bean-curd dregs" (which hardly conveys its utter deliciousness) and the third with a pungent soup-stew containing pork, seafood, onions and chilies. Also excellent is chung-kook-jang, soybean-paste stew with an elemental flavor, and doo-boo doo-roo-chi-gi, a combination of pork, pan-fried kimchi, clear vermicelli and big triangles of bean curd. **Price range:** Entrees, $6.95–$29.95.

Chola ☆☆ $$ INDIAN
232 East 58th St. (between Second and Third Aves.)   (212) 688-4619
Credit cards: All major   Meals: L, D

The menu at this modest, crowded restaurant roams across the Subcontinent, offering special dishes from the Jews of Calcutta, fiery dishes beloved by the English and wonderful vegetarian dishes like dosa from South India. Start with Mysore masala dosa, a thin, crisp, lacy crepe stuffed with a hot and fragrant potato mixture. You might also consider idli, little steamed cakes that come to life when dipped into sambar and chutney. Uthappam is a scallion-laced vegetable pancake that is among the great pancakes of the world. Having started in southern India, continue with a fine dish from Kerala, konju pappas, shrimp in a chili-laden sauce. Among the excellent desserts are kulfi, a grainy frozen dessert flavored with nuts and saffron, and rasmalai, an addictive, sweet sort of homemade cheese. Best of all is the extraordinary Indian coffee: strong, milky and sweet. **Price range:** Entrees, $10.95–$24.95.

Christer's ☆☆ $$$$ SCANDINAVIAN

145 West 55th St. (between Sixth and Seventh Aves.)   (212) 974-7224
Credit cards: All major   Meals: L, D

This relaxed, upscale Scandinavian restaurant shows how a fine chef translates his love for American ingredients and ideas into traditional dishes. The chef and owner specializes in seafood, salmon in particular. Everything he makes from salmon is good, from seared smoked salmon with black beans, corn, avocado and tomatillo salsa—more Southwestern than Scandinavian—to gentle citrus-glazed salmon. His smorgasbord is wonderful, while his fricadelles, Swedish meatballs made of veal, are hearty and comforting. Desserts like Pavlova, an airy confection of ice cream, fruit and meringue, and a tart of poached apples are perfect endings. **Price range:** Entrees, $18–$26.

Churrascaria Plataforma ☆☆ $$$ LATIN AMERICAN/
STEAK HOUSE

316 West 49th St. (between Eighth and Ninth Aves.)
(212) 245-0505
Credit cards: All major   Meals: L, D, LN

Two things are required to truly appreciate this all-you-can-eat Brazilian restaurant: a large appetite to keep you eating and a large group to cheer you on. A caipirinha or two, the potent Brazilian drink, doesn't hurt either. The salad bar is extraordinary, a long two-sided affair anchored at the corners by four hot casseroles. Go easy: This is only the appetizer, and it takes stamina to do justice to the main part of the meal. The waiters will entice you with ham, sausage, lamb, wonderfully crisp and juicy chicken legs, pork ribs, even the occasional side of salmon, which is delicious in its caper sauce. But it is beef that has pride of place: sirloin, baby beef, top round, skirt steak, brisket, short ribs, special top round. **Price range:** All-you-can-eat rodizio meal, $27; children under 12, $13.

Circus Restaurant ☆☆ $$$ BRAZILIAN

808 Lexington Ave. (near 62d St.)   (212) 223-2965
Credit cards: All major   Meals: L, D, LN

An upscale Brazilian restaurant that turns into a party every night. Circus serves the food your mother might cook if you were raised in São Paulo or Bahia. It is a warm and cozy place, usually packed with Brazilians eager for a taste of home. The camarao na moranga is excellent, a heap of tiny, tender rock shrimp sautéed with fresh corn, hearts of palm, shallots, peas and coconut milk, mixed with cheese and baked in an acorn squash. Another satisfying dish is an appetizer, bolo de milho e rabada, little polenta cakes baked with Manchego cheese and served with a robust oxtail sauce. Among the sweet, tropical desserts, the best is caramelized bananas with ice cream. **Price range:** Entrees, $15–$23.

City Hall ☆ ☆ $$$ AMERICAN
131 Duane St. (near Church St.)   (212) 227-7777
Credit cards: All major   Meals: L, D, LN

The cavernous dining room has the spare quality of an old steakhouse; the clean details, loud music and hip clientele give it an up-to-date air. The menu includes all the old classics, from iceberg lettuce to baked Alaska, but there is more to City Hall than old-fashioned fare. The plateau de fruits de mer, which feeds six to eight, is a $98 behemoth so impressive that people invariably gasp as it is carried across the room. You also can't go wrong with oysters at City Hall, raw or cooked. Among the meat dishes there is a huge double steak, still on the bone and served for two. For dessert, the apple bread pudding made with brioche is very, very good. **Price range:** Entrees, $18–$32.

Clementine ☆ ☆ $$$ NEW AMERICAN
1 Fifth Ave. (at 8th St.)   (212) 253-0003
Credit cards: All major   Meals: L, D, LN

This casual, noisy restaurant with a young scene serves great, affordable food. The kitchen favors big flavors and quirky combinations. Squid is stuffed with a mixture of couscous and spicy sausage, then sliced into pretty rings and set in a colorful tomato-cumin broth. Spareribs are stripped from the bone and served as a salad, mixed with white beans, watercress and fried green tomatoes. Impressive main dishes include chili-rubbed pork loin, a tasty steak, grilled lamb chops, roasted cod and Buffalo mahi-mahi, a humorous take on the famous chicken wings. Desserts are also impressive, especially the splendid lemon icebox cake. **Price range:** entrees, $14–$24.

Commune ☆ $ $ ITALIAN/NEW AMERICAN
12 East 22d St. (between Broadway and Park Ave. South)
(212) 777-2600
Credit cards: All major   Meals: L, D, LN

Commune may come up short as a temple of fine cuisine, but it shows enormous vitality as a social gathering place. It is loud. It is young. It is crowded. The food is just good enough to hold its own against the decor, but food is not really the main thing. Commune leans away a bit from the Mediterranean flavors and spices that dominated Chef Matthew Kenney's earlier restaurants in favor of simpler, homier food. Lemon pops up in the surprising spoonful of preserved-lemon purée alongside a hefty slab of hot-smoked salmon. Warm shrimp pick up a good, smoky bite from their bacon wrappers, nicely accentuated by a small dollop of thick tomato and chili jam. But many of the entrees suffer from the blahs. The main reason to order roasted rack of lamb is for the suave-textured

Parmesan polenta, one of several featured side dishes, like truffled macaroni and cheese, that can be ordered on their own. Saffron pasta with tender chunks of lobster poached in butter, rich and mildly exotic, has a whiff of distinction. **Price range:** Entrees, $18–$26.

Coup ☆ $$ FRENCH/NEW AMERICAN
509 East Sixth St. (Between Avenues A and B)   (212) 979-2815
Credit cards: All major   Meals: D

Like the rest of the East Village, Coup takes an ascetic stand on visual stimulation. Somehow, this sensory deprivation induces a feeling of tranquility. Beneath the cloak of mystery lies a deceptively normal neighborhood restaurant, one that fits stylistically with the blocks around it. The food does not aim too high, but what it aims at, it hits. It's the kind of place that always seems like a good idea. The roast Cornish hen takes some beating. Brown as a berry and pleasingly plump, it's packed with chunks of coarse-grained sourdough bread and Michigan cherries. The stuffing is beyond praise. Coup also has a deeply limey Key lime pie and an honest, homey pineapple upside-down cake. **Price range:** Entrees, $16–$21.

Cuba Libre $25 & Under LATIN AMERICAN
200 Eighth Ave. (at 20th St.)   (212) 206-0038
Credit cards: All major   Meals: Br, L, D.

The combination here of loud voices, hard surfaces and raucous music is enough to make you want to scream, but you may give up on talking entirely: while the food is not always consistent, some dishes are so good that you simply want to eat and sigh. An appetizer of oysters, coated in blue cornmeal and fried, would have been tasty left at that, but they are perched on smoky collard greens and served with a mildly spicy salsa. The resulting combination is superb. Peruvian ceviche, made with bass marinated in lime juice and served with a salad of cubed peppers spiked with the pungent ají amarillo chili, is fresh, tangy and delicious. Among the main courses, the best is the pork tenderloin. A fine piece of tuna is glazed with honey and red wine, giving it an unusual, brisk, lively flavor that goes well with its accompaniment of quinoa salad. **Price range:** Entrees, $14.95–$18.95.

Cyclo $25 & Under VIETNAMESE
203 First Ave. (at 12th St.)   (212) 673-3957
Credit cards: All major   Meals: D, LN

This stylish little East Village restaurant serves some of the best Vietnamese food in New York City: It is inventive, impeccably fresh and meticulously prepared, while service is friendly and informative. Try cha gio, crisp and delicate spring rolls, and chao tom, grilled shrimp paste wrapped around sugar cane. Don't hesitate to order fruit for dessert, like cubes of wonderfully fresh mango that are the perfect end to a stellar meal. **Price range:** Entrees, $10–$15.

Daniel ☆ ☆ ☆ $$$$ FRENCH

60 East 65th St. (between Park and Madison Aves.)   (212) 288-0033
Credit cards: All major   Meals: L, D   Closed Sun.

There's a headlong inventiveness to chef Daniel Boulud's cuisine, but at heart,
he is a classicist who prizes harmony, refinement and restraint. His oxtail terrine
is a dish that could inspire a crime of passion—all the more thrilling for being a
little cheeky. Mr. Boulud also has a knack for transforming low-rent ingredients.
He bathes mackerel in a soy-ginger marinade and gently applies a mustard dressing. If you prefer elegance, he is happy to oblige, with a pure, intense, chilled
oyster velouté. When the kitchen is firing on all cylinders, immortality seems
within reach. One bite of the wickedly rich squab stuffed with foie gras, morels
and lamb's-quarter greens, and you can feel the heart attack coming on, but it
doesn't matter. Some things are worth dying for. The best dessert by far is the
chocolate-caramel bombe, a gorgeous chocolate-dusted dome with a heart of passion fruit crème brûleé. Daniel's exemplary service and impressive and adventurous wine list, with a large number of bargains, make diners feel coddled. **Price
range:** 3-course prix-fixe, $68; tasting menus, $90–$120.

Danube ☆ ☆ ☆ $$$$ AUSTRIAN

30 Hudson St. (at Duane St.)   (212) 791-3771
Credit cards: All major   Meals: L, D

David Bouley does not do things in a small way. Using fin-de-siécle Vienna as a
culinary source, and a repository of romantic images, he has created Danube,
the most enchanting restaurant New York has seen in decades. This is an opiate
dream of lush fabrics, deeply saturated decadent colors and lustrous glazed surfaces. It's a swirl of opulent patterns and textures, dominated by the large,
unabashedly excessive Klimts on the walls. If ever a restaurant was made for a
four-hour meal, Danube is it.

   In some cases, Mr. Bouley insists on authenticity. The kavalierspitz, a man-
size slab of boiled beef shoulder served with puréed spinach, looks like a middle-
class Sunday dinner. But Mr. Bouley was not put on earth to boil beef. After
anchoring the menu with a handful of classics, he has conjured up his own private Austria or, in some cases, taken leave of the country altogether. One of the
most impressive appetizers on the menu is a delicate, complexly orchestrated
dish of raw tuna and shrimp, with marinated fennel in a Key lime dressing.
More typically, Mr. Bouley has lightened, modernized and personalized traditional dishes, or invented new ones using traditional ingredients, often with
stunning results: the ravioli stuffed with Yukon Gold potatoes and braised veal
is a triumph, coated in a powerfully reduced, syrupy veal stock and served with
braised sunchokes.

   Desserts tend to be overly complex, but two traditional desserts are both
impeccable: a Czech palacsintak, or crêpe, and a Salzburger nockerl, a mound-
shaped soufflé dusted in confectioners' sugar and served with raspberries. **Price
range:** Entrees, $29–$35.

Dawat ☆ $$$ INDIAN

210 East 58th St. (between Second and Third Aves.)   (212) 355-7555
Credit cards: All major   Meals: L, D

Most of the vegetable dishes here—the small baked eggplant with tamarind
sauce, the potatoes mixed with ginger and tomatoes, the homemade cheese in
spinach sauce—are excellent. The set lunches are a bargain. Cornish hen with
green chilies offers heat balanced by the sweet and sour flavor of tamarind. And
sarson ka sag, a sour, spicy, buttery puree of mustard greens, is extremely flavorful. Bhaja are also impressive: Whole leaves of spinach, battered so lightly that
the green glows through the coating, are paired with light little potato-skin fritters. **Price range:** Entrees, $15.95–$23.95.

Della Femina ☆ $$$$ NEW AMERICAN

131 East 54th Street;   (212) 752-0111
Credit cards: All major   Meals: L, D   Closed Sun.

Della Femina attracts a tony Upper East Side clientele with its cool, restrained,
Yankeefied setting straight out of Martha Stewart. It looks like a television commercial for the good life, late 1990's style. The style of cooking is usually
described as American with international accents: perfectly poached, unusually
flavorful chunks of lobster stand out in a cool salad of young greens, herbs and
mango, dressed with a basil-caviar vinaigrette. Roasted turbot, rich and firm,
gets just the right support from spring-fresh green peas, morels and a tomato-tar-
ragon essence. There can be inconsistencies but when the kitchen is on its
game, Della Femina is very good indeed. Desserts, however, are consistently
outstanding, especially the steamed lemon pudding. **Price Range:** Entrees,
$26–$42.

Delmonico's ☆ $$$ ITALIAN/NEW AMERICAN

56 Beaver St. (at Williams St.)   (212) 509-1144
Credit cards: All major   Meals: L, D

Opulent, old-fashioned and dignified, the huge rooms at this American icon are
rich with stained wood and soft upholstery, and the tables are swathed in oceans
of white linen. The best dishes are in the section headed "Pasta, Risotti." Linguine with clams is a classic that is very well done. Ricotta and spinach ravioli
may lack delicacy, but they are generous little pockets topped with clarified butter and fresh sage, and they make a satisfying meal. The rib-eye may not have
the pedigree of a porterhouse or Delmonico, but it is big, tasty and perfectly
cooked. **Price range:** Entrees, $21–$34.

Deniz à La Turk ☆☆ $$ TURKISH

400 East 57th St. (between First Ave. and Sutton Pl.)   (212) 486-2255
Credit cards: All major   Meals: D

While the kitchen concentrates on food from the sea, the menu is laden with
Turkish dishes that would make people who don't eat fish happy. The salty little

rolls of phyllo-wrapped feta cheese are crunchy and delicious, the yogurt with cucumbers is irresistible and the grilled chicken is fine. But it would be a shame to visit Deniz and miss the fish. So few restaurants in New York City serve whole fish, and here they are beautifully charred with nothing more than lemon and a small onion-and-parsley salad. **Price range:** Entrees, $13–$22.50.

Destinée ☆☆ $$$$ FRENCH

134 East 61st St. (between Lexington and Park Aves.)   (212) 888-1220
Credit cards: All major   Meals: L, D

Fancy French food, an intimate room, relatively reasonable prices: no wonder this small restaurant has been such a hit. This is food so decorative that each plate makes you gasp. The chartreuse of herring, with dots of concentrated beet that sparkle like garnets, looks like an intricate piece of jewelry. Calamari are gorgeous too, quickly seared and set on a green tangle of herbed pasta. Some main dishes feel fussy, but many are excellent, like the sea bass served in a crust of shellfish and capers richly scented with Indian spices. For dessert, the apricot tarte tatin is another jewel. **Price range:** Entrees, $14–$23.

Dock's Oyster Bar ☆ $$ SEAFOOD

633 Third Ave. (at 40th St.)   (212) 986-8080
2427 Broadway (at 89th St.)   (212) 724-5588
Credit cards: All major   Meals: Br, L, D, LN

These bustling fish houses are crowded fish emporiums that give you your money's worth, with sparkling shellfish bars from which to choose shrimp or lobster cocktails or oysters and clams on the half shell. Favorites among starters are the Docks clam chowder, Maryland crab cakes and steamers in beer broth. Engaging entrees include grilled red snapper with coleslaw and rice, grilled salmon steak with coleslaw and steamed potatoes and Caesar salad with grilled tuna. Steamed lobsters come in one- to two-pound sizes, and there is a New England clambake on Sunday and Monday nights. **Price range:** Entrees, $18–$22.

Eight Mile Creek ☆☆ $$$ AUSTRALIAN

240 Mulberry St. (at Prince St.)   (212) 431-4635
Credit cards: All major   Meals: D

Eight Mile Creek is cheery, outgoing and warm, with a bar scene enlivened by a scattering of Australian expats. But when a restaurant announces that it will be serving Australian cuisine, you expect good comic material, not good food. The joke stops when the kangaroo salad arrives: large cubes of the tender, richly flavored loin languish in a marinade flavored with coriander seed, smoked paprika and poached garlic, and then are seared and served on lettuce-leaf wrappers. The menu is short, but the chef makes every dish count. Oyster pie is a pastry-wrapped stew of precisely cooked oysters, still plump and juicy, suspended in a cream sauce chunky with salsify and leeks. Australia without lamb is an impossibility, and the chef does not fool around too much with this sacred national trust, merely braising a whopping big shank and surrounding it with parsnips, chanterelles and roasted apple. The desserts often limit themselves to one thrilling twist, like the pavlova dotted with pink peppercorns for a touch of perfumed sweetness. **Price range:** Entrees, $17–$23.

Eleven Madison Park ☆ ☆ $$$ CONTINENTAL
11 Madison Ave. (at 24th St.)   (212) 889-0905
Credit cards: All major   Meals: L, D   Closed Sun.

Eleven Madison Park occupies the stately ground floor of a grand Art Deco building near the Flatiron building. The restaurant is a conscious homage to the area's past, and the menu is a thoughtful return to Continental cuisine. It could be seriously scary to an audience raised on new American cooking: appetizers include an astonishing amount of offal. It took courage to put a terrine of beef shank, veal feet and foie gras on the menu, but it is a beautiful dish. Sweetbreads are spectacular, too. The best main courses are skate grenobloise and the choucroute of salmon and trout. Desserts are irresistible, especially the plate of lemon desserts and butterscotch pot de crème. **Price range:** Entrees, $19–$32.

El Fogon $25 & Under   SPANISH/PUERTO RICAN
183 East 111th St. (between Lexington and Third Aves.)
(212) 426-4844
Credit cards: Cash only   Meals: L, D   Closed Sun.

The Puerto Rican specialties are fabulous at this friendly neighborhood hangout, which generally offers two interesting main courses each day. Corned beef is ground fine and served in a rich sauce with olives, squash, peppers and onions, enhancing its briny, smoky flavor. Roasted pork is moist and garlicky and chicken fricassee is a beautifully flavored stew. Each dish comes with white rice and plump red beans; for an extra $1, try a remarkably flaky and crisp pastelillo, the Puerto Rican version of empanadas. **Price range:** Avg. entree, $6.

El Pollo $25 & Under   LATIN AMERICAN
1746 First Ave. (at 91st St.)   (212) 996-7810
Credit cards: All major   Meals: L, D

Nobody makes roast chicken better than El Pollo. Each whole chicken is rich, juicy and imbued with the flavors of garlic, lemon, herbs and spices. Many of the unusual Peruvian side dishes are also fine. Try mote, puffs of corn with a pleasantly firm texture, and papa rellena, mashed potatoes stuffed with ground beef, olives and hard boiled eggs, then deep-fried. **Price range:** Entrees, $4–$9.75.

Emily's $25 & Under   SOUTHERN
1325 Fifth Ave. (at 111th St.)   (212) 996-1212
Credit cards: All major   Meals: Br, L, D, LN

This pleasant but institutional restaurant offers a diverse Southern menu and draws an integrated crowd. If you go, go for the meaty, tender baby back pork ribs, subtly smoky and bathed in tangy barbecue sauce, or the big plate of chopped pork barbecue. The best sides include savory rice and peas (actually red beans) and peppery stuffing, and all dishes come with a basket of fine corn bread. Sweet potato pie is the traditional dessert, and Emily's version is nice and nutmeggy. **Price range:** Entrees, $10.25–$24.95.

Empire Diner $ $ DINER
210 10th Ave. (at 22d St.)   (212) 243-2736
Credit cards: All major   Meals: B, Br, L, D, LN

One of the early entries in the modern revival of America's love affair with diners was this campy Art Deco gem that attracted a hip late-night crowd in the 1980's. Nowadays, the Empire is a tourist destination. The up-to-date diner basics with some Mediterranean touches are not bad at all—better than at most diners, in fact—which is reflected in the prices. **Price range:** Entrees, $10–$17.

EQ ☆ ☆ $$$ FRENCH
267 West 4th St. (at Perry St.)   (212) 414-1961
Credit cards: All major   Meals: D, LN   Closed Sun.

Everything about this restaurant seems small, from the intimate dining room (it seats just 40) to the menu. But the first bite tells you that when it comes to cooking, the kitchen thinks big. It favors clear tastes, contrasting textures and unusual ingredients. Steamed cockles are tossed with fresh noodles and sections of pink grapefruit. Foie gras, cabbage and red pepper are another odd threesome, but once again it works. Saddle of rabbit, grilled and served with crisp slices of summer truffles and sweet onions, is truly delicious. Roasted chicken is such a crisp and juicy bird that it tastes as if it were cooked entirely to order. Best among the desserts is the chocolate praline royale. **Price range:** Entrees, $22–$28.

Esca ☆ ☆ $$$ ITALIAN/SEAFOOD
402 West 43rd St. (at Ninth Ave.) (212) 564-7272
Credit cards: All major Meals: L, D Closed Sun.

At Esca—the name means "bait"—the most important word in the Italian language is *crudo*. It means raw, and that's the way the fish comes to the table in a dazzling array of appetizers that could be thought of as Italian sushi. The *crudo* appetizers at Esca are the freshest, most exciting thing to happen to Italian food in recent memory. By changing olive oils, adding a bitter green, or throwing in a scattering of minced chilies, the chef works thrilling variations on a very simple theme. The menu changes daily depending on what comes out of the sea. Look hard enough, and you can find a dish like guinea hen or roast chicken, but it seems perverse to order anything but seafood. Often a single, standout ingredient carries an entire dish. Baked branzino, or sea bass, a special one evening, looked as plain as a sheet of blank paper, nothing more than a big deboned fish with some olive oil, caperberries and a handful of giant Sicilian olives. But oh, those olives. Baking had turned them into 100-megaton flavor bombs that released a complex, ravishing juice, earthy, winy and spicy all at once. About half the menu consists of knockouts. Half is rather ordinary, although the surroundings at Esca can trick any diner into believing otherwise. The lemon-yellow walls and sea-green tiles give it a bright, cool look, and the solid wooden table in the center of the dining room, loaded down with vegetable side dishes, strikes a rustic note while communicating the food philosophy: fresh from the market, and prepared without fuss. **Price range:** Entrees, $17—$26.

Esperanto $25 & Under   PAN-LATIN
145 Avenue C (at Ninth St.)   (212) 505-6559.
Credit cards: AE   Meals: D, LN

This is a warm and welcoming place with Latin food that can be surprisingly subtle and delicate. Bolinho de peixe, deep-fried balls of codfish, are exceptionally light, crisp and flavorful, with a terrific dipping sauce galvanized by spicy mustard. Esperanto's main courses are sturdy and hard to mess up, like a good and beefy steak bathed in chimichurri, the Argentine condiment of garlic and parsley. Feijoada, the Brazilian stew of black beans and smoked meats, has a nice, gritty texture and an almost yeasty flavor. Esperanto serves potent caipirinhas or mojitos, a sort of Cuban mint julep—and don't miss the stellar coconut flan. **Price range:** Entrees, $9 to $14.

Estiatorio Milos ☆ ☆ $$$$ GREEK
125 West 55th St. (between Sixth and Seventh Aves.)   (212) 245-7400
Credit cards: All major   Meals: L, D, LN   Closed Sun.

The restaurant is clean, spare, blindingly white, and the entire focus is on the display of gorgeous fish by the open kitchen. Choose one and it is grilled simply and brought to the table. If you like big fish, like striped bass, bring a crowd. All the fish are cooked whole. And the lamb chops, a concession to meat eaters, are excellent. Appetizers are wonderful, too. The grilled sardines are oily and flavorful, and the octopus, charred and sliced, mixed with onions, capers and peppers, is truly delicious. Thick homemade yogurt is the ideal way to end these meals. **Price range:** fish for main courses is sold whole and by weight, from $20–$32 a pound.

Etats-Unis ☆ ☆ $$$ NEW AMERICAN
242 East 81st St. (between Second & Third Aves.)   (212) 517-8826
Credit cards: All major   Meals: D

This family-run restaurant with only 31 seats serves terrific, eclectic food. The menu is handwritten each day and comes wrapped up in one of the quirkiest, most personal wine lists in the city. The food is astonishingly exuberant, accepting no limits and recognizing no boundaries; yet it also has the appealingly rustic character of the best home cooking. One evening, we began with homemade gnocchi, so light they literally seemed to float off the plate into your mouth. The best entree was slow-cooked pork, so tender that it fell apart at the approach of a fork. Desserts wear their plainness with pride: an apple pie that tastes as if it has just won a blue ribbon at a county fair and a rich, warm and fabulous chocolate soufflé. **Price range:** Entrees, $23–34.

Evergreen Shanghai $25 & Under   CHINESE
63 Mott St. (near Bayard St.)   (212) 571-3339
10 East 38th St. (between Fifth and Madison Aves.)   (212) 448-1199
Credit cards: Cash only at Mott St.   Meals: L, D, LN

Concentrate on the long menu's Shanghai specialties, like cold appetizers of aromatic beef, a Chinese version of barbecued brisket, and smoked fish, sweet with light, smoky notes and hints of star anise. Great main courses include bean curd with crab sauce and yellowfish with seaweed. The staff is friendly, with enough English speakers to help with the selections. **Price range:** Entrees, $5.95–$24.

Felidia ☆ ☆ ☆ $$$$ NORTHERN ITALIAN
243 East 58th St. (between Second and Third Aves.)   (212) 758-1479
Credit cards: All major   Meals: L, D   Closed Sun.

Felidia is an old-fashioned restaurant, comfortable and rustic, and largely oblivious to food fashions. The seasonal menu concentrates on the foods of Italy's northeast: Friuli, the Veneto as well as Istria, now part of Croatia, and the home of owners Felice and Lidia Bastinich. This is robust food served in generous portions, revolving around game, organ meats, and slow-cooked sauces. Homemade cotechino is highly spiced pork with mustard sauce; venison comes with wild rice, Swiss chard, and a thin puree of apples. The plate of venison osso buco is piled high with quince, cranberries and spatzle so soft and light they seem to float off your plate into your mouth. This is not to say you can't eat lightly. Felidia serves lots of seafood, including lobster and crabmeat salad, and an impressive octopus and potato salad. Roasted fish arrives at the table with its head and tail; filleted, slicked with olive oil and served with grilled tomatoes, it is simple and satisfying. Try to sit downstairs; the second floor dining room can be crowded and noisy. **Price range:** Entrees, $27–$28.

Fifty Seven Fifty Seven ☆ ☆ ☆ $$$$ AMERICAN
57 East 57th St., Four Seasons Hotel
(between Park and Madison Aves.)   (212) 758-5757
Credit cards: All major   Meals: B, L, D

With its solicitous service in a memorable public space, Fifty Seven Fifty Seven is setting a new standard for an old tradition. The menu changes frequently with a different prix-fixe offering every day, but it still offers something for absolutely every taste. The food is decidedly American with a modern bent. Vegetarians will find many choices: soups, large salads, even a sampling tray of five vegetable dishes big enough to feed two. Dieters will find starred offerings low in fat and salt. And those with an appetite for meat and potatoes have many options from rack of veal in a red wine sauce to grilled beef tenderloin with rosemary cream potato pie. One of the finest dishes, offered on occasion, is cured swordfish, sliced very thin and served with asparagus, greens and cherries. The visually restrained desserts are

rich in flavor and texture, but the chocolate desserts are the greatest triumph.
Price range: Entrees, $19–$30.

F.Illi Ponte ☆ ☆ $$$$ ITALIAN

39 Desbrosses St. (between Washington St. and West Side Hwy.)
(212) 226-4621
Credit cards: All major   Meals: L, D   Closed Sun.

This is a great, rustic room with bare brick walls, beamed ceilings and a fabulous
view of the Hudson. The menu features admirable Italian fare and fine spicy
lobster. The porchetta, spit-roasted baby pig, is superb. Fried calamari are sweet,
crisp, irresistible. Shrimp cocktail is just about perfect. There is an excellent
veal chop and good (if expensive) broccoli rape. Even if the menu were not
filled with dishes that I love, I'd go to F.illi Ponte for the sheer pleasure of sitting
in that beautiful old room watching the light fade over the Hudson River and to
bask in the extraordinary service. **Price range:** Entrees, $22–$38.

Firebird ☆ ☆ $$$ RUSSIAN

365 West 46th St. (between Eighth and Ninth Aves.)   (212) 586-0244
Credit cards: All major   Meals: L, D

When the Russian Tearoom closed, the crowd moved to this jewel box of a
restaurant. With a room as ornate and luxurious as a Fabergé egg, and a staff so
polished, it really does seem that you have entered some more serene and lavish era. The caviar arrives with its own private waiter who turns the service
into a performance, pouring hot butter onto the plate, spooning on the caviar
and then delicately twirling the blini around the roe. The wild mushroom
zhulien, roasted beet and walnut phkali and Georgian chicken satsivi, are delicious appetizers. Among the first courses, the manti, hearty steamed lamb
dumplings, and the herring are worth ordering. If you want to eat lightly, try
the grilled sturgeon in a creamy mustard sauce. Desserts, unfortunately, are a
disappointment. **Price range:** Entrees, $25–$30.

First $25 & Under NEW AMERICAN

87 First Ave. (between 5th and 6th Sts.)   (212) 674-3823
Credit cards: All major   Meals: D, LN

Ambitious, creative contemporary American fare at relatively modest prices,
served late into the night. First also offers an intelligently chosen list of wines
and beers and worthwhile weekly specials, like its Sunday night pig roast. **Price
range:** Avg. entree, $17.

Flor's Kitchen $25 & Under VENEZUELAN

149 First Ave. (near 9th St.)   (212) 387-8949
Credit cards: All major   Meals: L, D, LN

Tiny, bright and colorful, this new Venezuelan restaurant offers many snacking
foods like empanadas criollas, smooth, crisp pastries with fillings like savory

shredded beef or pureed chicken. The arepas—corncakes with varied fillings—include my favorite, chicken and avocado salada. Two sauces—one made with avocado, lemon juice and oil; the second, a hot sauce—make dishes like chachapas (corn pancakes with ham and cheese) taste even better. Soups are superb, and desserts are rich and homespun. **Price range:** Entrees, $4–$9.

Follonico ☆☆ $$$ ITALIAN
6 West 24th St. (near Fifth Ave.)   (212) 691-6359
Credit cards: All major   Meals: L, D   Closed Sun.

Follonico serves terrific Tuscan food from a wood-fired oven in a casually elegant atmosphere. The straightforward Italian fare here is the perfect antidote to too much fancy food. One bite of its spaghetti Genovese is enough to restore your faith in simplicity. What next? Perhaps a whole fish, roasted in a rock-salt crust with only broccoli rape and a few potatoes on the side. It's comforting to know that I can always walk into this restaurant and find a wonderful fritto misto of seafood. But when I think of Follonico, what I really crave is pasta or risotto. Try the malloreddus ("little bulls" in Sardinian dialect), small, ridged curves of pasta, lightly tossed with crumbles of sweet sausage, bits of broccoli rape and diced fresh tomatoes. Desserts are the least impressive section of the menu. **Price range:** Entrees, $16.25–$29.

The Four Seasons ☆☆☆ $$$$ NEW AMERICAN
99 East 52d St. (between Park and Lexington Aves.)   (212) 754-9494
Credit cards: All major Meals L, D   Closed Sun.

In a time of know-nothing waiters and deafening dining rooms, the Four Seasons is a gracious reminder that restaurants can still be comfortable and relaxing. The Grill room is still the power lunch place for those who count in fashion, finance and publishing. At lunch the menu is straightforward: begin with a big baked potato, served with its own bottle of olive oil, followed by meaty crab cakes or the bunless burger with creamed spinach and crisp onions. The Pool Room is at its best with unfussy food like broiled dover sole or rack of lamb and the perfect steak tartare. My favorite is the perfect duck—a bird with a skin so crisp it crackles invitingly with each bite. But wherever you are seated, it is hard to eat at the Four Seasons without luxuriating in an extraordinary sense of privilege. In the many years that the Four Seasons has been pampering its patrons, it has learned how to send each one out the door with a sense of having lived, if only for a few hours, the life of the very rich. **Price range:** Entrees, $34–$55.

Frank $25 & Under   ITALIAN
88 Second Ave. (near 5th St.)   (212) 420-0202
Credit cards: Cash only   Meals: Br, L, D, LN

This sweet, unpretentious restaurant, with its crowded, ragtag dining room, has been packed from the moment it opened. Start with an order of insalata

Caprese, ripe tomatoes and mozzarella di bufala, and you may forget the tight surroundings. Among the entrees, I loved polpettone, a savory meatloaf, with a classic, slow-cooked gravy, and orecchiette with fennel and pecorino Toscano. If you go early, you can expect special touches, like a free plate of tiny potato croquettes, or a dish of olive oil flavored with orange rind with your bread. **Price range:** Entrees, $6.95–$14.95.

Frank's ☆ $$$ STEAKHOUSE
85 10th Ave. (at 15th St.)   (212) 243-1349
Credit cards: All major   Meals: L, D

A paradise for carnivores and smokers. The bare brick walls and long bar announce this as a restaurant whose only desire is to serve big portions to hungry people. Three or four shrimp in a cocktail would probably provide enough protein for an average person: they are giant creatures of the sea, and absolutely delicious. The T-bone steak has the fine, funky flavor of meat that has been dry-aged for a long time and the steak fries are long and thick. The same family has been running Frank's since 1912; they want you to feel at home, and you will. **Price range:** Entrees, $18–$29.

Fresco By Scotto ☆ ☆ $$$ ITALIAN
34 East 52d St. (between Park and Madison Aves.)   (212) 935-3434
Credit cards: All major   Meals: L, D   Closed Sun.

At this political hangout in the middle of midtown, power lunchers eat grilled pizza and great Tuscan food. Fresco is an entirely new take on the old Italian mom-and-pop place. The heart and generosity of the red-sauce restaurants have been blended with the sophistication of a new generation. The grilled pizza is irresistible; so are most of the appetizers. But it's the pasta that you find yourself remembering. All are served in staggering portions. Entrees are equally massive. **Price range:** Avg. $45–$60 per person.

Funky Broome $25 & Under CHINESE
176 Mott St. (bet. Broome & Kenmare Sts.)
(212) 941-8628 Credit cards: All major   Meals: L, D, LN

From its odd name, which connotes the irreverence of those nonsensical Japanese T-shirts, to its brightly colored interior, Funky Broome suggests youth and energy rather than conformity. The staff is young, and so is the owner. Though the menu is largely Cantonese and Hong Kong, Funky Broome has stirred it up a bit with some Thai touches and by making mini-woks centerpieces. The small woks are set over Sterno flames, which keep everything bubbling hot. Some of the dishes are unusual and good, like a delicious vegetarian casserole of nutty-tasting fried lotus roots in a gingery sauce with dried cherries, and plump and flavorful oysters stuffed with green onions and steamed in a red wine sauce. Seafood dishes are excellent. Salt and pepper seafood, a familiar Cantonese dish of fried shrimp, scallops and squid, is flawless. Funky Broome can breathe new life into hoary old dishes like crisp and tender beef with broccoli, while shredded chicken with Chinese vegetables is full of distinct and honest flavors. **Price range:** Entrees, $6.95-$15.95.

Gabriela's $25 & Under   MEXICAN
685 Amsterdam Ave. (at 93d St.)   (212) 961-0574
311 Amsterdam Ave. (at 75th St.)
Credit cards: All major   Meals: B, L, D

There really is a Gabriela, and she makes terrific, authentic Mexican dishes. Taquitos al pastor, tiny corn tortillas topped with vinegary roast pork, pineapple salsa and cilantro, are a wonderful Mexican street dish. Gabriela's pozole, the traditional Mexican soup made with hominy, is an entire meal in itself, served in a huge bowl with chunks of tender pork or chicken. Entrees all come with tortillas so fragrant that the aroma of corn rises with the steam. Gabriela's also offers superb desserts, including capirotada, a buttery bread pudding with lots of honey. **Price range:** Entrees, $5.95–$14.95.

Gabriel's ☆ ☆ $$$ ITALIAN
11 West 60th St. (between Broadway and Columbus Ave.)
(212) 956-4600
Credit cards: All major   Meals: L, D   Closed Sun.

This clubby and comfortable restaurant offers great big portions and fabulous friendly service. Although the food is called Tuscan, it is far too American for that, too original. What Tuscan restaurant ever made tuna into a sausage, grilled it over a wood fire and then served it with a pile of peppers glistening with olive oil? The dish on almost every table is an earthy and seductive buckwheat polenta. None of the pastas are ordinary, either. The real winner here is homemade gnocchi, little dumplings so light they float into your mouth and down your throat. Among the entrees, the best dish is the sea bass cooked in a terra cotta casserole. Desserts, with the exception of the wonderful sorbets and gelatos, are not very exciting. **Price range:** Entrees, $17–$27.

Garrick $25 & Under   NEW AMERICAN
242 West 49th St. (between Eighth Ave. and Broadway)
(212) 489-8600
Credit cards: All major   Meals: B, L, D

This handsome, clubby little restaurant is my new answer to the question, "Where can I eat inexpensively near the theater district?" Named after the 17th-century Shakespearean actor David Garrick, it has wood-paneled walls covered with wonderful 1940's-era celebrity photographs; its menu is also largely a retrospective of 1940's favorites. One of the best, oysters Rockefeller, is incredibly rich and luxurious. Some old Provençal favorites also show up, like puff-pastry pissaladière topped with olives, caramelized onions and garlicky snails. Desserts are quite good, especially the dense chocolate pot de crème. **Price range:** Entrees from $8.50.

Good $25 & Under   LATIN AMERICAN
89 Greenwich Ave. (at Bank St.)   (212) 691-8080
Credit cards: All major   Meals: L, D   Closed Mon.

It's possible to eat unusually, eclectically and very well here. Crisp peanut chicken is a welcome old dish, while grilled calamari, a newcomer, takes its cue from Asia, arriving in a lime-and-mint dressing. Also good are the grilled flank steak with parsley-garlic sauce and sauteed rock shrimp, flavored with garlic and served over gloriously mushy grits with corn relish. The service is warm and professional. The signature dessert, house-made doughnuts, are rather dry and tasteless, although the demitasse of Oaxacan chocolate served with them is delicious. **Price range:** Entrees, $10–$17.

Good World Bar and Grill $25 & Under SCANDINAVIAN
3 Orchard Street (at Division St.)   (212) 925-9975.
Credit cards: All major   Meals: D, LN

Good World Bar and Grill beckons because it's a bar in an old barbershop near Chinatown that serves Scandinavian food. It offers a spirit of adventure, a departure from the routine, that makes Good World's world a good world indeed. Basic dishes like Swedish meatballs and potato pancakes can be unpredictable; Good World is on far firmer ground with seafood. Skagen is shrimp with créme fraîche and dill, served on toast. It's pretty good, a nice prelude for the exceptionally tender and tasty sautéed squid, or the fabulous fish soup, a bisque that tastes like the essence of the sea. **Price range:** Medium and large plates, $8 to $16.

Goody's ☆ $ CHINESE
1 East Broadway (at Chatham Sq.) Chinatown   (212) 577-2922
Credit cards: All major   Meals: L, D

Goody's pride is the crab meat version of soup dumplings, xiao long bao, tinted pink by the seafood that glows through the sheer, silky skin. But there are other unusual dishes, like fabulous turnip pastries, yellowfish fingers in seaweed batter, and braised pork shoulder, a kind of candied meat. This dish is so rich that it must be eaten in small bites. Goody's kitchen also works magic with bean curd, mixed with crab meat so it becomes rich and delicious. **Price range:** $15–$20.

Gotham Bar and Grill ☆ ☆ ☆ $$$$ NEW AMERICAN
12 East 12th St. (between Fifth and University Pl.)   (212) 620-4020
Credit cards: All major   Meals: L,D

Gotham Bar and Grill is a cheerful, welcoming restaurant in an open, high-ceilinged room with a lively bar along one side. Through some trick of design, each table offers intimacy: seated, you have the sense of watching without being watched. Waiters take their cues from the customer—anticipating their every wish and making diners feel remarkably well cared for. And then there's the food. The chef, Alfred Portale, famous for his vertical dishes, is working with an architecture of flavor, composing his dishes so that each element contributes something vital. His food seems modern but is almost classic in its balance. His signature dish is seafood salad, a spiral of scallops, squid, octopus, lobster and avocado that swirls onto the plate like a mini-tornado. Main courses are more straightforward. Rosy slices of duck breast might be set off by a single caramelized endive and a sweet potato puree, or by bok choy and caramelized mango. Squab topped with foie gras may be accompanied by sweet corn, polenta and cranberry beans or pureed potatoes. Desserts, like the wonderful chocolate cake, are intense and very American. **Price range:** Entrees, $26–$34.

Gramercy Tavern ☆ ☆ ☆ $$$$ NEW AMERICAN
42 East 20th St. (between Broadway and Park Ave. S.)   (212) 477-0777
Credit cards: All major   Meals: L, D

The large and lively tavern has redefined grand dining in New York. Chef Tom Colicchio cooks with extraordinary confidence, creating dishes characterized by bold flavors and unusual harmonies. Marinated hamachi is brushed with lemon and olive oil; roast beets and herbs are scattered across the top. The clean, fresh taste of the fish comes soaring through with the clarity of a flute. Salmon is baked in salt until the flesh has the texture of velvet. A silky, just-cooked breast of chicken with truffles stuffed under the skin in a lively broth perfumed with rosemary is chicken soup raised to an entirely new level. To experience Mr. Colicchio's cooking at its best, consider the chef's extraordinary market menu. At $90, it is expensive, but perfect for special occasions. For a less expensive alternative, the handsome bar in front offers a casual but excellent menu. **Price range:** 3-course prix-fixe, $62; vegetarian tasting menu, $68; 3-course seasonal tasting menu, $78.

Grand Sichuan $25 & Under   CHINESE
229 Ninth Ave. (at 24th St.)   (212) 620-5200
Credit cards: All major   Meals: L, D

The owner of this terrific restaurant hands out a 27-page pamphlet that explains five Chinese regional cuisines and describes dozens of dishes the restaurant serves. The eating is as interesting as the reading, with wonderful dishes like sour stringbeans with minced pork and tea-smoked duck. While Sichuan food is indeed spicy, that is only part of the story, as you see when you taste a fabulous cold dish like sliced conch with wild pepper sauce, coated with ground Sichuan peppercorns, which are not hot but bright, effervescent and almost refreshing. **Price range:** Entrees, $5.95–$16.95.

Grange Hall $25 & Under   AMERICAN

50 Commerce St. (at Barrow St.)   (212) 924-5246
Credit cards: AE   Meals: Br, L, D

Grange Hall celebrates Depression-era American food of the Midwest with flair, from fat little loaves of white bread to succotash, pork chops and lake fish. The food is usually pretty good, the décor is inspiring and the all-American wine and beer list is appealing. **Price range:** Entrees, $10.50–$21.

Grill Room ☆ ☆ $$$ NEW AMERICAN/SEAFOOD

2 World Financial Center   (212) 945-9400
Credit cards: All major   Meals: L, D

Wall Street has changed, and the Grill Room means to feed modern traders with up-to-date appetites. The menu is straightforward American fare with no exotic ingredients. Meals begin with warm biscuits so rich and crumbly they're impossible to stop eating. Many of the first courses are spectacular. Crab cakes wrapped into a spring roll are light and perfectly right. The dense chowder is the essence of corn, beautifully swirled with vegetable purees. The American theme continues with the main courses, which are heavy on protein. Of all the meats, pot-roasted short ribs are the best. The desserts are rich and wonderful. **Price range:** Entrees, $14–$28.

Guastavino's ☆ ☆ $$$$ ENGLISH/FRENCH

409 East 59th St. (between First and York Aves.)   (212) 980-2455
Credit cards: All major   Meals: L, D

Sir Terence Conran's dazzling transformation of the Queensboro Bridge vaults gives New Yorkers their first glimpse of a swaggering new international restaurant style where the scenes are loud, lively and up to the minute, and the food often runs second to the design. Guastavino's fits the pattern. The raw, almost brutal granite blocks that make up the caissons of the bridge have been left exposed. But the overall design is as sleek and international as the Concorde. It's not so much a restaurant as an opportunity to live, for two or three hours, a certain mood, and a certain sense of style, that suits every time zone and speaks every language.

   A long, low-slung bar on the main level pulls a large Upper East Side crowd. Guastavino Restaurant, on the first floor, is a 300-seat brasserie, clamorous and casual, with a glorious brasserie-style shellfish display in front of the kitchen. Up a curved marble staircase, the more formal and intimate Club Guastavino, which seats 100, hangs over the first floor like a giant balcony, soaking up noise and energy from below, but retaining a swaddled sense of isolation and privilege, enhanced by more luxurious materials and boothlike velvet-upholstered sofas. Guastavino's two kitchens feed a lot of people out there, and considering the number of diners swarming into the two restaurants, they do a more than respectable job. The food may not light up the night, but at its best, these are well-conceived, well-executed dishes that really can compete with the surroundings. **Price range:** Guastavino Restaurant: $14–$30. Club Guastavino: Dinner, three courses, $65.

Gus's Figs Bistro and Bar $25 & Under   MEDITERRANEAN
250 West 27th St. (between Seventh and Eighth Aves.)
(212) 352-8822
Credit cards: All major   Meals: L, D, LN

This restaurant captures the dreamy, generous, sun-soaked aura that makes the
Mediterranean so endlessly appealing. The chef excels at blending flavors and
textures in main courses like moist, flavorful chicken, braised in a clay pot and
served over creamy polenta. Top dishes include tender pieces of lamb served
over a soft bread pudding made savory with goat cheese and pine nuts and
sweetened with figs; and pan-roasted cod with grilled leeks, orange sections
and pomegranate vinaigrette. **Price range:** Entrees, $13–$19.50.

Habib's Place $25 & Under   MIDDLE EASTERN
438 East 9th St. (between First Ave. and Ave. A.)   (212) 979-2243
Credit cards: Cash only   Meals: B, Br, L, D, LN

A tiny North African and Middle Eastern restaurant that is a neighborhood
hangout for anybody carrying a guitar in the East Village. The owner, Habib
Belkadi, cooks by whim, using the ingredients he has fresh, pricing dishes off
the top of his head. One dish almost always available is the terrific falafel
sandwich, a big yet manageable concoction that is a perfect quick meal. Triangular wedges of baklava are often available, as are other less characteristic
desserts, like an intensely rich chocolate-walnut pie. **Price range:** Entrees,
$6–$9.

Hangawi ☆☆ $$ KOREAN/VEGETARIAN
12 East 32d St. (between Fifth and Madison Aves.)   (212) 213-0077
Credit cards: All major   Meals: L, D

Hangawi leaves you feeling cleansed and refreshed, as if you had come from a
spa instead of a vegetarian Korean restaurant. Eating in this calm, elegant
space with its smooth wooden bowls and heavy ceramic cups is utterly peaceful. Diners remove their shoes on entering and sit at low tables with their feet
dangling comfortably into the sunken space beneath them. They are surrounded by unearthly Korean music, wonderful objects and people who move
with deliberate grace. Many of the exotic greens, porridges and mountain
roots on the menu can be sampled by ordering the emperor's meal, which
includes a tray of nine kinds of mountain greens surrounded by 10 side dishes:
water kimchi, cold spinach, sweet lotus root with sesame, chili cabbage and
the like. **Price range:** Entrees, $14.95–$19.95.

Han Sung Garden $25 & Under   KOREAN
42 West 35th St. (between Fifth and Sixth Aves.)   (212) 563-1285
Credit cards: All major   Meals: L, D

The menu at this handsome Korean restaurant is 24 pages long, but some of the
finest dishes are the free condiments that come automatically when you order.

What makes Han Sung special are the lesser-known dishes that epitomize Korea's gutsy, assertive cuisine: modeum jun, a selection of seafood, beef and vegetables dipped in egg batter and carefully fried, or yang nyum dooboo, tofu poached in soy sauce, a remarkably refreshing dish. Topping everything off is persimmon broth, a lively mix of sweet and spicy that captures in a cup the lively contrasts in Korean cuisine. **Price range:** $10–$25.

Hatsuhana ☆☆ $$$ JAPANESE/SUSHI
17 East 48th St. (between Fifth and Madison Aves.)   (212) 355-3345
237 Park Ave. (at 46th St.)   (212) 661-3400
Credit cards: All major   Meals: L, D   Closed Sun.

Of all the city's sushi bars, Hatsuhana is the one that best bridges the gap between East and West. It is a comfortable and welcoming restaurant where you can depend on being served high-quality sushi whether you speak Japanese or not. Real connoisseurs sit at the downstairs sushi bar and enjoy extraordinary chu toro, tuna that is richer than maguro but less rich than toro, and ika uni, pure white squid cut into long strips as thin as spaghetti. The quality of the cooked food is excellent, too. The Park Avenue location is not nearly as good as the 48th Street location. **Price range:** Avg. entree, $30.

Havana NY $25 & Under   LATIN AMERICAN
27 West 38th St. (between Fifth and Sixth Aves.)   (212) 944-0990
Credit cards: All major   Meals: L, D   Closed Sat. & Sun.

There's little not to like about this bustling Cuban restaurant, a lunchtime hot spot serving tasty, inexpensive food in pleasant surroundings. The food is typically robust, flavored with lusty doses of garlic and lime, yet it can be delicate, too, as in an octopus salad, which is marinated in citrus until tender like a ceviche. Chilean sea bass, is moist and subtly flavored, not the sort of dish that would succeed in an assembly-line kitchen. Grilled skirt steak is excellent, served with a pungent chimichurri sauce, essentially garlic and parsley, that is delicious spread over the steak. All the main courses are enormous, served with rice, beans and sweet plantains—so appetizers are usually unnecessary. Service is swift and likable. **Price range:** Entrees, $8.95–$12.95.

Heartbeat ☆☆ $$ NEW AMERICAN
149 East 49th St. (at Lexington Ave.)   (212) 407-2900
Credit cards: All major   Meals: B, Br, L, D

New York's hippest spa food brings models to mingle with moguls in a slick setting. You could describe Heartbeat that way, but it would be doing the restaurant a disservice; this is a very comfortable, crowded and surprisingly quiet room with good service and good food. This approach works best when the food is simply left alone, like whole roasted quail with a mushroom-and-fig hash. Try the simple grills, the good meats and the Japanese-accented dishes. Be prepared for the tea sommelier to show up at the end of the meal. **Price range:** Entrees, $20–$29.

Hell's Kitchen $25 & Under   MEXICAN
679 Ninth Ave. (near 47th St.) (212) 977-1588
Credit cards: All major Meals: D, LN

For almost three years, Sue Torres was the chef at Rocking Horse Cafe Mexicano in Chelsea, a showcase for the possibilities of Mexican food beyond the tyranny of nachos, burritos and refried beans. In her new restaurant, she has continued her creative use of Mexican flavorings and cooking techniques and added ingredients and dishes from the global palette of contemporary American cooking. But if you're interested in what Ms. Torres can do when she's inspired, head directly for the interpretations of Mexican dishes. Her appetizer of tuna tostadas is brilliant. The small rounds of fresh fish are imbued with coriander and seared, then planted on crisp corn tortillas with guacamole and pineapple, a combination that melds effortlessly. Ms. Torres devotes part of her menu to quesadillas, house-made flour tortillas layered with cheese and other fillings. In size, they are like small main courses; in spirit, they succeed because they retain their clear Mexican identity even with creative enhancements. The best main course is a pork loin flavored with chili and set over steamed corn and pineapple. For dessert try the sorbets, which are wonderfully intense, made of different fruits each night and served over fruit with a surprising touch of chili. Other good choices include a fabulous coconut flan and a sweet banana empanada. In atmosphere, Hell's Kitchen is international, with music that is more Cuban than Mexican. The loud music and hopping bar suggest that ordinary conversations will be difficult, but once you sit down the acoustics are surprisingly good. **Price range:** Entrees, $13—$18.

Hog Pit $25 & Under   SOUTHERN
22 Ninth Ave. (at 13th St.)   (212) 604-0092
Credit cards: All major   Meals: D, LN   Closed Mon.

Nothing remarkable about this small bar in the meat-packing district, except that the kitchen unexpectedly turns out fine Southern food. The baby back ribs are terrific: meaty, tender enough to fall off the bone and bathed in a peppery sauce sweetened by molasses and brown sugar. Hush puppies are the real thing: cornmeal blended with garlic, celery and onion, and deep-fried until crisp, and the tart fried green tomatoes come with a crisp, greaseless cornmeal crust. The staff is friendly, the jukebox is loud, the room is smoky and the beer is cold. **Price range:** Entrees, $6.25–$12.95.

Holy Basil $25 & Under   THAI
149 Second Ave. (between 9th and 10th Sts.)   (212) 460-5557
Credit cards: All major   Meals: D, LN

This is one of the best Thai restaurants in the city, turning out highly spiced, beautifully balanced dishes like green papaya salad, elegant curries and delicious noodles. The dining room looks more like a beautiful church than a restaurant, jazz usually plays in the background and the wine list offers terrific choices. **Price range:** Entrees, $8–$16.

Home $25 & Under   AMERICAN
20 Cornelia St. (between Bleecker and West 4th Sts.)   (212) 243-9579
Credit cards: AE   Meals: B, Br, L, D

This little storefront makes creative interpretations of Middle American dishes like short ribs, pork chops and even fondue. The husband-and-wife owners, who also own Drovers Tap Room nearby, make their own sausages and ketchup and are thoroughly interesting and unconventional. **Price range:** Entrees, $16–$18.

Honmura An ☆ ☆ ☆ $$$ JAPANESE/NOODLES
170 Mercer St. (between Houston and Prince Sts.)   (212) 334-5253
Credit cards: All major Meals L, D   Closed Mon.

Making the buckwheat noodles known as soba is not easy. The Japanese say it takes a year to learn to mix the dough, another year to learn to roll it, a third to learn the correct cut. The soba chefs at Honmura An have clearly put in their time—the soba in this spare, soothing space is wonderful and worth the high price. Many appetizers, as well as good tempura, are worth trying here, including edamame (salted soybeans) and tori dongo, lightly fried balls of ground chicken. But nothing is remotely on a par with the noodles. To appreciate how fine they are, you must eat them cold. The noodles are earthy and elastic, and when you dip them into the briny bowl of dashi (dipping sauce), land and sea come, briefly, together. Honmura An also makes the best udon—the fat wheat noodles—I've ever eaten. Served cold with a sesame dipping sauce, they snap when you bite into them. Served hot, in the dish called nabeyaki (a staple of cheap noodle shops), they virtually redefine the dish. **Price range:** entrees, $13–$22

Hudson River Club ☆ ☆ $$$$ NEW AMERICAN
250 Vesey St., 4 World Financial Center   (212) 786-1500
Credit cards: All major   Meals: Br, L, D

This very sedate, very expensive restaurant has upscale American food, a dazzling view of the river, a largely male clientele and a great bar. Despite its spectacular setting, Hudson River Club is not a romantic restaurant. Everything about the place makes it a perfect place for a business meeting. It is also one of the few waterfront restaurants in which seafood is not the main draw. The kitchen makes some delicious hearty stews, like a braised rabbit pot pie with wild mushrooms and wine hidden beneath a great puff of pastry. Or try one of the dishes from the game menu. To end the meal with a laugh, try the white chocolate teacup filled with cheesecake, with a cookie spoon and a phyllo teabag. **Price range:** Entrees, $29–$36.

Icon ☆ ☆ $ $ NEW AMERICAN
130 East 39th St. (between Lexington and Park Aves.)   (212) 592-8888
Credit cards: All major   Meals: B, Br, L, D

Icon is swanky, slinky, murky. Located in the W Court Hotel, it has a mildly lurid décor and a lighting philosophy perfectly designed for illegal trysts and furtive meetings. It comes with a boutique hotel attached, ensuring a steady flow of youngish, stylish diners. Visually, it is soothing to the nerves. Aurally, it's touch and go. As the evening progresses, a thumping rock soundtrack forces diners to shout across the table, and the whoops and shouts of gaiety from Wet Bar across the lobby become intrusive.

The food at Icon is better than the setting might suggest. Warm Fishers Island oysters, for example, are served on the half shell, swathed in a luxurious saffron cream, with crisp strands of leek for textural contrast, and they are sublime. Braised oxtail, presented in a fat, round slice, is tender and deeply flavored, and seared foie gras in a hard-cider reduction is another winner, set off by tart Fuji apples and cranberries. Desserts are not flashy; quiet good taste is more the style. **Price range:** Entrees, $19–$25.

Il Mulino $ $ $ $ ITALIAN
86 W. 3d St. (between Sullivan & Thompson Sts.)   (212) 673-3783
Credit cards: All major   Meals: L, D, LN   Closed Sun.

Big portions, long waits, a halcyon atmosphere. No wonder New Yorkers are so enthralled with this garlic haven. While the portions are large, so are the prices. Dinner might begin with a dish of shrimp fricassee with garlic; bresaola of beef served over mixed greens tossed in a well-seasoned vinaigrette, or aromatic baked clams oreganato. The pasta roster includes fettuccine Alfredo; spaghettini in a robust Bolognese sauce; trenette tossed in pesto sauce; and capellini all'arrabbiata, or in a spicy tomato sauce. The menu carries a dozen veal preparations, along with beef tenderloin in a shallot, white wine and sage sauce; and broiled sirloin. **Price range:** Entrees, $24 and up.

Il Valentino ☆ ☆ $ $ ITALIAN
330 East 56th St., Sutton Hotel (between First and Second Aves.)
(212) 355-0001
Credit cards: All major   Meals: Br, L, D

In a city where purely pleasant restaurants have become increasingly rare, Il Valentino feels like an oasis. The food is reliable, you don't have to wait for your table and you know you will be able to hear your friends when they talk. The timbered ceiling and terra cotta floor give the room a cool rustic feeling, and the food is simple, tasty Tuscan fare. The artichoke salad is delicious, and the Caesar salad is impressive. But it is the pastas that really shine. My favorite is handmade garganelli, little quills tossed in a classic white veal, prosciutto and mortadellaragu. Marinated grilled lamb chops in a mustard seed sauce and osso buco are also excellent. **Price range:** entrees, $13–$22.

'ino $25 & Under   ITALIAN/SANDWICHES
21 Bedford St. (between Sixth Ave. and Downing St.)   (212) 989-5769
Credit cards: Cash only   Meals: B, Br, L, D

This inviting little Italian sandwich shop and wine bar offers intensely satisfying variations on three types of sandwich: panini, sandwiches made with crusty toasted ciabatta; tramezzini, made with untoasted white bread, crusts removed and cut into triangles, and bruschetta, in which ingredients are simply placed atop a slice of toasted bread. One dish that doesn't fall into any category but is nonetheless wonderful is truffled egg toast, a soft cooked egg served on top of toasted ciabatta with sliced asparagus and drizzled with truffle oil. It's like warm, delicious baby food. **Price range:** Entrees, $2–$10.

Island Spice $25 & Under   CARIBBEAN
402 West 44th St. (between Ninth and 10th Aves.)   (212) 765-1737
Credit cards: All major   Meals: L, D

This little storefront offers refined Caribbean cooking to a steady stream of show business types. Little beef patties, gently spiced bits of ground beef encased in half-moons of flaky dough, are a savory way to begin, and earthy red bean soup has a long, lingering, slightly smoky flavor. Island Spice's jerk barbecue (pork or chicken) is excellent. Island Spice serves beer and wine as well as Caribbean concoctions like sorrell, a tart, refreshing deep-red beverage made from hibiscus. **Price range:** Entrees, $8.95–$21.95.

Isola $25 & Under   ITALIAN
485 Columbus Ave. (between 83d and 84th Sts.)   (212) 362-7400
Credit cards: All major   Meals: Br, L, D

When Isola is crowded, its dining room, full of hard surfaces, can be unbearably loud, but the restaurant offers some of the best Italian food on the Upper West Side, with lively pastas like spaghetti in a purée of black olives and oregano, and fettuccine with crumbled sausages and porcini mushrooms. The wine list is nicely chosen. **Price range:** Entrees, $9.95–$18.

I Trulli ☆ ☆ $$$ ITALIAN
122 East 27th St. (between Lexington Ave. and Park Ave. S.)
(212) 481-7372
Credit cards: All major   Meals: L, D   Closed Sun.

This is New York City's best and most attractive restaurant dedicated to the cooking of Apulia. It serves interesting, unusual food in an understated room that is both elegant and warm; there is also a beautiful garden for outdoor dining. The rustic food from Italy's heel does not have the subtle charm of northern Italian food or the tomato-and-garlic heartiness of Neapolitan cuisine. The menu relies on bitter greens (arugula, dandelions, broccoli rape) and many foods that Americans rarely eat. The pastas have a basic earthy quality; orechiette are a house staple made by the owner. **Price range:** Entrees, $18–$29.

Jack Rose ☆ $$$ NEW AMERICAN/STEAKHOUSE
771 Eighth Ave. (at 47th St.) (212) 247-7518
Credit cards: All major   Meals: L, D

Jack Rose is an artful exercise in nostalgia. The smooth, dark wood floors and brown leather booths feel like the 1930's. The huge horizontal stone fireplace, the polished driftwood accents and the rec room paneling evoke postwar suburbia with a touch of lounge. It's a classic, four-square, no-punches-pulled all-American joint that specializes in seafood, steaks, chops and no funny stuff. Scallops wrapped in good, strong bacon delivers a gutsy American flavor, and the spicy mayonnaise on the side of the plate doubles the pleasure. Pan-roasted halibut, a generous snow-white slab with a golden-brown crust, could not be simpler, but it gets the job done. Although Jack Rose reserves a lot of room on the menu for steaks, Peter Luger has nothing to fear. The beef covers the plate, but it makes a pretty feeble impression on the palate. The kitchen can still win you over. At one meal it might be the oysters Rockefeller, topped with lovely fresh cress and piqued with just the right touch of Pernod. At lunch it could be a plump, moist chicken, roasted to a crisp mahogany. Aside from the bread pudding and a more than respectable crème brûlée, the desserts never quite hit the spot. Jack Rose seems about halfway there. When you hit, you hit big. When you don't—nothing. **Price range:** Entrees, $10.95—$28.50.

Jean Claude $25 & Under   BISTRO/FRENCH
137 Sullivan St. (between Prince and Houston Sts.)   (212) 475-9232
Credit cards: Cash only   Meals: D

The bustling dining room is authentically Parisian, with the scent of Gitanes and the sound of French in the air. For these low prices you don't expect to find appetizers like seared sea scallops with roasted beets or main courses like roasted monkfish with savoy cabbage, olives and onions. **Price range:** Entrees, $12–$16.

Jean Georges ☆ ☆ ☆ ☆ $$$$ NEW AMERICAN
1 Central Park West, Trump Hotel (at 60th St.)   (212) 299-3900
Credit cards: All major   Meals L, D   Closed Sun.

Chef and co-owner Jean-Georges Vongerichten has created an entirely new kind of four-star restaurant. He has examined all the details that make dining luxurious, and refined them for an American audience. Most important, he has returned the focus to the food. And he is at the top of his form. The austerity of the design of the restaurant, on Central Park West, also puts the focus on food. And while some restaurants are more concerned with who is in the room than what is on the plate, the people at Jean Georges neither fawn nor intimidate. This is no celebrity restaurant; all over the dining room, waiters bend over the food, carving or pouring, intent only on their guests' pleasure. **Price range:** 3 courses, $85; 8-course tasting menu, $115.

Joe Allen $ $ NEW AMERICAN
326 West 46th St. (between Eighth and Ninth Aves.)   (212) 581-6464
Credit cards: All major   Meals: Br, L, D

Chili and celebrities in the heart of Broadway. The food's not great, but it's not expensive either. If you're looking for safe, unpretentious American food in the high-rent Restaurant Row, this is the place. **Price range:** Entrees, $9–$19.50.

Joe's Shanghai ☆☆ $ CHINESE
24 West 56th St. (between Fifth and Sixth Aves.)   (212) 333-3868
9 Pell St., Chinatown   (212) 233-8888
Credit cards: Cash only   Meals: L, D

These spartan restaurants serve awesome xiao lung bao—Shanghai soup dumplings, modestly listed on the menu as "steamed buns". The chef has perfected the art of wrapping hot liquid in pastry: the filling is rich, light and swimming in hot soup. Everybody orders them, but there are many other wonderful dishes, including smoked fish, strongly flavored with star anise, vegetarian duck, thin sheets of braised tofu folded like skin over mushrooms, and drunken crabs, raw marinated blue crabs with a musty, fruity flavor that is powerful and unforgettable. **Price range:** A la carte $9.50 and up.

Jo Jo ☆☆☆ $$$$ FRENCH
160 East 64th St. (between Lexington and Third Aves.)
(212) 223-5656
Credit cards: All major   Meals: L, D   Closed Sun.

Jo Jo's alluring Parisian décor, in a handsome townhouse setting, is the perfect background for Jean Georges Vongerichten's sophisticated, beguiling cuisine. The restaurant is not new, but the dishes, which change frequently, still taste fresh and exciting. A dish described as 27 vegetables simmered in their own juice is an ode to the garden, a little essay on the individuality of vegetables. Entrees are equally stunning. And though Mr. Vongerichten made his reputation with light dishes and Asian accents, his Alsatian roots show up in foie gras sprinkled with grains of sea salt. After several visits I discovered that I would rather eat upstairs than down and that I like just about everything Mr. Vongerichten cooks. **Price range:** Entrees, $19–$36.

Josie's $25 & Under   NEW AMERICAN
300 Amsterdam Ave. (at 74th St.)   (212) 769-1212
Credit cards: All major   Meals: L, D, LN

Much of the food at Josie's is billed as organically raised; the surprise is that so much of the food is so good, with highlights like light potato dumplings served in a lively tomato coulis spiked with chipotle pepper, ravioli stuffed with sweet potato purée, superb grilled tuna with a wasabi glaze and wonderful gazpacho. Josie's offers about two dozen reasonably priced wines, some organic beers and freshly squeezed juices, including tart blueberry lemonade. Even the organic hot dogs are good. **Price range:** Entrees, $9.50–$16.

Jubilee $25 & Under   FRENCH
347 East 54th St. (between First and Second Aves.)   (212) 888-3569
Credit cards: All major   Meals: L, D

Small, crowded and exuberant, this is a great East Side find. It offers simple and good bistro food, like steak frites and roast chicken. The restaurant makes something of a specialty of mussels, offering them in five guises with terrific french fries or a green salad, all for reasonable prices. **Price range:** Entrees, $13.50–$24.

Judson Grill ☆ ☆ ☆ $$$$ NEW AMERICAN
152 West 52nd St. (bet Sixth and Seventh Aves.)   (212) 582-5252
Credit cards: All major   Meals: L,D   Closed Sun.

Judson Grill is big, bright and utterly urban, a mature restaurant with none of the irritating glitches of a new establishment. Its lighting is right, they've got the service down pat, and the wine list has had time to develop its own quirky personality. In the skillful hands of the chef, Bill Telepan, the food is unassuming but extremely eloquent, so roaring with flavor that the minute you finish one bite you instantly want another. Consider the vegetable soup—a clear golden broth filled with tenderly poached peas, beans and mushrooms. The liquid is alive with flavor, and the vegetables are faintly crisp and sweet. The organically grown meats are especially impressive. Pork is wrapped in a black mustard crust and lamb is coated with herbs and served with wild greens and potatoes. Desserts include the restaurant's Jack Daniel's ice cream soda and its chocolate sampler. Both are good, but the fruit concoctions appeal to me most. **Price range:** Entrees, $20–$34.

Kang Suh ☆ ☆ $$ KOREAN
1250 Broadway (at 32d St.)   (212) 564-6845
Credit cards: All major   Meals: B, L, D   Open 24 hours

This is the most accessible of the Korean restaurants in the small Koreatown locally known as Sam Ship Iga (32nd Street). Downstairs is a sushi bar, upstairs a huge menu of Korean dishes. Two things make this special: it's open 24 hours and you grill your own food over live charcoal at the table. **Price range:** Entrees, $6.99–$30.

Katsu-Hama $25 & Under   JAPANESE
11 East 47th St. (between Madison and Fifth Aves.)   (212) 758-5909
Credit cards: All major   Meals: L, D

Katsu-Hama doesn't offer much in the way of atmosphere or creature comforts, but it is an authentic Japanese experience. To enter it, you need to walk through a takeout sushi restaurant (Sushi-Tei) and pass through a curtain divider; there, you encounter an almost entirely Japanese crowd who've come for the restaurant's specialty: tonkatsu, or deep-fried pork cutlets. The best variation is unadorned, dipped into a special condiment that resembles freshly made Worcestershire sauce blended with sesame seeds. **Price range:** $8.95–$13.95, including soup, shredded cabbage and rice.

Katz's Deli $ DELI
205 East Houston St. (at Ludlow St.)   (212) 254-2246
Credit cards: All major   Meals: B, Br, L, D, LN

A wonderful Lower East Side artifact and originator of the World War II slogan, "Send a salami to your boy in the Army." While Katz's looks as if it hasn't been cleaned since then, it is one of the very few New York City delis that still carves pastrami and corned beef by hand, which makes for delicious sandwiches. **Price range:** Entrees, $5–$10.95.

Komodo $25 & Under   JAPANESE/LATIN AMERICAN
186 Avenue A (between 11th and 12th Sts.)   (212) 529-2658
Credit cards: All major   Meals: D   Closed Mon.

With a shared taste for ingredients like cilantro, chilies and rice, Mexico and Asia have more grounds for compatibility than most. Komodo's small storefront dining room is clean, simple and cool; the fusion idea never outweighs the flavors on the plate, so the food never seems forced or needlessly flamboyant. A simple appetizer like beef satay is rubbed with ground ancho chilies and served with peanut sauce, a combination that differs so subtly from the original that it seems effortlessly natural. Even better are Asian guacamole rolls, in which the avocado is flavored with ginger and wasabi and combined with sweet potato and cumin. The list of main courses is small, but I can't imagine tiring of the grilled sirloin topped with oysters tempura and crisp fried leeks. Good dessert choices include a rich chocolate pot de créme flavored with black litchi tea, and an apple empanada. **Price range:** Entrees, $9.75–$15.95.

Kori $25 & Under   KOREAN
253 Church St. (near Leonard St.)   (212) 334-0908
Credit cards: All major   Meals: L, D, LN

Kori is unusual, a Korean restaurant that succeeds in merging East and West, old and new. Kori seems a wholly personal expression of its owner and chef, Kori Kim: up-to-date and appealing to Americans but tied to Korean traditions. She learned to cook in a big, traditional Korean family in Seoul, but it is hard to imagine Ms. Kim serving food at home as polished as her dubu sobegi, a tofu croquette stuffed with savory ground Asian mushrooms and beautifully presented like a rectangular gift box, sliced diagonally into four pieces and held together with a seaweed ribbon. Galbi jim is a wonderful stew of short ribs with sweet dates, chestnuts and turnips, and bibimbop, a signature Korean dish of rice, beef, eggs and vegetables, served sizzling, is fresh and enjoyable. **Price range:** Entrees, $12.95–$21.

Kuruma Zushi ☆ ☆ ☆ $$$$ SUSHI
7 East 47th St., 2d Floor   (212) 317-2802
Credit cards: All major   Meals: L, D   Closed Sun.

Few restaurants are more welcoming to diners who do not speak Japanese, and few chefs are better at introducing people to sushi than Toshiro Uezu, proprietor of Kuruma Zushi. One of New York City's most venerable sushi bars, it serves only sushi and sashimi and is, admittedly, expensive. But after eating at Kuruma Zushi it is very hard to go back to ordinary fish. **Price range:** Entrees, $25–$45.

La Caravelle ☆☆☆ $$$$ FRENCH
33 West 55th St (near Fifth Ave.)   (212) 586-4252
Credit cards: All major   Meals: L, D   Closed Sun.

La Caravelle is a French restaurant of the old school, a great social stage
where people go to look at one another. The pretty murals and flattering
lighting make everyone look good, and the captains—busy carving ducks,
boning fish and flaming crepes at the table—are skilled at making their customers feel as good as they look. No restaurant in New York does a better job
at guarding tradition while honoring the present. If you are searching for solid
French cooking—airy quenelles in a creamy, rich lobster sauce, filet of Dover
sole meuniere or a truly satisfying vol-au-vent—you will find it here. And
nobody does classic dishes like roasted chicken with Champagne sauce or
canard a l'orange better.

But that is just one part of the menu. New inventions are scattered among
these old dishes, and the food changes with the seasons. For dessert, the mar-
quise au chocolat is intense enough to make a chocaholic swoon and soufflés
are excellent. Calorie watchers will find that a bavaroise of yogurt and rhubarb
is a wonderful way to end a meal. **Price range:** Prix-fixe dinner, $65. Tasting
menus, $75 and $90; pre-theater dinner, $44.

La Côte Basque ☆☆☆ $$$$ FRENCH
60 West 55th Street   (212) 688-6525
Credit cards: all major   Meals: L, D

For 36 years La Côte Basque was a bastion of civility on East 55th Street. After
settling gracefully into intimate new quarters, the food is still well-prepared and
well-presented, but rarely so unmannerly as to call undue attention to itself.
Similarly, the menu is smaller, more modern and easier to read than the one in
the old restaurant. The daily seafood special is often a discreet heap of fresh crab
meat and lobster daintily topped with grains of black caviar. The most exciting
entree is cassoulet, a splendid pile of white beans cooked with pork loin, duck
confit and fat chunks of garlic sausage until each bean bursts with fat and flavor.
Dover sole, a frequent special, is the best of the fish. The fillet of black bass
wrapped in "scales" of potato and served in a classic red wine sauce is a close
second. These dishes are extremely well executed. And large. Each plate is piled
with food, making the $63 prix-fixe dinner menu a good deal. **Price range:**
Prix-fixe dinner $63, with supplements.

L'Actuel ☆☆ $$$ FRENCH
145 East 50th St.   (212) 583-0001
Credit cards: All major   Meals: B, Br, L, D   Closed Sun.

Behold the brasserie of the future. It feels French. It sounds French. But there's
an unmistakable, enticing whiff of Spain, Italy, North Africa and the Caribbean
in the air. The name of this sparkling brasserie can be translated as "right now,"

and the restaurant is up-to-the-minute in a very French way, which is to say that it is pointedly international, while hanging on for dear life to the essential qualities that define a brasserie. It has an Alsatian choucroute, of course, but also a tapas menu—French tapas, like marinated grilled zucchini stuffed with goat cheese. There are plates of fruits de mer, because there must be, but you get a superior American cocktail sauce along with the mignonette, not to mention chewy, saline seaweed bread. The chef also makes a place on his menu for tartes flambées, the thin-crust pizzas of his native Alsace, but side by side with an orthodox cheese, onion and bacon tart smeared with a layer of créme fraîche, he offers a wild-card tart topped with wasabi and bluefin tuna. The place looks like several restaurants merged into one. But like the menu, everything seems to make sense in an indefinable way. Fish dishes are impressive; desserts are intriguing, including an excellent apple tart and warm chocolate cake with a molten center. **Price range:** Entrees, $17–$24.

La Grenouille ☆ ☆ ☆ $$$$ FRENCH
3 East 52nd St. (off Fifth Ave.)   (212) 752-1495
Credit cards: All major   Meals: L, D   Closed Sun. & Mon.

La Grenouille is the most frustrating restaurant in New York. This is not because the food is bad or the service unpleasant. Just the opposite, in fact, the restaurant displays such flashes of brilliance that each failure is a deep disappointment. It is also one of the few New York restaurants that still serves many of the French classics, including quenelles de brochette, perfectly grilled Dover sole and the best souffles in New York. La Grenouille could so easily be a four-star establishment with its golden light, magnificent floral displays and professional and caring staff. Each meal offers moments of joyful excellence, but unfortunately many dishes are entirely forgettable. You can count on a good meal at La Grenouille. If you're lucky, however, you may get a great one. **Price range:** Three course prix-fixe dinner $80; lunch $45, Tasting menu $100.

La Locanda   **$25 & Under**   ITALIAN
737 Ninth Avenue (near 50th St.)   (212) 258-2900
Credit cards: All major   Meals: L, D

La Locanda serves pastas and meat dishes that stand out for their simplicity and flavor, and offers an enticing and unusually arranged wine list. Start with the basket of bread and focaccia, freshly baked at La Locanda's bakery, Il Forno, which is just around the corner. Second, try one of the large and alluring salads, like insalata rifredda, essentially an Italian version of the frisée salad. Pastas can be excellent, either as a shared appetizer or as a main course. Penne alla Genovese is perfectly al dente, with carrots, celery and onions cooked until meltingly sweet and flavored with a sprinkle of herbs. Orecchiette with broccoli rape and house-made sausage is excellent, with the mellow meat rounding off the bitterness of the green. Sliced leg of lamb, served like all the main courses with roasted potatoes and sauted broccoli rape, is past the point of pink, but the sauce, simply lamb juices and herbs, imbues the meat with flavor. The same is true of veal shoulder, aromatic and delicious in its sauce of herbs, white wine and veal juices. Because La Locanda has its own bakery, it makes its own desserts, some of which are quite good. Skip tiramisu and profiteroles, and opt instead for the rustic blueberry tart or the compact French-style strawberry tart. **Price range:** Pastas and entrees, $11—$21.50.

La Nonna ☆ $$$ ITALIAN
133 West 13th St. (between Sixth and Seventh Aves.)   (212) 741-3663
Credit cards: All major   Meals: L, D

La Nonna is a warm, inviting place with a no-nonsense menu of thoroughly traditional Tuscan dishes, with an emphasis on meat and fish roasted or grilled in a wood-burning oven. The appetizers at La Nonna can be as simple as pink slices of prosciutto draped on thick slices of Tuscan bread coated with olive oil, or crostini piled high with chicken liver pâté. A moist and tender marinated Cornish hen makes the best advertisement for the oven, but pasta turns out to be the most dependable category on the menu. The Gorgonzola gnocchi are as light as whipped cream. Another standout is strozzapreti, slightly sticky dumplings of Swiss chard and spinach firmed up with ricotta and Parmesan cheese, then doused with butter and sage. By some mysterious process, the trippa alla Fiorentina becomes a deeply satisfying, earthy mix of sharp tomato flavor, fragrant rosemary, white wine and sweetly rich vegetables wrapped around chewy slivers of tripe. **Price range:** Entrees, $16.50–$24.50.

L'Ardoise $25 & Under   FRENCH
1207 First Ave. (between 65th and 66th Sts.)   (212) 744-4752
Credit cards: All major   Meals: L, D

This unfashionable little restaurant is not much to look at, but the well-prepared traditional French food and the quirky charm of the proprietor more than make up for this. Bistro favorites like warm frisée salad with lardons, steamed mussels, duck confit and steak frites are all good bets. **Price range:** Entrees, $6.50–$7.95.

Lavagna $25 & Under   MEDITERRANEAN
545 East 5th St. (at Ave. B)   (212) 979-1005
Credit cards: Cash only   Meals: D, LN   Closed Sun.

Lavagna's food is fresh and generous, with honest, straightforward flavors. The simple rectangular dining room is casual and inviting, but can get loud when it's crowded. Pastas are best, both simple dishes like rigatoni with crumbled fennel sausage, peas, tomatoes and cream, and more complicated ones like fresh pappardelle with rabbit stew. Cacciucco, the Tuscan fish soup scented with saffron and anise, and served with mussels, cockles and chunks of fish, is a great value. **Price range:** Entrees, $11–$16.50.

Layla ☆☆ $$$ MIDDLE EASTERN
211 West Broadway (at Franklin St.)   (212) 431-0700
Credit cards: All major   Meals: L, D

Layla is a hip downtown setting for the Arabian nights, complete with broken pottery shards on the wall and a belly dancer twirling through the room after 9 P.M. The restaurant is tasty and lots of fun, featuring good Middle Eastern food from a wood-burning oven. The smooth baba gannouj, briny taramosalata and tzatziki are seductively delicious dips. The phyllo-wrapped sardines are fabulous. The lobster pastilla is one of those sweet, spicy Moroccan dishes that everybody loves. Desserts are original and delicious, especially the eggy orange blossom crème brûlée. **Price range:** Entrees, $20–$28.

Le Bernardin ☆☆☆☆ $$$$ FRENCH/SEAFOOD
155 West 51st St. (between Sixth and Seventh Aves.)   (212) 489-1515
Credit cards: All major Meals L,D   Closed Sun.

Most restaurants grow into their stars. Not Le Bernardin: at the ripe old age of three months, it had all four stars bestowed upon it. The restaurant has been in the spotlight ever since. In 1986, the brother-and-sister team of Gilbert and Maguy Le Coze moved from Paris to New York, and Mr. Le Coze's cooking changed American dining. His style, impeccably fresh fish cooked with respect and simplicity, was so widely copied that people forgot who had invented it. When Mr. Le Coze died unexpectedly at 48 in 1994, Miss Le Coze hired Eric Ripert, a talented 33-year-old chef, and together they gave the restaurant an infusion of energy.

Most of the problems that plague other great establishments are solved here: there are no rude reservations takers, no endless waits for tables, no overcrowding in the dining room. The waiters know their jobs and keep their distance. Dinners are appropriately paced. When you reserve a table at Le Bernardin, you can count on being seated promptly, served beautifully and fed fabulously. Le Bernardin once showed New York how to eat fish; now it is showing the city how a four-star restaurant should behave. **Price range:** Dinner prix-fixe, $70; tasting menu, $125.

Le Cirque 2000 ☆☆☆☆ $$$$ NEW AMERICAN
455 Madison Ave. (in the Palace Hotel)   (212) 303-7788
Credit cards: All major   Meals: L, D

LOOK! Wasn't she on the cover of Vogue last month? Over there, the movie star! Isn't that the former Mayor at the corner table? The diva? The billionaire? Heads swivel, eyes turn. We are at Le Cirque, relocated a couple of years ago to the landmarked Villard houses where designer Adam Tihany simply unpacked a circus. The new Cirque is still a club, but now it welcomes everyone. The brash and garish design creates a kind of loony luxury that seems right for an endless party. And here comes the ringmaster, Sirio Maccioni. He is pulling tricks out of his sleeve and his charm is hard to resist as he produces a basket of truffle, a special cheese, a long-lost friend. But his best trick was persuading his sous-chef,

Sottha Khunn, to take charge of the kitchen when he moved the restaurant. It was an improbable choice. Mr. Khunn's cooking is shy and restrained. It never attempts to compete with the eager atmosphere of the dining room; it couldn't. But although Mr. Khunn does not show off, his subtle but brilliant food quietly makes a statement. **Price range:** Entrees, $28–$39.

Le Colonial ☆☆ $$ VIETNAMESE
149 East 57th St. (between Lexington and Third Aves.)
(212) 752-0808.
Credit cards: All major   Meals: L, D

Nostalgic for the old days when the French filled Saigon and the wind whispered in the palm trees? Here you'll find beautiful people and refined Vietnamese food for the not terribly adventurous. Vietnamese cuisine, as interpreted here, is sedate Asian fare that is more delicate than Chinese food, less spicy than Thai and notable mostly for its abundance of vegetables and its absence of grease. Spring rolls at Le Colonial are so delicate you tend to forget that they are fried. I loved the beef salad, the only really spicy dish here. **Price range:** Entrees, $14–$23.

Le Gigot $25 & Under   FRENCH
18 Cornelia St. (between 4th and Bleecker Sts.)   (212) 627-3737
Credit cards: AE   Meals: Br, L, D   Closed Mon.

This little restaurant pulses with the welcoming spirit of a Parisian hangout. The Provence-inflected food adds to the illusion, with excellent bistro fare like leg of lamb in a red wine reduction; lamb stew; endive salad with apples, walnuts and Roquefort, and rounds of baguette smeared with goat cheese and smoky tapenade. The best desserts are the sweet, moist, caramelized tarte Tatin, the excellent bananas flambé, and the great little cheese course, not usually available in a restaurant like this. **Price range:** Entrees, $12–$17.

Lenox Room ☆☆ $$$ NEW AMERICAN
1278 Third Ave. (near 73d St.)   (212) 772-0404
Credit cards: All major   Meals: Br, L, D

Some of the most inventive food on the Upper East Side is served in this loud, lively room. The eye-catching raw bar is lovely and expensive. The main dishes are largely straightforward and satisfying, and the kitchen does a very nice job with risotto. Decoration plays a big part in the desserts, though many of the concoctions look better than they taste: pretty desserts for pretty people. The kitchen clearly has its finger on the New York pulse. **Price range:** Entrees, $19–$28.

Lespinasse ☆☆☆☆ $$$$ FRENCH
2 East 55th St. (off Fifth Ave., in the St. Regis Hotel)   (212) 339-6719
Credit cards: all major   Meals: B, L, D   Closed Sun & Mon.

If the dining room at Lespinasse were a person, it would be smiling today. After a long marriage with a chef determined to put the décor in the shadows, it has finally found a compatible partner. Christian Delouvrier cannot match his predecessor's pyrotechnics. But in his own quiet way he has done something entirely different, creating a sumptuous menu so right for this staid, extravagant room that he is likely to be revered by his guests.

Open the door and be dazzled by the golden light of chandeliers and intoxicated by the aroma of white truffles. Flowers from lavish bouquets bend to caress your shoulders as you pass. Numerous servers hover nearby, eager to anticipate every wish. In this rarefied atmosphere, the butter never gets warm and no glass is ever empty. As you might expect, the menu descriptions are elaborate, the prices stratospheric. When was the last time anybody charged $35 for soup in New York? The only strategy is to abandon yourself to the experience and pretend, if only for a few hours, that money has no meaning.

Mr. Delouvrier has transformed the restaurant. The combination of his food, the quiet setting and the solicitous service create an experience so opulent and old-fashioned that it can be a serious shock to walk outside and find no coach waiting to take you home. **Price range:** entrees, $34–$46.

Le Tableau $25 & Under   MEDITERRANEAN
511 East 5th St. (between Aves. A and B)   (212) 260-1333
Credit cards: Cash only   Meals: Br, D   Closed Mon.

This simple storefront restaurant turns out superb Mediterranean fare. Unconventional dishes stimulate the mouth with new flavors and textures, like a spicy calamari tagine that incorporates anchovies, hummus and olive purée. Main courses are familiar, yet they are presented in inventive ways. Desserts can be excellent, like a mellow pumpkin bread pudding, a honey-nut tart and an apple tajine. The dining room is dimly lighted with candles and can become noisy, especially when a jazz trio begins playing in the late evening. **Price range:** Entrees, $9.50–$14.75.

Le Zie $25 & Under   ITALIAN
172 Seventh Ave. (at 20th St.)   (212) 206-8686
Credit cards: Cash only   Meals: L, D

This modest little trattoria offers some terrific Venetian dishes, like an inspired salad that features pliant octopus and soft potatoes acting in precise textural counterpoint. The chef has a sure hand with pastas like rigatoni with rosemary, served al dente in a perfectly proportioned sauce. Risotto with squid is also superbly cooked. Striped bass fillet with fennel and white beans is moist and wonderfully flavorful. Desserts are a weak point. **Price range:** Entrees, $8.50–$16.95.

Le Zoo $25 & Under   BISTRO/FRENCH
314 West 11th St. (at Greenwich St.)   (212) 620-0393
Credit cards: All major   Meals: D, LN

This popular little restaurant can get crowded, loud and zoolike, but the food is good and often creative. Where you might reasonably expect to find steak frites, roast chicken and pâté de campagne, there are instead such combinations as monkfish with honey and lime sauce, or wonderfully flavorful sliced scallops served in puff pastry with a leek-and-chive coulis. The dessert selection is small and classically French, offering satisfying choices. The restaurant does not take reservations, but once you are seated, the atmosphere becomes relaxed, casual and unrushed, though not quiet. **Price range:** Entrees, $12.50–$16.

Little Basil $25 & Under   THAI
39 Greenwich Ave. (at Charles St.)   (212) 645-8965
Credit cards: All major   Meals: D

Little Basil serves dishes with exquisite balance, Western touches and a beautiful presentation. Dishes like lamb shank draped in herbs and delicate steamed dumplings strewn with dried shrimp are not exactly Thai home cooking, yet the food remains true to the essence of Thai cuisine, with salty, sour, hot and sweet flavors unfurling in careful relation to one another. **Price range:** Entrees, $9–$16.

Little Dove ☆☆ $$$ NEW AMERICAN
200 East 60th St. (At Third Ave.)   (212) 751-8616
Credit cards: All major   Meals: L, D

The tiny dining room here looks like a cross between an antiques store and the drawing room of a dotty old aunt, but it has a civilized charm and genuine character. The menu is a brief document, presented in a folder hardly bigger than a greeting card, but each dish counts. It stresses high-quality ingredients and simple, strong, clearly defined flavors. A little casserole of roasted bread and tomatoes makes a robust, cold-weather appetizer, and a no-fuss vegetable tart, bound with clean-tasting Vermont goat cheese, is a textbook study in how to let raw ingredients shine. Roasted guinea hen, with a crackling crisp skin, takes an unusual accompaniment of braised root vegetables packed into a casing of caul fat. The crust on an unassuming lemon tart with pineapple meringue is thick and flaky, the filling tartly voluptuous, the meringue lighter than air. **Price range:** Entrees, $22–$32.

Lobster Club ☆☆ $$$ NEW AMERICAN
24 East 80th St. (between Fifth and Madison Aves.)   (212) 249-6500
Credit cards: All major   Meals: L, D   Closed Sun.

Anne Rosenzweig's creative American menu and wine list filled with bottles from boutique wineries make this a neighborhood favorite. She permits herself humor, odd adventures (skewers of grilled duck hearts stuffed with foie gras) and strange combinations (potatoes, apples and gingerbread). But mostly she sticks to comfort food, reinventing the everyday foods of many countries, such as matzoh brei and congee. Her Provençal fries and crisp rock shrimp are irresistible, and Mom's meatloaf is terrific. There's not a loser among the desserts, but avoid the awkward downstairs dining room. **Price range:** Entrees, $18–$29.

Local ☆☆ $$$ NEW AMERICAN

224 West 47th St. (between Broadway and Eighth Ave.)
(212) 921-2005
Credit cards: All major   Meals: L, D

A pretentious mission statement bills Local as a casual hangout, the late 20th-century equivalent of a corner cafe. Padded booths run all along the perimeter of the dining room, and the open kitchen, where you can sit down and order a meal, looks a little like a very elegant diner. But Franklin Becker, the executive chef, is doing a little more than slinging hash. He cooks with good taste, a respect for basic ingredients, properly integrated flavors and a sure hand. He is imaginative without being outlandish. Raw sea scallops are tenderized to the melting point in a lemon-truffle vinaigrette that's acidic and earthy. A straightforward tart of sweet Vidalia onions, goat cheese and pungent black olives in puff pastry cannot be improved on. The loin of rabbit, which is simply seared, comes with the leg meat done confit-style and delicately spiced with curry, ginger and garlic. Desserts are first-rate—and pay attention to the presentation of the tea board: precious it may be, but the teas have been chosen to complement the desserts, and they do. **Price range:** Entrees, $20–$34.

Los Dos Rancheros $25 & Under   MEXICAN

507 Ninth Ave. (at 38th St.)   (212) 868-7780
Credit cards: Cash only   Meals: B, L, D

The dining room may be bare-bones (unpretentious is an understatement), but the restaurant serves authentic, delicious Mexican fare, like pollo con pipián, chicken with a fiery green sauce made of ground pumpkin seeds, and excellent soft tacos with fillings ranging from chicken to braised pork to tongue and goat. **Price range:** Entrees, $2–$7.50.

Lupa $25 & Under   ITALIAN

170 Thompson Street (Houston Street),   (212) 982-5089.
Credit cards: All major   Meals: L, D   Closed Mon.

Crowded and clamorous, Lupa serves intensely delicious Roman trattoria food. Appetizers range from the classic to the bizarre: Prosciutto di Parma arrives in thin, nutty slices, a reminder of why this combination became popular in the first place, while beet carpaccio is not only amusing, but also delicious. Pastas are simple and tasty, and saltimbocca, thin slices of veal layered with prosciutto, is good and juicy. The resident wine expert takes great delight in directing you to the perfect choice on Lupa's 130-bottle wine list, and the best dessert choice is something from the cheese tray. **Price range:** Entrees, $9–$15.

Lutèce ☆☆☆ $$$$ FRENCH

249 East 50th St. (between 2nd and 3rd Aves.)   (212) 752-2225
Credit Cards: All major   Meals: L, D   Closed Sun.

No matter where you are seated, Lutèce makes you feel royal. The staff flutters about anticipating every wish, and the wine list is filled with surprises; good

wines at reasonable prices mingle with great ones. Chef Eberhard Müller works
in a pared-down fashion; his seasonal menu, driven by the produce raised on
his New Jersey farm, features vegetables and fruits at the peak of their flavor.
His fish soup is intense and delicious. He is rightly proud of his scallops, too:
large, soft, meaty creatures that become wondrously crisp. He sets them on a
bed of mashed potatoes and swathes them in a black truffle vinaigrette. His
grilled squab comes with a fine fricassee of artichokes and chanterelles. In summer, farm-raised rhubarb is baked in a tart accompanied by créme fraîche ice
cream; winter desserts focus on chocolate and nut confections and on dishes
made with exotic fruits like those in a mango papaya tart with passion fruit ice
cream. **Price range:** dinner prix-fixe, $65 with many supplements.

Luzia's $25 & Under   PORTUGUESE
429 Amsterdam Ave. (between 80th and 81st Sts.)   (212) 595-2000
Credit cards: All major   Meals: Br, L, D   Closed Mon.

Luzia's began life as a takeout place. Then the neighborhood fell in love with
the cozy restaurant and started staying for dinner. Luzia's serves wonderful Portuguese comfort food, like caldo verde, shrimp pie and cataplana, the soupy stew
of pork and clams. It also produces remarkably delicious non-Portuguese dishes,
like beef brisket that is tender and peppery. Luzia's has a great flan, and a nice
list of Portuguese wines. **Price range:** $20–$25.

Manhattan Ocean Club ☆☆ $$$ SEAFOOD
57 West 58th St. (between Fifth and Sixth Aves.)   (212) 371-7777
Credit cards: All major   Meals: L, D

Tony, comfortable and trim as a luxury yacht, this is the steakhouse of fish restaurants. Eating here is an indulgence, and the prices are high. Soups like the
creamy clam chowder are less expensive but no less delicious (the fish soup is so
intense it is almost a meal in itself). Simple preparations are the most appealing
but one of the best dishes is the oysters buried in tiny morels covered with cream
and baked in the shell. The dish is an edible definition of luxury. Desserts are
almost all big and sweet. **Price range:** Entrees, $22.50–$29.75.

March ☆☆☆ $$$$ NEW AMERICAN
405 East 58th St. (near First Ave.)   (212) 754-6272
Credit cards: All major   Meals: D

When everything is clicking, there are few places I would rather eat than this
cozy, antique-filled town house. The usual three-course restaurant menu is
replaced with one that allows you to choose either four or seven smaller
courses. At March, no dish is more than a few bites, but those are so pretty and
powerful that you are almost always satisfied. Mr. Nish has a Japanese bent,
and many dishes are his variations on sushi and sashimi. They are so beautiful
they look more like jewelry than food. More robust dishes include lobster and
shrimp in a sauce made with the sweet wine, Muscat de Beaumes-de-Venise;

two kinds of foie gras, one sliced and served with a spicy coulis of concord grapes, the other made into a terrine, dusted with garam masala and served with papadums and a pear-and-quince chutney; and grilled and braised duck, its richness underlined by dates and an exotic spinach puree with a confit of turnips. The most popular items are Beggars' purses, diminutive dumplings filled with caviar, truffles or foie gras. **Price range:** Four-course menu, $68 (with specially selected wines, $93); seven-course menu, $90 (with specially selected wines, $125).

Maritime ☆ $$$ SEAFOOD
1251 Sixth Ave. (At West 49th St.)   (212) 354-1717
Credit cards: All major   Meals: L, D

As a piece of design, Maritime is one slippery fish: gleaming white wall tiles suggest an urban fish market, but the dark, solid wood wainscoting and cabinets feel more like a men's club. The menu is not easy to get a handle on, either. The oysters are straightforward enough; so are the two-fisted lobster and corn chowder and a crowd-pleasing shrimp cocktail. A fair number of the dishes at Maritime, however, are overthought and overwrought, but some results can be terrific. Lobster in a Portuguese tomato sauce is plump and flavorful, and the spicy chorizo "tater tots" that dot the plate make a witty point. Seared sea scallops are just rich enough to carry pumpkin ravioli and a porcini truffle sauce, thanks to an offsetting, neutralizing layer of wilted Swiss chard. Two desserts break out of the pack: the Southwestern banana split and a florid apple crisp. **Price range:** Entrees, $16–$25.

Mark's ☆ ☆ $$$$ AMERICAN
The Mark Hotel, 25 East 77th St. (between Fifth and Madison Aves.)
(212) 879-1864
Credit cards: All major   Meals: B, Br, L, D, LN

Comfort, tranquillity and refined contemporary fare are offered at this hotel restaurant. Appetizers include warm lobster and mushroom salad; pan-seared foie gras; crab cakes, and a ragout of chanterelles and cepes. Roast pheasant, whole roasted black sea bass, grilled filet of beef with oxtail rillettes and pan-roasted medallions of veal are among the main dishes. For dessert, there are petits fours, black-and-white-chocolate gâteau St. Honore and caramelized apple tart. **Price range:** Entrees, $27–$36.

Marumi $25 & Under JAPANESE/SUSHI
546 La Guardia Pl. (between 3d and Bleecker Sts.)   (212) 979-7055
Credit cards: All major   Meals: L, D

This versatile, reliable Japanese restaurant near NYU offers a cross-section of casual Japanese dining. The service is swift, efficient and charming and will even go the extra mile in preventing bad choices. It's rare that you get such an interesting assortment of sushi at an inexpensive restaurant, like mirugai, or geoduck clam. Other worthwhile dishes are broiled eel, noodle soups and the economic bento box meals. **Price range:** Entrees, $9–$15.

Match Uptown ☆☆ $$$$ PAN-ASIAN/FUSION
33 East 60th St. (between Park and Madison Aves.)   (212) 906-9177
Credit cards: All major   Meals: L, D, LN

A casual, expensive restaurant for the ruling class, especially rich, young Europeans, Match has a chic bar scene and two attractive rooms. The noise level is very high, but the Asian-accented food is really good. Chicken satay, lamb samosas and steamed Japanese dumplings are all excellent, as are giant shrimp in a citrus vinaigrette. For dessert don't miss the mango sundae, the perfect cross-cultural dessert. **Price range:** Entrees, $23.50–$29.50.

Matthew's ☆☆ $$$ MEDITERRANEAN
1030 Third Ave. (at 61st St.)   (212) 838-4343
Credit cards: All major   Meals: Br, L, D, LN

Matthew's is a decorator's dream. White linen, rattan chairs, big baskets of fruit and white ceiling fans lazily cutting through the air give the restaurant a summery rustic feel. It looks like a coffee table book come to life. There is nothing here that leads you to expect the kind of sophistication coming out of the kitchen, but with Matthew Kenney in charge, you will always find something interesting on the menu. **Price range:** entrees, $20–$30.

Mavalli Palace $25 & Under   INDIAN/VEGETARIAN
46 East 29th St. (between Park and Madison Aves.)   (212) 679-5535
Credit cards: All major   Meals: L, D   Closed Mon.

This low-key Indian restaurant turns out terrific vegetarian fare that is exciting and full of flavor, like rasa vada, savory lentil doughnuts in a spicy broth, and baingan bharta, a fiery blend of eggplant and peas. Mavalli means mother goddess, and the restaurant's symbol is a goddess figure, hand out, waiting to serve. The staff, though merely mortal, takes orders efficiently and brings food out swiftly. **Price range:** $4.25–$16.75.

Max $25 & Under   ITALIAN
51 Avenue B (near 4th St.)   (212) 539-0111
Credit cards: Cash only   Meals: L, D, LN

A tiny Italian restaurant wholly without pretensions, Max is packed nightly. Max's draw is exactly what has always attracted people to neighborhood restaurants: well-prepared food, served with warmth. Best of all, Max is cheap, with only one appetizer approaching $9 and one main course nearing $15. Max's buffalo-milk mozzarella is fresh, nutty and slightly salty, and a perfect partner for prosciutto. Fettuccine al sugo Toscano has a wonderfully mellow meat sauce with layers of flavor that unfold in the mouth, while rigatoni Napoletano is served southern Italian style, with meatballs and sausages left intact in the sauce. Order the sauce on the side of the Neopolitan-style meatlof, because the meatloaf is fascinating, stuffed with mozzarella, hard-boiled egg and prosciutto, making for a savory, moist and delicious combination. Max has a brief list of wines under $25 and desserts include a good tiramisu and an excellent caramel panna cotta. **Price range:** Entrees, $8.95–$14.95.

Maya ☆☆ $$$ MEXICAN/TEX-MEX
1191 First Ave. (between 64th and 65th Sts.)   (212) 585-1818
Credit cards: All major   Meals: D, LN

Some of New York's most interesting Mexican food is served in this bright, festive but often noisy room. Although you can stick to margaritas and guacamole, you'll miss the best part if you don't try some of the more unusual dishes, like rock shrimp ceviche, seafood salad, and roasted corn soup with huitlacoche dumpling. The most impressive main courses are chicken mole (the dark sauce is truly complex) and pipian de puerco, grilled pork marinated in tamarind and served on a bed of puréed roasted corn. Desserts are not impressive. **Price range:** Entrees, $14.95–$21.95.

McHale's $$ BAR SNACKS/HAMBURGERS
750 Eighth Ave. (at 46th St.)   (212) 246-8948
Credit cards: Cash only   Meals: L, D, LN

This neighborhood bar has a single specialty: great hamburgers that are big and juicy. There's really no point in ordering anything else, except maybe a beer or two. A nice place in which to be a regular. **Price range:** Entrees, $10–$18.

Mee Noodle Shop $25 & Under   CHINESE
219 First Ave. (at 13th St.)   (212) 995-0333
547 Second Ave. (between 30th and 31st Sts.)   (212) 779-1596
922 Second Ave. (at 49th St.)   (212) 888-0027
795 Ninth Ave. (at 53d St.)   (212) 765-2929
Credit cards: AE   Meals: L, D

A little chain of Chinese restaurants that is a cut above takeout, with huge portions of cheap, tasty noodles. Ingredients are fresh, and dishes like lo mein with roast pork and mee fun with chicken are carefully prepared. Mee offers seven kinds of noodles. The portions are huge—complete meals in themselves—and delicious. **Price range:** $3.75–$12.

Meigas ☆☆ $$$ SPANISH
350 Hudson St. (Between King and Charlton Sts.)   (212) 627-5800
Credit cards: All major   Meals: L, D   Closed Sat., Sun.

Meigas (may-EEH-gus) is Galician for sorceresses, and one appears in a mural at the back of this large restaurant, a spooky figure who conjures from the sea an enormous table, laden with savory dishes. Chef Luis Bollo, a Basque, has done several tours of duty at forward-looking restaurants in Spain. He is cultivating homier virtues here, with judiciously applied modern touches. It's possible to order something as simple as baby squid cooked in its own ink, a traditional Basque specialty, or giant prawns grilled on a wood plank and served with lemon and olive oil. An exceptionally fruity Caroliva olive oil transforms humble fillets of grilled mackerel into a memorable, two-fisted dish, enlivened with garlic and a sharp, tingling dose of chili and Rioja vinegar. The pastry chef does some brilliant work, especially with his bread pudding, crunchy at the edges with baked sugar, and topped with a wonderfully dense, sourish ice cream. **Price range:** Entrees, $17–$27.

Meltemi $25 & Under   GREEK/SEAFOOD

905 First Ave. (at 51st St.)   (212) 355-4040
Credit cards: All major   Meals: L, D

This attractive neighborhood Greek restaurant offers big portions of simply prepared seafood, like grilled octopus with oil and lemon, and typical Greek offerings like grilled whole porgy and red mullet. Appetizers are generous, and two portions can easily feed four people. Grilled seafood is the centerpiece here; try the grilled shrimp, served butterflied, full of flavor and so delicate you can even eat the shell. The enthusiastic staff adds to Meltemi's enjoyable atmosphere. **Price range:** Entrees, $14.95–$28.95.

Mercer Kitchen ☆☆ $$$$ FRENCH

Mercer Hotel, 99 Prince St. (at Mercer St.)   (212) 966-5454
Credit cards: All major   Meals: L, D, LN

Jean-Georges Vongerichten strikes again in this chic SoHo restaurant filled with models and movie stars. The space is so mysteriously beautiful it makes each vegetable shimmer like a jewel in the dark. The food is equally innovative: mushrooms set into a marinade of white raisins and coriander; slowly baked rabbit with farfalle, olives and radicchio; and serious snacks like black sea bass with lime juice, coriander and mint. The kitchen occasionally spins out of control, but desserts are simple and appealing, especially the fruit terrines and the rich and fascinating custard with a slice of carmelized pineapple. **Price range:** Entrees, $18–$35.

Mesa Grill ☆☆ $$$$ SOUTHWESTERN

102 Fifth Ave. (between 15th and 16th Sts.)   (212) 807-7400
Credit cards: All major   Meals: Br, L, D

An instant hit on opening its doors in 1991, Mesa Grill is still a downtown favorite, crowded and clamorous at lunch, and even more crowded and clamorous at night. Despite the cookbooks, the television shows, and a second restaurant, Bolo, chef-owner Bobby Flay has somehow managed to keep Mesa Grill alive and kicking.

Two things set Mr. Flay apart. First, he goes after big flavors and he knows how to get them. Second, he uses chilies and spices for flavor, not for heat. Sixteen-spice chicken sounds like a tongue-scorcher. It turns out to be a subtly handled, tingling orchestration of flavors, with an off-sweet sauce of caramelized mangos and garlic. New arrivals have kept the menu fresh, like a crispy whole fish with a winningly simple sauce of roasted tomatillos, ancho chilies and chipotle peppers, served with a side dish of smoky, spicy black rice. The margarita list is an inspirational document, with a list of fine tequilas that can either be sipped on their own or used to upgrade a standard margarita. **Price range:** Entrees, $24–$39.

Metisse $25 & Under   BISTRO/FRENCH
239 West 105th St. (between Amsterdam Ave. and Broadway)
(212) 666-8825
Credit cards: All major   Meals: D

A true neighborhood restaurant with an owner who prowls his small dining room relentlessly to make sure all is well. Main courses seem less consistent than the appetizers, but roast chicken is superior, flavored with rosemary and served in a vinaigrette with crisp sliced potatoes and braised carrots. Roast leg of lamb and pork medallions are also good. Desserts count for something, too, especially the warm chocolate cake with the runny inside, and the brioche topped with caramelized apples and caramel sauce. **Price range:** Entrees, $12.50–$19.50.

Metsovo $25 & Under   GREEK
65 West 70th St. (near Columbus Ave.)   (212) 873-2300
Credit cards: All major   Meals: D

Metsovo's dim, romantic dining room is a far cry from the usual bright blue and white artifact-bedecked Greek restaurant. Instead of seafood, this restaurant, named after a town in northwestern Greece, specializes in hearty stews, roasts and savory pies from the hills that form a spine through the region. The house specialties form the heart of the menu and are the best choices. Try Epirus mountain pies, which are offered with different fillings each day. They are all delicious and, served with a small green salad, make an excellent meal. Tender chunks of baby lamb and a mellow stew of robust goat blended with thick yogurt and rice were also very good. Once you get through the house specialties, though, you're back in familiar territory. With the appetizers this is not a problem, but the grilled dishes are overcharred and dry. You may never receive the same selection of desserts twice, so hope for the luscious fig compote, or the wonderfully thick and fresh yogurt. **Price range:** Entrees, $10.50–$23.95.

Michael Jordan's Steak House ☆☆ $$$$ STEAKHOUSE
23 Vanderbilt Ave. (in Grand Central Terminal)   (212) 655-2300
Credit cards: All major   Meals: L, D

Despite a celebrity owner and a big-deal designer (David Rockwell), the real star of this place is Grand Central Terminal. You sit in comfort on the balcony gazing at the starry ceiling while harried commuters dash madly through the marble halls below. The menu is what you would expect, but the food, for the most part, is equal to the space. Shrimp cocktail is excellent, the meat robust, prime, aged and old-fashioned. All the standard cuts are available, but the flavorful rib eye steak is best. The hamburger, made from chopped prime sirloin, is absurd; it's so enormous it looks more like an inflated basketball. Desserts are not inspiring. **Price range:** Entrees, $16.95–$35.

Michael's ☆☆ $$$$ NEW AMERICAN

24 West 55th St. (between Fifth and Sixth Aves.)   (212) 767-0555
Credit cards: All major   Meals: B, L, D   Closed Sun.

Home of the power lunch. All of publishing goes to Michael's because the room is attractive and filled with good art. The menu offers one of the city's finest selections of fancy salads (some large enough to feed a small nation). The best food on the menu is unabashedly American, including grilled chicken, grilled lobster, good steaks and chops, and California cuisine. There are several daily fish selections. For dessert, the classic collection of tarts and cakes is very enticing. **Price range:** Entrees, $22–$34.

Mi Cocina ☆☆ $$ MEXICAN

57 Jane St. (at Hudson St.)   (212) 627-8273
Credit cards: All major   Meals: D

If you're looking for real Mexican food, you can't do better than this small Greenwich Village storefront. Floor-to-ceiling windows open up the slender rectangular space of the restaurant, with its sparkling kitchen framed in colorful tiles. A superior starter is the empanaditas de picadillo: little turnovers filled with shredded beef, raisins and olives. Main courses include chicken enchiladas and fajitas, made with grilled skirt steak or breast of chicken, onions, peppers, guacamole, black beans and salsa. Desserts include white almond flan, chocolate mousse cake and crepes filled with brandied raisins and walnuts. **Price range:** Entrees, $12–$21.

Molyvos ☆☆☆ $$$ GREEK

871 Seventh Ave. (near 55th St.)   (212) 582-7500
Credit cards: All major   Meals: L,D, LN

Casual, hospitable and lively as a Greek taverna, Molyvos offers food by people who passionately want you to love it. The friendly, caring service begins with mezedes, little tastes that captivate with the intensity of their flavors. They make a marvelous meal all by themselves. But that would mean missing the rest of the large menu with fine dishes from all the Greek islands. There are unusual dolmades—leaves of lettuce stuffed with salt cod and rice and served in an egg-lemon sauce. Marinated lamb shank, braised in wine with orzo and tomatoes, is soft, savory and delicious. Even Greek standards like moussaka and pastitsio are impressive.

Portions are huge, and much of this food is straightforward, relying primarily on good ingredients. Fresh fish are simply grilled whole over wood. The grill gives shrimp, with the heads still on, a fine char without robbing them of their juiciness. Desserts are as good (and as big) as everything else. The light, honey-drizzled fritters would easily feed an entire table. Custard comes wrapped in that fabulous phyllo, and mastic ice cream, which has a faint flavor of pine, is served with fresh and marinated figs. **Price range:** Entrees, $18.50–$27.50.

Montrachet ☆ ☆ ☆ $$$$ FRENCH

239 West Broadway (near White St.)   (212) 219-2777
Credit cards: All major   Meals: L (Fri. only), D   Closed Sun.

After 14 years, TriBeCa's first serious restaurant has achieved a pleasant patina of age without losing its casual charm and thoughtful service. Montrachet is more Gallic than ever with muscular French cooking that seems just right for the small bistro-like dining rooms. Start with the cool terrine of foie gras set off by a quince confit and crisp little haricots verts. Afterward, try the memorable roast chicken served with a rich potato purée and a robust garlic sauce. Then, of course, some cheese, and perhaps a subtle tart Tatin made with seasonal fruits. Fancier fare includes lightly poached oysters set in a creamy Champagne sauce, and braised short ribs dusted with orange peel, served with beets and embellished with a truffle vinaigrette. Main dishes tend to be straightforward, relying on excellence of execution rather than originality. **Price range:** Entrees, $22–$32.

Moomba ☆ ☆ $$$$ NEW AMERICAN

133 Seventh Ave. S. (near West 10th St.)   (212) 989-1414
Credit cards: All major   Meals: D, LN

If you simply must see Leonardo DiCaprio or Laurence Fishburne, this is probably your best bet, provided you can get a reservation, which is doubtful unless you have pull. If you do wangle a seat, you'll find a noisy, fairly dreary place but with surprisingly good modern American food. The tuna tartare laced with the spicy heat of wasabi is wonderful, and sweetbreads are carved into nuggets and cooked until each is no more than a crisp little bit, tossed with frisée in a hazelnut vinaigrette touched with blue cheese. Squab with sweet potato spatzle and a small lamb shank the restaurant calls "osso buco" are absolutely delicious. There is only one dessert you need to remember: Moomba bar. A cross between cake and candy, it is completely over the top. **Price range:** Entrees, $21–$32.

Moustache $25 & Under MIDDLE EASTERN

90 Bedford St. (between Grove and Barrow Sts.)   (212) 229-2220
265 East 10th St. (between First Ave. and Ave. A)   (212) 228-2022
Credit cards: Cash only   Meals: L, D, LN

These small, excellent Middle Eastern restaurants specialize in "pitzas," exceptional pizzalike dishes made with pita dough, including lahmajun, the Turkish specialty with a savory layer of ground lamb on crisp crust, and zaatar, a crisp individual pizza topped with a smoky, aromatic combination of olive oil, thyme, sesame seeds and sumac. Falafel is run-of-the-mill, but a sandwich of sliced lamb in pita bread with onion and tomato is brought to life by a minty lemon mayonnaise. **Price range:** $3–$12.

Mughlai $25 & Under   INDIAN
320 Columbus Ave. (at 71st St.)   (212) 724-6363
Credit cards: All major   Meals: L, D

Mughlai offers tantalizing glimpses of the pleasures of Indian food. Its menu offers the litany of familiar dishes, yet it also invites diners to try uncommon regional dishes, which are almost always better. Dal papri, potatoes and chickpeas blended in a tangy tamarind-and-yogurt sauce and served cool, is a superb appetizer. Pepper chicken, a dish from the southwestern state of Kerala, is another adventure: the pieces of stewed chicken, coated in ground black pepper, seem to dance invitingly across the mouth. Also excellent are baghare baigan, small eggplants in an aromatic sauce of ground peanuts, sesame, tamarind and coconut. **Price range:** Entrees, $6.95–$18.95.

Nadaman Hakubai ☆ ☆ $$$$ JAPANESE
Kitano Hotel, 66 Park Ave. (at 38th St.)   (212) 885-7111
Credit cards: All major   Meals: B, L, D

New York City's most expensive restaurant serves kaiseki cuisine in private, brightly lighted tatami rooms. A visit to this restaurant is like a quick trip to Japan. Kaiseki cuisine, associated with the tea ceremony, is food for the soul as well as the body, meant to feed the eye with its beauty and the spirit with its meaning. The courses follow a strict order and each is intended to introduce the coming season. The way to enjoy this is to abandon yourself to the experience, appreciating the peace, the subtlety of the flavors and the sense that you are being pampered as never before. Unless you are an extremely adventurous eater, you will probably not like every dish you are served. But in spite of the occasional disappointment, an evening in one of the private tatami rooms can be an immensely rewarding experience. Kaiseki dinners in the main restaurant are not particularly recommended. **Price range:** $100 minimum per person, for a minimum of four people.

New York Noodle Town ☆ ☆ $ CHINESE
28 1/2 Bowery (near Bayard St.), Chinatown   (212) 349-0923
Credit cards: Cash only   Meals: B, L, D, LN

New York Noodle Town, with its bustle and clatter, its shared tables and its chefs wreathed in billows of steam rising from the cauldrons of soup in the front of the restaurant, is as close as you can get to Hong Kong without leaving Manhattan. It serves Chinatown's most delicious food. Everything is good, from the superb roast suckling pig to the superlative deep-fried soft-shell crabs. All the noodle dishes are wonderful, and the roasted meats are also amazing. No meal at

Noodle Town is complete without one of the salt-baked specialties. **Price range:** Entrees, $4–$20.

Next Door Nobu ☆ ☆ ☆ $$$$ JAPANESE

105 Hudson St. (near Franklin St.)   (212) 334-4445
Credit cards: All major   Meals: D, LN

Slightly more casual than Nobu, Next Door Nobu takes no reservations and does not serve lunch. To dine here, come early: later arrivals may wait up to 90 minutes for a table. But the food is as accomplished (and as expensive) as Nobu's. And while the menu features many of the same dishes, it strives for its own identity, with an emphasis on raw shellfish, whole fish served for an entire table, noodles, and texture. Noodles range from the portly white udon, which slip sinuously into your mouth, to the more austere soba with their subtle chewiness. The few meat dishes on the menu are memorable. The sliced Kobe beef tataki comes with little side dishes—grated daikon, scallions and sliced garlic—that add both flavor and texture. And this textural roller coaster continues with mochi ice cream balls, the most appealing way to end a meal. Mochi, the pounded rice candy of Japan, is stretchy and sticky when warm, but hardens into a cold tackiness when frozen. This one dessert says it all: texture is an important part of Japanese cooking, and Next Door Nobu does it very well. **Price range:** Noodle dishes, $10–$15; hot dishes, $8–$32; sushi and sashimi, $3–$6 a piece.

Nha Trang $25 & Under   VIETNAMESE

87 Baxter St., Chinatown   (212) 233-5948
148 Centre St. (at Walker St.)   (212) 941-9292
Credit cards: Cash only   Meals: B, Br, L, D

Nha Trang was one of the pioneering Vietnamese restaurants in Chinatown, and it's still one of the best. Spring rolls are perfectly fried, while steamed ravioli, glistening paper-thin rice noodle crepes wrapped around minced pork and ground mushrooms and served with slices of smooth, mild Vietnamese pork sausage, is another excellent appetizer. Vietnamese rice noodle soups like pho tai, a huge bowl of noodles and tender slices of beef in a coriander-scented broth, are big enough to be an entire meal. A new branch opened on Centre St. in 2000. **Price range:** Entrees, $5–$11.

Nick & Toni's ☆ ☆ $$$ MEDITERRANEAN

100 West 67th St. (between Broadway and Columbus)   (212) 496-4000
Credit cards: All major   Meals: L, D

A great neighborhood restaurant, Nick & Toni's is a lot like the neighborhood it serves: casual, crowded and noisy. But there is one thing that sets it apart from most of the neighborhood's restaurants: the food is really delicious. Nick & Toni's starts with good ingredients and leaves them alone. The menu changes constantly, but there are a few perennials, like the mussels and the impeccable

Caesar salad. Often there is a fine pasta with just the right number of baby clams. Desserts are simple and seasonal. **Price range:** Entrees, $11–$25.

Nicole's ☆☆ $$$ ENGLISH
10 East 60th Street;   (212) 223-2288
Credit cards: All major   Meals: L, D

Nicole's is the New York twin of its London namesake in the Nicole Farhi store on Bond Street. At lunch, it hums and buzzes. It's filled with stylish, well-heeled diners, nearly all of them women. At night, the store closes, shadows descend, and Nicole's light and airy downstairs dining room takes on a somber tinge. The chef has developed a bright, appealing menu with a shrewd minimalist touch and just the right English notes. The smoked haddock chowder, more of a stew than a soup, thrives on the interplay between good-size, chewy nuggets of haddock with a smoky tang, and kernels of fresh corn that burst with sweetness. Nicole's does not go in for big, flashy effects. It's happy with clever little touches. The roasted duck breast is a good example: it derives just enough sweetness from a handful of baked figs, a small pile of roasted onions, and a little balsamic vinegar. The Moroccan cumin and lemon chicken is also irresistible. Nicole's wisely steers toward simple, homey sweets like lemon pudding, and also offers cheeses from Neal's Yard Dairy in London. **Price range:** Entrees, $20 to $32.

Nobu ☆☆☆ $$$$ JAPANESE
105 Hudson St. (at Franklin St.)   (212) 219-0500
Credit cards: All major   Meals: L, D

Chic, casual and pulsing with energy, Nobu cannot be compared with any other restaurant. The spirit of invention of its chef-owner, Nobuyuki Matsuhisa—incorporating new ingredients into old dishes or retooling traditional recipes—lighted a spark in the kitchen, igniting each chef to new and increasingly daring feats. The result is something that seems like a Japanese dish but is not.

The best time to eat at Nobu is lunchtime. Order an Omakase meal and let the chefs choose your meal for you. If dishes like Funazushi, a freshwater trout buried in rice for a year, do not appeal to you, just tell the waiter the foods you do not eat. A finicky child could eat happily at Nobu, munching skewers of grilled chicken, beautifully rendered fried tempura and toro, the richest of tuna. No kitchen turns out a more spectacular plate of sushi. And sake lovers, once they have tasted Hokusetsu sake, will find it almost impossible to drink the stuff served in other restaurants. Desserts include a warm chocolate soufflé cake with siso syrup and green tea ice cream that comes in a bento box. **Price range:** Avg. $60–$65 per person.

Oceana ☆☆☆ $$$$ SEAFOOD
55 East 54th St. (between Park and Madison Aves.)   (212) 759-5941
Credit cards: All major   Meals: L, D   Closed Sun.

Oceana's downstairs dining room is small and pretty, with an old-fashioned air. The intimate upstairs dining room is as handsome and luxurious as the dining room on a private yacht. Service is excellent, and you feel that you are about to set sail on a special voyage. You are. Oceana's viewpoint is global—dishes are inspired by a wide variety of cuisines—while firmly rooted in an American idiom. What's more, the menu changes daily as chef Rick Moonen continues to experiment with new combinations. His careful spicing and the extremely intelligent use of ethnic accents brings out the essential nature of the fish. In summer, there is a huge variety of fruit desserts like rhubarb crumble or raspberry gratin with coconut and pineapple. One of the winter standards is sticky toffee pudding with vanilla ice cream. **Price range:** 3-course prix-fixe, $65; tasting menu, $90 ($135 with wines).

Odeon ☆ ☆ $ $ BISTRO/NEW AMERICAN
145 West Broadway (at Thomas St.)   (212) 233-0507
Credit cards: All major   Meals: Br, L, D, LN

SoHo's first great American bistro is still cooking after all these years. The neighborhood has certainly changed, but time has stood still in the dining room. It is still unpretentious and comfortable, and it still feels as if it is filled with artists. It's great for burgers, omelets, pasta and roast chicken in a slightly funky setting; it's even greater for a martini. And it's still a destination until 3 A.M. **Price range:** Avg. entree, $18.

One If By Land, Two If By Sea ☆ $$$$ CONTINENTAL
17 Barrow St. (between West 4th St. and Seventh Ave. S.)
(212) 255-8649
Credit cards: All major   Meals: D

Considered by many to be the most romantic restaurant in New York, it is almost always booked. The lights are low, the gas fireplaces burn even in the summer and a pianist serenades you with music. Known mainly for the 1950's specialty Beef Wellington, the food has grown more ambitious of late. Wild field greens with Champagne vinaigrette and quenelles of Roquefort mousse is a perfectly fine salad. The seared tuna is fresh and rosy, and the lightly smoked and roasted rack of lamb is a fine piece of meat. Even the poached peaches with pistachio ice cream are good. **Price range:** Entrees, $23–$39.

Osteria Del Circo ☆ ☆ $$$ ITALIAN
120 West 55th St. (between Sixth and Seventh Aves.)   (212) 265-3636
Credit cards: All major   Meals: L, D

Circo (pronounced CHEER-co) means "circus" in Italian. The festive atmosphere includes flying panels of red and yellow striped cloth near the ceiling and metal monkeys moving around a pole in the middle of the room. The key to ordering from its menu is to look for the name Egidiana, sometimes shortened to Egi, who is the owner's mother. Every dish attributed to her is superb, including her zuppa alla frantoiana, a thick, flavorful purée of 30 vegetables, and cacciucco, a Tuscan fish soup. Among the main courses, try the tender roast squab with braised radicchio, a simple rotisserie chicken, red snapper served with capers, onions and artichokes and the expertly made risottos. Should there be the special chocolate polenta cake, don't miss it; it is just the thing to send you off with a smile. **Price range:** Entrees, $22–$29.

Otabe ☆ ☆ $$$ JAPANESE

68 East 56th St. (between Park and Madison Aves.)   (212) 223-7575
Credit cards: All major   Meals: L, D

Two separate dining rooms offer two different dining experiences. In the teppan room in the back it is a very upscale Benihana; the elegant front dining room serves kaiseki-like cuisine. The kaiseki dinner is a lovely and accessible introduction to the most poetic food of Japan, a ceremonial cuisine that is traditionally served in many small courses meant to reflect the season. Less ambitious eaters might want to sample fewer dishes. Desserts are the big surprise at Otabe; more French than Japanese, they are original, beautiful and very delicious. The teppan room has a separate menu, and each course is cooked before your eyes by your personal chef. **Price range:** Entrees, $14.50–$60.

Our Place Shanghai Tea Garden $25 & Under CHINESE

141 East 55th St. (At Third Ave.)   (212) 753-3900
Credit cards: All major   Meals: L, D

With its elevated service, the ornate birds carved out of radish and turnip that adorn serving plates, and the thick linens, Our Place has the feel of a fine yet informal banquet. The Shanghai dishes are rich and satisfying, beautifully rendered, yet accessible to Americans, who make up most of the clientele. The waiters are supremely attentive, dividing portions onto plates, putting umbrellas into drinks for young children and generally offering to do anything short of feeding you. Silver-dollar-size steamed soup dumplings are well-seasoned and nicely textured, and pieces of crunchy smoked fish are not really smoky but sweet. The kitchen excels at tofu dishes, and noodle dishes are superb. **Price range:** Entrees, $9.95–$24.95.

Palio ☆ ☆ $$$$ ITALIAN

151 West 51st St. (between Sixth and Seventh Aves.)   (212) 245-4850
Credit cards: All major   Meals: L, D   Closed Sun.

The murals by Sandro Chia make the bar at Palio one of New York City's most magical spaces. The upstairs dining room is entirely formal, and a man's world. The elegant Italian fare can be New York City's finest; it can also let you down. A fabulous puréed Tuscan bean soup with sage and olive oil is everything you expect from great Tuscan cooking. Main courses can be disappointing, but some dishes were really impressive, such as the lobster ravioli and salmon wrapped in spinach in a creamy caviar sauce. **Price range:** Pasta, $19–$25; entrees, $25–$38.

Palladin ☆ ☆ $$$ NEW AMERICAN

224 West 49th St. (between Broadway and Eighth Ave.)
(212) 320-2929
Credit cards: All major   Meals: L, D   Closed Sun.

In this casual, breezy restaurant, white-clad chefs work in a brightly lighted open
kitchen that seems like a stage. Palladin is a techno-bistro with enough sass and
style to divert attention from its mild identity crisis: it looks as though it should be
feeding supermodels but what it gets is a theater crowd. Jean-Louis Palladin is a
feisty chef with plenty of ideas so he finesses the situation skillfully. His plain-
sounding pea soup delivers every ounce of sweetness a pea possibly can, along with
soft truffle dumplings that bob on their little green sea. The oxtail crépinette with
bone marrow flan, a signature dish, deserves its fame. Pierce the pastalike wrapping
of caul fat, and you strike a compact mass of wine-braised oxtail swimming in a
thick veal stock. This is the greatest meatball known to humanity, a small bomb
capable of stunning a vegetarian at 100 paces. **Price range:** Entrees, $22–$28.

Palm $$$ STEAKHOUSE

837 Second Ave. (between 44th and 45th Sts.)   (212) 687-2953
250 W. 50th St. (between Broadway and Eighth Ave.)   (212) 333-7256
Credit cards: All major   Meals: L, D

Great steak, rude waiters and the world's best hash brown potatoes. The walls
are covered with caricatures, the floor is covered with sawdust and if you want
to experience the real New York rush, this is the place for you. **Price range:**
Entrees, $16–$35.

Panaché $25 & Under   BISTRO/FRENCH

470 Sixth Ave. (near 12th St.)   (212) 243-2222.
Credit cards: All major   Meals: L, D, LN

Panaché is an unpretentious place with a wood floor, leather banquettes and
brass lighting fixtures. With little flash, the food is the thing at Panaché, and
the chef has put together a menu that is generally down to earth and well-
anchored in bistro traditions. Appetizers are pretty and delicious, like potatoes
lyonnaise, flecked with smoky bacon and red wine vinegar, piled into a wide
column and crowned with the head of a portobello mushroom touched with
truffle oil. Main courses include a satisfying roast chicken with pearl onions,
mushrooms and mashed potatoes and salmon, cooked perfectly and enlivened
by a heady horseradish sauce. Crème brûlée is excellent and mango cake with
passion fruit sauce is a decent second choice. **Price range:** Entrees, $12–$27.50.

Pão $25 & Under   PORTUGUESE

322 Spring St. (at Greenwich St.)   (212) 334-5464
Credit cards: All major   Meals: L, D, LN

The small menu in this small restaurant offers traditional Portuguese cuisine
with a contemporary touch. To begin, try roasted quail on cabbage braised with

mild Portuguese sausage and black grapes. Main dishes include pork and clams in a roasted-red-pepper sauce, and grilled shrimp served with a clam-and-shrimp-studded lemony bread pudding. Desserts are not to be missed, particularly the pudding with port-and-prune sauce and the rice pudding with citrus, nutmeg and cinnamon. **Price range:** Entrees, $13.95–$16.95.

Paola's ☆☆ $$ ITALIAN
245 East 84th St. (between Second and Third Aves.)   (212) 794-1890
Credit cards: All major   Meals: L, D

Everybody in New York seems to be looking for the perfect neighborhood restaurant. This may be it. Paola's is one of the city's best and least-known Italian restaurants. It makes some of the city's finest pasta, and the wine list is wonderful. No regular would even consider starting a meal here without an order of carciofi alla giudea, a fine version of baby artichokes fried in the style of the Roman ghetto. But pastas are the soul of the menu. Filled pastas such as cazunzei and pansotti are wonderful. Desserts, except the ricotta cake, seem like an afterthought. **Price range:** Pastas, $12.95–$14.95; entrees, $16.95–$26.95.

Parioli Romanissimo ☆☆ $$$$ ITALIAN
24 East 81st St. (between Fifth and Madison Aves.)   (212) 288-2391
Credit cards: All major   Meals: D   Closed Sun.

One of New York City's most civilized restaurants, Parioli Romanissimo offers stunningly expensive Italian food in an elegant town house. The old-fashioned table-side cooking sends seductive aromas into the air. The rack of lamb is spectacularly good. Some of the other dishes are, too. The chef clearly cooks each risotto to order, and each one, whether it is asparagus, seafood or a simple Milanese, is perfect. Pastas are also exemplary. But the wine list is the major argument against a meal here: finding a good bottle at a reasonable price is extremely difficult. **Price range:** Entrees, $28–$38.

Park Bistro ☆☆☆ $$$ BISTRO/FRENCH
414 Park Ave. S. (between 28th and 29th Sts.)   (212) 689-1360
Credit cards: All major   Meals: L, D

A classic French bistro, from the décor (photos of Paris in the 1950's) to the menu (magret, onglet and so forth). It offers seductive Gallic fare, good wines at reasonable prices and a cozy setting. Openers include house-cured salmon, gratin of fresh mussels, guinea-hen terrine, and a ragout of calamari, white beans and peppers. Among the entrees are grilled escalope of salmon, veal medallion, roasted and caramelized shoulder of pork with carrots and fennel, and a daube of beef with potato gnocchi. There is a daily selection of imported cheeses, and to top off the meal, thin warm apple tart with Armagnac and vanilla ice cream; fresh roasted fig tart, or the ubiquitous crème brûlée. There is a large and interesting selection of tea in addition to several coffees. **Price range:** Avg. app., $9; entree, $14–$20; dessert, $6.50. Wheelchair access: Not accessible. Services: Delivery, takeout, catering, private parties.

Park View at the Boathouse ☆☆ $$$ NEW AMERICAN
Loeb Boathouse, Central Park, East 72d St. entrance   (212) 517-2233
Credit cards: All major   Meals: L, D

Is this Manhattan's most romantic spot? Very possibly. Situated in the Loeb Boathouse next to Central Park's prettiest lake, it combines country charm with views of skyscrapers peeking over the trees. There is interesting, eclectic food and a good wine list here. The setting is so swell that you feel lucky to be there. Live jazz at the adjacent café is a real bonus. And if you end your meal with the sweet, rich tres leches cake topped with white chocolate mousse and a raspberry coulis, or caramelized mango with coconut sorbet and macadamia crunch, you might just go dancing off into the dark. **Price range:** Entrees, $18–$30.

Pastis ☆ $$$ BISTRO/FRENCH
9 Ninth Ave. (at Little West 12th St.)
(212) 929-4844
Credit cards: All major   Meals: L, D, LN

Those who can't get into Balthazar now crowd into Pastis, expecting to see the shiny Balthazar crowd but instead seeing one another in large numbers. What do diners get for their suffering? A meal that's as good as it needs to be, but no better. Virtually every dish could qualify for protection by the French Ministry of Culture. It's a deliberate invitation to simple pleasures. And all are good. Pastis needs to work a little harder on its steak frites, but rabbit pappardelle is a pleasant surprise, a superior plate of firm pasta with a sweetly meaty sauce. For dessert, the crêpes suzette rise up in glory, and the floating island floats, a cloud with just enough substance to support its light custardy sauce. **Price range:** Entrees, $14–$17.

Patria ☆☆☆ $$$ LATIN AMERICAN
250 Park Ave. S. (at 20th St.)   (212) 777-6211
Credit cards: All major Meals L, D

With its colorful food and boisterous atmosphere, Patria feels like a party every night—one that celebrates Latin tastes and seduces customers with its flavors. The menu offers exuberant, outrageous nuevo Latino combinations with names like Honduran fire and ice, an extravagant tuna ceviche marinated with chilies, ginger and coconut milk. Each dish explodes in the mouth with a rich variety of tastes. At many restaurants, the main dishes are less interesting than the appetizers, but here the larger plates offer a greater opportunity for creativity. Guatemalan chicken is a gorgeous combination of grilled white meat and deep fried leg on a bed of green rice decorated with dots of mole sauce and an avocado salad. Rib-eye steak was so deeply smoked the taste seemed to fill the mouth. Sweets are visually restrained but each has a surprising intensity of flavor. Lunchtime is quieter and the menu is slightly different, but the food is always interesting, and I always leave with the desire to return. **Price range:** Three-course prix-fixe, $54.

Patroon ☆☆☆ $$$$ NEW AMERICAN
160 East 46th St. (between Lexington and Third Aves.)   (212) 883-7373
Credit cards: All major   Meals: L, D   Closed Sun.

When Ken Aretsky opened Patroon intending to create a contemporary "21,"
businessmen were charmed with the luxurious clubhouse atmosphere, the low
lights, neutral colors and smooth textures, and the extremely professional service. Many gourmets, however, found the food predictable. Chef Geoffrey
Zakarian (who has since left the restaurant) put an end to that. He invented a
few truly brilliant dishes: Duck a l'orange Patroon, served as an appetizer, is a
stunning rendition of an old standard. He introduced a similarly innovative
take on lamb breast, cooking it into a rich terrine enlivened with accents of
mango and tomato. It, too, makes an ideal appetizer. The menu is remarkably
smart, American without being hokey, rich without being fussy. **Price range:**
Entrees, $23–$38.

Payard Pâtisserie ☆☆ $$$ BISTRO/FRENCH
1032 Lexington Ave. (at 73d St.)   (212) 717-5252
Credit cards: All major   Meals: Br, L, D   Closed Sun.

This is the ultimate Upper East Side bistro, a whimsical belle epoque cafe
and pastry shop, complete with mirrors, mahogany and hand-blown lamps.
Just about everything here is extraordinary, from the inventive bistro menu
to the amazing pastries sold in the bakery. There is, however, a drawback: the
sound level can be excruciating. The menu is confident, centered, straightforward, offering French bistro fare with no apologies: steak frites, sweetbreads, even pigs' feet. Appetizers and desserts are terrific. **Price range:**
Entrees, $17–$25.

Peacock Alley ☆☆☆ $$$$ FRENCH
Waldorf-Astoria Hotel, 301 Park Ave. (at 50th St.)   (212) 872-4895
Credit cards: All major   Meals: B, Br, D, LN

What's going on at the Waldorf-Astoria? After the departure of its previous
chef, the hotel went shopping. They found a truly great chef in France, Laurent
Gras. Mr. Gras does not try to dazzle you with exotic ingredients and no Asian
accents find their way into his dishes. Dishes here change frequently—not only
with the seasons, but weekly—sometimes even daily—allowing Mr. Gras to
offer diners a varied menu. In one 10-day period, to take advantage of the spring
crop, he offered five different asparagus dishes. A few desserts from previous
menus appear from time to time, but a new pastry chef, working with Mr. Gras,
is developing a different and equally kaleidoscopic range of desserts. The wine
list, which once offered only high-priced selections, has been expanded to
include affordable bottles. The quiet, comfortable—even serene—dining room
has little character but the staff has been invigorated, and everyone seems
intent on providing diners with an extraordinary experience. **Price range:** Avg.
entree, $32; 6-course tasting menu, $80.

Pepe Verde $25 & Under   ITALIAN
559 Hudson St. (near Perry St.)   (212) 255-2221
Credit cards: Cash only   Meals: L, D

Pepe Verde is a slightly larger version of Pepe Rosso to Go, the excellent take-out shop in SoHo. It has tables where you can sit comfortably, but the idea is the same: freshly prepared Italian food several notches above the typical takeout fare, including excellent boneless chicken breasts, marinated in lemon and grilled; rigatoni with deliciously earthy meat sauce, and a rustic, enjoyable pear tart. **Price range:** Entrees, $4.95–$10.95.

Pepolino $25 & Under   ITALIAN
281 West Broadway (near Lispenard St.)   (212) 966-9983
Credit cards: AE   Meals: L, D, LN

There's a lot to like about Pepolino. The small, cheerful dining room seems to glow with warmth, the greeting is friendly, and the service is good-natured. The gnocchi at Pepolino are ethereal, as light as miniature clouds, making up with intense flavor what they lack in mass. Whether as malfatti, gnocchi made with spinach and served in a simple sauce of butter and sage, or in their more common potato incarnation, they are meltingly good. The chef also makes a glorious pappa al pomodoro, the Tuscan specialty of ripe tomatoes, shreds of stale bread and fragrant olive oil, cooked into a delicious mush. Pastas are marvelous, and one dessert stands out: a dense chocolate cake, intensely flavored with coffee. **Price range:** Entrees, $11–$19.

Periyali ☆ ☆ ☆ $$$ GREEK
35 West 20th St. (between Fifth and Sixth Aves.)   (212) 463-7890
Credit cards: All major   Meals: L, D   Closed Sun.

Periyali used to be the best Greek restaurant in the city, and even now with so much new competition it is still a great place to go. The atmosphere is rustic, and the food is made with good ingredients. Recommended starters are the avgolemono soup (a rich chicken soup smoothed with lemon, egg and semolina); the plate of three spreads, and especially the tender and fresh octopus marinated in red wine and grilled over charcoal. Grilled lamb chops with fresh rosemary, baked fillet of striped bass, rabbit stew, and garides Santorini—baked shrimp with tomato, scallions, brandy and feta cheese—are some of the entrees. For dessert, the creamy, lemon-scented rice pudding; moist orange semolina cake, walnut cake, and the deep-fried pastry twists called thiples. **Price range:** Entrees, $17–$25.

Petrossian ☆ ☆ $$$$ NEW AMERICAN/RUSSIAN
182 West 58th St. (at Seventh Ave.)   (212) 245-2214
Credit cards: All major   Meals: Br, L, D

Nobody in New York City serves better caviar, and nobody does it with more style. The dark room is covered with Art Deco splendor, the waiters wear blue blazers and an obsequious air, and the caviar arrives with warm toast, blini and beautiful little spoons. Vodka is served in icy little flutes that make it taste somehow better. Should you desire something else, the food is good and surprisingly affordable. **Price range:** Entrees, $24–$34.

Picholine ☆ ☆ ☆ $$$$ MEDITERRANEAN/FRENCH
35 West 64th St. (between Broadway and Central Park. West)
(212) 724-8585
Credit cards: All major   Meals: L, D   Closed Sun.

Picholine, named after a Mediterranean olive, focuses on the food of southern France, Italy, Greece and Morocco. Meals begin with good house-made breads, bowls of the tiny olives and olive oil. There is beautifully cooked whole fish for two, boned at the table. Salmon in horseradish crust is a signature dish and it is excellent. But there are also robust dishes from the north, like daube of beef short ribs with a horseradish potato puree, and a hearty cassoulet. The kitchen also has a way with game. Homey dishes—chestnut and fennel soup dotted with sausage, cassoulet rich with duck confit, and Moroccan spiced lamb, served on a bed of couscous with minted yogurt—are all wonderful. Finally, don't miss the wonderfully extravagant cheese cart, worth considering if only to hear the lovingly detailed descriptions of each cheese. **Price range:** Entrees, $26–$36; prix-fixe, $58; four-course tasting menu, $70 ($90 for seven courses).

Pig Heaven $25 & Under   CHINESE
1540 Second Ave. (near 80th St.)   (212) 744-4333
Credit cards: All major   Meals: L, D

Pig Heaven has a new, sleekly modern look, with a handsome bar, almond-shaped hanging lamps and a table of ceramic and carved decorative pigs. Its terrific Chinese-American food is spiced and presented in ways that please westerners, yet it is fresh and prepared with finesse. The best place to start is the pork selection, particularly roasted Cantonese dishes like suckling pig, strips of juicy meat under a layer of moist fat and wafer-thin, deliciously crisp skin. Most of the supposedly spicy Sichuan dishes here are good, but actually quite mild, and dumplings are excellent. **Price range:** Entrees, $7.95 to $18.95.

Ping's Seafood ☆ ☆ $$ CHINESE
22 Mott St. (bet. Worth & Mosco Sts.) (212) 602-9988
Credit cards: All major Meals: Br, L, D

Near the door, a high-rise of stacked fish tanks offers the menu headliners, a stellar cast that includes but is by no means limited to lobsters, eels, scallops, sea bass and shrimp. The seafood in the tanks ends up on your plate, pretty much short-cutting the freshness issue. The preparations are minimal—a ginger-garlic sauce for the lobster, for example, or black bean sauce for the eel—and the results are maximal. Shrimp in the shell, crackling crisp and salty, come to the table piping hot, exhaling a delicate, fragrant steam. Scallops, quickly steamed, come in three choices of sauce: garlic, black bean or XO, a Hong Kong innovation that's sweet and sour, hot and salty. Unusual for a Chinatown restaurant, they dare you to try things. For the adventurous eater, the quirky and often experimental food of Hong Kong always stands as a welcome challenge. One of the house signatures, a rather simple stir-fry of squid cut into long strands woven together with dried fish and crunchy matchsticks of jicama and celery is a winner.

One of the more appealing rituals at Ping's is winter melon soup. You must call a day ahead, since the melon, which flourishes in the summer despite its name, has to steam for six hours. It comes as a bulging green bowl brimming with what initially seems to be nothing more than a mild-flavored chicken stock. The melon flesh, similar in color and texture to honeydew, is also subtly flavored and slightly sweet. As the ladle dips deeper into the gourd, interesting things begin to emerge—bits of fresh scallop and dried scallop, ham, dried white fungus, shrimp, frog and crab. This seems like the perfect emblem for Ping's, an exotic package with thrilling secrets inside. **Price range:** Entrees, $6.95-$30.

Pongal $25 & Under   INDIAN/KOSHER/VEGETARIAN
110 Lexington Ave. (near 27th St.)   (212) 696-9458
Credit cards: All major   Meals: L, D

The delectable vegetarian cuisine of South India is the specialty at Pongal, where the food is kosher as well. The centerpiece dishes are the daunting dosai, huge crepes made of various fermented batters that are stuffed and rolled into cylinders that can stretch two-and-a-half feet. But they are light and delicious, filled with spiced mixtures of potatoes and onions. Pongal also serves a wonderful shrikhand, a dessert made of yogurt custard flavored with nutmeg, cardamom and saffron. **Price range:** Entrees, $7.95–$13.95.

Pop ☆ $$$ PAN-ASIAN/BISTRO
127 Fourth Avenue (12th Street);   (212) 767-1800
Credit cards: All major   Meals: D

Pop is a bright, happy place with a noncommittal, nonemotive décor and a crowd-pleasing menu that hips and hops from one culinary source to another. The result is toe-tapping food. Pop feels just right, within fairly narrow limits, like an episode of "Friends." Chef Brian Young sprinkles his plates with little surprises—fun, palate-pleasing footnotes like the ingenious slaw of fine-shaved brussels sprouts that comes with a thick, juicy veal chop in quince and pomegranate sauce. For dessert, try the caramel bread pudding and the strawberry cream cake, an all-out assault on the pleasure zones. **Price range:** Entrees, $24 to $36.

Provence ☆ $$$ FRENCH
38 MacDougal St. (near Prince St.)   (212) 475-7500
Credit cards: AE   Meals: L, D

A charmingly crowded French cafe straight out of the French countryside. The wine list is interesting and a few dishes work well. Mussels gratinées, baked on the half shell and sprinkled with almonds and garlic, are very tasty. Bourride, a pale fish soup, is thickened with aioli; don't miss it. Pot au feu, a sometime special, is also a fine example of hearty country cooking, and the bouillabaisse, served only on Fridays, is superb. **Price range:** Entrees, $15.50–$26.

Prune $25 & Under   ECLECTIC
54 East First St. (near First Ave.)   (212) 677-6221.
Credit cards: Major   Meals: D   Closed Mon.

The idiosyncratic name (the chef and owner's childhood nickname) is perfect for this unconventional little place. You could describe the food as homey, or as faintly European. Like pastrami, thin slices of duck breast taste deliciously of smoke, vinegar and black pepper, and are served with a small omelet flavored with rye. Voilá! Pastrami on rye. Roasted capon is as conventional a dish as Prune offers, yet it is marvelously juicy, served over a slice of toast imbued with garlic. Desserts are terrific, like cornmeal poundcake drenched in a sweet rosemary syrup, with a poached pear. **Price range:** Entrees, $10–$17.

Puttanesca $25 & Under   ITALIAN
859 Ninth Ave. (at 56th St.)   (212) 581-4177
Credit cards: AE   Meals: L, D

At Puttanesca the rule is, the simpler the better. Uncomplicated dishes, made with exceedingly fresh ingredients, include an excellent Caesar salad, perfectly grilled vegetables and mussels steamed in white wine and garlic. The room is large and it can get very noisy when the pre-theater crowd arrives. **Price range:** Entrees, $6.95–$16.95.

Quilty's ☆☆ $$$ NEW AMERICAN
177 Prince St. (near Sullivan St.)   (212) 254-1260
Credit cards: All major   Meals: L, D

The cooking at this spare, elegant restaurant is quirky and often exciting, and it deserves a more serene setting. One of the best appetizers is a salad of lettuces, fennel and sliced blood oranges tossed with big, warm squares of toasted hominy. There is occasionally one ingredient too many in the dishes, but not in the case of the shiitake, sage and tangerine peel sprinkled on the delicate pappardelle served with braised rabbit. Try the frozen nougat for dessert. **Price range:** Entrees, $17.50–$29.

Quince ☆☆ $$$$ FRENCH
33 West 54th St. (Between Fifth and Sixth Aves.)   (212) 582-8993
Credit cards: All major   Meals: L, D

Quince is not a shoot-for-the-moon sort of restaurant. It's a place of quiet, modest pleasures. It's in a town house with murals depicting gentle scenes of rolling countryside and happy birds, an ingenious and desperately needed device to suggest space where none exists. It is a cozy place where the floors creak underfoot, the lighting is subdued and the outside world seems very far away. Morgen

Jacobson, the chef and owner, says that he chose the name for the simple reason that he likes quinces. He has also worked them into several of the better dishes on the menu. Quince pancakes come with the confit of duck; it also shows up on the dessert menu in a frangipani tart with slices of roast quince and a scoop of almond ice cream. **Price range:** Dinner, three courses, $58.

Rafina $25 & Under   GREEK/SEAFOOD
1481 York Ave. (near 78th St.)   (212) 327-0950
Credit cards: All major   Meals: D

At this elemental Greek restaurant specializing in seafood, you know exactly what you'll get: simple ingredients, simply prepared. Charcoal-grilled octopus is crunchy outside, tender within, while grilled whole fish like porgy, red snapper and striped bass are enhanced by their simple marinade of olive oil, lemon juice, oregano and garlic, and they arrive moist and delicious. The pleasant, bright room is decorated in blue and white and bedecked in Greek seafood décor. **Price range:** Entrees, $12.95–$24.95.

Ratner's Dairy $ KOSHER/VEGETARIAN
138 Delancey St. (between Norfolk and Suffolk Sts.)   (212) 677-5588
Credit cards: All major   Meals: B, Br, L, D, LN   Closed 3 P.M. Fri.
to sundown Sat.

If you're eager to taste a real cheese blintz, this is the place to do it. The Lower East Side may be changing, but Ratner's soldiers on, serving Jewish dairy food with a snarl. **Price range:** Avg. dinner, $15–$20.

The Red Cat ☆ $$ BISTRO/AMERICAN
227 10th Avenue (near 23d St.)   (212) 242-1122
Credit cards: All major   Meals: D, LN

A lot of restaurants make a big noise about being warm, welcoming and accessible. The Red Cat, with little ado, manages to be all three. It is stylish, but not snooty, cool but relaxed. The menu reflects the spirit of the place with a lineup of solid, well-executed American bistro dishes, with a little trick or twist on each plate. The sweet-pea risotto cake is served with poached oysters and charred corn and a touch of Champagne and cream. The obligatory steak dish comes with a ragout of roasted shallots, tomatoes and cracked olives. The short dessert list does not disappoint. **Price range:** entrees, $15–$24.

Redeye Grill ☆ $$$ NEW AMERICAN
890 Seventh Ave. (at 56th St.)   (212) 541-9000
Credit cards: All major   Meals: Br, L, D, LN

The boisterous room seems as big as Grand Central Terminal and is lively at almost any hour. There's something for everyone on the vast menu, from smoked fish to raw clams, Chinese chicken, pasta, even a hamburger—late into the night. The small grilled lobster, served with a little potato cake and pristine haricots verts, is lovely. The steak of choice here would be the hanger steak, tender slices piled onto a biscuit. The plain Jane cream-cheese bundt cake is usually the best of the desserts. **Price range:** Entrees, $18–$29.

Remi ☆☆ $$$ ITALIAN

145 West 53d St. (between Sixth and Seventh Aves.)   (212) 581-4242
Credit cards: All major   Meals: L, D

Remi's stunning Gothic interior and the kitchen's enticing and inventive Northern Italian fare make it easy to understand its continued popularity. The diverse menu includes starters of roast quail, wrapped in bacon, drizzled with a balsamic reduction and cushioned on grilled polenta; warm shrimp cakes garnished with mixed baby greens and grilled mushrooms, and grilled octopus paired with radicchio, dressed with a sun-dried tomato-and-celery vinaigrette. Enticing pastas and main courses include garganelli blended with Coho salmon in balsamic sauce; veal-and-spinach-filled cannelloni in rosemary sauce; and salmon in a horseradish crust, finished with red wine sauce. **Price range:** Entrees, $16–$28.

Rinconcito Mexicano $ MEXICAN/TEX-MEX

307 West 39th St. (between Eighth and Ninth Aves.)   (212) 268-1704
Credit cards: All major   Meals: L, D   Closed Sat., Sun.

This tiny restaurant is little more than a smoky aisle in the garment center. English is barely spoken, but the food needs no translation: soft tacos with the freshest and most authentic ingredients, like sautéed pork, calf's tongue, goat, chorizo and pork skin. The aroma of corn rises from the steamed tacos, and the refried beans are still pleasantly grainy. **Price range:** Avg. entree, $8.

Rocking Horse Café $25 & Under   MEXICAN

182 Eighth Ave. (near 19th St.)   (212) 463-9511
Credit cards: All major   Meals: L, D

This bright, crowded restaurant serves some of the most exciting Mexican food in New York City: not exactly authentic, but interpretations in the best sense of the word, using Mexican ingredients and techniques to create appealing food for a New York audience. The playful dining room is colorful and light, with bold murals and folk art adorning the marigold walls. An intelligently chosen wine list may convince you that wine is a proper drink with Mexican food. **Price range:** Entrees, $12.95–$20.95.

Rosa Mexicano ☆☆ $$$ MEXICAN/TEX-MEX

1063 First Ave. (at 58th St.)   (212) 753-7407
51 Columbus Ave. (between W. 61st and 62nd Sts.)   (212) 977-7700
Credit cards: All major   Meals: D, LN

Rosa Mexicano has been one of the city's reigning Mexican restaurants for more than a decade. It's also one of the most expensive, but Rosa is also a proud proponent of Mexico's place among the world's leading cuisines. Rosa's renowned guacamole is prepared at tableside, and other top-flight dishes include sautéed marinated shrimp, taquitos de moronga, in which blood sausage is served in corn tortillas with coriander, and pozole, the soothing, earthy soup. Menudo, an earthy tripe stew, and prawns sautéed with garlic and parsley are also winners. **Price range:** Entrees, $16–$26.

Royal Siam $25 & Under THAI
240 Eighth Ave. (between 22d and 23d Sts.)   (212) 741-1732
Credit cards: All major   Meals: L, D

Royal Siam's generic décor of mirrored walls, Thai posters and glass-topped tables belie some of the most flavorful and attractively prepared Thai cooking around. Dishes to look for include tom yum koong, or shrimp and mushroom soup in a lemony seafood broth; tod mun pla, fish cakes paired with a bright peanut sauce; and nuur yunk namtok, or grilled steak served sliced on a bed of mixed greens with cucumber and tomato. **Price range:** Entrees, $8.95–$14.95.

Ruby Foo's ☆☆ $ $ PAN-ASIAN
1626 Broadway (between West 49th and 50th Sts.)   (212) 489-5600
2182 Broadway (at 77th St.)   (212) 724-6700
Credit cards: All major   Meals: Br, L, D, LN

The Upper West Side branch has everything it takes to make the neighborhood happy: fabulous décor, interesting pan-Asian food and the sort of atmosphere that appeals to families with children as well as singles on the prowl. The new location in Times Square, cheek by jowl with cartoon operations like the World Wrestling Federation restaurant, fits right into the area, with a décor that suggests the mysterious East as imagined by a 1940's B-movie producer. The menu offers everything from dim sum to sushi with side trips through Thailand, tailored to American tastes. With the exception of dim sum, the weakest link in the menu, the Chinese food is seductive. A memorable Japanese dish is the miso-glazed black cod. But it is the Southeast Asian dishes that really sing. The green curry chicken has a fiery coconut-based sauce that is irresistible. Desserts are purely American and purely wonderful, especially the raspberry-passion fruit parfait. **Price range:** Entrees, $9.50–$19.50.

Russian Tea Room $$$$ RUSSIAN
150 West 57th St. (between Sixth and Seventh Aves.)   (212) 974-2111
Credit cards: All major   Meals: L, D

The Russian Tea Room of old is no more. But the new-model Tea Room that has sprouted in its place shows every sign of robust life. The solid line of limousines on 57th Street and the nightly horde of tourists and misty-eyed locals of a certain age suggest that, at least as a brand name, the Russian Tea Room may be on the verge of its most glorious era. The downstairs looks much the same, although much brighter and shinier. But upstairs, the new owner has pulled out the stops: the room is meant to conjure up the glittering halls of the Peterhof Palace and the magic world of Afanasyev's fairy tales. It feels more like a pinball machine.

More than ever, the Russian Tea Room is not about the food. Still, some of the
charms of Russian cuisine are on display here, notably in a thick, no-holds-
barred borscht, packed with braised meats, fragrant with dill (and oddly enough,
cilantro) and outfitted with horseradish dumplings. Siberian veal and beef
dumplings, or pelmeni, are nicely done, and Pozharsky cutlets combine minced
veal and chicken in a soft, ovoid slab perked up with puréed beets. The caviar, a
fail-safe choice, makes a luscious appetizer, swaddled in buckwheat blini and
smothered in sour cream and butter. **Price range:** Entrees, $19.75–$32.50.

Salaam Bombay Indian Cuisine ☆ ☆ $ $ INDIAN
317 Greenwich St. (near Duane St.)   (212) 226-9400
Credit cards: All major   Meals: L, D

Salaam Bombay looks much like every other upscale Indian restaurant in New
York City, large and pleasant. But it departs from tradition and showcases the
richness of regional Indian cooking. At lunch there's a big, affordable buffet. At
dinner an interesting assortment of vegetable dishes is where this kitchen really
shines. My favorite is ringna bataka nu shaak, a Gujarati eggplant and potato
dish cooked with curry leaves and lots of spices. I loved kadhai jhinge, shrimp
stir-fried with tomatoes, onions and lots of fresh and fragrant spices. For dessert,
shrikhand, a dreamy, custardlike dessert, has a mysterious flavor that imparts a
certain sense of wonder. **Price range:** entrees, $9.95–$19.95.

San Domenico ☆ ☆ ☆ $$$$ ITALIAN
240 Central Park S. (between Broadway and Seventh Ave.)
(212) 265-5959
Credit cards: All major   Meals: L, D

San Domenico is dignified and comfortable. Menu descriptions are long and complicated. The wine list has the weight of the Manhattan phone book, service is
sedate and the food is fabulous. It is one of a handful of American restaurants trying to showcase the cooking of the aristocratic northern Italian kitchen, the cuisine known as alta cucina. Give this staid restaurant a chance and it will manage
to capture your heart. I have found most of the appetizers so seductive that I have
eaten every meal in a flush of joyful anticipation. The restaurant's signature dish is
uovo in ravioli con burro nocciola tartufato: a single large puff filled with ricotta
and spinach perfumed with truffle butter. Snuggled inside is an egg that spurts
golden yolk as you begin to eat. But the kitchen does not need luxury ingredients
to show its stuff. You could come to San Domenico and treat it like a trattoria,
choosing only simple dishes and enjoying the care with which they are cooked.

Savoy ☆ ☆ $$$ NEW AMERICAN
70 Prince St. (at Crosby St.)   (212) 219-8570
Credit cards: All major   Meals: L, D

Savoy looks like a funky old aluminum-sided diner. So it is surprising to walk into
the upstairs dining room, where cooking is done right in the fireplace, and find

one of the city's coziest rooms. The menu is another surprise, dancing around the globe, borrowing where it will. The results can be wildly uneven but are usually charming. If you are unlucky you may end up with one of the occasionally gummy risottos or doughy pastas. Order a salad, however, and you will instantly be seduced. Desserts are excellent and change with the market. If you have an adventurous spirit, you will discover a sense of fun that is missing in most modern restaurants. **Price range:** Entrees, $19–$26.

Scalini Fedeli ☆ $$ ITALIAN

165 Duane Street (Hudson Street);   (212) 528-0400
Credit cards: All major   Meals: L, D

Scalini Fedeli (which means "steps of faith") has no edge. What it has, instead, is old-fashioned grace. The dining room, with its well-spaced tables and conservative country-Italian décor, is as soothing as massage. The food is pleasing, for the most part, but it rarely takes flight, and when it does, the dish is likely to be disarmingly simple. The pappardelle with a sauce of Scottish hare and venison is a small feast of gloriously rich, dark meats finished off with cream and truffles. The main courses are satisfying, decorous and rather unassuming. A good-size fillet of roasted Patagonian toothfish (Chilean sea bass), for example, finds an ideal matchup in a sauce of sun-dried tomatoes and Sicilian and Greek olives, and saddle of rabbit, swaddled in pancetta and served with a black olive sauce, makes a simple, pleasing entrée. For dessert, the panna cotta takes a back seat to the dense chocolate tart, and to the clever miniature cannoli, filled with espresso-flavored mascarpone cream. **Price range:** Dinner, three courses, $60.

Screening Room ☆ ☆ $$$ NEW AMERICAN

54 Varick St. (below Canal St.)   (212) 334-2100
Credit cards: All major   Meals: Br, L, D

It's a bar. It's a restaurant. It's a movie theater. The slightly funky bar serves appealing snacks like lobster rolls, onion rings and Philadelphia cheese steaks. The restaurant offers serious American food on the order of grilled duck and spectacular desserts. The best appetizer is the pan-fried artichokes, served on lemony greens topped with shavings of Parmesan cheese. The simplest dishes are the most impressive: roast chicken with potatoes and escarole; a fine piece of grilled tuna; cedar-planked salmon with chard, tomatoes and parsley purée. The pastry chef does not have a loser on the list, but the best desserts are lemon icebox cake and toasted angel food cake. **Price range:** Entrees, $13–$22.

Sea Grill ☆ ☆ $$$ SEAFOOD

19 West 49th Street, Rockefeller Center;   (212) 332-7610
Credit cards: All major   Meals: L, D   Closed Sun.

A refiguring of the Rockefeller Center concourse has made the Sea Grill smaller, and a redesign by Adam Tihany has given it a cooler, cleaner and snappier appearance. But the main draw, a view of the Rockefeller Center skating

rink, remains unchanged. In warm weather, the skating rink becomes an outdoor extension of the restaurant, with canvas umbrellas and potted shrubs.
Much of the menu, with trimmed-back prices, has a brasserie feel to it, with a
changing daily menu of day-boat fish that are simply grilled, sauteed or seared.
There's a fresh new breeze blowing over the rest of the menu as well, with the
accent on vibrant flavors and simple preparations. Fat, rosy mussels come in a
subtly spiced Thai curry broth. A translucent sheet of striped sea bass carpaccio
needs no more than a sprinkling of baby cilantro and a slick of olive oil and
lime juice to come alive. The crab cake is justly renowned: a lumpy-looking
thing, more ball than patty, displaying the rough-hewn virtues that distinguish a
real crab cake from a thousand prettified pretenders. **Price range:** Entrees,
$21–$29.

71 Clinton Fresh Food ☆☆ $$ BISTRO/NEW AMERICAN

71 Clinton St. (near Rivington St.)   (212) 614-6960
Credit cards: All major   Meals: D   Closed Sun.

Cool, understated and hip, this makes every other restaurant in New York
look as if it's trying too hard It's the kind of place that diners want to keep
as their little secret. It would be hard to exaggerate Chef Wylie Dufresne's
virtues. He starts with wonderful ingredients, and when manipulating
them, he shows a purist's respect for clean flavors and harmonious combinations. He has a fresh, original take on every dish, but an innate sense of
rigor tells him when enough is enough. And he excels at striking visual
presentations. The menu is tiny. Diners can choose from six appetizers,
seven entrees and four desserts, with a special or two thrown in from time
to time. The wine list, too, is short. But then the restaurant itself is tiny.
The goat cheese tart is superior, with a flawless crust and an earthy note
provided by a drizzling of arugula oil. Root-vegetable lasagna is a perfect
cube made of layer after paper-thin layer of vegetables, topped with a colorful corsage of sharp and bitter cresses and surrounded by a tingling
mushroom vinegar broth. At the savage end of the spectrum lie beer-
braised short ribs and a juicy venison chop. Desserts are simple, like a
straightforward warm pineapple tart with coconut ice cream. **Price range:**
Entrees, $15–$22.

Shun Lee Palace ☆☆ $$$ CHINESE

155 East 55th St. (between Lexington and Third Aves.)
(212) 371-8844
Credit cards: All major   Meals: L, D

No restaurant in New York City can produce better Chinese food. And no
restaurant in New York City does it so rarely. Shun Lee is a New York institution, with a cool opulence that is almost a caricature of a Chinese-American
palace. Regular customers are so pampered that first-timers look on enviously
as they are shunted off to a table in the far less luxurious bar area. The
spareribs are long, meaty, almost fat-free and perfectly cooked. The chefs do
impressive things with whole fish, and the restaurant's owner likes to appear at

the table with live fish and suggest various ways the kitchen might prepare them. **Price range:** Entrees, $8.75–$29.95.

Shun Lee West $$$ CHINESE
43 West 65th St. (at Columbus)   (212) 595-8895
Credit cards: All major   Meals: Br, L, D, LN

A cavernous Chinese restaurant near Lincoln Center that is always packed. The kitchen can do great things, but they are rarely produced for a clientele that sticks mostly to the familiar. If you want the best food, call ahead and discuss the menu. Good Peking duck. **Price range:** Avg. entree, $19.

Silver Swan $25 & Under GERMAN
41 East 20th St. (between Broadway and Park Ave. S.)   (212) 254-3611
Credit cards: All major   Meals: L, D, LN

The excellent selection of more than 75 beers and ales is reason enough to enjoy Silver Swan's solid German fare in a friendly atmosphere. Rauchbier, or smoked beer, made with smoked malt, goes perfectly with kassler rippchen, smoked pork chops served with vinegary sauerkraut, while any of more than a dozen Bavarian wheat beers are just right with weisswurst, mild veal sausage, or bratwurst, juicy pork sausage. This is not the place to eat if you are longing for vegetables, which run the gamut from cabbage to potatoes, cooked until soft. Meat is another matter, however, starting with five varieties of schnitzel and ending with a satisfying sauerbraten. **Price range:** Entrees, $14–$27.

Smith & Wollensky ☆☆ $$$$ STEAKHOUSE
797 Third Ave. (at 49th St.)   (212) 753-1530
Credit cards: All major   Meals: L, D, LN

This is a place for two-fisted eating. It is also one of the few steakhouses that never lets you down: the service is swell, the steaks are consistently very, very good (if rarely great) and the portions are huge. The sirloins are aged for around two weeks to intensify the flavor and give the meat a dry edge. Beyond that, if you have noncarnivores to feed, the restaurant knows how to do it. The lobsters, clams, oysters and chicken are excellent too. Desserts, unfortunately, leave a great deal to be desired. **Price range:** Entrees, $18.50–$65.

Soho Steak $25 & Under BISTRO/FRENCH
90 Thompson St. (near Spring St.)   (212) 226-0602
Credit cards: Cash only   Meals: Br, D

This thoroughly French little restaurant, drawing a young, good-looking crowd, emphasizes meat but is no simple steakhouse. It is a cleverly conceived, bustling bistro that serves creative dishes for lower prices than you might imagine. Steak frites, of course, is top-notch. Few places offer this much value for this kind of money. **Price range:** Entrees, $14–$16.

Solera ☆☆ $$$ SPANISH
216 East 53d St. (between Second and Third Aves.)   (212) 644-1166
Credit cards: All major   Meals: L, D, LN   Closed Sun.

Solera looks so cozy it is almost impossible not to be drawn into the long room,
with its terra-cotta tiles and romantic lighting. Pull up a chair and prepare to be
seduced by the food and wine of Spain. The appetizers are all fine, but the octopus with paprika and olive oil is consistently amazing—it is as tender as marrow.
There are several versions of paella, all delicious but the seafood is the most
impressive. Best of all are the crisp little lamb chops served with a ragout of
beans and polenta laced with cheese. **Price range:** Entrees, $25–$35; tapas,
$3–$9.50.

Sono ☆☆ $$$$ JAPANESE/FRENCH
106 East 57th St. (At Lexington Ave.)   (212) 752-4411
Credit cards: All major   Meals: L, D

Sono—which means "garden enhanced by man"—is a showcase for Tadashi
Ono, the longtime executive chef at La Caravelle, and in his own culinary
theater, he has developed an idiosyncratic, very persuasive blend of French
and Japanese cooking. It would be absurd to call the style at Sono "no frills,"
but there is a disarming simplicity to the menu. The excitement comes from
unexpected pairings, or the sheer, inexhaustible pleasure of directly commu-
nicated taste sensations, or arresting visual presentations. The chef's assortment, an appetizer, offers a whirlwind tour through Mr. Ono's mind. The
lineup varies from day to day, but it's always a carousel of tastes and textures.
Roasted duck breast, served with a confit of the leg, starts out French but
takes a sudden turn with a sublime watercress and wasabi sauce, subtly sweet
and hot at the same time. It's enough that Mr. Ono has given the world his
roasted squab smeared with a paste of kaffir lime, a kind of hollandaise made
with sake and white miso that transforms the dark, gamy birds into luscious
little balls of opulent flavor. It has a counterpart on the dessert menu, an
impressively tall cheesecake made with kabocha squash (Japan's favorite
pumpkin) and coconut. **Price range:** Dinner, three courses, $52; seven course
tasting menu, $78.

Surya ☆☆ $$ INDIAN
302 Bleecker St. (between Seventh Ave. S. and Grove St.)
(212) 807-7770
Credit cards: All major   Meals: Br, D

The restaurant named for the sun (in Tamil) actually has a small garden in
the back along with a sleek interior. Its menu features mostly south Indian
dishes, often filtered through the technique of France. The main courses
have a bold freshness. But what is most splendid about Surya is the entirely
meatless side of the menu. It is, in fact, difficult to come up with a more
exciting place to eat vegetables in New York City. Don't eat a meal at Surya

without ordering the okra, sautéed in a thick mixture of tomatoes, onion, garlic and kokum (a sour Indian fruit). Try the dosai, too, and the exceptional desserts. **Price range:** Entrees, $11–$24.

Sushi Hatsu ☆ ☆ ☆ $$$$ JAPANESE/SUSHI

1143 First Ave. (near 62d St.)   (212) 371-0238
Credit cards: AE/Diner's   Meals: D, LN   Closed Mon.

With a modest sushi bar in front, and a few tables in the rear, Sushi Hatsu serves breathtakingly good fish of an astonishing purity. It is so light, you feel you could go on eating forever. The bill will be huge; good sushi is never cheap. But if you've got the money, they've got the fish. **Price range:** $30 minimum at the sushi bar, but expect to spend $75 to $100 a person.

Sushi Masa $25 & Under JAPANESE/SUSHI

141 East 47th St. (between Lexington and Third Aves.)
(212) 715-0837
Credit cards: All major   Meals: L, D   Closed Sun.

The small bright dining room here is extremely inviting, the service warm and pleasant. But what makes this restaurant special is the combination of high quality ingredients and the reasonable prices. At lunch order the specialty of the house, Sushi Masa gozen, an assortment of dishes that is like a small banquet (salad, dobin soup, sashimi, broiled tuna and pickled vegetables). At dinner try chirashi sushi, raw fish on top of vinegared rice. The sushi and sashimi assortments are all fresh and attractively presented. **Price range:** Dinner, $12–$25.

Sushi Yasuda ☆ ☆ ☆ $$$ JAPANESE/SUSHI

204 East 43rd St. (between Second and Third Aves.)   (212) 972-1001
Credit cards: All major   Meals: L, D   Closed Sun.

In one of the city's dreariest restaurant neighborhoods, Sushi Yasuda glows like a strange mineral, with a cool, celery-green façade. Inside, the refusal to decorate is almost palpable. The mood is quiet, contemplative, austere. But Sushi Yasuda has a lot of downtown in its soul. The manager and the waitresses are young. The exemplary service has an open, friendly quality to it. At the same time, the menu is dead serious, a purist's paradise of multiple choices among fish species— nearly 30, a startling number for a small restaurant—and elegantly presented appetizers and side dishes. Sushi Yasuda makes a point of carrying fish that most sushi restaurants either can't get their hands on or don't want to bother with. But sushi is only half the story. The daily menu includes a small, transparent sheet of special appetizers, and they are worth jumping for. The selection may include a textural medley of six seaweeds, arranged like small tumbleweeds on a white rectangular plate, or deep-fried eel backbones, as salty and crunchy as crisp bacon, but with a rich fish flavor. **Price range:** Sushi, $3–$6.50 a piece.

Sweet 'n' Tart Café $25 & Under   CHINESE
76 Mott St. (south of Canal St.), Chinatown   (212) 334-8088
Credit cards: Cash only   Meals: B, L, D, LN

The specialty here is tong shui, a range of sweet tonics intended to benefit
specific parts of the body or to balance one's yin and yang. But Sweet 'n'
Tart's more typical dishes are terrific as well, like Chinese sausage and taro
with rice, served in a tall bamboo steamer, and congee with beef, pork and
squid. Little English is spoken here, but waitresses describe dishes as well as
they can. **Price range:** $5–$14.

Tabla ☆☆☆ $$$$ AMERICAN-ASIAN FUSION
11 Madison Ave. (near 25th St.)   (212) 889-0667
Credit cards: All major   Meals: L, D   Closed Sun.

The newest of Danny Meyer's restaurants, Tabla vibrates with sound and sizzles
with color. At the bar downstairs, cooks grill roti and naan in odd and interesting flavors. Upstairs, the dining room is darkly sensuous with walls stained in
shades of jade and coral. Then the food arrives—American food, viewed
through a kaleidoscope of Indian spices. The powerful, original and unexpected
flavors evoke intense emotions.

   Those who do not like Tabla tend to dislike it with a passion. I have learned
to ignore them and to abandon myself to the joys of veal loin served with diced
sweetbreads, gingered greens and a marrow bone or spiced oxtails on a bed of
tapioca and roasted beets. Braised red onion stuffed with eggplant is an extraordinarily fine vegetarian dish. For me, Tabla was love at first bite. **Price range:**
Three-course prix-fixe dinner, $52 (plus a few supplements).

Tapika ☆☆ $$$ SOUTHWESTERN
950 Eighth Ave. (at 56th St.)   (212) 397-3737
Credit cards: All major   Meals: L, D, LN   Closed Sun.

This is a casual, comfortable restaurant with tongue-in-cheek references to the
West. It is an urban fantasy, a New York dream about what the West might be,
with delightfully inventive Southwestern fare. Start with an order of green chili
corn fries. The Tapika salad, a spicy take on Caesar salad, is irresistible—if you
can take the heat. Some of the main courses are a letdown, but the chile relleno
is an amazing tapestry of tastes and textures, the sort of thing you could happily
go on eating forever. All the meats are good, too, including the fine steak. **Price
range:** Entrees, $18–$29.

Tavern on the Green ☆ $$$$ NEW AMERICAN
Central Park West (at 67th St.)   (212) 873-3200
Credit cards: All major   Meals: Br, L, D

This is America's largest-grossing restaurant, a wonderland of lights, flowers,
chandeliers and balloons that can make a child out of the most cynical adult.
Patrick Clark, who died in February 1998, was a terrific chef, and he's left a culi-

nary legacy for his successors to follow. But even he was not able to overcome the tavern's unaccountably rude and lax service. Even so, the people keep coming, for the glittery setting and for dishes like mustard-and-herb-crusted rack of pork, served with braised red cabbage and potatoes mashed with horseradish. The trick is simply getting the food. **Price range:** Entrees, $21.75–$34.

Thalia ☆☆ $$$ NEW AMERICAN
828 Eighth Ave. (At West 50th St.)   (212) 399-4444
Credit cards: All major   Meals: L, D

Thalia is the Muse of comedy, and also a confusing name for a serious restaurant in a neighborhood that is rapidly losing its hard-won reputation as a joke when it comes to food. Executive chef Michael Otsuka practices an intelligent form of fusion cooking, with a strong Asian influence. He has faith in the power of simple ingredients and flavors, and the wit to use them in inventive ways. A small spoonful of wasabi granita, cold and crunchy, with a piercing heat, sets off Kumamoto oysters brilliantly. Foie gras fatigue disappears the moment you lay eyes on foie gras mousse, sprinkled with chopped pistachio and accompanied by figs drenched in port. It looks like dessert but it's twice as rich—damnation on a small plate. **Price range:** Entrees, $17–$29.

Tiffin $25 & Under   INDIAN/VEGETARIAN
18 Murray St. (between Church St. and Broadway)   (212) 791-3510
Credit cards: All major   Meals: L, D   Closed Sun.

At best, the vegetarian Indian food at Tiffin is fascinating and delicious, and should be a must-try for anybody curious about the range and breadth of Indian flavors. Almost nothing is familiar about the food, which abounds in herbs and spices not found in the usual Indian curry blends. Try the exceptional samosas, the smoked tomato rasam, and the undhiya, a Gujarati melange of potatoes and vegetables with adzuki beans and plantains, strongly flavored with mustard and anise seeds. **Price range:** Prix-fixe dinner, $20.

Tocqueville ☆☆ $$$ FRENCH
15 East 15th St. (between Fifth Ave. and Union Sq West)
(212) 647-1515
Credit cards: All major   Meals: L, D   Closed Sun.

Tocqueville is a quiet haven of good taste, good food and good service. Scallops have a concentrated richness that helps them hold their own when paired with foie gras. The lamb has the herbal flavor that American lamb usually doesn't. Billy Bi soup, the oddly named classic from France's Atlantic coast, is beyond praise. Fat mussels float languidly in a concentrated saffron meuniere broth with a briny tang and just the right citric spark. The roasted rack of lamb is surrounded by braised artichokes, mushrooms and fava beans in a red-wine reduction, and to show off the meat. Desserts also do honor to the menu. Warm chocolate cake, just gooey enough on the inside, comes with a scoop of green ice cream permeated with a pristine mint flavor. Upside-down banana tart is a little marvel, a small palisade of fat banana chunks encircling a disk of almond shortbread, teamed up with a ball of brown-sugar ice cream. **Price range:** Entrees, $22–$28.

The Tonic ☆☆ $ $$ NEW AMERICAN
108 West 18 St. (between Sixth and Seventh Aves.)   (212) 929-9755
Credit cards: All major   Meals: L, D   Closed Sun.

A tony restaurant that perfectly exemplifies New York in the late 1990's, Tonic has a raucous, old-fashioned tavern in front, and in back a tranquil restaurant filled with beautiful light that makes all the patrons look lovely. Excellent waiters serve robust American food like a wonderful pumpkin bisque, ravioli filled with sweetbreads and salsify, and scallop velouté. And who could resist sautéed fois gras set on chestnut purée? Not me. The menu changes seasonally. **Price range:** Entrees, $25–$28.

Tribeca Grill ☆☆ $$$ NEW AMERICAN
375 Greenwich St. (at Franklin St.)   (212) 941-3900
Credit cards: All major   Meals: Br, L, D

Robert De Niro's first venture into the restaurant business in what the neighbors sometimes call Bob Row is a cool, casual outpost of modern American cuisine with an almost constant flow of celebrity guests. And the food's good. The big, airy space with exposed bricks, colorful banquettes and comfortable tables centers on a massive handsome mahogany bar many may remember as the original bar of Maxwell's Plum. The beguiling fare remains a steady lure. **Price range:** Entrees, $12–$29.

"21" Club ☆☆ $$$$ AMERICAN
21 West 52d St. (between Fifth and Sixth Aves.)   (212) 582-7200
Credit cards: All major   Meals: L, D   Closed Sun.

Of all the restaurants in New York City, none has a richer history. American royalty has been entertaining at "21" for most of this century. The restaurant continues to be operated like a club where unknowns are led to the farthest dining room as the more favored clients are pampered and petted. Nothing much else has changed either: the tablecloths are still red and white checked, the toys are still hanging from the ceiling, and it still looks like the speak-easy it once was. The menu has been modernized but with mixed results. The basics are still superb, however. Great steak, rack of lamb, Dover sole, and the "21" burger, and several traditional desserts such as rice pudding and crème brûlée are all worthwhile. **Price range:** Entrees, $24–$39.

27 Standard ☆☆ $ $ NEW AMERICAN
116 East 27th St. (between Park and Lexington Aves.)   (212) 576-2232
Credit cards: All major   Meals: L, D   Closed Sun.

Part jazz club (in the basement), part casually elegant restaurant, 27 Standard is large and airy, with an interesting wine list and unusual, tasty American food. Salads are superb and main courses imaginative. Don't miss the roasted oysters with braised leeks and chives. The large Black Angus sirloin steak is bathed in a fine red wine sauce and served on a lively watercress and onion relish. Desserts are the most ornate section of the menu. **Price range:** Entrees, $16–$27.

Union Pacific ☆ ☆ ☆ $$$$ FRENCH/ASIAN
111 East 22d St. (near Park Ave. S.)   (212) 995-8500
Credit cards: All major   Meals: L, D   Closed Sun.

Union Pacific occupies one of the most beautiful, comfortable and soothing environments in Manhattan. Its curtain of falling water at the entrance has the cool, calm look of Japan. Service is professional and enthusiastic, and chef Rocco di Spirito has invented an exciting menu. Despite Asian touches in the main part of the menu, the focus here is largely French. The unusual wine list adds another dimension, emphasizing bright wines with enough acidity to make them friendly to this food. Desserts are as interesting as entrees. **Price range:** 3-course prix-fixe, $65 with supplements; 5-course prix-fixe, $85; flight of three or five little dishes, $20 and $30; 21 little dishes (requires advanced booking), $135.

Union Square Café ☆ ☆ $$$ NEW AMERICAN
21 East 16th St. (between Fifth Ave. and Union Square West)
(212) 243-4020
Credit cards: All major   Meals: L, D

This is one of the city's most beloved dining spots, and a top destination for tourists. The restaurant makes its guests feel welcome by catering to their every whim in an openhanded, Midwestern manner that disguises a disciplined, highly professional understanding of service that broke the mold in New York. Union Square's pioneering fusion of fine food and wine, casual atmosphere and stellar service has made it the most influential restaurant of its time in the city, and certainly one of the most popular. The wine list is still outstanding and still full of bargains. The signature fried calamari, a dull cliché elsewhere in town, come out golden brown, perfectly cooked outside and inside, and nicely complemented with an incisive, creamy anchovy mayonnaise. Although there are several foreign accents heard on the menu, Italian dominates, especially in the pasta dishes, which put many Italian restaurants to shame. Desserts aim for an artful blend of homey and exotic, most memorably in the banana tart with a caramel shellac, a Union Square standby. **Price range:** Entrees, $18.50–$28.

Vatan $25 & Under   INDIAN/VEGETARIAN
409 Third Ave. (at 29th St.)   (212) 689-5666
Credit cards: All major   Meals: D, LN   Closed Mon.

This astounding Indian restaurant transports you to a bright, animated Indian village with thatched roofs and artificial banyan trees. Vatan specializes in the rich, spicy yet subtle vegetarian cuisine of Gujarat. For one price, a parade of little dishes is served, which might include khaman, a delicious fluffy steamed cake of lentil flour with black mustard seeds; delicate little samosas; patrel, taro leaves layered with spicy chickpea paste and steamed, and much more. **Price range:** $19.95.

Velli $25 & Under   ITALIAN
132 West Houston St. (near Sullivan St.)   (212) 979-7614
Credit cards: Cash only   Meals: Br, L, LN

The newest of Jean-Claude Iacovelli's group of sophisticated, casually lively, moderately priced restaurants is a French bistro disguised as a trattoria. It is filled with people who have come to enjoy good food and good talk. Yes, the menu is Italian, but the vibe is decidedly French. The philosophy is clear: keep the menu and wine list short, the ingredients top quality and the prices reasonable. Appetizers are exceptional. **Price range:** Entrees, $12–$15.

Verbena ☆ ☆ $$$ NEW AMERICAN
54 Irving Pl. (at 17th St.)   (212) 260-5454
Credit cards: All major   Meals: Br, L, D

The dining room is small, elegant and beautifully lighted to give it a romantic glow. The food is fresh, seasonal and original American fare. Verbena also has one of the city's loveliest gardens and a wonderful small room for private parties. If it were a little less expensive, it would be the very model of a modern American restaurant. Like the dining room, the small menu seems entirely personal. While some appetizers are too complicated, the entrees are disarmingly simple. Portions are generous and many people seem to skip dessert, but it would be a shame to miss the crème brûlée. **Price range:** Entrees, $23–$29.

Veritas ☆ ☆ ☆ $$$$ NEW AMERICAN
43 East 20th St. (near Park Ave. S.)   (212) 353-3700
Credit cards: All major   Meals: L, D   Closed Sun.

Small, spare and elegant, Veritas could be called a wine cellar with a restaurant attached, because at Veritas, the wine is more important than the food. The 1,300 entries on its wine list include such rarities as a Chateau Margaux 1900, a Mouton Rothschild 1945 and Lafite-Rothschild 1953, and they are offered at extremely reasonable prices. The room often seems overcrowded and patrons sometimes feel rushed, but Veritas offers clean and unfussy food that works well with its wine. The chef serves food that is quietly sly: you barely notice that you are tasting chili peppers, ginger and vanilla in a delicious pineapple compote served with seared foie gras. Main courses, to suit the powerful wines, are robust, powerful and simple—with surprisingly little red meat on the menu. The intensity does not abate with desserts. Try warm chocolate cake (called a soufflé here), or a startlingly delicious praline parfait with a polished reduction of clementines so good that it eases you right into sweet wine. **Price range:** Prix-fixe dinner, $62.

Viceversa ☆ $ $ ITALIAN

325 West 51st St. (Between Eighth and Ninth Aves.)   (212) 399-9265
Credit cards: All major   Meals: L, D

With its crisp earth-colored awnings and gleaming façade, Viceversa (pronounced VEE-chey-VAIR-suh) stands out on one of Manhattan's grungier
blocks like a Versace suit. Managers and wait staff project an unmistakable Italian warmth. The menu, too, is honest and unpretentious, a solid lineup of
mostly northern Italian dishes presented in a perfectly straightforward manner.
Casoncelli alla bergamasca deserves star billing in Viceversa's strong ensemble
cast of pastas: it is a ravioli filled with chopped veal, crushed amaretti, raisins
and Parmesan, then topped with butter, crisped sage leaves and crunchy bits of
fried pancetta—a salty, herbal sauce that offsets the sweetness of the stuffing.
Price range: Entrees, $16.50–$22.50.

Virgil's Real BBQ $25 & Under BARBECUE

152 West 44th St. (between Broadway and Sixth Ave.)
(212) 921-9494
Credit cards: All major   Meals: L, D, LN

With its framed photographs of restaurants, cattle and pigs, aprons and other
artifacts covering the walls, Virgil's is a wildly popular shrine to barbecue joints
around the country. If the food isn't quite authentic, the formula comes close
enough and it works. And the place smells great, as any barbecue place should.
Highlights on the menu include hush puppies served with a maple syrup butter;
smoked Texas links with mustard slaw; crab cakes; barbecued shrimp and Texas
red chili with corn bread. For main fare, big barbecue platters carry enticing
selections of Owensboro lamb, Maryland ham, Carolina pork shoulder, Texas
beef brisket and more. **Price range:** Entrees, $10.95–$18.95.

Water Club ☆ ☆ $ $ $ $ NEW AMERICAN

500 East 30th St. (at the East River)   (212) 683-3333
Credit cards: All major   Meals: Br, L, D

The view from the Manhattan side is not nearly as enticing as the view that its
sibling, the River Cafe, has in the other direction. But it is peaceful on the water,
and the food is fine. While many waterside restaurants attempt a hokey romanti-
cism, the Water Club has a straightforward American quality that is very appealing. The emphasis, of course, is on seafood, and it is done with flair. The kitchen
is at its best when it sticks to the basics. A great appetizer is clams on the half
shell, and lobster is perfectly steamed. **Price range:** Entrees, $23–$35.

West 63rd Street Steak House ☆ $ $ $ $ STEAKHOUSE

44 West 63d St. (near Broadway)   (212) 246-6363
Credit cards: All major   Meals: D   Closed Sun.

This restaurant turns the New York steakhouse experience on its head. It is
quiet and restful, and the service is solicitous. As plush and comfortable as a

rich man's library, it has an attractive view of Lincoln Center and serves big potent drinks and excellent shrimp cocktail. Unfortunately the steaks aren't always very good. The porterhouse and T-bone are sometimes aged to perfection, sometimes not; you just can't count on them. The veal chop, however, is a fine piece of meat and the roasted baby chicken is flavorful. Among the many side dishes the french fries are excellent, and so is the nutmeg-free creamed spinach, but the home fries are unimpressive. Desserts are not recommended; just stick to the sorbet. **Price range:** Entrees, $21–$30.

Wild Blue ☆ $$$ NEW AMERICAN

1 World Trade Center (between Liberty and Vesey Sts.)
(212) 524-7107
Credit cards: All major   Meals: D   Closed Sun.

This intimate, romantic new restaurant atop the World Trade Center offers spectacular views over New York Harbor. On a clear evening you can almost see the Earth curve. The down-the-middle American menu walks a thin line between simple and austere. In spirit it is an updated chophouse for the weary business diner, with a few interesting twists, just enough to keep you from dozing off. The dessert menu throws off a few sparks. Try the Napa Valley chocolate cake or a scoop of luscious banana-passion fruit sorbet and a pool of tangy mango sauce. **Price range:** Entrees, $20–$30.

Windows on the World ☆ ☆ $$$$ NEW AMERICAN

1 World Trade Center (between Liberty and Vesey Sts.)
(212) 524-7000
Credit cards: All major   Meals: Br, D

The food is better now that the kitchen features regional American favorites. Still, despite good appetizers like short ribs with blue cheese and a fabulous, well-priced wine list, the view continues to be the main draw. The comfortable chairs and pleasantly muted twilight colors combined with the view create the illusion of being in an airliner hovering magically over Manhattan. **Price range:** Entrees, $25–$35.

Wu Liang Ye $25 & Under   CHINESE

338 Lexington Ave. (between 39th and 40th Sts.)   (212) 370-9647
215 East 86th St. (at Third Ave.)   (212) 534-8899
36 West 48th St. (between Fifth and Sixth Aves.)   (212) 398-2308
Credit cards: All major   Meals: L, D, LN

Though each of these branches of a Chinese restaurant chain differs slightly in menu and atmosphere, they all specialize in lively, robust Sichuan dishes, notable for their meticulous preparation. Sliced conch is one of their more unusual dishes, firm, chewy and nutty, served with spicy red oil. Four kinds of dumplings are all delicate and flavorful. **Price range:** $7.50–$20.

Zarela ☆☆ $$ MEXICAN/TEX-MEX
953 Second Ave. (between 50th and 51st Sts.) (212) 644-6740
Credit cards: All major Meals: L, D

Bright, bold and raucous as a party, the sort of place that looks like a typical Mexican taquería. Happily, it is not. Zarela Martinez has written several excellent Mexican cookbooks, and she serves some of the city's most exciting and authentic Mexican food. Among the best dishes are a fiery snapper hash, crisp flautas, tamales and fajitas. Good side dishes include creamy rice baked with sour cream, cheddar cheese, corn and poblano chilies, and pozole guisado, in which hominy kernels are sautéed with tomatoes, onions, garlic and jalapeño peppers. **Price range:** Avg. entree, $20.

Zuni $25 & Under SOUTHWESTERN
598 Ninth Ave. (at 43d St.) (212) 765-7626
Credit cards: All major Meals: Br, L, D, LN

The original focus at this appealing little restaurant was Southwestern, and the atmosphere still reflects this, but the current menu is all over the map, with Southwestern dishes like chili-rubbed rib-eye steak, New Orleans specialties like jambalaya and geographically indecipherable offerings like sesame-crusted salmon with mango-and-black-bean salsa and basmati rice. If it's too confusing, settle for meatloaf and garlic mashed potatoes. It's usually all pretty good. **Price range:** Entrees, $7.50–$14.95.

A Guide to Restaurants by Cuisine

AMERICAN
An American
 Place ☆☆
Fifty Seven
 Fifty Seven ☆☆☆
Mark's ☆☆

ARGENTINE
Chimichurri Grill

AUSTRALIAN
Eight Mile Creek ☆☆

AUSTRIAN
Danube ☆☆☆

BARBECUE
Virgil's Real BBQ

BISTRO
Panache
Pastis ☆
Pop ☆

CAJUN
Bayou

CARIBBEAN
Bambou ☆☆
El Fogon
Island Spice

CHINESE
Big Wong
Evergreen Shanghai
Joe's Shanghai ☆☆
Mee Noodle Shop

New York Noodle
 Town ☆☆
Our Place
Pig Heaven
Ping's ☆☆
Shanghai Tang
Shun Lee Palace ☆☆
Shun Lee West
Sweet-N-Tart Cafe
Wu Liang Ye

DELI
Artie's
Carnegie Deli
Katz's Deli

EAST EUROPEAN
Danube ☆☆☆

ENGLISH
Guastavino's ☆☆
Nicole's

FRENCH
Alison on
   Dominick   ☆☆
Alouette
Avenue
Balthazar ☆☆
Bandol
Bistro Le Steak
Blue Hill ☆☆
Bouley
   Bakery ☆☆☆☆
Bouterin ☆
Brasserie ☆☆
Café Boulud ☆☆☆
Cello ☆☆☆
Chanterelle ☆☆☆
Chelsea Bistro
   & Bar ☆☆
Chez Josephine ☆☆
Chez Louis ☆☆
Coup ☆
Daniel ☆☆☆
Destinée ☆☆
Guastavino's ☆☆
Jack's Fifth ☆☆
Jean Claude
JoJo ☆☆☆
Jubilee
La Caravelle ☆☆☆
La Côte Basque ☆☆☆
L'Actuel ☆☆
La Grenouille ☆☆☆
L'Ardoise
Le Bernardi ☆☆☆☆
Le Gigot
Lespinasse ☆☆☆☆
Le Tableau
Lutèce ☆☆☆

Mercer Kitchen ☆☆
Montrachet ☆☆☆
Odeon ☆☆
One If By Land ☆
Palladin ☆☆
Panache
Park Bistro ☆☆☆
Pastis ☆
Payard Pâtisserie ☆☆
Peacock Alley ☆☆☆
Picholine ☆☆☆
Provence ☆
Quince ☆☆
Restaurant
   Raphael ☆☆
Sono ☆☆
Tocqueville ☆☆
Trois Marches ☆
Union Pacific ☆☆☆

GREEK
Avra ☆
Christos Hasapo-
   Taverna
Estiatorio Milos ☆
Il Mulino
Meltemi
Metsovo
Molyvos ☆☆☆
Periyali ☆☆☆
Rafina

HAMBURGERS
McHale's

INDIAN
Chola ☆☆
Dawat ☆
Mavalli Palace
Mughlai
Pongal
Salaam Bombay ☆☆

Surya ☆☆

INDONESIAN
Bali Nusa Indah

ITALIAN
Al Di La
Arqua ☆☆
Babbo ☆☆☆
Bar Pitti
Bice ☆☆
Campagna ☆☆
Chianti ☆☆
Commune ☆
F.Illi Ponte ☆☆
Felidia ☆☆☆
Follonico ☆☆
Frank
Fresco By Scotto ☆☆
I Coppi ☆☆
I Trulli ☆☆
Il Valentino ☆☆
Il Mulino
'ino
Isola
La Nonna ☆
Le Zie
Lupa
Max
Osteria Del Circo
   ☆☆
Palio ☆☆
Paola's ☆☆
Parioli
   Romanissimo ☆☆
Pepe Verde
Pepolino
Puttanesca
Remi ☆☆
San Domenico
   ☆☆☆
Scalini Fedeli ☆

Note: Restaurants in **boldface italics** are Eric Asimov's choices for the best inexpensive restaurants in New York.

Velli
Viceversa ☆

JAPANESE
Blue Ribbon Sushi ☆☆
Hatsuhana ☆☆
Honmura An ☆☆☆
Katsu-Hama
Komodo
Kuruma Zushi ☆☆☆
Marumi
Nadaman
    Hakubai ☆☆
Next Door Nobu
    ☆☆☆
Nobu ☆☆☆
Otabe ☆☆
Sono ☆☆
Sushi Hatsu ☆☆
Sushi Masa
Sushi Yasuda ☆☆

KOREAN
Cho Dang Gol ☆☆
Han Sung Garden
Hangawi ☆☆
Kang Suh ☆☆
Kori

KOSHER
Pongal
Ratner's Dairy
Sammy's

LATIN AMERICAN
Asia de Cuba ☆
Boca Chica
Bolivar ☆☆
Chicama ☆☆
Chimichurri Grill
Churrascaria
    Plataforma ☆☆
Circus ☆☆
Coco Roco
Cuba Libre

El Pollo
Flor's Kitchen
Good
Havana NY
Komodo
Patria ☆☆☆
Pio Pio

MEDITERRANEAN
Acquario
Café Fès
Gus's Figs Bistro & Bar
Lavagna
Layla ☆☆
Matthew's ☆☆
Nick & Toni's ☆☆
Picholine ☆☆☆
Savoy ☆☆

MEXICAN/TEX-MEX
Café Frida
Casa Mexicana
Gabriela's
Los Dos Rancheros
Maya ☆☆
Mi Cocina ☆☆
Rinconcito Mexicano
Rocking Horse Cafe
Rosa Mexicano ☆☆
Zarela ☆☆

MIDDLE EASTERN
Habib's
Layla ☆☆
Moustache

NEW AMERICAN
Alley's End
An American
    Place ☆☆
Aureole ☆☆
Bayard's ☆☆
Bright Food Shop
Chat 'n Chew
City Hall ☆☆

Clementine ☆☆
Della Femina ☆
Delmonico's ☆
Etats-Unis ☆☆
First
The Four
    Seasons ☆☆☆
14 Wall Street ☆
Garrick
Gotham Bar
    and Grill ☆☆☆
Gramercy
    Tavern ☆☆☆
Heartbeat ☆☆
Hudson River
    Club ☆☆
Icon ☆☆
Joe Allen
Josie's
Judson Grill ☆☆☆
Le Cirque 2000
    ☆☆☆☆
Lenox Room ☆☆
Little Dove ☆☆
Lobster Club ☆☆
Local ☆☆
Michael's ☆☆
Moomba ☆☆
Odeon ☆☆
Park View ☆☆
Patroon ☆☆☆
Philip Marie
Quilty's ☆☆
The Red Cat ☆
Redeye Grill ☆
River Cafe ☆☆
Screening Room ☆☆
Tavern on the Green ☆
Thalia ☆☆
The Tonic ☆☆
Tribeca Grill ☆☆
21 Club ☆☆
27 Standard ☆☆
Union Square
    Cafe ☆☆☆

Verbena ☆ ☆
Veritas ☆ ☆ ☆
Water Club ☆ ☆
Wild Blue ☆
Windows on the
    World ☆ ☆

PAN ASIAN
Asia de Cuba ☆
Pop ☆
Ruby Foo's ☆ ☆
Tabla ☆ ☆ ☆

PAN-LATIN
Boca Chica
Bolivar ☆ ☆
Calle Ocho ☆
Esperanto
Patria ☆ ☆ ☆

PORTUGUESE
Pao

RUSSIAN
Firebird ☆ ☆
Petrossian ☆ ☆
Russian Tea Room

SCANDINAVIAN
Aquavit ☆ ☆ ☆
Christer's
    Restaurant ☆ ☆
Good World Bar & Grill

SEAFOOD
Aquagrill ☆ ☆

Atlantic Grill ☆
Avra ☆
Blue Water Grill ☆
Bongo
Cello ☆ ☆ ☆
Dock's ☆
Estiatorio Milos ☆ ☆
Le Bernardin ☆ ☆ ☆ ☆
The Little Place
Manhattan Ocean
    Club ☆ ☆
Maritime ☆
Meltemi
Oceana ☆ ☆ ☆
Rafina
Sea Grill ☆ ☆

SOUTHERN
Amy Ruth's
Emily's

SOUTHWESTERN
Mesa Grill ☆ ☆
Tapika ☆ ☆

SPANISH
Meigas ☆ ☆
Solera ☆ ☆

STEAKHOUSE
Bistro Le Steak
Churrascaria
    Plataforma ☆ ☆
Frank's ☆
Michael Jordan's ☆ ☆
Palm

Smith &
    Wollensky ☆ ☆
Soho Steak
West 63rd Street ☆

SUSHI
Donguri
Hatsuhana ☆ ☆
Inagiku ☆ ☆
Marumi
Sugiyama ☆ ☆
Sushi Hatsu ☆ ☆
Sushi Masa
Sushi of Gari
Sushi Yasuda ☆ ☆ ☆

THAI
Holy Basil
Little Basil
Ubol's Kitchen

TURKISH
Kazan
The Sultan

VEGETARIAN
Hangawi ☆ ☆
Mavalli Palace
Pongal
Tiffin

VIETNAMESE
Cyclo
Le Colonial ☆ ☆
Nha Trang

Note: Restaurants in **boldface italics** are Eric Asimov's choices for the best inexpensive restaurants in New York.